THE WALL STREET JOURNAL.

NATIONAL
BUSINESS
EMPLOYMENT
WEEKLY

JOBS RATED
ALMANAC

THE NATIONAL BUSINESS EMPLOYMENT WEEKLY PREMIER GUIDES SERIES

Published:

Resumes,   ISBN# 0-471-31029-8 cloth;
                              ISBN# 0-471-31028-X paper

Interviewing,   ISBN# 0-471-31024-7 cloth;
                              ISBN# 0-471-31025-5 paper

Networking,   ISBN# 0-471-31026-3 cloth;
                              ISBN# 0-471-31027-1 paper;

Forthcoming:

Cover Letters,   ISBN# 0-471-10671-2 cloth;
                              ISBN# 0-471-10672-0 paper

Alternative Careers,   ISBN# 0-471-10919-3 cloth;
                              ISBN# 0-471-10918-5 paper

THE WALL STREET JOURNAL.

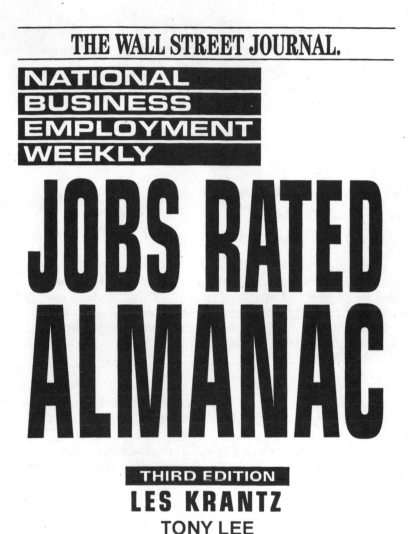

NATIONAL
BUSINESS
EMPLOYMENT
WEEKLY

JOBS RATED
ALMANAC

THIRD EDITION

LES KRANTZ

TONY LEE
(Contributor)

John Wiley & Sons, Inc.
New York • Chichester • Brisbane • Toronto • Singapore

Les Krantz: *Editor & Publisher*, Facts That Matter, Inc.
Contributor: Tony Lee. *Senior Editors:* Sharon Exley, Mark Mravic.
Associate Editiors: Adrienne Brown, Charley Custer.

Special Acknowledgement: Ruth Mills and Karen Caruso of John Wiley & Sons for their help and support.

National Business Employment Weekly and *The Wall Street Journal* are registered trademarks of Dow Jones & Company, Inc.

Published by John Wiley & Sons, Inc.

Produced by Facts That Matter, Inc.

All rights reserved. Published simultaneously in Canada.

Library of Congress Cataloging-in-Publication Data:

Krantz, Les.

The national business employment weekly jobs rated almanac/ Les   Krantz

p. cm.

ISBN 0-471-05495-X

Printed in the United States of America

10 9 8 7 6 5 4 3 2 1

CONTENTS

IN SEARCH OF PERFECTION   1

Searching for Satisfaction   2
New Career Shapes   3
Work vs. Family   4
The Bottom Line   5

CAREER CHANGING   6

The New Trend   6
Match Your Personality   8
Achieving Success   10

ENVIRONMENT AND JOB DESCRIPTIONS   12

The Environment Duality   12
Environment Factors   12
The Ranking System   13
250 Jobs Ranked by Environment Scores   14
The Lonely List   18
The Longest Work Weeks   18
250 Job Descriptions and Environment Information   19

INCOME   81

Growth Potential   81
Income Levels   82
The Ranking System   82
250 Jobs Ranked by Income Scores   83

CONTENTS

Highest Starting Pay 87

Top Bucks 87

250 Job Incomes from Starting to Top 88

OUTLOOK 127

The Four Outlook Factors 127

Graphic Symbols 128

Common Threads 128

250 Jobs Ranked by Outlook Scores 130

Jobs With the Most Employment Growth 134

Greatest Potential Income For Beginners 134

250 Job Outlooks 135

PHYSICAL DEMANDS 183

The Physical Factors 183

The Ranking System 183

250 Jobs Ranked by Physical Demands Scores 185

The White-Collar Weary 189

The Blue-Collar Sedentary 189

250 Job Demands Relating to Physical Factors 190

SECURITY 229

The Three Security Factors 229

Common Threads 230

250 Jobs Ranked by Security Scores 231

The Unemployment Line 235

CONTENTS

Lowest Unemployment 235

250 Job Security Descriptions 236

STRESS 271

The 21 Stress Factors 271

Graphics Representations 272

250 Jobs Ranked by Stress Scores 273

The Competitors 277

Clock Watchers 277

250 Job Stress Descriptions 278

EXTRAS, PERKS AND AMENITIES 320

Enumeration of Extras 322

TRAVEL OPPORTUNITIES 327

Enumeration of Travel Opportunities 329

OVERALL RANKINGS 333

250 Jobs Ranked by Cumulative Scores 333

250 Jobs Ranked Within Categories 337

Agriculture 337

The Arts 337

Athletics 337

Business/Finance 337

Communications 337

Construction Trades 338

CONTENTS

Health Care/Medicine 338

Math/Science 338

Personal Services 339

Production/Manufacturing 339

Public Sector 339

Social Sciences 340

Technical/Repair 340

Travel/Food Service 340

In Search of Perfection

How do you know when you've found the perfect job? Is it when you enjoy your work so much that you can't wait to start each day? Or when your job pays so well, you can afford many of life's luxuries? Perhaps you're dedicating your career to helping others, which brings all the fulfillment you need.

If you've reached such a high level of job satisfaction, consider yourself very lucky. The vast majority of working Americans aren't so happy. In fact, a recent national survey found that less than 30 percent say they're completely satisfied in their positions. Most admit that they'd change jobs tomorrow if given the opportunity. Labor Secretary Robert Reich admits that as baby boomers age, many find the careers they chose after college hold little attraction today.

"The baby-boom generation could create the largest midlife crisis in America's history," Reich says. "I can't tell you how many lawyers I've met who cannot stand to take one more deposition."

Unfortunately, the world is full of people who embarked on promising careers, only to discover years later that they made the wrong choice and are now profoundly unhappy. They say they're trapped by mortgage payments and tuition bills and can't afford to make a career or job change into a position they'd truly enjoy. And even if they're willing to try, many argue that the demands of learning a new field and finding a company that will hire them are too difficult to overcome. So they settle for less, do everything they can to make their weekends more fulfilling, and count the years until retirement. It's a sad way to live.

Sure, you can make fun of the situation. A good bumper sticker might help, like the one that reads, "A bad day fishing is still better than a great day at work." Or the ever-popular, "I owe, I owe, so off to work I go." You can share your woes with other unhappy commuters, or you can break away from the pack and take action.

That's what Tom Reid did, and he's never been happier.

As a sheet-metal worker in Local #25 in suburban New York, Reid enjoyed shaping structures with his hands, as well as the camaraderie he developed with fellow union members. But the lack of stability in his career was a constant worry.

"Sometimes you do well in sheet metal, and other times you're jobless for many months," Reid says. "It was very unpredictable." Rather than hang out at the union hall between jobs, Reid used the downtime to pursue his childhood hobby: Collecting baseball cards and comic character items. When funds were tight, he'd set up a table at a baseball card show on the weekend to earn a few bucks and add to his collection. But he never considered leaving his true craft.

"A lot of the sheet-metal jobs were very interesting and when I was younger, I liked the cocky, macho image of the profession," he explains. "Then, when I was out of work, I could look for collectibles."

Reid's life changed dramatically in the mid-1980s. Sheet-metal work slowed, but the collectibles field exploded. Items he'd bought for a dollar here and five dollars there, then put away, were starting to fetch hundreds.

"It was a Hollywood story," he says. "With high inflation, people were throwing money at me for the stuff I'd find. So I decided that something I loved as a kid should become my business." Reid opened a retail collectibles store in Nutley, N.J., and cashed in on the boom that followed.

Reid knew other sheet-metal workers who also collected. Why didn't they follow his lead and switch careers? Reid says fear was the greatest barrier. Most people wouldn't take a shot because they're afraid of not being able to pay the mortgage or feed their kids, even if they're unhappy with their 9-to-5 life. But unless you try, you'll never get out of your grind or be successful at something you really enjoy.

Reid also offers a philosophical perspective."You're supposed to have a steady job in this country, work 40 hours a week, then go home and cut the grass," he says. But it doesn't have to be that way if you don't want it to be. While switching careers at mid-life can be a financial risk, Reid says, "Life gets pretty boring if you don't take some risks."

Searching for Satisfaction

Whether you're a new college graduate trying to decide on a career direction, an early retiree not yet ready to leave the business world, or an unhappy mid-career-ist eager to try something new, it's critical that you research career fields to determine where your level of satisfaction will be high.

That's why the rankings in this book can be especially helpful. If you daydream about becoming an open-road truck driver because you imagine having great freedom to roam the highways and take in the sights, you'll be rudely awakened by the tight deadlines and incredibly long hours most truckers log. Or if you're fed up with the volatile corporate world and selling real estate is your idea of a stable environment, think again. Turnover among real-estate agents is sky-high, and only the savviest salespeople earn six-figure paychecks.

Both of these professions are ranked in the following pages, along with 248 other jobs. Before making a switch, however, be sure that the job you have now (or held most recently) isn't what you really want after all. Perhaps several specific aspects of your work need changing, not the job itself. A bad boss or heavier workload after a company reorganization can turn even the best position into a horrible chore that you dread waking up to each morning. A lateral transfer into another department or different company location might make the difference. Even volunteering for new duties or a new department may solve your dilemma as you're exposed to new projects and people.

To make certain a career change is truly necessary, consider the following tips offered by Dr. Don Bagin, publisher of Communications Briefings, a monthly newsletter published out of Alexandria, Va.:

- Consider what's really important. To determine your real priorities, ask yourself such questions as what you'd do if you only had six months to live, and how you'd want your obituary to read. "When considering career options, trust your gut," says Dr. Bagin.

- Think about the greater good your work does. For example, if you're in advertising, picture how the products you promote help consumers, and how the products' increased sales create jobs for people who manufacture and distribute them.

- Enjoy the process of doing your job, rather than focusing only on the outcome. Also, take time to revel in your accomplishments and take pride in the quality of your work. Remember how great you felt when you earned promotions and awards early in your career. What might you do now in your current job to generate such good feelings again?

New Career Shapes

If you're still eager to try something else after reviewing your present situation, you must think of your career in a new way before starting your search. Dr. Betsy Jaffe, president of Career Continuum, a New York City career-management consulting firm, has identified five new shapes that careers are taking in the '90s. By understanding them, you can see where you might fit in best, and develop a strategy for building on that base.

The New Classic Career. The old corporate career ladder that stretched to the executive suite is gone. Today's career ladder has fewer rungs and may lie sideways rather than point upward. To survive, let alone advance, your skills must be portable across many functions.

"Instead of looking to fill a box on an organizational chart, look for situations where you can build your repertoire of knowledge, skills and experience," Dr. Jaffe says. The key is that you must make it happen. To fare well in a large organization in the '90s, you'll need the abilities to adapt, handle a steep learning curve and play on ever-changing teams, she says.

The Concentric Career. If you imagine a bull's-eye, you'll see the basis for a concentric career. It is built on a core, such as a specific business or product line, and grows from there, Dr. Jaffe explains. Your main product or area of expertise is in the center. As you expand your product line or skills, concentric circles are added beyond the core. Typical careers in this mode include sales representative and product or service manager.

Dr. Jaffe identifies a former IBM employee in Michigan who began her second career by developing a line of home-security items, which she marketed through catalogs. As the business grew, she added guard services and home-security audits, and acted as a consultant to businesses on security issues. She expanded on her core business by weeding out financial losers and adding potential cash cows.

The Combination Career. If you enjoy variety and yearn for the chance to balance lots of very different jobs simultaneously, then you're ready for a combination career. While your resume may look like a hodge-podge of activities, you can vary your workload and keep boredom at bay.

Professional temps, freelancers, consultants, and interim executives are good examples of people with combination careers, but perhaps the best examples are spouses of executives who frequently relocate. They become accustomed to taking part-time jobs, volunteering, and starting small businesses, all of which require a degree of self-promotion.

Of course, having a combination career is easier when there's another source of family income and health-care coverage, but it's not mandatory if you know how to hustle while balancing family demands.

The Contingency Career. The typical contingency career resembles the broken lines on a highway, says Dr. Jaffe, because it's full of stopgaps and backtracks to earn money while hoping to get a break doing what you love. We've all heard about actors and musicians who wait tables and work in bookstores while auditioning and building a portfolio. Now many white-collar professionals are doing it, too, before making a major career change.

The Concurrent Career. If you can balance two completely separate careers at the same time, you're a prime candidate for a concurrent career. The obvious example is someone who holds down a full-time job while earning a college or graduate-school degree. Other examples include an art director at a Texas advertising agency who also designs and sells T-shirts to local merchants, and a bank executive who leads paid fishing expeditions in the wilds of Wisconsin every weekend.

Work vs. Family

Seeking a balance between work demands and family life may be your most important consideration when deciding whether to change careers. In fact, it could be your principal motivation for making a switch. But if you haven't yet really considered the effect your potential realignment will have on your family, you'd better start now.

You may be suffering high anxiety as you test new waters, but rest assured that your spouse and kids will be equally stressed. Even if you aren't married, friends and relatives may wonder what you're up to and how they can help. Thus, it pays to discuss your plans with people close to you before taking action.

There are many specific work/family questions you should answer when weighing new career directions. According to Stephen George, a vice president with MD Resources, a Miami-based health-care recruiting firm, the four most important are:

(1) How many hours per week do I want to work?
(2) How much do I need to earn to live comfortably?
(3) Will I be satisfied with the social status of my new company, position, and title?

(4) How complex does my new career need to be to keep me challenged?

In addition to balancing work and family demands, George suggests balancing your need for interaction with others with your desire (or lack of it) to work with technology.

Most positions either are people-oriented or technology-oriented, or include an equal share of dealing with people and technology, he says. If you relish product features and changes, then target a technology-driven industry. If you prefer dealing with people more than performing certain tasks, choose a career where you'll interact personally with others. And, if you like and are effective in both areas, he suggests considering a management position, noting that few jobs are more complicated — and challenging — than having to motivate others.

Each time Judy Koblentz of New York has considered a career change, the critical issue has been finding the right career balance between technology and people, and between her vocation and the demands of raising a son. Koblentz began as a reporter for *Forbes* magazine in Manhattan, a job she describes as "exciting, challenging and a perfect fit for my skills and talents." But after having a child, she found that trying to work a strenuous schedule and spend time with her son was impossible.

"I realized that I couldn't have it all, so I had to make choices," she says. Those included the decision to spend the following four years raising her son. She returned to the workforce slowly with a job as a freelance writer, which led to her first career change: a vice president's position at an investor relations firm.

"The job focused on making bad corporate-revenue pictures look good, and I was good at it," says Koblentz. "Plus, they agreed that child-rearing was important, so

I could work on a flex-time schedule when I needed to."

Culturally, she says, "the job was a big step from magazine journalist. But skill-wise, it really broadened the skills I already had and helped me learn new ones."

Two years later, another career shift beckoned. Koblentz was recruited to become a partner at a Manhattan public relations firm, where she spent another six years. "The firm agreed that child-rearing was important, so they allowed me to work till 5 p.m. and rarely travel," Koblentz explains. "But I never loved PR as much as journalism or parenting. A piece was missing, so I quit and spent a year trying to decide what I really wanted to do next."

Following a thorough self-assessment of her likes, dislikes, skills, and experiences, she began investigating career options with the fervor of an investigative reporter on the trail of a swindler. She networked with everyone she could, including complete strangers whose names she was given by other contacts. And she read incessantly, focusing on trade journals and magazine articles on various careers. The result of her in-depth research? She decided that the career-guidance field offered all she wanted in a perfect job.

"It's everything I've ever done wrapped up in one," she says. "You have to understand interviewing, how companies work, and how to sell yourself and your ideas to others. You even have to be a great listener, which is what you learn from parenting."

Now a vice president with Right Associates Inc., a Philadelphia-based outplacement consulting firm, Koblentz says the key to her career success was that she was always clear about her priorities and values: "You need to be prepared for your career to evolve. I picked up new skills at each step, and given how the business world continues to evolve, there's no telling where I may show up to contribute next."

The Bottom Line

When you've heard from every specialist and processed every fact, you'll find that the most important issue when deciding to change careers doesn't involve a market basket of plans and procedures. Instead, it'll be a straightforward decision based on the type of job that would bring you the most happiness and greatest fulfillment.

As Philadelphia career consultant and author Douglas B. Richardson explains, most career changers are faced with two options. "You can bag your existing set of technical skills and acquire a new set, like the person who used to be a pharmacist but is now a CPA," he says. "Or, you can bag your old set of technical skills and redefine yourself in terms of your transferable abilities," such as the writer who moved from a brokerage firm to a movie studio. In either case, Richardson says, old stereotypes don't apply anymore, and the job market will be forced to look at you through new eyes.

Career Changing

When Wendell Hall was asked to relocate for the 13th time in 31 years, he realized how demanding and unfulfilling his corporate life had become.

As a vice president of operations for General Motors Acceptance Corp., Hall oversaw lending activities among GM dealers throughout the western United States. The job required a good deal of travel and, at age 55, another transfer — this time from northern New Jersey to Detroit.

"I wasn't willing to do that again, so I left," Hall says.

Hall accepted an early-retirement offer, then wasted little time before launching what he considers his second career. "During all those moves, I always liked buying and selling homes," he explains. "It's a hell of an interesting business, so I decided to give it a try."

Hall completed a real-estate course and earned his license in less than a month, then signed on with a local realtor as a sales associate. How did he manage such a major change — from corporate bigwig to lowly sales associate? Hall says that taking a complete inventory of his strengths and having a strong motivation to succeed were key ingredients. Now, 10 years later, he co-owns a multisite brokerage firm, Prudential Lambert Real Estate Inc., based in Oakland, N.J. The firm employs dozens of sales associates.

"I enjoy working with people, and that's the greatest similarity between the two careers," Hall says. "In both, it's important to build trust and mutual respect with others, which I like doing." Hall adds that if he were an engineer or scientist who enjoyed working alone, "real estate wouldn't be a good career choice."

How he earns a paycheck is one of the biggest differences between Hall's two careers, and it reveals a source of his strong motivation. "In a corporation, you're paid a salary whether you have a good year or not," he notes, "so some people lay back on the oars if they want to. In real estate, everything is on commission, so you've got a real incentive to do well. If you're not a self-starter, you won't earn any income."

Inevitably, there are trade-offs. "What I really miss most about corporate life is that I have to do my own photocopying," Hall says with a laugh.

The New Trend

It seems everyone is changing careers these days. Teachers become stockbrokers. Airline pilots buy fast-food franchises. Middle managers learn to write software programs and sell them at trade shows. The litany goes on, and for good reason: There's no excuse for sticking with a career that you no longer enjoy or aren't good at anymore—or one that has been taken away from you.

The massive restructuring of Corporate America has hastened this trend. Companies are eliminating entire layers of management, as well as whole departments. As a result, long-tenured employees from all levels find themselves thrust into a volatile job market.

6

Some of these displaced workers are so eager to find new corporate homes that they're squeezing themselves into restrictive job requirements just to earn paychecks. However, many more are putting a positive spin on the situation. They see it as a chance to launch more meaningful, exciting, and potentially challenging careers.

Of course, choosing which career to try next often isn't an easy process, whether you're 25 or 65. Some laid-off workers have second jobs that can be expanded to fill their now-available time, but most find themselves at loose ends. However, understanding the process makes selecting a new career direction less difficult, and more rewarding.

"If you're conducting a fundamental career reappraisal, you must pay attention to three distinct areas of inquiry," says career consultant Doug Richardson in Philadelphia. Those areas are:

1) What am I capable of doing?

2) What am I temperamentally suited to do?

3) What will the world let me do, given what I've done before?

This last point often is ignored by idealistic or highly motivated career changers," says Richardson, who has worn many occupational hats in his career, including lawyer, headhunter, and outplacement executive. "They overlook the fact that their future career options are dramatically limited by past choices."

Richardson says that overcoming other people's stereotypes of what you're capable of achieving will probably be the biggest obstacle you'll face as you attempt to change careers. It's easy for potential employers to hire known quantities: A tax accountant at an automobile dealership can probably handle the taxes for a nursing home without much difficulty. But would he succeed as an emergency medical technician? And would any ambulance company give him a chance to try?

Perhaps the best way to boost your odds in a new career field is to research it so thoroughly before making your entry that you know as much about it as people who have been in the field for years. That approach worked well for Gary Blum, a financial planner in Los Angeles. Blum, a lawyer by training, spent four years trading options on the Chicago Board Options Exchange, and he saw an opportunity to enter a new career just as demand was growing.

"I could see lots of people gathering lots of wealth at young ages but not knowing what to do with that money," he says. "They needed financial counseling, especially in regard to tax issues."

Blum didn't know very much about financial consulting or estate planning, but from his law-school days he did know how to learn, so he started cramming. He attended multiple seminars and read every book he could find on both subjects. Then he did lots of networking, which included several informational interviews—meetings with people primarily to pick their brains about a specific career field, and to gather names of others who can help.

Blum's career shift was complicated by his decision to move to California from the Midwest with his wife and infant child without having a job lined up. Nevertheless, it wasn't long before he convinced a financial-planning firm to take a chance on him to handle legal duties, with the understanding that he'd quickly move into estate planning, which he did. After two years, Blum rounded up a group of clients and went solo. He now teaches a course in estate planning in addition to working on his consulting practice.

"Its important to keep your eyes open to all possibilities and expect the unexpected," Blum says. "Determine what potential problems are out there, and what you can do to help solve them. Then you'll create a career based on consumer demand for your services."

Researching the market is critical at this stage, and there's no better source for help than your local public or university library. Paula Azar, a reference librarian with the Providence, R.I., public library system, says many reference librarians get their greatest satisfaction from helping career changers explore new job possibilities.

Once you decide on a career direction and are ready to identify companies that may hire you in that field, the best sources for information are three directories that are carried by practically every library worth its salt. Azar notes that these directories provide detailed company data, such as addresses, telephone and fax numbers for each division and many departments, data on number of employees, annual sales (sometimes by product or service), and the names of key executives. They are:

- *The Career Guide, Dun's Employment Opportunities Directory*, published by Dun & Bradstreet Information Services. In addition to providing basic company facts, this guide focuses on the type of information you'll find most helpful when exploring career options. "Employers are listed alphabetically, and each entry includes a list of educational and experience specialties generally hired by the company," Azar says. "A description of present career opportunities, recruiting and hiring practices, training and career-development programs, and benefits also are included."

- *Moody's Manuals*, published by Moody's Investors Service. This eight-volume set features information from each company's annual and quarterly reports, proxy statements, and regulatory filings. It is published annually, with frequent updates, and its primary focus is on financial information, says Azar. The eight subject areas in the se-

ries include: Banking and Finance, Industrial, International, Municipal and Government, Over-the-Counter Industrial, Over-the-Counter Unlisted, Public Utilities, and Transportation.

- *Standard & Poor's Register of Corporations, Directors and Executives*, published by Standard & Poor's. This guide includes an alphabetical listing of more than 55,000 companies, of which more than 75 percent are privately owned. Since the vast majority of new U.S. jobs are being created by companies with fewer than 200 employees, this directory is an important resource. S&P has also compiled data on more than 70,000 officers, directors, trustees, and partners of the firms, including their titles, addresses, years and places of birth, and college affiliations, says Azar.

Azar notes that electronic sources of information also are widely available in libraries, including CD-ROMs and on-line databases. While you may be charged for usage, electronic services can save lots of time and offer key information not found in conventional reference materials.

Match Your Personality

Researching potential new careers and employers is critical, but it's even more important to make sure the career is a match with your personality. Many people would like to be famous entrepreneurs, but few have the ability to take risks and live with uncertainty without looking back. A job as CEO of a major company might sound ideal, but what if that position requires constant travel, separating you from your family for weeks on end? The money and benefits may be great, but would you still be willing to make the time and travel commitment, and sacrifice some family time?

There are many ways to determine whether you have the right personality for a particular job. Some work in the field on a part-time or temporary basis just to develop a feel for its pace. Others complete career-assessment tests that measure personality traits and match them against job classifications (with the help of a career counselor). Many simply have a gut feel for what they enjoy doing based on duties they've enjoying handling in the past.

That was the case for Mark Evans, 42, who has made two significant career changes in the past 15 years. He started his working life as an eighth-grade social studies teacher in upstate Bergen, N.Y., a job in which he "didn't have a happy day in two years."

Desperate to find a career better suited to his skills, Evans completed a free series of skills and personality assessment tests at a local community college. The results told him he'd make a great librarian. Evans enrolled in a one-year Master's program in the field, followed by two and a half years as a library director in a nearby town.

Evans thrived in his new career—so much so that he soon was tapped to become director of the public library system for two neighboring counties. Throughout the 13 years that followed, he excelled in the public relations aspects of his job, devising unique PR campaigns and developing new customer services and revenue sources. He loved staffing a booth at state library conventions and finding new products to sell for fundraisers. However, a lack of revenues to maintain his system during the last recession proved too much for Evans to endure.

"We were swimming upstream against declining funding from the state, which made my job impossible," Evans says. His office eventually was merged with another 50 miles away. He says, "I decided that I didn't want to move or commute that far each day, so I gave notice." Evans considered joining another library system, but limited funding statewide made it clear that he'd "have to do the work of three people just to earn one salary."

Not sure which direction to head next, Evans talked with a friend in Houston, and the conversation opened his eyes to a new career direction.

"My friend had recently bought an advertising specialty company, and he asked if I'd like to be his New York state sales representative," Evans says. "I realized it would involve all the aspects of my former job that I really enjoyed, so I agreed."

Evans spent a year establishing a local office and learning how to manage a promotional products business. When sales volume wasn't enough to justify his full-time position, Evans jumped at the chance to become regional sales manager of ad specialties for a local printing and publishing company.

"This career was a natural transition for me, because I was able to build on my strong points, such as customer relations and putting out brushfires," he says. "It was also important to me that I wasn't becoming just an order-taker, but someone who matches products to client needs. I also enjoy the creative end of devising slogans and ad campaign ideas."

Evans admits he couldn't have accomplished such major career changes — either financially or emotionally — without the help of his wife, who provided moral support and a steady income as a librarian herself. "It was great to have her salary to count on while I was experimenting," he says.

In retrospect, Evans says the vocational tests and counseling he'd received 18 years ago were important to his successful transitions. "I remember the counselor saying that I should find a career where I could work closely with others, and that stuck with me."

Achieving Success

Identifying the psychological ingredients that determine your career success isn't hard. The more demanding task, according to Eugene Raudsepp, a consultant and president of Princeton Creative Research in Princeton, N.J., lies in applying those traits consistently.

"Comprehending why we succeed or fail in our jobs is important, since we can learn as much from what works as from what doesn't," he says. Raudsepp cites eight traits as being most critical to succeeding in whatever job you try. Those eight include:

- Self-confidence: The feeling that you can cope with problems, master challenges, and overcome obstacles and barriers.

- Personal esteem: What we believe we can do directly influences our actions and determines the outcomes of our plans. "A person who's convinced he's attained his career limits will stop striving," says Raudsepp.

- Persistence and perseverance: Having staying power in the face of failure is critical—frequently even more important than talent or special skills, according to Raudsepp.

- Enthusiasm: When you're enthusiastic, your perception of the number of available opportunities is much greater, as is your ability to pursue them. "Sustained, steady enthusiasm packs a powerful force that propels us towards accomplishing what we set out to do," Raudsepp explains.

- Good luck: "Luck is essentially a readiness to perceive opportunities, coupled with a willingness to take advantage of them," he says. While there's no accounting for a string of misfortunes, continuing to see the bright side will help pave the way for Lady Luck to return.

- Response to failure: If you see problems as temporary setbacks that must be overcome, you'll greatly enhance the odds that failure won't occur again soon. And if you use failure as a chance to analyze what you did wrong, you can learn from the experience.

- Be concerned, not worried: Worry creates a sense of fear that stops you from achieving your goals. Concern, on the other hand, is a realistic expectation that a problem may arise, which prompts you to prepare to handle that problem now, before it can become serious.

- Flexibility: In the volatile job market of the '90s, knowing how to shift gears quickly is a critical attribute. By welcoming change, you'll stand out from the crowd of job hunters and company managers who grasp at the status quo in hope of maintaining what they've already built for themselves. What today's workplace needs and rewards are people who can embrace the latest developments and make something out of them.

Once you've adopted most of these traits, you can effectively target jobs you'd enjoy tackling. You'll also be able to convince hiring managers that you're well-suited to handle the position, even if you've never before performed its required functions.

Take the case of Susan Holman. She says trying to match her personal traits more closely to her career interests was a primary reason she shifted gears recently. Trained as a special education teacher, Holman spent the first six years of her career instructing elementary students in the Lewisville, Texas, public school system, about 20 miles north of Dallas.

About that time, Holman developed an itch to try something new. Her brother was majoring in computer science, and so she decided to enroll in several technical courses herself. This was the early '80s, and computer technology still was in its infancy, but Holman quickly developed a love for learning about new technologies. When her courses ended, she quit her job and began searching for a training position with a major computer manufacturer. She reasoned that it would allow her to combine her love of teaching and with her newfound interest in computers.

Holman soon landed a job as a computer trainer, a position she says she truly loved. Six years later, the training field had ballooned into a billion-dollar industry, and Holman felt she needed to return to school for a Master's degree in training and development. As a part-time student who taught high school students on the side to earn a living, Holman needed four years to graduate. But her persistence and determination paid off. She's now a training instructor and documentation writer for the Dallas Independent School District, one of the nation's largest school systems.

"I had to take a pay cut and sell my house when I went back to school, but it was worth it," she says. "Where I am right now really incorporates all of my best skills and my strongest interests."

Certainly, not everyone can afford to return to college and live on a part-time income. But the alternative usually requires an even greater sacrifice. It's never too late to look at other types of jobs. Holman advises seeing the sometimes difficult moves toward a new career as learning experiences, not as steps backward, and she adds that making a career change is probably easier than you think. Don't stay someplace where you're not happy. You don't have to settle for less.

Environment and Job Descriptions

When choosing an occupation, too few aspirants ask the elementary but essential question: What will I be doing all day? Often it isn't at all what they may think. Since most of us spend more time at work than at home, other essential questions might be: What will my surroundings be like? Who will I interact with? What kind of company will employ me in this particular career field? The answers are often surprising to people who do not have the benefit of close contact with individuals in an occupation they may be considering. This chapter can help eliminate the surprises.

THE ENVIRONMENT DUALITY

Also addressed in this chapter are the physical and emotional environments in which one is likely to work. In white-collar occupations, are the settings plush offices, or do most workers find themselves forced to make do with the bare-bones essentials? In the trades or in technical fields, can you expect to work on a job site, in a factory, in a lab, or in the great outdoors? The work environment might not always be what you think, unless you've been there on a regular basis to see for yourself how things can change from day-to-day, year-to-year, or company-by- company.

A job's emotional environment cannot be as easily perceived as its physical settings. One should take into account considerations such as: What's the "feel?" Do workers in a particular field function harmoniously, or is there heated competi-

tion between workers in rival firms, or even within the same firm? Does gloom or danger hang heavy in the air? At some jobs it does, but that fact is not always obvious to outsiders, even those who are physically present to observe activities.

ENVIRONMENT FACTORS

The ranking system used to evaluate a job's environment considers and measures two basic factors of every work environment: the physical and the emotional components. For each occupation, points were assigned for any adverse working condition typically encountered in that job. Thus the greater number of points a job scores, the worse the rank; the fewer points awarded, the better the rank.

The following categories and points were used to rate the physical work environment:

The "necessary energy" component	0-5
Physical demands (crawling, stooping, bending, etc.).	0-12
Work conditions (toxic fumes, noise, etc.)	0-13
Physical environment extremes	0-10
Stamina required	0-5
Degree of confinement	0-5
TOTAL MAXIMUM POINTS	50

These categories were used to assess the emotional environment:

Degree of competitiveness	0-15
Degree of hazards personally faced*	0-10
Degree of peril faced by others	0-8
Degree of public contact	0-8
TOTAL MAXIMUM POINTS	41

* i. e. coworkers, customers including medical patients, outside stressful situations of all kinds, etc.

THE RANKING SYSTEM

The ranking system is designed so that the higher point totals reflect lower quality environments. After the raw scores are added together, they are mathematically adjusted to reflect average work-hours per week. This adjustment provides that jobs which require longer working hours than most have the point total adjusted upward on a scale that escalates proportionally with the number of hours worked.

The ranking system is designed to give slightly greater weight to the physical factors, with 50 maximum points, than emotional factors, with 41 maximum points. Therefore, jobs that have adverse emotional conditions often rank as low as those with poor physical conditions.

The most adverse physical conditions are for firefighters, who fare poorly in both the physical and emotional categories, and therefore are near the bottom of the list of environment scores. Below fireman, in last place, is President of the U.S. Although the position may seem outwardly cushy, the Presidency has such a poorly scoring emotional environment that it drags the position into dead-last on our list. Also consider the physical dangers involved; there's a reason the President is accompanied by a large contingent of Secret Service agents wherever he goes.

In contrast, statisticians enjoy the best working environment, according to the rankings. Statisticians earned a mere one point in the physical component and one in the emotional component. When adjusted for the relatively short work week (slightly less than 45 hours) the career entails, statisticans scored 89.52 in the environmental rankings. In comparison, the Presidency, with its very high scoring emotional component and grueling physical factors — including high travel, confinement, and very long hours — scored more than 3,600 points.

250 Jobs Ranked by Environment Scores

RANK		SCORE	RANK		SCORE
1	STATISTICIAN	89.52	32	ASTRONOMER	314.37
2	ACTUARY	89.72	34	JEWELER	316.40
2	MATHEMATICIAN	89.72	35	SOCIOLOGIST	318.29
4	COMPUTER SYSTEMS ANALYST	90.78	36	ELECTRICAL ENGINEER	318.92
			37	MEDICAL SECRETARY	322.24
5	HOSPITAL ADMINISTRATOR	93.14	38	PETROLEUM ENGINEER	322.42
6	HISTORIAN	136.41	38	CIVIL ENGINEER	322.42
7	SOFTWARE ENGINEER	150.00	38	NUCLEAR ENGINEER	322.42
8	ASTROLOGER	160.00	41	DIETICIAN	334.40
8	TYPIST/WORD PROCESSOR	160.64	42	BROADCAST TECHNICIAN	351.76
			43	SET DESIGNER	354.00
10	MEDICAL RECORDS TECHNICIAN	165.20	44	ZOOLOGIST	356.72
			45	BOOKBINDER	359.20
11	INDUSTRIAL DESIGNER	177.00	46	PHYSIOLOGIST	359.28
12	METEOROLOGIST	179.64	46	URBAN/REGIONAL PLANNER	359.28
13	POSTAL INSPECTOR	195.28			
14	BOOKKEEPER	204.40	48	PHILOSOPHER	361.44
15	NEWSWRITER (RADIO/TV)	221.25	48	STENOGRAPHER/COURT REPORTER	361.44
15	TECHNICAL WRITER	221.25			
17	ARCHITECTURAL DRAFTER	222.95	50	MEDICAL TECHNOLOGIST	371.70
			50	OPTICIAN	371.70
18	ECONOMIST	227.35	52	PAROLE OFFICER	381.06
19	INSURANCE UNDERWRITER	228.10	53	LIBRARIAN	385.20
			54	BANK OFFICER	390.56
20	AEROSPACE ENGINEER	230.30	55	FLORIST	398.25
20	INDUSTRIAL ENGINEER	230.30	56	PHOTOGRAPHIC PROCESS WORKER	404.10
22	PURCHASING AGENT	230.85			
23	MUSICAL INSTRUMENT REPAIRER	234.70	56	DENTAL LABORATORY TECHNICIAN	404.10
24	FILE CLERK	248.22	58	INDUSTRIAL MACHINE REPAIRER	422.46
25	PARALEGAL ASSISTANT	263.82			
26	LITHOGRAPHER/ PHOTOENGRAVER	264.54	59	MUSEUM CURATOR	428.00
			60	SCHOOL PRINCIPAL	432.99
27	COMPUTER PROGRAMMER	265.08	61	COMPOSITOR/ TYPESETTER	440.90
28	PHYSICIST	269.46	62	CARTOONIST	442.50
29	MOTION PICTURE EDITOR	274.68	63	CHEMIST	449.10
30	ACCOUNTANT	276.78	63	GEOLOGIST	449.10
31	MECHANICAL ENGINEER	278.46	63	TAX EXAMINER/ COLLECTOR	449.10
32	BIOLOGIST	314.37			

RANK		SCORE	RANK		SCORE
66	HOME ECONOMIST	451.80	101	DENTAL HYGIENIST	593.25
67	MEDICAL LABORATORY TECHNICIAN	454.30	102	CASHIER	595.36
68	FORKLIFT OPERATOR	454.50	103	SHOE MAKER/REPAIRER	597.24
69	AUDIOLOGIST	463.43	104	APPLIANCE REPAIRER	610.22
69	SPEECH PATHOLOGIST	463.43	104	COMPUTER SERVICE TECHNICIAN	610.22
71	VENDING MACHINE REPAIRER	469.40	104	COMMUNICATIONS EQUIPMENT MECHANIC	610.22
72	COMPUTER OPERATOR	477.73	107	OFFICE MACHINE REPAIRER	611.91
73	SECRETARY	483.36	108	PROTESTANT MINISTER	626.52
74	PUBLICATION EDITOR	486.75	109	HEATING/REFRIGERATION MECHANIC	633.50
75	ARTIST (FINE ART)	486.75	110	PRECISION ASSEMBLER	639.45
76	JANITOR	489.60	110	AUTOMOBILE ASSEMBLER	639.45
77	ENGINEERING TECHNICIAN	493.79	112	BANK TELLER	642.56
78	AGRICULTURAL SCIENTIST	494.01	113	JUDGE (FEDERAL)	655.98
79	ANTHROPOLOGIST	500.17	114	TELEPHONE INSTALLER/ REPAIRER	657.16
79	POLITICAL SCIENTIST	500.17	114	ELECTRICAL EQUIPMENT REPAIRER	657.16
81	ELECTRICAL TECHNICIAN	502.26	116	PHOTOGRAPHER	663.75
82	FURNITURE UPHOLSTERER	504.36	117	RECEPTIONIST	665.21
83	OCCUPATIONAL THERAPIST	505.56	118	COOK/CHEF	666.06
84	SHIPPING/RECEIVING CLERK	520.32	119	AUTOMOBILE BODY REPAIRER	669.90
85	CATHOLIC PRIEST	522.10	120	CONSERVATIONIST	673.65
85	RABBI	522.10	121	MAID	682.02
87	ARTIST (COMMERCIAL)	531.00	122	WAITER/WAITRESS	687.42
88	OPTOMETRIST	538.34	123	AGENCY DIRECTOR (NONPROFIT)	700.00
89	OCCUPATIONAL SAFETY/ HEALTH INSPECTOR	538.92	124	DRESSMAKER	704.31
90	ARCHAEOLOGIST	545.64	125	TEACHER	709.60
91	TEACHER'S AIDE	546.78	126	PHYSICAL THERAPIST	716.21
92	TICKET AGENT	547.82	127	TELEPHONE OPERATOR	719.82
93	FINANCIAL PLANNER	550.00	128	MILITARY (WARRANT OFFICER)	720.00
94	SOCIAL WORKER	550.42	128	EXECUTIVE SEARCH CONSULTANT	720.00
95	VOCATIONAL COUNSELOR	556.40	130	PSYCHOLOGIST	727.52
96	PIANO TUNER	563.28	131	DRILL-PRESS OPERATOR	728.32
97	BARBER	575.12	132	SEWAGE PLANT OPERATOR	734.24
98	COSMETOLOGIST	581.14			
99	OCEANOGRAPHER	583.83			
100	CHIROPRACTOR	587.28			

RANK	SCORE	RANK	SCORE
133 PERSONNEL RECRUITER	737.85	169 CARPENTER	973.36
134 TOOL-AND-DIE MAKER	740.55	170 DRYWALL APPLICATOR/ FINISHER	973.94
135 AUTHOR (BOOKS)	752.25	171 VETERINARIAN	978.80
136 MACHINE TOOL OPERATOR	753.10	172 AIRCRAFT MECHANIC	981.20
137 MACHINIST	756.80	173 BUTCHER	987.80
138 MILITARY (COMMISSIONED OFFICER)	760.00	174 ADVERTISING ACCOUNT EXECUTIVE	1010.10
139 ANTIQUE DEALER	765.00	175 UNDERTAKER	1015.40
140 PODIATRIST	783.04	176 NURSE (REGISTERED)	1018.75
141 PHARMACIST	788.64	177 PAINTER	1034.02
142 BARTENDER	796.74	178 STATIONARY ENGINEER	1055.47
143 CARPET INSTALLER	796.86	179 DISK JOCKEY	1062.00
143 GLAZIER	796.86	180 AIRPLANE PILOT	1064.16
145 FLIGHT ATTENDANT	803.00	181 BOILERMAKER	1079.62
146 HOTEL MANAGER	807.12	182 NURSE (LICENSED PRACTICAL)	1080.00
147 GUARD	812.06	183 STEVEDORE	1084.59
148 NUCLEAR PLANT DECONTAMINATION TECHNICIAN	821.88	184 INSURANCE AGENT	1085.52
		185 AUTOMOBILE MECHANIC	1100.55
149 RAILROAD CONDUCTOR	830.28	186 CHOREOGRAPHER	1106.25
150 PLUMBER	836.38	186 REPORTER (NEWSPAPER)	1106.25
151 SALESPERSON (RETAIL)	836.43	188 BUYER	1108.08
152 ELECTRICIAN	855.76	189 DENTIST	1119.75
153 MARKET RESEARCH ANALYST	863.93	190 BUS DRIVER	1124.48
		191 METER READER	1127.36
154 DISHWASHER	868.32	192 TRAVEL AGENT	1134.77
155 NURSE'S AIDE	872.96	193 CONGRESSPERSON/ SENATOR	1135.42
156 RESPIRATORY THERAPIST	884.73		
157 RECREATION WORKER	889.14	194 CONSTRUCTION MACHINERY OPERATOR	1136.25
158 CONSTRUCTION FOREMAN	923.21	195 AUTOMOBILE PAINTER	1148.40
159 NEWSCASTER	929.25	196 MUSICIAN	1150.50
159 FASHION DESIGNER	929.25	197 BRICKLAYER	1151.02
161 PLASTERER	929.67	198 STOCKBROKER	1155.75
162 SPORTS INSTRUCTOR	931.48	199 BASEBALL UMPIRE (MAJOR LEAGUE)	1170.00
163 ORTHODONTIST	940.59		
164 CHAUFFEUR	945.80	200 MILLWRIGHT	1173.50
165 CHILD CARE WORKER	947.25	201 WELDER	1180.14
166 COLLEGE PROFESSOR	948.78	202 SINGER	1194.75
167 SURVEYOR	956.97	203 ARCHITECT	1195.00
168 TRUCK DRIVER	968.20	204 MAYOR	1212.57

RANK	SCORE	RANK	SCORE
205 SYMPHONY CONDUCTOR	1239.00	227 DAIRY FARMER	1474.48
206 AIR TRAFFIC CONTROLLER	1241.52	228 ROOFER	1481.20
207 PUBLIC RELATIONS EXECUTIVE	1247.13	229 CORPORATE EXECUTIVE (SENIOR)	1540.00
208 ATTORNEY	1261.50	230 CONSTRUCTION WORKER (LABORER)	1555.85
209 FARMER	1263.84	231 BASKETBALL COACH (NCAA)	1572.12
210 SHEET METAL WORKER	1266.14	232 IRONWORKER	1593.72
211 MILITARY (ENLISTED PERSON)	1280.00	233 EMERGENCY MEDICAL TECHNICIAN	1610.70
212 ADVERTISING SALESPERSON	1293.57	234 COWBOY	1615.79
212 REAL ESTATE AGENT	1293.57	235 FISHERMAN	1640.21
214 SALES REPRESENTATIVE (WHOLESALE)	1293.84	236 CORRECTION OFFICER	1646.75
215 PHYSICIAN ASSISTANT	1295.80	237 SEAMAN	1660.56
216 PHOTOJOURNALIST	1327.50	238 DANCER	1725.75
217 GARBAGE COLLECTOR	1368.32	239 ROUSTABOUT	1731.45
218 ACTOR	1371.75	240 HIGHWAY PATROL OFFICER	1733.40
219 BASKETBALL PLAYER (NBA)	1380.00	241 LUMBERJACK	1817.53
220 AUTOMOBILE SALESPERSON	1389.39	242 POLICE OFFICER	1877.85
221 PSYCHIATRIST	1417.00	243 SURGEON	1962.00
222 FASHION MODEL	1450.10	244 JOCKEY	2079.75
223 MAIL CARRIER	1461.24	245 ASTRONAUT	2270.84
224 BASEBALL PLAYER (MAJOR LEAGUE)	1470.00	246 TAXI DRIVER	2317.21
225 OSTEOPATH	1471.50	247 FOOTBALL PLAYER (NFL)	2401.85
225 PHYSICIAN (GENERAL PRACTICE)	1471.50	248 RACE CAR DRIVER (INDY CLASS)	2522.25
		249 FIREFIGHTER	3314.03
		250 PRESIDENT (U.S.)	3630.00

THE LONELY LIST

Some jobs, such as that of cashiers or taxi drivers, are confining, but workers at least have the opportunity to interact with people. Other jobs are downright lonely; that is, workers are not only confined, but they have little or no contact with the outside world. Below is a list of those jobs, the loneliest ones of them all. At right of the job title is its "Environment" rank.

Job	Rank	Job	Rank
AUTHOR (BOOKS)	135	DRILL-PRESS OPERATOR	131
AUTOMOBILE ASSEMBLER	110	GUARD	147
AUTOMOBILE PAINTER	195	MACHINE TOOL OPERATOR	136
CARTOONIST	62	MACHINIST	137
COMPUTER OPERATOR	72	MEDICAL LABORATORY TECHNICIAN	67
COMPUTER PROGRAMMER	27		
COOK/CHEF	118	PHOTOGRAPHIC PROCESS WORKER	56
DENTAL LABORATORY TECHNICIAN	56	PRECISION ASSEMBLER	110
DISHWASHER	154	SHOE MAKER/REPAIRER	103
DISK JOCKEY	179	SOFTWARE ENGINEER	7
DRESSMAKER	124	TOOL-AND-DIE MAKER	134

THE LONGEST WORK WEEKS

Some say the myth that hard work pays has been exposed long ago. Statistics, however tell us the contrary. The majority of jobs below, the ones at which workers are most likely to burn the most midnight oil, are among the highest paying.

	Hours Wkly.		Hours Wkly.
PRESIDENT (U.S.)	65.00	JUDGE, FEDERAL	50.00
FIREFIGHTER	55.00	ATTORNEY	50.00
CORPORATE EXECUTIVE (SENIOR)	55.00	SOFTWARE ENGINEER	50.00
		FINANCIAL PLANNER	50.00
PSYCHIATRIST	55.00	AGENCY DIRECTOR (NONPROFIT)	50.00
OSTEOPATH	55.00		
PHYSICIAN (GENERAL PRACTICE)	55.00	ROUSTABOUT	50.00
		PHARMACIST	50.00
RABBI	55.00	PERSONNEL RECRUITER	50.00
SURGEON	55.00	OPTOMETRIST	50.00
FARMER	52.50	CHIROPRACTOR	50.00
DAIRY FARMER	52.50	PODIATRIST	50.00
CATHOLIC PRIEST	52.50	VETERINARIAN	50.00
PROTESTANT MINISTER	52.50	RAILROAD CONDUCTOR	50.00
UNDERTAKER	50.00	SEAMAN	50.00

ACCOUNTANT

Ranking: 30

Score: 276.78

Hours Weekly: 45

Duties: Preparing and analyzing financial reports to assist managers in business, industry and government.

Employers are businesses, industry, federal, state, and local governments, and colleges and universities. Approximately one-tenth of all accountants are self-employed. Many accountants assist organizations by ordering financial data to facilitate sound business practices by managers. Others advise clients as to the advisability of certain investments, and may make recommendations about efficiency and compliance with laws and government regulations. Accountants work indoors, usually at a desk, and rely increasingly on computers to organize financial reports and prepare income tax returns. Although most accountants work forty-hour weeks, long hours during tax seasons are common in this profession. Heavy pressures, particularly at these times of the year, can be extremely stressful; patience, a good attention span, and an eye for detail are very important in this field. Because so many people trust and rely upon accountants for the soundness of their recommendations, integrity is also critical. Beginning accountants usually work under the direction of supervisors or managers.

ACTOR

Ranking: 218

Score: 1,371.75

Hours Weekly: 45

Duties: Entertains, informs, and instructs audiences by interpreting dramatic roles on stage, film, television, or radio.

Actors and actresses may be self-employed or under contract to a television or movie studio. They communicate feelings and moods through facial expressions, speech, or physical gestures. This career requires a great deal of self-discipline and patience; relatively few individuals achieve professional renown and the great financial remuneration that some more visible members of the profession possess. Because the work is frequently unsteady, many actors and actresses often find themselves out of work. During these times, they fall back on a variety of odd jobs, including waiting tables, or retail sales. Physical stamina is necessary for actors and actresses; they must often work outside in uncomfortable weather conditions, or in hot studios under glaring lights.

Twelve to fourteen hour days are not uncommon for those working on television serials. Frequent contacts of actors and actresses include agents, script managers, casting directors, and producers.

ACTUARY

Ranking: 2

Score: 89.72

Hours Weekly: 45

Duties: Interprets statistics to determine probabilities of accidents, sickness, and death, and loss of property from theft and natural disasters.

Most actuaries are employed by insurance companies in large cities throughout the United States. Government agencies and private organizations also employ actuaries to work on pension and welfare plans. Actuaries use information they assemble to calculate expected losses through personal injury or disability, or material loss by fire or other natural hazards. They use data to insure claim coverage, and ensure a profitable yet competitive edge for their employers. Actuaries work in offices and use computers and charts to assist in calculations. Work weeks consist of approximately 45 hours, except during busy periods. Inactivity and pressure of deadlines are common to this profession. Contacts include statisticians and insurance sales personnel.

ADVERTISING ACCOUNT EXECUTIVE

Ranking: 174

Score: 1,010.10

Hours Weekly: 47.5

Duties: Negotiates to procure accounts, and supervises advertising campaigns for products, companies, and organizations.

Advertising account executives are employed by advertising agencies and companies of all sizes. Most large ad agencies servicing national accounts are located in major cities. Account executives coordinate all aspects of an advertising campaign, from bringing in new accounts, through implementation of advertising ideas, to the purchasing of air time and ad space. Account executives work with clients, copywriters, and artists to develop marketing strategies for products, services, and corporate images. Account executives make periodic presentations to clients for approval of specific ideas and advertising concepts. The environment in advertising is fast-paced and high-pressured. Overtime may be required to meet deadlines. Imagination, creativity, and tact are all essential to success in this field.

Advertising account executives work with graphic artists, television directors, and marketing executives and top management at their clients' firms.

ADVERTISING SALESPERSON

Ranking: 212

Score: 1,293.57

Hours Weekly: 47.5

Duties: Negotiates contracts with clients for advertising in publications and on radio and television.

Some advertising salespeople are employed by newspapers, magazines, and other publications, as well as radio stations, and local, network and cable television broadcasters. A small number work for firms involved in specialty fields of advertising, such as selling space on billboards and airplane banners. Advertising sales representatives generate income for media outlets through the sale of ad space or airtime. They collect ad material from advertisers, negotiate rates and contracts, and work with editors to schedule advertisements. At some publications and stations, advertisers approach sales representatives to inquire about rates and demographics, and to arrange for ad placement. Other ad salespeople spend long hours on the phone and in meetings with potential clients. Ad salespeople may work with clients to gear advertising strategies toward particular readers or audience. This can be a fast-paced, hectic profession. Ad sales workers are often under extreme pressure to meet publication deadlines and sales quotas. Members of this profession work closely with advertising account executives, as well as editors, station managers, and graphic artists.

AEROSPACE ENGINEER

Ranking: 20

Score: 230.30

Hours Weekly: 45

Duties: Designs, develops, and tests new technologies concerned with the manufacture of commercial and military aircraft and spacecraft.

Most aerospace engineers are employed by aircraft and space vehicle industries. Approximately one-fifth work for the agencies of the federal government, including the Department of Defense and NASA. Aerospace engineers analyze aeronautical principals to resolve problems and better adapt new designs to aircraft, missiles, and space systems. Members of this profession use computers to design and analyze data, and consultation with customers is a routine part of aero-

space engineers' jobs. Stresses of this job include working long hours to meet deadlines. Aerospace engineers commonly have contact with corporation executives and design personnel.

AGENCY DIRECTOR (NOT-PROFIT)

Ranking: 123

Score: 700.00

Hours Weekly: 50

Duties: Executive director, a title that usually goes with the job, is the public figurehead and is responsible for the public image, fundraising, and the overall day-to-day managerial responsibility of the organization.

The highly visible director's duties are somewhat vague due to the expectations of the board or supervisory committee that the director will make things happen. The agency director will project a new image, institute new programs, connect with the community, supervise staff and fund raise in cooperation with the board of directors (who frequently act in a volunteer capacity). Directors need excellent people skills, diplomacy, energy and genuine desire to work with volunteers and donors for the mission and cause of their institutions. They are highly team oriented. As the profession becomes more sophisticated the ability to work with high level community leaders as well as advanced computer systems are also increasingly important. Access to a network of colleagues and leaders in a non-profit field is a major attribute in order to keep at the forefront of this executive position. Non-profit agencies are as competitive as those in the corporate market, therefore excellent fund-raising abilities become an extraordinary asset to the individual seeking to excel in this field.

AGRICULTURAL SCIENTIST

Ranking: 78

Score: 494.01

Hours Weekly: 45

Duties: Researches methods to improve quantity and quality of yields from farm crops and livestock, and attempts to find practical solutions to problems in agriculture.

Agricultural scientists are employed primarily by local, state, and federal government, and by colleges and universities. In the private sector, agricultural researchers can find job opportunities with agricultural service firms and fertilizer companies. Agricultural scientists conduct laboratory and field research, and act as consultants to businesses and government. Areas of specialty in agricultural research include animal husbandry, horticulture, and entomology. In each of these fields, scientists propose specific lines of research to seek solutions to inherent agricultural problems, such as crop yield and soil conservation. Most agricultural scientists work regular hours, in either an office or a laboratory setting. Others work outdoors, under various weather conditions. Agricultural scientists regularly come in contact with farmers, veterinarians and conservationists.

AIR TRAFFIC CONTROLLERS

Ranking: 206

Score: 1,241.52

Hours Weekly: 45

Duties: Routes the flow of air traffic in and out of airports, and through stations along the way.

Air traffic controllers are employed by the federal government, and selected through the federal civil service system. They route several aircraft at any given time, and must often make quick decisions based on the activities of each plane. Controllers also alert pilots about adverse weather conditions and other potential hazards. Air traffic controllers work a 40-hour week, but due to the constant scheduling of flights throughout the day and night, they usually rotate night and weekend shifts. In addition to strict physical and psychological testing, age limitations exist in this field. Skills such as the ability to reason abstractly, and three-dimensional spatial visualization are measured prior to employment. Controllers rely on complex navigational systems, as well as state-of-the- art communications equipment to do their jobs efficiently. Air traffic controllers usually begin as ground controllers, and advance to positions as local controller, departure controller, and arrivals controller, respectively. Frequent contacts include airline-radio operators and dispatchers.

AIRCRAFT MECHANIC

Ranking: 172

Score: 981.20

Hours Weekly: 45

Duties: Performs scheduled inspections, maintenance and repairs on commercial and private aircraft.

Over half of all aircraft mechanics work for the transportation industry, primarily for commercial airlines. About one-quarter are employed by the federal government. Others work for aircraft assembly firms, independent repair shops, and private companies that operate their own planes.

Aircraft mechanics perform routine inspections on planes following a schedule based on aircraft flying time. Mechanics examine engines, landing gear, instrumentation, and other parts and systems. Necessary maintenance, including replacing worn or defective parts, is carried out. Often, mechanics diagnose problems following pilots' reports during pre-flight checks. Aircraft mechanics use hand and power tools and precision X-ray and magnetic equipment. This work is usually performed in hangars but may take place outdoors and at airline terminals under time constraints. Mechanics lift and pull heavy loads and are exposed to noise and vibration from engines. These workers come in contact with pilots, service managers, and other airline personnel.

AIRPLANE PILOT

Ranking: 180

Score: 1,064.16

Hours Weekly: 45

Duties: Operates an aircraft to transport passengers and cargo to appointed destinations.

Three-fifths of all pilots work for the airlines. Others are employed by air freight companies and air taxi services. On large aircraft, two pilots normally make up the cockpit crew. Before departure, pilots check weather information, and plan the best route, speed and altitude. Instrumentation and equipment is checked thoroughly to insure that it functions properly. Take-off and landing require a high degree of cooperation and communication between pilot and co-pilot. During flight, pilots constantly monitor instruments, fuel consumption, and weather conditions to insure safe flight. Flying time for pilots is limited by law, and most airline pilots log approximately 80 hours in the air each month. Work schedules for pilots are irregular, and often involve layovers in cities away from home. Pilots on long domestic or international flights often suffer from jet lag. Pilots carry responsibility for the lives of passengers and crew, and this can be stressful. This profession requires extensive training and skill, physical fitness, and mental acuity. Pilots work closely with flight attendants, air traffic controllers, meteorologists, and airline executives.

ANTHROPOLOGIST

Ranking: 79

Score: 500.17

Hours Weekly: 45

Duties: Studies the social customs, language, and physical attributes of people throughout the world.

Anthropologists contribute to our understanding of the world around us by studying and analyzing the customs and values of persons from archaic, non-industrialized societies, or modern urbanized cultures. They work with educators, government officials, and world leaders to increase our understanding of our own way of life in relation to the broader range of our global environment. Anthropologists are employed by government agencies as well as colleges and universities, and work in laboratories, offices, or out in the field, collecting data and organizing research and records with the help of computers. Pressures of deadlines and tight schedules are common to members of this profession, as is adjustment to foreign cultures and climates.

ANTIQUE DEALER

Ranking: 139

Score: 765.00

Hours Weekly: 45

Duties: Provides a source for clients collecting interests within particular fields (period furniture, vintage toys or historical memorabilia, for example).

Antiques/collectibles dealers seek out and purchase antiques within their specialty and either maintain an in-store inventory of items, deal by appointment or through shows. Many dealers begin as avid collectors and opt to turn their hobbies into a business, selling what they collect, becoming acknowledged experts in their fields. Their key to continued success is thoroughly researching the market and maintaining a good customer base. Newcomers to the antiques business must stay on top of market trends by reading books, visiting museums, talking to other dealers and generally exploring the field. In addition to selling antiques, a significant proportion of a dealer's time is spent in acquiring pieces for an inventory and also maintaining a network of clients and lists of their interests and wish-lists.

APPLIANCE REPAIRER

Ranking: 104

Score: 610.22

Hours Weekly: 47.5

Duties: Performs major and routine maintenance on a variety of electrical home appliances.

Home appliance repairers—often known as service technicians, treat the ills of household machines, from refrigerators and freezers to toasters and food processors. Appliance repairers use hand tools, power tools, and schematic wiring diagrams to locate and repair faulty electrical and mechanical components. Repairers employed at large repair shops tend to be highly specialized, while workers in smaller shops are "jacks of all trades." Appliance repair shops are generally well-lighted and clean, but workers who make frequent home repair visits may be exposed to considerable dirt and dust.

ARCHEOLOGIST

Ranking: 90

Score: 545.64

Hours Weekly: 45

Duties: Studies, analyzes, and collects data based on research of ancient, often preliterate cultures.

Employed by universities and colleges, as well as government agencies, archeologists conduct research into extinct cultures. They collect and study artifacts and architectural structures uncovered by excavation to determine cultural identity and age of their subjects, and frequently specialize in a specific geographical area or time period. In addition to shovels, trowels, maps, and survey equipment, archeologists use computers to assist in recording and analyzing data. Work is done in the field, as well as in offices and laboratories. This is difficult, physically draining work which can be tedious during periods of infrequent finds. Contacts include ed-ucators and government officials.

ARCHITECT

Ranking: 203

Score: 1,195.00

Hours Weekly: 47.5

Duties: Plans and designs spaces to be constructed or remodeled according to specifications of clients.

Architects, either self-employed or working for a firm, design residential or industrial spaces. Taking into account aesthetic and utilitarian concerns, architects apply scientific and mathematical theories to plan spaces, and consider any special needs of clients when designing. Architects work in offices, usually at a desk or drafting table during the early planning stages. Consultation with clients and engineers takes place inside, while latter stages of a job often take them outdoors, where they consult with surveyors and contractors during the actual construction of a structure. Architects frequently work long hours, including nights and weekends, to complete a project before its deadline. Drafting tools and computers are among the equipment architects use; a thorough knowledge of structural materials is also a necessary tool. Architects' contacts include drafters, civil engineers, and urban planners.

ARCHITECTURAL DRAFTER

Ranking: 17

Score: 222.95

Hours Weekly: 45

Duties: Prepares drawings according to the specifications of scientists, architects, and engineers.

Engineering and architectural firms are the most frequent employers of drafters. Others in this profession work for manufacturing companies and construction, transportation, communications, and utilities industries. Work is done indoors, usually at a desk or a drafting table, using compasses, protractors, triangles, and a variety of writing implements. Drafters also use calculators and tables to help in their computations, and computer-aided design systems are becoming increasingly standard in this field. Before buildings and other materials can be constructed, designers must carefully follow the detailed specifications of the plans developed by drafters. Because of the complex nature of the work, which often involves many hours bending over a drafting table or seated before a computer, individuals in this field sometimes complain of stiffness and eyestrain. Persons just starting out as drafters usually work as junior drafters under the supervision of individuals with more experience. Contacts include engineering technicians, architectural assistants, and industry managers.

ARTIST (COMMERCIAL)

Ranking: 87

Score: 531.00

Hours Weekly: 45

Duties: Designing and/or illustrating materials to sell a product or concept to a specific audience.

Graphic artists can include medical, scientific, and fashion illustrators, cartoonists, and editorial artists. They are usually salaried employees who work in studios or offices, often at a drafting table. Designers use a variety of special pens, brushes, and other equipment to achieve a desired effect. Many graphic artists are self-employed, and may work on several different assignments according to the needs of individual clients. Free-lancers establish their own hours and working conditions, but there are often frequent lags in employment, especially until one's reputation is firmly settled and referrals are constant. Deadlines and long, irregular hours are also common to this field. Competition is strong, and the most talented individuals have the greatest chances of success. Con-

tacts include art directors, photographers, and editors.

ARTIST (FINE ART)

Ranking: 75

Score: 486.75

Hours Weekly: 45

Duties: Creates artwork, usually in the form of painting, drawing, sculpture, or related visual art mediums.

Painters use a variety of colorful substances such as acrylic and oil paints; sculptors use steel or stone and clay to create artistic images. Most fine art painters are self-employed and sell their pieces to museums, galleries and private collectors. A few are hired as artists-in-residence by museums or universities who subsidize their living expenses. Painters often endure long periods of poverty and fierce competition. They sell their pieces through art galleries or agents and rely on contacts and publicity to advance their careers. Painters become successful as their work builds a reputation and their styles become unique. Many businesses purchase paintings as investments toward the painter's future success. Contacts include art critics, gallery owners, collectors and other artists.

ASTROLOGER

Ranking: 8

Score: 160.00

Hours Weekly: 40

Duties: Attempts to divine the future and fortunes of individuals through observation of the positioning and movement of heavenly bodies.

Many astrologers are self-employed, and work as consultants. Some in this occupation work for carnivals or traveling shows. A small number have horoscopes or astrological columns in newspapers and other publications. Astrologers give advice on current and future events by observation of planets, stars and constellations. An individual's birth date places the person under the influence of particular heavenly bodies. All those born during a specific period have the same zodiacal sign, and are said to have similar fortunes and similar types of behavior. Astrologers make daily predictions and observations, called horoscopes, for each sign of the zodiac. Many people are skeptical about this ancient art, while others consult horoscopes constantly for guidance. Some astrologers may work long hours to create a good business volume, while those employed by publications work regular hours. Astrologers meet people from all walks of life. Those on publications work closely with editors.

ASTRONAUT

Ranking: 245

Score: 2,270.84

Hours Weekly: 45

Duties: Serves as a crew member on space flights, operating craft and conducting experiments in space.

U.S. astronauts are employed by the National Aeronautics and Space Administration. In the past, astronauts been drawn from the military. More recently, as crews become larger and duties are diversified, private citizens have joined the ranks of the nation's astronauts. The American manned space program currently is centered around the space shuttle. Shuttle crews consist of pilot and co-pilot, who fly the craft, and several others who are responsible for payload, cargo and experiments. In flight, astronauts place satellites into orbit, and perform classified military duties. Crew members also conduct research and experiments on the effects of weightlessness, and make meteorological observations from space. This is a hazardous profession. Mishaps during flight can endanger the lives of crew members. Astronauts undergo intense physical and psychological testing and training before being selected to serve in this profession. Astronauts work with flight support personnel, government officials, and members of the media.

ASTRONOMER

Ranking: 32

Score: 314.37

Hours Weekly: 45

Duties: Uses principles of physics and mathematics to understand the workings of the universe.

Colleges and universities, and the federal government are the largest employers of astronomers. Individuals in this profession use tools such as telescopes, radio telescopes, and sophisticated photographic equipment to assist them in research and analysis of data. Astronomers spend only a few weeks each year in actual observation of the solar system, and contrary to popular opinion, rarely look directly through a telescope due to the greater effectiveness of modern photographic and electronic equipment. Although astronomers usually work regular hours, observation takes place at night. Contacts include educators and physicists.

ATTORNEY

Ranking: 208

Score: 1,261.50

Hours Weekly: 50

Duties: Counseling clients in legal matters; using interpretation of laws and rulings to advise and represent businesses and individuals.

Lawyers are employed by industry, federal, state, and local governments, universities, and large and small law firms; most are in private practice. Attorneys apply laws to specific situations and advise their clients with regard to previous judicial rulings. Lawyers also act as executors, trustees, or guardians. Since a great deal of research is required in this profession, work involves many long hours in law libraries to prepare a case. For this reason, graduates of law schools often begin their careers as research assistants to partners in law firms. Meetings with clients take place in offices, but lawyers also spend time outside in conferences with other attorneys and in judge's chambers; contrary to popular opinion, few attorneys spend much time in courtrooms. Lawyers frequently come into contact with bankers, medical professionals, and corporate managers.

AUDIOLOGIST

Ranking: 69

Score: 463.43

Hours Weekly: 42.5

Duties: Diagnoses and treats hearing problems by attempting to discover the range, nature, and degree of hearing function.

Audiologists are usually employed by elementary and secondary schools and colleges and universities. Hospitals and nursing homes also employ audiologists to evaluate hearing disorders. Audiologists use electro-acoustical instrumentation and speech audiometers as they plan and conduct rehabilitation programs. They assist in hearing aid selection and orientation, and counsel individuals with varying degrees of hearing loss. Audiologists work indoors, in comfortable surroundings. A great degree of mental concentration is needed, and this is frequently stressful for members of this profession. Lack of progress in patients can also be frustrating. Contacts are maintained with speech pathologists, occupational therapists, and rehabilitation counselors.

AUTHOR (BOOKS)

Ranking: 135

Score: 752.25

Hours Weekly: 45

Duties: Creates fiction and non-fiction books, either on assignment from editors, or independently.

Most book authors are self-employed, and hire literary agents to acquire writing assignments and negotiate publishing contracts for them. Authors also submit unsolicited manuscripts to publishing houses in hopes of being published. Authors of fiction develop story ideas, and use imagination, creativity, and writing skills to produce short stories or novels. Non-fiction authors select a topic, or are assigned one by publishers. These writers conduct research and interviews to assemble pertinent information, and transform this information into prose, often adding personal observations to provide the reader with insight and illumination. Non-fiction books cover a wide range of topics, from academic to popular subjects. After a manuscript is completed, editors make changes, and return the manuscript to the author for final approval before publication. This process can be very lengthy. Authors set their own hours, but face pressure from publishing deadlines. Writers work closely with editors, publishers, and typists.

AUTOMOBILE ASSEMBLER

Ranking: 110

Score: 639.45

Hours Weekly: 42.5

Duties: Assembles parts or contributes to the final assembly of automobiles and trucks.

Large automotive manufacturers are the primary employers of automotive assemblers. Individuals in this profession work indoors, in vast plants. They work on subassemblies, or on the final line, assisting in the assemblage of the complete product. Most jobs require a great deal of precision, and assemblers must use a variety of automotive tools and measuring devices. Work is often repetitive, and lifting and straining can cause physical hardships. Noise, as well as frequent contact with grease and oil, accompany work in this field. Shift work, including nights and weekends, is standard in this profession. Contacts commonly include plant supervisors and managers.

AUTOMOBILE BODY REPAIRER

Ranking: 119

Score: 669.90

Hours Weekly: 47.5

Duties: Mends cosmetic and structural damage to car, truck, and bus chassis .

Automotive body repairers remove dents and creases; fill and sand rust and puncture holes; replace broken or pitted windows and windshields; straighten bent bodies and fenders; and replace irreparable body panels. Body repairers use a variety of hand, power, pneumatic, and welding tools. They generally work in well ventilated, indoor body shops, where they are frequently exposed to dust, dirt, rust, grease, and excessive noise. Body repairers often work in awkward or cramped positions, and they are sometimes required to lift heavy parts such as auto doors and quarter panels. Most repairers are employed by small, owner operated auto repair garages.

AUTOMOBILE MECHANIC

Ranking: 185

Score: 1,100.55

Hours Weekly: 47.5

Duties: Diagnoses problems with automotive vehicles, makes repairs, and performs routine maintenance.

Automotive dealers, auto repair shops, and service stations are the primary employers of automotive mechanics nationwide. Others in this occupation work for federal, state or local governments, auto rental and leasing companies, and organizations that perform in-house repairs on automotive fleets. About one in six mechanics is self-employed. Mechanics diagnose automotive troubles, using a variety of tools and instruments. Adjustments and repairs are made to problematic equipment, and damaged or worn parts are replaced. Mechanics also perform preventive maintenance, repairing or replacing parts such as belts, hoses or wires before they break down. These workers use a variety of hand and power tools, such as screwdrivers, pneumatic wrenches, jacks and hoists. Garages may be noisy, drafty and dirty. Minor cuts, bruises and burns are common in this work. Automotive mechanics regularly come in contact with auto dealers, insurance estimators, and service managers.

AUTOMOBILE PAINTER

Ranking: 195

Score: 1,148.40

Hours Weekly: 47.5

Duties: Restores by repainting damaged or time-worn finish of trucks and automobiles to bring back the original luster of these vehicles.

The majority of automotive painters are employed by auto body repair and paint shops throughout the country. Using tools such as power-sanders and spray guns, they first remove the original paint before applying primer coats. After each application of primer dries, painters sand the surface to rid it of irregularities. Finally, a sealer and the final topcoat is applied. Automotive painters work indoors, and the fumes from paints and paint-mixing can be hazardous, especially without proper ventilation. Long periods spent standing can also be uncomfortable. Contacts commonly include automotive body repairers and mechanics.

AUTOMOBILE SALESPERSON

Ranking: 220

Score: 1,389.39

Hours Weekly: 47.5

Duties: Shows and demonstrates new and used cars to prospective buyers, and negotiates prices of vehicles and service contracts.

The large majority of automotive salespersons work for automobile dealerships across the country. Some own and operate their own new or used car dealerships. When a customer enters the dealership, salespersons inquire about the type of car, van or truck the customer is looking for, and about the amount the customer is willing to spend. Salespersons then show the customer various makes, models and colors, and discuss options available on the vehicles. Salespersons accompany customers on test drives, and answer customer inquiries. Prices for vehicles are negotiated, and service contracts arranged. This profession requires knowledge of automotive products, a personable manner, and tact. Evening and weekend work is common in this field. Salespeople spend a good deal of time on their feet. Auto sales is a highly competitive field, and sales pressure can cause stress for some individuals. Automobile salespeople work with sales and service managers, and with dealership owners.

BANK OFFICER

Ranking: 54

Score: 390.56

Hours Weekly: 42.5

Duties: Oversees the successful operations by assisting in the direction of policies and procedures for a financial institution.

Employers are banks, savings and loans, and mortgage companies throughout the United States. Bank officers plan and direct financial practices, and work within an existing framework of regulations established by a board of directors. Members of this profession use computers for account information and credit histories, and frequently rely on computer systems to tie into other branch offices or the main office of the companies for which they work. Regular work weeks consisting of about 40 hours are common in this profession, although attendance at civic functions and organization meetings are often encouraged. Contacts include government officials, business executives, and attorneys.

BANK TELLER

Ranking: 112

Score: 642.56

Hours Weekly: 40

Duties: Cashing checks, making deposits and withdrawals, and handling a variety of other transactions for bank customers.

Employed by banks, savings and loans, and credit agencies, tellers perform a wide range of duties for their customers. They issue savings bonds and traveler's checks, handle loan payments, sell foreign currencies, check savings and checking balances, and add interest to accounts. Tellers use calculators, typewriters, coin machines, and computers to help facilitate their work. They work thirty- five to forty hour weeks; evening and saturday hours are often required. Workers spend most of their time standing at teller windows while servicing indoor and drive-up or walk-up customers, and many complain of the long hours on their feet, or of the routine nature of the work. However, this job can be rewarding for those individuals who enjoy talking to people and who are detail-oriented. Tellers are supervised by a teller supervisor, or a head teller, who distributes cash and money orders to each teller on a daily basis. The head teller is also responsible for assisting inexperienced employees in balancing procedures, and for maintaining an adequate central cash fund. Frequent contacts include savings officers, mortgage and consumer loan officers, and bank managers.

BARBER

Ranking: 97

Score: 575.12

Hours Weekly: 42.5

Duties: Shampoos, trims, cuts, and styles hair according to the desires of customers.

Many barbers are employed by barbershops or unisex salons. Others work for beauty salons, department stores, hospitals, and hotels, and almost two out of three barbers are self-employed. In addition to basic cuts and trims, offers of scalp treatments and shaves are common. Barbers use tools such as scissors, electric razors, and combs to improve the appearance of their customers. A great deal of time is spent standing, with arms raised to shoulder level. Contacts include wholesale distributors and cosmetologists.

BARTENDER

Ranking: 142

Score: 796.74

Hours Weekly: 37.5

Duties: Mixes and serves drinks to customers of a tavern, restaurant, or lounge.

Bartenders are employed by restaurants, hotels, and private clubs. Some work for recreation and amusement facilities. Relatively few bartenders are self-employed, and most work part-time. Individuals in this field mix and pour drinks according to established recipes, or to suit the tastes of particular customers. They are frequently responsible for keeping the bar stocked with liquor and garnishes, and for collecting payment from customers. Common contacts include waitresses and restaurant or hotel managers.

BASEBALL PLAYER (MAJOR LEAGUE)

Ranking: 224

Score: 1,470.00

Hours Weekly: 30

Duties: Bats and fields in games between major league baseball teams.

Major league baseball players are on the rosters of the teams making up the National and American Leagues. Before becoming a major leaguer, players normally spend several, often many, years in the minor leagues, where skills are refined and evaluated. Very talented players make the major leagues after tryouts in spring training. Players specialize in a particular position, in the outfield or infield, or pitching or catching. Players who combine great batting ability and fielding skills can become stars, commanding high salaries and heavy media exposure. Those who can play a number of positions are also valuable, since rosters are limited to 24 players for most of the season. Baseball players can suffer minor and major injuries, and fatigue, over the course of the season. This profession involves extensive travel. Games are played both day and night, and on weekends and holidays. In addition to team personnel, major leaguers come in contact with sportswriters, broadcasters, and fans.

BASEBALL UMPIRE (MAJOR LEAGUE)

Ranking: 199

Score: 1,170.00

Hours Weekly: 30

Duties: Referees monitor play in a major league baseball game, making judgments on pitched and batted balls, and on the legality of plays.

Major league umpires are employed by the National and American Leagues in professional baseball. In a regular-season game, four umpires are used, one behind home plate, and one located near each of the three bases. Foursomes normally work together for a series of games, and rotate positions game to game. The primary responsibility of the home plate umpire is to determine balls and strikes on pitched balls. He also keeps the pitcher supplied with new balls, rules on fair and foul batted balls, and keeps play moving. Umpires in the field make calls on plays at their respective bases, and in the outfield. Umpiring requires good eyesight and quick judgment, as well as a thorough knowledge of baseball rules. Players and managers occasionally engage umpires in heated arguments over disputed calls, and umpires are subject to jeers and taunts from fans. In important games, umpire decisions sometimes come under intense media scrutiny. This profession involves extensive travel during the baseball season. Most games are played outdoors, and weather conditions vary. In addition to players and managers, umpires regularly come in contact with league officials, and media personnel.

BASKETBALL COACH (NCAA)

Ranking: 231

Score: 1,572.12

Hours Weekly: 45

Duties: Directs player recruitment, and the practice and play of college basketball teams.

NCAA Division I basketball coaches are hired by the athletic departments of colleges with very strong intercollegiate basketball programs. Coaches take part in recruitment of players, often traveling to high schools to evaluate talent and meet with prospects. Before and during the season, coaches schedule and supervise team practices, developing individual skills of players, and molding team cooperation. In games, head and assistant coaches call offensive plays and defensive formations, and make substitutions. Strategy is adjusted as the opposition's own strategy becomes clear, and as the game unfolds. Successful basketball programs can gain exposure and revenue for colleges, and thus there may be great pressure on coaches to win. Coaching at the Division I level requires extensive travel, and schedules are often hectic. In addition to players and assistants, coaches work with athletic directors, college administrators, and the media.

BASKETBALL PLAYER (NBA)

Ranking: 219

Score: 1,380.00

Hours Weekly: 30

Duties: Plays one of five positions on teams in the National Basketball Association.

Basketball players in the NBA are part of 12-man rosters for teams that make up the National Basketball Association. NBA players normally are drafted after displaying talent on college teams. Since NBA rosters are small, very few drafted players actually are selected to the final rosters of NBA teams. Players attend practices to get in shape and prepare for games. In games, each teams places five players on the court: two guards, two forwards, and a center. Guards tend to be smaller, and are better ball-handlers and outside shooters. Forwards and centers are larger, and are responsible for scoring, rebounding, and defense close to the basket. Action during games is continuous and physical, and coaches substitute players often. The schedule of traveling and playing can be grueling over the course of the season for even the best-conditioned athletes. Injuries, especially to feet and knees, are common in this sport. NBA players regularly come in contact with team personnel, agents, and members of the media.

BIOLOGIST

Ranking: 32

Score: 314.37

Hours Weekly: 45

Duties: Studies the relationship of plants and animals to their environment.

Biological scientists are employed by colleges and universities, private research firms, hospitals, and non-profit agencies. About one-quarter work for the federal government. Biological scientists conduct research as a means of understanding living organisms. They use laboratory equipment in testing, and computers to help with statistics and in writing of reports. They are frequently specified according to their particular area of expertise; ornithologists, botanists, and zoologists are all subdivisions of biological science. While most individuals work in laboratories, where contact with dangerous chemicals is possible, others work in the field, observing and collecting data. Contacts include health professionals, farmers, and educators.

BOILERMAKER

Ranking: 181

Score: 1,079.62

Hours Weekly: 47.5

Duties: Assembles and repairs industrial vats, boilers, and tanks.

Nearly one-half of all boilermakers work for the construction industry. Others work for steel plants, railroads, petroleum refineries, and electric power companies. Boilermakers erect and maintain large tanks which hold liquids and gases used for industrial purposes. They use instruments such as gauges, compasses, and scales to make the precise measurements necessary for cutting metal parts for assembly or repair of boilers and vats. Work is frequently done in cramped, damp surroundings, or at high altitudes, and exposure to dangerous equipment makes this work hazardous at times. Contacts include mechanics and industrial equipment operators.

BOOKBINDER

Ranking: 45

Score: 359.20

Hours Weekly: 45

Duties: Participates in the assembly of books or magazines for commercial printing companies.

Some bookbinders work for libraries, small shops, or publishing companies. The majority, however, work for outside firms that contract with publishers to do commercial printing. Some bookbinders take a book through all stages of production, trimming pages, sewing signatures, and gluing covers. In large firms, workers have more specialized jobs, involving paper cutting, or running a gathering machine. This work can be physically demanding: bending, lifting, and long periods of standing amid loud noise levels is common. Contacts may include paper making machine and press operators.

BOOKKEEPER

Ranking: 14

Score: 204.40

Hours Weekly: 42.5

Duties: Maintains financial records and prepares statements of a company's income and daily operating expenses.

Most bookkeepers work for wholesale and retail firms. Others work for small businesses, hospitals, and government agencies. Members of this profession use calculators and sometimes computers to analyze and record financial transactions. Responsibilities may include payroll disbursement, billing, and interest computation. Long hours spent sitting before computer screens can cause eye strain and back discomfort, and intense concentration on details may also be stressful. Bookkeepers maintain daily contact with other office personnel, including receptionists, typists, and computer operators.

BRICKLAYER

Ranking: 197

Score: 1,151.02

Hours Weekly: 45

Duties: Erects structures such as fireplaces and walls with brick and other masonry materials.

Most bricklayers work for building, trade, and contracting firms; a smaller number are employed by government agencies, industrial plants, and businesses that do their own construction and repair work. Approximately one-quarter of all bricklayers are self-employed. Bricklayers use trowels, levels, hammers and chisels, and jointing tools to build walls and floors and to enhance the beauty of existing structures. Most of their work is done outdoors, and a great deal of time is spent standing, bending, and lifting heavy materials. Bricklayers are also subject to falling debris and injuries from tools. They are frequently assisted by hod carriers, and contact with other construction workers is common.

BROADCAST TECHNICIAN

Ranking: 42

Score: 351.76

Hours Weekly: 45

Duties: Runs and maintains the equipment used to transmit radio and television messages.

Broadcast technicians are employed by radio and television studios throughout the country. They use electronic equipment such as microphones, video and sound tape recorders, and television cameras to relay material being broadcast. Broadcasters operate equipment that regulates sound and color clarity. They also use hand signals and wear headsets to relay messages to other workers in television and radio studios. Most work is done indoors, but some technicians work outdoors, in unfavorable weather conditions. Long hours spent standing, and lifting and carrying heavy equipment is common to this profession. Contacts include disk jockeys, television announcers, and station managers.

BUS DRIVER

Ranking: 190

Score: 1,124.48

Hours Weekly: 40

Duties: Transports passengers according to a specific schedule along metropolitan and community routes.

The majority of bus drivers work for school systems or companies under contractual agreement for school bus service. Others are employed by private and local transit systems and interstate and charter bus services. In addition to transporting passengers, bus drivers collect fares and give advice about scheduling and routes. They must exercise particular caution, especially under adverse weather conditions, to insure the safety of passengers. Many drivers must report for work on extremely short notice; other problems include mental stress and fatigue. Contact is maintained with supervisors and ticket agents.

BUTCHER

Ranking: 173

Score: 987.80

Hours Weekly: 45

Duties: Preparing meat for sale to distributors, supermarket customers, and other consumers.

Approximately half of all butchers work for retail stores. Others are employed by packing houses, restaurants, and hotels. Butchers use knives, power-blades, and saws to cut and trim meat. They use trimmings to make sausages and luncheon meats. Butchers who work in food stores are frequently responsible for display of meat products in refrigerated cases. They also answer questions and prepare special cuts according to the request of customers. Butchers spend much of their time standing in refrigerated rooms designed to prevent spoilage. Injuries from sharp tools are common in this profession, and the work is often physically draining. Contacts include supermarket personnel and wholesale distributors.

BUYER

Ranking: 188

Score: 1,108.08

Hours Weekly: 45

Duties: Orders merchandise and maintains inventory control for wholesale and retail sales firms.

Approximately two-thirds of all buyers work for retail establishments. Retail buyers purchase merchandise from wholesale firms or from the manufacturer for resale to directly to consumers. Wholesale buyers purchase goods from other wholesalers or from manufacturers for sale to retail or commercial establishments. Buyers rely heavily on the use of computers to facilitate inventory control and to assist in the selection of goods. Long hours, frequently including evenings and weekends, are common. To undergo the rigor of this highly competitive field, intense concentration and patience are necessary. Contacts include store executives, and advertising and sales personnel.

CARPENTER

Ranking: 169

Score: 973.36

Hours Weekly: 42.5

Duties: Assists in the construction, repairing, and remodeling of buildings and other structures.

Contractors are the largest employers of carpenters; others in this profession work for government agencies, utility companies, and manufacturing firms. Approximately one-third of all carpenters are self-employed. Workers' responsibilities vary according the needs of their employers. Some individuals frame houses and install doors and woodwork; others pour forms for concrete construction, erect scaffolding, and install flooring. Some industries employ carpenters to assist in the manufacture of pre-fab houses and furniture. Although duties vary, all carpenters must follow a blueprint and, using a variety of special tools, such as levels, planes, saws, and drills, take measurements and perform jobs as stipulated in the original plan. Work can be done indoors or outdoors, and adverse weather can be an unpleasant aspect of this career. The work is frequently strenuous; long periods standing, bending, and kneeling are common in this field.

Misuse of sharp tools and power equipment can cause injury to workers. Carpentry supervisors oversee the work of carpenters. Contacts include bricklayers, electricians, pipe fitters, and plumbers.

CARPET/TILE INSTALLER

Ranking: 143

Score: 796.86

Hours Weekly: 45

Duties: Lays tile or carpets in homes and businesses.

Over one-half of all carpet installers are self-employed; others work for carpet flooring contractors throughout the country. After inspecting the floor to determine its condition, installers plan the layout of carpeting in consideration of traffic patterns and unsightly seams. They then tack a foam pad on the floor before laying the carpet. Installers must first measure and cut the carpet, allowing for extra carpet on each side. Sections must also be joined in some rooms, and workers use large needles and special thread or heat-seam tapes and irons to unite pieces of carpet. Installers use a variety of other tools, including hammers, drills, and staple guns in their work. This job takes place indoors, under more comfortable conditions than most construction work. The hours are usually regular, however special circumstances might call for evening or weekend hours. Some individuals complain of the physical discomfort of this job; a great deal of kneeling, bending, and lifting is necessary. Minor injuries, such as cuts and burns can also accompany this work. Supervisors or installation managers oversee the work of carpet and tile installers; other contacts include painters and business managers.

CARTOONIST

Ranking: 62

Score: 442.50

Hours Weekly: 45

Duties: Draws political cartoons and comic strips for publication in newspapers, magazines, and other periodicals.

Many syndicated cartoonists are employed by newspaper syndicates and major magazines. Others are self-employed, and work out of private offices or studios. Political cartoonists work with themes drawn from current affairs. These cartoonists attempt to convey a message, attack an issue or attitude, or express concern, through humorous or satirical drawings and captions. This requires a thorough knowledge of politics and current events, a sharp wit, imagination, and creativity. Comic strip cartoonists create daily or on-going stories, using a continuing set of characters. The work of comic strip cartoonists is normally less topical than political cartoons, and is intended mainly to humor readers. Some cartoonists work with others who create ideas, stories, and captions. This job requires artistic talent, in addition to a sense of humor. Cartoonists, like others in publishing, regularly face the pressure of publication deadlines. Cartoonists come in contact with editors, publishers, and public officials.

CASHIER

Ranking: 102

Score: 595.36

Hours Weekly: 37.5

Duties: Receives payments, makes change, and provides receipts for goods sold.

Cashiers are employed by retail establishments such as food stores, restaurants, department stores, and gas stations. Responsibilities of cashiers depend on the needs of their employers; some workers answer telephone inquiries, arrange displays, and mark merchandise in addition to performing other cashiering duties. Cashiers use sophisticated machinery including scanners and computerized cash registers. They may also use adding machines to assist in payment calculations and balancing procedures. Problems include long hours standing in small spaces, and extremes in temperature while working near doors in the summer and winter. Contacts include store managers and sales personnel.

CATHOLIC PRIEST

Ranking: 85

Score: 522.10

Hours Weekly: 52.5

Duties: Attends to spiritual, moral and educational needs of Catholic church members.

Priests serve in cities and towns across the country. Positions in this field are especially concentrated in major cities with large Catholic populations. Priests prepare and deliver sermons, administer the sacraments, preside at weddings and funerals, comfort the sick, and counsel those in need of help or spiritual guidance. Diocesan or secular priests serve in parishes designated by bishops, while religious priests are members of particular orders, such as the Jesuits or Franciscans. In addition to serving parishioners, priests may teach in seminaries, perform missionary work, or work with community and charitable organizations. Priests take vows of poverty, and their expenses, food, and clothing are provided by the Church. Strong religious faith is a fundamental necessity in this line of work, as is compassion and understanding. The ability to communicate effectively with people of all ages and types is essential. Priests work closely with church and community leaders, and with administrators of charitable organizations.

CHAUFFEUR

Ranking: 164

Score: 945.80

Hours Weekly: 47.5

Duties: Drives limousines or other vehicles to transport passengers to and from specified locations.

Chauffeurs are employed by livery services, the government, and private individuals. Many livery companies specialize in airport transportation. Chauffeurs for these companies operate limousines or vans along selected routes, making stops by request to pick up and drop off passengers. These drivers may also collect fares from passengers. Other chauffeurs for livery services drive hired limousines for weddings, funerals, parades, and other social occasions. Many high-ranking government officials use limousines for basic transportation. Chauffeurs employed by private individuals may have other responsibilities, including domestic chores, and may be on call at irregular hours. Chauffeurs must have excellent driving skills, and must be able to cope with stressful situations, such as heavy traffic or hectic schedules. Interpersonal skills and tact are needed in this profession. Limousine passengers may include corporate executives, entertainment personalities, and foreign diplomats.

CHEMIST

Ranking: 63

Score: 449.10

Hours Weekly: 45

Duties: Develops substances through research of properties and composition; assists industry and individuals by study of chemical structures of products.

Private industry, state and federal governments, universities, and high schools employ chemists to study and communicate the physical properties of substances. Members of this profession usually work regular hours in laboratory settings, although many chemists work in offices, where they prepare reports and analyze data. The job can be hazardous, especially when proper procedures are not followed in the handling of dangerous substances. Chemists usually specialize in a specific area of chemistry; biochemists and organic chemists are examples of these subdivisions. Most individuals work in product development, where their energies are concentrated on creating new products or improving existing ones. Some chemists are involved in inspecting those products to ensure proper usage by industrial workers. Frequent contacts include occupational safety workers and chemical engineers.

CHILD CARE WORKER

Ranking: 165

Score: 947.25

Hours Weekly: 37.5

Duties: Cares for infants and toddlers when parents are at work or are unable to do so for other reasons.

Approximately two-thirds of all child care workers are self-employed. Others work for child care centers, residential institutions, government agencies, and hospitals. Child care workers tend to the basic care of young children during their parents' absence. They provide nutritious meals, and structure play and educational activities. They also watch for physical or developmental problems so these can brought to the attention of a child's parents. Some workers have administrative duties, such as the paying bills, and program development. Child care workers should have a great deal of physical stamina; they must also remain alert at all times to avoid accidents and deal with disruptive children. Contacts may include health care professionals and administrators.

CHIROPRACTOR

Ranking: 100

Score: 587.28

Hours Weekly: 50

Duties: Treating physical problems by manipulating various parts of the body, especially the spinal column.

Chiropractors are often self-employed, or work in small chiropractic clinics. A relatively small number of individuals teach or conduct research at chiropractic colleges. Chiropractors use a variety of techniques to diagnose and treat impairments of the nervous system, which they believe to be at the root of most physical problems. They take detailed patient histories and use X-rays to determine the source of difficulties, and treat patients primarily by manual manipulation of the spinal column. Chiropractors also use water and heat massage, along with ultrasound and light therapy to relieve distress in patients. By law, they cannot prescribe surgery or drugs to their patients, but they can and do prescribe exercise, rest and proper diet to alleviate physical problems. Chiropractors work indoors, in a clean, well-lit environment. Their work weeks are about forty hours, although many work evenings and weekends to accommodate individuals who cannot visit their offices during daytime hours. The ability to work independently and keen observation skills are necessary to this profession, as are empathy and understanding.

CHOREOGRAPHER

Ranking: 186

Score: 1,106.25

Hours Weekly: 45

Duties: Instructs performers and develops and interprets routines for stage and other presentations.

Employed by dance companies and educational institutions, choreographers teach students ballet, stylized, traditional, and modern dance techniques. Individuals in this profession might also work for television and movie studios, or for community organizations. Work is frequently performed indoors, in a rehearsal studio or perhaps in a theater. To interpret and arrange new dances, choreographers use sound systems and musical instruments, such as pianos to assist them. They may also rely on movies, plays, and other dramatic presentations to provide them with inspiration for their work. Since many choreographers begin as dancers, physical stresses such as arthritis can accompany them throughout their careers. Long hours spent in rehearsal and presentation can also be very trying. Since this work is often dependent upon the favorable reviews of critics and the public, bad notices can be a tremendously stressful part of this job. Those with developed visual tastes, feeling for rhythm and music, and a strong creative sense are most likely to be successful. Frequent contacts include musicians, dance instructors, and critics.

CIVIL ENGINEER

Ranking: 38

Score: 322.42

Hours Weekly: 45

Duties: Plans and supervises the building of roads, bridges, tunnels, and buildings.

Manufacturing industries, engineering and architectural firms, management consulting companies, and federal, state, and local governments are among employers of civil engineers. They put scientific and mathematical theories to work to design and implement plans for structures which make our lives easier and more efficient. To do this, they must consider factors such as cost, safety, and reliability. Engineers are also involved in testing, operations, and maintenance of the structures they design. They may work in an office or outdoors in the supervision of a project. Others work in research labs or industrial plants. They use calculators and computer-assisted design programs to facilitate their work. Supervisory engineers are responsible for overseeing the production of entire projects. Civil engineers are frequently in close contact with managers, government officials, and other engineers.

COLLEGE PROFESSOR

Ranking: 166

Score: 948.78

Hours Weekly: 45

Duties: Instructs college and university students according to a particular area of expertise and within a prescribed curriculum.

Community colleges, private and state colleges, and universities employ professors to teach undergraduate and graduate students. In addition to teaching responsibilities, professors prepare lectures, develop and administer exams, grade papers, and stimulate class discussion. They use computers, closed-circuit television, and slides to assist in classroom presentation. At college and university levels, professors regularly conduct research; there is frequently intense pressure to publish, even in the face of conflicting teaching responsibilities. Work hours are somewhat flexible, and most faculty members work evenings and weekends to prepare classes and grade exams. Colleges professors come into contact with teaching assistants, librarians, and school administrators.

COMMUNICATIONS EQUIPMENT MECHANIC

Ranking: 104

Score: 610.22

Hours Weekly: 47.5

Duties: Installs, repairs and maintains residential and commercial phone systems.

The large majority of communications equipment mechanics work for local and long-distance telephone companies. A small number in this field are employed by cable television and related companies. Communications equipment mechanics install and repair complex telephone switching systems, working either in telephone company central offices, or on customers' premises. These workers follow circuit diagrams, blueprints and electrical plans to install wiring and telephones, and to locate trouble in communications systems. Mechanics use a variety of tools and equipment, including screwdrivers, soldering guns, and oscilloscopes. Evening and weekend work is normal in this profession, and mechanics may be on-call 24 hours a day to perform emergency repairs on communications equipment. Workers in this field are subject to electrical shocks, and to cuts from tools. Communications equipment mechanics come in contact with maintenance managers, electricians, and telephone company personnel.

COMPOSITOR/TYPESETTER

Ranking: 61

Score: 440.90

Hours Weekly: 45

Duties: Typesetters operate keyboards to prepare print to the specified column width, hyphenating and adjusting space accordingly. Compositors may lay out pages, check page proofs for errors, and make corrections as instructed by editors.

Over half of all compositors and typesetters work in newspaper or commercial printing plants. Others work for graphic design and commercial art firms, publishing companies, and other firms which do their own printing. In large printing shops and plants, compositors prepare preliminary printing plates, using linotype or monotype machines, or computerized phototypesetting systems and electronic pagination equipment. In more advanced systems, justification of text and other typesetting tasks are performed by computers, and typesetters simply enter desired specifications into the machine. Some may perform repairs on equipment. Printing shops using linotype or monotype machines may be noisy and dirty. Shift work to meet publication deadlines is common in this profession. Compositors and typesetters work closely with printers, editors and plant personnel.

COMPUTER OPERATOR

Ranking: 72

Score: 477.73

Hours Weekly: 42.5

Duties: Operates a computer according to an instruction manual, and monitors to respond to operating and error messages.

Computer operators can be found in almost any industry, but are especially prevalent in banks, insurance companies, hospitals, and government agencies. Operators run consoles and sometimes peripheral equipment. They load computers with tapes, disks, and paper, and record malfunctions in log books. Computer operators must respond to all messages displayed, locate problems, and find solutions or terminate the program. Although operators work in well-lighted, comfortable surroundings, computer noise is a constant companion. Many large computer systems operate 24 hours a day, 7 days a week, and shift work is common in this field. Contacts include computer programmers and service technicians.

COMPUTER PROGRAMMER

Ranking: 27

Score: 265.08

Hours Weekly: 45

Duties: Organizes and lists the instructions for computers to process data and solve problems in logical order.

Manufacturing firms, banks, educational institutions, and government agencies are among the employers of computer programmers. They use languages such as BASIC or COBOL to write detailed instructions for computers according to the specific needs of organizations. Programmers often insert comments so that other programmers can also work with the system. They then test the operation of the program to be sure that it is understandable and working according to the specifications of users. Frequent contacts include systems analysts and operations research analysts.

COMPUTER SERVICE TECHNICIAN

Ranking: 104

Score: 610.22

Hours Weekly: 45

Duties: Repairs malfunctions, maintains service according to manufacturers' schedules, and sometimes installs computers and peripheral equipment.

Wholesalers and computer manufacturers are the largest employers of computer service technicians. Others work for large companies that own and operate their own computer systems. Technicians consult maintenance manuals to diagnose and correct computer malfunctions. They employ a variety of hand tools, including wire-strippers, needle-nosed pliers, and soldering equipment to repair parts. Technicians are also responsible for keeping all equipment in good running order. They must frequently be on call 24 hours a day to repair breakdowns. Unless proper safety procedures are followed, small burns and electrical shocks can occur. Contacts include computer programmers and engineers.

COMPUTER SYSTEMS ANALYST

Ranking: 4

Score: 90.78

Hours Weekly: 45

Duties: Plans and develops computer systems for businesses and scientific institutions.

Many computer systems analysts are employed by durable goods manufacturers, banks, insurance companies, and government agencies. Companies hire analysts to develop computer applications for better management of their operations. After assessing the needs of a business, analysts use charts and diagrams to show managers how a particular system has been developed and what it can accomplish. Most computer systems analysts specialize in either business, engineering, or scientific applications, because of the varied and complex uses of computers. The pressure of deadlines can mean evening and weekend overtime, which is usually not compensated for except for those who provide outside services for their clients rather than working directly for the owner of the system.

CONGRESSPERSON/SENATOR

Ranking: 193

Score: 1,135.42

Hours Weekly: 45

Duties: Represents a constituency in one of the houses of Congress, introducing, debating, and voting on legislature to enact laws.

U.S. Senators are elected by the voters of a state to serve them in Washington, D.C. U.S. Representatives are elected by the voters of congressional districts. Legislators introduce bills and resolutions into debate to achieve specific legislative results, such as the creation of new laws and regulations, or to implement broad-ranging social, economic, or political policies. Legislators serve on various committees of the House and Senate, which conduct regular and special hearings on judicial matters, budget policy, foreign relations, and other topics. Work days for federal legislators are normally long, and schedules are hectic. Campaigning for office can be stressful, fatiguing, and financially draining. Members of the House and Senate meet with top-ranking business, military, and educational leaders, and with lobbyists, foreign diplomats, and members of the other branches of the government.

CONSERVATIONIST

Ranking: 120

Score: 673.65

Hours Weekly: 45

Duties: Conducts research into range problems, and manages range lands to make efficient use of livestock and wildlife without destroying their habitat.

The Department of Agriculture employs almost half of the conservationists and range managers in this country. Others work for state and local governments; a small portion are employed by private firms. Range managers study range lands to determine optimal grazing seasons and the number and kind of animals to graze. They also direct improvements such as corralling and building of water reservoirs. Some range managers plan for reseeding and plant growth in relation to environmental suitability; they also protect range lands from fire and rodent damage. Much of this work is done outdoors, frequently in uncomfortable weather conditions and in remote surroundings. Contacts include farmers, ranchers, and foresters

CONSTRUCTION FOREMAN

Ranking: 158

Score: 923.21

Hours Weekly: 50

Duties: Supervises the work of employees and ensures that equipment and materials are being used properly and effectively.

Foremen or forewomen, otherwise known as blue-collar supervisors, are employed by manufacturing, service, and construction industries. They oversee the work of employees on production lines in manufacturing plants, or outside on construction sites. Supervisors are responsible for training employees, reinforcing safety procedures, and recommending workers for promotions. Discipline of poorly performing employees and hostility of workers envious of supervisors' positions as "boss" are considered negative aspects of this job by some individuals. Most supervisors work regular 40 hour weeks, but shift work is common in this field. In companies where employees have labor unions, supervisors spend time in consultation with union representatives to discuss work problems and grievances.

CONSTRUCTION MACHINERY OPERATOR

Ranking: 194

Score: 1,136.25

Hours Weekly: 45

Duties: Operates one or more machines used in extractive or construction work.

Construction machinery operators usually work for contracting firms that specialize in construction, extractive and foundation work, or structural steel building. Some workers operate only one type of machinery; bulldozers, for example. Others run a number of construction machines, including trench excavators, tower cranes, and air compressors. Workers are classified according to the type of machine they operate. They frequently toil under extreme heat or cold, and are subject to injuries from falling debris or machinery. The shaking and jostling of some equipment can be physically draining. Construction machinery operators have regular contact with construction workers and heavy equipment mechanics.

CONSTRUCTION WORKER (LABORER)

Ranking: 230

Score: 1,555.85

Hours Weekly: 42.5

Duties: Assists construction trade workers by performing a wide variety of tasks requiring physical labor.

Construction contractors are the major employers of trades helpers, or laborers. Construction laborers' responsibilities depend on the type of construction project with which they are involved and the work they are assigned to do. Workers may dig trenches or operate machinery including cement mixers and mechanical hoists. They might also lift and carry construction materials such as wood or cement mixes and equipment to carpenters and masons. This work is done outdoors, often under adverse weather conditions, and involves a great deal of lifting, bending, and straining. Sore muscles are common after a hard day's work on a construction site. Injuries from falls, cuts, and burns are also relatively prevalent.

COOK

Ranking: 118

Score: 666.06

Hours Weekly: 40

Duties: Plans menus for restaurants or private individuals and prepares meals.

Cooks are employed by restaurants, hotels, hospitals, universities, culinary institutes, the federal government, and a variety of other establishments. A small number of cooks work for private individuals. Large restaurants have several chefs; in these establishments, the head cook supervises the work of other members of the kitchen staff, including assistant chefs and pastry chefs. Head cooks plan menus, determine meal portions, and often purchase food supplies. The degree of skill and innovation chefs display in preparing dishes plays a large role in establishing a restaurant's reputation. Talented haute cuisine cooks are in great demand among prestigious establishments. Work environments for cooks vary widely. Some kitchens may be large and uncluttered, while others are cramped, dirty, and poorly organized. Cooks spend long hours on their feet, in hot, often hectic conditions. Minor cuts and burns are common to workers in this profession. Restaurants regularly operate during evenings, weekends and holidays, and chefs may work irregular hours, including overtime during busy periods. Cooks work closely with waiters and waitresses, restaurant managers, and other food service personnel.

CORPORATE EXECUTIVE (SENIOR)

Ranking: 229

Score: 1,540.00

Hours Weekly: 55

Duties: Formulates the policies and directs the operations of private and publicly-held companies.

Senior corporate executives try to ensure that their organizations meet fundamental objectives, such as maintaining efficiency and profitability, bringing high technology into service, and competing successfully in aggressive markets. They must implement programs to keep their companies at the forefront of their industry while keeping them within budgetary constraints, doing so in conjunction with the chief executive officer (CEO), a board of directors as well as other senior level executives. The scope of their responsibility often depends upon the size of the organization. Some executives will manage operational divisions, head up new ventures, find new markets or develop new applications for their products. A senior corporate excutive will have departments under his tutelage attempt to meet their goals as quickly and economically as possible. In smaller organizations, this role is sometimes referred to

as General Manager. Coming from many backgrounds and fields all senior corporate executives need to establish successful track records with an astute understanding of finance, technology and ongoing developments in their field. Senior corporate executives work closely with their departments, and network closely with other executives. Executives are being sought in all fields and functions, with demand being the greatest for financial and technical managers.

CORRECTION OFFICER

Ranking: 236

Score: 1,646.75

Hours Weekly: 47.5

Duties: Supervises inmates' activities and enforces regulations in jails, prisons, and other correctional facilities.

Employed by federal, state, and local governments, correction officers monitor the behavior of persons who are incarcerated and awaiting trial. They supervise inmates at work, recreation, eating, and bathing, and make sure that order is maintained during all times. They also make periodic checks to assure that no individual is absent. In some institutions, correction officers help inmates adjust to incarceration, talk over personal problems which may have led to criminal behavior, and discuss ways in which inmates can avoid future transgressions following their release. Officers are supervised by correction sergeants, who oversee security maintenance in prisons and jails. Workers in many large state and federal institutions monitor activities from a central location, such as a control tower, using sophisticated technical equipment. According to their specific responsibilities, officers may work indoors or outdoors, and working conditions can vary with surroundings. Work is often stressful; noise, overcrowding, and other disagreeable conditions can be a regular part of this job. Frequent contacts include recreation leaders and probation and parole officers.

COSMETOLOGIST

Ranking: 98

Score: 581.14

Hours Weekly: 42.5

Duties: Creates hair styles, and advises clients about caring for their hair between appointments.

Almost one-half of all cosmetologists are self-employed. Others work for beauty salons, department stores, hospitals, and hotels. Some individuals teach in cosmetology schools. Also called beauty operators, hair stylists, or beauticians, cosmetologists shampoo, cut, and style hair and have as their central objective helping people look more attractive. They frequently add coloring, and do permanents or body waves to add flair to an individual's appearance. It is very important to keep current with new fashions and updates in hair treatment; cosmetologists frequently attend workshops and classes to remain knowledgeable about advances in the field. Individuals in this profession work in clean, well-ventilated and well-lit surroundings, using a variety of special tools to cut and style hair. Among the physical stresses inherent to this career are many hours spent standing with raised arms; complaints of clients dissatisfied with new hair styles can be another problem in this field. Contacts include manicurists and make-up artists, as well as beauty suppliers and store managers.

COWBOY

Ranking: 234

Score: 1,615.79

Hours Weekly: 45

Duties: Oversees the grazing and round-up of livestock and takes part in other activities on ranches.

The traditional role of the cowboy lives on today on cattle, sheep and horse ranches of various sizes in the American West and Southwest. Cowboys perform a variety of duties around the ranch and out on the range. These workers keep track of grazing animals, recover strays, round up and herd livestock into pens or corrals, and sometimes prepare animals for slaughter or shearing. In addition, cowboys monitor food and water levels on range lands, and deliver hay and water in cold weather and when levels are low. Cowboys also mend fences, perform repairs to corrals and ranch buildings, and care for equipment and their horses. In addition to riding the range on horseback, cowboys may use trucks, off-road vehicles, and even helicopters to patrol vast grazing lands. This work is strenuous and takes place in all weather conditions. Cowboys must have excellent strength and stamina, in addition to riding skills. These workers come in contact with ranchers, range managers, and livestock breeders.

DAIRY FARMER

Ranking: 227

Score: 1,474.48

Hours Weekly: 52.5

Duties: Directs and takes part in activities involved in the raising of cattle for milk production.

Dairy farmers may be self-employed operators of their own farms, or may work as farm managers on larger farms. Dairy farmers raise cattle to produce milk for consumption, and for use in dairy products, such as cheese and cream. Farm operators plan for the breeding, feeding and milking of dairy cattle. Depending on the size of the farm, a farmer may operate field machinery and milking equipment, repair and clean barns, and build fences and sheds. On larger farms, hired hands may perform these tasks. Dairy farm operators must plan for optimum yield from cattle, keep financial records, and oversee marketing activities. A good degree of business sense and financial skill is required in this profession. On large farms run by management firms, a farm manager may oversee one aspect of operations, such as feeding or milking. Dairy farmers work long hours year-round. These workers face the danger of injury from machinery, and illness from farm animals. Dairy farmers come in contact with agronomists, animal breeders, and dairy buyers.

DANCER

Ranking: 238

Score: 1,725.75

Hours Weekly: 45

Duties: Engages in stylized artistic movement, solo or as part of a group, usually to instrumental accompaniment.

Approximately half of all major dance companies in the country are located in New York City. Many other major cities, including Los Angeles, Chicago and Pittsburgh, support full-time dance troupes. Those dancers not employed full-time with companies may be employed periodically for musical shows, television productions, or other entertainment events. Dancers in classical ballet perform a traditional repertory, while modern dance allows for innovatively choreographed routines set to contemporary music. Dancers attempt to interpret and idea or story, or express rhythm and sound, through physical movement. Performers work either in groups, or solo. This profession is strenuous, and training, rehearsal and performance schedules are rigorous. Long hours are common in this profession. Some companies may go on tour for parts of the year, requiring extensive periods away from home for dancers. Members of this profession work closely with instructors, choreographers and musicians.

DENTAL HYGIENIST

Ranking: 101

Score: 593.25

Hours Weekly: 40

Duties: Assists dentists in diagnostic and therapeutic aspects of a group or private dental practice.

Most dental hygienists are employed by private dental offices. Others work for schools, hospitals, clinics, and public health agencies. Hygienists are licensed to clean teeth by removing deposits and stains through use of rotating brushes, rubber caps, and cleaning compounds. Hygienists also take medical and dental histories, operate X-ray equipment and develop films, and instruct patients about proper practice of oral hygiene. Some hygienists remove sutures and administer anesthesia to patients. Exposure to infections through patient contact can be hazardous. Dental hygienists come into contact with dental assistants, educators, and medical personnel, depending on their place of employment.

DENTAL LABORATORY TECHNICIAN

Ranking: 56

Score: 404.10

Hours Weekly: 45

Duties: Makes and repairs dentures, crowns, and orthodontic devices.

Dental laboratory technicians work for commercial dental laboratories, dentists' offices, hospitals and federal agencies. Approximately one of five technicians is self-employed. Dental laboratory technicians use hand tools, molding equipment, bunsen burners, and bench fabricating machines to fabricate and repair dental appliances according to written prescriptions of dentists. Using stone or plaster models of dental impressions, technicians work with ceramics, metals, and acrylics to make and repair teeth. According to their area of specialization, technicians may be dental ceramists or orthodontic technicians. Excessive noise levels generated by frequent use of power machines can be uncomfortable for some workers. There is also some pressure to meet deadlines imposed by dentists. Workers have regular contact with supervisors and other laboratory technicians.

DENTIST

Ranking: 189

Score: 1,119.75

Hours Weekly: 45

Duties: Examines, cleans, and repairs teeth, and diagnoses and treats diseases and abnormalities of the mouth.

Responsible for educating patients about oral hygiene, including the care and maintenance of teeth. Dentists take X-rays, and use a wide variety of specialized equipment to fill cavities, repair decayed teeth, and perform surgical procedures. They also educate patients about preventative measures and provide instructions for self-care. While most dentists are general practitioners, others specialize in orthodontia, pedodontics (treatment of children), and periodontics (treatment of gum disease). Most dentists work five days each week; many have evening and Saturday hours. Approximately nine out of ten dentists are in private practice. Scientific ability, good spatial perception, and manual dexterity are all necessary to be successful in this career.

DIETITIAN

Ranking: 41

Score: 334.40

Hours Weekly: 42.5

Duties: Assesses patients' dietary needs, plans menus, and instructs patients and their families about proper nutritional care.

Clinical dietitians are employed by hospitals, nursing homes, and clinics. Dietitians consult with physicians, nurses, and social service personnel to determine patients' dietary habits and needs. Members of this profession use computer programs to devise nutritional care plans and to coordinate food intake with institutional menus. Dietitians also instruct patients in proper diet and food selection and provide nutritional therapy for individuals who are critically or terminally ill. They inspect meals served for conformance to dietary standards, and are sometimes subject to the discomfort of hot, steamy kitchens. Dietitians also spend a lot of time on their feet. Contacts include medical personnel and educators.

DISHWASHER

Ranking: 154

Score: 868.32

Hours Weekly: 35

Duties: Cleans the plates, glasses and silverware used by patrons of an eating establishment, and the pots, pans and cooking utensils used by chefs.

Dishwashers are employed in most establishments which provide food and beverage service, including restaurants, bars, hotels, cafeterias and hospitals. These workers clean dishes and utensils by hand, using soap, sponges and scouring pads. In kitchens with automatic dishwashing machines, dishes are rinsed and cleaned before being loaded into machines. Dishwashers then monitor machine operation. Dishwashers keep cooks and servers provided with an ample supply of clean plates, glasses and utensils. These workers may also mop floors, clean kitchen equipment, stock refrigerators, and assist in food preparation. Many dishwashing jobs are part-time, and include evening and weekend shifts. Dishwashers spend a great deal of time on their feet, often in hot, uncomfortable kitchens. This work involves exposure to grease, food refuse, and foul odors. Dishwashers work with cooks and chefs, waiters and waitresses, and food service managers.

DISK JOCKEY

Ranking: 179

Score: 1,062.00

Hours Weekly: 45

Duties: Selects and plays records or tapes; comments on areas of interest to a particular radio audience.

Disk jockeys are employed by large and small radio stations throughout the country. They announce radio programs and select musical entertainment in accordance with audience tastes. In small radio stations, disk jockeys may also announce the news, weather, and sports. Interviews with music and entertainment personalities are a common staple of some disk jockeys' repertoires. Most disk jockeys specialize in a particular type of music: rock, jazz, country, or classical, for example. The timing of live broadcasts can be physically and mentally draining; some members of this profession complain of the irregular hours and disrupted personal lives. Contacts include program managers and broadcast technicians.

DRESSMAKER

Ranking: 124

Score: 704.31

Hours Weekly: 40

Duties: Follows design instructions, operates a sewing machine to join, reinforce, and decorate parts of garments or other textiles.

Dressmakers, often referred to as "seamers" in the apparel trade are employed by clothing manufacturers, and other segments of the textile industry. Garment seamers follow a pattern to assemble parts of an article of clothing, such as legs, arms, collars, and pockets. These parts are then attached to the main body of the coat, jacket, shirt, or dress. Other seamers work on household articles, such as bedspreads, linens, and curtains. Seamers guide material under a sewing machine needle, or between feed cups, stitching parts together, reinforcing edges, and adding decoration. These workers may also be responsible for oiling machines, changing needles, and placing modifying attachments on equipment. Though the "sweat shop" days of the garment industry are generally part of the past, seamers still normally work in hectic, noisy surroundings. This work can be monotonous and repetitive. Cuts from needles are common. Seamers come in contact with supervisors, and with other textile workers.

DRILL PRESS OPERATOR

Ranking: 131

Score: 728.32

Hours Weekly: 45

Duties: Operates drilling machines to place holes in metal or nonmetal pieces according to predetermined specifications.

Drill press operators work in plants that manufacture metal products, transportation equipment, and machinery. Operators lift machines, either by hand or with hoists, and place them on work areas. They feed metal or plastic material into presses on which sequence and speeds have already been set. Drill press operators monitor machine operation, and measure finished pieces for conformance to specifications using calipers, fixed gages, and micrometers. Some skilled workers set up the sequence of operations using blueprints and other instructions. This work is repetitive, and physical stamina is required since so much time is spent standing. Operators come into contact with set-up operators and machinists.

DRYWALL APPLICATOR/ FINISHER

Ranking: 170

Score: 973.94

Hours Weekly: 45

Duties: Installs and prepares surfaces of drywall panels for commercial or residential interiors.

Drywall applicators and finishers work for construction contractors throughout the country. Applicators fasten drywall panels to the framework of buildings. Drywall finishers ready wall surfaces for painting or papering. Installers use tape measures and straightedges to determine the exact dimensions of surfaces. Hand and power-tools, hacksaws, knives, trowels, and electric mixers are also used in hanging drywall and preparing wall surfaces. This work involves many hours of standing, bending, and heavy lifting. Injuries from power tools and falls are not uncommon. Drywallers often work side by side with other members of the construction trades, including electricians and insulation workers.

ECONOMIST

Ranking: 18

Score: 227.35

Hours Weekly: 45

Duties: Studies and analyzes the effects of resources such as land, labor, and raw materials, on costs and their relation to industry and government.

Economists, employed by private industry or by federal and state governments, collect data and prepare charts to illustrate costs. They work in a particular area of expertise (finance, insurance, labor, or government), and advise clients of cost benefits based on statistical study of raw resources. Responsibilities also include analysis and review, and report preparation. Economists have structured work schedules; they may work alone in an office, or as members of teams oriented towards a solution to particular sets of problems. Economists' equipment includes statistical charts, calculators, and computers. The pressures of deadlines and heavy workloads are common to members of this profession. Some might also consider the frequent travel to attend conferences and seminars to be a hindrance. Contacts include industry management personnel, accountants, and government officials.

ELECTRICAL ENGINEER

Ranking: 36

Score: 318.92

Hours Weekly: 45

Duties: Conducts research and plans and directs design, testing, and manufacture of electrical equipment.

Electrical equipment manufacturers, engineering and business consulting firms, and government agencies employ electrical engineers to develop and supervise the manufacture of electrical equipment. Electrical engineers design new products, test equipment, and direct the installation of systems and facilities. Most electronics engineers specialize in a particular area, which might include electrical energy generation, instrumentation, computers, or communications. While many engineers spend a great deal of time working at a desk, others spend time on site, solving problems or coordinating the activities of installation workers. Although regular hours are the norm in this field, overtime is sometimes required to meet the pressures of deadlines. Frequent contacts of electrical engineers include business managers, as well as other engineers and scientists.

ELECTRICAL EQUIPMENT REPAIRER

Ranking: 114

Score: 657.16

Hours Weekly: 47.5

Duties: Installs and repairs electronic equipment for military installations, manufacturers, and businesses.

The Department of Defense is the major employer of electronic equipment repairers. Other employers include hospitals and telephone companies. Repairers follow blueprints and use diagnostic tools such as voltmeters and oscilloscopes to locate and correct malfunctions in electronic control panels, X-ray equipment, and transmitters. In accordance with preventative maintenance procedures, many workers keep logs to show servicing dates and indicate schedules for reservicing. Discomfort from long periods of standing, bending, and kneeling is common to this profession. Some repairers work shifts, including nights and weekends; other individuals are on call during non-working hours to correct malfunctions in emergency equipment. Contacts include managers and hospital administrators.

ELECTRICAL TECHNICIAN

Ranking: 81

Score: 502.26

Hours Weekly: 45

Duties: Develops, assembles, and tests electrical equipment according to principles of electrical engineering.

Using a practical knowledge of electrical principles, electrical technicians manufacture, diagnose, and repair electrical equipment according to theoretical designs by scientists and engineers. Employers include manufacturing firms, research and development organizations, and public utilities companies. Some technicians also work for the federal and state governments. Individuals in this field work closely with electrical engineers to assemble and maintain electrical machinery. They rely on wiring diagrams and engineering specifications to install, maintain, and modify electrical equipment. Most electrical technicians work regular hours. Electric shocks from equipment can be hazardous to some workers.

ELECTRICIAN

Ranking: 152

Score: 855.76

Hours Weekly: 45

Duties: Maps layout and installs and repairs electrical wiring and fixtures.

Approximately half of all electricians are employed by the construction industry. Others work for manufacturers, public utilities, and federal and state governments. Electricians follow blueprints or prepare sketches to indicate location of wiring prior to construction of walls, ceilings, and floors. They use a variety of hand-tools to assemble and install wiring and electrical conduits in residential and commercial structures. Electricians also test circuitry to ensure safety and electrical compatibility. This work is sometimes uncomfortable, entailing many hours in cramped or awkward positions. Injuries from falls and electrical shocks can occur, and electricians wear protective clothing and follow safety procedures to avoid these mishaps. Engineers and engineering technicians, as well as members of the construction trades are frequent contacts of electricians.

EMERGENCY MEDICAL TECHNICIAN

Ranking: 233

Score: 1,610.70

Hours Weekly: 40

Duties: Attends to situations which demand immediate medical attention, such as automobile accidents, heart attacks, and gunshot wounds.

Emergency medical technicians, once known as ambulance attendants, are often the first professionals on the scene of an accident or unexpected illness. They must use their medical training to determine the nature of the problem and provide the care necessary to sustain patients until they reach the nearest hospital. They are responsible for making sure all equipment is functioning properly, and for the smooth operation of the ambulances they drive. EMT's are employed by fire departments, private ambulance services, police departments, and hospitals. Speed and the ability to work as a member of a team are vitally important in this field, as life-and-death decisions are often a part of an EMT's job. Workers must be equipped to work both indoors and outdoors, and they are frequently exposed to adverse

weather conditions. Straining, bending, lifting, and kneeling can cause discomfort, and the quick reaction time demanded of EMT's under severely stressful circumstances make this job very difficult at times. Forty hour weeks are standard, however, many EMT's are on call during their off hours, and must be available at all hours of the day and night. Contacts include police officers, firefighters, and nurses.

ENGINEERING TECHNICIAN

Ranking: 77

Score: 493.79

Hours Weekly: 45

Duties: Assists engineers in planning, design, and development by applying a practical knowledge of civil, mechanical, or industrial engineering.

Engineering technicians are employed by manufacturing and engineering firms throughout the country. Some members of this profession work for federal and state agencies. Engineering technicians set up experiments, conduct research, and prepare reports, often under the direct supervision of engineers. Computers are sometimes used to design equipment and record the results of engineering experiments. Engineering technicians help study efficiency through analysis of production costs, as well prepare layouts of machinery and equipment. Most engineering technicians work regular hours in laboratories, offices, or industrial plants. Frequent contacts include supervisors and laboratory technicians.

EXECUTIVE SEARCH CONSULTANT

Ranking: 128

Score: 720.00

Hours Weekly: 45

Duties: Assists corporations or other clients in locating ideal executives suited to parameters determined by the company.

Like a broker, putting buyer and seller together, these "headhunters" often meet with a good deal of controversy. The executive search firm or consultant is compensated in contractual terms; typically on contingency or retainer basis. Contingency search firms operate more like employment agencies searching for candidates to fill vacancies and they are only paid when someone is hired. They maintain a large database of candidates and market those people to corporate clients. Those executive search consultants "retained" are paid in advance or in progress payments whether job placement occurs or not.

The retainer firm is granted exclusivity, thereby searching for appropriate candidates often working with the client directly. They may work with the client's board of directors analyzing specific needs or review the corporate climate and culture. Contingency consultants perform in a highly competitive market, often trying to locate a match quicker than the competition. Those retained, locating high level CEO's or senior executives for example, may have a consultant working on a fee based on a percentage of the candidate's starting salary. The search in this case will tend to be slower, more deliberate and with greater care and emphasis on identifying those who are best qualified. Executive search consultants work closely with their corporate clients, candidates and network with other professionals.

FARMER

Ranking: 209

Score: 1,263.84

Hours Weekly: 52.5

Duties: Manages the successful operation of a crop, livestock, dairy, or poultry farm.

Operators may be farm owners or tenant farmers. Responsibilities vary greatly with the size and type of farm they operate, and may range from planting, tilling, and harvesting on a crop farm to feeding, and cleaning and repairing farm buildings on a poultry or livestock farm. On smaller farms, operators carry out many of the duties themselves, but larger farms frequently require these individuals to supervise the activities of many other workers. Operators must often make managerial decisions, such as when to seed, and what type and amount of feed to purchase; they must also plan ahead to take advantage of better prices as farm economy changes. Farm operators secure bank loans, finance the purchase of machinery, and maintain records of farm operations. Because of the seasonal nature of farming, work is long and arduous during planting and harvesting seasons, with workdays lasting from dawn until dusk, seven days a week. Many crop farm operators take second jobs during winter months; workers in livestock farms must be available throughout the year. Injuries from machinery, and illnesses incurred through contact with diseased animals and pesticides, make this a dangerous job. Contacts include farm worker supervisors and feed and farm management advisors.

FASHION DESIGNER

Ranking: 159

Score: 929.25

Hours Weekly: 45

Duties: Designs articles or complete lines of clothing for men, women, or children.

Fashion designers work with a thorough knowledge of their markets (obtained through analysis of trends, activities, and predictions) to design apparel. They take into account their own, as well as their clients' tastes and interests as they design and construct garments for the marketplace. Designers compare fabrics and color schemes, meet with executives in sales and management, and coordinate clothing workers' efforts to achieve their objectives in garment design. Fashion designers work in offices, where they use sewing equipment, pens and pencils, fabrics, and measuring devices to achieve desired effects. Designers may be designated as to their areas of expertise (swim wear, outer wear, lingerie, for example), or by the audience for whom they design (such as women or children). This career involves long hours and frequent travel to attend fashion shows and sales meetings. Contacts include models, garment manufactures and fashion models.

FASHION MODEL

Ranking: 222

Score: 1,450.10

Hours Weekly: 42.5

Duties: Wears garments in fashion shows and advertisements to exhibit style, fabric, and quality of clothing.

The majority of fashion models are employed by modeling agencies, which contract with garment designers, retail establishments, and advertising agencies. Models wear dresses, suits, coats, and undergarments to display innovations in style and fabric in new fashion designs, and to demonstrate the range of sizes and colors for a line of clothing. In fashion shows, models dress in a particular garment, and display it by walking, turning, and standing in view of observers, such as retail and wholesale buyers, sales personnel, and customers. These models may be responsible for answering questions about price and availability of clothing. In print and broadcast advertising, models, under the direction of photographers, strike interpretive poses to enhance the appearance of the garments being worn. Fashion modeling can be a high-pressure occupation. Many models enter the profession at a very young age. Extensive travel, tight schedules, and constant concern about physical appearance can be stressful to some in this field. Models work varied and flexible schedules. Some may find employment only periodically, while others are in constant demand. Fashion models regularly work with clothing designers, retailers, photographers, and advertising personnel.

FILE CLERK

Ranking: 24

Score: 248.22

Hours Weekly: 40

Duties: Maintains business records, such as invoices, receipts, and correspondences, in specified order.

File clerks are employed in most businesses and organizations which require records maintenance, including private business, government agencies, and educational and health care institutions. Clerks file correspondences, financial records, contracts and other documents according to a specific filing system. Filing may be done by by alphabetical, numerical or chronological order, or by some other pertinent method, such as subject matter. File clerks locate and remove materials as requested, and may classify and file new material as it comes in. Workers in this occupation may also perform other clerical or office tasks. In establishments with advanced filing systems, clerks may operate computers to retrieve files or other data. File clerks regularly come in contact with secretaries, bookkeepers, and other office personnel.

FINANCIAL PLANNER

Ranking: 93

Score: 550.00

Hours Weekly: 50

Duties: Related to careers in portfolio management, the financial planner offers a broad range of services aimed at assisting individuals in managing and planning their financial future.

Planners study a client's present retirement program, level of income, and their savings and investments. Also analyzing a client's wish list for retirement, such as the age they would like to retire, how much income they would like at that point and how much of that income would derive from Social Security and or pensions. The financial planner would also look at current or future financial burdens such as mortgages, college educations or financial objectives such as sabbaticals. Reviewed as well is the client's insurance coverage and will to see if these are adequate. This review leads to a strategy plan for the client to best meet his goals through savings and investments, including bank certificates of deposit, mutual funds, or management of portfolios of stocks and bonds. Personal finance planners can work for brokerage firms or are self- employed. Coming from many backgrounds; accountants, securities, stockbrokers or corporate executives, financial planners must have an acute understanding of finance as well as good marketing sense. Financial planners work closely with their individual clients, and network with other professionals.

FIREFIGHTER

Ranking: 249

Score: 3,314.03

Hours Weekly: 55

Duties: Protects individuals and saves lives and property from the ravages of fire.

Most jobs for firefighters can be found in municipal fire departments, although opportunities also exist in state and federal installations, such as military bases and aeronautical sites. Private firefighting units employ a relatively small number of workers. A firefighter's job can be complicated and dangerous and individuals must be able to work as team players; heavy reliance on the support of other firefighters in emergencies fosters a communal spirit among members of this profession. Specific duties are assigned by officers such as lieutenants, captains, and chiefs, and responsibilities can include educating students and civic groups about safety procedures and inspecting public buildings for hazardous conditions. Firefighters spend much of their time at fire stations, where they share meals and sleeping quarters with other firefighters. They must be prepared to respond to emergencies at any hour of the day or night regardless of weather conditions. Risks in this job are great; many firefighters die each year from injuries sustained by collapsing walls and roofs, or by explosions or smoke inhalation. Contacts include emergency medical technicians and police officers.

FISHERMAN

Ranking: 235

Score: 1,640.21

Hours Weekly: 45

Duties: Hunts and catches fish, shellfish and other marine life for consumption.

Large commercial fishing fleets employ fishermen on ocean-going vessels. Other workers in this occupation operate their own small fishing fleets, or work as crew members on independently-owned boats. Commercial fishers work either aboard a boat or from shore. Using nets, pots, cages, rods and other equipment, members of this profession gather a variety of aquatic life. In commercial fishing, fin-fish are caught using nets. After a school of fish has been located, nets are assembled, lowered into the water, and either towed or anchored. Crew members haul nets aboard manually or using a winch. A crew member's duties may include sorting the catch, cleaning fish, and repairing nets and other equipment. Fishers work long hours, often rising early in the morning. Some fishing is seasonal. Vessels and equipment must be kept in proper working order to prevent breakdowns or accidents on the open seas. Some types of fishing are highly regulated by the government. Workers in this occupation come in contact with buyers, government officials, and harbor personnel.

FLIGHT ATTENDANT

Ranking: 145

Score: 803.00

Hours Weekly: 40

Duties: Tends to the care and comfort of passengers on commercial and corporate aircraft.

Prior to each flight, attendants receive information about weather conditions and special passenger problems from the flight captain. They prepare the cabin for boarding, make sure that adequate supplies such as food, beverages, and reading materials are aboard, and greet passengers and check tickets as they enter the aircraft. Before taking off, attendants instruct passengers on the use of emergency equipment; during the flight, they answer questions and serve meals and drinks. After the flight has arrived at its destination, attendants assist passengers as they leave the plane, and prepare reports on equipment conditions. Since flights are made 24 hours a day, seven days a week, persons in this field must frequently work evenings, weekends, and holidays. Attendants are away from home approximately one-third of the time. Although this is considered a glamorous job because of inherent travel opportunities, it can often be stressful, especially during adverse weather and when working with fatigued, demanding, passengers. Contacts include ticket and gate agents and flight crew members.

FLORIST

Ranking: 55

Score: 398.25

Hours Weekly: 45

Duties: Cuts and arranges flowers for special events according to the wishes of customers.

Most floral designers are employed by retail flower shops throughout the country. Individuals in this profession fashion floral arrangements for special events such as weddings, birthdays, anniversaries, and funerals. Florists use cutters and wire and work with live or artificial flowers to evoke particular sentiments of customers. For this reason, a good deal of a designer's time is spent discussing desired costs and types of arrangement with clients. Holiday seasons in retail flower shops can be extremely busy and stressful, and many hours of overtime work is necessary to keep up with great demand for special arrangements during these times of year, which include Christmas and Mother's Day. In addition to other retail personnel, floral designers have contact with craft and plant and garden suppliers.

FOOTBALL PLAYER (NFL)

Ranking: 247

Score: 2,401.85

Hours Weekly: 45

Duties: Plays one of a number of positions as a member of a professional football team.

The 28 football teams in the National Football League are the primary, and most stable, employers of professional football players. Other professional leagues include Arena Football and the Canadian Football League. An NFL team carries an active roster of 45 players. Each week, coaches devise a game plan, based on the strengths and weaknesses of the team and the opponent. 11 players each are fielded on offense and defense. On the offense, linemen, running backs, receivers and quarterbacks implement plays in an attempt to score points. The defense, consisting of linemen, linebackers and defensive backs, uses its own strategy to prevent scoring. Teams also include punters, place-kickers, and backup players. Play on the field is regulated by referees. Players wear protective equipment, including pads, helmets and facemasks, but minor and major injuries are common. Some injuries, such as those to the knee, back, and neck, can end a player's career, and even cause permanent disability. Media attention, sudden wealth, and the pressure to win can all be sources of stress in this profession. Drug and alcohol abuse remains a problem among some professional football players. In addition to team personnel, players come in frequent contact with sportswriters, broadcasters, agents, and fans.

FORK-LIFT OPERATOR

Ranking: 68

Score: 454.50

Hours Weekly: 45

Duties: Operates industrial trucks and tractors to move products and raw materials for manufacturing firms.

Most industrial truck and tractor operators work for manufacturing firms, such as automobile, paper, and building material producers. Others are employed by warehouses, shipping yards, and lumber yards. The typical industrial truck, also known as a fork-lift, is equipped with hydraulic lifting devices and used to carry cargo or pull trailers loaded with materials. Besides operating machinery, operators must be fully aware of lifting capabilities, to avoid damage to the trucks they are driving. Some operators are expected to perform routine maintenance keep their vehicles clean and well oiled. Falling objects and collisions can be hazardous for truck operators; extreme safety precautions must be followed at all times. Contacts include supervisors and dock workers.

FURNITURE UPHOLSTERER

Ranking: 82

Score: 504.36

Hours Weekly: 42.5

Duties: Builds new furniture and restores worn furniture using a thorough knowledge of fabrics and manufacturing techniques.

Most furniture upholsterers work in small shops of three or fewer workers. Others are employed by furniture stores or by businesses such as hotels, that repair their own furniture. Upholsterers use a variety of hand-tools, including hammers, staple removers, and shears to remove old fabric and rebuild furniture. To upholster new furniture or restore old pieces, upholsterers first install webbing. Springs are attached, burlap is tacked to the furniture's frame, and heavy cloth is added before the fabric covering is fitted. Upholsterers add embellishments such as fringe or buttons as a final step in the upholstery process. Individuals in this profession stand to do their work, and frequent bending, stooping, and kneeling can make this work uncomfortable at times.

GARBAGE COLLECTOR

Ranking: 217

Score: 1,368.32

Hours Weekly: 42.5

Duties: Collects refuse on a designated municipal route, and transports trash to disposal plants or landfill areas.

Garbage collectors are employed by city governments, or by private garbage collection contractors. These workers ride either in the cab or on the outside of a garbage truck. The truck follows a specific route, making stops as warranted to collect trash, garbage, branches, discarded appliances and other refuse. Trash cans and bags are lifted by hand and loaded into an opening in back of the truck. For larger refuse bins, some trucks

are equipped with a hoist, which lifts the container and deposits its contents into the vehicle. A hydraulic system then compacts refuse inside the storage area of the truck. Refuse is unloaded at collection facilities, such as trash dumps, municipal landfills, or waste disposal plants. Garbage collectors wear uniforms, gloves, and masks as protection from dirt, filth, and disease. These workers are often exposed to foul odors and other unpleasant conditions. Refuse collection involves heavy lifting, and requires physical strength and stamina. Garbage collectors come in contact with supervisors, disposal plant personnel, and vehicle maintenance workers.

GEOLOGIST

Ranking: 63

Score: 449.10

Hours Weekly: 45

Duties: Studies and analyzes the physical properties of the earth's surface, adding to our knowledge of oil and gas exploration techniques.

Geologists are employed by oil industries, federal and state agencies, and colleges and universities throughout the country. About 1 out of 6 is a self-employed consultant to industry or government. Geologists use X-ray equipment to study mineral and fossil specimens. They prepare reports, conduct surveys, and make maps of findings to assist in locating future drilling sites for natural gas, oil, and water reservoirs. Geologists often advise contractors and government officials as to the suitability of particular sites for construction of dams, highways, and buildings. Much of geologists' time is spent on site at remote locations, necessitating time away from family and friends.

GLAZIER

Ranking: 143

Score: 796.86

Hours Weekly: 45

Duties: Measures, cuts, and installs glass in residential and commercial buildings.

Glaziers work for construction contractors, government agencies, and businesses that do their own construction. They select glass for use in windows, display cases, walls, or ceilings. Glaziers use cranes to lift glass to elevated spots before guiding glass surfaces with their hands to prevent cracking. They then spread putty or use metal clips to secure the glass before installing molding that will hold the glass in place. Sometimes, glaziers use metal wheels to cut glass manually prior to installation. Much of this work is done outdoors, often under adverse weather conditions. Injuries from falls, and cuts from glass and hand-tools are among the hazards of this profession. Contacts include other members of the construction trades, including carpenters and electricians.

GUARD

Ranking: 147

Score: 812.06

Hours Weekly: 42.5

Duties: Protects property from damages incurred by theft, fire, and vandalism.

Approximately one-half of all guards work for industrial security firms or guard services throughout the country. Others work in-house in banks, insurance companies, government agencies, and retail establishments. Guards frequently patrol properties on foot, although in some larger spaces they use scooters or automobiles to check for disturbances. Guards often wear uniforms and carry nightsticks and guns as they patrol properties. Some individuals sit behind desks and use surveillance monitors to check for intruders. This can be a lonely profession; much of the work is done at night when businesses are closed. Those who work during daytime hours have frequent contact with customers and industry personnel.

HEATING/REFRIGERATION MECHANIC

Ranking: 109

Score: 633.50

Hours Weekly: 45

Duties: Installs and services air-conditioning and furnace systems in businesses and residences.

Heating and refrigeration mechanics work for cooling and heating contractors, retail food chains, school systems and hospitals. Mechanics diagnose problems, make repairs, and perform off-season maintenance on heating and cooling systems. They use a variety of tools, including hammers, wrenches, pipe cutters, and torches. Most mechanics specialize in the installation and servicing of certain equipment, furnaces or air-conditioning systems, for example. Heating and refrigeration mechanics work in homes, offices, and commercial establishments, often under uncomfortable temperature conditions. A great deal of this work is done in cramped spaces where systems are located. Contacts include sheet-metal workers and pipe-fitters.

HIGHWAY PATROL OFFICER

Ranking: 240

Score: 1,733.40

Hours Weekly: 47.5

Duties: Patrols roads and highways, and enforces traffic regulations and criminal statutes.

State police officers and state highway patrol officers are employed across the country. States with large populations and heavy motor vehicle traffic have the highest concentration of jobs in this field. State police officers stop motorists who violate traffic regulations on state or interstate highways, and issue tickets. These officers assist at accident scenes, administering first aid and radioing for ambulances. State police direct traffic during road construction. Troopers also assist motorists whose vehicles have broken down, by radioing for service. Troopers may also check the weight of trucks to enforce compliance with state regulations. In communities without a local police force, state police are the primary law enforcement officials. Troopers investigate crimes and apprehend criminal suspects. State police normally work 40-hour weeks in shifts, including nights, weekends, and holidays. State police face the threat of injury during high speed chases, or dealing with criminals. Members of this profession work with local and federal law enforcement personnel.

HISTORIAN

Ranking: 6

Score: 136.41

Hours Weekly: 45

Duties: Analyzes and records historical information from a specific era or according to a particular area of expertise.

Historians work for colleges and universities, museums, research organizations, and government agencies. Individuals in this profession collect data and organize information in narrative or outline form. Historians may work in specific areas of expertise, including sociology, economics, or art. They study indexes, catalogues, news reports, court documents, and miscellaneous published material to compile briefs as a written record of their findings. Historians rely heavily on computers to do research and to store information, as well as to prepare final narratives. They must be extremely disciplined, because wading through tedious documents in search of pertinent data requires a great deal of time and concentration. Contacts include librarians and research assistants.

HOME ECONOMIST

Ranking: 66

Score: 451.80

Hours Weekly: 45

Duties: Studies and instructs about efficiency in homemaking, and develops economical household budgets.

Home economists are employed by schools, home health care agencies, nursing homes, and other health care establishments, and social service agencies. Some work as consultants to hotels and restaurants, food service organizations, and companies involved in the manufacture of household products. In schools, home economists instruct students on the proper use of household equipment and appliances, teach cooking, help students develop household budgets, and instruct on nutrition, health, and hygiene. Home economists with health care and social service agencies assist individuals who are disabled, ill, or of limited means in the efficient use of resources, the preparation of meals, and the performance of household chores. They may also assist in rehabilitation, prepare menus, and test new household products and equipment. Most work in offices, but some may work in clinics, or in residential centers. Members of this profession come in contact with school administrators, social workers, and health professionals.

HOSPITAL ADMINISTRATOR

Ranking: 5

Score: 93.14

Hours Weekly: 47.5

Duties: Responsible for the effective management of programs, staff, and budgets of health care establishments.

Only about half of all those trained as hospital administrators work for hospitals. With the consolidation of hospitals, many now work for health maintenance organizations, physicians' offices, and outpatient facilities which often have similar facilities to hospitals. Hospital administrators oversee the work of associates and department heads to ensure that services and programs are running smoothly. They plan budgets and frequently organize in-service training programs. Some administrators perform community outreach functions and meet with government regulatory boards to communicate program policies and procedures. Most administrators work long hours, and are constantly under pressure from outside agencies to meet regulatory requirements. Contacts include community and business leaders and public health officials. Hospital administrators oversee the work of associates and department heads to ensure that services and programs are running smoothly. They plan budgets and frequently organize in-service training programs. Some administrators perform community outreach functions and meet with government regulatory boards to communicate program policies and procedures. Administrators work long hours, and are constantly under pressure from outside agencies to meet regulatory requirements. Contacts include community and business leaders and public health officials.

HOTEL MANAGER

Ranking: 146

Score: 807.12

Hours Weekly: 45

Duties: Oversees the successful and profitable operation of hotels and motels.

Hotel managers may be employed by large national chains, or by small motels or hotels, and their responsibilities vary accordingly. They can include the supervision of staff, organization of recreational activities, and managing of marketing and accounting services for the hotel. Duties might include handling of customer complaints, and the processing of reservations in small establishments. Computers are increasingly used in this field for budget management as well as for housekeeping and reservations, and managers should be proficient in their use. Managers work most frequently indoors, and often from offices. However, they must be available for problem-solving throughout areas of the establishments they serve. Work weeks are often unstructured, and evening and weekend work is necessary, especially during busy seasonal periods. Special events, such as conventions, can also be stressful, and good managers need exert a great deal of self-discipline to counter problems that might occur during these times. Hotel managers' contacts include sales and marketing professionals and wholesaling and retailing suppliers.

INDUSTRIAL DESIGNER

Ranking: 11

Score: 177.00

Hours Weekly: 45

Duties: Designs and develops manufactured products.

Industrial designers work for wholesale and retail trade organizations, manufacturers, service, and construction firms. They consider customer preferences for style and utility as they design products for the marketplace. Designers usually specialize in one type of product, automobiles or home appliances, for example. They use measuring devices, pens and pencils, and rely heavily on computer-aided design systems to do their work. Designers must stay cognizant of customer preferences for color, size, and material as they prepare sketches or models for completed designs. Industrial designers generally work regular hours, but must sometimes work overtime to meet deadlines for product designs. Constant pressure to please clients is stressful to some members of this profession. Contacts include engineers and drafting personnel.

INDUSTRIAL ENGINEER

Ranking: 20

Score: 230.30

Hours Weekly: 45

Duties: Plans for optimum use of facilities and personnel to improve industrial efficiency.

Approximately 75 percent of industrial engineers are employed by manufacturing firms. The remainder work for a variety of enterprises, including banks and retail organizations. Industrial engineers work to find ways to improve operational efficiency. They use organization charts and study the functions and responsibilities of workers before making recommendations to management on manpower utilization, including worker motions, and space layout. Industrial engineers work more closely with people than do other members of the engineering profession. They spend much of their time in industrial plants, where noisy surroundings are sometimes stressful. Individuals in this field have frequent contact with business administrators and consultants.

INDUSTRIAL MACHINE REPAIRER

Ranking: 58

Score: 422.46

Hours Weekly: 47.5

Duties: Maintains, inspects, and repairs industrial machinery.

Well over half of all industrial machinery repairers work for manufacturing firms, where a great deal of industrial machinery is used. Industrial machinery repairers make periodic checks to keep vital industrial machinery from breaking down. To keep machines in good working order, they clean parts and make sure machines are well oiled and greased. When breakdowns occur, repairers use hoists to lift heavy machinery and hand-tools such as wrenches and screwdrivers to correct problems. Repairers keep detailed logs of preventative maintenance procedures, and refer to blueprints and engineering specifications when fixing broken equipment. Workers frequently toil in cramped spaces, and must be on call evenings and weekends in the event that machinery breaks down during peak production periods. Contacts include machinists, tool-and-die workers, and millwrights.

INSURANCE AGENT

Ranking: 184

Score: 1,085.52

Hours Weekly: 45

Duties: Sells insurance and advises clients about amount and type of coverage based on needs and circumstances.

Approximately one out of three insurance agents is self-employed. Others work for headquarters of large insurance firms. Most agents work for local insurance agencies throughout the country. Insurance agents use adding machines and rate books to calculate insurance rates for individuals and businesses based on risks and insurance requirements. Three types of insurance coverage are commonly offered: casualty, health, and life, and agents are often designated according to the type of insurance they sell. Those individuals who are self-employed frequently set their own hours, but evening and weekend work is necessary to consult with clients not available during regular weekday hours. Contacts of insurance agents include business managers and underwriters.

INSURANCE UNDERWRITER

Ranking: 19

Score: 228.10

Hours Weekly: 45

Duties: Assesses and analyzes the risks inherent in insuring potential policy holders before making recommendations to the insurance companies that employ them.

Employed by insurance agencies throughout the country, individuals in this field spend their time reviewing applications, loss and medical reports, and actuarial studies to determine the feasibility of insuring groups and individuals. They may specialize in property and liability, life, or health insurance, and in some companies must be familiar with all of these when "package policies", covering all three are issued. Underwriters work in offices at a desk, and their work week usually consists of thirty five to forty hours. They use a variety of small office equipment to perform their jobs. Initially, those just starting out in this field are assigned to an experienced risk appraiser. They are given more responsibilities as they become familiar with types of losses. Those who are successful in this profession are detail-oriented and good communicators. Contacts include policyholders, agents, and managers.

IRONWORKER

Ranking: 232

Score: 1,593.72

Hours Weekly: 45

Duties: Raises the steel framework of buildings, bridges, and other structures.

Most ironworkers are employed by construction contractors to erect the steel frames of buildings or to do repair work on bridges. Ironworkers also install steel stairs and window reinforcements. Workers start by moving steel to the construction site with cranes and derricks. They then connect the sections of steel, beams, and girders before lifting steel parts via cables to other workers who will put them into place. Ironworkers use handtools to align holes in the steel bars with those in the framework. Finally, workers check alignment before bolting steel permanently into place. Ironworkers do most of their work outside, frequently in uncomfortable weather. They wear protective devices such as safety belts and use netting to avoid injury from falls. Contacts include welders and crane operators.

JANITOR

Ranking: 76

Score: 489.60

Hours Weekly: 40

Duties: Cleanes offices and other spaces within buildings, and keeps areas in good condition.

Janitors work in almost every type of industry, including schools, hospitals, businesses, and restaurants. About one of every six janitors is employed by a contract maintenance firm. Janitors use a variety of tools, such as mops, cleaners, polishing machines, and vacuums to clean spaces. Some janitors perform other duties, including painting, restocking supplies, and shoveling snow or mowing lawns. Although most janitors work in comfortable temperatures indoors, many work outside during adverse weather conditions. Some jobs, such as cleaning rest rooms, can also be unpleasant. In the course of their work, janitors come into contact with any number of other workers, including educators and hospital personnel.

JEWELER

Ranking: 34

Score: 316.40

Hours Weekly: 45

Duties: Manufactures and repairs rings, bracelets, pins, and necklaces using precious or semi-precious metals and stones.

Approximately forty percent of all jewelers are self-employed, operating jewelry retail or repair shops. Others work for jewelry manufacturing firms. Jewelers alter rings sizes, reset stones, and replace broken clasps. Some jewelers repair watches and do engraving. A few design jewelry and are qualified to do appraisals. Jewelers use a variety of small hand tools, such as pliers, files, and soldering irons. They use special cleaning compounds and polishes to restore worn jewelry to its original luster. Although most jewelers work in clean, quiet surroundings, the extreme detail of their work, coupled with pressure to please clients, can be stressful. Contacts include wholesale representatives, gem cutters, and engravers.

JOCKEY

Ranking: 244

Score: 2,079.75

Hours Weekly: 45

Duties: Rides thoroughbred horses in sweepstakes, derbies, and other professional races.

Professional jockeys are hired by horse owners to race their horses at tracks across the country. Jockeys are skilled equestrians and good athletes. These individuals often assist in the training and conditioning of horses, and successful jockeys become familiar with the abilities, tendencies, and temperaments of the horses they ride. Some horses have great initial speed, while others are slower, but possess better endurance over the length of the race. Jockeys employ skill and strategy to make best use of their horses' assets during thoroughbred races. Some jockeys travel extensively over the course of the racing season, and are in great demand by horse owners for their experience and reputations for success. Jockeys normally receive a share of the winnings of the horses they ride. Members of this profession can suffer minor and major injuries in spills during racing or training. Jockeys come in contact with horse owners, trainers, groomers, and racing officials.

JUDGE (FEDERAL)

Ranking: 113

Score: 655.98

Hours Weekly: 50

Duties: Arbitrates legal matters coming under the jurisdiction of the federal government, using a thorough knowledge of federal statutes and legal precedent.

Federal judges work in the U.S. government's federal court systems, such as the U.S. District Courts, the Courts of Appeals, or Bankruptcy Courts. These judges are nominated by the president and must be confirmed by the U.S. Senate. Federal judges preside over cases lying outside the jurisdiction of local or state courts. These include cases concerning interstate commerce, federal regulations, civil rights, and federal taxation. Federal judges also hear cases in which the constitutionality of state and local statutes, and of lower court rulings, is disputed. Federal judges rely on knowledge of federal statutes and legal precedent, and on an interpretation of the U.S. Constitution, to assist in deciding cases. Judicial opinions are written and published for the public record. In cases where no clear precedent exists, or where legal precedent has been overturned, these opinions have the power to shape and direct law. In some cases, political pressure on judges for a certain ruling can be strong. Judges work in comfortable surroundings. Federal judges work with attorneys, educators, and government officials.

LIBRARIAN

Ranking: 53

Score: 385.20

Hours Weekly: 42.5

Duties: Selects and organizes materials to make information available to the public.

Librarians are designated according to the type of institution in which they work, such as public, school, and academic libraries. Librarians are classified according to two functions: user and technical services. Workers in user services, for example, reference librarians, work more closely with the public than do technical services workers, such as acquisitions librarians. Responsibilities of librarians vary according to the size of collections with which they work. Libraries are often busy and stressful; individual demands can also be taxing for librarians, who must often attend to several projects at one time. In addition to these hardships, there is a great deal of reaching, lifting, and stooping involved in this job.

Librarians work a 35-40 hour week, which often includes evenings and weekends. Computers are increasingly used to catalogue and control circulation. Frequent contacts include publishers' representatives and educators.

LITHOGRAPHER/ PHOTOENGRAVER

Ranking: 26

Score: 264.54

Hours Weekly: 45

Duties: Prepares material for printing through use of cameras and metal printing plates.

Lithographers work for commercial printing plants, newspapers, and printing trade service firms. They photograph material to be printed before making a plate from the film which is then inked and pressed through rollers to print on paper. These professionals tend to specialize, especially in large companies, and may be designated as camera operators, strippers, or platemakers. Intense concentration is required to attend to fine details, and this is stressful for some workers. Exposure to toxic chemicals can also be hazardous, and lithographers must practice careful safety procedures to avoid burns and other skin irritations. Since many large newspaper services operate around the clock, shift work, including evenings and weekends, is common in this field. Lithographers have contact with editors and printing press operators.

LUMBERJACK

Ranking: 241

Score: 1,817.53

Hours Weekly: 45

Duties: Fells, cuts, and transports timber to be processed into lumber, paper, and other wood products.

Lumberjacks are employed by forestry companies, and by federal and private conservation agencies. Workers are categorized according to duties performed in the process of harvesting timber. Applying knowledge of tree characteristics and cutting techniques, fellers use axes and chain saws to cut down trees. These specialists control the direction of fall to minimize tree damage and avoid danger to other workers. Buckers saw timber into log lengths, cutting limbs, tops, and roots from felled trees. Logs are then secured by cable to tractors, and skidded to awaiting trucks. Workers load logs onto trucks by hand or using a winch, and the wood is transported to processing facilities. This work is performed outdoors, often in poor weather conditions. Lumber work involves operating large chain saws and lifting heavy branches and logs. Consequently, physical strength and stamina are needed in this line of work. Injuries from falling debris, and from equipment, are common among workers in this field. Lumberjacks come in contact with foresters, conservationists, and rangers.

MACHINE TOOL OPERATOR

Ranking: 136

Score: 753.10

Hours Weekly: 45

Duties: Operates computerized machines in the manufacture of industrial parts.

Numerical-control machine tool operators are employed by metal working, aircraft, and construction equipment manufacturers. Operators tend one or more machines according to written instructions or the directions of supervisors. They position work pieces and attach tools before feeding programs into machines. Since these machines work only by computerized instructions, positioning is extremely important to avoid problems with future sequencing. Operators monitor machines and use gauges and micrometers to ensure completed parts meet specifications. Workers wear protective clothing to avoid injuries from moving parts, and stamina is required for long hours spent standing or lifting heavy work pieces. Contacts include machinists and computer programmers.

MACHINIST

Ranking: 137

Score: 756.80

Hours Weekly: 47.5

Duties: Operates machinery in manufacturing plants for fabrication of industrial parts.

Machinists set up and operate the machinery used to make metal parts for industrial machinery, motor vehicles, and aircraft manufacturing firms. They begin a project by looking over blueprints or written specifications to plan the sequence of machine operations. Machine controls must then be set before machinists can mark and guide work pieces for cutting and boring. Machinists use micrometers and gauges to check completed pieces for adherence to specifications. Workers must wear safety glasses and ear-plugs to avoid injuries from flying metal parts and loud machinery. shift work, including evening and night shifts, is common in this field. Machinists have

frequent contact with tool-and-die workers and tool programmers.

MAID

Ranking: 121

Score: 682.02

Hours Weekly: 37.5

Duties: May perform a variety of services, including cleaning and upkeep for residential and institutional employers.

Hotels, hospitals, and individuals homeowners employ maids to perform various tasks; members of this occupational group are often jacks-of-all-trades. Some employers might expect maids to be responsible for cleaning; mops, pails, commercial cleansers, and polishing equipment are among the many tools maids use to clean commercial and residential establishments. Maids may also perform a myriad of other tasks, including running errands and answering phones. Maids in private homes sometimes do the work of other service professionals, and may cook meals, for example. Individuals in this field often spend a great deal of time on their feet; heavy lifting and frequent stooping and bending to clean in cramped spaces can also be very uncomfortable. Maids have frequent contact with house cleaners, cooks, and restaurant and hospital personnel.

MAIL CARRIER

Ranking: 223

Score: 1,461.24

Hours Weekly: 45

Duties: Delivers and collects mail along prearranged rural and urban routes.

Mail carriers are employed by the federal government to cover routes by foot, vehicle, or a combination of both. Carriers usually begin work very early in the morning. They begin their days by arranging their mail for delivery. Carriers who walk their routes push carts or carry heavy satchels full of mail. Individuals who serve rural customers usually drive postal vehicles. Some carriers make more than one trip daily; routes serving several businesses require two or three pickups each day. When their daily work is completed, mail carriers return to the post office and turn in receipts and money collected along their routes. Carriers must work under all kinds of weather conditions, and spend a great deal of time on their feet carrying heavy loads. During the course of their work, mail carriers answer questions and have other contact with individuals from all walks of life.

MARKET RESEARCH ANALYST

Ranking: 153

Score: 863.93

Hours Weekly: 45

Duties: Collects and evaluates data to make recommendations to businesses concerning trends in consumer purchasing.

Market research analysts work for management consulting firms and for other businesses that rely on data collected to assist in management decisions. Research analysts conduct surveys and prepare reports to determine cost benefits for employers who are considering developing new products and making sales forecasts. Analysts depend on computers to do computations and prepare tables, charts, and reports for presentation to business managers. Research analysts spend a great deal of time at desks, with only charts, calculators, and computers as companions. Although analysts usually work a regular forty hour week, overtime is sometimes necessary to meet deadlines. In addition to corporate contacts, research analysts also meet with health services professionals and urban planners to devise marketing strategies.

MATHEMATICIAN

Ranking: 2

Score: 89.72

Hours Weekly: 45

Duties: Applies mathematical theories and formulas to teach or solve problems in a business, educational, or industrial climate.

Employers are often corporations or government agencies, but can also be colleges and universities. Chief responsibilities include application of mathematical formulas and processes to solve management problems in private firms or industry. Work is solitary and performed in a structured setting, frequently at a desk, using computers, calculators, and mathematical tools as companions. Deadlines and overtime work, as well as travel to attend workshops and conferences, may add to their responsibilities. Members of the profession may be involved in research with scientists and engineers; communication skills are important to relay solutions to common problems to nonmathematicians. Frequent contacts include engineers, computer programmers, and systems analysts.

MAYOR

Ranking: 204

Score: 1,212.57

Hours Weekly: 45

Duties: Oversees the administration of city services and programs, and presides over the activities of city legislatures.

Most every city, town and village in the country elects a mayor, or someone in a similar capacity. The mayor is the highest-ranking official in city government. Mayors preside over city council meetings, and may cast votes on legislature to break ties. Often, mayors are elected on a platform to modify city services and enact new municipal programs. Mayors introduce legislation to city councils, or institute policies and procedures on their own authority. Mayors oversee the development of city budgets. Many have the power to appoint heads of city departments and programs, such as chief of police, and to hire and fire other city employees. Depending on the size of the city and the range of mayoral duties, mayors may work extremely long hours and keep very hectic schedules. Those holding this office suffer from stress, fatigue or overwork. Mayors regularly meet with civic leaders, city and state officials, and members of the news media.

MECHANICAL ENGINEER

Ranking: 31

Score: 278.46

Hours Weekly: 45

Duties: Develops mechanical products and coordinates the operation and repair of power-using and power-producing machinery.

Over half of all mechanical engineers work for manufacturing industries. Others are employed by businesses, government agencies, and engineering consulting firms. Members of this profession use engineering principles to design mechanical systems and products. They direct the testing and repair of such machinery, and coordinate the operation and maintenance to ensure optimum usage. Individuals may specialize in particular products, such as internal combustion engines, or refrigeration and air-conditioning equipment. Intense concentration is necessary to handle frequent problems that occur in product development. Mechanical engineers often consult with industry managers to determine specifications and design.

MEDICAL LABORATORY TECHNICIAN

Ranking: 67

Score: 454.30

Hours Weekly: 40

Duties: Conducts routine laboratory tests and analyses used in the detection, diagnosis, and treatment of disease.

Most medical laboratory technicians are employed in hospitals. Others in the occupation work for independent laboratories, public health care agencies, pharmaceutical firms, and research institutions. Jobs in this field are concentrated in metropolitan areas. Medical laboratory technicians perform tests on body fluids and tissues to detect changes in cell structures, changes in red or white blood cell count, or the presence of parasites, viruses, or bacteria. This information aids physicians in diagnosing and treating illnesses. Technicians use a wide array of lab equipment, including microscopes and diagnostic machines. Work schedules in this occupation may include nights and weekends. The work pace may be very hectic. Technicians must follow proper sterilization and handling procedures to reduce the possibility of exposure to infectious substances. Medical laboratory technicians work closely with medical technologists, physicians, and medical researchers.

MEDICAL RECORDS TECHNICIAN

Ranking: 10

Score: 165.20

Hours Weekly: 40

Duties: Maintains complete, accurate, and up-to-date medical records for use in treatment, billing, and statistical surveys.

Over three-quarters of all medical record technicians are employed by hospitals and other health care institutions and agencies. A number of workers in this field are employed by insurance firms, law firms, and accounting firms, as well as manufacturers of medical record systems. Medical record technicians code symptoms, diseases, and treatments, and record patients' medical histories. Records are coded and filed using a standardized system, often on computers. Technicians assist medical staff, insurance companies, and law firms in statistical research, by tabulating data and compiling information. Medical record technicians often work shifts, including nights and weekends. The accuracy and attention to detail are the watchword of their occupation. On the job they come in contact with physicians, and with hospital and health care administrators.

MEDICAL SECRETARY

Ranking: 37

Score: 322.24

Hours Weekly: 40

Duties: Transcribes dictations, prepares correspondence, and assists physicians and other medical scientists in compiling reports, articles, speeches and conference proceedings.

Medical secretaries must have a broad understanding of technical terminology and a general familiarity with hospital, laboratory and clinical procedures, to intelligently assimilate and process the information which they receive. Secretaries routinely use dictating machines, and electric typewriters, as well as computer-based word processors and related electronic office systems. They usually work in well lighted, well-ventilated offices, and encounter nominal environmental stress. Long periods of sitting and close eye work, however, can create eye and back strain.

METEOROLOGIST

Ranking: 12

Score: 179.64

Hours Weekly: 45

Duties: Studies the physical characteristics, motions and processes of the earth's atmosphere.

Workers who attempt to forecast the weather are known as operational or "synoptic meteorologists." They collect data on air pressure, temperature, humidity and wind velocity and apply statistical and physical principles to make long and short-term predictions. Workers who study the effects of the atmosphere on transmission of light, sound and radio waves, and who investigate the factors affecting the formation of clouds, storms and tornadoes, are known as "physical meteorologists." Workers who study trends in climate and analyze historical records of temperature, wind, rainfall and sunshine to characterize the climate of a particular region (or era) are referred to as climatologists. Meteorologist work irregular hours, during times of weather emergency, and they may be exposed to inclement or health- threatening weather conditions.

METER READER

Ranking: 191

Score: 1,127.36

Hours Weekly: 42.5

Duties: Monitors public utility meters, and records volume of consumption by customers.

Meter readers are employed by public utility companies throughout the country. Workers in this occupation read electric, gas, water, and steam consumption meters at private residences and commercial establishments. Levels are recorded, and used by utility companies to determine service charges for customers. Meter readers drive or are passengers in utility company vehicles. Meters may be located indoors, sometimes in cramped or hard-to-reach locations. Some residential and commercial utility meters are located outdoors, and meter readers may be required to perform their duties in adverse weather conditions, such as snow, rain or extreme cold. Meter readers come in contact with supervisors and other utility company employees, and customers.

MILITARY (COMMISSIONED OFFICER)

Ranking: 138

Score: 760.00

Hours Weekly: 40

Duties: Supervises enlisted personnel, and performs a variety of military tasks in defense of the nation, from combat leadership to support functions.

Commissioned officers in the military are members of one of the branches of the Armed Forces. Officer training is provided by the Service Academies, the ROTC, Officer Candidate Schools, and other programs. Applicants to Service Academies normally must be nominated by a member of Congress. The ROTC provides training and financial assistance to students while in college, while college graduates and enlisted personnel can receive commissions through OCS programs in each of the branches of service. Officers are concentrated in administration, medical specialties, and combat activities. These military personnel may hold positions as ship's officers, aircraft pilots, or as infantry, intelligence or communications officers. Officers undergo basic training, and in combat use their leadership abilities and military training to gain strategic objectives. Officers follow the strict disciplinary code of the military, and must maintain a standard of physical fitness. Officers work with enlisted personnel, and with other military specialists.

MILITARY (ENLISTED PERSON)

Ranking: 211

Score: 1,280.00

Hours Weekly: 40

Duties: May perform any number of military tasks involved in the defense of the nation, from engaging in combat to working as a payroll clerk in an office.

Enlistees in the U.S. Armed Forces choose a branch of the service, from the Army, Navy, Air Force, Marines, Coast Guard and National Guard. Nearly three out of ten enlisted persons are involved in the operation, maintenance and repair of electrical, mechanical or electronic equipment. Approximately 15% are in combat roles, as foot soldiers, members of gun crews, or seamanship specialists. Other soldiers serve in support roles, such as supply, personnel, communications and administration. All enlistees undergo a rigorous period of basic training, including physical conditioning and weapons instruction, before being assigned to permanent duty at military installations throughout the world. Military life is highly disciplined. Grooming and dress codes must be followed, as must orders from those of higher rank. Even non-combat military jobs may be extremely hazardous. Enlisted personnel work with officers and soldiers from a variety of fields.

MILITARY (WARRANT OFFICER)

Ranking: 128

Score: 720.00

Hours Weekly: 40

Duties: May perform any number of specialized duties in the military, from combat support to conducting military bands.

There are three types of licenses for military service—enlistment contracts, commissions, and warrants. Warrant officers generally hold the ranks between non-commissioned and commissioned officers. To qualify for a warrant, individuals normally must fulfill requirements concerning knowledge or experience in a particular field of expertise. Warrants, however, generally do not require the advanced education needed for commissions. Warrant officers may be flight specialists, supply officers, or medical experts, work in food preparation and distribution, or perform any number of other functions. These officers generally enjoy the rank and privileges accorded other officers in the branches of the military. Occasionally, enlisted personnel can receive warrants after pertinent training and experience. Warrant officers must follow the codes of military discipline, and keep a standard of physical fitness. All military positions carry a degree of danger or hazard. Warrant officers work with enlisted personnel, non-commissioned officers, and commissioned officers.

MILLWRIGHT

Ranking: 200

Score: 1,173.50

Hours Weekly: 47.5

Duties: Installs or dismantles industrial machinery and heavy equipment.

When equipment arrives at a manufacturing site, millwrights scrutinize layout plans, blueprints and other schematic drawings to determine work procedures. They utilize hoists, dollies, pulleys, cables and fork lifts to move the unassembled equipment into proper position. Then they use simple hand-tools to uncrate machinery components, and they use a variety of hand and power instruments for final assembly. Most millwrights are employed by a single factory, and work year round. Others are employed by tool manufacturers or construction firms, and travel between many sites. Millwrights are often exposed to excessive noise, and they are subject to injury from falling or malfunctioning equipment.

MOTION PICTURE EDITOR

Ranking: 29

Score: 274.68

Hours Weekly: 45

Duties: Supervises the filming and editing of motion pictures for entertainment, business, and educational purposes.

Motion picture editors are employed by large and small movie production studios. Those in the entertainment industry normally work out of studios in Los Angeles. Along with the picture's directors, editors oversee all aspects of the filming of motion pictures. The film producer provides the director with a screenplay, actors, and a budget. The editor must familiarize himself with the screenplay, and interpret it in his own manner. Though directors set up scenes to be filmed, establishing the locations of cameras and lights, instructing actors on how to move through a scene and deliver lines, editors play a large role by choosing the "cuts" to be used in the the final version. The director may shoot a scene repeatedly, or in a number of different ways, until satisfied. In large-budget productions for major studios, filming often takes place "on location," in areas all over the world. After filming is completed, directors also supervise the editing process. The pressure for success in the entertainment industry can be strong, and tight schedules and budgets can add to stress in this profession. In addition to working with directors, film editors work closely with producers, actors, writers, and other motion picture personnel.

MUSEUM CURATOR

Ranking: 59

Score: 428.00

Hours Weekly: 42.5

Duties: Plans and directs activities of workers and arranges for the exhibition of articles of interest to museum visitors.

Museum curators are employed by federal, state, and local governments, private museums, and colleges, universities, and libraries throughout the country. Curators coordinate educational, research, and public interest concerns of art museums and science and historical institutions. In addition to obtaining new acquisitions, curators often direct restoration procedures and supervise the installation of exhibits. Frequent travel is necessary for some curators of larger museums. Lifting of heavy objects in preparation for exhibition can also be physically taxing. Curators have contact with registrars, museum directors, and educators.

MUSICAL INSTRUMENT REPAIRER

Ranking: 23

Score: 234.70

Hours Weekly: 47.5

Duties: Maintains and repairs band and orchestral instruments of all kinds.

Almost half of all instrument repairers are self-employed. Others work in music stores, and in musical instrument repair shops. Repairers first inspect instruments to determine problems. Using a variety of small hand tools, workers then dissemble the instrument and remove defective parts. Frequently, replacement pieces must be carved by hand, before being fitted into new sections with glue and clamps. Instrument repairers also decorate and protect instruments by varnishing and buffing. This work is normally done in comfortable, quiet surroundings. Members of this profession can suffer small cuts and bruises while working on the strings and wooden bodies of instruments. Precision repair requires intense concentration. This is a solitary occupation, but repairers sometimes come in contact with music store owners and instrument manufacturers.

MUSICIAN

Ranking: 196

Score: 1,150.50

Hours Weekly: 45

Duties: Plays musical instruments, conducts, composes or performs musical or vocal pieces.

Musicians and singers usually specialize in either classical or popular styles, although many perform in both genres. Musicians play instruments in orchestras, bands, jazz "combos" or solo performances for public entertainment, radio or television soundtracks and commercials. Singers interpret music with accompaniment or a cappella (voice alone). They are classified according to vocal ranges such as soprano, alto, tenor, baritone or bass, and by the style in which they sing. Few musicians work full-time. They generally perform at night and on weekends and are often traveling. Many are hired on the basis of reputations and genre and so must work to gather a following. Unionized musicians receive a minimum fee per performance.

NEWSCASTER

Ranking: 159

Score: 929.25

Hours Weekly: 45

Duties: Prepares and delivers news and related presentations over the air on radio and television.

Newscasters deliver programming on subjects such as current events, sports, weather, or politics. Radio announcers and newscasters are often disc-jockeys as well. Newscasters usually specialize in a particular kind of programming. News anchors, or co-anchors, present the day's top news stories, broadcast news analysts and commentators interpret or discuss stories in greater detail, sports commentators discuss sporting events. Most announcers prepare their own material and some even write advertising copy. Clear delivery and a sense of timing are essential for all newscasters, as well as a pleasing appearance for television announcers. Job hazards in the broadcasting studio are few, but on-scene reporters risk injury when reporting from dangerous areas.

NEWS WRITER (RADIO/TV)

Ranking: 15

Score: 221.25

Hours Weekly: 45

Duties: Writes news items for newspapers, magazines, and radio and television news departments.

News writers employed by large corporations work with stories supplied by reporters or international wire services, or research them in libraries. Writers for wire services and city news bureaus research local stories and condense them into concise articles for national or international use. News writers must learn special writing techniques to capture attention, and relay facts in an objective, non-biased manner. Reporters and news writers often work under heavy deadline pressure and may be required to work overtime, on weekends or during holidays to finish late-breaking stories. The work often requires travel to conduct interviews, or gather research materials.

NUCLEAR ENGINEER

Ranking: 38

Score: 322.42

Hours Weekly: 45

Duties: Conducts research, designs, and monitors the operation and maintenance of nuclear reactors and power plant equipment.

Over one-quarter of all nuclear engineers are federally employed by the Nuclear Regulatory Commission, the Tennessee Valley Authority, or the Department of Energy. Others work for public utilities, nuclear power equipment manufacturers, or engineering consulting companies. Nuclear engineers develop nuclear power plants to generate electricity. They also conduct research and prepare reports on experiments in radiation and nuclear energy. Some individuals coordinate the maintenance and operation of nuclear power plants, during which time they must employ every precaution to avoid the constant threat of nuclear accidents. Plant supervisors and engineering technicians are some of the people who are in regular contact with nuclear engineers.

NUCLEAR PLANT DECONTAMINATION TECHNICIAN

Ranking: 148

Score: 821.88

Hours Weekly: 45

Duties: Cleanses nuclear power plant equipment and personnel of irradiated material.

Nuclear decontamination technicians are employed in nuclear power plants operated by both private utilities and the federal government. These workers use water, cleansing solutions, brushes, and chemical sprays to decontaminate plant equipment that has been exposed to radiation. Workers in nuclear facilities also are normally cleansed at the end of shifts, and decontamination technicians supervise this process. Technicians wear lead-lined protective suits to prevent exposure to irradiated particles on plant equipment or in the air. Large spills or accidents can require extended periods of time in the presence of harmful radiation. Even with protective gear, workers run the risk of illness or injury if radiation levels are very high. Decontamination technicians must be on call 24 hours a day to handle emergency situations. Shift work is common in this line of work. Members of this profession come in contact with plant supervisors, and workers.

NURSE (LICENSED PRACTICAL)

Ranking: 182

Score: 1,080.00

Hours Weekly: 40

Duties: Assists doctors and registered nurses in the care of physically or mentally ill patients.

LPNs work in hospitals, clinics, schools, and other institutions, such as nursing homes and prisons. Other employers include state and local governments and home health care agencies. They take blood pressures and temperatures, administer medicines, chart patients' progress and perform other bedside functions, such as changing dressings and assisting with personal hygiene. Individuals who work in private homes may prepare meals, provide companionship and boost patients' morale and teach family members how to provide basic care for patients. LPNs use sophisticated technical equipment to assist in complex medical procedures. Individuals in this profession usually work forty hour weeks, although many LPNs work part-time. Evening and weekend work is frequently required of nurses, since ailing patients need constant medical attention. This work involves many hours of standing and walking; bending, straining, and lifting can also be physically taxing. Some nurses complain of emotional strain while attending to the demands of severely sick and dying patients. Supervisors include registered nurses and physicians.

NURSE (REGISTERED)

Ranking: 176

Score: 1,018.75

Hours Weekly: 40

Duties: Assists physicians in administering holistic medical care and treatment to assigned patients in clinics, hospitals, public health centers, and health maintenance organizations.

Hospital nurses provide skilled bedside care, and execute individualized programs of treatment prescribed by physicians. They commonly specialize in a single area of medical treatment—such as surgery, pediatrics, or obstetrics. Private duty nurses provide 'one-on-one' care—most often in private residences—for patients requiring intensive treatment and supervision. Community health nurses provide group care for patients in public schools, clinics, and retirement and life-care homes, and office nurses assist physicians and dental surgeons in private practice. Nurses are often required to stand for long periods of time, and they are exposed to a variety of biological and chemical hazards.

NURSE'S AIDE

Ranking: 155

Score: 872.96

Hours Weekly: 40

Duties: Assists practical nurses in caring for patients.

Nursing homes and hospitals are the primary employers of nurse's aides. Most of the time on the jobs is spent doing routine tasks for patients who are convalescing and include assisting in dressing and undressing, mobilizing patients, feeding them and other common tasks that cannot be performed by patients unassisted. Irregular hours are common. Work loads can be very heavy at times. Nurse's aides work closely with patients, registered nurses, therapists and licensed practical nurses. Contact with doctors varies from institution to institution.

OCCUPATIONAL SAFETY/ HEALTH INSPECTOR

Ranking: 89

Score: 538.92

Hours Weekly: 45

Duties: Examines places of business to ensure that equipment and work conditions do not endanger the health and safety of employees.

Occupational safety and health inspectors are employed by the U.S. Department of Labor, as well as by state governments. Inspectors are trained in applicable state and federal laws governing safety in the workplace, and in proper inspection procedures. Members of this profession visit places of employment, from manufacturing and industrial plants to restaurants and hospitals, to detect unsafe work equipment, machinery and procedures, and unhealthy work conditions. Inspectors discuss findings with employers or managers, advising on steps to correct violations, and urging compliance with regulations. Inspectors also prepare reports, and compile evidence in the event that legal action must be taken to enforce laws. This job involves considerable travel and fieldwork. Many occupational safety and health inspectors work long or irregular hours. Members of this profession come in contact with plant supervisors, business managers, and government officials.

OCCUPATIONAL THERAPIST

Ranking: 83

Score: 505.56

Hours Weekly: 42.5

Duties: Develops individualized programs of activity for mentally, physically, developmentally and emotionally impaired persons, to aid them in in achieving self-reliance.

Most occupational therapists work in concert with other health care professionals, to formulate reasonable, holistic programs of treatment for their patients. Occupational therapists use a variety of routine chores to encourage motor skills, concentration, and motivation in patients, as well as to prepare them for the rigors of independent living. Most therapists are employed by hospitals. Others work for school systems, nursing homes, private health care agencies, community mental health centers and out-patient programs.

OCEANOGRAPHER

Ranking: 99

Score: 583.83

Hours Weekly: 45

Duties: Studies the physical characteristics of marine environments, and the organisms that inhabit the seas.

A large number of oceanographers serve on the faculties of colleges and universities, or on the staffs of research institutes. Others work for government agencies, private research firms, or museums. A few are self-employed consultants. Physical or geological oceanographers study ocean currents, the topography of the ocean floor, and the chemical composition of sea water. Marine biologists study the interaction between marine life and marine environments. Most oceanographers divide time between laboratory work and research at sea. These researchers use a variety of tools and equipment, including underwater diving gear and wet suits. Working below the surface is hazardous and extremely strenuous activity, and requires excellent physical conditioning. Oceanographers doing field work occa-

sionally travel to remote regions, and may spend extended periods away from family and friends. Members of this profession regularly come in contact with geologists, biological scientists, and environmentalists.

OFFICE MACHINE REPAIRER

Ranking: 107

Score: 611.91

Hours Weekly: 47.5

Duties: Repairs and maintains business machines

Most office machine repairers do much of their work in the customer's office. Some repairers perform routine maintenance on business machines, while others provide emergency service for malfunctioning machines. Most repairers specialize in one particular machine, such as copiers, calculators, typewriters, cash registers or postage meters. They generally work with common handtools like screwdrivers, pliers and wrenches and wear business clothing. Office machine repairers generally work a 40- hour work week during business hours. Repairers must travel a great deal between customers' offices. Some employers require repairers to be bonded because they work with expensive machines and are exposed to the inner workings of the office. Job-related injuries are rare.

OPTICIAN

Ranking: 50

Score: 371.70

Hours Weekly: 40

Duties: Fills lens prescriptions, and fits eyeglasses and contact lenses.

Most opticians work for optical shops, or for department stores or other retail outlets with optical departments. About one-third work for optomologists or optometrists who sell glasses directly to patients. Some opticians own their own shops, or operate franchise stores of large optical chains. Opticians use optometrists' or ophthalmologists' prescriptions to order the necessary laboratory work for eyeglasses and contact lenses. Opticians assist customers in the selection of eyeglass frames, and perform measurements on the eyes to determine placement of lenses, or to prepare specifications for contact lens manufacturers. Opticians check orders that return from the lab, and make adjustments to ensure proper and comfortable fit. This work takes place indoors, in quiet, comfortable surroundings. Evening and weekend work may be required in some optical shops. Members of this profession work closely with ophthalmologists, optometrists, and optical laboratory technicians.

OPTOMETRIST

Ranking: 88

Score: 538.34

Hours Weekly: 50

Duties: Diagnoses visual disorders and prescribes and administers corrective and rehabilitative treatments.

Optometrists check eyes for signs of cataracts and other disease, and test for depth perception, color differentiation, focus, and coordination. They prescribe glasses, contact lenses and other optical aids, and design exercises to develop and strengthen ocular coordination and muscular control. Most optometrists maintain private practices, although the number involved in partnerships and group practices is steadily rising. Others are employed by eye-care clinics, health maintenance organizations, and a few work as consultants for insurance companies and manufacturers of eye care products.

ORTHODONTIST

Ranking: 163

Score: 940.59

Hours Weekly: 45

Duties: Diagnoses and corrects deviations in dental growth, development and position.

Orthodontists design, fabricate and install braces, space maintainers, space retainers, bite planes, labial and lingual arch wires, head caps and other intra- and extra-oral appliances, to alter the positions and relationships of teeth and jaws, and restore maintain normal appearance and function. Orthodontists use x-ray machines and a wide variety of specialized hand and power tools. Nine out of ten are in private practice, while the remainder are primarily employed by dental schools, private hospitals, and health maintenance organizations. Orthodontists often spend evenings and weekends at the office, in addition to traditional work hours.

OSTEOPATH

Ranking: 225

Score: 1,471.50

Hours Weekly: 55

Duties: Performs medical examinations, diagnoses illnesses, and treats patients with ailments of the muscular and skeletal system.

Licensing requirements for osteopaths differ from state to state. The large majority of positions in this occupation are in states where osteopathic hospitals are located. Over 60 percent of all osteopaths work in Florida, Michigan, Pennsylvania, New Jersey, Ohio, Texas, and Missouri. More than half work in cities and towns of less than 50,000 people. Doctors of Osteopathy (D.O.'s) differ from M.D.'s in that they place special emphasis on the muscular and skeletal systems, and attempt to correct ailments and relieve pain by manipulating body parts with the hands. In addition, D.O.'s prescribe drugs, perform surgery, and counsel patients on preventative health care. Osteopaths work in quiet, well-lit, sterilized environments in offices, hospitals, and clinics. These professionals may spend a good deal of time on their feet, or sitting at desks meeting with patients. Osteopaths often work evenings and weekends to accommodate patients. Members of this profession come in contact with nurses and other health care professionals.

PAINTER

Ranking: 177

Score: 1,034.02

Hours Weekly: 40

Duties: Prepares surfaces, and applies paints, varnishes, and finishes to the interiors and exteriors of houses and other structures.

House painters work for contractors engaged in construction, restoration, repair, or remodeling. Large institutions, such as schools or housing complexes, also employ painters. A number of workers in this profession are self-employed. Before applying paint and finishes, house painters prepare surfaces, stripping old paint with power sanders, wire brushes, and chemical solvents. Nails, grease, and dirt also are removed from surfaces. Painters use rollers, brushes, and spray guns to apply paints to interior walls and ceilings, and exteriors of buildings. Painters may stand for long periods of time. This work involves climbing on ladders or scaffolds to dangerous heights. Painters often suffer serious injuries from falls. These workers need strong arms to carry materials, and to paint for long periods. Painters work closely with paperhangers, painting contractors, and members of the construction trades.

PAROLE OFFICER

Ranking: 52

Score: 381.06

Hours Weekly: 42.5

Duties: Monitors, counsels, and reports on the progress of individuals who have been released from correctional institutions to serve parole.

Parole officers are employed by municipal, state, and federal departments of corrections. The primary responsibility of parole officers is to monitor parolees to insure that terms of parole are not being violated. Parole boards grant parole to inmates based on good behavior and degree of rehabilitation. Terms of parole normally involve regular meetings with parole officers. In addition to checking on the progress of parolees, parole officers may provide counseling on educational and employment opportunities, assist with family and social adjustment, and otherwise help parolees enter the mainstream of society. Officers prepare reports, and work with other correction officials to track parole violators. This work may involve frequent visits to parolees' homes or places of employment. Budget constraints may create heavy workloads for parole officers. Members of this profession work with law enforcement personnel, social workers, and corrections officers.

PARALEGAL ASSISTANT

Ranking: 25

Score: 263.82

Hours Weekly: 45

Duties: Assists attorneys in preparation of legal documents; collection of depositions and affidavits; and investigation, research and analysis of legal issues.

Paralegals work directly under the supervision of licensed attorneys. While they cannot accept clients, set legal fees, or present cases in court, experienced paralegals may perform any other function traditional relegated to lawyers. Skilled workers write motions, take depositions, conduct independent legal research, and file court papers, as well as performing less critical clerical tasks such like typing, word processing, and file management. Paralegals generally work regular hours, in plush, well-lighted offices, but they may be required to work substantially longer during to meet deadlines in major cases.

PERSONNEL RECRUITER

Ranking: 133

Score: 737.85

Hours Weekly: 50

Duties: Interviews prospective employees, administers tests, and provides information about company policies and available jobs.

The large majority of personnel recruiters are employed in private industry. A number in this field work for consulting and outplacement firms. Personnel recruiters spend a good deal of their time traveling to college campuses, job fairs, and conventions to meet with job candidates. Recruiters may conduct screening interviews, or discuss in depth the educational background, work experience, and career goals of prospective employees, in relation to what the company is looking for and has to offer. Recruiters judge candidates, and usually pass recommendations on to personnel offices or hiring committees for final determination. Some may be authorized to make job offers on the spot. Recruiters should have excellent communication skills and the ability to judge character accurately. Overnight travel is very common in this occupation. Personnel recruiters work closely with college placement counselors and personnel managers.

PETROLEUM ENGINEER

Ranking: 38

Score: 322.42

Hours Weekly: 45

Duties: Plans drilling locations and effective production methods for optimal access to oil and natural gas.

The majority of petroleum engineers are employed by major oil companies. Others work for independent oil firms, government agencies, or private consulting firms. Petroleum engineers use maps of subsurfaces to determine exact locations of natural gas and oil reservoirs. They evaluate production costs and drilling rates to establish effective recovery methods. Petroleum engineers spend the great majority of their time on-site, often at remote locations off-shore or in isolated areas of the country. Large amounts of time away from home and frequent traveling is stressful for some individuals. Petroleum engineers' responsibilities include consultation with managers about operational problems.

PHARMACIST

Ranking: 141

Score: 788.64

Hours Weekly: 50

Duties: Advises physicians and patients on the affects of drugs and medications; prepares and dispenses prescriptions.

Hospitals, pharmaceutical companies, and community pharmacies are among those who employ pharmacists as integral members of their professional staffs. Pharmacists counsel patients about the functions of prescribed medications and drug treatments, and about the proper storage of medicines. They also make certain that patients understand the instructions for proper use of such medications. The mixing of ingredients to form ointments, powders, and capsules (known as compounding) constitutes little of today's pharmacists responsibilities, because this function has been taken over by large pharmaceutical companies. Responsibilities of pharmacists employed by chain drug stores include hiring and supervision of personnel. The use of computers facilitates pharmacists' jobs; they use them to record prescriptions and maintain inventory. Recent grads often begin their employment under the supervision of licensed pharmacists. Among the problems encountered by pharmacists are irregular hours, which often include nights and weekends; they also spend much of their time standing. Work is performed indoors, in a clean, laboratory-like setting. Contacts include medical professionals, sales personnel, and pharmaceutical wholesalers.

PHILOSOPHER

Ranking: 48

Score: 361.44

Hours Weekly: 45

Duties: Studies questions concerning the nature of intellectual concepts, and attempts to construct rational theories concerning our understanding of the world around us.

Professional philosophers are employed almost exclusively in colleges and universities throughout the country. A very few work as educational consultants, or in the fields of applied business or medical ethics. Philosophers examine the nature of certain ideas, concepts and theories, such as the relation of body to mind, the function of language and other symbol systems, and the justification for moral or ethical systems. These professionals also study the history of philosophical thought, and its effect on the development of social, economic and scientific trends through history. Specialists in this discipline may study ethics, metaphysics, logic, political philosophy, or other fields. Theories are published in books and journal articles. This profession is intellectually demanding. Teaching loads, combined with the pressure to publish, can cause stress for some faculty members. Philosophers come in contact with librarians, university administrators, and faculty from other disciplines.

PHOTOGRAPHER

Ranking: 116

Score: 663.75

Hours Weekly: 45

Duties: Uses shutter-operated cameras and photographic emulsions to visually portray a variety of subjects.

Still photographers utilize a wide variety of mechanical and optical instruments to achieve specific graphic effects, and adapt to differential lighting conditions. Scientific, medical and engineering photographers use magnifying lenses to photograph facets of the physical realm which are usually invisible to the naked eye. Advertising and catalog photographers provide illustrations of commercial wares. Photojournalists capture news-worthy events for newspaper and magazine publication, and portrait photographers take pictures of individuals or groups in a variety of posed settings.

PHOTOGRAPHIC PROCESS WORKER

Ranking: 56

Score: 404.10

Hours Weekly: 45

Duties: Develops photographic film, makes prints and slides, prepares enlargements, and retouches photographs.

Approximately half of all photographic process workers are employed in photo-finishing labs that work with amateur and professional photographers. Others work for portrait photographers, commercial studios, motion picture producers, and newspapers. All-around darkroom technicians follow developing and printing procedures to create prints and slides. This involves exposing film to chemical solutions and using projection printers. In small labs, work is done by hand, while workers in larger labs operate automated equipment. Specialists in this field include airbrush artists, photographic retouchers, colorists, and color laboratory technicians. Photo labs are normally clean and air-conditioned. In large labs, work can be fast-paced and repetitive. During holidays and summer, overtime may be required in this occupation. Many photographic process workers come in contact with professional photographers, and with photojournalists.

PHOTOJOURNALIST

Ranking: 216

Score: 1,327.50

Hours Weekly: 45

Duties: Photographs newsworthy events for publication in newspapers and magazines.

Some photojournalists are salaried employees on the staffs of newspapers, news magazines, and other publications. Many others work free-lance. Photojournalists cover news events, supplying photographs to accompany reporter' stories. News photographers receive assignments from editors, and normally travel with reporters to news sites. At the scene, news photographers attempt to capture visually striking images which help convey the meaning of the particular story. On newspaper and magazine feature articles, photojournalists take a series of photographs to illustrate and elaborate upon the story. This work often takes news photographers into war zones, scenes of disasters, and other hazardous situations. Photojournalism requires a keen sense for news, and a good eye for the visual image. Some workers in this occupation develop and print their own film. This work involves irregular hours and schedules, and the pressure of deadlines common to all journalists. Photojournalists work closely with editors, reporters, and photographic process workers.

PHYSICAL THERAPIST

Ranking: 126

Score: 716.21

Hours Weekly: 42.5

Duties: Plans and directs treatment to improve mobility and alleviate pain in persons disabled by injury or disease.

While hospitals are the largest single employer of individuals in this profession, others work in rehabilitation centers, nursing homes, and home health agencies. Therapists work with persons recovering from debilitating accidents and afflictions such as multiple sclerosis, cerebral palsy, and heart disease. Since mutual cooperation is so important to the recovery rate in this area, it is important for therapists to work hard to develop a good rapport with each patient. Treatments include exercise, electrical stimulation, heat massage, and ultrasound to relieve pain and promote muscle and skin development. Therapists may work in physical therapy departments of hospitals, or at patients' homes. Some individuals work evenings and weekends, especially if they are in private practice. Long hours spent standing, bending, and straining can be difficult for some members of this profession. Lifting of heavy equipment, and the physical support of patients is also a demanding characteristic of this job. Contacts include physicians, counselors, and occupational therapists.

PHYSICIAN (GENERAL PRACTICE)

Ranking: 225

Score: 1,471.50

Hours Weekly: 55

Duties: Performs examinations, diagnoses medical conditions, and prescribes treatment for individuals suffering from injury, discomfort or disease.

The overwhelming majority of doctors practice in groups of several physicians. Approximately one-quarter are on staffs of hospitals, either as residents or on a full-time basis. General practitioners take patients' medical histories, order tests such as X-rays, and analyze medical reports before prescribing treatments and medications; they also advise patients in proper diet and other preventative health measures. Stethoscopes, and thermometers are among the many instruments physicians use to assist in their diagnoses. Members of this profession work long hours, including evenings and weekends, and are frequently on-call 24 hours a day in case of medical emergencies. General practitioners consult with surgeons and other specialists on a daily basis.

PHYSICIAN ASSISTANT

Ranking: 215

Score: 1,295.80

Hours Weekly: 42.5

Duties: Aids in the performance of essential procedures which free physicians to attend to more specialized aspects of their work.

Physicians in private practice employ the largest number of physician assistants; hospitals, clinics, and HMO's also present opportunities for PA's. Physician assistants take medical histories, perform physical exams and laboratory tests, and sometimes prescribe treatments. As they perform these duties, they are under the supervision of a licensed "supervising physician." They work in well-lit, sterile environments, and due the nature of their work, PA's must spend many hours on their feet. Individuals in this profession use a wide range of equipment to assist them in various complex medical procedures. Work weeks are usually forty hours; however some PA's, especially those who work in emergency rooms, may work two 24-hour shifts weekly. Others work 12-hour shifts three times each week. They frequently work evenings and weekends to make hospital rounds or to accommodate schedules of patients who work. Patience, stability, and the ability to work well with all types of persons are requisites of this career. Contacts include nurses, technicians, and medical therapists.

PHYSICIST

Ranking: 28

Score: 269.46

Hours Weekly: 45

Duties: Researches and develops theories concerning the physical forces of nature.

Most physicists study one or more branches of the field, including elementary-particle physics, atomic or molecular physics, optics, acoustics, or the physics of fluids. Most work in universities, but some work for the federal government and in private industry. Some do consulting work. Much of federal grant money given to physicists is based on research for military applications. Physicists are highly trained and often use specialized and delicate instruments like lasers, particle accelerators, computers, or semiconductors. Physicists are usually expected to publish scientific papers about the results of their research. They usually work regular hours in laboratories or classrooms, but often travel to conferences or to use large facilities unavailable to them at home.

PHYSIOLOGIST

Ranking: 46

Score: 359.28

Hours Weekly: 45

Duties: Studies the life functions of plants and animals, both in their natural habitats, and under experimental or abnormal conditions.

A large number of physiologists hold teaching and research positions on the faculties of colleges and universities. Many work in the private sector, for commercial research and development companies, and the food industry. Others are employed by the Departments of Agriculture and the Interior, and other government agencies. Physiologists study all aspects of the life cycles of organisms. These include growth, reproduction, photosynthesis, and metabolism. Physiolo-gists also analyze the function of organic systems in plants and animals, such as the circulatory, nervous, and immune systems in animals, and the root systems of plants. This work may be performed in offices, laboratories or classrooms, or in the field, to observe organisms in their natural environment and collect specimens. Researchers may be exposed to toxic substances, disease, and dangerous animals. Physiologists work closely with other biological scientists, as well as government officials and educators.

PIANO TUNER

Ranking: 96

Score: 563.28

Hours Weekly: 47.5

Duties: Adjusts piano strings to achieve proper musical pitch.

The large majority of piano tuners work in music stores. Of these, about half are self-employed. Others in this profession work for musical instrument manufacturers. Most positions are in large metropolitan areas. Piano tuners help maintain instruments in proper performing condition, by insuring that piano strings emit the correct note when keys are struck. The pitch of a string is determined by how quickly it vibrates, and this is connected to its tension. Piano tuners compare the pitch of the "A" or "C" string to that of a tuning fork or electronic tone, and adjust the string accordingly by tightening or loosening steel pins with a tuning hammer or wrench. This work is not overly strenuous, but tuners must have a sharp musical ear to be able to distinguish subtle variations in pitch. In addition, mechanical aptitude and manual dexterity are helpful. Tuners normally perform their work in customers' homes, or in music studios. Members of this profession come in contact with musicians, music store owners, and piano repairers.

PLASTERER

Ranking: 161

Score: 929.67

Hours Weekly: 45

Duties: Applies the plaster finish to interior walls and ceilings, and cement finish and stucco to exterior surfaces.

The majority of plasterers work for independent contractors in the construction and home improvement industries. About one-third of the workers in this field are self-employed. Plasterers normally apply several different plaster coats to surfaces of cinder block, gypsum lath, or wire mesh. A single coat may be applied to interior masonry surfaces, such as specially prepared drywall or wallboard. In addition to preparing smooth, durable finishes on surfaces, plasterers also install insulation systems, using insulation board, Fiberglas and plaster. Some specialize in decorative or ornamental work, such as molding intricate designs and patterns for walls and ceilings. This requires special skill, and the ability to work from architects' blueprints. Plasterers use trowels, mixing tools, and plastering materials such as lime and Plaster of Paris. This work can be strenuous. Stucco work takes place outdoors, but only in favorable weather. Plasterers work with painters and other members of the construction trades.

PLUMBER

Ranking: 150

Score: 836.38

Hours Weekly: 45

Duties: Plumbers build and repair water, waste disposal, drainage, and gas delivery systems for residential, commercial, and industrial structures.

Plumbers use hand and power tools to cut and fit pipes, and they frequently consult blueprints and drawings, indicating the location of these pipes. They must stand for long periods in cramped quarters, while being exposed to dirt, moisture, rust, and noxious fumes. Most plumbers are employed by mechanical or plumbing contractors; one out of six is self-employed.

PODIATRIST

Ranking: 140

Score: 783.04

Hours Weekly: 50

Duties: Diagnoses and treats problems of the feet, through corrective devices, medication, therapy, and surgery.

Most podiatrists own or are employed in private practices. Others work for hospitals, HMOs, podiatric medical colleges, and public health agencies. Podiatrists treat foot ailments, such as corns, bunions, ingrown toenails, and skin and nail diseases. Some specialize in podiatric surgery, or orthopedics (treatment of bone, joint and muscle disorders). Podiatrists use X-rays and laboratory reports to aid in diagnosis. Treatment may include prescribing and fitting corrective devices or implants, performing hospital or outpatient surgery, recommending programs of therapy, or referring patients with arthritis or other diseases to physicians. Podiatrists most often work 40-hour weeks, frequently accommodating patients with evening and weekend hours. Required training and education normally includes a degree from a college of podiatric medicine, classroom and laboratory

study, and clinical experience. Members of this profession come in contact with physicians, nurses, and other health care professionals.

POLICE OFFICER

Ranking: 242

Score: 1,877.85

Hours Weekly: 47.5

Duties: Provides protection against crime, investigates criminal activity, and works with the public on crime-prevention measures.

Police officers are employed by cities and towns across the country. Large cities maintain police forces of hundreds or thousands of officers, while small rural communities may employ only a few officers. After completing training, new recruits normally begin on patrol duty, monitoring surroundings, reacting to suspicious or dangerous situations, and responding to radio instructions from police headquarters. In large forces, patrol officers are supplemented by mounted and canine corps, firearms and fingerprint experts, mobile rescue and SWAT teams, laboratory experts, and numerous other specialists. Plainclothes detectives investigate criminal activity, gathering facts and evidence, performing surveillance on suspects, and conducting raids and arrests. Police work is performed around the clock. Officers must be physically fit, and face dangerous and even deadly situations on the job. Police officers work with community leaders, educators, and corrections workers.

POLITICAL SCIENTIST

Ranking: 79

Score: 500.17

Hours Weekly: 45

Duties: Studies the origin, development and operation of political institutions, in order to formulate, develop and validate political theories.

Political scientists conduct research into political processes, using public opinion data and narrative historical accounts They are generally associated with institutions of higher learning, though many are employed by consulting firms, political organizations and government intelligence agencies. They typically work in comfortable, well-lit offices, and and encounter few environmental stresses. Many political scientist specialize in a specific geographical, political, or philosophical aspect of political behavior.

POSTAL INSPECTOR

Ranking: 13

Score: 195.28

Hours Weekly: 45

Duties: Monitors the function of the postal system, insuring smooth, safe, and legal postal service operations.

Postal enspectors are employed in regional and district offices of the U.S. Postal Service. Postal inspectors enforce the laws and regulations governing the operation of the postal system. Responsibilities in this occupation include investigating criminal activities, such as theft of mail or use of the postal system for fraudulent purposes. Inspectors conduct investigations into mismanagement, perform financial audits, and work with the Internal Revenue Service and other agencies on special projects. In addition, inspectors recommend improvements in postal procedures, and receive and respond to customer complaints. Postal inspectors must be well-trained in applicable laws and regulations, as well as in inspection procedures. This job often requires travel and field work. Postal inspectors involved in criminal investigations may face danger in dealing with suspected lawbreakers. Members of this profession come in contact with mail carriers and other postal workers, and with government officials.

PRESIDENT (U.S.)

Ranking: 250

Score: 3,630.00

Hours Weekly: 65

Duties: Serves as Chief Executive Officer of the federal government, administrative head of the executive branch of the government, and commander in chief of the armed forces of the nation.

Woodrow Wilson, the 27th President, said that the President was to be as big as he could, in law and conscience. With a vast multitude of duties and responsibilities, the President meets with advisors, determines policy and courses of action and works out a legislative program. The oath the President takes on assuming office states that he will protect and preserve the Constitution and enforce the laws of the land. The President also influences the economic life of the United States as well as directing the foreign policy in its political, economic and commercial aspects. Work days are normally long and stressful for the President. As Commander-in-Chief, he is actually considered working and on duty 24 hours a day, 7 days a week. The presidential schedule is hectic, filled with meetings with his staff, the Cabinet, top-ranking business, educational and military leaders, lobbyists, foreign diplomats and members of the other branches of the government.

PRECISION ASSEMBLER

Ranking: 110

Score: 639.45

Hours Weekly: 42.5

Duties: Works on subassembly or final assembly of products such as machinery, electronic equipment, or aircraft.

Large and small manufacturing firms throughout the United States employ precision assemblers to produce working products. Members of this profession often undergo many months of training, during which time they may learn to read blueprints, and to use a wide variety of special tools and precision measuring equipment. Although working conditions vary according to the type of industry in which they are employed, common problems include heavy lifting, noisy surroundings, and monotonous and repetitive tasks. Work takes place indoors, most frequently in large factories. Shift work is common is this field, and night and weekend work is standard. Contacts include engineers, technicians, and machine operators.

PROTESTANT MINISTER

Ranking: 108

Score: 626.52

Hours Weekly: 52.5

Duties: Leads a congregation in worship services and rites of the church in Protestant congregations.

Many Protestant ministers write articles, participate in community and charitable activities or teach in seminaries and schools. Although Protestant congregations differ from branch to branch, most ministers traditionally focus on biblical study, preparing sermons and being spiritual leaders of the community. In smaller or rural communities, ministers may work more individually with parishioners, but in urban areas ministers often have opportunities in management or organizing church affairs. Ministers often work with volunteer laity members who perform non-liturgical functions such as preparing church budgets or office work. Travel is required by some ministers who are assigned to new congregations every few years.

PSYCHIATRIST

Ranking: 221

Score: 1,417.00

Hours Weekly: 55

Duties: Studies, diagnoses, and treats mental, emotional and behavioral disorders.

Psychiatrists study the psychological and biological pathology of human thought processes, in order to explain and remedy behavioral abnormalities. They employ a wide variety of therapies—from dream interpretation to programs of psychoactive medication—to modify aberrant or destructive patterns of behavior in their patients. Psychiatrists work regular hours, but they may be called at any time in case of emotional crisis or medical emergency. Most psychiatrists are self-employed, but many others work for hospitals, universities, crisis centers, public mental institutions and health maintenance organizations. A small number of psychiatrists are employed as salaried workers or consultants to private industry.

PSYCHOLOGIST

Ranking: 130

Score: 727.52

Hours Weekly: 45

Duties: Studies human behavior, emotion, and mental processes, and provides counseling and therapy for individuals.

Over one-quarter of the psychologists in the U.S. are in private practice or are otherwise self-employed. Others work in education, health care, social service organizations, private businesses, and government agencies. Psychologists may perform research through experiments, tests, interviews, surveys, and clinical studies. Experimental psychologists study motivation, learning, perception, and neurological factors in behavior. Developmental psychologists investigate patterns of change that occur in the maturing and aging processes. Clinical psychologists assist the emotionally or mentally disturbed in adjusting to life, often through psychotherapy. Therapists normally work their own hours in comfortable offices, while clinical psycholo-gists may occasionally work evenings and weekends. Those in government and health care services normally have more structured schedules. Heavy workloads, deadline pressures, and the difficulty of working with disturbed patients can all lead to stress for members of this profession. Psychologists may work with physicians, psychiatrists, and educators.

PUBLIC RELATIONS EXECUTIVE

Ranking: 207

Score: 1,247.13

Hours Weekly: 45

Duties: Helps governmental bodies, businesses and individuals maintain a positive image with the public.

Communicating prevalent perceptions of customers, employees, and other affected individuals to those with decision-making powers is an important aspect of a public relations specialist's job. They may work with the press, community organizations, and special interest groups to assess popular reaction to a company's policies. They are also responsible for promoting communication and understanding among various factions of our society. Because each employer's needs are different, public relations department heads must develop specific programs dependent on these ends. Deadlines and varied hours, which include evening and weekend meetings and speeches, are common in this field. Travel is frequent, and flexibility is very important. Frequent contacts corporate clientsand media personnel.

PUBLICATION EDITOR

Ranking: 74

Score: 486.75

Hours Weekly: 45

Duties: Plans and directs the editorial activities of various publications.

Approximately 40 percent of all publication editors work for newspapers, magazines, or book publishers. Others are employed by businesses and nonprofit organizations. Responsibilities include supervising writers and other workers, assigning material to be researched and written, and organizing material for page layouts. Editors meet frequently with publishers and editorial staff to establish policies and solve publication problems. Some individuals work in quiet offices, while others are surrounded by other writers and editors working on word processing equipment. Stresses related to frequent travel and constant problem-solving are difficult for some members of this profession, and pressure of deadlines is a constant companion to editors.

PURCHASING AGENT

Ranking: 22

Score: 230.85

Hours Weekly: 45

Duties: Assesses an establishment's needs and available products, and buys raw materials, equipment and machinery, furniture, and other supplies accordingly.

Almost half the positions for purchasing agents are in manufacturing, primarily in the machinery and transportation equipment industries. Others are in construction companies, schools, advertising firms, and government agencies, especially the Department of Defense. Purchasing agents buy supplies based on predetermined reorder schedules or departmental requests, or by examining computerized inventory reports. Agents compare supplier catalogs and price lists, meet with salespeople, and invite bids from suppliers on large orders. In addition, purchasing agents may negotiate long-term contracts based on projected needs and resources. Many agents arrange for services such as office maintenance and waste disposal. Purchasing agents must have a thorough knowledge of specific products and suppliers they work with, as well as the needs of their own companies. Some travel may be necessary in this profession. Purchasing agents work with business managers, sales representatives, and inventory control personnel.

RABBI

Ranking: 85

Score: 522.10

Hours Weekly: 55

Duties: Acts as spiritual leader of Jewish communities; advising, teaching, and leading religious services.

Most rabbis serve congregations, many of which are relatively small. Others teach, work as chaplains in the Armed Forces, or work in hospitals and other institutions. They conduct weddings and funeral services, supervise spiritual education programs, visit the sick and bereaved, and work with various community organizations in the interests of their congregations. Rabbis are also involved in administrative duties, and may supervise assistants. Others write for religious publications or teach in colleges and universities. Rabbis spend much of their time among members of their communities, and are not confined to an office as an essential ingredient of their jobs. However, long, irregular hours, and sedentary activity in pursuit of religious teachings and writing can be a problem for some individuals. Like other clergy members, rabbis have a great deal of autonomy. They are responsible only to their congregations and to the board of trustees of those congregations. A strong desire to serve the needs of others, combined with good communication skills and deep, enduring spiritual beliefs are necessary attributes of this profession. Contacts include members of social service professions, community leaders, educators, and other religious workers.

RACE CAR DRIVER (INDY CLASS)

Ranking: 248

Score: 2,522.25

Hours Weekly: 45

Duties: Drives specially designed automobiles in tournament races of various distances.

Most professional race car drivers are members of racing teams. These can range in size from two- or three-person operations, to large, corporate-sponsored organizations with many drivers, mechanics, and designers. Drivers race against each other in different categories of automobile, including Indy cars, stock cars, and dragsters. Tournament races begin with time trials, where the vehicle is constantly refined and tested to maximize performance. During the race, driving skill and knowledge of the machine are essential to successful performance. Drivers must know when to accelerate, when to pass, and when to stop for fuel and repairs. Often, members of the same racing team will work together to ensure that one member finishes high in the standings. Auto racing is an extremely dangerous profession. Cars can travel in excess of 200 miles per hour on some courses. At such speeds, machine malfunctions can be deadly. Crashes during training and races can cause critical or fatal injuries. The profession requires very high degrees of mental acuity and physical stamina. Indy drivers work closely with mechanics, pit crew, and corporate sponsors.

RAILROAD CONDUCTOR

Ranking: 149

Score: 830.28

Hours Weekly: 50

Duties: Operates an electric, diesel-electric, or gas-turbine-electric locomotive to transport passengers and freight.

Railroad conductors and engineers are employed by private rail transport companies, local rail transit lines, and Amtrak. Before leaving on a run, conductors and locomotive engineers inspect the train to insure a proper amount of fuel, water, and other supplies. Conductors and engineers synchronize watches in accordance with departure times and schedules. The engineer receives the starting signal from the conductor, and controls train speed using throttles and air-brakes. During a passenger trip, the conductor moves through the cars, collecting tickets and answering passenger inquiries. Conductors and engineers receive signals from a traffic control center concerning stops, delays, and oncoming trains. Strict attention must be paid to all train signals, orders, and safety regulations. Obstructions on the track, misinterpreted information, and malfunctioning equipment, can all lead to railroad accidents. On longer runs, shift work is necessary for engineers, and evening and weekend work is common in this profession. Conductors and engineers come in contact with dispatchers, freight handlers, and other rail workers.

REAL ESTATE AGENT

Ranking: 212

Score: 1,293.57

Hours Weekly: 47.5

Duties: Acts as intermediary between buyer and seller in real estate transactions, usually by being the prime salesperson of a property.

Real estate agents are usually independent salespersons who work for licensed brokers. Large firms and national franchises employ sales or general managers, who act in a supervisory capacity to sales agents. Agents and brokers usually sell residential properties, although some specialize in industrial or agricultural real estate. A thorough knowledge of client's needs (budget, proximity to schools, shopping, and religious institutions) is necessary for an agent who specializes in residential real estate. Agents should also know where to obtain financing, and have a good understanding of local zoning and tax laws. Although agents use an office as the base of their operations, their work involves property showings and meetings with clients, which frequently take them outside their offices. Long hours, including evening and weekend work, are common to this profession. However, the flexibility of work schedules makes this an attractive career to homemakers and retired persons. Computers are increasingly employed in this field to obtain listings and research sources of available financing. Frequent contacts include mortgage bankers, lawyers, and city officials.

RECEPTIONIST

Ranking: 117

Score: 665.21

Hours Weekly: 40

Duties: Greets visitors to offices, answers questions, and refers customers to appropriate staff.

Nearly half of all receptionists are employed in health care facilities, such as doctors' and dentists' offices, hospitals, and clinics. Others work in business offices of real estate, insurance, manufacturing, and other types of companies. Receptionists usually sit at desks in central locations in offices, near entrances or elevators. These workers greet customers and visitors, inquire about the purpose of the visit, and direct them to the proper individuals. Receptionists may also keep logs of phone calls and visitors, perform clerical tasks such as typing and filing, and serve a security function. Receptionists may use advanced office technology, such as word processors, personal computers, and PBX systems to facilitate tasks. A receptionist is often the first personal contact a client has with a business, so these workers must be pleasant, personable, and knowledgeable. Most receptionists work normal daytime hours, but those in hospitals may work evenings and weekends. Receptionists come in contact with secretaries, office managers, and other office personnel.

RECREATION WORKER

Ranking: 157

Score: 889.14

Hours Weekly: 42.5

Duties: Organizes and supervises a variety of leisure activities, including sports, arts, crafts, drama, singing, dancing, and story telling.

Recreation workers range from camp counselors instructing children in nature-related, athletic, and academic activities, to industrial recreation workers organizing leisure activities, fitness programs, and social functions for employees. State and municipal park systems employ nearly 40 percent of all recreation workers. Twenty-five percent find jobs with social organizations like the YMCA, YWCA, and Red Cross; while 15 percent work for social service establishments, such as day care centers, nursing homes, and half-way houses. Recreation workers spend much of their time outdoors, and must have excellent physical stamina and coordination.

REPORTER

Ranking: 186

Score: 1,106.25

Hours Weekly: 45

Duties: Covers newsworthy events for newspapers, magazines, and television news programs.

Nearly three-quarters of all reporters work for newspapers, either large city or suburban dailies, or small town weekly papers. Others work for news magazines, local and network broadcasters, and wire services. General assignment reporters cover local events as assigned by editors, writing and filing stories, broadcasting live from the news site, or taping reports for later airing. "Beat" reporters cover specific assignments, such as police headquarters or city hall, on a regular basis. Investigative reporters go into stories in depth, often filing series reports to cover a particular angle, or uncover injustice or corruption. Reporters with special backgrounds or interests are assigned fields such as science, health and military affairs. This work may take reporters to distant countries to cover fast-breaking stories. Reporters may be assigned to war zones, crime scenes, neutral disasters, or other dangerous situations. Reporters need good writing and interviewing skills. Journalists can suffer stress and fatigue from working long, irregular hours under deadline pressure. Reporters work closely with editors, photojournalists and newsmakers.

RESPIRATORY THERAPIST

Ranking: 156

Score: 884.73

Hours Weekly: 42.5

Duties: Treats and rehabilitates patients suffering from cardiopulmonary (heart and lung) ailments which interfere with normal breathing.

Respiratory therapists administer a variety of routine and emergency treatments. They dispense pure oxygen and oxygen mixtures, use water vapor and aerosol sprays to moisten the respiratory tract, coach patients in performing breathing exercises, and operate mechanical breathing aids. Respiratory therapists configure, operate, and monitor a variety of special medical devices, including oxygen tents, ventilators, and breathing machines. Nine out of ten respiratory therapists are employed by hospitals. Others provide in-home care, or are employed in private clinics or nursing homes.

ROOFER

Ranking: 228

Score: 1,481.20

Hours Weekly: 42.5

Duties: Installs roofs on new buildings, performs repairs on old roofs, and re-roofs old buildings.

The majority of roofers are employed by roofing contractors. A number work for businesses and government agencies which do in-house construction and repair work on facilities. Approxi-

mately one-third of all roofers are self-employed. On flat roofs of commercial and industrial buildings, roofers install layers of insulation, sealer, and roofing felt, before glazing the top layer with gravel. On the pitched roofs of most houses, roofers fit and nail shingles. Roofers use hammers, nails, shovels, and mops. This work is extremely strenuous, involving carrying heavy loads of shingles and tar up ladders to work sites. Roofers suffer a high degree of injury from slips and falls from roofs, scaffolds, and ladders, and are susceptible to burns from hot tar or bitumen. Working on hot roofs in the summer can be extremely uncomfortable. Roofers work closely with building contractors, and with members of other construction trades.

ROUSTABOUT

Ranking: 239

Score: 1,731.45

Hours Weekly: 50

Duties: Performs routine physical labor and maintenance on oil rigs and pipelines, both on and off shore.

The large majority of roustabouts work for companies in the oil and gas field services industry. Roustabouts provide labor for numerous tasks related to oil and gas extraction, including digging foundations or drainage ditches, loading and unloading trucks and boats, mixing concrete, and clearing trees. In addition, roustabouts connect pipes, and assemble and repair oil rig equipment, such as pumps, boilers, drills, and engines. These workers use hand and power tools, motorized lifts, and electronic testing equipment. A number work for drilling contractors involved directly in the oil or gas extraction process. This work is physically strenuous, and hazards include falls from rigs, and cuts, abrasions, and burns from tools and heavy machinery. Workers may be exposed to adverse weather and sea conditions. Offshore roustabouts work 7-day, 12-hour shifts every other week. Others may work night and weekend shifts on wells. Roustabouts come in contact with truck and boat operators, and drilling contractors.

SALES REPRESENTATIVE (WHOLESALE)

Ranking: 214

Score: 1,293.84

Hours Weekly: 47.5

Duties: Represents wholesalers who distribute products to stores, manufacturers, and businesses.

The primary employers of wholesale trade sales workers are firms that sell machinery, equipment and other products to business and industrial users. Others in this profession work for food product companies, hardware distributors, and companies that sell electrical goods. Wholesale trade salespeople simplify the process of moving products from manufacturers to consumers. These workers often represent a large array of products. Salespersons meet with buyers to discuss the buyers' inventories and needs, and how various products can meet those needs. Sales pressure in this profession is not strong. Rather, salespeople attempt to develop good working relations with buyers, to create lasting and dependable clients. Salespeople in wholesale trade keep financial records, contact potential clients, and advise on marketing and advertising strategies. This profession often demands long hours and extensive travel. Salespeople must be personable and tactful. Salespersons in wholesale trade come in contact with buyers, and with wholesale distributors.

SALESPERSON (RETAIL)

Ranking: 151

Score: 836.43

Hours Weekly: 40

Duties: Provides courteous and efficient service to customers in retail stores.

Retail sales workers are employed in a wide range of establishments, from drug, grocery and department stores, to specialized shops for home entertainment equipment, clothing and furniture. These workers provide information on products, give demonstrations of available models, discuss prices, and otherwise assist potential buyers. Since many retail salespeople work on commission, interesting the customer in products is a major concern for these workers. Most retail workers also keep count of inventory, and insure that merchandise is displayed properly. For some, though, the job consists primarily of handling transactions and wrapping purchases. Retail sales workers generally work indoors, spending much of their time on their feet. Evening and weekend work is common in this occupation, as is overtime or extended hours during the holiday shopping season. A large number of retail sales workers are part-time employees. Sales staff often enjoys discounts on store merchandise. These workers come in contact with cashiers, inventory clerks, and store managers.

SCHOOL PRINCIPAL

Ranking: 60

Score: 432.99

Hours Weekly: 47.5

Duties: Supervises the educational curricula and programs in elementary and secondary schools.

Public and private school systems across the country employ principals in schools to oversee the administration of educational programs. Many secondary schools also employ assistant principals to handle some of the duties this job entails. Principals are the highest authority in schools, and provide leadership for faculty and students. These professionals plan and institute curricula, and visit classrooms to evaluate teachers and learning material. Principals meet with faculty to discuss teaching strategies and skills. Principals also prepare and manage school budgets, oversee allocation and requisitioning of supplies, and meet with students, parents, and community leaders. Assistant principals may handle disciplinary matters, counsel students, administer various programs, and monitor maintenance of buildings and grounds. Principals often work over 40 hours a week, 11 months a year. Members of this profession work with school administrators, civic leaders, and other educators.

SEAMAN

Ranking: 237

Score: 1,660.56

Hours Weekly: 50

Duties: May perform any number of tasks involved in the operation of ships, boats, barges, or dredges.

Sailors are employed on cargo vessels, passenger ships, ferries, and other forms of marine transportation. Sailors stand deck watch, and perform a variety of duties on ships. These may include painting and chipping rust from decks and superstructures, operating engines, maintaining lines and equipment, measuring water depth, and steering the vessel. Seamen also break out, rig, and store cargo loading and handling gear. Mates supervise and coordinate the activities of crew, under the direction of the captain. The work of sailors can be strenuous. Some jobs, such as standing watch or chipping rust, are tedious. Sailors must perform duties in all weather conditions, from extreme heat to extreme cold. In foul weather, such as storms, sailors are in danger from drowning if they fall overboard, or if the vessel capsizes. Members of this profession spend long stretches at sea, away from families. Sailors come in contact with stevedores, harbor personnel, and other ship crew members.

SECRETARY

Ranking: 73

Score: 483.36

Hours Weekly: 40

Duties: Acts as the center of communication, processes and disseminates information throughout an organization.

Employers are organizations of all types; businesses, educational institutions, government agencies, and hospitals need secretaries to facilitate smooth operations and sustain objectives. The work of secretaries is highly dependent on the kind of organization for which they work; they may organize and maintain files, answer questions of callers and schedule appointments, type and perform word processing functions, and take dictation for employers. In some organizations, secretaries work in small groups, forming a "secretarial pool," where all work to together to perform specific functions. Secretaries usually work in an office, and have a standard work week, consisting of forty hours; overtime work is sometimes necessary to meet deadlines. Many secretaries work part-time, or on a temporary basis. Individuals who want to work as secretaries must be organized and have strong communications skills. Good typing speed and word processing talents are also important in this field. Many people find the long hours sitting behind a desk, and the eyestrain created by constant viewing of a video display terminal distressing parts of this job. Unappreciative employers can also be a negative force. Contacts include office managers and receptionists.

SET DESIGNER

Ranking: 43

Score: 354.00

Hours Weekly: 45

Duties: Plans and assembles theatrical sets for film, television and stage productions.

Set designers may work as salaried employees of television or movie studios, or work on an independent basis. Jobs are concentrated in entertainment centers, especially New York and Los Angeles, but many opportunities also exist with local, community or university theater groups. Set designers meet with directors, producers and screenwriters to plan stage and studio layouts, based on the settings and themes of the production in question. Designers supervise the construction of sound stages, the painting of backdrops, and the assembly or purchase of props. Since many stage productions require numerous sets during the course of an evening, designers develop systems, such as rotating sets or multi-purpose props, to facilitate scene changes. This work is fast-paced, and requires design talent and aesthetic sense, in addition to basic construction and carpentry skills. Designers may work long hours to meet production schedules. Members of this profession work with entertainment industry personnel, and with construction trade workers.

SEWAGE PLANT OPERATOR

Ranking: 132

Score: 734.24

Hours Weekly: 45

Duties: Monitors and controls processes and equipment to remove harmful waste materials from sewage.

The large majority of sewage plant operators work in treatment plants operated by local governments. A small number work for private chemical or waste management companies, or for the federal government. Operators monitor and maintain the pipes, pumps, gauges, valves, and other equipment in sewage treatment facilities, in order to insure the proper removal of solid materials, organisms, and chemicals from waste water. Sewage that is rendered harmless is recirculated into waterways. Operators read gauges and meters, adjusting controls as needed, and may take water samples and perform chemical and biological analyses on sewage. These workers use wrenches, pliers, and other hand tools, and more specialized equipment. Sewage plant operators may be exposed to foul odors, toxic substances, and noise. Shift work, including nights and weekends, is common in this occupation, as is overtime during emergencies. Sewage plant operators work with plant supervisors, and with government regulatory officials.

SHEET METAL WORKER

Ranking: 210

Score: 1,266.14

Hours Weekly: 45

Duties: Constructs, installs, and maintains sheet metal products for home, commercial, and industrial use.

Sheet metal workers are employed by construction contractors, primarily those specializing in roofing, heating and air-conditioning, and by general contractors engaged in residential, commercial and industrial construction. These workers follow blueprints or other instructions, and cut, bend, and fasten pieces of sheet metal to construct ducts, roofs, gutters, kitchen counters, and other custom products, which are then installed at construction sites. Often, sheet metal workers operate computerized metal working equipment, in addition to using saws, shears, presses, hammers, drills, and measures. This work entails a good deal of bending, lifting, and standing, often in awkward positions or at great heights. Workers may suffer injury from falls, or cuts from tools, machinery, and sharp metal edges. Sheet metal workers normally wear gloves and eye protection. Members of this profession work closely with other construction trade workers.

SHIPPING/RECEIVING CLERK

Ranking: 84

Score: 520.32

Hours Weekly: 42.5

Duties: Monitors the movement of shipments of merchandise into and out of places of business.

Approximately half of all shipping and receiving clerks work for wholesale establishments or retail stores. Over one-third are employed in factories. Most jobs in this field are located in urban areas. Shipping clerks are responsible for all shipments to consumers or retailers that leave an establishment. Receiving clerks monitor the arrival of merchandise shipments from suppliers. Clerks check shipments against invoices to insure that orders have been properly filled. Shipping clerks compute freight or postal rates, address shipments, and direct or assist in loading trucks. Receiving clerks may unload material and route it to appropriate locations. In smaller businesses, all of these duties may be handled by one individual. Some clerks may operate computerized inventory control systems. Shipping clerks must be familiar with postal regulations. These workers may spend long periods on their feet, in cold and drafty warehouses. Shipping and receiving clerks regularly come in contact with inventory and warehouse managers, and with truckers.

SHOE MAKER/ REPAIRER

Ranking: 103

Score: 597.24

Hours Weekly: 42.5

Duties: Refurbishes and mends worn shoes, saddles, and boots.

The most common tasks performed by shoe repairers are heel and sole replacement. Shoe repairers use hand-tools, such as hammers, awls, and knives; and power tools, including sewing machines, heel nailing machines, hole punching machines, and sole stitchers. Most shoe repairers work in small, crowded shops. They are often exposed to noxious fumes from leather dyes and stains, and they are required to stand for long periods. About one in four shoe repairers are self-employed. Most others are employed in large shops which provide both shoe repair and general leather repair services.

SINGER

Ranking: 202

Score: 1,194.75

Hours Weekly: 45

Duties: Performs vocal compositions solo or as part of a group, often to instrumental accompaniment.

Professional opera singers are employed by opera companies in major cities across the country. Classical singers work with orchestra choruses. Other singers are members of rock, pop, country, or folk groups, and perform in concert halls, nightclubs, churches, and at social gatherings. Singers perform vocal arrangements, using knowledge of melody and harmony, and employing personalized style. Operatic and choral singers are classified according to vocal range, from soprano to bass. Virtuosos and choral singers perform traditional repertory pieces, while popular contemporary singers often perform their own compositions. Talented singers may be offered recording contracts, go on concert tours, and perform on television. Formal training is helpful in this profession. Performance schedules for singers often include evenings, weekends, and holidays. Lack of success can be stressful in this field. Professional singers work closely with musicians, talent agents, and members of the media.

SOCIAL WORKER

Ranking: 94

Score: 550.42

Hours Weekly: 42.5

Duties: Assists individuals, families, and groups in need of counseling and special social services.

State, county, and local government agencies employ a large percentage of social workers. Positions in the public sector are located in departments of social service, human resources, housing, education, and mental health. In the private sector, social workers are employed with charitable and non-profit agencies, hospitals and nursing homes, and community and religious organizations. Responsibilities in social work are broad, and include providing counseling on specific problems, such as alcoholism, housing, and child care, and referring individuals to available resources and agencies. Social workers may specialize in family counseling, child welfare, mental health, or care of the elderly, among many options. This work requires compassion, understanding, and the ability to communicate effectively. Some in this profession can suffer stress, frustration or "burn-out" from constant subjection to difficult situations. Social workers come in contact with health care workers, psychologists, and social service administrators.

SOCIOLOGIST

Ranking: 35

Score: 318.29

Hours Weekly: 45

Duties: Studies human behavior by examining the interaction of social groups and institutions.

Employers include government agencies, research firms, corporations, and welfare organizations. Sociologists collect, analyze, and assess information gathered through surveys or direct observation. They rate the efficiency of various social programs, such as job training or remedial education. The results of their efforts assist educators, government officials, and physicians in developing and implementing social reforms. Members of this profession rely on statistical and computer techniques to analyze and disseminate data collected. Some sociologists act in an administrative capacity, directing services in welfare agencies or youth organizations, while others are employed as consultants, advising and evaluating social programs. Most sociologists work at a desk writing reports and analyzing data. Pressures of deadlines and heavy workloads are endemic to this profession. Travel is often required to gather data and attend meetings.

SOFTWARE ENGINEER

Ranking: 7

Score: 150.00

Hours Weekly: 50

Duties: Researches, designs, develops and maintains software systems along with hardware development for medical, scientific, and industrial purposes.

With the explosive growth and development of computer applications, the problems of creating programs and software systems have become intense and crucial. Software engineers analyze software requirements to determine whether a product under design is feasible and within what time and cost restraints. Formulating and designing a software system, software engineers use scientific analysis to predict and measure both the outcome and consequence of a design. They develop and direct software testing procedures, programming, and documentation. Recognizing that the kinds of real-world problems systems were designed to handle may change over time, software engineers define ways to modify programs. Often, they consult with customers concerning maintenance of the software system and may coordinate the actual installation of software system. Employed within the computer industry itself as well as within business, industry and government, it is a comfortable and secure work environment. This is in contrast to the intense, creative and analytical work involved. Difficulties and "bugs" within systems may create some overtime in this profession. Software engineers work closely with other engineers and programmers.

SPEECH PATHOLOGIST

Ranking: 69

Score: 463.43

Hours Weekly: 42.5

Duties: Assesses hearing, speech, and language disabilities and provides treatment. Assists individuals with communication disorders through diagnostic techniques.

Responsibilities vary according to education and employer. Individuals who work in hospitals diagnose and identify speech abnormalities, and work closely with physicians and other professionals to develop therapeutic programs to treat those with speech disorders. Pathologists who are employed by school systems have a wider range of responsibilities, including consultation with parents and school administrators. They also instruct classroom teachers on development of communication skills in students. Work is usually done in an office, and much of a speech pathologist's time is spent in preparing reports and treatment plans. Intense concentration and close attention to detail are important in this profession. Often the rewards of seeing improvement in a patient's speech are slow in developing, but positive changes can also be highly satisfying.

SPORTS INSTRUCTOR

Ranking: 162

Score: 931.48

Hours Weekly: 42.5

Duties: Teaches, coaches and develops the athletic talent of individuals or groups for health, recreation, or professional purposes.

Sports instructors are employed by elementary and secondary schools, colleges and universities, recreational facilities, and private individuals. In schools, sports instructors teach students athletic skills to maintain health and for recreation. In gym classes, these workers instruct students on how to perform calisthenics and other exercises, and supervise the play of particular sports and games, such as basketball, volleyball, and soccer. Sports instructors may also coach varsity or intercollegiate teams. In health clubs, golf courses, and tennis clubs, instructors advise members and customers in proper conditioning and play. Professional athletes, such as tennis players, hire coaches to aid in performance. Sports instructors may suffer minor injuries, such as pulled muscles. Instructors must take care to insure that recreational activities are safe. Sports instructors come in contact with school staff, recreational facility managers, and professional athletes.

STATIONARY ENGINEER

Ranking: 178

Score: 1,055.47

Hours Weekly: 45

Duties: Operates, monitors, and repairs power plants and industrial heating, cooling, and ventilation systems.

Stationary engineers tend and control generators, pumps, turbines, compressors, condensers, boilers, and diesel engines, in order to meet consumer and industrial power, heating, refrigeration, and ventilation needs. Periodically, they monitor meters, gauges, and other mechanical indicators to assess the condition and performance of their equipment. When a mechanical fault is detected, stationary engineers often use hand and power tools to make repairs. In large plants a stationary engineer may command a staff of boiler tenders, assistant stationary engineers, turbine operators, and air-conditioning and refrigeration operators and mechanics. In a small plant a stationary engineer may be the lone worker.

STATISTICIAN

Ranking: 1

Score: 89.52

Hours Weekly: 45

Duties: Tabulates, analyzes, and interprets the numeric results of experiments and surveys.

Statisticians attempt to predict the behavior of large groups by studying the numeric characteristics of small segments of those groups, called statistical samples. Statistical methods are often applied in academic areas like economics, psychology, engineering, physics, and genetics. Statistician frequently employ computers to aid in monotonous calculations. Private industry provides two out of three jobs for statisticians—primarily in finance, manufacturing, insurance, and business service. Most other statisticians are employed by State, Federal, and municipal agencies, and universities. Employment in this field is available throughout the United States, but most openings are in major metropolitan centers.

STENOGRAPHER/COURT REPORTER

Ranking: 48

Score: 361.44

Hours Weekly: 40

Duties: Transcribes testimony, judicial decisions, and other proceedings of a court of law.

Federal, state, and local courts, and legislatures and agencies of the executive branch of government employ court reporters to record statements made during legal proceedings. Court reporters use typewriters, recording machines, and stenotype machines to report testimony, judicial opinions, or judgments of the court. Reporters also take shorthand, and are frequently responsible for reading transcripts or clarifying inaudible statements at the judge's request. Court reporters work a standard forty-hour week in clean, comfortable surroundings. Contacts include attorneys and law enforcement personnel.

STEVEDORE

Ranking: 183

Score: 1084.59

Hours Weekly: 40

Duties: Loads and unloads cargo from vessels, routes cargo to proper locations.

Stevedores work on loading docks at port facilities throughout the nation. Major port cities are located on the Atlantic and Pacific coasts, as well as on the Gulf of Mexico, the Great Lakes, and major inland waterways, such as the Mississippi River. Under the direction of supervisors, stevedores operate fork-lifts, tow motors, and trucks to transport cargo from dock facilities. These workers load and unload cargo, including raw materials, manufactured products, and foodstuffs, from ships and barges. Stevedores use hoists, winches, ropes, and cables to raise cargo into and out of ships' holds. This is physically strenuous work, involving lifting and carrying heavy loads, and operating heavy machinery and equipment. Good health and stamina are needed, as stevedores spend long periods on their feet. Work is performed outdoors, occasionally in inclement weather. Stevedores regularly come in contact with transportation workers, ships' crews, and loading dock supervisors.

STOCKBROKER

Ranking: 198

Score: 1,155.75

Hours Weekly: 45

Duties: Facilitates the purchase and sale of stocks, bonds, and other securities for individual and institutional clients.

Stockbrokers are employed by brokerage houses, investment firms, and financial management companies. A large number of these positions are located in New York City, though small firms and branch offices are located across the country. Stockbrokers spend much of their time on the telephone, discussing stock options with clients and placing orders. Brokers buy and sell securities through representatives on the floors of securities exchanges, or over-the-counter directly with dealers. In addition, many brokers provide full financial services to clients, including offering advice on other investment opportunities, and managing financial portfolios. Brokers work in noisy, active offices, constantly monitoring stock prices on computer terminals or quote boards. Sudden market changes can cause hectic reaction, and ill-advised investments can cost clients and brokers alike very large sums of money. Brokers must be able to handle this type of pressure. These professionals often work with attorneys, bankers and other financial service workers.

SURGEON

Ranking: 243

Score: 1962.00

Hours Weekly: 55

Duties: Diagnoses ailments and performs operations to repair, reconstruct, remove, or replace organs, limbs, and bodily systems.

Most surgeons are affiliated with hospitals or other large health care establishments, such as research institutions. Some surgeons work for outpatient clinics, surgical centers, health maintenance organizations, or private practices. Surgeons treat major physical illnesses and trauma through surgical procedures. They use precision instruments and diagnostic equipment, including scalpels, sutures, and lasers. Many highly-trained individuals specialize in one area of treatment, such as heart surgery, brain surgery, or orthope-

dics, among many fields of expertise. Plastic surgeons reconstruct body parts using prosthetic or artificial devices, repair birth defects or damage from accidents, and enhance the physical appearance of patients. Surgeons undergo many years of rigorous training and education. These professionals must have the ability to handle the pressure of dealing daily with life-and-death situations. Surgeons work closely with anesthesiologists, nurses, and other health care professionals.

SURVEYOR

Ranking: 167

Score: 956.97

Hours Weekly: 45

Duties: Establishes official land and aquatic boundaries, measures construction and mining sites, writes technical property descriptions for deeds and leases, and prepares maps and charts.

Federal, state, and municipal governments employ 25% of all surveyors, while engineering, architectural, and surveying firms employ an additional 50 percent. Most state and municipal surveyors work for highway or urban planning agencies. The work of surveyors is frequently physically strenuous. Surveyors often walk long distances while carrying heavy instruments, and are exposed to hot or inclement weather. Although the majority of surveying tasks are performed outdoors, surveyors prepare reports, plot charts, perform computations and plan surveys in traditional offices. Many computational, mapping, and drafting

SYMPHONY CONDUCTOR

Ranking: 205

Score: 1,239.00

Hours Weekly: 45

Duties: Auditions and selects members of an orchestra; organizes musicians to obtain optimum balance and harmony of musical selections.

Orchestra conductors direct performances for large and small local, regional, and national orchestras. Musicians who perform in this capacity are also frequently employed by colleges and universities. Conductors use music theories and conducting techniques to ensure a desired balance of musical effects. In addition to the direction of individual performances, conductors also lead rehearsals and select music appropriate to the talents of the concert musicians. Orchestra conductors position members of the orchestra to achieve harmony of musical selections; they must also consider the mood of the performance when selecting music to be performed. Since this profession requires a great deal of travel, physical stamina is needed to withstand the long hours spent waiting in airports and other transportation terminals. Evening and weekend work is common to those involved in music careers. Self-discipline and versatility are skills that enable conductors to spend long hours in study of musical compositions and theory. Frequent contacts include musicians, symphony patrons and educators.

TAX EXAMINER/COLLECTOR

Ranking: 63

Score: 449.10

Hours Weekly: 45

Duties: Determines tax liability and collects taxes from individuals or businesses.

Tax examiners and collectors are employed by federal and state internal revenue departments, and work in government offices nationwide. Members of this profession examine the financial records of businesses and individuals. Examiners go over tax statements and returns to determine liability, and compare these figures with actual taxes paid. Examiners look at receipts, canceled checks, payroll statements, and other pertinent documents. Examiners and collectors prepare reports, and impose penalties for unreported income or unpaid taxes. These workers also collect evidence in the event that legal action is necessary to enforce laws and regulations. This profession requires accounting skills, and a broad knowledge of state and federal tax codes. Working extensively with numbers can be stressful or tedious for some in this occupation. Tax examiners and collectors come in contact with accountants, and with other government officials.

TAXI DRIVER

Ranking: 246

Score: 2,317.21

Hours Weekly: 47.5

Duties: Operates a taxi cab over the streets and roads of a municipality, picking up and dropping off passengers by request.

Taxi drivers are employed by cab companies in major metropolitan areas. Small cab companies also operate in some suburban communities. Some cabbies own and operate their vehicles independently. Cab drivers patrol city streets in their vehicles, picking up fares who hail them, or following the radio instructions of dispatchers. Drivers load baggage, and transport passengers to requested locations. At the end of the ride, cabbies collect fares, make change, and receive tips. In most cities, rates for taxi service are strictly regulated, as are the number of taxi permits or "medallions." Acquiring a medallion can be a lengthy and expensive process for those wishing to operate their own taxis. Many cab drivers work long hours, including nights, evenings, and weekends. Stamina, good health, and excellent driving skills are needed in this profession. In addition to passengers, taxi drivers come in contact with dispatchers and auto mechanics.

TEACHER

Ranking: 125

Score: 709.60

Hours Weekly: 45

Duties: Introduces children to the basics of mathematics, language, science, and social studies, and assists other aspects of child development.

Kindergarten and elementary school teachers work public and private schools across the country. Approximately 15% of all teachers at these levels are employed by private schools. Kindergarten and elementary school teachers instruct children in the fundamentals of math, reading, writing, science, and other fields. Teachers may use visual instruction aids, such as films and slides, to help children become interested in learning. Teachers also observe and assist in students' social and emotional development, and monitor health. Teachers meet with parents and school officials to discuss progress or problems of students. Much work in this profession, such as preparing lessons, grading papers, and attending meetings, is done after the school day has ended. Teachers spend long periods of time on their feet. Working with rambunctious children can be fatiguing and stressful. Teachers work with other faculty members, school administrators, and principals.

TEACHER'S AIDE

Ranking: 91

Score: 546.78

Hours Weekly: 42.5

Duties: Supervises elementary school students in the classroom, school yard, and in the cafeteria, operates audio-visual equipment, records grades, and prepares educational materials.

The responsibilities of a teacher's aide vary greatly between school districts. In some systems, aides provide supplementary instruction for students, individually or in small groups. Often, these aides organize special projects and demonstrations, while the teacher attends to the primary curriculum. In other districts, aide's responsibilities are limited to nonteaching tasks, such as grading tests, correcting homework, and maintaining health and attendance records. Occasionally aides perform secretarial tasks—typing, filing, and photocopying for teachers and administrators. A few teacher's aides assist special education teachers with handicapped students.

TECHNICAL WRITER

Ranking: 15

Score: 221.25

Hours Weekly: 45

Duties: Transforms scientific and technical information into readily understandable language.

A large number of technical writers work for companies which produce electronics and computer equipment, and by aircraft, chemical, and pharmaceutical companies. Communications and computer software firms also employ a substantial number of technical writers. Some in this field are free-lancers. Technical writers prepare instruction manuals, catalogs, parts lists, and brochures for use by sales representatives and technicians. Writers assemble information on machinery, scientific equipment, software, and other merchandise, and put this data into clear, concise instructions, or describe products or procedures. Background in a particular scientific or technical field is helpful in this profession. Technical writers normally work in quiet, comfortable offices. Work occasionally can be tedious. Publication deadlines can cause stress for technical writers. These workers come in contact with sales personnel, editors, and equipment manufacturers.

TELEPHONE INSTALLER/ REPAIRER

Ranking: 114

Score: 657.16

Hours Weekly: 47.5

Duties: Installs, services, cleans, tests, and repairs telephones and switchboard systems.

The majority of work full time for public telephone companies. Since service interruptions can occur at any time, these workers are subject to year round 24-hour call, and often perform emergency repairs under adverse weather conditions. When customers move or upgrade their service, installers relocate telephones or make improvements to existing systems. Before performing a requested task, installer-repairers often consult service orders, circuit diagrams, and technical manuals. Telephone installers, like all repair professionals, need excellent problem solving skills.

They must also be adept with small tools and be comfortable working in cramped quarters.

TELEPHONE OPERATOR

Ranking: 127

Score: 719.82

Hours Weekly: 40

Duties: Operates manual or computerized telephone switchboards and assists in the placement of local and long distance calls.

Roughly half of the nation's operators are employed by public telephone companies. Central office operators help place person- to-person, coin-phone, and collect calls. Directory assistance operators answer customer number inquiries, and long-distance operators make intra-area connections. Most privately employed operators man PBX (private branch exchange) switchboards, and many double as receptionists. Work is performed in well-lighted, air-conditioned surroundings. Little physical exertion is required, but operators need excellent eye-hand coordination and general dexterity to maintain their hectic pace during peak hours. Operators must also be alert, polite listeners and possess excellent spelling and arithmetic abilities.

TICKET AGENT

Ranking: 92

Score: 547.82

Hours Weekly: 40

Duties: Vends tickets for transportation agencies.

Ticket agents are employed by airline, railroad, bus , and steamship companies to collect fares, and assist customers in making travel arrangement. There are three basic specialties within this field: reservation agents (who process advance reservation by telephone), gate agents (who distribute airline boarding passes), and ticketing clerks (who issue tickets at the point of departure). Because the transportation industry operates around-the-clock, ticketing agents usually work extended or irregular hours. They must spend long hours on their feet, and they are sometimes required to lift heavy pieces of passenger luggage.

TOOL-AND-DIE MAKER

Ranking: 134

Score: 740.55

Hours Weekly: 45

Duties: Constructs and repairs precision tools, gauges, holding devices and stamping tools for the machine industry.

Tool makers produce jigs and fixtures to exact specifications and also make and calibrate gauges and measuring devices. Die makers design and construct metal dies which shape metal when it is stamped or punched. Tool-and-die makers work closely from blueprints and must have a broad knowledge of machine operations, mathematics and metallurgic properties such as heat tolerance. Workers are usually employed in machine shops, but do their specialized work in "tool rooms" which are separated from the production floor. Workers are on their feet most of the day and lift moderately heavy objects. Tool-and-die makers must wear protective clothing like safety glasses, helmets and ear plugs. They often work overtime to meet production deadlines.

TRAVEL AGENT

Ranking: 192

Score: 1,134.77

Hours Weekly: 40

Duties: Makes arrangements for travel according to the specific needs of individuals and businesses.

Keeping in mind the travel requirements of individual clients, agents use their expertise to arrange flights, make hotel accommodations, and schedule tourist packages. They provide information on customs regulations, travel documents, and exchange rates for international travelers. Travel agents consult various sources to familiarize themselves with their markets, and frequently do promotional work, such as slide presentations and speeches to special interest and business groups. There has been an increasing reliance on computers in this field, to meet complex scheduling and financial criteria. Agents spend much of their work week at a desk, and hours may be long, especially for those who are self-employed. Peak vacation times can be particularly stressful for individuals in this profession; however, among the rewards are reduced rates and promotional trips for agents. Frequent contacts include reservation agents, and travel counselors.

TRUCK DRIVER

Ranking: 168

Score: 968.20

Hours Weekly: 47.5

Duties: Operates 16-wheeled tractor-trailer, to transport durable and perishable goods from producers to consumers.

Truck drivers spend the majority of their time on the job behind the wheel. Under the law they cannot drive more than 60 hours in 7 days or more than 10 consecutive hours without an eignt-hour rest. Long-haul drivers, carrying specialty cargo, often load and unload their own cargo, when experienced helpers are not available. Drivers of refrigerated trucks must frequently monitor the temperature and condition of their loads. Wholesale driver-salesmen study the inventory of client stores, and may recommend changes in client orders or recruit new clients. On very long, "sleeper" routes, one trucker drives while his partner sleeps in a berth behind the cab.

TYPIST/WORD PROCESSOR

Ranking: 8

Score: 160.64

Hours Weekly: 40

Duties: Prepares and edits typed or electronic copies of handwritten, printed, or magnetically recorded documents. Junior typists create custom headings for form letters, transcribe from handwritten drafts, and address envelopes.

Typists and word processors often perform related office chores, including filing, photocopying, and answering telephones. Senior typists—those who have developed exceptional speed, accuracy, and discretion—often work with technical materials and rough drafts, which may be difficult to interpret. Typing clerks often tabulate data and type applications for insurance companies. Note readers transcribe the notes of stenographic court reporters, and word processors use electronic keyboards and display screens (CRTs) to quickly compile and edit large documents.

UNDERTAKER

Ranking: 175

Score: 1,015.40

Hours Weekly: 50

Duties: Prepares bodies for burial, and arranges and directs funerals.

Most morticians own or are employed in private funeral homes throughout the country. Others work for municipal governments, and for the military. After bodies are delivered to funeral homes, morticians treat them with embalming fluid to prevent decomposition. Morticians discuss funeral arrangements with relatives or friends of the deceased, in order to decide on type of casket, funeral procedures, and the physical appearance of the body. In religious ceremonies, funeral directors consult with priests, ministers, or rabbis on rites and methods of procedure. When the body is laid out for viewing, funeral home workers greet mourners, and answer inquiries. These workers often accompany mourners to the church and the burial site, assisting clergy in directing ceremonies. This profession requires a great deal of tact and sensitivity in dealing with mourning relatives and friends of those recently passed away. Morticians work with potentially dangerous chemical solutions. Caution must be used to prevent infection or disease from bodies. Morticians regularly come in contact with hospital personnel and members of the clergy.

URBAN/REGIONAL PLANNER

Ranking: 46

Score: 359.28

Hours Weekly: 45

Duties: Plans the use of land for public and industrial sites through collection and analysis of data.

Employment is by appointment of local governments and is aimed at serving the interests of businesses and individuals. Urban planners work with government officials, business leaders, and community members to anticipate changes in the development of land for public and private use. They must be aware of shifts in the economy and population and develop programs according to specific needs of the individuals within a community. Urban planners work in offices and have regular hours, although attendance at evening community meetings and conferences is often required of members of this profession. Pressures of tight schedules and deadlines are inherent to this job, as is overtime spent during special projects. Interviews and surveys are tools that urban planners use to assist them in their assessment of land use.

VENDING MACHINE REPAIRER

Ranking: 71

Score: 469.40

Hours Weekly: 47.5

Duties: Performs maintenance and repairs on coin operated vending and amusement machines.

The majority of vending machine operators work for vending machine companies that operate machines to sell food and other items. Others work for soft-drink companies, or for firms that operate mechanical amusement equipment, such as pinball machines and juke boxes. Repairers perform maintenance on vending machines in the field or shop, checking springs, coin mechanisms, and plungers, and oiling and cleaning parts. If machines break down, repairers determine the cause,

employing circuit diagrams and electric circuit testers. Repairs and adjustments are made, using hand and power tools, such as wrenches, torches, and pipe cutters. Vending machine repairers may also perform clerical work, collect money, and stock machines. Some repairers may work overtime, or shifts, including evenings and weekends. These workers are subject to electrical shocks, and to cuts and burns from tools. Vending machine repairers come in contact with service managers, and with business owners.

VETERINARIAN

Ranking: 171

Score: 978.80

Hours Weekly: 50

Duties: Ministers to the care of animals through the use of preventative and diagnostic techniques.

Veterinarians are frequently self-employed, although many work for small hospitals, colleges and universities, and health agencies. Veterinarians work in various areas of expertise, such as dogs, cats, and other small animals, or with livestock, caring for injured or diseased cattle, horses, sheep, or poultry. Research and teaching can also constitute a large part of a veterinarian's job, which includes diagnosis, surgery, and the administration and prescription of medicines to animals in their care. Veterinarians also perform autopsies and are increasingly employed by the federal government to inspect livestock and help to control the passage of diseases through food products. Recent grads usually begin as employees of or partners to established veterinarians, because great financial expense is involved in setting up a private practice. Work is often done from an examining room or in a surgical setting, but those veterinarians who specialize in the treatment of livestock can spend several hours daily traveling to and from rural sites. They must frequently work outside at night or during inclement weather to care for injured or diseased animals. Contacts include veterinary assistants, farmers, and health agency officials.

VOCATIONAL COUNSELOR

Ranking: 95

Score: 556.40

Hours Weekly: 42.5

Duties: Helps students with educational and social problems, and provides vocational guidance.

Employers are elementary and secondary schools and colleges and universities throughout the country. School counselors use records, tests, and interviews to assess the mental, emotional, social, and educational status of students. They use this information to assist students and to work with parents and other professionals to find solutions to special problems. College counselors spend much of their time measuring vocational skills to assist in career planning. Most counselors work standard 40-hour weeks, although many college counselors work overtime to attend career fairs or hold special office hours. Elementary and secondary school counselors frequently have summers free. Contacts include social service professionals, teachers, and school administrators.

WAITER/WAITRESS

Ranking: 122

Score: 687.42

Hours Weekly: 35

Duties: Takes customer orders, serves food and drink, and prepares meal checks.

Eight out of ten waiters and waitresses are employed in bars and restaurants. A waiter's duties sometimes include setting and clearing tables, and transporting soiled linen to the kitchen. In large or expensive restaurants these tasks are usually performed by bus boys. Waiters and waitresses are on their feet at most times, and often carry heavy trays and dishes. Accidental slips and falls are common work hazards. Frequently waiters and waitresses are expected to work on holidays and weekend. Split shifts at which waiters work for several afternoon hours and return to their jobs for the evening hours, are also very common.

WELDER

Ranking: 201

Score: 1,180.14

Hours Weekly: 45

Duties: Joins or repairs metal surfaces through the application of heat.

Most welders are employed in the manufacture of durable goods including boilers, trucks, farm machines, ships and, large consumer appliances. Others work in the repair and construction of bridges, steel-framed buildings, pipelines, and power plants. Welders use gas and electric torches to heat and fuse metal parts. Precision welders, who labor in nuclear plants, submarines, and ships, possess a thorough knowledge of metallurgical properties and often work from blueprints and technical diagrams. Factory welding machine operators perform repetitive tasks and are usually less skilled. Welders encounter many potential health hazards. Protective clothing and headgear must be worn to prevent burns and eye injuries; and proper ventilation is essential to diffuse the toxic fumes which some metals emit as they melt.

ZOOLOGIST

Ranking: 44

Score: 356.72

Hours Weekly: 45

Duties: Studies the behavior, life processes, origins, and diseases of animals.

Many zoologists concentrate their attentions on a single animal group. Ornithologists study birds, mammalogists study mammals, herpetologists study reptiles, and ichthyologists study fish. Some zoologists work exclusively with live animals, in natural and artificial habitats (zoos). Others investigate the anatomy and physiology of animal species, through dissections performed in biological laboratories. Zoologists take frequent field trips, and are sometimes exposed to inclement weather and dangerous animals. Most zoologist are involved in research, but a few serve exclusively as zoo and park administrators. Many zoologists are employed by the Department of the Interior.

Income

If you've ever wondered what your neighbors earn but don't have the gall to ask, this chapter will more than satisfy your curiosity. It also will provide a valuable lesson about what various jobs pay and will keep paying as you get better at performing them.

GROWTH POTENTIAL

Overall, Americans working at the jobs rated in this book can increase their annual incomes 391 percent (almost four-fold) if they are good at what they do. To illuminate this point, an important but frequently overlooked statistic is computed for each job entry in this chapter: "Growth Potential."

The career-by-career potential for growth in income is surely one of the most valuable pieces of information in this volume. This important consideration is defined simply as the percentage difference between the average starting income and the top income. For example, the highest growth potential among all 250 jobs is for a race car driver; such athletes can increase their income more than 200-fold as they rise to the top of the profession. The job with the worst growth potential? President of the United States; income in that position is set by legislation at $200,000 annually. Just imagine the political fallout if Bill Clinton beseeched Congress for a raise.

* See "Top" definition the following page.

Growth potential in this chapter is expressed as a percent. For example, a real estate agent will earn a modest $12,000 the first year. However, the position carries a fairly good growth potential of 475%, which would allow for an increase in earnings of $57,000. "Top" * real estate agents can expect to earn about $69,000.

Generally speaking, doing something well is the key to getting more money, an elementary but frequently overlooked principle. For example, a corporate executive who has the staying power to reach a senior-level position will earn about $50,000 annually when he or she first reaches that status—not much more than an average plumber, who earns $45,000. However, if an executive is proficient enough to rise to a "mid-level" senior position, earnings average $100,000; a "top-level" executive position demands about $300,000; and those who reach the pinnacle, of course, earn millions. Most white-collar jobs and many technical and scientific occupations are good examples of this principle of "better pay for better work."

One the other hand, some career paths do not have a built-in compensation factor to reward a job well done. Governmental jobs, with their highly structured promotion system and fairly low salary ceilings, are the worst offenders in this regard. Even white-collar and professional jobs in civil service have little room for income growth. Some nontraditional occupations, even those among the best career choices, have similar drawbacks. A person whose main interest is climbing the income ladder would be well advised to carefully check out the income growth potential in various occupations. They vary widely from field to field and are often not commonly known—or worse, they are overlooked by outsiders aspiring to enter the field.

INCOME LEVELS

We provide three figures on incomes in each of our 250 occupations: starting, mid-level, and top incomes. Figures for each entry in this chapter are based on the latest available statistics, principally from the Bureau of Labor Statistics, an arm of the U.S. Department of Labor. In many cases they come from professional organizations, as diverse as the Society of Actuaries to the National Football League. When reliable data could not be found, estimates were culled from professionals familiar with incomes in the given field. All annual incomes shown in this volume have been systematically updated to reflect estimated incomes for 1995, using a cost-of-employment index computed by economists at the Bureau of Labor Statistics.

The starting figure is that of the lowest-paid workers in the field, or in cases such as fashion model or actor, the lowest earnings that those calling themselves "professionals" might make.

"Mid-level" income, as expressed in this volume, reflects what the average worker is paid. In many cases the phrase "average" is exactly that: the average of the income of all workers in the field. Some income figures we encountered are quoted as "medians"— meaning half the workers in the field make less, and half make more. When averages were not available, median incomes were used.

The "Top" figure means earnings in the 90th percentile in the occupation. We feel this reflects the level that the most talented or experienced workers might reasonably expect to make. It does not represent the highest or near-highest income in the field. For example, the top movie stars earn some $10 million per film, but that is not reflected in our "top" income for actors; rather, the top is a mundane $39,000 — what a successful actor in the 90th percentile of his or her profession might earn.

THE RANKING SYSTEM

The scores shown in the ranking tables might look like average incomes to those familiar with pay levels in the jobs to which they relate. However, the scores are actually a derivative of mid-level incomes, and not the average income at all. Since all incomes shown in this chapter are estimates rounded to the nearest $1,000, there would be many ties if the mid-level income was the sole basis of the score. Instead, the score was computed by adding the estimated mid-level income and the Growth Potential. For example, a physicist with a mid-level income earns $67,000. His or her income Growth Potential is 138%. Adding these two, yields a score of $67,138. As you can see, this very closely resembles an average dollar-denominated income as if it was computed in an income survey. Therefore the dollar-sign precedes the score as an accommodation to someone who wishes to get at-a-glance estimates of average incomes.

250 Jobs Ranked by Income Scores

RANK		SCORE	RANK		SCORE
1	BASKETBALL PLAYER (NBA)	$1,560,833	32	NUCLEAR ENGINEER	$68,206
			33	MECHANICAL ENGINEER	$68,197
2	BASEBALL PLAYER (MAJOR LEAGUE)	$1,188,845	34	ASTRONOMER	$68,077
			35	ELECTRICAL ENGINEER	$67,200
3	FOOTBALL PLAYER (NFL)	$655,055	36	PHYSICIST	$67,138
4	RACE CAR DRIVER (INDY CLASS)	$420,832	37	EXECUTIVE SEARCH CONSULTANT	$65,567
5	PRESIDENT (U.S.)	$200,000	38	INDUSTRIAL ENGINEER	$64,206
6	SURGEON	$194,144	39	AEROSPACE ENGINEER	$64,203
7	ORTHODONTIST	$193,247	40	RABBI	$64,137
8	BASEBALL UMPIRE (MAJOR LEAGUE)	$140,192	41	PHILOSOPHER	$63,183
			42	COLLEGE PROFESSOR	$62,193
9	CONGRESSPERSON/ SENATOR	$134,019	43	HOTEL MANAGER	$61,168
10	JUDGE (FEDERAL)	$127,041	44	CIVIL ENGINEER	$58,203
11	DENTIST	$111,155	45	SHEET METAL WORKER	$58,138
12	PSYCHIATRIST	$110,134	46	SOCIOLOGIST	$57,254
13	PHYSICIAN (GENERAL PRACTICE)	$104,977	47	SOFTWARE ENGINEER	$57,153
14	PODIATRIST	$104,346	48	SCHOOL PRINCIPAL	$57,038
15	SYMPHONY CONDUCTOR	$101,900	49	AIR TRAFFIC CONTROLLER	$56,226
16	CORPORATE EXECUTIVE (SENIOR)	$100,500	50	PHYSIOLOGIST	$56,196
			51	OCEANOGRAPHER	$56,171
17	ATTORNEY	$86,267	52	GEOLOGIST	$55,300
18	AIRPLANE PILOT	$85,291	53	CHEMIST	$55,265
19	STOCKBROKER	$83,453	54	MATHEMATICIAN	$55,204
20	CHOREOGRAPHER	$83,241	55	ZOOLOGIST	$55,196
21	FINANCIAL PLANNER	$82,647	56	STATISTICIAN	$54,219
22	OSTEOPATH	$80,240	57	MUSICIAN	$53,900
23	OPTOMETRIST	$80,198	58	SINGER	$53,233
24	AGENCY DIRECTOR (NONPROFIT)	$80,176	59	AGRICULTURAL SCIENTIST	$52,213
25	PETROLEUM ENGINEER	$79,195	60	ACCOUNTANT	$52,203
26	FASHION MODEL	$76,900	61	MARKET RESEARCH ANALYST	$52,192
27	ASTRONAUT	$76,080	62	ARCHEOLOGIST	$52,169
28	CHIROPRACTOR	$75,823	62	ANTHROPOLOGIST	$52,169
29	ACTUARY	$70,288	64	GLAZIER	$52,084
30	ECONOMIST	$69,219	65	METEOROLOGIST	$50,910
31	VETERINARIAN	$69,197	66	HOSPITAL ADMINISTRATOR	$50,750

RANK		SCORE	RANK		SCORE
67	POSTAL INSPECTOR	$50,045	101	AUDIOLOGIST	$38,058
68	MOTION PICTURE EDITOR	$48,431	102	OCCUPATIONAL THERAPIST	$38,050
69	PUBLICATION EDITOR	$48,192	103	CONSTRUCTION FOREMAN	$37,244
70	CONSERVATIONIST	$48,176	104	BIOLOGIST	$37,177
71	PHARMACIST	$48,125	105	BANK OFFICER	$37,161
72	UNDERTAKER	$47,247	106	NURSE (REGISTERED)	$37,135
73	PUBLIC RELATIONS EXECUTIVE	$47,200	107	TEACHER	$37,091
74	MUSEUM CURATOR	$47,161	108	TECHNICAL WRITER	$37,071
75	OCCUPATIONAL SAFETY/ HEALTH INSPECTOR	$46,139	109	INSURANCE UNDERWRITER	$36,131
76	DAIRY FARMER	$45,900	110	TOOL-AND-DIE MAKER	$36,117
77	URBAN/REGIONAL PLANNER	$45,226	111	FIREFIGHTER	$35,175
78	POLITICAL SCIENTIST	$45,170	112	TELEPHONE INSTALLER/ REPAIRER	$35,171
79	INDUSTRIAL DESIGNER	$45,167	113	AIRCRAFT MECHANIC	$35,168
80	COMPUTER SYSTEMS ANALYST	$45,159	114	ARTIST (COMMERCIAL)	$35,129
81	PLUMBER	$45,113	115	MAIL CARRIER	$35,044
82	BUYER	$44,142	116	SEAMAN	$34,337
83	PLASTERER	$44,103	117	SALES REPRESENTATIVE (WHOLESALE)	$34,288
84	PHYSICIAN ASSISTANT	$44,063	118	DENTAL LABORATORY TECHNICIAN	$34,280
85	RAILROAD CONDUCTOR	$44,045	119	POLICE OFFICER	$34,175
86	BASKETBALL COACH (NCAA)	$43,252	120	RESPIRATORY THERAPIST	$34,122
87	CHAUFFEUR	$43,066	121	PHOTOJOURNALIST	$33,655
88	ADVERTISING ACCOUNT EXECUTIVE	$42,228	122	MILLWRIGHT	$33,147
89	PERSONNEL RECRUITER	$42,164	123	DENTAL HYGIENIST	$33,094
90	MILITARY (COMMISSIONED OFFICER)	$41,226	124	ROUSTABOUT	$33,068
91	SET DESIGNER	$41,100	125	DRILL-PRESS OPERATOR	$33,067
92	ARCHITECT	$40,312	126	NEWSWRITER (RADIO/TV)	$32,392
93	ANTIQUE DEALER	$40,220	127	FASHION DESIGNER	$32,343
94	LIBRARIAN	$40,071	128	INSURANCE AGENT	$32,331
95	HISTORIAN	$39,284	129	ADVERTISING SALESPERSON	$32,253
96	MEDICAL TECHNOLOGIST	$39,044	130	VOCATIONAL COUNSELOR	$32,189
97	COMPUTER PROGRAMMER	$38,195	131	SOCIAL WORKER	$32,104
98	PHYSICAL THERAPIST	$38,195	132	PAROLE OFFICER	$32,100
99	STATIONARY ENGINEER	$38,194			
100	SPEECH PATHOLOGIST	$38,111			

RANK	SCORE	RANK	SCORE
133 MEDICAL SECRETARY	$32,072	163 COMMUNICATIONS EQUIPMENT MECHANIC	$27,171
134 DIETICIAN	$32,048	164 JEWELER	$27,159
135 JOCKEY	$31,500	165 COMPUTER SERVICE TECHNICIAN	$27,116
136 NEWSCASTER	$31,405		
137 PSYCHOLOGIST	$31,320	165 OFFICE MACHINE REPAIRER	$27,116
138 AUTOMOBILE SALESPERSON	$31,118	167 COSMETOLOGIST	$27,100
139 ELECTRICAL TECHNICIAN	$31,100	168 BARBER	$27,090
139 ENGINEERING TECHNICIAN	$31,100	169 ASTROLOGER	$26,525
		170 APPLIANCE REPAIRER	$26,207
141 BOILERMAKER	$31,096	171 HIGHWAY PATROL OFFICER	$26,132
142 ELECTRICIAN	$30,172	172 AUTHOR (BOOKS)	$26,100
143 MILITARY (WARRANT OFFICER)	$30,128	173 TAX EXAMINER/ COLLECTOR	$26,060
144 PARALEGAL ASSISTANT	$30,028		
145 PROTESTANT MINISTER	$29,488	174 PURCHASING AGENT	$25,220
146 ARCHITECTURAL DRAFTER	$29,171	175 CARTOONIST	$25,188
		175 ARTIST (FINE ART)	$25,188
146 EMERGENCY MEDICAL TECHNICIAN	$29,071	177 CORRECTION OFFICER	$25,180
		178 COWBOY	$25,171
148 LITHOGRAPHER/ PHOTOENGRAVER	$29,064	179 MEDICAL LABORATORY TECHNICIAN	$25,163
149 ELECTRICAL EQUIPMENT REPAIRER	$29,035	180 FORKLIFT OPERATOR	$25,121
150 BROADCAST TECHNICIAN	$28,664	181 MEDICAL RECORDS TECHNICIAN	$25,045
151 REAL ESTATE AGENT	$28,475	182 CARPENTER	$24,207
152 INDUSTRIAL MACHINE REPAIRER	$28,169	183 CONSTRUCTION MACHINERY OPERATOR	$24,200
153 SURVEYOR	$28,165	184 WELDER	$24,150
154 HEATING/REFRIGERATION MECHANIC	$28,156	185 PHOTOGRAPHER	$23,300
155 SEWAGE PLANT OPERATOR	$28,147	186 DRYWALL APPLICATOR/ FINISHER	$23,269
		187 STEVEDORE	$23,240
156 TRUCK DRIVER	$28,139	188 AUTOMOBILE MECHANIC	$23,215
157 SECRETARY	$28,081	189 STENOGRAPHER/COURT REPORTER	$23,212
158 AUTOMOBILE ASSEMBLER	$28,050		
159 OPTICIAN	$28,045	190 MACHINE TOOL OPERATOR	$23,200
160 IRONWORKER	$28,033	191 REPORTER (NEWSPAPER)	$23,182
161 BRICKLAYER	$27,214		
162 MACHINIST	$27,180	192 FLORIST	$23,169

RANK		SCORE	RANK		SCORE
193	NURSE (LICENSED PRACTICAL)	$23,113	219	BOOKBINDER	$19,227
194	BUS DRIVER	$22,264	220	DISK JOCKEY	$18,243
195	TICKET AGENT	$22,260	221	PRECISION ASSEMBLER	$18,173
196	AUTOMOBILE BODY REPAIRER	$22,208	222	PHOTOGRAPHIC PROCESS WORKER	$18,142
197	COMPUTER OPERATOR	$22,193	223	TAXI DRIVER	$17,230
198	TRAVEL AGENT	$22,108	224	GARBAGE COLLECTOR	$17,200
199	HOME ECONOMIST	$22,106	225	BUTCHER	$17,169
200	NUCLEAR PLANT DECONTAMINATION TECHNICIAN	$22,100	226	RECEPTIONIST	$17,167
			227	DANCER	$17,075
200	COMPOSITOR/ TYPESETTER	$22,100	229	WAITER/WAITRESS	$17,075
			229	FILE CLERK	$17,013
202	FARMER	$21,970	230	SPORTS INSTRUCTOR	$16,263
203	CARPET INSTALLER	$21,290	230	RECREATION WORKER	$16,263
204	PAINTER	$21,255	232	LUMBERJACK	$16,244
205	AUTOMOBILE PAINTER	$21,240	233	BANK TELLER	$16,136
206	PIANO TUNER	$21,231	234	ROOFER	$15,264
206	MUSICAL INSTRUMENT REPAIRER	$21,231	235	MILITARY (ENLISTED PERSON)	$15,210
208	FLIGHT ATTENDANT	$21,207	236	JANITOR	$15,160
209	TELEPHONE OPERATOR	$21,138	237	NURSE'S AIDE	$15,150
210	FISHERMAN	$21,119	238	CHILD CARE WORKER	$14,213
211	TYPIST/WORD PROCESSOR	$21,067	239	SALESPERSON (RETAIL)	$14,200
212	MAYOR	$20,682	240	CONSTRUCTION WORKER (LABORER)	$14,189
213	VENDING MACHINE REPAIRER	$20,236	241	BARTENDER	$14,140
			242	COOK/CHEF	$13,330
214	SHIPPING/RECEIVING CLERK	$20,192	243	GUARD	$13,178
			244	CASHIER	$12,188
214	METER READER	$20,192	245	DRESSMAKER	$12,100
216	BOOKKEEPER	$20,100	246	TEACHER'S AIDE	$12,045
217	SHOE MAKER/REPAIRER	$20,040	247	CATHOLIC PRIEST	$10,343
218	FURNITURE UPHOLSTERER	$19,236	248	MAID	$10,138
			249	DISHWASHER	$10,022
			250	ACTOR	$7,850

HIGHEST STARTING PAY

Not all of the highest starting salaries are available to everyone who aspires to enter a profession, such as professional athletics or the presidency. Some, however are. Below are the jobs with the highest starting pay.

PRESIDENT (U.S.)	$200,000	ASTRONAUT	$51,000
BASKETBALL PLAYER (NBA)	$150,000	CORPORATE EXECUTIVE (SENIOR)	$50,000
CONGRESSPERSON/ SENATOR	$134,000	OPTOMETRIST	$48,000
SURGEON	$117,000	ASTRONOMER	$48,000
BASEBALL PLAYER (MAJOR LEAGUE)	$109,000	OSTEOPATH	$47,000
		SCHOOL PRINCIPAL	$47,000
FOOTBALL PLAYER (NFL)	$108,000	AIRPLANE PILOT	$45,000
JUDGE (FEDERAL)	$98,000	POSTAL INSPECTOR	$44,000
PSYCHIATRIST	$94,000	PETROLEUM ENGINEER	$43,000
ORTHODONTIST	$75,000	RABBI	$41,000
BASEBALL UMPIRE (MAJOR LEAGUE)	$60,000	ATTORNEY	$39,000
DENTIST	$53,000	AGENCY DIRECTOR (NONPROFIT)	$38,000

TOP BUCKS

Those who reach the pinacle of their profession almost always earn big incomes. Below are incomes of those who are in the 90th percentile of the earnings scale in the highest paying jobs.

FOOTBALL PLAYER (NFL)	$5,567,000	EXECUTIVE SEARCH CONSULTANT	$200,000
RACE CAR DRIVER (INDY CLASS)	$5,233,000	AIRPLANE PILOT	$176,000
BASKETBALL PLAYER (NBA)	$4,400,000	BASEBALL UMPIRE (MAJOR LEAGUE)	$175,000
BASEBALL PLAYER (MAJOR LEAGUE)	$4,300,000	CONGRESSPERSON/ SENATOR	$171,500
SYMPHONY CONDUCTOR	$700,000	STOCKBROKER	$166,000
PHYSICIAN (GENERAL PRACTICE)	$334,000	PODIATRIST	$165,000
CORPORATE EXECUTIVE (SENIOR)	$300,000	OSTEOPATH	$160,000
		ATTORNEY	$143,000
SURGEON	$285,000	OPTOMETRIST	$143,000
ORTHODONTIST	$260,000	FINANCIAL PLANNER	$142,000
HOSPITAL ADMINISTRATOR	$238,000	JUDGE (FEDERAL)	$138,000
PSYCHIATRIST	$220,000	DENTIST	$135,000
METEOROLOGIST	$212,000	ACTUARY	$132,000
CHIROPRACTOR	$203,000	PETROLEUM ENGINEER	$127,000
PRESIDENT (U.S.)	$200,000	MUSICIAN	$120,000
FASHION MODEL	$200,000		

ACCOUNTANT

Ranking: 60

Starting: $29,000

Mid-level: $52,000

Top: $88,000

Growth Potential: 203%

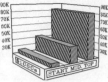

Salaries for accountants in the public sector usually lag significantly behind their private counterparts. The average annual salary for accountants in large public accounting firms is usually higher than those employed by smaller firms.

ACTOR

Ranking: 250

Starting: $2,000

Mid-level: $6,000

Top: $39,000

Growth Potential: 1,850%

The life of an actor can be one of glamour and renown, and a successful actor can earn an impressive income. However, only a very small number of those who enter this highly competitive field go on to achieve recognition and fame, and command top salary. Many are forced to leave the profession because they cannot earn a living, and even the most well-known actors can suffer long periods without work. Actors for whom salary is not important can find opportunities in local or amateur theater companies.

ACTUARY

Ranking: 29

Starting: $34,000

Mid-level: $70,000

Top: $132,000

Growth Potential: 288%

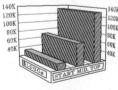

Both salary and advancement for actuaries depend on experience, and on progress through a series of actuarial examinations. Individuals entering the field who have passed the first examination can command annual salaries which are significantly higher than entry-level applicants with no examination record.

ADVERTISING ACCOUNT EXECUTIVE

Ranking: 88

Starting: $25,000

Mid-level: $42,000

Top: $82,000

Growth Potential: 228%

In the high-pressure, fast-paced field of advertising, the career of an account executive can be made or broken on a single ad campaign. Earnings in smaller advertising agencies normally combine salary with commission. In larger agencies handling major national accounts, compensation is normally salary plus bonus.

ADVERTISING SALESPERSON

Ranking: 129

Starting: $17,000

Mid-level: $32,000

Top: $60,000

Growth Potential: 253%

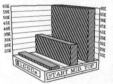

Income for advertising sales workers normally combines a base salary with commission on revenue generated. Consequently, earnings in this profession are linked directly to job performance. Advertising salespeople with larger, more popular stations and publications enjoy greater income potential.

AEROSPACE ENGINEER

Ranking: 39

Starting: $34,000

Mid-level: $64,000

Top: $103,000

Growth Potential: 203%

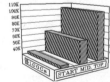

Demand for aerospace engineers is cyclical and depends largely on political factors, such as defense budgets and funding for space programs. The industry can experience long periods of sustained growth, and equally long periods of decline. Because of the unstable nature of the aerospace industry, earnings for some engineers may be affected by the need to look for a new job in mid-career.

AGENCY DIRECTOR (NONPROFIT)

Ranking: 24

Starting: $38,000

Mid-level: $80,000

Top: $105,000

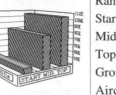

Growth Potential: 176%

Nonprofit agency directors are typically well paid. The high security cost of living in a metropolitan area and frequent entertaining expenses associated with this type of job can affect the buying power of earnings. Highest salaries are within the educational, private or health areas with the less stable arts or controversial non-profit charities offering less. Also, earnings tend to reflect what an organization can afford; those non-profits with more money to spend can offer a higher range of executive salaries.

AGRICULTURAL SCIENTIST

Ranking: 59

Starting: $23,000

Mid-level: $52,000

Top: $72,000

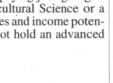

Growth Potential: 213%

Earnings for agricultural scientists depend on degree level, with the highest-paying jobs going to those with a Ph.D. in Agricultural Science or a related field. Job opportunities and income potential for applicants who do not hold an advanced degree are limited.

AIR TRAFFIC CONTROLLER

Ranking: 49

Starting: $23,000

Mid-level: $56,000

Top: $75,000

Growth Potential: 226%

Air traffic controllers are well-compensated for the high-pressure jobs they perform. Since many lives daily depend on the performance of air traffic controllers, these workers must undergo an extensive period of training and testing, during which pay is lower. After moving into positions of responsibility, salaries for air traffic controllers increase.

AIRCRAFT MECHANIC

Ranking: 113

Starting: $19,000

Mid-level: $35,000

Top: $51,000

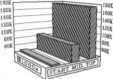

Growth Potential: 168%

Aircraft mechanics employed by companies where workers are unionized enjoy greater salaries and benefits than non-unionized members of this occupation. Mechanics who work for major airlines receive reduced fares.

AIRPLANE PILOT

Ranking: 18

Starting: $45,000

Mid-level: $85,000

Top: $176,000

Growth Potential: 291%

Salaries for pilots vary depending on the employer. Pilots working for commercial airlines earn the highest salaries in this profession. In fact, commercial airline pilots are some of the highest-paid of all professionals.

ANTHROPOLOGIST

Ranking: 62

Starting: $29,000

Mid-level: $52,000

Top: $78,000

Growth Potential: 169%

Nearly all anthropologists are associated with academic institutions. Salary scales in this profession are typical for faculty in colleges and universities. Employment and income potential for anthropologists depend on academic achievement. The highest paying positions at the most prestigious schools go to those who have earned the Ph.D. from a top graduate program.

ANTIQUE DEALER

Ranking: 93

Starting: $25,000

Mid-level: $40,000

Top: $80,000

Growth Potential: 220%

Financial compensation is tied to the total sales amount for merchandise inventoried and resold. For that reason, dealers of high profile antiques and collectibles earn the highest salaries in this profession. Some dealers may work for a gallery on a commission system or fixed salary plus incentives, although typically most antique dealers are self-employed. Experts in this field frequently interconnect dealing with promoting antique shows focusing on their specialty and writing or lecturing on their expertise to supplement income.

APPLIANCE REPAIRER

Ranking: 170

Starting: $14,000

Mid-level: $26,000

Top: $43,000

Growth Potential: 207%

While some home appliance repairers work in union shops, where wages are determined by experience, most in this profession are not union members, and many are self-employed. Wages for appliance repairers vary from region to region, and also by the type of appliance repaired.

ARCHEOLOGIST

Ranking: 62

Starting: $29,000

Mid-level: $52,000

Top: $78,000

Growth Potential: 169%

As in most other social sciences, the highest salaries in archeology go to holders of advanced degrees. Only professional archeologists whose research has produced remarkable findings can command the top salaries. Those with bachelor's degrees generally find temporary work on short-term projects, and must continue their education to be successful in the field.

ARCHITECT

Ranking: 92

Starting: $26,000

Mid-level: $40,000

Top: $107,000

Growth Potential: 312%

Architects can establish private practices, or work as salaried employees of an established firm. The potential for earnings as a partner or owner of a private practice is greater, but this venture can be risky. Income for most salaried architects with established firms in large, urban areas depends on level of experience.

ARCHITECTURAL DRAFTER

Ranking: 146

Starting: $17,000

Mid-level: $29,000

Top: $46,000

Growth Potential: 171%

Most drafters work in industries where the amount of work for drafters fluctuates seasonally and with economic conditions. Those entering this occupation should expect the possibility of periodic layoffs. Earnings in this field rise regularly, and in substantial increments, as drafters become more experienced. Drafting can be a stepping stone to architecture or engineering for some individuals, with potential for higher earnings.

ARTIST (COMMERCIAL)

Ranking: 114

Starting: $24,000

Mid-level: $35,000

Top: $55,000

Growth Potential: 129%

More than half of all commercial and graphic artists are self-employed, and earnings depend almost entirely on the reputation and clientele they have been able to develop. Well-established free-lance artists can earn comfortable incomes, but free-lancers lack the benefits associated with a full-time job. Salaried positions for artists exist in advertising agencies, graphic art companies, consulting firms, and other businesses. Earnings in these positions depend on the artist's experience, and on the type of employer.

ARTIST (FINE ART)

Ranking: 175

Starting: $16,000

Mid-level: $25,000

Top: $46,000

Growth Potential: 188%

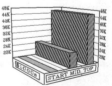

Since most artists are self-employed, their earnings are dependent upon the number of works they sell. As only the most successful are able to support themselves by their work, many fine artists augment salaries by working part-time at other occupations, such as art instructors and graphic illustrators.

ASTROLOGER

Ranking: 169

Starting: $4,000

Mid-level: $25,000

Top: $65,000

Growth Potential: 1,525%

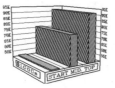

The great majority of astrologers are self-employed, and their earnings depend on the quality of their predictions, and the sizes of their clientele. A small number of workers augment their incomes by authorizing astrology columns for newspapers and magazines.

ASTRONAUT

Ranking: 27

Starting: $51,000

Mid-level: $76,000

Top: $92,000

Growth Potential: 80%

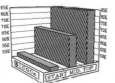

In the past, astronauts were almost without exception members of the armed services. As such, their salaries are tied to military pay scales, with higher-ranking officers earning more. Many astronauts are expert pilots, and space shuttle astronauts often have specialized training in some area of science. These highly specialized skills can earn astronauts much higher pay in the private sector. In recent years, shuttle crews have been drawn from the ranks of science and academia.

ASTRONOMER

Ranking: 34

Starting: $48,000

Mid-level: $68,000

Top: $85,000

Growth Potential: 77%

Employers of astronomers include federal government agencies, private research and development laboratories, observatories, and colleges and universities. Salaries are about equal throughout the field. A Ph.D. in physics or astronomy is essential to permanent, well paying employment in astronomy. Many students work as research assistants at relatively low salary for several years while earning a degree.

ATTORNEY

Ranking: 17

Starting: $39,000

Mid-level: $86,000

Top: $143,000

Growth Potential: 267%

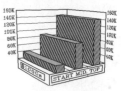

Salaries for lawyers vary widely depending on legal specialty, academic and professional qualifications, and type of employer. Graduates from top law schools who are hired by large law firms in major cities, large corporations, and financial institutions command extremely high starting salaries. For those with degrees from less prestigious schools, those working for local or state governments, or those in smaller practices, salaries will be lower. Establishing a private legal practice may take several years, and beginning lawyers who choose this path must often supplement their income with other work.

AUDIOLOGIST

Ranking: 101

Starting: $31,000

Mid-level: $38,000

Top: $49,000

Growth Potential: 58%

Professional audiologists must meet minimum licensing requirements to practice. The vast majority of audiologists are employed by hospitals, clinics, public health care agencies, and schools. Income is fairly consistent throughout this profession. A very small number of audiologists are in private practice, and may enjoy better-than-average incomes.

AUTHOR (BOOKS)

Ranking: 172

Low: $5,000

Mid-level: $25,000

Top: $60,000

Growth Potential: 1,100%

Best sellers are the only books that can earn an author a good deal of money. The difficulty of turning a written work into a best seller in this highly-competitive field is reflected in the high income differential for this occupation. Writing talent and quality of work often take a back seat to other factors in determining an author's success.

AUTOMOBILE ASSEMBLER

Ranking: 158

Starting: $22,000

Mid-level: $28,000

Top: $33,000

Growth Potential: 50%

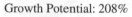

Automotive assemblers are usually members of labor unions, and pay and benefits for these workers are determined by union contracts with automobile manufacturers. Pay raises and promotions normally depend on seniority in this field, with the exception of workers who specialize in highly technical components. This work requires the greatest skill, and commands the highest wages.

AUTOMOBILE BODY REPAIRER

Ranking: 196

Starting: $13,000

Mid-level: $22,000

Top: $40,000

Growth Potential: 208%

Like automobile painters, those who repair automobile bodies often rely on commissions for earnings. Thus, income in this field varies widely depending on the volume of business and the affluence of the area in which the repairer works. Repairers in union shops generally earn steadier wages, though those who are self-employed, and who have gained a reputation for excellent work quality, enjoy greater earning potential.

AUTOMOBILE MECHANIC

Ranking: 188

Starting: $13,000

Mid-level: $23,000

Top: $41,000

Growth Potential: 215%

Automobile dealerships generally pay mechanics better than do independent shops. Mechanics working in repair shops are often paid a commission on work performed. The size and type of clientele of a shop can thus affect a mechanic's earnings considerably.

AUTOMOBILE PAINTER

Ranking: 205

Starting: $10,000

Mid-level: $21,000

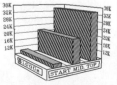

Top: $34,000

Growth Potential: 240%

Automotive painters have employment opportunities in automotive assembly plants, automobile dealerships, and independent paint shops. Earnings in this occupation depend on experience, and on place of employment. Unionized factory painters earn the most in wages, but an accomplished painter in a shop can supplement income considerably with commissions.

AUTOMOBILE SALESPERSON

Ranking: 138

Starting: $22,000

Mid-level: $31,000

Top: $48,000

Growth Potential: 118%

Automobile salespersons average considerably higher incomes than sales personnel in other industries. This is not unexpected, since commission normally accounts for a large percentage of a salesperson's earnings, and for those who work with high-priced merchandise, such as automobiles, earnings from commission will be greater.

BANK OFFICER

Ranking: 105

Starting: $28,000

Mid-level: $37,000

Top: $73,000

Growth Potential: 161%

Salaries for bank officers are fairly consistent throughout the profession. An M.B.A. in finance or economics translates into higher starting salaries for bank employees. Banking skills, administrative abilities, and experience are generally more important than educational background in determining advancement. Banks promote officers from within, and often provide training for well-qualified employees.

BANK TELLER

Ranking: 233

Starting: $11,000

Mid-level: $16,000

Top: $26,000

Growth Potential: 136%

Salaries for bank tellers are uniform throughout the industry. Training for qualified applicants is usually provided on the job. Bank teller positions do not command high salaries, but banks often promote experienced tellers to higher-level positions, such as loan officer, with better compensation.

BARBER

Ranking: 168

Starting: $21,000

Mid-level: $27,000

Top: $40,000

Growth Potential: 90%

The work of a barber is considered a personal service, and like many such services, tips may comprise a significant portion of earnings. Because earnings from tips depend not only on volume, but on a barber's clientele, shops in more affluent areas generally provide for greater income. Many barbers own their own shops, while others work for a small salary and a commission on work performed.

BARTENDER

Ranking: 241

Starting: $10,000

Mid-level: $14,000

Top: $24,000

Growth Potential: 140%

Most bars pay starting bartenders minimum wage, or slightly higher. Tips account for a significant percentage of earnings for a large majority of bartenders. Depending on a bar's clientele and volume of business, bartenders' total income can be considerably more than the wages paid by the employer.

BASEBALL PLAYER (MAJOR LEAGUE)

Ranking: 2

Starting: $109,000

Mid-level: $1,185,000

Top: $4,300,000

Growth Potential: 3,845%

Baseball players command some of the highest salaries in professional sports. A player's salary is tied closely to performance on the field. Most stars supplement their salaries significantly through product promotion and advertising. However, very few of those who attempt a professional career make it to the major leagues, and even fewer become stars, with long, illustrious careers. Major league players are unionized, and

collective bargaining agreements with owners have established excellent minimum salaries and good retirement plans for players.

BASEBALL UMPIRE (MAJOR LEAGUE)

Ranking: 8

Starting: $60,000

Mid-level: $140,000

Top: $175,000

Growth Potential: 192%

The earnings of major league umpires are exceptionally high, relative to the modest educational requirements of the field. There is little distinction between the income and benefits of novice and experienced workers in this field.

BASKETBALL COACH (NCAA)

Ranking: 86

Starting: $27,000

Mid-level: $43,000

Top: $95,000

Growth Potential: 252%

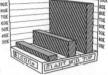

High-profile coaches at prominent basketball schools are handsomely paid. Successful basketball teams earn large amounts of money for the school through fees paid by television networks. The importance of winning, however, means that successive poor seasons can be grounds for a coach's dismissal. Assistant coaches usually specialize in a particular aspect of the game, such as defensive or offensive strategy, and are less well-paid. Many assistant coaches with successful programs go on to head coaching positions at other schools.

BASKETBALL PLAYER (NBA)

Ranking: 1

Starting: $150,000

Mid-level: $1,558,000

Top: $4,400,000

Growth Potential: 2,833%

Teams in the National Basketball Association carry rosters of only 12 players at any one time during the season. As a result, salaries for basketball players are generally higher than those for other professional athletes. However, smaller rosters make it extremely difficult to secure a position on a pro team, and only the most superbly gifted athletes become NBA players. The average NBA career is very short for less gifted players.

Famous players can supplement their income substantially with product endorsements and promotions.

BIOLOGIST

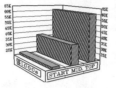

Ranking: 104

Starting: $22,000

Mid-level: $37,000

Top: $61,000

Growth Potential: 177%

The highest paid biologists hold Ph.D. degrees, and conduct or administer independent research, teach in colleges and universities, or work for federal government agencies. Hospitals and private laboratories offer jobs with modest salaries to applicants with bachelor's degrees, but promotion and higher pay normally require advanced degrees.

BOILERMAKER

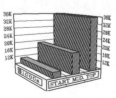

Ranking: 141

Starting: $28,000

Mid-level: $31,000

Top: $55,000

Growth Potential: 96%

Boilermaking is a heavily unionized occupation. Wages for boilermakers are higher than the average for non-supervisory workers. Industries which employ boilermakers are subject to the effects of recessions or other economic downturns. During these times, boilermakers can experience layoffs, and total annual income will drop.

BOOKBINDER

Ranking: 219

Starting: $11,000

Mid-level: $19,000

Top: $36,000

Growth Potential: 227%

Wages for bookbinders in large printing plants depend on an individual's level of training. Some plants are unionized. A small percentage of bookbinders work for libraries, book shops specializing in restoring old books, or the hand binderies of small, specialized publishing houses. These workers may earn a salary, rather than hourly wages.

BOOKKEEPER

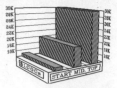

Ranking: 216

Starting: $15,000

Mid-level: $20,000

Top: $30,000

Growth Potential: 100%

Bookkeepers and accounting clerks are employed in businesses, schools, hospitals, government, and almost all other segments of the marketplace. Earnings in this occupation vary by industry, with public utilities paying the highest salaries in the field.

BRICKLAYER

Ranking: 161

Starting: $14,000

Mid-level: $27,000

Top: $44,000

Growth Potential: 214%

Although bricklayers command relatively high wages, yearly income in this profession can be lower than these wages would suggest. In most sections of the country, poor weather restricts the number of hours bricklayers work, and thus limits overall income.

BROADCAST TECHNICIAN

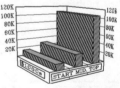

Ranking: 150

Starting: $14,000

Mid-level: $28,000

Top: $107,000

Growth Potential: 664%

Broadcasting stations in large cities pay more than those in smaller cities. Hours are generally shorter, and overtime is compensated, at larger stations. Competition for positions at stations in larger markets is extremely strong. Applicants in smaller cities generally have better chances of gaining entry-level positions. Television broadcasting equipment is more complicated than that for radio, and workers in television usually command higher wages.

BUS DRIVER

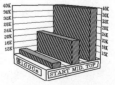

Ranking: 194

Starting: $11,000

Mid-level: $22,000

Top: $40,000

Growth Potential: 264%

Nearly three-fourths of all bus drivers work for school systems, or for companies that contract to operate school buses. These positions are part-time, and school bus drivers earn lower wages than local transit or commercial bus line drivers. Drivers in cities with populations over one million can earn as much as $3 per hour more than drivers in smaller cities. Drivers on interstate lines command the highest salaries.

BUTCHER

Ranking: 225

Starting: $13,000

Mid-level: $17,000

Top: $35,000

Growth Potential: 169%

Butchers who are members of the United Food and Commercial Workers Union can expect to earn higher wages than non-unionized butchers. Earnings in this occupation vary according to place of employment. Butchers working in meat processing and packaging plants generally have less opportunity to develop meat-cutting skills than those working in supermarkets. As a result, their wages and earning potential are lower.

BUYER

Ranking: 82

Starting: $26,000

Mid-level: $44,000

Top: $63,000

Growth Potential: 142%

Salaries for retail and wholesale buyers are often tied to the total sales amount for the merchandise purchased and inventoried. For that reason, buyers for wholesale or large volume retail businesses, or buyers specializing in very expensive items, earn the highest amounts in this profession.

CARPENTER

Ranking: 182

Starting: $14,000

Mid-level: $24,000

Top: $43,000

Growth Potential: 207%

Wages in carpentry are relatively high. Like members of other construction trades, carpenters may experience periods of unemployment during economic downturns. Poor weather also restricts work time for carpenters in most areas of the country. The majority of carpentry projects are short-term. Maintenance carpenters enjoy steadier income than do journeymen.

CARPET/TILE INSTALLER

Ranking: 203

Starting: $10,000

Mid-level: $21,000

Top: $39,000

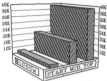

Growth Potential: 290%

Many carpet and tile installers work under union contracts which govern wage scales and benefits. Under union contracts, apprentices earn about half the amount of experienced workers in this occupation. The highest earnings are enjoyed by independent contractors who have established reputations for doing quality work.

CARTOONIST

Ranking: 175

Starting: $16,000

Mid-level: $25,000

Top: $46,000

Growth Potential: 188%

The work of popular syndicated cartoonists can be carried by dozens of papers across the country, reaching millions of people, and these cartoonists enjoy extremely high incomes. However, the number of cartoonists who gain nationwide prominence is small, and many in this occupation must leave the field when they find they cannot make a living in it.

CASHIER

Ranking: 244

Starting: $8,000

Mid-level: $12,000

Top: $23,000

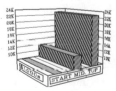

Growth Potential: 188%

Wages for cashiers vary widely, depending on whether or not their place of employment is unionized. Members of the United Food and Commercial Workers International Union earn relatively high wages for a job that requires little or no experience or training. Over half of all cashiers' jobs are part-time.

CATHOLIC PRIEST

Ranking: 247

Starting: $7,000

Mid-level: $10,000

Top: $31,000

Growth Potential: 343%

Because priests take vows of poverty, income is not a primary concern for those entering the priesthood. However, the church provides for priests' basic needs, such as room and board.

CHAUFFEUR

Ranking: 87

Starting: $32,000

Mid-level: $43,000

Top: $53,000

Growth Potential: 66%

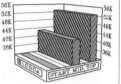

Most chauffeurs do not have special training, but those who have attended a school which teaches defensive driving command the highest salaries. The few chauffeurs who work for a single private individual, as opposed to a livery service, may also receive a housing allowance.

CHEMIST

Ranking: 53

Starting: $26,000

Mid-level: $55,000

Top: $95,000

Growth Potential: 265%

Chemists are employed in greater numbers outside of academic settings than those in any other occupation requiring formal knowledge and training in the physical sciences. A bachelor's degree is often sufficient to obtain a well-paying job, though chemists with advanced degrees enjoy higher salaries, better advancement potential, and greater prestige.

CHILD CARE WORKER

Ranking: 238

Starting: $8,000

Mid-level: $14,000

Top: $25,000

Growth Potential: 213%

Entry-level positions in child care often require little training or experience. These positions do not pay as well as entry-level jobs in other occu-

pations for those with no experience. Members of this profession who operate small, independent child care centers often earn more than those working in larger facilities.

CHIROPRACTOR

Ranking: 28

Starting: $22,000

Mid-level: $75,000

Top: $203,000

Growth Potential: 823%

Nearly all chiropractors are in private practice, where earnings depend on an established clientele and a good reputation. New chiropractors often work as salaried employees at established practices. Those opening new practices can expect several years of relatively low income.

CHOREOGRAPHER

Ranking: 20

Starting: $27,000

Mid-level: $83,000

Top: $92,000

Growth Potential: 241%

Choreographers, like dancers or other performing artists, must successfully establish themselves in their profession before earnings become consistent and significant. Choreographers may have to supplement income in other jobs until they reach a certain level of fame and success. Renowned dancers who become choreographers enjoy the highest earnings in this field.

CIVIL ENGINEER

Ranking: 44

Starting: $31,000

Mid-level: $58,000

Top: $94,000

Growth Potential: 203%

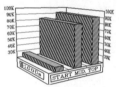

Because civil engineers work in a construction-related profession, these professionals may experience a drop in employment opportunities, and income potential, during economic downturns. Civil engineers in private firms earn more than do those in government agencies.

COLLEGE PROFESSOR

Ranking: 42

Starting: $29,000

Mid-level: $62,000

Top: $85,000

Growth Potential: 193%

Salaries for college professors depend on an individual's area of expertise and standing in the profession. Professors in the sciences tend to earn more than those in the humanities; professors whose published work gains national recognition are better-paid than those who are simply good teachers. College instructorships are low-paying, entry-level positions. These jobs almost always require a master's degree. Very few professors who do not hold a Ph.D. gain permanent jobs or tenured positions at the university level.

COMMUNICATIONS EQUIPMENT MECHANIC

Ranking: 163

Starting: $17,000

Mid-level: $27,000

Top: $46,000

Growth Potential: 171%

A large number of communications mechanics work for utilities and phone companies which offer liberal benefits packages in addition to employee salaries. These packages usually include excellent insurance, stock buying and retirement plans, and tuition reimbursement.

COMPOSITOR/TYPESETTER

Ranking: 200

Starting: $15,000

Mid-level: $22,000

Top: $30,000

Growth Potential: 100%

Because technology is changing rapidly in this field, differences in overall earnings are especially marked for compositors. Many older machines are much more complicated than newer models, and require higher degrees of skill to operate. The most skilled operators, of course, earn the best wages. As the technology in this field becomes more sophisticated, making equipment easier to use, earnings in this occupation may decrease.

COMPUTER OPERATOR

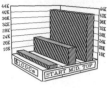

Ranking: 197

Starting: $14,000

Mid-level: $22,000

Top: $41,000

Growth Potential: 193%

Almost every industry employs computer operators. Earnings for these workers are fairly consistent across all industries. Operators in banks and other financial institutions, however, do tend to earn less than those in other businesses, and computer operators in the South average lower salaries than those in other areas of the country.

COMPUTER PROGRAMMER

Ranking: 97

Starting: $21,000

Mid-level: $38,000

Top: $62,000

Growth Potential: 195%

Experience with particular systems and hardware is usually a prerequisite for advancement for computer programmers. Most programmers are salaried employees, but some talented individuals write programs, or code, on a free-lance basis, and enjoy the possibility of higher earnings.

COMPUTER SERVICE TECHNICIAN

Ranking: 165

Starting: $25,000

Mid-level: $27,000

Top: $54,000

Growth Potential: 116%

Because many businesses rely on the proper operation of computer equipment 24 hours a day, computer service technicians often are on call after normal working hours, and can supplement income with overtime. Employers normally reimburse computer service technicians for travel expenses, and occasionally provide cars to these workers.

COMPUTER SYSTEMS ANALYST

Ranking: 80

Starting: $27,000

Mid-level: $45,000

Top: $70,000

Growth Potential: 159%

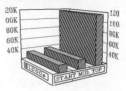

Analysts who are certified by various software companies can command higher salaries. These privatized certifications can often be more prized than academic credentials. Earnings are highest among those who are self-employed. As professionals branch out to service the new, more sophisticated PC-networks springing up in small businesses, more income opportunities exist for those with entrepreneurial skills.

CONGRESSPERSON/SENATOR

Ranking: 9

Starting: $133,600

Mid-level: $133,600

Top: $171,500

Growth Potential: 27%

Legislative salaries are determined by federal law. Senators and members of the House of Representatives earn the same amount: $133,600. In the Senate and House, higher pay is earned by the Majority and Minority Leaders: $148,400. Top Congressional pay is earned by just one person, the Speaker of the House: $171,500.

CONSERVATIONIST

Ranking: 70

Starting: $21,000

Mid-level: $48,000

Top: $58,000

Growth Potential: 176%

Over 70 percent of all positions in conservation and range management are with federal or state governments. Starting salaries in this profession are highest for those with advanced degrees. Governmental salary scales provide for regular pay increases for government employees. Forestry and paper companies do not have congressionally mandated salary limits, and experienced conservationists working for such companies have the potential to earn more than colleagues working for governmental agencies.

CONSTRUCTION FOREMAN

Ranking: 103

Starting: $34,000

Mid-level: $37,000

Top: $117,000

Growth Potential: 244%

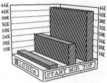

Experience brings greater responsibility on larger jobs for foremen, and earnings increase accordingly for workers in this occupation. Some construction supervisors go into business for themselves as independent contractors. Self-employed contractors with good business sense can earn substantially more than even the highest-paid construction foreman.

CONSTRUCTION MACHINERY OPERATOR

Ranking: 183

Starting: $14,000

Mid-level: $24,000

Top: $42,000

Growth Potential: 200%

Average wages in this occupation are not quite as high as those in other construction specialties. As with others in construction related jobs, employment for construction machinery operators is subject to weather, and to and the economic condition of the construction industry. Poor weather, or slowdowns in new construction starts, can limit earnings for machinery operators.

CONSTRUCTION WORKER (LABORER)

Ranking: 240

Starting: $9,000

Mid-level: $14,000

Top: $26,000

Growth Potential: 189%

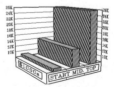

In general, construction wages are highest on the West coast, and lowest in the South. Earnings for apprentices are usually about half those of experienced workers, and all construction laborers are subject to seasonal layoffs during inclement weather.

COOK

Ranking: 242

Starting: $10,000

Mid-level: $13,000

Top: $43,000

Growth Potential: 330%

A renowned chef in a well-known hotel or expensive restaurant can earn several times that of his counterpart at an establishment catering to a working-class clientele. The best jobs are usually given to those who possess refined skills and who have worked at a number of different establishments, each time for higher pay. Uniforms and free meals are usually provided.

CORPORATE EXECUTIVE (SENIOR)

Ranking: 16

Starting: $50,000

Mid-level: $100,000

Top: $300,000

Growth Potential: 500%

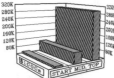

Senior corporate executives are among the highest paid workers in the nation. However, salary levels will vary greatly depending upon level of responsibility, how long they have been at this position and most importantly the size, type and location of the organization. Most senior level corporate executives are also rewarded when they perform well. In addition to their top level salaries, they have some, if not all, of the following: front-end bonuses, annual incentive bonuses, stock options, pension plans, fully covered insurance programs, partial personal accounting and legal services as well as coverage for car leasing and miscellaneous club memberships.

CORRECTION OFFICER

Ranking: 177

Starting: $20,000

Mid-level: $25,000

Top: $56,000

Growth Potential: 180%

Earnings for correction officers are fairly consistent throughout the occupation. Raises come regularly for all officers, and are normally based on seniority. Employers provide training for most correction officers, and no formal experience is required to enter this profession. However, government agencies, which hire over half of all correction officers, pay higher starting salaries to applicants with degrees in criminology, psychology, personal counseling, or related fields.

COSMETOLOGIST

Ranking: 167

Starting: $21,000

Mid-level: $27,000

Top: $42,000

Growth Potential: 100%

Weekly earnings for cosmetologists include tips, which can vary depending on the type of beauty salon in which they are employed, and its location. Skilled beauticians, and those with interpersonal skills that make them popular with customers, can build an extensive and loyal clientele, increasing earnings. Those owning their own salons enjoy the greatest income potential.

COWBOY

Ranking: 178

Starting: $14,000

Mid-level: $25,000

Top: $38,000

Growth Potential: 171%

Earnings for cowboys are low, but meals and a place to sleep (even if only a tent) are usually provided. Because employment in this occupation is seasonal, cowboys often work at other jobs for parts of the year. Some cowboys are employed year-round on ranches, and a few are able to save enough money to purchase ranches of their own.

DAIRY FARMER

Ranking: 76

Starting: $10,000

Mid-level: $45,000

Top: $100,000

Growth Potential: 900%

Market conditions, such as milk prices, have a significant effect on earnings for dairy farmers. Dairy production requires large capital investments in equipment, structures, and livestock. Operating costs for dairy farmers are also high, and very few small operations yield high earnings for owners. However, large farms can be quite profitable. Some large farms hire workers to assist in production. These positions generally offer low wages, but may include meals and housing.

DANCER

Ranking: 227

Starting: $4,000

Mid-level: $16,000

Top: $47,000

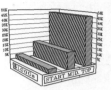

Growth Potential: 1,075%

Many professional dancers belong to one of three main unions or dancers' guilds, and rates for these dancers are governed by union scales. Performance rates are normally quite generous. However, many professional dancers find dancing jobs only periodically, and must supplement income with unrelated work. Competition is high for permanent positions with established dance companies.

DENTAL HYGIENIST

Ranking: 123

Starting: $18,000

Mid-level: $33,000

Top: $35,000

Growth Potential: 94%

Earnings for dental hygienists are consistent throughout the trade. Because many dentists do not require the services of a hygienist full-time, members of this occupation must often hold more than one part-time job to realize full earning potential.

DENTAL LABORATORY TECHNICIAN

Ranking: 118

Starting: $10,000

Mid-level: $34,000

Top: $38,000

Growth Potential: 280%

Learning the skills to become a competent, fully independent dental laboratory technician takes approximately three to four years. Those who operate their own laboratories enjoy greater earnings.

DENTIST

Ranking: 11

Starting: $53,000

Mid-level: $111,000

Top: $135,000

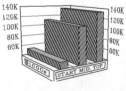

Growth Potential: 155%

Like other health professionals, dentists achieve their highest earnings after establishing successful practices. Dentists who work in affluent areas with stable economic conditions earn the most money. Those who start practices in small towns with less competition can build a clientele faster.

DIETITIAN

Ranking: 134

Starting: $27,000

Mid-level: $32,000

Top: $40,000

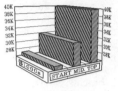

Growth Potential: 48%

A bachelor's degree with concurrent on-the-job training is usually required for entry into this profession. Because pay scales for jobs with the federal government are tied to levels of education, beginning salaries for dietitians working for agencies of federal government are generally less than those for their colleagues in private hospitals and clinics.

DISHWASHER

Ranking: 249

Starting: $9,000

Mid-level: $10,000

Top: $11,000

Growth Potential: 22%

Uniformly low earnings, which begin at minimum wage, reflect the rather temporary nature of this occupation. There are few requirements to become a dishwasher. Pay increases in this occupation are almost always tied to experience and seniority.

DISK JOCKEY

Ranking: 220

Starting: $14,000

Mid-level: $18,000

Top: $48,000

Growth Potential: 243%

Income potential for disc jockeys depends almost entirely on the size of the audience individual disk jockeys are able to generate. Most start at small stations, where pay is low. Those who demonstrate the ability to attract listeners can move to stations in larger markets, where salaries are substantially higher. Larger audiences allow stations to increase advertising rates, and this added results in higher pay for successful DJs.

DRESSMAKER

Ranking: 245

Starting: $12,000

Mid-level: $12,000

Top: $24,000

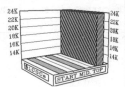

Growth Potential: 100%

The highest-paid dressmakers enjoy established reputations for skill and imagination in design, and make individualized dresses for a wealthy clientele. Many dressmakers, however, are employed by clothing companies and work in garment factories. The best-paid of these are covered by union contracts which govern wages, pay increases and benefits.

DRILL-PRESS OPERATOR

Ranking: 125

Starting: $21,000

Mid-level: $33,000

Top: $35,000

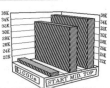

Growth Potential: 67%

Hourly wages for drill press operators are about equal to the average for all production workers. Most workers in this occupation are affiliated with unions, such as the International Association of Machinists and Aerospace Workers, and wages and promotions are tied to seniority. The increased use of robotics in some areas of production may affect future earning potential in this trade.

DRYWALL APPLICATOR/ FINISHER

Ranking: 186

Starting: $13,000

Mid-level: $23,000

Top: $48,000

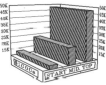

Growth Potential: 269%

Unlike other construction workers, drywall applicators and finishers, who normally work indoors, seldom lose work time because of poor weather. However, periods of sluggish growth in the housing construction industry can lead to layoffs of drywallers. During their two-year training periods, apprentices in this trade usually earn about half the wages of more experienced workers.

ECONOMIST

Ranking: 30

Starting: $26,000

Mid-level: $69,000

Top: $83,000

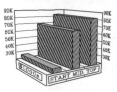

Growth Potential: 219%

Starting salaries for economists reflect an individual's level of education, with holders of advanced degrees commanding the larger salaries. Economists are employed in many areas of the private sector, as well as government agencies and colleges and universities. Most positions for economists, particularly those in government, are located in large urban areas, where costs of living are high.

ELECTRICAL ENGINEER

Ranking: 35

Starting: $36,000

Mid-level: $67,000

Top: $108,000

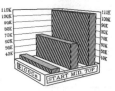

Growth Potential: 200%

Most jobs for electrical engineers are in manufacturing. Defense contractors may experience periodic drops in the number and size of orders from the government, and may be forced to lay off engineers as a consequence. Electrical engineering technology changes rapidly, and those in this profession who do not keep up will suffer decreased earning potential.

ELECTRICAL EQUIPMENT REPAIRER

Ranking: 149

Starting: $17,000

Mid-level: $28,900

Top: $40,000

Growth Potential: 135%

Electrical equipment repairers serve as apprentices for three or four years before gaining certification as journeymen. Wages for apprentices are considerably lower than for certified repairers. Jobs in this occupation are concentrated in large urban areas, where living costs are high, or in the military.

ELECTRICAL TECHNICIAN

Ranking: 139

Starting: $22,000

Mid-level: $31,000

Top: $44,000

Growth Potential: 100%

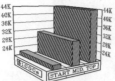

Despite the the different paths available for candidates entering this occupation, beginning salaries are fairly consistent. The federal government directly employs only a small percentage of all electrical technicians, but many more are employed by defense contractors. Should federal defense spending be cut, electrical technicians in defense-related industries may experience layoffs.

ELECTRICIAN

Ranking: 142

Starting: $18,000

Mid-level: $30,000

Top: $49,000

Growth Potential: 172%

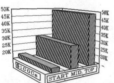

Apprenticeships for electricians can last as long as four years, during which time apprentices earn less than half the amount of journeymen electricians. Electricians' earnings are not as affected by poor weather as are the earnings of others in construction related jobs. Electricians tend to earn more than carpenters or masons.

EMERGENCY MEDICAL TECHNICIAN

Ranking: 146

Starting: $21,000

Mid-level: $29,000

Top: $36,000

Growth Potential: 71%

Emergency medical technicians at the highest level of registration can earn as much as $4,000 more annually than colleagues at lower levels. Those technicians employed by fire departments in large cities can earn a third more than those working in small towns

ENGINEERING TECHNICIAN

Ranking: 139

Starting: $22,000

Mid-level: $31,000

Top: $44,000

Growth Potential: 100%

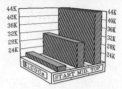

There are a wide variety of tasks technicians may be required to perform, and the backgrounds of those entering the profession may be substantially different. Those with excellent training, education, and experience can command starting annual salaries as much as $3,000 higher than those with less background in the field.

EXECUTIVE SEARCH CONSULTANT

Ranking: 37

Starting: $30,000

Mid-level: $65,000

Top: $200,000

Growth Potential: 567%

Financial compensation is often tied to the number of matches made, candidates located or client searches retained. For consultants working on the retainer system, compensation is often based on the level of executive located. For that reason, typically those retained receive the higher salaries with an individual consultant commanding as much as 30 or 40 percent of their candidate's first year salary package as their share of the fee. Often consultants supplement this by becoming partners or senior executives in executive search firms.

FARMER

Ranking: 202

Starting: $10,000

Mid-level: $21,000

Top: $107,000

Growth Potential: 970%

Income for farmers is highly dependent on the market for particular agricultural produce. Each year, weather conditions, crop yields, produce prices, and consumer demands combine to determine earnings for farmers. The right combination of these factors can lead to a profitable year; a change in these factors could mean a net loss. Each year many farmers are forced into bankruptcy; at the same time some farmers work profitably for many years and can become quite wealthy.

FASHION DESIGNER

Ranking: 127

Starting: $14,000

Mid-level: $32,000

Top: $62,000

Growth Potential: 343%

Designers who own their own businesses tend to make more money than salaried employees of garment manufacturers or design houses. Independence, however, brings greater risks along with greater earning potential.

FASHION MODEL

Ranking: 26

Starting: $10,000

Mid-level: $75,000

Top: $200,000

Growth Potential: 1,900%

Successful, popular fashion models can command extremely high daily or hourly wages. However, very few in the profession gain this prominence, and, like actors, most fashion models work irregularly. Often, models must supplement their incomes with employment in other occupations. The majority of modeling jobs are located in large cities, where the buying power of a model's earnings may be decreased.

FILE CLERK

Ranking: 229

Starting: $16,000

Mid-level: $17,000

Top: $18,000

Growth Potential: 13%

Although earnings for file clerks rise slowly with experience, most in this field achieve greater earnings only by using the job as a stepping stone to other positions. Businesses and other employers with complex or computerized filing systems pay file clerks more.

FINANCIAL PLANNER

Ranking: 21

Starting: $19,000

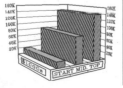

Mid-level: $82,000

Top: $142,000

Growth Potential: 647%

Financial compensation is tied into the way planners work and bill their time. Some receive commissions from investment firms for the investments that are recommended to clients and others receive only client compensation for services provided, an option many clients prefer, feeling it means that the planner has no financial interest in recommending one investment over another. Planners may also opt for receiving a combination of fees and commissions. There are large differences in salaries depending upon the scope of work performed by financial planner. Some financial planners charge by the hour at rates going from $75.00 to $250.00 per hour.

FIREFIGHTER

Ranking: 111

Starting: $20,000

Mid-level: $35,000

Top: $55,000

Growth Potential: 175%

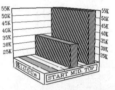

Salaries for firefighters are usually linked to the size of the particular city or town. Larger cities generally pay more for this essential service, although higher pay for big-city firefighters can be offset by a higher cost of living. Firefighters enjoy excellent pension plans, and many firefighters can receive full retirement benefits at age 50, or after 25 years of service.

FISHERMAN

Ranking: 210

Starting: $16,000

Mid-level: $21,000

Top: $35,000

Growth Potential: 119%

Earnings for fishermen vary with the seasons, and are tied to the size and type of catch. Poor weather, overfishing, and bad luck can all limit the size of catches. In smaller commercial fishing fleets, each crew members' share of the catch depends on expertise; the captain of the boat receives the larger share. Crew members on large commercial fishing vessels may be paid a salary or an hourly wage.

FLIGHT ATTENDANT

Ranking: 208
Starting: $14,000
Mid-level: $21,000
Top: $43,000
Growth Potential: 207%

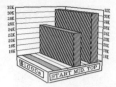

Because training for flight attendants is fairly standard throughout the airline industry, salaries are consistent throughout the occupation. Recessions may limit profits for airlines. This could lead to layoffs, lower salaries, and decreases in benefits for flight attendants.

FLORIST

Ranking: 192
Starting: $13,000
Mid-level: $23,000
Top: $35,000
Growth Potential: 169%

Volume and overhead are critical factors in determining income for florists. Shops in suburban locations generate more income, as customers are more affluent, and store rents are lower than in business districts of large cities. Floral designers average lower earnings than designers in other businesses.

FOOTBALL PLAYER (NFL)

Ranking: 3
Starting: $108,000
Mid-level: $650,000
Top: $5,567,000
Growth Potential: 5,055%

Collective bargaining agreements between the National Football League Players' Association and team owners have established minimum salaries in professional football. The debacle of the 1987 players' strike, however, has weakened the union's bargaining strength on issues affecting player salaries, such as free agency. The average salary for NFL players is lower than the average for baseball or basketball players. Talented, popular players still earn extremely large salaries, and supplement this income through product endorsements. Careers tend to be short in this hazardous, highly competitive profession.

FORK-LIFT OPERATOR

Ranking: 180
Starting: $14,000
Mid-level: $25,000
Top: $31,000
Growth Potential: 121%

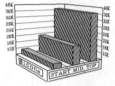

Earnings for fork-lift operators generally are about the same or slightly above the average for non-supervisory manufacturing occupations. Those operators who are unionized earn better wages in this profession.

FURNITURE UPHOLSTERER

Ranking: 218
Starting: $11,000
Mid-level: $19,000
Top: $37,000
Growth Potential: 236%

Trainee upholsterers generally earn minimum wage. After approximately three years, upholsterers are considered experienced, and pay increases accordingly.

GARBAGE COLLECTOR

Ranking: 224
Starting: $10,000
Mid-level: $17,000
Top: $30,000
Growth Potential: 200%

The collection of garbage is an essential service, and in large cities, garbage collectors are relatively well-paid. In smaller cities and towns, earnings are lower. Some garbage collectors in less-populated areas may earn little more than minimum wage. Private garbage collecting services yield substantial income for their owners.

GEOLOGIST

Ranking: 52
Starting: $27,000
Mid-level: $55,000
Top: $108,000
Growth Potential: 300%

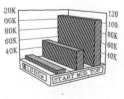

Starting salaries for geologists in the petroleum industry should begin to rise in the mid-1990's, as the current oil glut levels off. Geologists who work in academic settings should expect salaries similar to those specializing in other physical sciences.

GLAZIER

Ranking: 64

Starting: $31,000

Mid-level: $52,000

Top: $57,000

Growth Potential: 84%

Glaziers belonging to the International Brotherhood of Painters and Allied Trades generally work in construction. Unionized glaziers in construction earn much more than non-union glaziers.

GUARD

Ranking: 243

Starting: $9,000

Mid-level: $13,000

Top: $25,000

Growth Potential: 178%

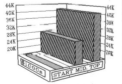

Although most guards work for private security firms, those working for other employers, such as banks, offices and retail stores, earn more. Security guards in the federal government earn the best salaries, but must have military training. In the private sector, guards working for manufacturers earn the most money.

HEATING/REFRIGERATION MECHANIC

Ranking: 154

Starting: $16,000

Mid-level: $28,000

Top: $41,000

Growth Potential: 156%

The learning period for heating and refrigeration mechanics is generally four or five years. Earnings in this period increase from about 40 percent of average in the first year to 85 percent of average in the fourth year. More than half of those employed in this occupation work in construction, where earnings may be effected by downturns in the industry.

HIGHWAY PATROL OFFICER

Ranking: 171

Starting: $19,000

Mid-level: $26,000

Top: $44,000

Growth Potential: 132%

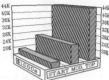

Salaries of state police officers are generally determined by the state population. The population of some states is similar to that of a major city, and thus the tax base is equivalent. As a result, the average salary for state troopers is about that for police officers in large cities. Salaries for state police officers are higher in heavily-populated states. Pay increases in this occupation come with experience and rise in rank.

HISTORIAN

Ranking: 95

Starting: $19,000

Mid-level: $39,000

Top: $73,000

Growth Potential: 284%

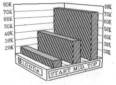

The large majority of historians work as faculty members in colleges or universities. Salaries are equivalent to those in other social science disciplines. The earning potential for the few historians working for museums, historical societies, and other areas outside of academia is limited by funding and budget constraints.

HOME ECONOMIST

Ranking: 199

Starting: $17,000

Mid-level: $22,000

Top: $35,000

Growth Potential: 106%

Most positions for home economists are with state and local governments. Salaries in this profession vary slightly from state to state, with positions located in the north and the west paying the most.

HOSPITAL ADMINISTRATOR

Ranking: 66

Starting: $28,000

Mid-level: $50,000

Top: $238,000

Growth Potential: 750%

The chief administrator of a hospital with more than 1,000 beds can earn as much as three times the salary of a colleague at a hospital with fewer than 100 beds. Because of stiff competition for jobs, new administrators will likely be offered lower-ranking and lower-paying positions than those who entered the profession a few years ago.

HOTEL MANAGER

Ranking: 43

Starting: $34,000

Mid-level: $61,000

Top: $91,000

Growth Potential: 168%

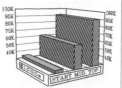

Salaries for different managerial positions within the same hotel vary widely, depending on duties. Earnings in this field also vary with the size and type of hotel. Larger chains generally pay well and demand that their managers have degrees in business- related areas. Applicants with specific degrees in hotel management have the best chance at landing these jobs.

INDUSTRIAL DESIGNER

Ranking: 79

Starting: $30,000

Mid-level: $45,000

Top: $80,000

Growth Potential: 167%

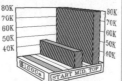

Familiarity with computer-aided design techniques will become increasingly important in realizing top earnings in this occupation. Qualifications for entry into this profession are not standardized, and therefore earnings vary somewhat throughout the field. "Hot" industries, of the time pay the best.

INDUSTRIAL ENGINEER

Ranking: 38

Starting: $34,000

Mid-level: $64,000

Top: $104,000

Growth Potential: 206%

Industrial engineers are employed not only by manufacturers, but by many other businesses and industries which require efficient and economical use of labor, material and capital in production and operation. Since the importance of the role of the industrial engineer grows during economic

downswings, these professionals are relatively safe from layoffs even during recessions.

INDUSTRIAL MACHINE REPAIRER

Ranking: 152

Starting: $16,000

Mid-level: $28,000

Top: $43,000

Growth Potential: 169%

Most industrial machine repairers work in heavy industries that are concentrated near large urban areas. Living costs in these areas can affect the buying power of wages. The industries employing repairers are almost always unionized, and consequently, wages for industrial machine repairers increase with experience.

INSURANCE AGENT

Ranking: 128

Starting: $16,000

Mid-level: $32,000

Top: $69,000

Growth Potential: 331%

After a training period of about six months, insurance agents earn a commission on the policies they sell. Because agents continue to earn a percentage on premiums paid over the life of a policy, an agent's total yearly earnings increase with each new policy sold.

INSURANCE UNDERWRITER

Ranking: 109

Starting: $29,000

Mid-level: $36,000

Top: $67,000

Growth Potential: 131%

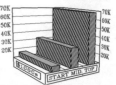

As an underwriter's training and experience grows, income increases regularly. Excellent benefits packages, including good insurance coverage and liberal vacations, add to the value of salaries in this occupation.

IRONWORKER

Ranking: 160

Starting: $24,000

Mid-level: $28,000

Top: $32,000

Growth Potential: 33%

Most ironworkers are employed in the construction industry, and can suffer lost work time due to poor weather. Extensive travel to new job sites is often required in this occupation, and this can cut into net income. Many positions are located in urban areas, where costs of living are high.

JANITOR

Ranking: 236

Starting: $10,000

Mid-level: $15,000

Top: $26,000

Growth Potential: 160%

Industries in which janitors are unionized pay these workers much more than non-unionized industries. A non-union janitor who is not a supervisor often earns little more than the minimum wage.

JEWELER

Ranking: 164

Starting: $22,000

Mid-level: $27,000

Top: $57,000

Growth Potential: 159%

Starting jewelers in unionized factories earn about half that of experienced workers. Pay raises for unionized jewelers come regularly. Non-unionized jewelers working in manufacturing and repair earn less than those who belong to unions. Jewelers who own their own shops have the highest income potential.

JOCKEY

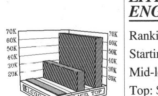

Ranking: 135

Starting: $11,000

Mid-level: $31,000

Top: $66,000

Growth Potential: 500%

Earnings for jockeys are tied to winnings in races. Purses in big-time horse racing are quite high, and jockeys can earn as much as ten percent of the take. However, earnings can be much lower in local racing, where prizes are smaller.

JUDGE (FEDERAL)

Ranking: 10

Starting: $98,000

Mid-level: $127,000

Top: $138,000

Growth Potential: 41%

Top salaries for federal government officials, including judges, are mandated by law. Salaries in bankruptcy court are somewhat lower than in other federal courts. Congress is expected to increase judicial salaries in the next few years. Though a federal judgeship is very prestigious, qualified candidates can usually earn more in private law practice.

LIBRARIAN

Ranking: 94

Starting: $28,000

Mid-level: $40,000

Top: $48,000

Growth Potential: 71%

Librarians with specialized backgrounds in fields other than library science earn more than colleagues who have no such training. Those working for the federal government average as much as $4,000 more per year than those working for colleges and universities, or for locally funded libraries.

LITHOGRAPHER/PHOTO ENGRAVER

Ranking: 148

Starting: $22,000

Mid-level: $29,000

Top: $36,000

Growth Potential: 64%

Although employers often provide on-the-job training for lithographers, applicants with postsecondary training in this trade normally earn higher starting salaries. In general, lithographers who operate more sophisticated equipment earn higher salaries.

LUMBERJACK

Ranking: 232

Starting: $9,000

Mid-level: $16,000

Top: $31,000

Growth Potential: 244%

Unionized lumberjacks can expect regular pay increases with experience, as well as benefits governed by collective bargaining agreements. Smaller lumber companies generally pay lumberjacks less than large forestry companies. Independent lumberjacks who are highly-skilled and own their own equipment have the potential for significant earnings.

MACHINE TOOL OPERATOR

Ranking: 190

Starting: $13,000

Mid-level: $23,000

Top: $39,000

Growth Potential: 200%

Machine tool operators average one dollar per hour over the median wage for all hourly workers. Earnings for machine tool operators vary depending on the complexity of machine being operated. Workers in this trade who take computer programming courses increase their earning potential.

MACHINIST

Ranking: 162

Starting: $15,000

Mid-level: $27,000

Top: $42,000

Growth Potential: 180%

Average wages for machinists vary by as much as $6 per hour depending on geographic region. Machinists in western states earn the most. Average wages for all machinists can be as much as $4 per hour more than that for other non-supervisory workers.

MAID

Ranking: 248

Starting: $8,000

Mid-level: $10,000

Top: $19,000

Growth Potential: 138%

Earnings for maids vary with types of employer. Non-unionized employees of smaller hotels and motels earn the least in this field. Private maids working for wealthy households are often well-compensated, with living expenses included in salaries.

MAIL CARRIER

Ranking: 115

Starting: $25,000

Mid-level: $35,000

Top: $36,000

Growth Potential: 44%

Because mail carriers are all employed by the U.S. Postal Service, salaries are consistent throughout the country. Carriers can attain maximum earnings with ten years of service. Benefits for mail carriers, as for other federal government employees, are excellent.

MARKET RESEARCH ANALYST

Ranking: 61

Starting: $25,000

Mid-level: $52,000

Top: $73,000

Growth Potential: 192%

Although most analysts have a knowledge of research techniques, those who also bring with them a specialized background in a particular market can start at higher salaries. Market research generally pays more than other social science-related fields, since most positions are in the private sector.

MATHEMATICIAN

Ranking: 54

Starting: $28,000

Mid-level: $55,000

Top: $85,000

Growth Potential: 204%

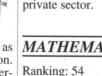

About three-fifths of all mathematicians work as college professors. Salaries for mathematics faculty average slightly higher those for faculty in the humanities and social sciences. Mathematicians with a Ph.D. can earn more in private sector research and development than in education.

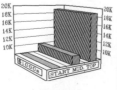

MAYOR

Ranking: 212

Starting: $11,000

Mid-level: $20,000

Top: $86,000

Growth Potential: 682%

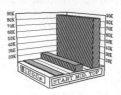

Mayor of can be unpaid volunteers or highly-paid officials with massive administrative responsibility in large cities where most earn over $100,000 annually. Salaries for mayors are set by municipal law, and are normally linked to population size, administrative duties, and breadth of responsibilities.

MECHANICAL ENGINEER

Ranking: 33

Starting: $37,000

Mid-level: $68,000

Top: $110,000

Growth Potential: 197%

Mechanical engineers who work in construction-related fields run the risk of losing earnings during periodic downturns in the construction industry. Some mechanical engineers boost earnings and save on income taxes by working overseas.

MEDICAL LABORATORY TECHNICIAN

Ranking: 179

Starting: $16,000

Mid-level: $25,000

Top: $42,000

Growth Potential: 163%

In general, technicians in large cities receive the greatest wages, but income varies widely with employer and geographic location. Novice technicians employed by the federal government usually receive an annual average salary earn somewhat below that of those in the private sector, especially those at major hospitals.

MEDICAL RECORDS TECHNICIAN

Ranking: 181

Starting: $22,000

Mid-level: $25,000

Top: $32,000

Growth Potential: 45%

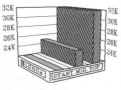

Formal education and a two- to four-year period of training are essential for securing a job as a records technician. Employers prefer applicants who are accredited by examination, and earnings are higher for accredited technicians.

MEDICAL SECRETARY

Ranking: 133

Starting: $25,000

Mid-level: $32,000

Top: $43,000

Growth Potential: 72%

The responsibilities, and thus the earnings, of medical secretaries vary from employer to employer, and from position to position. Experienced secretaries earn a broad range of salaries. Geographic location is one factor in this regard.

MEDICAL TECHNOLOGIST

Ranking: 96

Starting: $27,000

Mid-level: $39,000

Top: $39,000

Growth Potential: 44%

The duties of medical technologists are similar to those of medical technicians, but technologists generally are more highly trained and experienced. As a result, earnings for medical technologists are considerably higher than for technicians.

METEOROLOGIST

Ranking: 65

Starting: $21,000

Mid-level: $50,000

Top: $212,000

Growth Potential: 910%

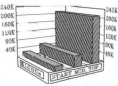

Academic performance and degree level determine both starting salaries and advancement potential for meteorologists. Beginning salaries for meteorologists vary by as much as $3,500 depending on grades alone. Meteorologists working as weather reporters for television stations can earn considerably more than their colleagues employed elsewhere.

METER READER

Ranking: 214

Starting: $13,000

Mid-level: $20,000

Top: $38,000

Growth Potential: 192%

Meter reading is an entry-level position, and pay is generally low. With training and experience, meter readers can advance to more lucrative positions with greater responsibility in public utility companies.

MILITARY (COMMISSIONED OFFICER)

Ranking: 90

Starting: $19,000

Mid-level: $41,000

Top: $62,000

Growth Potential: 226%

Federal government salary guidelines specify the top salaries for each rank in the military. Consequently, earnings are consistent throughout each rank in this occupation. Excellent retirement benefits, allowances for food and clothing, and free medical care add considerably to the value of a military income.

MILITARY (ENLISTED PERSON)

Ranking: 235

Starting: $10,000

Mid-level: $15,000

Top: $31,000

Growth Potential: 210%

Pay scales for military personnel are based on grade of rank. While experience is one of the most widely-applied criteria for promotions in grade, highly-qualified enlisted personnel may be promoted rapidly despite less experience. Excellent retirement benefits, allowances for food and clothing, and free medical care complement military salaries considerably.

MILITARY (WARRANT OFFICER)

Ranking: 143

Starting: $18,000

Mid-level: $30,000

Top: $41,000

Growth Potential: 128%

Warrant officers who work as civil servants usually earn good benefits in addition to salary. Some warrant officers are self-employed, and are paid for warrants served. This piecework may be lucrative, but self-employed warrant officers do not enjoy employee benefits.

MILLWRIGHT

Ranking: 122

Starting: $19,000

Mid-level: $33,000

Top: $47,000

Growth Potential: 147%

Requirements for millwrights range from a four-year apprenticeship program to up to eight years of on-the-job training. Earnings during this period are likely to be considerably lower than those for experienced millwrights. Wages also vary widely from region to region. Average wages for millwrights in the upper Midwest can be as much as $3.00 an hour higher than wages in other areas.

MOTION PICTURE EDITOR

Ranking: 68

Starting: $16,000

Mid-level: $48,000

Top: $85,000

Growth Potential: 431%

Box office performance is a greater factor than is skill or experience in determining earnings for film editors. Editors who have established a reputation for success, as well as quality, enjoy a better chance of being hired for a high-paying film project.

MUSEUM CURATOR

Ranking: 74

Starting: $23,000

Mid-level: $47,000

Top: $60,000

Growth Potential: 161%

The size, the prestige, and the funding base for a museum are the biggest contributing factors in determining the salaries of its curators. Curators generally advance, and gain higher earnings, by moving to more prestigious museums. Institutions sponsored by federal agencies pay more than state or locally-funded museums.

MUSICAL INSTRUMENT REPAIRER

Ranking: 206

Starting: $16,000

Mid-level: $21,000

Top: $53,000

Growth Potential: 231%

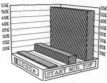

Musical instrument repairers involved in other aspects of the musical instrument business, such as sales, rental, or instrument making, enjoy better opportunity for high earnings. Established instrument repair businesses in affluent areas net the highest profits in this field.

MUSICIAN

Ranking: 57

Starting: $3,000

Mid-level: $50,000

Top: $120,000

Growth Potential: 3,900%

As with other performing artists, earnings for musicians vary considerably. While some musicians, such as those with popular recordings and big record contracts, earn large sums, others may go for long periods without employment or income from music. Musicians in major symphonies, and studio musicians, normally are union members. Their salaries are determined by union scales, and income generally is steadier for unionized musicians than for non-union members of this profession.

NEWSCASTER

Ranking: 136

Starting: $22,000

Mid-level: $31,000

Top: $111,000

Growth Potential: 405%

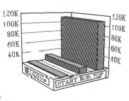

Salaries for newscasters vary with the size of market the station serves, and the ratings the newscaster can bring to the station. Successful newscasters in smaller markets can advance in pay and prestige by moving to stations having larger audiences.

NEWS WRITER (RADIO/TV)

Ranking: 126

Starting: $13,000

Mid-level: $32,000

Top: $64,000

Growth Potential: 392%

News writers' earnings vary widely. Skilled and experienced writers at large television stations are quite well-paid, while those at smaller stations make considerably less. Many news writers are unionized, and their salaries and benefits are determined by collective bargaining agreements.

NUCLEAR ENGINEER

Ranking: 32

Starting: $36,000

Mid-level: $68,000

Top: $110,000

Growth Potential: 206%

New orders for nuclear power plants in the United States have virtually ceased, and the demand for new nuclear engineers is low. Competition for openings in nuclear engineering among those entering the field will be strong. These factors will have the greatest impact on starting salaries in this profession in the coming years. Current members of this profession will be needed to maintain the safe and efficient operation of existing nuclear plants, but relatively few new openings are anticipated in the private sector.

NUCLEAR PLANT DECONTAMINATION TECHNICIAN

Ranking: 200

Starting: $16,000

Mid-level: $22,000

Top: $32,000

Growth Potential: 100%

Workers in this field receive premium wages, in compensation for the intrinsic hazards of their task and for the nearly constant travel that the occupation demands. Individuals who work hours in excess of safety guidelines are often paid as much as twice the customary hourly rate.

NURSE (LICENSED PRACTICAL)

Ranking: 193

Starting: $16,000

Mid-level: $23,000

Top: $34,000

Growth Potential: 113%

A drop in demand for licensed practical nurses may adversely affect starting salaries in this occupation. Regular pay increases are typical in health care occupations. Licensed practical nurses can expect increased earnings as experience grows.

NURSE (REGISTERED)

Ranking: 106

Starting: $23,000

Mid-level: $37,000

Top: $54,000

Growth Potential: 135%

Registered nurses who enter the field with a bachelor's degree in nursing start at higher salaries and have better opportunity for advancement than those entering with associate's degrees. Career advancement potential is somewhat limited, but nurses can expect regular pay increases with experience.

NURSE'S AIDE

Ranking: 237

Starting: $10,000

Mid-level: $15,000

Top: $25,000

Growth Potential: 150%

Nurse's aides employed in hospitals generally earn as much as $3.00 an hour more than those working in other establishments. This position provides experience which is helpful when aides pursue formal education to become eligible for better-paying jobs in the health care industry.

OCCUPATIONAL SAFETY/ HEALTH INSPECTOR

Ranking: 75

Starting: $23,000

Mid-level: $46,000

Top: $55,000

Growth Potential: 139%

Salaries are based on government service levels. Workers must meet minimum background requirements, and thus salaries are consistent throughout this profession. Liberal retirement plans and other benefits add considerably to the value of inspectors' salaries.

OCCUPATIONAL THERAPIST

Ranking: 102

Starting: $32,000

Mid-level: $38,000

Top: $48,000

Growth Potential: 50%

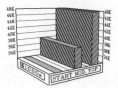

Increased demand for occupational therapists in the next decade will mean a rise in starting salaries for members of this profession. As in other health care occupations, therapists enjoy excellent benefits in addition to their regular earnings.

OCEANOGRAPHER

Ranking: 51

Starting: $31,000

Mid-level: $56,000

Top: $84,000

Growth Potential: 171%

Many positions in oceanography are in higher education and research institutes, and salaries for oceanographers are similar to those for faculty members in the natural and physical sciences. In the coming years, the demand for oceanographers in the private sector, especially in the petroleum industry, will decline. Consequently, salaries for oceanographers will be less competitive than they have been in recent years.

OFFICE MACHINE REPAIRER

Ranking: 165

Starting: $25,000

Mid-level: $27,000

Top: $54,000

Growth Potential: 116%

Many office equipment repairers are covered by union contracts which offer good wages and benefits. However, the highest earnings in this occupation are enjoyed by those who are self-employed. In some cases, office equipment repairers can build up a clientele while working for a larger company, and then open an independent service firm using this client base.

OPTICIAN

Ranking: 159

Starting: $22,000

Mid-level: $28,000

Top: $32,000

Growth Potential: 45%

Requirements for licensing or certification in this occupation, and consequently earnings, vary from state to state. In general, opticians who operate their own practices enjoy the highest earnings, while beginners, learning the trade on-the-job or in formal apprentice programs, earn the least.

OPTOMETRIST

Ranking: 23

Starting: $48,000

Mid-level: $80,000

Top: $143,000

Growth Potential: 198%

The growing number of eyeglass franchises is changing the way in which optometrists earn a living. These professionals may earn a salary, own a franchised store, or establish an individual practice. Although the first two options provide steadier incomes for beginning optometrists, those who establish private practices still enjoy the potential for greater long-term earnings.

ORTHODONTIST

Ranking: 7

Starting: $75,000

Mid-level: $193,000

Top: $260,000

Growth Potential: 247%

Like dentists, orthodontists may need several years to establish a profitable practice. Once established, orthodontists have the potential to make much more than dentists who are general practitioners.

OSTEOPATH

Ranking: 22

Starting: $47,000

Mid-level: $80,000

Top: $160,000

Growth Potential: 240%

Because most osteopaths are general practitioners, they tend to earn less than physicians with an M.D. The medical profession is becoming more popular as a career choice, and while earnings in this field are good in comparison to most other occupations, competition for jobs may cause a decline in starting salaries for osteopaths and other medical professionals.

PAINTER

Ranking: 204

Starting: $11,000

Mid-level: $21,000

Top: $39,000

Growth Potential: 255%

Although painters make more per hour than the average wage earner, total annual income for members of this profession can be affected by lost work time due to poor weather, and by periods of unemployment between contracts. Experienced painters often become individual contractors, with potential for much higher earnings.

PARALEGAL ASSISTANT

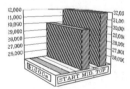

Ranking: 144

Starting: $25,000

Mid-level: $30,000

Top: $32,000

Growth Potential: 28%

There are no standard requirements for beginning paralegals. A number of schools do offer formal training in this field. Training, background, and expertise in relevant areas all affect starting salaries, which vary widely.

PAROLE OFFICER

Ranking: 132

Starting: $26,000

Mid-level: $32,000

Top: $52,000

Growth Potential: 100%

Because parole officers are paid by government agencies, earnings vary according to the size of the tax base. Officers in large urban areas earn considerably more than those in smaller cities and towns. On average, federal parole officers earn more than their colleagues working for state and local governments.

PERSONNEL RECRUITER

Ranking: 89

Starting: $22,000

Mid-level: $42,000

Top: $58,000

Growth Potential: 164%

As in other positions where entry requirements are not defined, earnings for personnel recruiters vary widely according to employer. Though many positions in this occupation are considered entry-level, experience may be required for some beginning jobs. Entry-level positions for personnel recruiters often lead directly to higher-paying, more responsible jobs with experience.

PETROLEUM ENGINEER

Ranking: 25

Starting: $43,000

Mid-level: $79,000

Top: $127,000

Growth Potential: 195%

Anticipated declines in the profit margins for oil companies may effect the starting salaries for petroleum engineers in the coming years, and may even lead to layoffs for some in this profession. However, as oil becomes increasingly difficult to recover, skilled petroleum engineers with excellent grasp of the discipline will have opportunity for increased earnings.

PHARMACIST

Ranking: 71

Starting: $28,000

Mid-level: $48,000

Top: $63,000

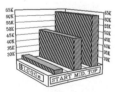

Growth Potential: 125%

The location and size of stores are often determiners of salaries for pharmacists employed by chain stores. Pharmacists can increase their earning potential by buying their own stores or moving into the management of large drugstore chains.

PHILOSOPHER

Ranking: 41

Starting: $30,000

Mid-level: $63,000

Top: $85,000

Growth Potential: 183%

Jobs for professional philosophers are almost exclusively in colleges and universities. Salaries in this field are on a par with those in other humanities disciplines. A very few philosophers, such as those who write extremely popular textbooks or treatises, can earn large amounts of money from book royalties. In the coming years philosophers with expertise in technical areas such as mathematics and computer science will be able to command quite high salaries, and opportunities may open up in the private sector for these specialists.

PHOTOGRAPHER

Ranking: 185

Starting: $13,000

Mid-level: $23,000

Top: $52,000

Growth Potential: 300%

Photography has a wide application, and professional photographers are employed in journalism, advertising, medicine and other fields. Salaries for photographers range broadly, according to the difficulty or complexity of the photographer's duties and assignments. Free-lance photographers have the potential to earn much more than salaried photographers. General talent, business sense, and sheer luck are all important for success as a free-lancer.

PHOTOGRAPHIC PROCESS WORKER

Ranking: 222

Starting: $12,000

Mid-level: $18,000

Top: $29,000

Growth Potential: 142%

The skills possessed by photographic laboratory workers vary widely, and wages accordingly span a broad range. Training can be acquired on the job. Talented and experienced individuals in this occupation can advance rapidly to higher-paying jobs.

PHOTOJOURNALIST

Ranking: 121

Starting: $11,000

Mid-level: $33,000

Top: $83,000

Growth Potential: 655%

Like other information- and media-related occupations, photojournalism pays the best in large urban areas. Photojournalists usually advance by moving to publications with larger circulations.

PHYSICAL THERAPIST

Ranking: 98

Starting: $19,000

Mid-level: $38,000

Top: $56,000

Growth Potential: 195%

The fees and clienteles of self-employed workers, who make up roughly 20% of this field, vary tremendously. Therapists with extensive practices in urban areas, generally enjoy the highest earnings.

PHYSICIAN (GENERAL PRACTICE)

Ranking: 13

Starting: $31,000

Mid-level: $104,000

Top: $334,000

Growth Potential: 977%

Like other health care professionals, doctors earn more as their practices become established. Doctors in private practice with a steady clientele generally earn more than those on salary. In the past, income for physicians has been higher than that for almost any other group. However, changes in health insurance policies and practices in the coming years may adversely effect earnings for physicians, as may competition from the large number of persons entering the field.

PHYSICIAN ASSISTANT

Ranking: 84

Starting: $35,000

Mid-level: $44,000

Top: $57,000

Growth Potential: 63%

Because this occupation is a relatively new one, requirements for practice, and insurance company policies on coverage to this profession, have not been established. Resolution of these issues will have a great impact on future earnings of physician's assistants. Assistants working in hospitals and clinics earn slightly more than those in other settings.

PHYSICIST

Ranking: 36

Starting: $32,000

Mid-level: $67,000

Top: $76,000

Growth Potential: 138%

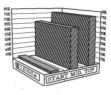

Physicists generally hold Ph.D. degrees and have substantial research experience. Consequently, these professionals command high salaries. Physicists working in colleges and universities earn about the same as professors in other sciences; those working in private research and development, or for the federal government, earn slightly more.

PHYSIOLOGIST

Ranking: 50

Starting: $28,000

Mid-level: $56,000

Top: $83,000

Growth Potential: 196%

Most starting jobs for physiologists require a master's degree in the field. This degree or a doctorate is necessary for advancement in this profession. College professors in physiology earn about the same as those in other biological science specialties. Government research positions for physiologists often pay slightly more than academic positions.

PIANO TUNER

Ranking: 206

Starting: $16,000

Mid-level: $21,000

Top: $53,000

Growth Potential: 231%

Self-employed piano tuners have the potential to make more than those working for music stores. Earnings for all piano tuners depend on clientele,

with those working in affluent areas earning the most.

PLASTERER

Ranking: 83

Starting: $33,000

Mid-level: $44,000

Top: $67,000

Growth Potential: 103%

Apprentice plasterers start at about half the pay earned by experienced plasterers, but receive 10 percent raises every six months. Plasterers are less affected by work stoppage due to poor weather than are those in other construction-related occupations. However, economic downturns can mean less construction, and less work.

PLUMBER

Ranking: 81

Starting: $23,000

Mid-level: $45,000

Top: $49,000

Growth Potential: 113%

In many areas, plumbers must be licensed, and training is often quite lengthy in this profession. As a consequence, wages are slightly higher than average for other construction- or maintenance-related occupations. Along with higher wages, plumbers can earn more annually because their work is less affected by downturns in new housing starts, or by poor weather.

PODIATRIST

Ranking: 14

Starting: $37,000

Mid-level: $104,000

Top: $165,000

Growth Potential: 346%

Like other health care professionals, podiatrists may take several years to establish a successful practice. A greater percentage of podiatrists than of physicians or dentists are in private practice, which can be extremely lucrative.

POLICE OFFICER

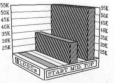

Ranking: 119

Starting: $20,000

Mid-level: $34,000

Top: $55,000

Growth Potential: 175%

Earnings for police officers vary according to the size of the community served. Within each community, salaries for police officers are quite consistent, with the range between lowest and highest annual averaging a few thousand dollars per year. Police officers earn more as they advance in rank and responsibility. Advancement depends both on length of service, and on performance on aptitude tests. Liberal retirement benefits add to the value of police officers' salaries.

POLITICAL SCIENTIST

Ranking: 78

Starting: $23,000

Mid-level: $45,000

Top: $62,000

Growth Potential: 170%

As in the other social sciences, job candidates in political science who hold a Ph.D. enjoy better employment and income potential than those with lesser degrees. Academic positions in political science pay about the same as those in other social science disciplines. Political scientists working for government agencies, lobbying groups, opinion pollsters, and related organizations can make considerably more than their colleagues in academia.

POSTAL INSPECTOR

Ranking: 67

Starting: $44,000

Mid-level: $50,000

Top: $64,000

Growth Potential: 45%

Postal inspectors are the highest paid of all government-employed inspectors. In addition to salary, postal inspectors enjoy liberal benefits, including excellent retirement packages.

PRECISION ASSEMBLER

Ranking: 221

Starting: $11,000

Mid-level: $18,000

Top: $30,000

Growth Potential: 173%

As with other heavily unionized occupations, wages and benefits for precision manufacturing assemblers depend on collective bargaining agreements between unions and management. Pay increases and promotions in unionized occupations normally are tied to seniority. Workers in areas which require greater skill to meet sophisticated and strict design requirements, such as aircraft assembly, command higher wages.

PRESIDENT (U.S.)

Ranking: 5

Starting: $200,000

Mid-level: $200,000

Top: $200,000

Growth Potential: 0%

The President's annual salary, determined by law, is currently $200,000 a year. Most entertainment and all travel costs are courtesy of taxpayers. Upon completing an elected term, the President receives a pension mandated by law, determined by prior federal service and equal to a designated cabinet level official, which is $143,800 per year. In addition to the salary, the President resides in and has the use of the White House, home to all of the U.S. presidents but one, complete with its full staff of over seventy.

PROTESTANT MINISTER

Ranking: 145

Starting: $8,000

Mid-level: $29,000

Top: $47,000

Growth Potential: 488%

Free housing and transportation are common benefits which can add considerably to the value of a minister's salary. Salaries in this occupation are determined to some extent by the size and wealth of a minister's congregation.

PSYCHIATRIST

Ranking: 12

Starting: $94,000

Mid-level: $110,00

Top: $220,00

Growth Potential: 134%

Net income for psychiatrists is about the same as that for others in the medical profession. Psychiatrists tend to be geographically more concentrated in urban areas than other doctors. As a consequence, both earnings and living expenses are higher.

PSYCHOLOGIST

Ranking: 137

Starting: $20,000

Mid-level: $31,000

Top: $84,000

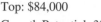

Growth Potential: 320%

Unlike psychiatrists, psychologists are not physicians, and many do not depend on private practice for income. As a result, earnings are generally less for psychologists than for psychiatrists. Many psychologists do, however, hold a Ph.D. and their earnings are similar to those of other professionals in the social sciences with advanced degrees.

PUBLIC RELATIONS EXECUTIVE

Ranking: 73

Starting: $22,000

Mid-level: $47,000

Top: $66,000

Growth Potential: 200%

Most public relations specialists work in large cities, where the high cost of living can affect the buying power of earnings. The highest salaries for public relations professionals are enjoyed by those employed in large organizations with substantial public relations departments.

PUBLICATION EDITOR

Ranking: 69

Starting: $25,000

Mid-level: $48,000

Top: $73,000

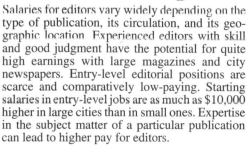

Growth Potential: 192%

Salaries for editors vary widely depending on the type of publication, its circulation, and its geographic location. Experienced editors with skill and good judgment have the potential for quite high earnings with large magazines and city newspapers. Entry-level editorial positions are scarce and comparatively low-paying. Starting salaries in entry-level jobs are as much as $10,000 higher in large cities than in small ones. Expertise in the subject matter of a particular publication can lead to higher pay for editors.

PURCHASING AGENT

Ranking: 174

Starting: $15,000

Mid-level: $25,000

Top: $48,000

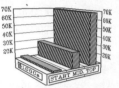

Growth Potential: 220%

Entry requirements for purchasing agents have in the past been quite wide-ranging, as have salary levels. As certain minimum requirements are more universally recognized for entry into the field, salaries will rise, and will become more consistent throughout the occupation. In general, purchasing agents' salaries do not reflect the difficulty of doing this job well.

RABBI

Ranking: 40

Starting: $41,000

Mid-level: $64,000

Top: $97,000

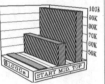

Growth Potential: 137%

Like protestant clergy, rabbis earn more in large synagogues in affluent areas than in smaller, poorer areas. The higher earnings for rabbis in larger synagogues reflect greater administrative duties and wider-ranging activities required in large congregations.

RACE CAR DRIVER (INDY CLASS)

Ranking: 4

Starting: $25,000

Mid-level: $400,000

Top: $5,233,000

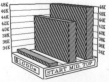

Growth Potential: 20,832%

Top money winning drives earn millions. As with most sports figures, the net earnings from competition are only a small percentage of a top driver's income. They add considerably to their income through endorsements.

RAILROAD CONDUCTOR

Ranking: 85

Starting: $33,000

Mid-level: $44,000

Top: $48,000

Growth Potential: 45%

Railroad occupations are highly unionized, and collective bargaining agreements between unions and management for the most part determine wages and benefits in this field. As a result, earnings are fairly consistent throughout the industry. Wages for rail conductors and engineers rise with seniority.

REAL ESTATE AGENT

Ranking: 151

Starting: $12,000

Mid-level: $28,000

Top: $69,000

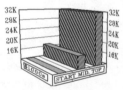

Growth Potential: 475%

A real estate agent's earnings are based on commissions from property sold. If the agent is working alone, a few large commercial or residential sales can add up to a very good annual income for the sales agent. As in most sales professions, income in realty is affected by changing economic conditions. A strong housing market means increased earning potential for agents; rising interest rates, a fall-off in new housing starts, and drops in personal income can all restrict the real estate market.

RECEPTIONIST

Ranking: 226

Starting: $12,000

Mid-level: $17,000

Top: $32,000

Growth Potential: 167%

Entry-level positions for receptionists require little training or professional background, and thus pay only modestly. Income rises moderately with experience in this occupation. Receptionists with clerical skills can advance to more lucrative work.

RECREATION WORKER

Ranking: 230

Starting: $8,000

Mid-level: $16,000

Top: $29,000

Growth Potential: 263%

Recreation workers employed in the private sector, including private health clubs and business-sponsored recreational programs for employees, earn more than those employed by city or state governments. This trend will continue through the coming decade. Income potential for recreation workers in the private sector will increase, as interest in health and physical fitness grows throughout the population.

REPORTER

Ranking: 191

Starting: $17,000

Mid-level: $23,000

Top: $48,000

Growth Potential: 182%

Income for reporters with particular publications is proportional to the circulation of the publication — the larger the paper, the higher the pay for reporters. Most reporters start out on smaller papers, and, given talent and experience, can move to larger newspapers in bigger markets. On a large and prestigious paper or magazine, reporters' earnings increase as they handle more important assignments.

RESPIRATORY THERAPIST

Ranking: 120

Starting: $23,000

Mid-level: $34,000

Top: $51,000

Growth Potential: 122%

Respiratory therapists beginning their careers by working for government agencies earn less than those starting in hospitals or other private health care institutions. Therapists usually receive excellent benefits in addition to their salaries.

ROOFER

Ranking: 234

Starting: $11,000

Mid-level: $15,000

Top: $40,000

Growth Potential: 264%

The starting salary for apprentice roofers is about half the salary of experienced workers in this occupation. Roofers can expect pay increases approximately every six months, and can expect to reach the average salary or above for this profession after three to five years of employment. Since roofing work cannot be performed in excessively cold or wet weather, roofers lose work time during the winter months.

ROUSTABOUT

Ranking: 124

Starting: $25,000

Mid-level: $33,000

Top: $42,000

Growth Potential: 68%

Earnings for roustabouts vary depending on the location of the job. Those working on offshore or Alaskan drilling operations earn considerably more than other members of the profession. Since these roustabouts work in isolated areas for long periods of time, they also enjoy the potential to save their earnings to meet special needs. Fluctuating economic conditions in the oil industry can lead to layoffs of roustabouts, affecting yearly income for these workers.

SALES REPRESENTATIVE (WHOLESALE)

Ranking: 117

Starting: $17,000

Mid-level: $34,000

Top: $66,000

Growth Potential: 288%

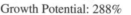

Earnings for wholesale salespersons are based largely on commissions for merchandise sold, and can vary from week to week. Some employers allow sales personnel to draw regular pay against their total expected annual earnings. Long-term recessions can seriously restrict earnings in particular areas of sales.

SALESPERSON (RETAIL)

Ranking: 239

Starting: $10,000

Mid-level: $14,000

Top: $30,000

Growth Potential: 200%

In retail sales, earnings can vary between different positions by more than $150 per week, depending on the merchandise sold. In general, sales of high-volume and high-priced merchandise earns the salesperson greater commission, and commission accounts for a significant percentage of income in this profession.

SCHOOL PRINCIPAL

Ranking: 48

Starting: $47,000

Mid-level: $57,000

Top: $65,000

Growth Potential: 38%

Earnings for school principals depend largely on the source of funding for the school system. Public school principals' salaries vary considerably from state to state. For those in private schools, the size of the school, its endowment, and its ability to attract funding from individuals and organizations, contribute to determining salaries.

SEAMAN

Ranking: 116

Starting: $19,000

Mid-level: $34,000

Top: $83,000

Growth Potential: 337%

Income for seamen is supplemented considerably by excellent benefits, such as room and board, and liberal retirement plans. In addition, seamen often spend a great deal of time on ship, where the opportunity to spend money is limited. Thus the potential for saving money, or for profligate spending, is greater in this than in other occupations at the same income level.

SECRETARY

Ranking: 157

Starting: $21,000

Mid-level: $28,000

Top: $38,000

Growth Potential: 81%

Many secretaries are affiliated with unions, where pay increases are based on seniority. The level of responsibility, and the number of duties a secretary is expected to perform, has a large impact on earnings in this occupation. Those working for top executives earn much more than lower-level secretaries, or those in secretarial pools.

SET DESIGNER

Ranking: 91

Starting: $27,000

Mid-level: $41,000

Top: $54,000

Growth Potential: 100%

Income for set designers, like that for others in the entertainment industry, can be unstable. Many begin their careers by working with small, local productions, at a very modest wage. However, a popular, long-running show can produce a great deal of prestige for all those associated with it. Reputation for success is as much a factor as is talent in determining a professional set designer's earnings.

SEWAGE PLANT OPERATOR

Ranking: 155

Starting: $17,000

Mid-level: $28,000

Top: $42,000

Growth Potential: 147%

Earnings for sewage plant operators are determined by the difficulty of duties performed, and by level of certification attained. With experience, training and certification, operators can advance to the plant supervisory positions, where salaries are higher.

SHEET METAL WORKER

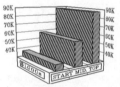

Ranking: 45

Starting: $37,000

Mid-level: $58,000

Top: $88,000

Growth Potential: 138%

Most sheet metal workers are union members. Since the availability of jobs in this occupation is tied to the volume of new construction, union assistance to sheet metal workers is helpful under certain economic conditions. When construction slows, and unemployment rises accordingly, sheet metal workers can draw a stipend from the union. Apprentice sheet metal workers start at about 40 percent of the wages paid to experienced workers. Wages in this occupation increase regularly with seniority.

SHIPPING/RECEIVING CLERK

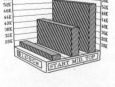

Ranking: 214

Starting: $13,000

Mid-level: $20,000

Top: $38,000

Growth Potential: 192%

Shipping and receiving clerks in the Midwest enjoy the highest average earnings in this occupation. Salaries for shipping clerks generally are greatest for those employed by utility companies.

Though this is often considered an entry-level position, earnings for shipping clerks are on a par with those for other non-supervisory workers in private industry.

SHOEMAKER/REPAIRER

Ranking: 217

Starting: $15,000

Mid-level: $20,000

Top: $21,000

Growth Potential: 40%

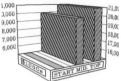

Shoe repairers who also specialize in making custom shoes for wealthy clients earn more than those relying on repair alone for their income. The lowest earnings in this occupation fall to those repairers who are employed in others' shops.

SINGER

Ranking: 58

Starting: $3,000

Mid-level: $50,000

Top: $100,000

Growth Potential: 3,233%

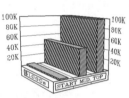

Like other performing artists, singers can experience a broad range of earnings. Very few professional singers gain the widespread recognition and popularity that leads to lucrative recording and concert contracts. Studio musicians, and singers working for opera companies and orchestras are usually members of unions, and their prospects for steady, long-term earnings are generally better than others in this profession.

SOCIAL WORKER

Ranking: 131

Starting: $26,000

Mid-level: $32,000

Top: $53,000

Growth Potential: 104%

Salaries for social workers depend on the availability of funding for public social work agencies. This in turn is determined by the size of the tax base supporting the agency. Thus, federal agencies pay social workers more than state agencies, and state agencies in heavily populated states pay higher salaries than those in sparsely populated states. Earnings for social workers in medical institutions generally lie between beginning salaries for federal workers and the average salary for all states.

SOCIOLOGIST

Ranking: 46

Starting: $24,000

Mid-level: $57,000

Top: $85,000

Growth Potential: 254%

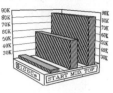

Sociologists employed as faculty at colleges and universities enjoy salaries on a par with other faculty members in the liberal arts. Many other sociologists work for government agencies, and earnings vary considerably depending on locale and type of job. Federal salaries, which depend on experience and level of academic degree, are the highest among government jobs for sociologists.

SOFTWARE ENGINEER

Ranking: 47

Starting: $38,000

Mid-level: $57,000

Top: $96,000

Growth Potential: 153%

The combination of high salaries, job security and comfortable working conditions make software engineering one of the most attractive jobs on the market today. A masters degree and often Ph.D. are almost always required to succeed in this relatively competitive environment. Innovators and particularly creative individuals with team leadership skills are most likely to command top salaries.

SPEECH PATHOLOGIST

Ranking: 100

Starting: $28,000

Mid-level: $38,000

Top: $59,000

Growth Potential: 111%

Because many speech pathologists must meet minimum licensing requirements to practice, earnings are fairly consistent throughout this occupation. Salaries for speech pathologists are largely determined by the funding or income base of the particular public agencies or health care institutions with which they are employed.

SPORTS INSTRUCTOR

Ranking: 230

Starting: $8,000

Mid-level: $16,000

Top: $29,000

Growth Potential: 263%

Many sports instructors are employed in schools and other public agencies. As with recreation therapists, sports instructors will see greater earning potential in the private sector, as the emphasis on health and fitness continues. A very few sports instructors, such as coaches of world-class tennis players, can achieve worldwide distinction. This fame can bring with it extremely high earnings.

STATIONARY ENGINEER

Ranking: 99

Starting: $17,000

Mid-level: $38,000

Top: $50,000

Growth Potential: 194%

Wages can vary by as much as $7.00 per hour from region to region. Almost all workers in this profession are union members, and can expect the normal benefits that accrue from collective bargaining, including negotiated pay increases, and insurance and retirement plans.

STATISTICIAN

Ranking: 56

Starting: $21,000

Mid-level: $54,000

Top: $67,000

Growth Potential: 219%

The federal government provides the best income opportunities for statisticians. Earnings for statisticians in federal agencies are based on government service classifications, which largely depend on level of education. Ph.D's in this field seeking faculty positions in higher education can expect to to earn about the same as their colleagues in other social science specialties.

STENOGRAPHER/COURT REPORTER

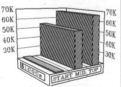

Ranking: 189

Starting: $17,000

Mid-level: $23,000

Top: $53,000

Growth Potential: 212%

While earnings in stenography as a whole vary widely according to industry, salaries for court reporters are fairly consistent throughout the profession. Earnings in this occupation increase with seniority.

STEVEDORE

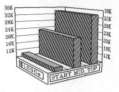

Ranking: 187

Starting: $10,000

Mid-level: $23,000

Top: $34,000

Growth Potential: 240%

Also called stevedores or longshoremen, they are members of a heavily unionized profession. As such, their wages are tied to seniority, and increase regularly with experience. Almost all jobs for dock workers are located in or near large cities, which serve as transportation and shipping hubs. The high cost of living in these cities may affect the buying power of wages for dock workers.

STOCKBROKER

Ranking: 19

Starting: $30,000

Mid-level: $83,000

Top: $166,000

Growth Potential: 453%

As a stock broker advances from servicing individual accounts to working on large, institutional accounts, earnings more than double. For established brokers, income derives from commissions on sales. Brokers often can draw on anticipated earnings during short-term market slowdowns in the number of market transactions being handled.

SURGEON

Ranking: 6

Starting: $117,000

Mid-level: $194,000

Top: $285,000

Growth Potential: 144%

Surgeons are the highest-paid medical specialists. For those with experience and expertise in sophisticated, complex, or ground-breaking surgical procedures, the income potential is especially great. However, the growing cost of malpractice insurance can take a large bite out of earnings for some surgeons in particular specialties, or in particular geographic locations.

SURVEYOR

Ranking: 153

Starting: $17,000

Mid-level: $28,000

Top: $45,000

Growth Potential: 165%

Entry-level surveyors' helpers can expect to earn $1,000 over the base salary in this profession for each year of training past high school. After two to four years of training, surveyors can be licensed, and this brings greater opportunity for higher earnings. Many surveyors work for the federal government, where retirement plans and other benefits are good.

SYMPHONY CONDUCTOR

Ranking: 15

Starting: $35,000

Mid-level: $100,000

Top: $700,000

Growth Potential: 1,900%

Because funding for symphony orchestras is derived virtually from the same sources as that of private institutions of higher education, salaries for symphony conductors are similar to those for university presidents. World-renowned orchestras in major cities generally have a broader base of funding support, and can thus attract the best conductors with generous salary offers.

TAX EXAMINER/COLLECTOR

Ranking: 173

Starting: $20,000

Mid-level: $26,000

Top: $32,000

Growth Potential: 60%

Tax examiners earn a salary which equals the average for financial inspectors in other fields. As employees of the federal government, tax inspectors enjoy an excellent benefits package in addition to their salaries.

TAXI DRIVER

Ranking: 223

Starting: $10,000

Mid-level: $17,000

Top: $33,000

Growth Potential: 230%

The rates taxi drivers can charge for service are fixed by law in each particular municipality. In addition to a modest salary, taxi drivers earn a percentage of of the fixed fare, and keep whatever tips they are paid. Thus, earnings in this occupation are directly tied to volume of business.

TEACHER

Ranking: 107

Starting: $22,000

Mid-level: $37,000

Top: $42,000

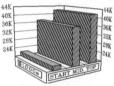

Growth Potential: 91%

Teacher's salaries vary enormously from state to state and city to city. The range is from very low to moderately high. Teachers in states with large urban populations generally earn higher salaries. Private schools pay considerably more than public schools.

TEACHER'S AIDE

Ranking: 246

Starting: $11,000

Mid-level: $12,000

Top: $16,000

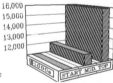

Growth Potential: 45%

Earnings for teacher's aides, as for teachers, vary widely from state to state, and from city to city. In some school systems, aides have made collective bargaining agreements, and enjoy benefits similar to those offered teachers.

TECHNICAL WRITER

Ranking: 108

Starting: $28,000

Mid-level: $37,000

Top: $48,000

Growth Potential: 71%

Writing is not a homogenous occupation in terms of required skill, experience, and knowledge. Thus, earnings vary widely in different areas of writing depending on these factors. The best-paid technical writers have formal education in engineering, science, or other technical specialties that can be applied to their work.

TELEPHONE INSTALLER/ REPAIRER

Ranking: 112

Starting: $17,000

Mid-level: $35,000

Top: $46,000

Growth Potential: 171%

The declining demand for telephone installers and repairers may adversely affect future earnings for those entering this profession. Most members of this occupation currently are covered by union contracts governing pay increases, insurance benefits, sick leave, and vacation time. Some workers in this field can also participate in stock-buying plans with their company.

TELEPHONE OPERATOR

Ranking: 209

Starting: $13,000

Mid-level: $21,000

Top: $31,000

Growth Potential: 138%

Telephone operators' salaries are about average for all non-supervisory workers. Phone company employees generally enjoy excellent benefits packages which significantly complement annual income. Stock ownership plans with phone companies are particularly valuable, and some companies purchase shares for employees as part of the benefits plan.

TICKET AGENT

Ranking: 195

Starting: $15,000

Mid-level: $22,000

Top: $54,000

Growth Potential: 260%

Earnings for airline ticket agents are the highest in this field, followed by Amtrak agents. Ticket agents for interstate bus lines earn the least of any in this profession. Most ticket agents benefit from union contracts which offer excellent insurance and retirement plans. Ticket agents usually also enjoy discounts on travel.

TOOL-AND-DIE MAKER

Ranking: 110

Starting: $23,000

Mid-level: $36,000

Top: $50,000

Growth Potential: 117%

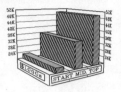

Tool and die makers in western states earn more than members of this trade working in other parts of the country. For instance, workers in the San Francisco region can average up to $6 per hour more than those in South Carolina. During apprenticeships, which can last as long as five years, earnings are lower.

TRAVEL AGENT

Ranking: 198

Starting: $13,000

Mid-level: $22,000

Top: $27,000

Growth Potential: 108%

Several factors can affect the earnings of agents. Independent agents earn a commission on tickets; thus, earnings for these agents is primarily determined by volume of sales. In addition, during recessions agents may earn less, as fewer people take personal trips requiring agents' services.

TRUCK DRIVER

Ranking: 156

Starting: $18,000

Mid-level: $28,000

Top: $43,000

Growth Potential: 139%

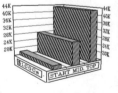

Union contracts determine earnings for nearly all drivers. Teamsters driving larger rigs generally earn more than those driving smaller ones. Drivers employed by trucking companies average higher pay than those working independently or for other types of companies.

TYPIST/WORD PROCESSOR

Ranking: 211

Starting: $15,000

Mid-level: $21,000

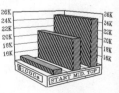

Top: $25,000

Growth Potential: 67%

Familiarity with word processing programs and systems can raise the earning potential of a typist considerably. The salaries of typists who operate word processing equipment average about $1000 per year more than typists using traditional equipment.

UNDERTAKER

Ranking: 72

Starting: $19,000

Mid-level: $47,000

Top: $66,000

Growth Potential: 247%

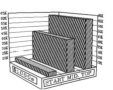

Undertakers are paid a fee for services performed, and also earn a commission on caskets and other funeral items which they sell. The fees and commissions an undertaker can expect will vary according to location. In affluent neighborhoods or areas, mourners generally will spend more for funeral goods and services.

URBAN/REGIONAL PLANNER

Ranking: 77

Starting: $19,000

Mid-level: $45,000

Top: $62,000

Growth Potential: 226%

Beginning urban planners holding a Ph.D. can earn as much as $12,000 more per year than those who start with a bachelor's degree. Many planners work as professors in colleges and universities; their salaries are typical for faculty in the social sciences.

VENDING MACHINE REPAIRER

Ranking: 213

Starting: $11,000

Mid-level: $20,000

Top: $37,000

Growth Potential: 236%

Wages and benefits for a large number of vending machine repairers are determined by union contracts, though some workers in this occupation are employed by non-unionized bottling or distribution companies. The low end of the income scale in this field is occupied by beginning laborers and non-union workers.

VETERINARIAN

Ranking: 31

Starting: $31,000

Mid-level: $69,000

Top: $92,000

Growth Potential: 197%

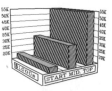

Like medical doctors, veterinarians may take a few years to establish a lucrative practice. Veterinarians who specialize can increase their earnings in private practice.

VOCATIONAL COUNSELOR

Ranking: 130

Starting: $19,000

Mid-level: $32,000

Top: $55,000

Growth Potential: 189%

With a master's degree in counseling, personnel services, psychology, or sociology, a counselor can expect his or her salary to rise to the average salary in a short while. Those specializing in psychological counseling are normally required to have a Ph.D. Geographic location has a greater effect on earnings than does experience. The highest salaries in this field are enjoyed by those working in the far west. Many counselors supplement their incomes by opening private practices.

WAITER/WAITRESS

Ranking: 229

Starting: $12,000

Mid-level: $17,000

Top: $21,000

Growth Potential: 75%

Tips comprise a significant percentage of earnings for waiters and waitresses. Earnings in this occupation can vary widely. Since tips are usually determined by the size of the bill, income for waiters and waitresses in more expensive restaurants can be significantly higher than for those at lower-priced establishments. Volume of business is also a factor affecting earnings in this field.

WELDER

Ranking: 184

Starting: $16,000

Mid-level: $24,000

Top: $40,000

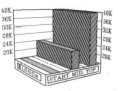

Growth Potential: 150%

Welders working in construction earn up to $2 per hour more than those in manufacturing or production. The highest-paid welders are those who specialize in stainless steel, as working with this material on equipment or components requires the highest degree of skill and experience.

ZOOLOGIST

Ranking: 55

Starting: $28,000

Mid-level: $55,000

Top: $83,000

Growth Potential: 196%

The highest-paid zoologists hold Ph.D. degrees and conduct or administer independent research, teach in college, or work for governmental or private agencies. Laboratories, hospitals, and industry offer jobs with modest salaries for zoologists with bachelor's degrees. Advanced degrees are usually required for promotion ins this field.

Outlook

In this chapter, "outlook" is defined roughly as the quality of a job's future. With the rapid changes in technology, this factor is hard to predict. For example, 20 years ago vocational counselors might have touted the future for computer operators. Then came the personal computer revolution. Less than 10 years later, almost anyone could operate an office computer, and the future of computer operators dimmed — so much so that the job has only the 228th-best outlook among the 250 jobs ranked in this chapter.

Other factors can come into play as well. For example, jobs in the U.S. military had some of the best outlook scores in the first edition of the *Jobs Rated Almanac* in 1988. Today, however, with the Cold War over and a 5% cutback in military jobs mandated to begin in 1997, military careers have slipped considerably in the "Outlook" rankings. If there ever are cures for cancers or heart disease — and there is reason to believe both may come about some day — the excellent outlook in many medical careers will slip in a similar fashion. And who knows what such careers hold if the long-discussed health care reform is as drastic as some proposals would have it?

It should be emphasized strongly that success in any occupation depends primarily upon a person's talents and efforts. There will always be four-star generals, well-paid computer operators, and medical personnel with good jobs. Occupational statistics do not always determine how successful someone is going to be in a career field. One can be in a field that is declining precipitously but still be at the top of the profession, happy and secure.

Nevertheless, anyone but the most casual worker should be concerned with the future of his or her career. Even the most motivated and competent employee will have difficulty if the status of his or her occupation is not healthy. While most of us know what makes a strong body, few know what elements contribute to a career field that has the promise of a good future. There are indeed several factors to look at when make such an evaluation.

THE FOUR OUTLOOK FACTORS

The ranking system used to evaluate job outlook awards higher scores to jobs with promising futures for those working in the field. Lower scores indicate a poorer outlook. Our ranking system considers four factors for each occupation. These factors, and the weights assigned to them in the ranking system, are:

(1) Unemployment rates from 1993 and 1994, based on an index from one to five. A score of one means a very low unemployment rate, two is low, three is moderate, four is high, and five is very high. Each point was multiplied by 50; hence the highest achievable score was 250.

(2) Expected employment growth through the year 2005, as forecast by the Department of Labor. This area, too, was factored so that the highest achievable score was 250. However, if the employment growth is negative, this score could fall below zero, and in many cases it did.

(3) Potential salary growth—that is, the percent of growth from the starting income to the top income. For example, the highest growth potential among all 250 jobs is for a race car driver, who can increase his or her income more than 200-fold if he or she gets to the top. The lowest is for the President of the U.S., whose income is legally mandated to stay at $200,000 annually. That career scored in the lowest level, receiving one point.

(4) Potential for promotion, which received points based on the number of possible promotions, or levels, one could occupy at a job. Jobs in the U.S. military, which has 19 possible levels, scored the maximum points, 250. The job of President, which has no promotion potential save a second term, scored the lowest. Scores were based on rating the potential for promotion from one to five (low to very high) and multiplying this figure by 50.

Each of the above four factors could score 250 points. While the first factor, unemployment rate, was treated as a negative number in the scoring, the others were treated as positive. This means that if a job received the highest points in all categories, the formula used to determine its score would look like this: -250 + 250 + 250 + 250 = 500. Thus, 500 is maximum number of achievable points. The highest actual score was achieved by computer systems analysts, at 441 points. The lowest was President, at a dismal -199.

Generally speaking, more than half the jobs achieved scores above zero and could be thought of as having at least some positive outlook—though relative to other occupations, they may be somewhat clouded. However, almost 100 jobs scored below zero, and the job seeker who is planning a long career in one of those chosen fields might be well advised to proceed with caution.

GRAPHIC SYMBOLS

A brief explanation of the symbols we used to illustrate job outlook for each of our 250 occupations follows. We used five different weather symbols to represent job prospects in each field—sunny, partly cloudy, cloudy and raining, cloudy with lightning, and a lightning bolt. Jobs scoring in the top fifth in outlook rankings—numbers 1 through 50—were given a "sunny" outlook, those in the next fifth a "partly sunny outlook," and so on. Of course, since we have 250 jobs and only five graphics, the symbols should be taken in conjunction with the numerical information and descriptions given for the jobs, in order to gain an accurate outlook picture.

COMMON THREADS

A forecast of job outlook is almost always a sign of the times, or more specifically, what people anticipate *at the time* to be around the corner. Job forecasters are anticipating growth in the medical fields, the public sector, and of course, the high-tech jobs for which so many individuals are training.

The rankings in this chapter for the most part confirm those forecasts. However, many high-tech jobs are not as high on the list as they previously were. Simply stated, forecasters anticipate a glut of qualified people in computers, engineering, communications and related fields. Only those who occupy very specialized niches — such as computer systems analysts (the top-ranked job in outlook) or software engineers (number 21) — are expected to enjoy excellent health in the high-tech fields.

On the opposite end of the spectrum are the declining jobs. Ironically, many of these occupations were once considered "high-tech," at least during their heyday decades ago. Among them are: semi-skilled manufacturing jobs, communications and electrical equipment repairers, telephone operators and installers, meter readers, word processors, compositors, and other jobs that today are either automated or can be performed by less-skilled workers on today's inexpensive and easy-to-operate equipment. And then there is the job of President of the U.S., which simply has no future.

250 Jobs Ranked by Outlook Scores

RANK		SCORE	RANK		SCORE
1	COMPUTER SYSTEMS ANALYST	441	33	NURSE'S AIDE	154
			34	DENTAL HYGIENIST	149
2	PHYSICAL THERAPIST	438	34	DIETICIAN	149
3	CHILD CARE WORKER	415	36	TAX EXAMINER COLLECTOR	143
4	CORRECTION OFFICER	380			
5	MEDICAL LABORATORY TECHNICIAN	305	36	NURSE (LICENSED PRACTICAL)	143
6	PAROLE OFFICER	281	36	PHYSICIAN (GENERAL PRACTICE)	142
7	NURSE (REGISTERED)	265			
8	OCCUPATIONAL THERAPIST	253	36	CHIROPRACTOR	142
9	PARALEGAL ASSISTANT	249	40	HOSPITAL ADMINISTRATOR	139
10	MEDICAL SECRETARY	232			
11	RACE CAR DRIVER (INDY CLASS)	211	41	PODIATRIST	138
			42	COMPUTER SERVICE TECHNICIAN	137
12	MILITARY (COMMISSIONED OFFICER)	193			
			43	ADVERTISING ACCOUNT EXECUTIVE	135
12	RESPIRATORY THERAPIST	193			
12	MILITARY (ENLISTED PERSON)	193	44	EMERGENCY MEDICAL TECHNICIAN	133
15	FIREFIGHTER	191	44	WAITER/WAITRESS	133
16	HIGHWAY PATROL OFFICER	185	46	PSYCHIATRIST	132
			47	PHYSICIAN ASSISTANT	129
16	AUDIOLOGIST	185	48	VETERINARIAN	128
18	OPTICIAN	183	49	COMPUTER PROGRAMMER	122
19	SURGEON	182	49	AUTOMOBILE BODY REPAIRER	122
20	ACCOUNTANT	176			
21	SOFTWARE ENGINEER	175	51	ACTUARY	120
21	VOCATIONAL COUNSELOR	175	52	FLIGHT ATTENDANT	119
21	PROTESTANT MINISTER	175	53	PHARMACIST	118
24	ATTORNEY	174	54	COLLEGE PROFESSOR	112
25	CATHOLIC PRIEST	173	54	REPORTER (NEWSPAPER)	112
26	SPEECH PATHOLOGIST	168	56	ELECTRICAL ENGINEER	108
26	GUARD	168	57	JUDGE (FEDERAL)	107
28	MEDICAL RECORDS TECHNICIAN	165	58	URBAN/REGIONAL PLANNER	106
29	PSYCHOLOGIST	163	59	MAIL CARRIER	104
30	DENTAL LABORATORY TECHNICIAN	162	60	ASTRONAUT	102
			61	FASHION MODEL	96
31	MEDICAL TECHNOLOGIST	158	61	MAID	96
32	OCEANOGRAPHER	157	63	UNDERTAKER	95

RANK		SCORE	RANK		SCORE
63	ENGINEERING TECHNICIAN	95	99	POLITICAL SCIENTIST	48
65	MILITARY (WARRANT OFFICER)	92	99	PHILOSOPHER	48
			102	HOME ECONOMIST	47
66	COOK/CHEF	91	103	INDUSTRIAL DESIGNER	46
67	OPTOMETRIST	90	104	ACTOR	45
68	SYMPHONY CONDUCTOR	85	105	SEWAGE PLANT OPERATOR	44
69	AIRPLANE PILOT	84	105	MUSEUM CURATOR	44
69	PERSONNEL RECRUITER	84	105	SHIPPING/RECEIVING CLERK	44
71	OSTEOPATH	83	108	BANK OFFICER	43
72	POLICE OFFICER	82	109	INDUSTRIAL ENGINEER	42
72	AIRCRAFT MECHANIC	82	109	SOCIAL WORKER	42
72	AGENCY DIRECTOR (NONPROFIT)	82	109	SPORTS INSTRUCTOR	42
			112	RECREATION WORKER	40
75	COSMETOLOGIST	81	113	INSURANCE AGENT	39
76	PHYSIOLOGIST	74	114	SALES REPRESENTATIVE (WHOLESALE)	37
77	MATHEMATICIAN	72			
78	POSTAL INSPECTOR	70	115	JOCKEY	36
79	METEOROLOGIST	66	115	AGRICULTURAL SCIENTIST	36
80	STATIONARY ENGINEER	65	117	FLORIST	35
81	DENTIST	64	117	ADVERTISING SALESPERSON	35
82	PUBLIC RELATIONS EXECUTIVE	63	119	SURVEYOR	32
83	BROADCAST TECHNICIAN	60	119	DISHWASHER	32
84	BIOLOGIST	59	121	RECEPTIONIST	30
85	CIVIL ENGINEER	58	122	TEACHER	29
86	INSURANCE UNDERWRITER	57	123	AIR TRAFFIC CONTROLLER	27
86	CASHIER	57	124	STATISTICIAN	24
88	AUTOMOBILE MECHANIC	56	125	FOOTBALL PLAYER (NFL)	23
89	GEOLOGIST	55	126	ZOOLOGIST	22
89	PUBLICATION EDITOR	55	126	TICKET AGENT	22
91	TECHNICAL WRITER	54	128	HEATING/REFRIGERATION MECHANIC	18
91	ELECTRICAL TECHNICIAN	54	129	AUTHOR (BOOKS)	16
93	HOTEL MANAGER	52	130	BASKETBALL COACH (NCAA)	15
94	FASHION DESIGNER	52	130	NEWSCASTER	15
93	TRAVEL AGENT	51	130	ORTHODONTIST	15
96	SOCIOLOGIST	49	130	PHOTOJOURNALIST	15
96	MECHANICAL ENGINEER	49	134	BASEBALL UMPIRE (MAJOR LEAGUE)	14
96	TEACHER'S AIDE	49			
99	ANTHROPOLOGIST	48	134	HISTORIAN	14

RANK	SCORE	RANK	SCORE
134 ARCHITECT	14	168 BOOKBINDER	-14
137 APPLIANCE REPAIRER	13	172 MARKET RESEARCH ANALYST	-15
138 PHOTOGRAPHIC PROCESS WORKER	12	172 BARTENDER	-15
138 CONSTRUCTION MACHINERY OPERATOR	12	174 AUTOMOBILE ASSEMBLER	-16
140 SECRETARY	11	175 STEVEDORE	-17
141 CONSTRUCTION FOREMAN	10	176 STOCKBROKER	-19
141 DISK JOCKEY	10	177 OCCUPATIONAL SAFETY/ HEALTH INSPECTOR	-20
143 MOTION PICTURE EDITOR	8	177 CONSERVATIONIST	-20
143 NEWSWRITER (RADIO/TV)	8	179 GARBAGE COLLECTOR	-21
145 CARTOONIST	5	179 FURNITURE UPHOLSTERER	-21
145 CARPET INSTALLER	5	181 ARCHITECTURAL DRAFTER	-22
145 ARTIST (COMMERCIAL)	5	182 MUSICAL INSTRUMENT REPAIRER	-26
148 NUCLEAR ENGINEER	4	182 PIANO TUNER	-26
148 SCHOOL PRINCIPAL	4	184 PLUMBER	-29
148 REAL ESTATE AGENT	4	184 RABBI	-29
148 MUSICIAN	4	184 BUTCHER	-29
152 IRONWORKER	2	184 OFFICE MACHINE REPAIRER	-29
153 CHEMIST	1	188 PAINTER	-31
153 MACHINIST	1	188 FORKLIFT OPERATOR	-31
153 BUS DRIVER	1	190 FINANCIAL PLANNER	-35
153 SALESPERSON (RETAIL)	1	190 WELDER	-35
157 CHAUFFEUR	-1	190 RAILROAD CONDUCTOR	-35
158 ARCHEOLOGIST	-2	193 FISHERMAN	-36
159 AEROSPACE ENGINEER	-3	193 EXECUTIVE SEARCH CONSULTANT	-36
160 SINGER	-4	195 BRICKLAYER	-37
160 PHYSICIST	-4	196 TRUCK DRIVER	-38
160 INDUSTRIAL MACHINE REPAIRER	-4	197 VENDING MACHINE REPAIRER	-39
160 JANITOR	-4	197 PHOTOGRAPHER	-39
164 BANK TELLER	-6	199 CHOREOGRAPHER	-40
164 FILE CLERK	-6	199 ECONOMIST	-40
166 ASTROLOGER	-8	201 BASEBALL PLAYER (MAJOR LEAGUE)	-42
167 TOOL-AND-DIE MAKER	-13	202 ROOFER	-46
168 PURCHASING AGENT	-14	203 STENOGRAPHER/COURT REPORTER	-48
168 CORPORATE EXECUTIVE (SENIOR)	-14	204 TAXI DRIVER	-49
168 ANTIQUE DEALER	-14		

RANK	SCORE	RANK	SCORE
205 PETROLEUM ENGINEER	-51	227 TYPIST/WORD PROCESSOR	-84
205 LITHOGRAPHER/ PHOTOENGRAVER	-51	228 COMPUTER OPERATOR	-85
205 CARPENTER	-51	228 DAIRY FARMER	-85
208 ASTRONOMER	-53	230 COWBOY	-88
208 BARBER	-53	230 CONSTRUCTION WORKER (LABORER)	-88
210 BASKETBALL PLAYER (NBA)	-54	232 ELECTRICAL EQUIPMENT REPAIRER	-90
210 ELECTRICIAN	-54	233 MAYOR	-91
210 JEWELER	-54	233 BOOKKEEPER	-91
213 BOILERMAKER	-57	235 AUTOMOBILE PAINTER	-94
213 DRESSMAKER	-57	236 ARTIST (FINE ART)	-95
215 NUCLEAR PLANT DECONTAMINATION TECHNICIAN	-59	237 METER READER	-97
216 PRECISION ASSEMBLER	-61	238 TELEPHONE INSTALLER/ REPAIRER	-101
217 PLASTERER	-62	239 SEAMAN	-106
218 DRYWALL APPLICATOR/ FINISHER	-63	240 SHEET METAL WORKER	-109
219 AUTOMOBILE SALESPERSON	-65	241 TELEPHONE OPERATOR	-110
220 BUYER	-68	242 ROUSTABOUT	-122
221 SET DESIGNER	-69	243 DRILL-PRESS OPERATOR	-125
222 LIBRARIAN	-71	244 COMMUNICATIONS EQUIPMENT MECHANIC	-133
223 MILLWRIGHT	-77	245 MACHINE TOOL OPERATOR	-134
223 COMPOSITOR/ TYPESETTER	-77	246 CONGRESSPERSON/ SENATOR	-142
225 GLAZIER	-80	247 LUMBERJACK	-162
225 DANCER	-80	248 FARMER	-184
		249 SHOE MAKER/REPAIRER	-193
		250 PRESIDENT (U.S.)	-199

JOBS WITH THE MOST EMPLOYMENT GROWTH

The rate at which the number of jobs is increasing is one of best barometers of an occupational field's health. Below, with the rate of growth at right, are the jobs that will have the greatest number of openings through the year 2005, according the Bureau of Labor Statistics.

COMPUTER SYSTEMS ANALYST	111%	MEDICAL RECORDS TECHNICIAN	50%
PHYSICAL THERAPIST	88%	PSYCHOLOGIST	48%
PARALEGAL ASSISTANT	86%	CONSTRUCTION MACHINERY OPERATOR	48%
CORRECTION OFFICER	70%		
CHILD CARE WORKER	66%	CONSTRUCTION FOREMAN	47%
TRAVEL AGENT	66%	OCEANOGRAPHER	46%
OCCUPATIONAL THERAPIST	60%	MEDICAL SECRETARY	45%
FASHION MODEL	54%	NURSE'S AIDE	45%
ACTOR	54%	HOTEL MANAGER	44%
AUDIOLOGIST	51%	DENTAL HYGIENIST	43%
SPEECH PATHOLOGIST	51%	DIETICIAN	43%
GUARD	51%	TEACHER'S AIDE	43%
FLIGHT ATTENDANT	51%	NURSE (REGISTERED)	42%
		PAROLE OFFICER	40%

GREATEST POTENTIAL INCOME FOR BEGINNERS

At some jobs, beginning pay is not bountiful. There are jobs, however, at which those who are willing to "pay their dues," can reap enormous increases. Below are the jobs with the greatest potential percentage increases relative to the starting pay and the top-level pay.

RACE CAR DRIVER (INDY CLASS)	20,932%	CHIROPRACTOR	923%
FOOTBALL PLAYER (NFL)	5,155%	HOSPITAL ADMINISTRATOR	850%
MUSICIAN	4,000%	MAYOR	782%
BASEBALL PLAYER (MAJOR LEAGUE)	3,945%	BROADCAST TECHNICIAN	764%
		PHOTOJOURNALIST	755%
SINGER	3,333%	FINANCIAL PLANNER	747%
BASKETBALL PLAYER (NBA)	2,933%	EXECUTIVE SEARCH CONSULTANT	667%
FASHION MODEL	2,000%		
SYMPHONY CONDUCTOR	2,000%	JOCKEY	600%
ACTOR	1,950%	CORPORATE EXECUTIVE (SENIOR)	600%
ASTROLOGER	1,625%	PROTESTANT MINISTER	588%
AUTHOR (BOOKS)	1,200%	REAL ESTATE AGENT	575%
DANCER	1,175%	STOCKBROKER	553%
PHYSICIAN (GENERAL PRACTICE)	1,077%	MOTION PICTURE EDITOR	531%
		NEWSCASTER	505%
FARMER	1,070%	NEWSWRITER (RADIO/TV)	492%
METEOROLOGIST	1,010%	PODIATRIST	446%
DAIRY FARMER	1,000%	CATHOLIC PRIEST	443%

ACCOUNTANT

Ranking: 20

Score: 176

Job Growth: 72%

Promotion Potential: Good

Promotion Opportunities: Within corporations advancement to chief accountant, controller, treasurer, or financial executive such as a CFO (chief financial officer) is the progression for successful individuals; within accounting firms: junior accountant, auditor, supervisor, manager, or partner.

Because of the integral role these professionals play in the development of industry and business, opportunities in this field are expected to be good for the next several years. Contributing to a positive job outlook for accountants are the size of the occupation and the complexity and growth of industry in this country. Changes in tax laws will also create openings for accountants. This profession is not as sensitive as most financial occupations to changes in the economy especially for those involved in tax preparation. Large cities throughout the United States present the best job opportunities for accountants.

ACTOR

Ranking: 104

Score: 45

Job Growth: 122%

Promotion Potential: Moderate

Promotion Opportunities: Actors often begin their careers with minor roles in non-equity productions. As they gather experience and notoriety, many actors advance to major roles in equity stage, cinematic and video productions.

Employment opportunities for actors are expected to increase very rapidly through the year 2005. However, job seekers will far outnumber paying positions in this field, and only the most talented individuals can reasonably expect steady employment.

ACTUARY

Ranking: 51

Score: 120

Job Growth: 65%

Promotion Potential: Moderate

Promotion Opportunities: Qualified workers in this occupation can move from assistant or associate to chief actuary within an insurance company or other organization.

Employment opportunities for actuaries will remain good through the next decade, as the volume of insurance sales increases, and pension plans are expanded and liberalized. The rising average age of the population will contribute to a greater need for health and pension benefits. Continuing diversity among types of insurance coverage (dental or malpractice, for example) will stimulate a growing demand for professional actuaries. Because insurance coverage is considered a necessity, members of this profession are not likely to be laid off during recessions.

ADVERTISING ACCOUNT EXECUTIVE

Ranking: 43

Score: 135

Job Growth: 81%

Promotion Potential: Good

Promotion Opportunities: Newly-hired account executives are usually assigned to relatively small accounts, and move to larger, more important accounts as they gain experience.

Outstanding executives may be rewarded with partnerships in their firms, or they may establish their own agencies. Employment opportunities for advertising account executives are expected to increase greatly over the next decade, as the new-found affluence of the U.S. population fuels demand for consumer products which require advertising and promotion, Most openings will occur in major urban financial centers.

ADVERTISING SALESPERSON

Ranking: 117

Score: 35

Job Growth: 81%

Promotion Potential: Moderate

Promotion Opportunities: Experienced advertising representatives with demonstrated sales ability may move up to the positions of advertising manager or director, or to more lucrative outlets. Employment opportunities for ad sales workers will grow rapidly over the next decade, as the print and broadcast media expands. Turnover in this profession is high, as many use it as a springboard to other media occupations. Competition for jobs at the upper levels of advertising sales is strong.

AEROSPACE ENGINEER

Ranking: 159

Score: -3

Job Growth: 43%

Promotion Potential: Low

Promotion Opportunities: Experienced professionals in this field can advance to executive positions in private companies, or to administrative or policy-making positions in government. Some opportunity for private consulting in this field does exist.

A cut in federal spending for military aircraft and aerospace systems will cloud opportunities in this once fast-growing field. In commercial aviation, engineers will also be needed to develop new designs for quieter and more fuel-efficient flight systems. The growing demand for business planes and helicopters will further contribute to a bright employment picture for aerospace engineers in the commercial sector. Competition from other areas of the profession, such as chemical or electrical engineering, could arise, as aircraft design and technology become more sophisticated. This occupation is somewhat sensitive to fluctuations in the economy, and a drop in federal spending can mean layoffs for aerospace engineers. Much of the aerospace and aviation manufacturing industry is concentrated in the western states, especially California and Washington.

AGENCY DIRECTOR (NONPROFIT)

Ranking: 72

Score: 82

Job Growth: 29%

Promotion Potential: Low

Promotion Opportunities: This is the position at the top and once there, directors may opt for moving to a larger or more prestigious organization, where their earnings will increase and their impact will be greater.

Some non-profit executives may move into government or foundation positions, to be on the giving rather than receiving end. Many individuals choose to stay within non-profit and carve out lifetime careers, finding immense job satisfaction in pursuing the goals of an organization whose motives and directives they are personally and professionally committed to. And in the top-level positions, the salaries become very respectable. The non-profit industry is one of the few industries experiencing significant growth. Tough times have not halted expansion of non-profit

organizations. Cities are also recognizing the importance of non-profits to their local economies, encouraging employment opportunities in these areas. Employment opportunities are good for the next decade.

AGRICULTURAL SCIENTIST

Ranking: 115

Score: 36

Job Growth: 32%

Promotion Potential: Low

Promotion Opportunities: New graduates usually start in lower-level research positions, and may advance to supervisory jobs in agricultural science.

The federal government is a major source of funding for agricultural research, and budget cutbacks could affect employment opportunities in this occupation. However, a drop in government spending on research will likely be offset by increased funding for agricultural science from the private sector, as advances in biotechnology open up new possibilities for the agricultural industry. Individuals with with advanced degrees should fare better than those with only bachelor's degrees, although entry-level positions, such as technician, purchasing agent, or agricultural products inspector, are often available.

AIR TRAFFIC CONTROLLER

Ranking: 123

Score: 27

Job Growth: 23%

Promotion Potential: Moderate

Promotion Opportunities: Many experienced workers in this field advance to supervisory and administrative positions. A few controllers are promoted to executive-level positions in the F.A.A.

Employment opportunities in this field are expected to increase very slowly through the year 2005, despite projected increase in air traffic. Competition for available positions will be keen, because the high pay and relatively modest educational requirements of the field attract a wealth of well-qualified candidates.

AIRCRAFT MECHANIC

Ranking: 72

Score: 82

Job Growth: 29%

Promotion Potential: Good

Promotion Opportunities: Mechanics with a few years experience often advance to more responsible and difficult assignments. Seasoned workers may be promoted to head mechanic, crew chief, inspector, head inspector, or shop supervisor. A few aircraft maintenance supervisors advance to executive positions. Most openings will occur in large cities with major airports.

AIRPLANE PILOT

Ranking: 69

Score: 84

Job Growth: 79%

Promotion Potential: Moderate

Promotion Opportunities: Newly hired airline pilots usually serve as co- pilots or flight engineers on domestic routes, and advance to full pilot status as they gain experience. Experienced workers may be promoted to chief pilot in charge of aircraft scheduling, maintenance, and flight procedures.

Employment opportunities in this field are expected to increase rapidly through the next decade, as the expected growth in passenger and cargo traffic creates additional demand aircraft and pilots.

ANTHROPOLOGIST

Ranking: 99

Score: 48

Job Growth: 45%

Promotion Potential: Moderate

Promotion Opportunities: Qualified anthropologists with universities and government agencies can advance to supervisory roles on major research projects, or to administrative and policy-making positions in educational or government institutions.

Keen competition for jobs will remain the norm in this field through the next decade, as the number of graduates continues to exceed the demand for new anthropologists. Declining college enrollment will minimize the number of available academic positions for members of Ranking:

ANTIQUE DEALER

Ranking: 168

Score: -14

Job Growth: 32%

Promotion Potential: Low

Promotion Opportunities: Antiques/Collectibles Dealers may open their own shop, manage an antique center or work from home.

Establishment of a reputable dealership can be a slow and lengthy process, however with patience and persistence and a real entrepreneurial talent, the rewards can be excellent.

APPLIANCE REPAIRER

Ranking: 137

Score: 13

Job Growth: 9%

Promotion Potential: Moderate

Promotion Opportunities: Home appliance repairers generally learn their trade on the job, as assistants to skilled workers. Employees of large shops are often promoted to supervisor, assistant service manager, or service manager. Some workers open their own repair shops.

Employment opportunities in this field are expected to decrease slightly through the year 2005, as the number of home appliances grows with the U.S. population. Repairers with extensive background in electronics should have the brightest employment prospects.

ARCHAEOLOGIST

Ranking: 158

Score: -2

Job Growth: 45%

Promotion Potential: Low

Promotion Opportunities: Researchers in this field can advance to administrative positions with universities, museums, and government agencies, or to supervisory roles on major research projects.

Archaeologists will face keen competition for employment in the coming years. Declining college enrollment, resulting in a sharp drop in available academic positions, will seriously affect employment opportunities for professional archaeologists. However, some jobs will open up as workers in this field retire or transfer to other occupations. Those with advanced degrees from more prestigious universities are likely to be most successful in the job search.

ARCHITECT

Ranking: 134

Score: 14

Job Growth: 59%

Promotion Potential: Moderate

Promotion Opportunities: Recent architectural graduates usually perform routine design tasks under the supervision of registered architects. As they gain experience, architects may accept partnerships in established firms, or open their own firms.

Employment opportunities for architects are expected to increase modestly through the next decade, as the expansion of the commercial sector creates new demand for office buildings, shopping centers, and factories. Most job opportunities in this field will occur in major urban centers.

ARCHITECTURAL DRAFTER

Ranking: 181

Score: -22

Job Growth: 25%

Promotion Potential: Moderate

Promotion Opportunities: Following experience, junior drafters may advance to senior drafting or supervisory positions.

Employment opportunities in this field are expected to grow with the demand for new products and more complex design solutions. A continuing reliance on computers may serve to increase productivity by assisting in the development of greater design variations; thus far only the most routine tasks have been eliminated by computers. This profession is sensitive to cyclical swings in the economy, since building and manufacturing are adversely affected by recessions.

ARTIST (COMMERCIAL)

Ranking: 145

Score: 5

Job Growth: 52%

Promotion Potential: Low

Promotion Opportunities: Entry-level workers often begin by assisting a more experienced artist. As skills develop, opportunities for more challenging assignments arise. Promotions to assistant art director and art director are also possible.

Because of the glamorous image associated with careers in the fine arts, competition is strong in this area. The supply of graphic artists exceeds the demand, and many artists spend time as free-lancers before finding full-time employment. Salaries vary according to the reputation and talents of designers. Employment in this field is geographically skewed to large cities.

ARTIST (FINE ART)

Ranking: 236

Score: -95

Job Growth: 52%

Promotion Potential: Low

Promotion Opportunities: The incomes and prestige of fine artists increase as their work circulates among galleries, museums, and collectors. The vast majority of artistic painters are self- employed.

An artist's earnings depend largely on the volume of his work and the the quality of his reputation. The supply of artistic goods clearly exceeds public demand, so competition for collectors' dollars and gallery exposure is intense. Painters with exceptional talent and good sales skills will enjoy the best employment prospects.

ASTROLOGER

Ranking: 166

Score: -8

Job Growth: 23%

Promotion Potential: Low

Promotion Opportunities: Advancement in this field generally comes in the form of larger clienteles and higher fee. A few astrologers find relatively prestigious employment as newspaper and magazine columnists.

Employment opportunities for astrologers are expected to increase modestly through the next decade, as the increasingly opulent U.S. population commits more of its disposable income to entertainment. Astrologers in densely populated areas will have the best earnings and employment prospects.

ASTRONAUT

Ranking: 60

Score: 102

Job Growth: 0%

Promotion Potential: Good

Promotion Opportunities: Experienced astronauts are usually rewarded with assignment to space missions (many astronauts and candidates never leave the Earth's atmosphere), or military promotions.

Employment opportunities for astronauts should increase very slowly over the next decade, as the U.S. space program recovers from the monumental setback of the shuttle crash. Astronauts with advanced scientific training and significant flight experience should have the best prospects for assignment to prestigious space missions.

ASTRONOMER

Ranking: 208

Score: -53

Job Growth: -5%

Promotion Potential: Low

Promotion Opportunities: Professionals in this field can advance to tenured positions in colleges and universities, or to administrative roles with NASA or other government agencies.

Job opportunities for astronomers will hold steady the decade. Most openings will be created as members of the profession retire or move into another field. Colleges and universities will remain the major employer of professional astronomers, and employment opportunities will be best in centers of research and development located in or near university communities.

ATTORNEY

Ranking: 24

Score: 174

Job Growth: 70%

Promotion Potential: Moderate

Promotion Opportunities: Successful attorneys of large firms may be rewarded with promotion to partner. Other experienced workers found their own firms or practices. A few attorneys are elected or appointed to judgeships.

Employment opportunities for attorneys are expected to increase very rapidly through the year 2005, as growth in U.S. population and business activity fuels unprecedented demand for legal services. However, job seekers in this field will significantly outnumber available positions, and even graduates of "top-flight" law schools will not be guaranteed employment.

AUDIOLOGIST

Ranking: 16

Score: 185

Job Growth: 115%

Promotion Potential: Low

Promotion Opportunities: Audiologists working in large institutions can advance to administrative positions, or transfer into research.

The rising number of middle-aged and elderly persons in the population will create greater demand for audiological services. This will present growing employment opportunities for audiologists over the next ten years. Referrals by family members, physicians, and other health care professionals should also open up new opportunities for audiologists. However, the high price of services, and cost-containment measures in health care, could curtail the demand for these professionals

AUTHOR (BOOKS)

Ranking: 129

Score: 16

Job Growth: 52%

Promotion Potential: Low

Promotion Opportunities: Advancement for authors usually comes through higher earnings and wider readership.

Employment opportunities for authors are expected to increase very rapidly through the year 2005, as the growing U.S. population creates new demand for non-fiction and entertainment literature. However, job seekers greatly outnumber available positions in this highly-competitive field, and only the most talented individuals can expect steady employment.

AUTOMOBILE ASSEMBLER

Ranking: 174

Score: -16

Job Growth: 32%

Promotion Potential: Moderate

Promotion Opportunities: Assemblers may advance to the positions of supervisor or inspector.

Employment opportunities in this field are highly dependent on the economic condition of the automotive industry. Layoffs are frequent during periods of recession. Jobs for assemblers are located in many large metropolitan areas, and are especially prevalent in major automotive manufacturing centers, such as Detroit. Automation is expected to reduce employment opportunities for automotive assemblers in the future, but the rate at which assemblers are replaced depends on the pace of techological advance in automobile manufacture.

AUTOMOBILE BODY REPAIRER

Ranking: 49

Score: 122

Job Growth: 68%

Promotion Potential: Moderate

Promotion Opportunities: Auto body repairers generally enter the occupation by transfer from related helper positions. Experienced repairers often advance to shop supervisor. Others establish their own repair shops, or are hired as automobile damage appraisers by insurance companies. Employment opportunities in this field are expected to increase modestly through the year 2005, as the number of vehicles in service grows with the national population. Positions for automobile body repairers are available in every area of the country.

AUTOMOBILE MECHANIC

Ranking: 88

Score: 56

Job Growth: 52%

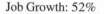

Promotion Potential: Moderate

Promotion Opportunities: Most workers enter this field as helpers, lubrication workers, or gasoline station attendants and gradually acquire skills through contact with experienced mechanics. Workers with one to two years experience are often promoted to service mechanic. Service mechanics with leadership skills may advance to shop supervisor or service manager, or they may open independent repair shops.

Employment opportunities for auto mechanics will increase rapidly through the year 2005, as the growing U.S. population spurs demand for automotive transportation. Positions should be most plentiful for individuals with formal training from technical or vocational schools.

AUTOMOBILE PAINTER

Ranking: 235

Score: -94

Job Growth: 2%

Promotion Potential: Low

Promotion Opportunities: Experienced automotive painters often advance to supervisory positions, or open their own automotive painting shops.

Job opportunities for members of this profession will increase, as the number of automobiles, and thus automobile accidents, continues to rise. This field is not greatly affected by swings in the economy, since the demand for automotive repair is steady. Prospects for work as an automotive painter are best in large urban areas of the country.

AUTOMOBILE SALESPERSON

Ranking: 219

Score: -65

Job Growth: 32%

Promotion Potential: Low

Promotion Opportunities: Experienced auto sales workers frequently advance to managerial and supervisory positions such as Customer Service Representative.

Employment opportunities for auto sales workers are expected to increase rapidly through the year 2005, as moderate fuel prices, population growth, and increased consumer affluence combine to create record demand for new cars. Workers with some college training or previous experience in retail sales should have the best prospects for employment.

BANK OFFICER

Ranking: 108

Score: 43

Job Growth: 90%

Promotion Potential: Low

Promotion Opportunities: Bank officers at smaller branch offices can advance to managerial positions at main offices, or at larger financial institutions.

Employment opportunities for bank managers will grow at a moderately fast rate over the next decade, as the financial services market continues to expand. However, because of the increasing number of qualified applicants, competition for managerial positions will become stronger within the next several years. Members of this fairly prestigious occupation are generally reluctant to leave the field, and the majority of positions for bank officers become available when managers retire.

BANK TELLER

Ranking: 164

Score: -6

Job Growth: -9%

Promotion Potential: Moderate

Promotion Opportunities: Bank tellers may aspire to supervisory or head teller positions. Promotions to managerial spots are not uncommon in the banking profession.

Job opportunities for tellers are expected to slow due to the proliferation of automatic teller machines, but openings will continue to be available for those with experience in this field. Length of service and the location and size of the hiring institution are factors in the earnings of tellers, although this field is, as a rule, a low-paying one. Fluctuations in the economy do not affect jobs in this area to a great degree; layoffs are rare.

BARBER

Ranking: 208

Score: -53

Job Growth: -5%

Promotion Potential: Low

Promotion Opportunities: Workers in this profession can advance to managerial positions in a barbershop or salon. Many open their own shops after gaining experience.

Although job prospects for barbers have been on the decline for the past several years, an increase in consumer spending on personal services over the next decade will help end this skid. Turnover in this field is relatively low. Many are self-employed, and tend to remain in the profession until retirement. Jobs for barbers are available throughout the country. Employment opportunities in this occupation are better in more heavily populated areas.

BARTENDER

Ranking: 172

Score: -15

Job Growth: -18%

Promotion Potential: Moderate

Promotion Opportunities: Experienced workers in this profession can advance to head bartender, wine steward, or beverage manager.

Employment opportunities for bartenders should remain plentiful through the next decade, due to an increase in consumer spending on entertainment outside the home. Turnover in this occupation is quite high, because many people take on this work as a means of supplementary income. Students often tend bar to help finance their college education. Bartending jobs can be found throughout the country, and are especially numerous in heavily populated areas.

BASEBALL PLAYER (MAJOR LEAGUE)

Ranking: 201

Score: -42

Job Growth: 11%

Promotion Potential: Low

Promotion Opportunities: Active players with exceptional leadership skills may advance to player/coach or player/manager. Retirees may advance to full-time coaching or management positions.

Employment opportunities for major league players are expected to remain constant through the next decade, unless a rule change permits an increase in the maximum size of team rosters. Competition in this field is extremely intense, and only extremely talented players can expect long-term employment.

BASEBALL UMPIRE (MAJOR LEAGUE)

Ranking: 134

Score: 14

Job Growth: 11%

Promotion Potential: Low

Promotion Opportunities: Experienced umpires occasionally advance to administrative positions within the Baseball Commission.

Employment opportunities for major league umpires are expected to remain constant through the next decade, unless a rule change permits an increase in the size of the league and in the number of games.

BASKETBALL COACH (NCAA)

Ranking: 130

Score: 15

Job Growth: 11%

Promotion Potential: Moderate

Promotion Opportunities: Most coaches begin their careers as assistants, and move to full coaching positions and more prestigious teams, as they gain experience and notoriety.

Employment opportunities for Division I coaches are expected to remain constant through the next decade, since (in all likelihood) no new teams will enter the division, and since the NCAA limits the number of assistants allowed for each program. Most openings in this field will occur as experienced workers retire, or transfer to new occupations.

BASKETBALL PLAYER (NBA)

Ranking: 210

Score: -54

Job Growth: 11%

Promotion Potential: Low

Promotion Opportunities: Active players with exceptional leadership skills may advance to player/coach or player/manager. Retirees may advance to full-time coaching or management positions. A few players find work as basketball commentators for radio and television.

Employment opportunities for NBA players are expected to remain constant through the next decade, unless a rule change permits an increase in the maximum size of team rosters. Competition in this field is extremely intense, and only extremely talented and motivated players can expect long-term employment.

BIOLOGIST

Ranking: 84

Score: 59

Job Growth: 56%

Promotion Potential: Low

Promotion Opportunities: Experienced researchers can advance to tenured positions in universities, or to administrative and policy-making positions in government agencies, or private health care organizations.

Job opportunities in this profession over the next decade will vary among particular specialties. Those who do research in cellular biology and genetics will have better employment prospects than those in other areas of expertise. However, cutbacks in federal funding for biological and medical research can have a negative impact on job availability in the biological sciences. Biologists can find employment opportunities in university communities and major research centers throughout the United States.

BOILERMAKER

Ranking: 213

Score: -57

Job Growth: -9%

Promotion Potential: Moderate

Promotion Opportunities: Competent workers in this profession can advance to supervisory positions.

Slowdowns in the chemical and petroleum industries may cause a slight drop in job opportunities for boilermakers over the next decade. However, increased construction of electrical power plants will offset these losses to some extent. During times of recession, layoffs in the industrial sector can affect some workers in this field, but the continuing need for maintenance and repair provides for relatively stable employment for most boilermakers.

BOOKBINDER

Ranking: 168

Score: -14

Job Growth: 32%

Promotion Potential: Low

Promotion Opportunities: Qualified workers in large commercial printing companies can advance to supervisory positions.

Employment opportunities for bookbinders will increase through the next decade, due to growth in commercial printing. The rising amount of leisure time available to consumers, and the demand it creates, will result in rapid expansion in the publishing industry. However, the book publishing industry has suffered in the early 1990s and press-runs of books have virtually been cut in half at many major publishing houses which has clouded the occupation's near term outlook.

BOOKKEEPER

Ranking: 233

Score: -91

Job Growth: 7%

Promotion Potential: Moderate

Promotion Opportunities: Qualified individuals in this profession can advance to head bookkeeper, or to other supervisory positions.

As the volume of business transactions grows through the next decade, the demand for individuals to perform bookkeeping functions will be steady. The majority of job opportunities for bookkeepers will arise from the need to replace workers who retire or leave the profession for other reasons. Since this is a relatively large employment field, this need to replace retiring or transferring workers results in many job openings each year. Employment opportunities for bookkeepers are available in both large and small communities throughout the country.

BRICKLAYER

Ranking: 195

Score: -37

Job Growth: 59%

Promotion Potential: Moderate

Promotion Opportunities: Competent workers in this occupation can advance to the positions of supervisor or estimator. Many bricklayers go into business for themselves after gaining experience.

Employment opportunities for bricklayers will grow moderately over the next decade, as more money becomes available for structural improvements to older buildings. Architects and planners are also showing an increased preference for the aesthetic qualities of brick and stonework in new designs, especially in structural elements such as sidewalks and interior walls. Consequently, demand for qualified bricklayers should remain steady. However, this trade is sensitive to economic fluctuations, and a downswing in the construction industry could result in layoffs of bricklayers. Job opportunities in this occupation can be found in all areas of the country, although most jobs are concentrated in more heavily populated areas.

BROADCAST TECHNICIAN

Ranking: 83

Score: 60

Job Growth: 9%

Promotion Potential: Moderate

Promotion Opportunities: Experienced broadcast technicians can advance to the positions of supervisory technician or chief engineer.

Job opportunities for broadcast technicians are best with local broadcasting outlets in smaller cities. In large metropolitan areas, the intense competition among highly qualified candidates for jobs in this field creates an inhospitable employment climate. The number of jobs for broadcast technicians will increase moderately over the next decade, due to longer broadcasting hours and a growth in the number of cable television systems. With the rise of computer-aided programming, employment emphasis in this profession is switching from operations to maintenance.

BUS DRIVER

Ranking: 153

Score: 1

Job Growth: 47%

Promotion Potential: Low

Promotion Opportunities: Experienced bus drivers can advance to positions as supervisor or dispatcher, or to management levels.

Jobs for bus drivers will remain plentiful through the next decade. New openings will be particularly abundant in the growing metropolitan areas of the West and Southwest. Employment opportunities for school bus drivers should increase, as enrollments in elementary and secondary schools rise. In major cities, automobile traffic congestion will become worse, creating demand for improved public transit services. As these services expand, the number of jobs for drivers with local transit systems will grow accordingly. This occupation is not particularly affected by recessions or other economic fluctuations. However, seasonal layoffs are common for school bus drivers and employees of charter services.

BUTCHER

Ranking: 184

Score: -29

Job Growth: -32%

Promotion Potential: Moderate

Promotion Opportunities: With experience, butchers can advance to positions as meat department managers or grocery store managers. Many choose to open their own shops.

Job opportunities for butchers will decline slightly over the next ten years, but many positions will still become available each year, as workers retire or leave the field. Overall consumption of meat and poultry will rise in coming years, with the increase in population. However, the trend toward prepackaging at meat plants will keep the demand for butchers down to some extent. Although automated cutting machines are currently being developed and tested by the meat packing industry, automation is not a threat to this profession in the near future. Through the next decade, skilled and knowledgeable butchers will still be needed to handle the many varied sizes and cuts of meat. Jobs for butchers are available in cities and towns throughout the country.

BUYER

Ranking: 220

Score: -68

Job Growth: 29%

Promotion Potential: Moderate

Promotion Opportunities: Individuals normally start as assistant buyers, and later can advance to buyer or to merchandise manager.

The number of qualified job candidates in this profession will exceed the demand for new workers over the next ten years. Although many buyers transfer to sales or managerial positions, the influx of recent college graduates to the retail field will offset the growing availability of positions for buyers. The use of computers has improved record-keeping and inventory control for wholesale and retail firms, and may affect employment prospects for buyers in the near future. Jobs in this occupation are primarily concentrated in major metropolitan areas.

CARPENTER

Ranking: 205

Score: -51

Job Growth: 45%

Promotion Potential: Moderate

Promotion Opportunities: Advancement to carpentry supervisor or general construction supervisor is possible with experience in this field.

Job opportunities are dependent on the degree of new construction and the need for remodeling and modernizing existing structures. Because this occupation is large and the turnover is relatively high, openings in this area are more frequent than in other craft careers. Periods of unemployment are to be expected in this occupation; many individuals become discouraged and leave the profession for this reason. Jobs in carpentry are sensitive to cyclical swings in the economy; interest rates and the availability of mortgage funds can predict the rate of building. Construction activity is dependent on the rate that individuals and businesses move to new geographic locations and jobs may fluctuate from one part of the country to another.

CARPET/TILE INSTALLER

Ranking: 145

Score: 5

Job Growth: 50%

Promotion Potential: Moderate

Promotion Opportunities: Installers may advance to positions of supervisor or installation manager. Others might go into business for themselves or become salespersons or estimators after gaining experience in this field.

Jobs are expected to be available for carpet installers as new construction and remodeling of old structures continue. The advent of plywood rather than hardwood floors calls for the use of carpeting in new homes and businesses; as new fabrics and colors are developed, carpet installers play a part in remodeling outdated interiors. This occupation is less sensitive to downturns in the economy than others in the construction industry, since most work is done in existing buildings. Jobs are found throughout the country, although better opportunities exist in areas undergoing heavy construction.

CARTOONIST

Ranking: 145

Score: 6

Job Growth: 52%

Promotion Potential: Low

Promotion Opportunities: Many cartoonists are with small circulation, non-paying publications. As they gain experience and notoriety, they may move to larger, paying publications.

Employment opportunities for cartoonists are expected to increase nicely through the next decade. Competition in this field, however, is extremely intense, and only the most talented, creative individuals can expect steady employment.

CASHIER

Ranking: 86

Score: 57

Job Growth: 54%

Promotion Potential: Moderate

Promotion Opportunities: With experience, competent workers in this field can move into bookkeeping or managerial positions.

Employment opportunities for cashiers should increase steadily in the next ten years, as the service sector expands. The turnover rate in this field is very high. Jobs will remain plentiful during heavy shopping seasons, and employment prospects will be excellent for part-time and temporary workers looking to earn extra money during busy holiday and vacation periods. The number of available positions in fast-food restaurants will also grow rapidly. Opportunities for cashiers exist throughout the country.

CATHOLIC PRIEST

Ranking: 25

Score: 173

Job Growth: 68%

Promotion Potential: Moderate

Promotion Opportunities: Experienced priests are often rewarded by being assigned to large or affluent parishes. Exceptional individuals may be promoted to Monsignor, Cardinal, Bishop, Archbishop or Pope.

Employment opportunities for priests will increase over the next decade, as the number of practicing U.S. Catholics grows. There is already an acute shortage of workers in this field. The number of newly ordained priests is insufficient to replace those who leave the work force, and many traditional priestly duties are now performed by lay deacons. Job openings will be concentrated in urban areas, where most Catholics reside.

CHAUFFEUR

Ranking: 157

Score: -1

Job Growth: 47%

Promotion Potential: Low

Promotion Opportunities: Generally, this occupation offers very few opportunities for advancement.

Employment opportunities for chauffeurs are expected to increase modestly through the year 2005, as the affluence of the U.S. population continues to increase. Most openings in this field will arise in major urban areas with large affluent populations.

CHEMIST

Ranking: 153

Score: 1

Job Growth: 47%

Promotion Potential: Low

Promotion Opportunities: Most recent chemistry graduates are assigned to relatively simple, routine research projects, and as they gain experience they advance to more responsible and complex assignments. Privately-employed chemists with exceptional leadership skills may advance to supervisory or administrative positions.

Employment opportunities for chemists are expected to increase slightly through the year 2005, with the slow expansion of the chemical and pharmaceutical industries. Openings in this field will be concentrated in large industrial areas.

CHILD CARE WORKER

Ranking: 3

Score: 415

Job Growth: 149%

Promotion Potential: Moderate

Promotion Opportunities: Experienced child care workers can advance to supervisory, administrative, or developmental positions. Many workers open their own child care centers.

Job opportunities in child care will continue to be plentiful through the next decade. Turnover is relatively high in this field, as many workers open their own child care services after gaining experience, or transfer to related professions. This work is sensitive to slowdowns in the economy, since unemployed or lower-income parents are either at home to attend to their children, or cannot afford professional services. Jobs for child care workers are located throughout the country, with the highest concentration of available positions to be found in heavily populated areas.

CHIROPRACTOR

Ranking: 36

Score: 142

Job Growth: 81%

Promotion Potential: Moderate

Promotion Opportunities: Newly licensed chiropractors often enter into partnership with established practitioners, until they acquire the experience and capital to fund their own practices.

Employment opportunities for chiropractors are expected to increase rapidly through the next decade, as the aging U.S. population creates an unprecedented demand for health care. However, the number of chiropractic graduates has increased fourfold since the 1970s, and new chiropractors can expect stiff competition for patients in densely populated areas.

CHOREOGRAPHER

Ranking: 199

Score: -40

Job Growth: 56%

Promotion Potential: Low

Promotion Opportunities: Most choreographers begin their careers creating pieces for amateur companies, and advance to assignments with more prestigious professional companies.

Employment opportunities opportunities for choreographers are expected to increase rapidly through the year 2005. However, competition in this field is extremely intense, and only the most talented and aggressive individuals can expect steady employment.

CIVIL ENGINEER

Ranking: 85

Score: 58

Job Growth: 54%

Promotion Potential: Low

Promotion Opportunities: Experienced employees of public agencies or major engineering firms may advance to a variety of supervisory and administrative positions.

Employment opportunities for civil engineers are expected to increase rapidly through the year 2005, as the nation allots more tax money to replace or improve its airports, roads, bridges, sewage systems and subways. Positions in this field will be concentrated in and around major industrial and commercial centers.

COLLEGE PROFESSOR

Ranking: 54

Score: 112

Job Growth: 59%

Promotion Potential: Good

Promotion Opportunities: New members of the academic profession normally start as instructors. With experience, teachers can advance from there to associate professor, assistant professor, and full professor. Qualified individuals often move into university administrative positions. In some areas of expertise, professors have the opportunity to do consulting work.

Declining enrollment at the college and university levels will result in a marked decrease in overall employment opportunities for professors through the next decade. Individuals in particular fields, such as engineering and mathematics, will fare somewhat better, as the great demand for college graduates in these areas continues. Universities often cannot match the high salaries offered in the private sector for individuals in particular areas of expertise, and many gifted scholars leave academic careers in pursuit of better pay.

COMMUNICATIONS EQUIPMENT MECHANIC

Ranking: 244

Score: -133

Job Growth: -86%

Promotion Potential: Moderate

Promotion Opportunities: Most workers enter this field as frame wirers. After one to two years on-the-job training, many wirers are promoted to trouble locator, central office repairer, or instrument repairer.

Employment opportunities for communications mechanics will decrease rapidly through the year 2005, as advances in automated telecommunications technologies improve worker efficiency. Workers with extensive formal training in digital electronics will have the best prospects for employment.

COMPOSITOR/TYPESETTER

Ranking: 223

Score: -77

Job Growth: -13%

Promotion Potential: Moderate

Promotion Opportunites: Most compositors learn their trade as assistants to skilled workers. Many eventually advance to shop foreman or supervisory positions.

The advent of the PC and its ability to produce camera-ready type has caused a decline in the field which is accelerating. Though jobs exist, those operators who can combine their skills with light graphic design will have the best opportunities.

COMPUTER OPERATOR

Ranking: 228

Score: -86

Job Growth: -88%

Promotion Potential: Low

Promotion Opportunities: Experienced operators can advance to the position of supervisor or computer programmer.

Employment opportunities will increase very sharply in this field over the next decade. Advances in computer technology will open up a wider range of computer applications for almost every field of endeavor. With the greater efficiency and lower costs these advances bring, computer technology will be implemented in a rapidly growing number of businesses and industries. Consequently, as the computerization of the work place continues, the demand for computer operators will rise accordingly. Jobs for computer operators are available throughout the country, and are especially abundant in major urban centers.

COMPUTER PROGRAMMER

Ranking: 49

Score: 122

Job Growth: 68%

Promotion Potential: Moderate

Promotion Opportunities: Beginning programmers often attend intensive training classes, and then work under the close supervision of more experienced workers. Promotions to lead programmer or systems programmers may occur after an individual becomes more skilled.

Jobs for programmers should be increasingly available as computer usage grows more commonplace. However, due to simplified programs and improved software, employment opportunities will not be as abundant as in the recent past. Recent graduates with a familiarity with several computer languages, especially the newest ones, will have the best chances for employment. Salaries vary according to employer, and opportunities for employment can be found throughout the country.

COMPUTER SERVICE TECHNICIAN

Ranking: 42

Score: 137

Job Growth: 34%

Promotion Potential: Moderate

Promotion Opportunities: Experienced technicians can become specialists, supervisors, or service managers.

Job opportunities for computer service technicians will continue to increase rapidly over the next ten years. Expansion in the business sector, and greater spending on business and personal computer systems, will foster employment growth for technicians, the need for maintenance on the rising number of new computer systems, and for repairs on older equipment, will keep the demand for qualified service technicians high. Some leveling off of job growth in this field might result from technological breakthroughs enabling computers to self-diagnose problems via telephone hook-up. Downturns in the economy could also limit hiring of new technicians to some ex-

tent. Employment opportunities for computer service technicians are primarily concentrated in large metropolitan areas.

COMPUTER SYSTEMS ANALYST

Ranking: 1

Score: 441

Job Growth: 250%

Promotion Potential: Moderate

Promotion Opportunities: Experienced systems analysts can advance to senior positions or corporate information managers. Some become high-level corporate communications managers, or open their own consulting practices.

Job opportunities for systems analysts will continue to increase in the coming years, as technological advances lead to more diverse applications for computer systems. A large percentage of job openings will arise as a result of companies adopting more sophisticated systems. Individuals in this occupation with degrees in computer science should fare considerably better than those with no college degree. Jobs for computer systems analysts are located throughout the country.

CONGRESSPERSON/SENATOR

Ranking: 246

Score: -142

Job Growth: 7%

Promotion Potential: Low

Promotion Opportunities: While senators and congressmen have no direct opportunities for promotion, they often advance by seeking higher elective or appointed offices.

Employment opportunities for senators and congressman should remain constant through the next decade, since the nation's political geography has essentially stabilized. Since this is a very volatile and competitive field, even the most talented individuals are not guaranteed continued employment.

CONSERVATIONIST

Ranking: 177

Score: -20

Job Growth: 27%

Promotion Potential: Low

Promotion Opportunities: Range managers can move into administrative or policy-making positions in government agencies, or into research positions.

Employment for range managers is expected to slow in the coming years, as state and federal spending on environmental protection drops. An increase in job opportunities in private industry may offset this decline somewhat, as range management of grazing and timber land becomes increasingly profitable. The majority of opportunities for range managers can be found in western states.

CONSTRUCTION FOREMAN

Ranking: 141

Score: 10

Job Growth: 106%

Promotion Potential: Moderate

Promotion Opportunities: Outstanding employees of large construction firms may advance to more responsible managerial positions. Employees of smaller firms may found their own contracting services.

Employment opportunities for foremen are expected to increase markedly through the next decade. The growing U.S. population will create significant demand for new housing, but economic fluctuations may cause periodic layoffs for workers in this field, which has recently clouded the field.

CONSTRUCTION MACHINERY OPERATOR

Ranking: 138

Score: 12

Job Growth: 108%

Promotion Potential: Moderate

Promotion Opportunities: Qualified workers in this field can advance to supervisory positions. A small number open their own businesses.

The rate of population and business growth determines the amount of new construction on factories, office complexes, and residential buildings, which in turn directly affects employment opportunities for machinery operators. As with the other construction trades, this field is sensitive to economic fluctuations. During recessions, construction slows, and many workers are laid off. Some construction work is seasonal. Spring and summer are normally the best times for construction machinery operators to find employment. Job opportunities in this occupation are located in all areas of the country.

CONSTRUCTION WORKER (LABORER)

Ranking: 230

Score: -88

Job Growth: 59%

Promotion Potential: Low

Promotion Opportunities: Competent workers in this occupation can take on more complex job assignments. Some advance to apprenticeships in a particular trade.

Despite the increase in residential and commercial construction expected through the year 2005, job opportunities for construction laborers will not grow accordingly. However, the seasonal nature of the work, and the abundance of temporary employees it attracts, such as college students, creates a high rate of turnover in this occupation. Employment in the construction trades is closely linked to the state of the economy, and recessions can mean periods of layoffs for workers. Job opportunities in this field are more concentrated in heavily populated areas of the country.

COOK

Ranking: 66

Score: 91

Job Growth: 86%

Promotion Potential: Moderate

Promotion Opportunities: Most cooks learn as assistants to skilled workers. Experienced cooks advance by moving to higher- paying positions at larger or more prestigious restaurants. Others open their own restaurants or catering businesses.

Employment opportunities for cooks are expected to increase rapidly through the next decade, as population growth and higher personal income fuel demand for restaurant meals. Workers with extensive experience with a variety of cuisines should have the brightest prospects for employment.

CORPORATE EXECUTIVE (SENIOR)

Ranking: 168

Score: -14

Job Growth: 29%

Promotion Potential: Moderate

Promotion Opportunities: Usually near the top already, senior corporate executives can either move into the number one spot, CEO, or move to a similar position at a larger organization. Employment is expected to grow slowly as companies continue to restructure themselves in an effort to curb rising costs. Some executives will be affected by these cost-cutting strategies but openings will still occur as executives transfer, go out on their own, or retire. Those whose accomplishments reflect their leadership and business acumen will have the best opportunities. Knowledge of and sensibility to global and multicultural issues are advantageous to a candidate as international markets continue to expand.

CORRECTION OFFICER

Ranking: 4

Score: 380

Job Growth: 158%

Promotion Potential: Good

Promotion Opportunities: Advancement to correction sergeant or other administrative positions is possible following additional training, education, or experience.

A dramatic increase in criminal behavior has led to a rise in job opportunities for correction officers. As prison facilities expand to accommodate an influx of offenders, positions become available for experienced workers to monitor these populations. High levels of stress and difficult working conditions contribute to a rapid turnover rate, which also creates good opportunities for those seeking work in this area. Employment is not usually affected by downswings in the economy, as security is always needed in correctional institutions. Jobs for correction officers can be found throughout the country, in small cities and towns as well as large metropolitan areas.

COSMETOLOGIST

Ranking: 75

Score: 81

Job Growth: 79%

Promotion Potential: Moderate

Promotion Opportunities: As individuals become more experienced, they can advance to salon management positions; many choose to open their own shops after they gain experience and a solid clientele.

Employment opportunities in this field are expected to remain good due to increasing numbers of working women and a rise in the middle-aged population, both groups among the most frequent users of cosmetologists' services. A continued interest in men's hair styling should also create

opportunities for operators, since many men frequent unisex salons rather than barber shops. Jobs for cosmetologists are continually created as individuals leave the work place to return to full-time homemaking duties; many persons in this field work part-time. Jobs are found throughout the country; major U.S. cities present the best opportunities for employment.

COWBOY

Ranking: 230

Score: -88

Job Growth: -41%

Promotion Potential: Low

Promotion Opportunities: Experienced employees of large ranches are often promoted to managerial positions such as trail boss and ranch manager. A small number of cowboys buy and establish their own ranches.

Employment opportunities for cowboys are expected to increase modestly through the next decade, as the the growing U.S. population creates additional demand for beef and other ranch products. Most openings, however, will result from the need to replace workers who transfer to other occupations.

DAIRY FARMER

Ranking: 228

Score: -85

Job Growth: -47%

Promotion Potential: Low

Promotion Opportunities: The majority of dairy farmers are self- employed, and their advancement comes primarily through increased farm profits. Business opportunities for dairy farmers are expected to rise through the year 2005, as the dairy industry has stabilized after a tumultuous period in the previous decade.

DANCER

Ranking: 225

Score: -80

Job Growth: 56%

Promotion Potential: Low

Promotion Opportunities: Most dancers begin their careers with small, amateur companies, and advance to positions with more prestigious companies.

Employment opportunities for dancers are expected to increase rapidly through the year 2005.

However, competition in this field is extremely intense, and only the most talented and aggressive individuals can expect steady employment.

DENTAL HYGIENIST

Ranking: 34

Score: 149

Job Growth: 97%

Promotion Potential: Low

Promotion Opportunities: Hygienists can advance to research and teaching positions, or may choose to continue their education in the dental field.

Job prospects for dental hygienists are expected to remain good over the next several years, due to the population's growing awareness of the importance of oral hygiene. A rise in personal income will lead to increased spending on dental care. In addition, the liberalization of dental insurance plans and benefits will make dental hygiene services available to a broader range of people. As a result, the demand for qualified hygienists is expected to be high in the coming years.

DENTAL LABORATORY TECHNICIAN

Ranking: 30

Score: 162

Job Growth: 7%

Promotion Potential: Good

Promotion Opportunities: Experienced technicians can become laboratory supervisors or managers. Many open their own dental labs.

Jobs as laboratory technicians will not increase as markedly as other fields in dentistry through the year 2005. Wider availability of dental insurance, and greater awareness of the importance of good dental hygiene, will lead to rapid expansion in the field of dental services. Growing use of orthodontic procedures in adults, as well as in adolescent patients, will also contribute to the rise in demand for experienced technicians. Positions for dental technicians are located throughout the country, and are most highly concentrated in areas of heavy population.

DENTIST

Ranking: 81

Score: 64

Job Growth: 11%

Promotion Potential: Low

Promotion Opportunities: Recent dental graduates usually enter into partnership with established practitioners, until they acquire the experience and capital to fund their own practices.

Employment opportunities for dentist are expected to increase through the year 2005, as the aging U.S. population creates an unprecedented demand for dental and orthodontal care. However, since the number of dental graduates has increased greatly over the last two decades, new dentists can expect stiff competition for patients.

DIETITIAN

Ranking: 34

Score: 149

Job Growth: 97%

Promotion Potential: Moderate

Promotion Opportunities: Experienced workers in this profession can advance to clinical director, or to administrative positions in health care agencies and institutions.

Rising need for dietary planning in hospitals, nursing homes, and social service agencies, will create an increase in employment opportunities for clinical dietitians through the next decade. Private and public health care services, especially in geriatrics, will expand in the coming years. In addition, there will be a broader awareness of the benefits of preventative medicine, and of prudent nutritional planning. Consequently, the demand for qualified clinical dietitians will grow steadily.

DISHWASHER

Ranking: 119

Score: 32

Job Growth: 81%

Promotion Potential: Low

Promotion Opportunities: Competent workers in this field often advance to higher-paying, more responsible food service positions such as busboy, cook, or waiter.

Employment opportunities for dishwashers are expected to increase modestly through the year 2005, as the additional leisure time and disposable income of the U.S. population creates additional demand for restaurant meals.

DISK JOCKEY

Ranking: 141

Score: 10

Job Growth: 56%

Promotion Potential: Low

Promotion Opportunities: Many successful disk jockeys often move on to higher-paying positions at radio stations in larger markets. Some experienced workers can advance to program or station manager.

Competition among disk jockeys for available jobs, especially with more popular radio stations in larger cities, will remain extremely strong through the next decade. Because radio broadcasting is perceived as a glamorous occupation, this field continually attracts far more job candidates than it can support. Most opportunities in the coming years will arise with small radio stations that are willing to hire beginners. These stations normally have very limited budgets, and salaries for disk jockeys in such stations are low. Radio stations are located in both rural and urban areas throughout the country.

DRESSMAKER

Ranking: 213

Score: -57

Job Growth: -4

Promotion Potential: Low

Promotion Opportunities: Workers with good management potential can advance to supervisory positions in shops and factories. Some can advance to production managers.

Foreign competition in the garment industry has seriously affected jobs in U.S. The "buy American" sentiment may help create jobs, but unless the momentum picks up, opportunities are expected to decrease percipitously.

DRILL-PRESS OPERATOR

Ranking: 243

Score: -125

Job Growth: -27%

Promotion Potential: Low

Promotion Opportunities: Some workers advance to supervisory positions. Others may train for jobs in skilled occupations such as machinist or tool-and-die worker.

Workers in this field face tremendous competition from overseas, as a result of advances in manufacturing technology, and management and marketing strategy, among foreign companies. In some industries, such as steel and automobile manufacturing, foreign firms have assumed large parts of the U.S. market, causing losses of jobs for American workers. Moreover, a number of U.S. firms have moved their production facilities to

foreign countries, in order to take advantage of the lower labor costs. Finally, the introduction of automated machinery has resulted in quicker, more efficient production, further hampering job opportunities for drill press operators and other manufacturing workers. Jobs in this occupation are concentrated in the major manufacturing centers.

DRYWALL APPLICATOR/ FINISHER

Ranking: 218

Score: -63

Job Growth: 83%

Promotion Potential: Low

Promotion Opportunities: With experience, workers can be promoted to supervisory positions. Some choose to go into business as contractors.

Job prospects for drywall applicators and finishers in the commercial construction industry are especially promising for the next decade. New office and industrial construction is expected to increase sharply in the coming years. However, like other construction trades, this profession is sensitive to swings in the economy. As building activity slows during recessions, some workers lose jobs. Others are laid off between construction projects. Unlike other members of the construction trades, drywallers are seldom idle during inclement weather, since most of their work is done indoors. Jobs in this field can be found throughout the country, but are concentrated primarily in metropolitan areas.

ECONOMIST

Ranking: 199

Score: -40

Job Growth: 56%

Promotion Potential: Low

Promotion Opportunities: Most economists begin their careers at small educational institutions as graduate assistants or associate professors. As they gain experience and recognition, they may move to higher-paying, more prestigious positions at well-known universities. Economists employed in the private sector often are promoted to senior-level, supervisory positions, or establish consulting practices.

Employment opportunities for economists are expected to increase modestly through the year 2005. Openings in the commercial sector should be more abundant than those at educational institutions, as the nation's student enrollments continues in decline.

ELECTRICAL ENGINEER

Ranking: 56

Score: 108

Job Growth: 54%

Promotion Potential: Moderate

Promotion Opportunities: Advancement in this field normally comes in the form of increased responsibility on research and development projects. Some possibility for business and military consulting exists in this profession.

Job opportunities in electrical engineering will rise steadily in the next ten years. The increased reliance in the business sector, and in government, on sophisticated communications and computer technology, will keep the demand for electrical engineers high. The growing consumer market for electronic hardware, especially entertainment equipment, will further contribute to the need for qualified electrical engineers in the years to come. Cutbacks in military spending could cause layoffs among members of this profession employed by defense contractors. Other engineers may see their roles become increasingly obsolete with advances in technology. As in other areas of engineering, jobs for electrical engineers are concentrated in major urban areas.

ELECTRICAL EQUIPMENT REPAIRER

Ranking: 232

Score: -90

Job Growth: 7%

Promotion Potential: Low

Promotion Opportunities: Competent workers in this profession can advance to positions as electronics technicians or engineering assistants.

An increase in the installation of new electronic equipment in business and industry will help alleviate the problem of slow job growth for equipment repairers in the coming decade. The trend toward sophisticated electronic production and manufacturing processes will keep the demand for qualified service personnel alive, as will the military's continuing dependence on electronic and computer-based hardware. Employment opportunities in this occupation are concentrated in the large industrial and business centers of the country.

ELECTRICAL TECHNICIAN

Ranking: 91

Score: 54

Job Growth: 52%

Promotion Potential: Moderate

Promotion Opportunities: Individuals normally enter this field as trainees, and may later advance to supervisory positions. Some eventually become electrical engineers.

Employment opportunities for electrical technicians will increase markedly over the next ten years. In business, industry, and the military, the growing use of sophisticated communications and computer technology will continue to spur demand for qualified electrical technicians. Cutbacks in military spending could jeopardize some jobs for electrical technicians working in the defense industry. Job opportunities in this field exist throughout the country, and are most abundant in major industrial and business centers.

ELECTRICIAN

Ranking: 210

Score: -54

Job Growth: 43%

Promotion Potential: Low

Promotion Opportunities: Experienced electricians can become supervisors. Some workers in this field start their own contracting businesses.

Job opportunities for electricians will remain good through the the coming decade, due to continued growth in the economy. As advances in electrical and electronic technology continue, a growing number of electricians will be needed to install wiring and cables for computer systems and telecommunications equipment. Employment opportunities in this profession are affected by fluctuations in the economy. As building slows during recessions, those electricians in the construction trades may experience periods of unemployment. Other industries in which technicians may feel the effects of economic slowdowns include automobile manufacturing, and steel production. Employment opportunities for electricians vary with local economic conditions, and reflect recent shifts in the population.

EMERGENCY MEDICAL TECHNICIAN

Ranking: 44

Score: 133

Job Growth: 81%

Promotion Potential: Low

Promotion Opportunities: Many experienced technicians often advance to medical technologist. A few are promoted to supervisory positions.

Although the demands of an aging population and developments in the field of emergency medicine might be considered positive factors in projected job opportunities for EMT's, the rising cost of training and equipping EMT's is likely to constrain job growth. The availability of unpaid volunteers and taxpayer's resistance to increasing government expenditures are also expected to contribute to a general decrease in opportunities in this area. Municipal governments and hospitals will continue to be the largest employers of EMT's, although competition will be stiff throughout the country for available jobs. Salaries depend on geographic location, as well as experience and training.

ENGINEERING TECHNICIAN

Ranking: 63

Score: 95

Job Growth: 43%

Promotion Potential: Low

Promotion Opportunities: Some experienced engineering technicians can advance to supervisory positions. With continued education, a few eventually become engineers.

Continued industrial expansion, and advances in technology, will cause steady growth in employment opportunities for engineering technicians over the next ten years. The call for more sophisticated industrial and mechanical designs, and an overall rise in the demand for technical products and services, will produce a corresponding need for a greater number of qualified engineering technicians. Like engineers, engineering technicians are employed in both large and small communities throughout the country. Jobs in this field are most abundant in major centers of industry and commerce.

EXECUTIVE SEARCH CONSULTANT

Ranking: 193

Score: -36

Job Growth: 56%

Promotion Potential: Low

Promotion Opportunities: Experienced and successful search consultants will be rewarded with partnerships, senior level positions or more lucrative searches to conduct.

Employment opportunities will increase steadily as the demand for skilled professionals increases. Those with degrees in economics, information systems or business administration have the best prospects.

FARMER

Ranking: 248

Score: -184

Job Growth: -47%

Promotion Potential: Low

Promotion Opportunities: The vast majority of workers in this field are self-employed, and thus advance only through increased farm earnings.

Opportunities for small farmers are expected to decline greatly through the year 2005, as low commodity prices and precipitate bankruptcies and foreclosures.

FASHION DESIGNER

Ranking: 94

Score: 52

Job Growth: 47%

Promotion Potential: Moderate

Promotion Opportunities: Fashion designers usually begin their careers performing relatively simple tasks as assistants to established, experienced workers. As they gain experience, fashion workers may be given more responsible, complex assignments, or they may establish their own clothing lines.

Employment opportunities for designers are expected to increase rapidly through the next decade, as the additional leisure time and disposable income of the U.S. population creates record demand for quality clothing. However, as job seekers in this field greatly outnumber available positions, only the most talented workers can reasonably anticipate steady employment.

FASHION MODEL

Ranking: 61

Score: 96

Job Growth: 122%

Promotion Potential: Low

Promotion Opportunities: Advancement for fashion models usually comes in the form of increased pay and appearances in prestigious shows and publications.

Employment opportunities for models are expected to increase rapidly through the next decade, as the additional leisure time and disposable income of the U.S. population create additional demand for fashion clothing and, therefore, modeling. However, job seekers in this field greatly outnumber available positions, and only the most talented, attractive workers can reasonably anticipate steady employment.

FILE CLERK

Ranking: 164

Score: -6

Job Growth: 43%

Promotion Potential: Low

Promotion Opportunities: Experienced clerks, in many businesses, may advance to supervisory or low-level managerial positions.

Employment opportunities in this field are expected to increase only slightly through the year 2005, as gains in office automation and worker efficiency offset the growing demand for information management. Workers with extensive experience with computerized systems will have the best prospects for continuing employment.

FINANCIAL PLANNER

Ranking: 190

Score: -35

Job Growth: 56%

Promotion Potential: Low

Promotion Opportunities: Assistant planner, certified planner, senior planner, firm partner or vice president.

Opportunities will increase steadily as the demand for skilled professionals increases. As awareness of this occupation grows, so will the opportunities. Planners may move from individual clients to working with financial counseling programs for banks, government or private agencies, working in health care industries, or directing finances for nonprofit organizations or corporations.

FIREFIGHTER

Ranking: 15

Score: 191

Job Growth: 38%

Promotion Potential: Good

Promotion Opportunities: Competent workers with exceptional leadership abilities may advance to Lieutenant, Captain, Battalion Chief, Assistant Chief, Deputy Chief or Chief.

Employment opportunities in this field are expected to increase modestly through the next decade as the growing U.S. population creates demand for fire protection. Most openings in this field will be concentrated in major urban centers.

FISHERMAN

Ranking: 193

Score: -36

Job Growth: 11%

Promotion Potential: Low

Promotion Opportunities: Most fishermen learn their trade informally, as assistants to skilled workers. As they gain experience, they may move to more responsible assignments. A few employees of large commercial fishing groups may be promoted to land-based managerial positions. Others purchase and operate their own fishing boats.

Employment opportunities in this field are expected to decline significantly through the year 2005 as worker efficiency and availability of fish substitutes increase.

FLIGHT ATTENDANT

Ranking: 52

Score: 119

Job Growth: 51%

Promotion Potential: Low

Promotion Opportunities: Experienced flight attendants may advance to crew chiefs or make better-paying lateral movies such as flight service instructors or recruiting representatives.

Employment opportunities are expected to increase rapidly as the U.S. population increases and travels more. The growth of smaller airlines, especially those specializing in commuter flights, will add to the momentum. Flight attendants with college educations will have the best chance to advance.

FLORIST

Ranking: 117

Score: 35

Job Growth: 32%

Promotion Potential: Moderate

Promotion Opportunities: Experienced floral designers may open their own retail flower shops.

Job opportunities for florists and floral designers will remain good over the next decade. Population growth, and a rise in expendable income, will contribute to greater demand for floral services in the coming years, and the need for talented floral designers will be strong. Design professions generally undergo a relatively high degree of turnover, and most new employment opportunities for florists will arise from the need to replace workers who retire or leave the field for other reasons.

FOOTBALL PLAYER (NFL)

Ranking: 125

Score: 23

Job Growth: 11%

Promotion Potential: Moderate

Promotion Opportunities: Many players enter the NFL's team roster as "second stringers" and eventually move on to starting positions. Retirees with leadership skills may advance to full- time coaching or management positions.

A few players find work as football commentators for radio and television. Employment opportunities for NFL players are expected to remain constant through the next decade, unless a rule change permits an increase in the maximum size of team rosters.

FORK-LIFT OPERATOR

Ranking: 188

Score: -31

Job Growth: 16%

Promotion Potential: Low

Promotion Opportunities: With experience, some truck operators can advance to supervisory positions.

Computerized handling, packing, and shipping systems in large industrial plants allow for more efficient transportation of goods and materials by truck and tractor. This improved efficiency results in the elimination of positions for truck operators. However, turnover in this occupation is high. Employment for industrial truck operators is sensitive to fluctuations in the economy, and many workers suffer layoffs during recessions. Employment opportunities are concentrated in major industrial centers.

FURNITURE UPHOLSTERER

Ranking: 179

Score: -21

Job Growth: 25%

Promotion Potential: Low

Promotion Opportunities: Individuals in this field often choose to go into business for themselves. Others can become supervisors in large upholstery shops or factories.

The majority of job opportunities for upholsters in the next decade will result from the need to replace workers who retire or leave the field for other reasons. Some new jobs will become available as the population grows, and as personal spending increases. However, the market for self-employed upholsterers has shrunk over the past several years, because consumers now tend to purchase new furniture rather than restore worn pieces. The demand for upholstery service is greatest in large metropolitan areas, and job opportunities are concentrated accordingly.

GARBAGE COLLECTOR

Ranking: 179

Score: -21

Job Growth: 25%

Promotion Potential: Low

Promotion Opportunities: Experienced employees of municipal sanitation services often advance to managerial or supervisory positions. A few workers establish private sanitation services.

Employment opportunities for garbage collectors are expected to remain fairly constant through the year 2005, as advances in sanitation disposal technology offset the increases in garbage volume created by U.S. population growth. Openings in this field should be concentrated in major urban areas.

GEOLOGIST

Ranking: 89

Score: 55

Job Growth: 50%

Promotion Potential: Moderate

Promotion Opportunities: Geologists can advance to project leader, program manager, or other research and management positions. The opportunity for independent consulting work also exists.

In the private sector, the availability of jobs for geologists is largely dependent on the status of oil and gas exploration in this and other countries. The current steady prices for petroleum indicate slow growth in this field over the next few years. However, new sources of oil and gas must eventually be found, as must more sophisticated techniques for locating deposits. Individuals who have advanced degrees, and who specialize in oil and gas exploration techniques, are expected to have the best employment opportunities. In colleges and universities, dropping enrollment will combine with budgetary constraints to limit the hiring of geologists, and create increased competition for available positions.

GLAZIER

Ranking: 225

Score: -80

Job Growth: 68%

Promotion Potential: Low

Promotion Opportunities: Experienced workers in this profession can advance to supervisory positions. Some become glazing contractors.

Although job prospects in this profession are good, the high wages glaziers enjoy lead to heavy competition for available jobs in this relatively small field. As the economy expands, a corresponding increase in commercial and residential building will create greater job opportunities for glaziers. Glass facades are becoming more popular in architectural designs, and this will further contribute to the growing demand for qualified glaziers. Glass construction is best suited to warm weather areas, and consequently, a high number of jobs for glaziers are concentrated in western and southern regions of the country.

GUARD

Ranking: 26

Score: 168

Job Growth: 115%

Promotion Potential: Moderate

Promotion Opportunities: Some security guards advance to positions in police departments. Other may take on administrative duties, or open their own security agencies.

Job prospects for security guards will be extremely good in the coming decade. In business and industry, huge capital investments in costly computer systems and plant equipment has heightened concern over theft, vandalism, and other loss or damage to expensive property. The need for intense security measures to protect these valuable assets will force the demand for security personnel to rise. The turnover rate in contract guard agencies is high. Security guards with in-house jobs, where wages and benefits are generally better, tend to stay with their jobs longer. Personnel employed by security agencies may lose jobs during recessions, while in-house security is needed to protect property even when busi-

nesses close or are shut down. Employment opportunities for security guards are widespread throughout the country.

HEATING/REFRIGERATION MECHANIC

Ranking: 128

Score: 18

Job Growth: 65%

Promotion Potential: Low

Promotion Opportunities: Experienced mechanics can become supervisors. Others can open their own cooling and heating contracting firms.

Heating and refrigeration mechanics will see a moderate growth in job opportunities over the next ten years. The amount of new commercial building is expected increase, and these new commercial structures will require expansive, well-maintained heating and cooling systems. Skilled service mechanics will be needed to install new systems, and repair older ones. Continuing concern about energy efficiency and conservation will lead to cost-containment measures on energy systems, further driving up the demand for qualified heating and refrigeration mechanics. Jobs in this occupation are available throughout the country. A growing number of job opportunities for mechanics are concentrated in warmer regions, where construction and air-conditioning installation are both on the rise.

HIGHWAY PATROL OFFICER

Ranking: 16

Score: 185

Job Growth: 32%

Promotion Potential: Excellent

Promotion Opportunities: Most workers in this field begin their careers as highway patrol officers. Experienced officers may advance to detective or supervisory posts such as captain, or superintendent.

Employment opportunities for state police officers are expected to increase steadily through the next decade, as the nation affirms its resolve to alleviate crime.

HISTORIAN

Ranking: 134

Score: 14

Job Growth: 59%

Promotion Potential: Low

Promotion Opportunities: Historians can advance to administrative positions in universities, museums, or government agencies.

The largest number of job openings for historians in the next decade will arise from the need to replace workers who retire or leave the profession for other reasons. The number of recent graduates in history will exceed job availability in this field by a wide margin. Faculty positions will be increasingly limited, as a result of the trend for students to move away from college liberal arts programs. Competition amongst historians for available positions will be heavy. Key factors in this competition will be geographical flexibility, salary requirements, and the level and quality of advanced degree.

HOME ECONOMIST

Ranking: 102

Score: 47

Job Growth: 45%

Promotion Potential: Moderate

Promotion Opportunities: Home economists with experience and skill can advance to program development and policy-making positions in social services and health care agencies. Those who teach can advance to department head, or to administrative positions in education.

Overall employment opportunities for home economists will decline slightly over the next decade. A slight rise in enrollment in secondary schools will be offset by tighter budgets for education and social service.

HOSPITAL ADMINISTRATOR

Ranking: 40

Score: 139

Job Growth: 79%

Promotion Potential: Moderate

Promotion Opportunities: Individuals in this profession can advance to administrative positions with greater responsibility and higher pay within health care organizations or agencies.

As hospitals and other health-care agencies continue to diversify, and to assume for-profit philosophies, effective health care management will become increasingly important. Sophisticated cost-containment measures will require the business expertise of skilled administrators. Consequently, employment opportunities for experienced hospital administrators will grow markedly over the next decade. Competition for upper-level administrative positions will remain strong. Jobs in this field are found throughout the country, and are most abundant in metropolitan areas.

HOTEL MANAGER

Ranking: 93

Score: 52

Job Growth: 99%

Promotion Potential: Low

Promotion Opportunities: Most managers begin their careers in junior-level positions, at relatively small hotels or motels. As they gain experience, they may advance to full-charge positions at larger institutions. A few managers advance to executive positions with hotel chains.

Employment opportunities for hotel managers are expected to increase rapidly through the next decade, as the U.S. population expends more of its disposable income on vacations. Graduates of university programs in hotel management should have the best prospects for advancement and continued employment.

INDUSTRIAL DESIGNER

Ranking: 103

Score: 46

Job Growth: 43%

Promotion Potential: Moderate

Promotion Opportunities: The majority of employment openings for industrial designers will result from the need to replace workers who retire or leave the profession for other reasons.

This is a highly competitive occupation. Job prospects will depend to a great extent on an individual's design talent and technical skill. The continuing need for technically sophisticated designs for the marketplace will help maintain a steady demand for industrial designers in the coming years. Growth in personal and business income should spur consumer spending, further sparking demand for industrial designers to develop new products. Jobs in this field are concentrated in metropolitan areas.

INDUSTRIAL ENGINEER

Ranking: 109

Score: 42

Job Growth: 38%

Promotion Potential: Low

Promotion Opportunities: Advancement in this occupation normally comes in the form of increased responsibility on research and design projects.

Employment opportunities in this field will remain good over the next several years. Industrial expansion, and the growing sophistication of business operations, will lead to a great demand for skilled industrial engineers to solve production problems and develop new designs. Industrial engineers will also be needed to implement scientific techniques for increasing efficiency and cost-effectiveness in production. This job is somewhat sensitive to economic downturns. Cutbacks in corporate or industrial spending could result in layoffs for some members of this profession. As in other areas of engineering, employment opportunities in industrial engineering are best in major industrial and commercial centers of the nation.

INDUSTRIAL MACHINE REPAIRER

Ranking: 160

Score: -4

Job Growth: -7%

Promotion Potential: Moderate

Promotion Opportunities: Advancement opportunities for industrial machine repairers are extremely limited. Experienced workers are often rewarded with responsibility for large or complex machinery, but very few supervisory or administrative positions are available in this field.

Employment opportunities for industrial repairers will increase very slowly through the next decade. Fewer new machine repairers are expected to be necessary as the general reliability of industrial systems increases. Employment in this field is concentrated in heavily populated areas.

INSURANCE AGENT

Ranking: 113

Score: 39

Job Growth: 34%

Promotion Potential: Moderate

Promotion Opportunities: Individuals who demonstrate good sales ability may advance to positions as sales manager, agency superintendent, or executive. Some open their own insurance agencies or brokerage firms.

Employment opportunities in the insurance profession will grow over the next ten years. Computers are being used more often to perform routine clerical tasks once handled by insurance agents. Moreover, consumers are becoming in-

creasingly dependent on group policies to meet insurance needs. As a result, the demand for new professionals in this field will be limited. Turnover in this occupation is high.

INSURANCE UNDERWRITER

Ranking: 86

Score: 57

Job Growth: 54%

Promotion Potential: Moderate

Promotion Opportunities: With experience, insurance underwriters can advance to the position of chief underwriter. Chief underwriters may move up to the position of underwriting manager.

As insurance sales continue to increase, so too will job opportunities for underwriters. Contributing to rising insurance sales is the need for home, life, health, and auto coverage by "baby boomers"—conspicuous consumers between 25 and 54 years old. New and growing businesses will also be in need of more insurance protection. Employment in this field is not particularly affected by changes in the economy, as insurance coverage is regarded as a necessity rather than a luxury. Most job opportunities exist in large cities, such as New York, Chicago, San Francisco, and Hartford, where insurance headquarters are based.

IRONWORKER

Ranking: 152

Score: 2

Job Growth: 50%

Promotion Potential: Low

Promotion Opportunities: With experience, workers in this field can advance to supervisory positions.

If a rise in the number of construction starts on non-residential buildings, and continuing need for construction and maintenance of highways and bridges gets back on track, it will lead to only a modest rise in job opportunities for ironworkers through the next decade. However, construction activity is affected by fluctuations in the economy, and some ironworkers will experience periods of unemployment during recessions, when building slows. The relatively high wages offered in this trade contribute to stiff competition for jobs. Employment opportunities in this occupation vary according to geographic area. The level of construction activity, and thus of construction hiring, reflects regional economic conditions.

JANITOR

Ranking: 160

Score: -4

Job Growth: 43%

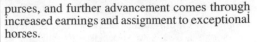

Promotion Potential: Low

Promotion Opportunities: Experienced janitors in large establishments can become supervisors. Some start their own building maintenance services.

An increasing number of companies are hiring outside personnel to perform cleaning services. The consequent growth in contract maintenance firms will offer the best employment opportunities for janitors over the next decade. Employment of janitors in almost all other areas will remain steady during this period. Requirements for entrance into this occupation are few. Janitors need little formal education or experience. Opportunities for part-time work in this field are abundant. Jobs for janitors are most plentiful in areas of heavy industry and commerce, such as major metropolitan centers.

JEWELER

Ranking: 210

Score: -54

Job Growth: 43%

Promotion Potential: Low

Promotion Opportunities: Jewelers who are employed by manufacturing firms can advance to positions as supervisors. Others can become store managers, or open their own jewelry shops.

This occupation will undergo relatively slow growth over the next ten years. Employment prospects for jewelers will be best in retail jewelry or repair shops. Increased automation in jewelry manufacture and repair, combined with competition from foreign manufacturers, will hinder job opportunities in jewelry manufacturing firms. Downswings in the overall economy can also contribute to slow growth or layoffs.

JOCKEY

Ranking: 115

Score: 36

Job Growth: 29%

Promotion Potential: Low

Promotion Opportunities: Aspiring jockeys usually enter the occupation as trainers assistants or general helpers. As they gain experience, talented newcomers may be allowed to compete for purses, and further advancement comes through increased earnings and assignment to exceptional horses.

Employment opportunities for jockeys are expected to remain fairly constant through the next decade. However, this is a competitive field, and only the most talented, dedicated workers can expect steady employment.

JUDGE (FEDERAL)

Ranking: 57

Score: 107

Job Growth: 5%

Promotion Potential: Moderate

Promotion Opportunities: While federal justices have no direct opportunities for promotion, historically many have been appointed to the United States Supreme Court.

Employment opportunities for federal judges are expected to grow rapidly through the next decade. Positions in this prestigious field are created when cases overload the system, as they invariably will through the decade.

LIBRARIAN

Ranking: 222

Score: -71

Job Growth: 27%

Promotion Potential: Low

Promotion Opportunities: Individuals with advanced degrees are most likely to be given promotions, especially in academic libraries. Entry level workers who have completed internship or work-study programs are apt to advance more quickly than other workers, and experienced librarians are often considered for administrative positions.

Many job opportunities will arise from nontraditional sources, such as information search services and bibliographic cooperatives; competition is expected to remain fierce for traditional library jobs. Individuals with experience in computer applications will have the greatest job opportunities. Those with specialized training in science and business are also expected to be in demand.

LITHOGRAPHER/PHOTO ENGRAVER

Ranking: 205

Score: -51

Job Growth: 47%

Promotion Potential:

Promotion Opportunities: Experienced lithographers can advance to supervisory positions in large printing plants, or go into business for themselves.

Growing use of color printing in newspapers, and in mail-order catalogues, will lead to expanded employment opportunities for lithographers in the next ten years. Technological advances in electronic equipment, such as scanners, may affect job prospects in some specialized areas of the profession. However, small businesses comprise much of this industry, and use of this costly equipment will not be widespread in the near future. Job opportunities for lithographers exist throughout the country.

LUMBERJACK

Ranking: 247

Score: -162

Job Growth: -16%

Promotion Potential: Low

Promotion Opportunities: Advancement opportunities in this field are extremely limited. However, a few experienced employees of large firms are promoted to supervisory and administrative positions.

Employment opportunities for lumberjacks are expected to decline slightly through the next decade, as improvements in logging technology offset growing demands for lumber. Workers in the Pacific Northwest should have the best prospects for continued employment.

MACHINE TOOL OPERATOR

Ranking: 245

Score: -134

Job Growth: -38%

Promotion Potential: Low

Promotion Opportunities: Workers with experience can advance to positions as supervisors or tool programmers.

Employment opportunities for numerical-control machine tool operators will decrease steadily over the next ten years. Competition from foreign manufacturers has forced growing reliance on sophisticated machinery for domestic manufacture of industrial parts. Demand for qualified operators for this equipment should be high. However, technological advances leading to computerized monitoring and operation in manufacturing could limit job prospects in this occupation to some extent. Fluctuations in the economy

tend to affect the manufacturing sector more severely than other industries, and economic downswings can slow hiring in this field. Jobs for machine tool operators are concentrated in the midwestern and northeastern manufacturing centers.

MACHINIST

Ranking: 153

Score: 1

Job Growth: -2%

Promotion Potential: Moderate

Promotion Opportunities: Some experienced machinists advance to positions as tool-and-die workers, tool programmers, or supervisors. Others go into business for themselves.

Job opportunities in this occupation will suffer somewhat from increasing reliance over the next decade on computer-controlled machine operations. Continuing technological advances will significantly reduce operational time in manufacturing, further contributing to a decline in job opportunities for machinists. In addition, heavy competition from foreign industries will hinder growth for American manufacturing companies. However, qualified machinists will still be needed to replace individuals who transfer or leave the profession for other reasons. Because manufacturing is sensitive to economic conditions, recessions can cause short layoffs for machinists. Most job opportunities in this profession are concentrated in major industrial centers, such as the Northeast and Midwest.

MAID

Ranking: 61

Score: 96

Job Growth: 43%

Promotion Potential: Low

Promotion Opportunities: Maids in commercial establishments can advance to supervisory positions. Some individuals open their own cleaning service companies.

Employment opportunities will grow at an average pace for members of this profession over the next decade. Job prospects for maids will be best with private firms that contract out for maid service. This occupation has a relatively high turnover rate. As formal education requirements for maids are usually minimal, the field is easy to enter. Technological developments are expected to exert negligible influence on employment for maids, and replacement with robots is not likely to occur within the near future. Economic factors do affect

OUTLOOK

this occupation, and and increase in personal wealth could spur consumer demand for maid services. Major metropolitan areas offer the best employment opportunities for maids.

MAIL CARRIER

Ranking: 59

Score: 104

Job Growth: 2%

Promotion Potential: Moderate

Promotion Opportunities: With seniority, carriers can obtain preferred routes, or can advance to positions as carrier technicians or supervisors.

An overabundance of applicants has led to intense competition for available jobs with the postal service over the past several years, and this situation will persist through the next decade. Postal workers enjoy relatively high salaries, excellent benefits, and a good degree of job security. In addition, educational requirements for mail carriers are modest. Consequently, this is an attractive occupation for many individuals. Turnover in this profession is low, as few workers leave the field in mid-career. Economic downturns do not normally result in layoffs of postal workers. Rather, cutbacks in spending are achieved by freezing the hiring of replacement workers for positions vacated by retiring employees. Mail carriers are employed in areas of the country.

MARKET RESEARCH ANALYST

Ranking: 172

Score: -15

Job Growth: 32%

Promotion Potential: Low

Promotion Opportunities: Those with advanced degrees usually qualify for more responsible research and administrative positions. Many business executives have experience as market researchers.

The employment outlook for market research analysts is expected to remain good over the next several years. Contributing to the demand for research analysts is the increasing reliance on quantitative analysis of trends in business, including sales forecasts and product development. Job prospects should be best in domestic and foreign manufacturing, financial services, and direct mail firms. Although employment opportunities are available throughout the country, prospects for market research analysts are best in large metropolitan areas.

MATHEMATICIAN

Ranking: 77

Score: 72

Job Growth: 18%

Promotion Potential: Moderate

Promotion Opportunities: Most mathematicians begin their careers at small educational institutions — as graduate assistants or associate professors. As they gain experience and recognition, they may move to higher-paying, more prestigious positions at well-known universities. Mathematicians employed in the private sector often are promoted to senior-level supervisory positions.

Employment opportunities for mathematicians are expected to increase rapidly through the year 2005. Positions in this field will be concentrated in "high-tech" industrial centers, and opportunities for Ph.D. graduates in applied mathematics should be especially plentiful.

MAYOR

Ranking: 233

Score: -91

Job Growth: 0%

Promotion Potential: Low

Promotion Opportunities: While mayors have no direct opportunities for promotion, they typically advance by running for higher elective office.

Employment opportunities for mayors should remain fairly constant through the next decade, since the nation's political geography has essentially stabilized. Since this is a very volatile and competitive field, even the most talented individuals are not guaranteed continued employment.

MECHANICAL ENGINEER

Ranking: 96

Score: 49

Job Growth: 45%

Promotion Potential: Low

Promotion Opportunities: Experienced mechanical engineers can advance to managerial positions.

An increased reliance on sophisticated mechanical systems in business and industry, and the overall trend toward automation, will lead to growth in employment opportunities for mechanical engineers over the next decade. Skilled professionals in this occupation will be needed to develop complex energy systems for industry and government, and to work on elaborate defense projects for the military. Manufacturing firms seeking to increase productivity will also require the services of engineers in the coming years. As with other engineering professions, job prospects in mechanical engineering are concentrated in heavily populated areas.

MEDICAL LABORATORY TECHNICIAN

Ranking: 5

Score: 205

Job Growth: 59%

Promotion Potential: Good

Promotion Opportunities: Many experienced technicians often advance to medical technologist. A few are promoted to supervisory positions in large laboratories.

Employment opportunities in this field are expected to increase nicely through the year 2005, as gains in laboratory automation and worker efficiency offset growing demand for health care services. Workers with extensive experience with computerized lab equipment will have the best prospects for continuing employment.

MEDICAL RECORDS TECHNICIAN

Ranking: 28

Score: 165

Job Growth: 113%

Promotion Potential: Low

Promotion Opportunities: Medical record clerks with exceptional work records frequently advance to medical record technicians. A few experienced record technicians are promoted to executive level medical administrative positions.

Employment opportunities for medical record technicians are expected to increase very rapidly through the year 2005, as the aging U.S. population creates unprecedented demand for health-care. Graduates of two-year vocational training programs will have the best prospects for employment.

MEDICAL SECRETARY

Ranking: 10

Score: 232

Job Growth: 101%

Promotion Potential: Moderate

Promotion Opportunities: Experienced medical secretaries with exceptional leadership skills may advance to positions in medical administration.

Employment opportunities for medical secretaries are expected to increase very rapidly through the year 2005, as the aging U.S. population creates unprecedented demand for health-care. Secretaries with word processing and related computer skills will have the brightest prospects for employment.

MEDICAL TECHNOLOGIST

Ranking: 31

Score: 158

Job Growth: 56%

Promotion Potential: Moderate

Promotion Opportunities: Experienced medical technologists can advance to supervisory positions in laboratories, or to the position of chief medical technologist in large hospitals. Those who earn advanced degrees in biological science enjoy the best advancement potential.

The volume of laboratory testing will increase sharply in the coming years and advances in medical technology will serve to create new tests and laboratory procedures perhaps even overloading the present capacity of the system. Workers and new laboratories are always in demand.

METEOROLOGIST

Ranking: 79

Score: 66

Job Growth: 54%

Promotion Potential: Moderate

Promotion Opportunities: Most novice meteorologists are involved in routine data collection. Experienced workers advance to more complex assignments, and may be promoted to supervisory or administrative positions.

Employment opportunities for meteorologists are expected to increase steadily through the next decade. Many new positions will be created as more organizations recognize the value of private weather forecasting.

METER READER

Ranking: 237

Score: -97

Job Growth: 0%

Promotion Potential: Low

Promotion Opportunities: Experienced workers in this field with exceptional management skills often advance to supervisory or management positions.

Employment opportunities in this field will decrease sharply through the next decade, as the growing U.S. population presents additional demand for public utilities. Workers with some college experience should enjoy the best prospects for advancement and steady employment.

MILITARY (COMMISSIONED OFFICER)

Ranking: 12

Score: 193

Job Growth: -11%

Promotion Potential: Excellent

Promotion Opportunities: Employment opportunities for military personnel are expected to decrease modestly through the year 2005. Though the military is scaling back on manpower, early retirements, and normal attrition are expected to increase the need for new personnel — about 15,000 new officers must be recruited annually. Workers with extensive university or on-the-job training will have the brightest prospects for advancement and continued advancement.

MILITARY (ENLISTED PERSON)

Ranking: 12

Score: 193

Job Growth: -11%

Promotion Potential: Excellent

Promotion Opportunities: Competent enlisted personnel may advance through a great variety of ranks and assignments. Exceptional individuals may be promoted to non-commissioned or commissioned positions.

Employment opportunities are expected to increase only modestly through the year 2005, even as the combined Armed Forces scales back its manpower.

MILITARY (WARRANT OFFICER)

Ranking: 65

Score: 92

Job Growth: -11%

Promotion Potential: Moderate

Promotion Opportunities: Competent warrant officers may be promoted to various warrant ranks and sometimes to commissioned positions.

Employment opportunities for warrant officer personnel are expected to increase modestly through the year 2005. Because many warrant officers come from those promoted from military ranks, job growth may be lower than the rest of the military, but the state of flux in the armed forces today, makes an accurate outlook prediction difficult.

MILLWRIGHT

Ranking: 223

Score: -77

Job Growth: 20%

Promotion Potential: Low

Promotion Opportunities: Most millwrights begin their careers as assistants to skilled workers and learn their trade informally over six to eight years. A few experienced millwrights advance to supervisory positions.

Employment opportunities in this field are expected to increase slowly through the next decade, as foreign industrial competition results in weakening demand for U.S. durable goods.

MOTION PICTURE EDITOR

Ranking: 143

Score: 8

Job Growth: 52%

Promotion Potential: Moderate

Promotion Opportunities: Editors usually begin their careers performing relatively simple tasks as assistant to established, experienced workers. As they gain experience, editors may be given more responsible, complex assignments on higher budget films.

Employment opportunities for film editors are expected to increase rapidly through the year 2005, as the increasingly affluent U.S. population commits more of its disposable income to entertainment. Positions in this field will be concentrated in New York and Los Angeles.

MUSEUM CURATOR

Ranking: 105

Score: 44

Job Growth: 41%

Promotion Potential: Moderate

Promotion Opportunities: In large museums, experienced curators can advance to positions of program planner or museum director.

The job outlook for museum curators will be hurt by government cutbacks in funding for museums, the arts, and other related fields over the next decade. The profession will remain highly competitive, as the number of qualified job candidates continues to exceed the demand for new workers. Those with substantial work experience in collection management and restoration should fare best in the competition for available curatorships.

MUSICAL INSTRUMENT REPAIRER

Ranking: 182

Score: -26

Job Growth: 20%

Promotion Potential: Low

Promotion Opportunities: Musical instrument repairers usually learn the trade on-the-job, by serving as assistants to skilled workers. Experienced repairers may advance to supervisory positions or establish their own repair services.

Employment opportunities in this field are expected to increase very slowly through the next decade, and most openings will arise to replace retiring workers. Repairers with knowledge of a variety of instruments will have the best employment prospects.

MUSICIAN

Ranking: 148

Score: 4

Job Growth: 56%

Promotion Potential: Low

Promotion Opportunities: Exceptionally accomplished orchestral musicians are often rewarded with soloist status. Others advance by transferring to larger or more prestigious orchestras A few become professional conductors.

Employment opportunities for musicians should increase through the 1990s, but competition for openings will be fierce.

NEWSCASTER

Ranking: 130

Score: 15

Job Growth: 59%

Promotion Potential: Low

Promotion Opportunities: Newscasters frequently begin their careers at small, rural stations, and advance by moving to larger metropolitan or network stations. Others may be promoted to station director or programming director.

Employment opportunities for newscaster will increase through the middle of the next decade. Competition for all newscasting positions will be intense, but jobs in radio should generally be easier to secure than those in TV. Almost all openings will arise to replace experienced newscasters who leave the work force.

NEWS WRITER (RADIO/TV)

Ranking: 143

Score: 8

Job Growth: 52%

Promotion Potential: Low

Promotion Opportunities: News writers usually begin their careers performing relatively routine duties for small or amateur stations. As they gain experience they may move to higher-paying, more responsible assignments at larger or more prestigious stations.

Employment opportunities for news writers are expected to increase rapidly through the year 2005, as the growing complexity of the "global community" fuels demand for radio and television news commentary.

NUCLEAR ENGINEER

Ranking: 148

Score: 4

Job Growth: 0%

Promotion Potential: Low

Promotion Opportunities: Nuclear engineers can advance to administrative and policy-making positions with federal agencies, or to managerial positions in nuclear power plants.

The continuing concerns over the safety of nuclear power, combined with the enormous construction costs of nuclear power plants, will limit new construction of atomic energy facilities over the next decade. In addition, conservation efforts will help lessen the overall demand for energy. As a result, employment prospects in nuclear engineering are not as good as in other branches of engineering for the near future. Nuclear engineers will still be needed to operate existing power plants, and to monitor safety measures. Military projects will remain a prime source of jobs for nuclear engineers, but cutbacks in defense spending could limit hiring in this field. Many nuclear engineers work in rural areas of the country, where nuclear power plants are located.

NUCLEAR PLANT DECONTAMINATION TECHNICIAN

Ranking: 215

Score: -59

Job Growth: -11%

Promotion Potential: Low

Promotion Opportunities: Decontamination technician have very few formal opportunities for promotion. A few employees of major decontamination firms, however, advance to managerial positions.

Employment opportunities for decontamination technicians are expected to increase rapidly through the year 2005, with the growing demand for inexpensive nuclear power. Openings in this field will be concentrated in heavily industrialized areas.

NURSE (LICENSED PRACTICAL)

Ranking: 36

Score: 143

Job Growth: 90%

Promotion Potential: Low

Job opportunities in this field are expected to change with an increasing orientation toward employment in nursing homes, psychiatric hospitals, and private duty nursing.

Because of technical advances, jobs that formerly went to LPN's are increasingly being delegated to registered nurses and physician assistants. An aging population is expected to present some opportunities for LPN's, since home care is experiencing rapid growth. .

NURSE (REGISTERED)

Ranking: 7

Score: 265

Job Growth: 95%

Promotion Potential: Moderate

Promotion Opportunities: Experienced nurses may be promoted from staff positions in hospitals to a variety of higher-paying, more responsible positions. Workers with exceptional management skills may advance to assistant head nurse or head

nurse. Nurses who receive advanced training in hospital administration may move to executive levels.

Employment opportunities in this field are expected to increase rapidly through the year 2005, as the aging U.S. population creates record demand for health care services.

NURSE'S AIDE

Ranking: 33

Score: 154

Job Growth: 101%

Promotion Potential: Low

Promotion Opportunities: Advancement opportunities in this field are very limited. Many nursing aides return to school to become registered or practical nurses.

Employment opportunities for nursing aides will increase dramatically through the mid-1990s. Positions at nursing homes and home care agencies will be especially plentiful, as the average age of the U.S. population climbs. Job opportunities for psychiatric nursing aides however, will be scarcer than in other fields, as funding for public and private mental institutions becomes increasingly tight.

OCCUPATIONAL SAFETY/ HEALTH INSPECTOR

Ranking: 177

Score: -20

Job Growth: -23%

Promotion Potential: Low

Promotion Opportunities: Experienced occupational safety and health inspectors may be appointed to senior supervisory or administrative positions. A few inspectors establish consulting practices to advise private corporations on government regulations.

Employment opportunities for occupational safety and health inspectors are expected to increase through the next decade. However, a cloud hangs over the horizon as government funding for regulatory programs shrinks.

OCCUPATIONAL THERAPIST

Ranking: 8

Score: 253

Job Growth: 135%

Promotion Potential: Moderate

Promotion Opportunities: Newly graduated therapists usually accept staff positions at large institutions. As they gain experience they may advance to supervisory or teaching positions.

Employment opportunities for occupational therapists are expected to increase very rapidly through the year 2005, as the growing U.S. population fuels demand for rehabilitative and long-term health care. Barring a significant increase in the size of educational programs, openings in this field should outnumber job seekers.

OCEANOGRAPHER

Ranking: 32

Score: 157

Job Growth: 104%

Promotion Potential: Moderate

Promotion Opportunities: Most oceanographers are initially employed as graduate assistants or associate professors at college and universities. Experienced workers may advance to full, tenured professorships or seek employment with private or non-profit research groups.

Employment opportunities for oceanographers will increase modestly through the next decade. The number of advanced degrees awarded, however, will probably exceed available academic positions, so competition will be severe.

OFFICE MACHINE REPAIRER

Ranking: 184

Score: -29

Job Growth: 18%

Promotion Potential: Moderate

Promotion Opportunities: Many advance to sales positions. Those with managerial potential may be promoted to service manager; a few open their own repair shops.

Employment opportunities for office machine repairers will grow over the next decade, as businesses purchase additional equipment to increase office productivity. Office machine services are employed throughout the nation, but openings are concentrated in major metropolitan areas.

OPTICIAN

Ranking: 18

Score: 183

Job Growth: 81%

Promotion Potential: Moderate

Promotion Opportunities: Most opticians learn their trade as assistants to skilled workers. Many experienced opticians go into business for themselves. Others become managers of retail optical stores or sales representatives for manufacturers of lenses and glasses.

Employment opportunities are expected to increase rapidly through the next decade, as the aging U.S. population will present record demand for corrective eye wear. Graduates of 2-year optical fabricating and dispensing programs will have the brightest prospects for employment.

OPTOMETRIST

Ranking: 67

Score: 90

Job Growth: 36%

Promotion Potential: Low

Promotion Opportunities: Most optometrists are self-employed and thus have few opportunities for advancement. Experienced workers, however, may act as consultants to industrial safety programs, insurance companies, and manufacturers of eye wear.

Employment opportunities for medical assistants are expected to grow through the year 2005, as the aging U.S. population creates unprecedented demand for optical goods and therapy. Since a third of all active optometrists are between 50 and 65 years of age, it's likely that a large number of experienced workers will leave the profession in the next decade.

ORTHODONTIST

Ranking: 130

Score: 15

Job Growth: 11%

Promotion Potential: Low

Promotion Opportunities: Most orthodontists begin their careers as assistants to experienced dentists to gain experience and save money to establish and equip their own offices.

Employment opportunities for orthodontists are expected to increase rapidly through the year 2005, as the baby-boom generation matures, and many middle-aged Americans become candidates for intensive dental care.

OSTEOPATH

Ranking: 71

Score: 83

Job Growth: 79%

Promotion Potential: Low

Promotion Opportunities: Most osteopaths begin their careers as interns at small osteopathic hospitals. Experienced workers may advance to positions of greater medical or administrative responsibility.

Employment opportunities for osteopaths are expected to rise rapidly through the year 2005, as the increasingly elderly U.S. population creates unprecedented demand for workers in all health care professions.

PAINTER

Ranking: 188

Score: -31

Job Growth: 65%

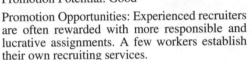

Promotion Potential: Low

Promotion Opportunities: Novice painters often undertake three- year, on-the-job apprenticeships. Experienced painters may advance to the position of painting foreman, or may establish their own contracting businesses.

There will be reasonable growth in painting trades through the next decade. Replacement needs will account for most of the positions available.

PARALEGAL ASSISTANT

Ranking: 9

Score: 249

Job Growth: 194%

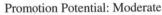

Promotion Potential: Moderate

Promotion Opportunities: As they gain experience, paralegal assistants are given successively more responsible, less- supervised assignments, but opportunities for promotion are severely limited. A few paralegals advance to administrative positions. Others return to school to earn legal degrees.

Employment opportunities for paralegals are expected to increase almost astronomically through the next decade, as Americans continue to air their grievances in court. Graduates of one-year training programs should have the best prospects for employment.

PAROLE OFFICER

Ranking: 6

Score: 281

Job Growth: 90%

Promotion Potential: Good

Promotion Opportunities: Experienced parole officers with exceptional leadership or organizational skills may advance to supervisory or administrative correctional positions.

Employment opportunities for parole officers are expected to increase rapidly through the year 2005, as America commits additional resources to relieving the overcrowding in its penal facilities.

PERSONNEL RECRUITER

Ranking: 69

Score: 84

Job Growth: 81%

Promotion Potential: Good

Promotion Opportunities: Experienced recruiters are often rewarded with more responsible and lucrative assignments. A few workers establish their own recruiting services.

Employment opportunities for personnel recruiters are expected to increase steadily through the year 2005, as U.S. demand for skilled professional employees mounts. College graduates with degrees in psychology or human resources management will have the best prospects for employment.

PETROLEUM ENGINEER

Ranking: 205

Score: -51

Job Growth: -5%

Promotion Potential: Low

Promotion Opportunities: Experienced professionals in this field can advance to managerial positions with energy companies.

Employment opportunities for petroleum engineers show almost on increase through the next decade. The development of new, more efficient techniques for recovery of oil and gas will be necessary to keep pace with the the energy demands created by economic expansion. Petroleum engineers will be needed to evaluate methods to improve production and refinery facilities, which currently can process only half the amount of all available oil. Jobs for petroleum engineers are concentrated in California, Louisiana, Oklahoma, and Texas. Many members of this profession work in oil-producing countries overseas.

PHARMACIST

Ranking: 53

Score: 118

Job Growth: 65%

Promotion Potential: Low

Promotion Opportunities: Most recent graduates of pharmaceutical programs find employment at community pharmacies. As they gain experience and amass capital, many pharmacist become owners or part-owners of their own establishments. Others advance to supervisory or administrative positions.

Employment opportunities for pharmacists are expected to increase modestly as the aging U.S. population creates record demand for prescription medications. Most openings will result from the need to replace retiring pharmacists.

PHILOSOPHER

Ranking: 99

Score: 48

Job Growth: 45%

Promotion Potential: Moderate

Promotion Opportunities: Most philosophers are initially employed as graduate assistants or assistant professors at colleges and universities. Experienced, talented workers may advance to full, tenured professorships.

Employment opportunities for philosophers will decrease modestly through the next decade. The number of advanced humanities degrees awarded will greatly exceed available academic positions, so competition in this field will be severe.

PHOTOGRAPHER

Ranking: 197

Score: -39

Job Growth: 56%

Promotion Potential: Low

Promotion Opportunities: Photographers with experience take on more demanding assignments, and may move to larger, more prestigious publications, eventually rising to photography editor or graphic arts department head. Some photographers open their own commercial studios.

Employment opportunities for photographers will increase in the coming years. Demand for photographic services in business and industry, as well as in scientific and medical research, will grow.

PHOTOGRAPHIC PROCESS WORKER

Ranking: 138

Score: 12

Job Growth: 59%

Promotion Potential: Low

Promotion Opportunities: Competent employees of large photo finishing labs often advance to supervisory positions. A few photographic process workers go on to become professional photographers.

Employment opportunities for photographic process workers will increase over the next decade. Growth in the number of small laboratories will account for most new openings. Although positions will be available throughout the country, opportunities will be concentrated in large metropolitan areas.

PHOTOJOURNALIST

Ranking: 130

Score: 15

Job Growth: 56%

Promotion Potential: Moderate

Promotion Opportunities: Newly hired workers in this field are given relatively routine, low-paying assignments. Experienced workers are given more responsible assignments and may transfer to larger newspapers or magazines.

Employment opportunities for in this field are expected to increase through the year 2005. Competition for positions in photojournalism should be extremely intense, and only the most talented individuals can expect to find steady employment.

PHYSICAL THERAPIST

Ranking: 2

Score: 438

Job Growth: 198%

Promotion Potential: Moderate

Promotion Opportunities: With experience and the proper education, an individual might advance to teaching, research, and administrative positions.

This field is expected to grow rapidly due to increasing emphasis on rehabilitation and long-term care. Anticipated growth in surgery for elderly patients should stimulate a need for therapists to assist in the recovery of hip and knee replacements; as baby-boomers age, there will also be an increase in heart disease and strokes, which will require treatment by experienced physical therapists. Opportunities for individuals in private practice should grow in coming years, as hospitals cut back on the length of patients' stays, and treatment becomes more intensive.

PHYSICIAN (GENERAL PRACTICE)

Ranking: 36

Score: 142

Job Growth: 79%

Promotion Potential: Low

Promotion Opportunities: After graduation from medical school, all physicians must complete a two year residency. Physicians who have completed this residency period may enter private practice, or accept salaried positions with hospitals, clinics, or health maintenance organizations. A small number of physicians advance to prestigious research or administrative positions.

Employment opportunities in this field are expected to increase rapidly through the year 2005, as the growing U.S. elderly population creates unprecedented demand for intensive health care.

PHYSICIAN ASSISTANT

Ranking: 47

Score: 129

Job Growth: 77%

Promotion Potential: Low

Promotion Opportunities: All physicians assistants must complete a four-year program of paraprofessional training. Experienced workers advance to more responsible assignments with higher earnings.

Employment opportunities for medical assistants are expected to increase very rapidly through the year 2005, as the growing U.S. elderly population creates unprecedented demand for intensive health care.

PHYSICIST

Ranking: 160

Score: -4

Job Growth: -7%

Promotion Potential: Moderate

Promotion Opportunities: Physicists with colleges and universities may advance to tenured faculty positions, and to supervisory or directorial

positions on research projects. In the private sector, some entrepreneurs form their own companies.

Funding for private sector research and development will increase slowly, opening up a minimum number jobs in this profession. Employment of physicists in defense-related research will depend on national political and economic factors.

PHYSIOLOGIST

Ranking: 76

Score: 74

Job Growth: 70%

Promotion Potential: Low

Promotion Opportunities: Fledgling physiologists are often assigned to relatively simple, routine research projects. Experienced workers receive more responsible assignments, and may transfer to larger, more prestigious institutions.

Employment opportunities in this field are expected to increase nicely through the year 2005. Workers with advanced degrees will have the best prospects for continued employment.

PIANO TUNER

Ranking: 182

Score: -26

Job Growth: 20%

Promotion Potential: Low

Promotion Opportunities: Piano tuners who work for large music shops or repair firms can advance to supervisory positions. Many others opt for self-employment.

Job opportunities for tuners will increase very slightly through the 1990s, with most openings occurring to replace retiring personnel. Ample demand will exist for highly trained workers, but there will be few positions for untrained or apprentice piano tuners. Most openings will occur in affluent areas with sizable populations.

PLASTERER

Ranking: 217

Score: -62

Job Growth: 36%

Promotion Potential: Moderate

Promotion Opportunities: Experienced workers in this field may be promoted to supervisor, superintendent, or contract estimator. Others establish their own contracting processes.

Employment opportunities for plasterers should will increase very slightly through the next decade.

Employment of plasterers declined substantially in the 1960s and 1970s, as many contractors switched to drywall construction. This decline has been halted recently, and employment of plasterers has remained fairly static.

PLUMBER

Ranking: 184

Score: -29

Job Growth: 18%

Promotion Potential: Moderate

Promotion Opportunities: Most competent apprentices become licensed plumbers after 4-5 years of on-the-job training. Many experienced plumbers advance to supervisory positions, or establish their own contracting companies.

Employment opportunities for plumbers will increase moderately through the year 2005. The high pay and modest educational requirements of this field attract many qualified applicants, so competition for plumbing apprenticeships will be intense.

PODIATRIST

Ranking: 41

Score: 138

Job Growth: 83%

Promotion Potential: Low

Promotion Opportunities: Most beginning practitioners establish their own practices or purchase existing practices. Those who begin in salaried positions usually branch out on their own after one or two years.

Employment opportunities will increase dramatically through the next decade. The growing popularity of fast-paced sports like soccer, jogging, fast-walking and running (and the accompanying growth of sports-related foot injuries) should fuel demand for podiatric care.

POLICE OFFICER

Ranking: 72

Score: 82

Job Growth: 29%

Promotion Potential: Moderate

Promotion Opportunities: Most individuals begin their careers as patrol officers. Experienced officers may advance to detective or supervisory posts such as Captain, or Superintendent.

Employment opportunities in this field are expected to increase steadily through the next decade, as the nation affirms its resolve to alleviate street crime. Most new positions will be concentrated in major urban centers.

POLITICAL SCIENTIST

Ranking: 99

Score: 48

Job Growth: 45%

Promotion Potential: Moderate

Promotion Opportunities: Most in this field begin their careers as graduate assistants or assistant professors at small colleges and universities. Experienced political scientists may transfer to more prestigious posts at larger institutions.

Employment opportunities in this field are expected to modestly increase through the next decade. However, the number of advanced degrees awarded in the social sciences will continue to outnumber available positions, so competition in this field will be intense.

POSTAL INSPECTOR

Ranking: 78

Score: 70

Job Growth: 18%

Promotion Potential: Moderate

Promotion Opportunities: Postal inspectors whose job performance is satisfactory, advance to a specified "full performance level". Beyond this level, advancement is merit-based, and extremely competitive.

Employment opportunities in this field are expected to increase slowly through the next decade, as strict controls on government spending continue.

PRECISION ASSEMBLER

Ranking: 216

Score: -61

Job Growth: -14%

Promotion Potential: Moderate

Promotion Opportunities: Competent workers in this profession can advance to the positions of inspector, supervisor, or product repairer.

Employment prospects will plummet occupation over the next decade. Movement of assembly operations to foreign countries, where labor is cheaper, may also adversely affect job opportunities for workers in this field in the near future. The trend toward automation will contribute to some loss of jobs, but the skills and precision of these workers is not easily duplicated by machine, and thus the effects of automation on employment in this profession will be limited.

PRESIDENT (U.S.)

Ranking: 250

Score: -199

Job Growth: 0%

Promotion Potential: None

Promotion Opportunities: While holding the highest elected office in the nation, the President has no direct opportunity for promotion. Often the President seeks re-election and will serve another four-year term.

This is the most sought after of all government positions and to even run for this office, one has already followed a most competitive path. Historically, presidents who completed a second term or were not elected a second time around take on advisory roles in assorted political and commercial arenas. This in addition to remaining a U.S. representative either in an official or non-official capacity. Many former presidents capitalize on their achievements to benefit charitable organizations and other philanthropic activities.

PROTESTANT MINISTER

Ranking: 21

Score: 175

Job Growth: 68%

Promotion Potential: Moderate

Promotion Opportunities: The church often rewards experienced ministers with assignment to large or affluent congregations.

Employment opportunities for Protestant ministers will increase very slightly over the next decade. The number of ordained divinity school graduates has grown markedly in recent years, so competition for ministries should be intense. Most openings in this field will arise from the need to replace retiring workers. Ministers willing to work in rural areas should have slightly better job prospects than those seeking metropolitan or suburban congregations.

PSYCHIATRIST

Ranking: 46

Score: 132

Job Growth: 79%

Promotion Potential: Low

Promotion Opportunities: After graduation from medical school, psychiatrists must complete a general medical internship, and a special rotation in psychiatric medicine. Psychiatrists who have completed this residency period, may enter private practice, or accept salaried positions with hospitals, clinics, or health maintenance organizations. A small number of psychiatrists advance to prestigious research or administrative positions.

Employment opportunities are expected to increase rapidly through the year 2005, as members of the "baby-boom" generation mature and become candidates for mental health care.

PSYCHOLOGIST

Ranking: 29

Score: 163

Job Growth: 108%

Promotion Potential: Moderate

Promotion Opportunities: Experienced psychologists often establish private practices. Others are promoted to senior or supervisory positions.

Employment opportunities for qualified psychologists will increase very rapidly through the year 2005. Although openings will be plentiful in most specialties, competition for academic positions will be very intense. Experienced individuals holding doctorates from major universities will have the best chance of securing these prestigious appointments.

PUBLIC RELATIONS EXECUTIVE

Ranking: 82

Score: 63

Job Growth: 59%

Promotion Potential: Moderate

Promotion Opportunities: Individuals starting in this profession usually begin in entry-level positions, and are later granted more difficult assignments. Promotions to supervisory positions develop as workers prove their capabilities, and some more experienced individuals start their own consulting firms.

Because individuals in this profession often move to related positions in management, turnover is relatively high in this field. However, this is a popular profession, due to the excitement that is often associated with its responsibilities, and the competition is sometimes fierce. Those with experience in media have the best edge in obtaining jobs in this field. Public relations specialists are concentrated in large cities throughout the United States.

PUBLICATION EDITOR

Ranking: 89

Score: 55

Job Growth: 52%

Promotion Potential: Good

Promotion Opportunities: Most individuals begin as proofreaders, researchers, or writers, and may advance to editorial positions after gaining experience. Some editors eventually become publishers. Others have the opportunity to teach in journalism schools.

The job outlook for editors is expected to remain strong over the next decade, due to the increasing communications needs of an information-based society. The turnover rate is relatively high in this field, because editors often transfer to other occupations. However, the number of aspirants seeking to enter this profession more than offsets the number of openings created by turnover. This field is highly competitive, and many persons hoping to enter this profession begin in low-paying, entry-level positions, such as proofreader or copy editor. Employment prospects for editors are best in large publishing centers such as New York, Chicago, and Los Angeles.

PURCHASING AGENT

Ranking: 168

Score: -14

Job Growth: 32%

Promotion Potential: Moderate

Promotion Opportunities: Experienced and highly competent purchasing agents can advance to the positions of assistant purchasing manager, purchasing manager, vice-president of materials management, and president of materials management.

Employment opportunities for purchasing agents will increase moderately through the year 2005, as the volume of consumer goods and services grows. Most new openings will occur in the manufacturing sector, and will be concentrated in heavily populated areas. Individuals holding

MBA's will have the best employment prospects in this profession in the coming areas.

RABBI

Ranking: 184

Score: -29

Job Growth: 68%

Promotion Potential: Low

Promotion Opportunities: Newly ordained rabbis often serve as assistants to more experienced clergy members. They frequently head small congregations until they gain the necessary experience to work with larger, more well-established congregations.

Job opportunities in this area are divided among the four major branches of Judaism. While competition is stiff among Orthodox clergy due to a rapid increase in enrollment rates in Orthodox seminaries, those members of the Reform, Conservative, and Reconstructionist branches should fare much better. Other opportunities for employment exist in Jewish social service agencies, educational institutions, and the U.S. military.

RACE CAR DRIVER (INDY CLASS)

Ranking: 11

Score: 211

Job Growth: 11%

Promotion Potential: Low

Promotion Opportunities: Race drivers usually begin their careers by competing in "open" races in less competitive divisions. As they gather experience they may advance by securing the requisite financial sponsorship to enter Indy Class races.

Employment opportunities for Indy drivers are expected to increase modestly through the next decade, as the growing U.S. population creates additional demand for all manners of entertainment. Competition in this field, however, is extremely intense, and only the most skilled workers can reasonably expect steady employment.

RAILROAD CONDUCTOR

Ranking: 190

Score: -35

Job Growth: 63%

Promotion Potential: Low

Promotion Opportunities: Experienced workers can advance to non- traveling supervisory positions.

Employment opportunities in this field are expected to decline significantly through the next decade, as more passengers opt for the speed and convenience of air travel. Most available positions will be found in major urban areas with large train yards.

REAL ESTATE AGENT

Ranking: 148

Score: 4

Job Growth: 47%

Promotion Potential: Moderate

Promotion Opportunities: Experienced agents in large firms often advance to sales manager or general manager. Others establish their own real estate agencies.

Employment opportunities in this field are expected to increase modestly through the next decade, with growing demand for sales and rental properties. Real estate positions are available throughout the nation, but most will be concentrated in large urban and suburban areas.

RECEPTIONIST

Ranking: 121

Score: 30

Job Growth: 77%

Promotion Potential: Low

Promotion Opportunities: Many receptionists advance to secretarial and clerical positions involving additional responsibilities.

Job opportunities for receptionists will increase markedly in the coming decade. The growth of the service sector of the economy will create an exceptional demand for full and part-time reception personnel. brightest job prospects.

RECREATION WORKER

Ranking: 112

Score: 40

Job Growth: 86%

Promotion Potential: Moderate

Promotion Opportunities: Recreation workers with experience, certification or Bachelor's degrees often advance to supervisory or administrative positions. Some work on development or institutional recreation programs.

Employment opportunities for recreation workers will grow rapidly in the coming years, due to increased leisure time among the population, and a rise in recreational demand in nursing homes and other health care facilities. Commercial recreation will offer the best job prospects, since government budget priorities often place parks and recreation funding among the first to be cut when resources are scarce.

REPORTER

Ranking: 54

Score: 112

Job Growth: 59%

Promotion Potential: Good

Promotion Opportunities: "Cub" reporters usually begin their careers with relatively routine assignments for small or amateur publications. As they gain experience and reputation, reporters usually move to more prestigious publications.

Employment opportunities for reporters are expected to increase through the year 2005, as the growing U.S. population creates new demand for news reportage. However, job seekers will continue to greatly outnumber available positions in this highly competitive field, and only the most talented, aggressive workers can expect steady employment.

RESPIRATORY THERAPIST

Ranking: 12

Score: 193

Job Growth: 90%

Promotion Potential: Moderate

Promotion Opportunities: Respiratory therapists often advance by switching from care of "general" to "critical" patients. Others may be promoted to supervisory and managerial positions.

Therapists with additional academic training may direct departments of respiratory therapy. Employment opportunities in this field will increase rapidly through the next decade, as the average age of the U.S. population rises. Many openings will occur in home therapy, and HMO's should also provide excellent job prospects.

ROOFER

Ranking: 202

Score: -46

Job Growth: 50%

Promotion Potential: Low

Promotion Opportunities: Roofers often advance to supervisory positions for roofing contractors. Others establish their own contracting businesses.

Employment opportunities in this field will increase modestly through the 1990s. Most openings will come in the summer and spring, since roofing work is difficult during inclement weather. Long-lasting, high-technology shingles will decrease the demand for re-roofing, but new construction will provide many new jobs. Roofers will be less affected by economic downturns than workers in other construction trades.

ROUSTABOUT

Ranking: 242

Score: -122

Job Growth: -74%

Promotion Potential: Moderate

Promotion Opportunities: As roustabouts gain experience, they are assigned to more complex skilled tasks. Those attached to maintenance crews may graduate to switcher, gager, oil pumper, or head maintenance operator. Drillers with 6 months experience can become floor hands, rotary helpers or roughnecks (pipe guiders).

Little growth in opportunities for roustabouts is expected through the next decade. Virtually all openings will arise from replacement needs. Approximately 85% of all roustabouts are employed in eight states: Texas, Louisiana, Oklahoma, California, Colorado, Wyoming, Kansas, and New Mexico.

SALES REPRESENTATIVE (WHOLESALE)

Ranking: 114

Score: 37

Job Growth: 32%

Promotion Potential: Moderate

Promotion Opportunities: Experienced wholesale trade workers with exceptional sales skills may advance to supervisor or sales manager. A few are promoted to executive marketing positions.

Employment opportunities for wholesale sales workers should increase rapidly through the mid-1990s, as the volume of goods produced in the U.S. economy grows. The turnover rate in this occupation is exceptionally high, so most openings will arise to replace those who leave the work force.

SALESPERSON (RETAIL)

Ranking: 153

Score: 1

Job Growth: 47%

Promotion Potential: Moderate

Promotion Opportunities: Inexperienced sales workers in large retail establishments are generally assigned to departments where customers need little assistance—like house wares and notions. As they gain experience they may move to more responsible assignments in departments like furniture and major appliances. Workers with exceptional leadership skills often advance to supervisory and administrative positions.

Employment opportunities for retail salespersons are expected to increase nicely through the year 2005, as the growing U.S. population creates new demand for retail goods. During peak sales periods, like the Christmas holiday, many additional temporary positions will be available in this field.

SCHOOL PRINCIPAL

Ranking: 148

Score: 4

Job Growth: 52%

Promotion Potential: Low

Promotion Opportunities: Experienced workers in this field may advance by moving to larger, more prestigious schools, or they may be promoted to school district superintendent.

Employment opportunities for school principals should increase nicely through the next decade. Public school enrollments, which declined substantially in the 1960s and 1970s, have begun to rise again, but most openings in this field will still arise to replace retiring workers.

SEAMAN

Ranking: 239

Score: -106

Job Growth: -11%

Promotion Potential: Low

Promotion Opportunities: Most workers enter this occupation as ordinary seamen or marine oilers, and eventually advance to the more skilled position of "able-bodied seaman." Seamen with exceptional leadership ability may be promoted to "mate."

Employment opportunities for seamen are expected to increase modestly through the year 2005, as expansion in the U.S. manufacturing sector creates new demand for freight transportation.

SECRETARY

Ranking: 140

Score: 11

Job Growth: 9%

Promotion Potential: Moderate

Promotion Opportunities: Advancement to positions such as administrative assistant, clerical or secretarial supervisor, or office manager are possible.

Technical developments, such as increasing reliance on personal computers to perform office tasks is expected to take jobs from secretaries in the coming years. The market for individuals in this field remains strong, however. The need for persons who can perform in an administrative capacity will continue because these duties require personal contact that computers cannot provide. Salaries vary with responsibilities and experience and type of employer. Jobs are found throughout the country.

SET DESIGNER

Ranking: 221

Score: -69

Job Growth: 29%

Promotion Potential: Low

Promotion Opportunities: Set designers may advance to supervisory positions, or transfer to other creative occupations.

Employment in design occupations will grow rapidly through the next decade. Competition for entry-level design positions, though, is fierce, and job seekers with only average talent or weak formal education will find placement very difficult. Because this is a very small field, most openings will arise to replace those who leave the work force.

SEWAGE PLANT OPERATOR

Ranking: 105

Score: 44

Job Growth: 41%

Promotion Potential: Low

Promotion Opportunities: Sewage plant operators with high school diplomas and several years ex-

perience may advance to the position of plant supervisor or superintendent. Educational prerequisites, though, are rising in modern sewage treatment centers; some require college degrees of their supervisory personnel.

Employment of sewage plant operators will increase steadily through 1995. Most future new workers will staff plants now under construction in major urban areas. Later, openings will primarily arise from the transfer of experienced workers to other industries.

SHEET METAL WORKER

Ranking: 240

Score: -109

Job Growth: 38%

Promotion Potential: Low

Promotion Opportunities: Seasoned sheet-metal workers often assume supervisory positions or establish their own contracting businesses.

Opportunities in this field will increase steadily through the next decade, with most openings arising from the departure of current workers. Although overall employment will rise, sheet-metal workers may be subject to long layoffs during periods of economic sluggishness. Seasonal unemployment of sheet-metal fabricators and installers, however, will will be substantially less severe than in other construction trades.

SHIPPING/RECEIVING CLERK

Ranking: 105

Score: 44

Job Growth: 41%

Promotion Potential: Moderate

Promotion Opportunities: Experienced workers in this field may advance to head traffic clerk, head shipping clerk, head receiving clerk, warehouse manager, or purchasing agent. A few outstanding workers enter the related field of industrial traffic management

Employment opportunities for shipping and receiving clerks should increase modestly through the next decade, as growth in the manufacturing sector lags behind that of the overall economy. Most openings will occur in heavily industrialized urban areas.

SHOE MAKER/REPAIRER

Ranking: 249

Score: -193

Job Growth: -45%

Promotion Potential: Low

Promotion Opportunities: Many experienced shoe repairers open their own repair and custom production shops. Others advance to managerial and supervisory positions at larger shops.

Employment opportunities for shoe repair workers should decline through the year 2005, as the availability of high-durability, low-cost footwear increases. Most openings will arise to replace experienced repairers who leave the work force. Job prospects in "while-you-wait" repair shops should be somewhat brighter than in other sectors of this industry.

SINGER

Ranking: 160

Score: -4

Job Growth: 56%

Promotion Potential: Low

Promotion Opportunities: Many experienced singers with formal musical training become full or part-time voice coaches.

Employment opportunities for singers will increase greatly through the next decade. However, there are many more job seekers than available positions in this competitive field, and only the most talented and persistent individuals can reasonably expect steady employment. Most singers reside in major metropolitan entertainment centers including New York, Los Angeles and Nashville, Tennessee.

SOCIAL WORKER

Ranking: 109

Score: 42

Job Growth: 90%

Promotion Potential: Moderate

Promotion Opportunities: Qualified social workers usually advance to supervisory, administrative, or directorial positions at social, educational, and welfare agencies.

A few experienced workers establish private practices. Employment opportunities in social work should increase quickly through the middle of the next decade, as the U.S. population ages. Openings in private agencies and health maintenance organizations (HMOs) will be plentiful.

Positions in public agencies, hospitals, and educational institutions will be slightly scarcer.

SOCIOLOGIST

Ranking: 96

Score: 49

Job Growth: 45%

Promotion Potential: Moderate

Promotion Opportunities: Sociologists on university faculties can advance to tenured teaching positions, or move into academic administration. Others may advance to policy-making positions in government.

Individuals with backgrounds in research and quantitative methods, including survey techniques and computer science, will find the most opportunities for employment. Sociologists with training in business administration and public policy are also attractive to employers.

SOFTWARE ENGINEER

Ranking: 21

Score: 175

Job Growth: 72%

Promotion Potential: Moderate

Promotion Opportunities: Advancing software engineers progress to senior then principal software engineers prior to deciding upon whether to specialize in more technical areas or leadership roles. Those taking the technical route become support supervisors and advance to support manager. Others following the leadership path become more senior project leaders and ultimately "systems architects."

Employment opportunities for software engineers are expected to increase very rapidly through the next decade, as computer usage and development continues to expand upon this discipline. Job prospects are brightest for those with a masters degree in computer science.

SPEECH PATHOLOGIST

Ranking: 26

Score: 168

Job Growth: 115%

Promotion Potential: Low

Promotion Opportunities: Experienced speech pathologists working for hospitals or other health care establishments can advance to administrative positions, or move into private practice.

Most new jobs for pathologists will be in hospitals, nursing homes, and rehabilitation centers. The number of speech pathologists in private practice is also expected to grow sharply, due to a rise in the incidence of home health care, and a commensurate need for professional consultants. Liberalized insurance plans will make speech therapy available to a wider range of people.

SPORTS INSTRUCTOR

Ranking: 109

Score: 42

Job Growth: 88%

Promotion Potential: Low

Promotion Opportunities: Employees of large gymnasiums, health clubs, or social clubs, or social centers may advance to supervisory or administrative positions.

Employment opportunities for sports instructors are expected to increase modestly through the next decade, as the health and fitness consciousness of the U.S. population increases. Residents of population centers should have the best prospects for employment and advancement.

STATIONARY ENGINEER

Ranking: 80

Score: 65

Job Growth: 11%

Promotion Potential: Moderate

Promotion Opportunities: Experienced stationary engineers are often rewarded with positions, such as supervisor. A few skilled workers may become boiler inspectors, plant engineers, examining engineers, or building and plant superintendents.

Employment opportunities for stationary engineers will hold steady through the year 2005. Technological advances, including computerization, will offset the growing industrial demand for mechanical and electrical energy anticipated in the coming decade. Most openings for stationary engineers will occur in heavily populated, industrial areas.

STATISTICIAN

Ranking: 124

Score: 24

Job Growth: 20%

Promotion Potential: Moderate

Promotion Opportunities: Experienced statisticians with advanced degrees often advance to supervisory positions.

Jobs for statisticians should be readily available through the end of the decade, especially for those with backgrounds in computer science. Most openings will come in large metropolitan areas, and will arise primarily to replace experienced statisticians who leave the work force. Federal and state agencies will require many statisticians, particularly those with expertise in agricultural, labor, educational, or health statistics.

STENOGRAPHER/COURT REPORTER

Ranking: 203

Score: -48

Job Growth: -2%

Promotion Potential: Low

Promotion Opportunities: Stenographers frequently advance to executive secretarial positions, and stenographers with a great deal of experience and exceptional dictation skills can also become executive secretaries or shorthand reporters.

Job opportunities for stenographers are projected to decrease very markedly within the next ten years, due in large part to the increased use of dictation machines. The demand for experienced stenographic court reporters, however, is actually projected to increase, as criminal and civil court case loads grow heavier.

STEVEDORE

Ranking: 175

Score: -17

Job Growth: 29%

Promotion Potential: Low

Promotion Opportunities: Experienced workers in this field occasionally advance to dock supervisor, but generally promotion opportunities are very limited.

Employment opportunities for longshoremen are expected to increase modestly through the year 2005, as expansion in the U.S. manufacturing sector creates new demand for transportation of raw materials and durable goods.

STOCKBROKER

Ranking: 176

Score: -19

Job Growth: 74%

Promotion Potential: Low

Promotion Opportunities: The principal form of advancement for stockbrokers is an increase in the number, importance and size of the accounts that they handle. A few brokers with exceptional managerial skills are promoted to branch office manager.

Employment opportunities for stock brokers should increase very rapidly through the next decade, as public interest in equity investment continues its astronomical growth. Workers with college-level degrees in economics and finance should have the best prospects for employment.

SURGEON

Ranking: 119

Score: 185

Job Growth: 35%

Promotion Potential: Low

Promotion Opportunities: Surgeons may advance to chiefs of staff at the hospitals at which they are affiliated.

Employment opportunities will reflect changing patterns in surgical practice over the next decade. As the population ages, the amount of surgical procedures will increase. Advances in out-patient and ambulatory surgery, which can often be performed in clinics or physicians' offices, will make surgery more palatable and cost effective for patients, hence more surgerical procedures are expected overall. Major surgery is expected to be unaffected by this trend. Insurance pay-out limitations may negatively affect incomes.

SURVEYOR

Ranking: 119

Score: 32

Job Growth: 29%

Promotion Potential: Moderate

Promotion opportunities: Individuals with training in surveying beyond the secondary level generally begin their careers as technicians. After a few years experience they may advance to a team chief of licensed surveying firm.

The slump in new construction is anticipated to slow growth in new job opportunities. Employment, however, will probably fluctuate considerably, since construction activity is highly cyclical.

SYMPHONY CONDUCTOR

Ranking: 68

Score: 85

Job Growth: 11%

Promotion Potential: Low

Promotion Opportunities: Most conductors begin their careers with small or amateur orchestras. As they gain experience and recognition they may advance to assignments with more prestigious professional symphonies.

Employment opportunities for conductors are expected to increase very slightly through the year 2005. However, competition in this field is extremely intense, and only the most talented and aggressive individuals can expect steady employment.

TAX EXAMINER/COLLECTOR

Ranking: 36

Score: 143

Job Growth: 41%

Promotion Potential: Moderate

Promotion Opportunities: Experienced workers in this field may be promoted to supervisory or executive positions in the Internal Revenue Service.

Employment opportunities for tax examiners are expected to increase modestly through the year 2005, with the expansion of the U.S. tax base. Workers with experience in commercial accounting should have the brightest prospects for employment.

TAXI DRIVER

Ranking: 204

Score: -49

Job Growth: 47%

Promotion Potential: Low

Promotion Opportunities: Experienced drivers with managerial ability occasionally advance to dispatcher or other taxi-related administrative position. Others purchase their own taxis and acquire independent operation permits.

Employment opportunities for taxi drivers should increase steadily through the next decade, with the additional transportation needs of the growing U.S. population. The great majority of openings in this field will arise in major urban areas.

TEACHER

Ranking: 122

Score: 29

Job Growth: 77%

Promotion Potential: Low

Promotion Opportunities: Experienced teachers may advance to administrative, supervisory, or specialized instructional positions. A few establish private schools, pre-schools, or day- care centers.

Employment opportunities for kindergarten, elementary, and secondary teachers should improve markedly through the year 2005, as school enrollments climb and pupil-teachers ratios are decreased. Positions for elementary teachers should be especially plentiful, as "grammar school" enrollment increases from 27.2 million to almost 32 million in the next decade.

TEACHER'S AIDE

Ranking: 96

Score: 49

Job Growth: 97%

Promotion Potential: Low

Promotion Opportunities: Many aides earn their bachelor's degree and become certified teachers. For others, advancement comes in the form of increased responsibility and additional earnings.

Employment of teacher's aides will increase rapidly through the end of the decade, reflecting the growing enrollment of the nation's elementary schools. Job opportunities will be especially plentiful in Southern states, which are expected to encounter heavy migration. occupations.

TECHNICAL WRITER

Ranking: 91

Score: 54

Job Growth: 52%

Promotion Potential: Low

Promotion Opportunities: Newly-hired technical writers are usually assigned relatively routine rewrites or administratvie editorial tasks. As they gain experience they move to more complex assignments and may be promoted to supervisory or administrative positions including editorships or publishers' positions.

Employment opportunities for technical writers are expected to expand rapidly through the year 2005, as the commercial sector struggles to explain its increasingly complex products to con-

sumers. Available positions in this field will be concentrated in heavily industrialized areas, particulary in the Northwestern United States.

TELEPHONE INSTALLER/ REPAIRER

Ranking: 238

Score: -101

Job Growth: -54%

Promotion Potential: Moderate

Promotion Opportunities: With supplementary training, telephone installer-repairers can advance to installation supervisor, sales or customer service representative, PBX installer, and switching equipment technician.

Employment of telephone installer-repairers will decline through the next decade, as technological advances and private phone ownership reduce the need for skilled repair personnel.

TELEPHONE OPERATOR

Ranking: 241

Score: -110

Job Growth: -63%

Promotion Potential: Moderate

Promotion Opportunities: After one or two years of experience, public telephone operators may be promoted to junior service assistant, service observer, or supervisor. Some public operators advance to technical positions such as installer and repairer . Experienced PBX operators, in large firms, often move to more responsible clerical positions.

Employment prospects for PBX operators will be good through the end of the decade, but jobs for telephone company operators will be hard to find. Employment for public operators has declined for the past 25 years, as technological innovations have increased operator efficiency and reduced the need for manual switching.

TICKET AGENT

Ranking: 126

Score: 22

Job Growth: 68%

Promotion Potential: Low

Promotion Opportunities: Experienced workers in this field, with excellent inter-personal skills, may advance to supervisory positions. A few skilled agents are promoted to field sales agent or district sales manager.

Employment opportunities for ticket agents should increase rapidly through the next decade, however, automation and other productivity improvements is likely to counteract the growing demand for their services, offering jobs, but lower, unskilled ones which will not pay well compared to other fields.

TOOL-AND-DIE MAKER

Ranking: 167

Score: -13

Job Growth: -16%

Promotion Potential: Moderate

Promotion Opportunities: Experienced employees of large tool- and-die firms often advance to supervisory and administrative positions. Others become tool designers, and a few establish their own tool-and-die shops.

Employment opportunities for tool-and-die makers will increase very slightly through the next decade. A growing national demand for motor vehicles, aircraft, and other machinery will create some new jobs; but increased use of non-metal parts in heavy manufacturing industries will ultimately limit growth in this field.

TRAVEL AGENT

Ranking: 93

Score: 51

Job Growth: 149%

Promotion Potential: Low

Promotion Opportunities: Individuals advance as they gain experience in this field. A skilled agent might become an office manager or attain a management position in a larger agency.

Deregulation and price wars should contribute to an increase in travel by the general public. However, travel is affected by swings in the economy, and long-distance travel may be particularly affected by downward trends. Salaries vary with experience of the worker, and size and location of the agency. Opportunities for agents exist throughout the country, but are most abundant in large metropolitan areas, where most corporate clients are based.

TRUCK DRIVER

Ranking: 196

Score: -38

Job Growth: 59%

Promotion Potential: Low

Promotion Opportunities: A few local, short-haul truck drivers are promoted to dispatching, managerial, and scheduling positions. Others advance to long-haul and specialty truck driving. Long-haul drivers occasionally purchase their own tractor-trailers.

The trucking industry provides thousands of job openings each year. Competition for these is intense, since earnings are high and little formal training is required. Demand for truck drivers should increase modestly through the 1990s, as U.S. freight volume increases. Most jobs will be concentrated in and around large cities.

TYPIST/WORD PROCESSOR

Ranking: 227

Score: -84

Job Growth: -36%

Promotion Potential: Moderate

Promotion Opportunities: Typists often transfer to other clerical occupations: secretary, statistical clerk, and stenographer. A small number go on to office supervisory positions.

Word-processing machines have greatly improved the productivity of individual typists, and have reduced the number of new personnel needed. Workers with high typing speed and a familiarity with popular word-processing systems will have the best prospects for employment.

UNDERTAKER

Ranking: 63

Score: 95

Job Growth: 41%

Promotion Potential: Low

Promotion Opportunities: Workers usually enter this occupation as assistants to experienced professionals, and learn their skills informally on the job. Some undertakers may advance to funeral director.

Employment opportunities are expected to increase only slightly through the year 2005, as life expectancies in the U.S. increase. Most openings in this field will arise in major population centers, to replace retiring workers.

URBAN/REGIONAL PLANNER

Ranking: 58

Score: 106

Job Growth: 52%

Promotion Potential: Moderate

Promotion Opportunities: Individuals entering this field normally start as assistant city planners, then advance to urban planner and planning director. Transferring to larger cities, where urban planning programs are more expansive, can offer opportunities for greater advancement.

Local government spending on urban planning will be very limited, and competition for available jobs in this profession will be strong. Urban planners with advanced degrees, and with good communication skills and analytical ability, will be most successful in finding jobs. Willingness to relocate will help urban planners in the job search.

VENDING MACHINE REPAIRER

Ranking: 197

Score: -39

Job Growth: 7%

Promotion Potential: Low

Promotion Opportunities: Skilled vending machine repairers and servicers often advance to supervisory positions. Some with good managerial abilities and professional contacts open their own companies.

Employment opportunities for vending machine repairers will increase modestly in the coming decade. Many jobs will open as workers retire or leave the profession. The demand for vending machine products, and the variety of products sold by this means, will grow. Repairers with training in electronics will enjoy the best job prospects in this field.

VETERINARIAN

Ranking: 48

Score: 128

Job Growth: 74%

Promotion Potential: Low

Promotion Opportunities: Newly licensed veterinarians often enter into partnership with established practitioners, until they acquire the experience and capital to fund their own practices.

Employment opportunities for veterinarians are expected to increase rapidly through the next decade, with the growing popularity of companion animals. However, the number of veterinary graduates has doubled since the 1960s, and new vets can expect stiff competition.

VOCATIONAL COUNSELOR

Ranking: 21

Score: 175

Job Growth: 72%

Promotion Potential: Good

Promotion Opportunities: Experienced counselors can advance to positions in educational administration. Some individuals become researchers, consultants, or teachers.

Employment opportunities for school and college counselors will increase nicely over the next ten years. Job prospects for counselors in elementary schools, where no enrollment drop is anticipated, will remain steady. However, student enrollment in secondary schools and colleges is expected to decline, and the number of jobs for counselors in these institutions will decrease accordingly. Counseling positions can be found throughout the nation, and are most concentrated in heavily populated areas.

WAITER/WAITRESS

Ranking: 44

Score: 133

Job Growth: 81%

Promotion Potential: Moderate

Promotion Opportunities: Because of the small size of most eating and drinking establishments, opportunities for advancement are very limited. A few experienced workers secure supervisory, host/hostess, and maitre d' positions.

Competition will be keen for positions in high-paying expensive eateries, but there will be many opportunities at more moderately priced establishments.

WELDER

Ranking: 190

Score: -35

Job Growth: -38%

Promotion Potential: Moderate

Promotion Opportunities: Welders' apprentices and assistants need several years of on-the-job training to master the skills of a precision welder. Precision welders may be promoted to welding inspectors, technicians, or supervisors.

The slump in construction, manufacturing and production has clouded the future for welders. The trend of using prefabricated steel will keep job growth low.

ZOOLOGIST

Ranking: 126

Score: 22

Job Growth: 18%

Promotion Potential: Moderate

Promotion Opportunities: Most recent zoology graduates are assigned to relatively simple, routine research projects, and as they gain experience they advance to more responsible and complex assignments. Employees of zoos and game reserves with exceptional managerial skills may advance to zoo manager or other administrative positions.

Recent interest in conservation and nature have increase demand for zoologists. Those with advanced, specialized academic degrees should have the best prospects for continued employment.

Physical Demands

Hard physical labor is not the only thing that makes us tired. Almost everyone who starts wading through his tax forms on April 14th, a day before the filing deadline, will attest to being as tired as a lumberjack when the job is done.

Some occupations, such as surveying or supervising a construction job, tax our bodies through exposure to weather. But even those jobs that seem largely based on brainpower can be physically draining. Desk-bound, sedentary workers who sit all day can experience fatigue, which can interfere with the ability to work. Ironically, desk jobs that require virtually no lifting or carrying may deprive us of valuable physical exertion. The current popularity of fitness sports, especially among white-collar workers, surely is a result of the realization of the body's need to get exercise. Feeling exhausted does make us feel good under certain circumstances — especially for those who don't have a job that requires physical activity.

THE PHYSICAL FACTORS

The idea of measuring work has long fascinated physicists. They have even devised formulas for it. The Bureau of Labor Statistics has also developed ways of measuring the physical demands of work, and in part, this was used to formulate the rankings in this chapter. One method the BLS employs is similar to that used by physicists. It relies on how much weight a person is normally required to lift on the job. Five categories are specified: (1) sedentary work, which requires the occasional lifting of 10 pounds or less; (2) light work, which requires lifting a maximum of 20 pounds; (3) medium work, defined as lifting a maximum of 50 pounds, but with frequent lifting of objects weighing up to 25 pounds; (4) heavy work, which requires lifting up to 100 pounds, maximum; (5) very heavy work, which requires lifting in excess of 100 pounds, with frequent carrying of objects weighing five pounds or more.

The BLS also considers other aspects of a job's demands, such as whether a job takes place indoors or outdoors, and whether or not it involves stooping, kneeling, climbing, or balancing. Only when all these factors are considered together can the true physical demands of an occupation be determined.

The ranking system for physical demands employed in the *Jobs Rated Almanac* uses many elements measured by the BLS. However, an important criterion is added: overtime — that is, work time in excess of eight hours daily. After all, an executive working until 10 p.m. can be as tired when he gets home as a construction worker who has knocked off at 5 p.m.

THE RANKING SYSTEM

In order to compute the physical demands of each of our jobs, we awarded higher scores to careers with greater physical demands and lower scores to those with lesser demands. We arrived at these scores by compiling data used by the BLS. One points was awarded for each physical com-

183

ponent of a job. These components include lifting, pulling, pushing, standing, walking, stooping, kneeling, crawling, climbing, crouching, and reaching. We also awarded points for hazards faced, exposure to various weather conditions, the need for stamina, and the work environment.

One to five points also was added for each degree of lifting required, based on the five categories at left, which range from 10- pound lifting at sedentary jobs to 100- pound lifting for very heavy work.

One point also was added for each hour, or fraction thereof, the average worker logs in excess of 40 hour a week. These determinations were based on U.S. Census data and sundry estimates provided by those familiar with work habits in various professions.

The point total accumulated is the score used to determine the rankings.

250 Jobs Ranked by Physical Demands Scores

RANK		SCORE	RANK		SCORE
1	ASTROLOGER	3.00	34	JEWELER	6.04
2	STATISTICIAN	3.95	36	INSURANCE AGENT	6.05
3	ACTUARY	3.97	37	SECRETARY	6.06
3	MATHEMATICIAN	3.97	37	MEDICAL SECRETARY	6.06
5	EXECUTIVE SEARCH CONSULTANT	4.00	39	ATTORNEY	6.09
			39	POLITICAL SCIENTIST	6.09
6	MARKET RESEARCH ANALYST	4.09	41	AEROSPACE ENGINEER	6.21
			41	NUCLEAR ENGINEER	6.21
3	ECONOMIST	4.09	43	HOSPITAL ADMINISTRATOR	6.31
8	ACCOUNTANT	4.23			
9	ADVERTISING ACCOUNT EXECUTIVE	4.62	44	DIETICIAN	6.36
			45	PAROLE OFFICER	6.47
10	BANK OFFICER	4.76	46	NEWSCASTER	6.85
11	PUBLICATION EDITOR	4.85	46	CARTOONIST	6.85
12	ASTRONOMER	4.98	46	AUTHOR (BOOKS)	6.85
12	URBAN/REGIONAL PLANNER	4.98	46	INDUSTRIAL DESIGNER	6.85
14	SOFTWARE ENGINEER	5.00	46	ARTIST (COMMERCIAL)	6.85
14	FINANCIAL PLANNER	5.00	51	ARCHITECTURAL DRAFTER	6.92
14	AGENCY DIRECTOR (NONPROFIT)	5.00	52	HOTEL MANAGER	6.97
			53	MAYOR	6.98
14	TICKET AGENT	5.00	53	METEOROLOGIST	6.98
18	TYPIST/WORD PROCESSOR	5.03	55	CASHIER	7.00
19	COMPUTER SYSTEMS ANALYST	5.08	55	DENTAL HYGIENIST	7.00
20	JUDGE (FEDERAL)	5.09	57	STENOGRAPHER/COURT REPORTER	7.03
20	HISTORIAN	5.09	58	PSYCHOLOGIST	7.09
20	SOCIOLOGIST	5.09	59	INSURANCE UNDERWRITER	7.12
23	BOOKKEEPER	5.18	60	MOTION PICTURE EDITOR	7.16
24	SOCIAL WORKER	5.47	61	PURCHASING AGENT	7.23
25	SCHOOL PRINCIPAL	5.62	62	PUBLIC RELATIONS EXECUTIVE	7.24
26	PARALEGAL ASSISTANT	5.79			
27	PERSONNEL RECRUITER	5.84	63	STOCKBROKER	7.25
27	COMPUTER PROGRAMMER	5.84	64	MEDICAL TECHNOLOGIST	7.26
29	TECHNICAL WRITER	5.85	64	MEDICAL RECORDS TECHNICIAN	7.26
30	CORPORATE EXECUTIVE (SENIOR)	6.00	64	MEDICAL LABORATORY TECHNICIAN	7.26
30	TRAVEL AGENT	6.00			
30	RECEPTIONIST	6.00	67	TEACHER'S AIDE	7.41
33	BANK TELLER	6.03	68	AUDIOLOGIST	7.43
34	PHILOSOPHER	6.04	69	PROTESTANT MINISTER	7.44

PHYSICAL DEMANDS

RANK		SCORE	RANK		SCORE
70	ARCHITECT	7.56	105	PHYSICIAN ASSISTANT	9.36
70	LIBRARIAN	7.56	106	MUSICAL INSTRUMENT REPAIRER	9.39
71	LITHOGRAPHER/ PHOTOENGRAVER	7.82	107	SPEECH PATHOLOGIST	9.43
72	NEWSWRITER (RADIO/TV)	7.85	108	SHOE MAKER/REPAIRER	9.53
72	DISK JOCKEY	7.85	109	MUSEUM CURATOR	9.56
75	ENGINEERING TECHNICIAN	7.98	110	ADVERTISING SALESPERSON	9.58
75	PHOTOGRAPHIC PROCESS WORKER	7.98	110	SALES REPRESENTATIVE (WHOLESALE)	9.58
75	DENTAL LABORATORY TECHNICIAN	7.98	112	SHIPPING/RECEIVING CLERK	9.67
75	BIOLOGIST	7.98	113	COMPUTER OPERATOR	9.69
75	PHYSIOLOGIST	7.98	114	POSTAL INSPECTOR	9.76
75	PHYSICIST	7.98	115	OPTOMETRIST	9.79
75	TAX EXAMINER/ COLLECTOR	7.98	116	FASHION DESIGNER	9.85
			116	REPORTER (NEWSPAPER)	9.85
82	COLLEGE PROFESSOR	8.04	116	ARTIST (FINE ART)	9.85
83	INDUSTRIAL ENGINEER	8.21	116	FLORIST	9.85
83	PETROLEUM ENGINEER	8.21	120	AIR TRAFFIC CONTROLLER	9.87
85	BUYER	8.23	121	DENTIST	9.96
86	OPTICIAN	8.26	122	CHEMIST	9.98
87	FILE CLERK	8.27	123	FLIGHT ATTENDANT	10.03
88	OCCUPATIONAL THERAPIST	8.43	124	CIVIL ENGINEER	10.21
89	RABBI	8.44	125	MECHANICAL ENGINEER	10.28
89	CATHOLIC PRIEST	8.44	126	PODIATRIST	10.79
91	VOCATIONAL COUNSELOR	8.56	127	COMPOSITOR/ TYPESETTER	10.82
92	REAL ESTATE AGENT	8.58	128	PHOTOGRAPHER	10.85
93	CONGRESSPERSON/ SENATOR	8.73	129	AIRPLANE PILOT	10.87
94	BROADCAST TECHNICIAN	8.79	130	PHYSICIAN (GENERAL PRACTICE)	10.90
95	ACTOR	8.85	131	WAITER/WAITRESS	11.00
95	SET DESIGNER	8.85	131	SALESPERSON (RETAIL)	11.00
97	PHARMACIST	8.86	131	MILITARY (COMMISSIONED OFFICER)	11.00
98	ORTHODONTIST	8.96	134	ELECTRICAL ENGINEER	11.11
99	BOOKBINDER	8.98	135	AUTOMOBILE SALESPERSON	11.58
100	TELEPHONE OPERATOR	9.00	136	CHOREOGRAPHER	11.85
101	ANTHROPOLOGIST	9.09	137	TEACHER	11.87
101	ARCHEOLOGIST	9.09	138	PSYCHIATRIST	11.90
103	BARBER	9.22			
104	COSMETOLOGIST	9.30			

RANK	SCORE
139 OCEANOGRAPHER	11.98
140 ANTIQUE DEALER	12.00
141 BUS DRIVER	12.03
142 HOME ECONOMIST	12.04
143 ELECTRICAL TECHNICIAN	12.13
144 COMPUTER SERVICE TECHNICIAN	12.39
145 OFFICE MACHINE REPAIRER	12.41
146 GUARD	12.55
147 CHIROPRACTOR	12.79
148 GEOLOGIST	12.98
149 BARTENDER	13.00
150 NURSE (REGISTERED)	13.15
151 DRESSMAKER	13.29
152 ELECTRICAL EQUIPMENT REPAIRER	13.39
152 PIANO TUNER	13.39
154 CORRECTION OFFICER	13.41
155 RESPIRATORY THERAPIST	13.43
156 CHAUFFEUR	13.46
157 PRECISION ASSEMBLER	13.53
157 AUTOMOBILE ASSEMBLER	13.53
157 FASHION MODEL	13.53
160 SINGER	13.85
161 AGRICULTURAL SCIENTIST	13.98
162 FORKLIFT OPERATOR	14.09
163 ZOOLOGIST	14.19
164 PRESIDENT (U.S.)	14.20
165 APPLIANCE REPAIRER	14.39
165 VENDING MACHINE REPAIRER	14.39
165 COMMUNICATIONS EQUIPMENT MECHANIC	14.39
168 FURNITURE UPHOLSTERER	14.41
169 TAXI DRIVER	14.46
170 RAILROAD CONDUCTOR	14.77
171 SYMPHONY CONDUCTOR	14.85
172 MACHINE TOOL OPERATOR	14.86

RANK	SCORE
173 OCCUPATIONAL SAFETY/ HEALTH INSPECTOR	14.98
174 COOK/CHEF	15.00
174 NURSE (LICENSED PRACTICAL)	15.00
174 MILITARY (WARRANT OFFICER)	15.00
177 UNDERTAKER	15.15
178 TELEPHONE INSTALLER/ REPAIRER	15.39
179 PHYSICAL THERAPIST	15.43
180 SPORTS INSTRUCTOR	15.47
181 BASKETBALL COACH (NCAA)	15.73
182 MUSICIAN	15.85
182 PHOTOJOURNALIST	15.85
184 SURGEON	15.90
184 OSTEOPATH	15.90
186 CONSERVATIONIST	15.98
187 JANITOR	16.16
188 INDUSTRIAL MACHINE REPAIRER	16.39
189 TOOL-AND-DIE MAKER	16.87
190 MAID	17.00
190 NURSE'S AIDE	17.00
192 DRILL-PRESS OPERATOR	17.10
193 MACHINIST	17.46
194 AUTOMOBILE BODY REPAIRER	17.57
195 HIGHWAY PATROL OFFICER	17.63
196 VETERINARIAN	17.79
197 CARPET INSTALLER	17.85
198 SEWAGE PLANT OPERATOR	18.18
199 RECREATION WORKER	18.47
200 GLAZIER	18.85
201 AIRCRAFT MECHANIC	18.92
202 CHILD CARE WORKER	19.00
203 BUTCHER	19.98
204 HEATING/REFRIGERATION MECHANIC	20.05

PHYSICAL DEMANDS

RANK	SCORE	RANK	SCORE
205 NUCLEAR PLANT DECONTAMINATION TECHNICIAN	20.13	228 STEVEDORE	28.03
206 CONSTRUCTION FOREMAN	20.72	229 CONSTRUCTION MACHINERY OPERATOR	28.09
207 ASTRONAUT	20.73	230 WELDER	29.08
208 EMERGENCY MEDICAL TECHNICIAN	21.26	231 FISHERMAN	29.87
		232 DAIRY FARMER	30.53
209 AUTOMOBILE MECHANIC	21.57	233 SHEET METAL WORKER	30.73
210 TRUCK DRIVER	21.68	234 SEAMAN	30.77
211 PLUMBER	21.80	235 RACE CAR DRIVER (INDY CLASS)	30.85
212 DISHWASHER	22.00	235 JOCKEY	30.85
213 ELECTRICIAN	22.01	237 BRICKLAYER	32.85
214 POLICE OFFICER	22.63	238 BASEBALL UMPIRE (MAJOR LEAGUE)	33.00
215 BOILERMAKER	23.39	239 ROOFER	33.46
216 AUTOMOBILE PAINTER	23.57	240 FARMER	34.53
217 DANCER	23.85	241 CONSTRUCTION WORKER (LABORER)	36.41
218 SURVEYOR	24.11		
219 CARPENTER	25.46	242 GARBAGE COLLECTOR	36.55
220 METER READER	25.67	243 IRONWORKER	36.85
221 PLASTERER	25.85	244 ROUSTABOUT	36.89
222 PAINTER	26.00	245 BASEBALL PLAYER (MAJOR LEAGUE)	37.00
222 MILITARY (ENLISTED PERSON)	26.00	246 BASKETBALL PLAYER (NBA)	38.00
224 STATIONARY ENGINEER	26.18	247 LUMBERJACK	38.87
225 MAIL CARRIER	26.86	248 COWBOY	41.00
226 MILLWRIGHT	27.39	249 FIREFIGHTER	43.23
227 DRYWALL APPLICATOR/ FINISHER	27.85	250 FOOTBALL PLAYER (NFL)	43.73

THE WHITE-COLLAR WEARY

Physical exertion is not necessarily the exclusive domain of tradespeople and laborers. Some white-collar jobs will make even the most physically-fit individuals dog-tired. Below are the jobs at which workers generate the most elbow grease. At right of the job title is the "Physical Demand" rank.

VETERINARIAN	196	SYMPHONY CONDUCTOR	171
CONSERVATIONIST	186	PRESIDENT (U.S.)	164
SURGEON	184	ZOOLOGIST	163
OSTEOPATH	184	AGRICULTURAL SCIENTIST	161
MUSICIAN	182	SINGER	160
PHOTOJOURNALIST	182	FASHION MODEL	157
BASKETBALL COACH (NCAA)	181	CHAUFFEUR	156
PHYSICAL THERAPIST	179	BARTENDER	149
UNDERTAKER	177	GEOLOGIST	148
OCCUPATIONAL SAFETY/HEALTH INSPECTOR	173	CHIROPRACTOR	147
		HOME ECONOMIST	142

THE BLUE-COLLAR SEDENTARY

A blue collar doesn't always translate to a physically demanding job. Some tradespeople and unskilled workers have jobs at which machines, or even robots, do most of the heavy work. Below are jobs at which individuals don't work up too much of a sweat on the job. At right of the job title is the "Physical Demand" rank.

BUS DRIVER	141	COOK/CHEF	174
OFFICE MACHINE REPAIRER	145	TELEPHONE INSTALLER/ REPAIRER	178
GUARD	146	JANITOR	187
ELECTRICAL EQUIPMENT REPAIRER	152	INDUSTRIAL MACHINE REPAIRER	188
CORRECTION OFFICER	154	TOOL-AND-DIE MAKER	189
PRECISION ASSEMBLER	157	DRILL-PRESS OPERATOR	192
AUTOMOBILE ASSEMBLER	157	MACHINIST	193
FORKLIFT OPERATOR	162	AUTOMOBILE BODY REPAIRER	194
APPLIANCE REPAIRER	165	CARPET INSTALLER	197
VENDING MACHINE REPAIRER	165	SEWAGE PLANT OPERATOR	198
COMMUNICATIONS EQUIPMENT MECHANIC	165	GLAZIER	200
FURNITURE UPHOLSTERER	168	BUTCHER	203
RAILROAD CONDUCTOR	170	HEATING/REFRIGERATION MECHANIC	204
MACHINE TOOL OPERATOR	172		

ACCOUNTANT

Ranking: 8

Score: 4.23

Basic Day: 9.0 Hours

Most accountants work regular 45-hour weeks, though extended hours to meet fiscal and tax deadlines increases their average work week considerably. Those who are self-employed or who work for large firms may work longer, more irregular hours, and may be required to travel. Accountants spend most of the day sitting at desks or computers, going over information and writing reports which can cause considerable eye and back strain. Accounting calls for stamina during the tax season, when accountants have heavy work loads.

ACTOR

Ranking: 95

Score: 8.85

Basic Day: 9.0 Hours

Actors work highly irregular hours, and in a variety of environments and situations. In the course of their work, they may be required to perform a wide range of physical activities. An actor must be physically fit and have a good command of both movement and speech. Stamina is essential in the acting business, film actors often spend long hours "on location," and stage actors spend long hours in rehearsal, and may have to perform a show several times a day.

ACTUARY

Ranking: 3

Score: 3.97

Basic Day: 9.0 Hours

Actuaries are confined to their desks most of the time, although they may have to travel occasionally to consult with clients or company employees. Constant work with probabilities and statistics, often at a computer terminal, can cause eye strain. Actuaries must be able to express themselves well verbally, because they advise and train others. They communicate with a wide variety of people, from policyholders to legislators, advising them in complicated insurance matters.

ADVERTISING ACCOUNT EXECUTIVE

Ranking: 9

Score: 4.62

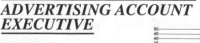

Basic Day: 9.5 Hours

Advertising account executives normally work in quiet, comfortable offices. Most of this office work is performed while sitting at desks. Heavy phone contact with clients is the norm in this profession. In the fast-paced, high pressure field of advertising, account executives are often required to travel extensively and to work overtime to meet deadlines. Consequently, account executives can suffer physical as well as mental fatigue.

ADVERTISING SALESPERSON

Ranking: 110

Score: 9.58

Basic Day: 9.5 Hours

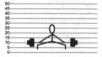

Most advertising sales representatives work a normal week of 40 hours, since advertisers and agencies generally operate during normal business hours. Salespeople may spend much of the day at desks, or moving from one business office to the next on sales calls. The pace in this profession can be fatiguing and emotionally draining. Though little physical labor is involved in this work, ad sales representatives need a personable manner, and good communication skills to negotiate and otherwise interact with advertisers and account executives.

AEROSPACE ENGINEER

Ranking: 41

Score: 6.21

Basic Day: 9 Hours

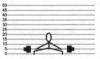

Aerospace engineers work both at desks in offices, and in labs or industrial plants. In some cases, they work at the actual construction sites where aircraft or missiles, for example, are assembled and tested. Extreme attention to detail is essential, because of the technical complexities and danger involved in space travel or weaponry. In most cases, inaccuracy in design can threaten the lives of many people. Mental and physical strain can result from this kind of pressure.

AGENCY DIRECTOR (NON PROFIT)

Physical Demands

Ranking: 14

Score: 5.00

Basic Day: 10 Hours

Long hours and frequent public presentations are offset by comfortable working environments and minimal physical exertion. Scheduling of events and meetings to coordinate with volunteers life-styles necessitates a great deal of flexibility and a commitment to work at all times. Stamina for repeated presentations and dealing with a variety of deadlines, situations and travel is essential.

AGRICULTURAL SCIENTIST

Ranking: 161
Score: 13.98
Basic Day: 9.0 Hours

Agricultural scientists work in labs, with a variety of chemicals and organic matter. They require manual dexterity in using specialized equipment to analyze plant and animal substances as part of their research in plant and animal growth. Some agricultural scientists, such as agronomists or horticulturalists, must conduct much of their research outdoors. Minimal physical exertion is required.

AIR TRAFFIC CONTROLLER

Ranking: 120
Score: 9.87
Basic Day: 9.0 Hours

Air traffic controllers sit at control panels throughout their shifts, working over 40 hours per week, on a rotating shift basis. They must have good observation skills and be able to listen and speak well in order to guide pilots in and out of airports, without mishap. Air traffic controlling calls for constant attention and complete concentration. Because air traffic controllers have so many planes, and the lives of so many passengers to think of, they suffer from considerable stress.

AIRCRAFT MECHANIC

Ranking: 201
Score: 18.92
Basic Day: 9.0 Hours

Aircraft mechanics work 40 hours per week, on day or night shifts. Most of the time in this occupation is spent in large, noisy hangars. Repairs to aircraft occasionally are performed outdoors, however, so aircraft mechanics are expected to work in a variety of weather conditions. Mechanics are required to stand, stoop, lie, stretch, climb, and lift or pull heavy objects. Good hand-to-eye coordination is necessary to make repairs accurately and safely, often under time constraints.

AIRPLANE PILOT

Ranking: 129
Score: 10.87

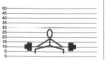

Basic Day: 9.0 Hours

Commercial airplane pilots spend about 80 hours per month in actual flight time. They must have 20/20 vision (with or without eyeglasses) and good hearing in order to operate flight equipment and insure safe air travel. Pilots are exposed to high levels of noise and vibration. They must operate under the stress of knowing that their lives, or the lives of the passengers, could be threatened at any time. Irregular hours and jet lag cause fatigue, so airplane pilots must have strong constitutions.

ANTHROPOLOGIST

Ranking: 101
Score: 9.09
Basic Day: 9.0 Hours

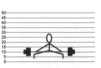

Anthropologists spend most of their time at a desk conducting research and writing about their findings. Sometimes they travel in order to gather first-hand information in remote areas, to attend meetings or to present papers. Therefore, their work requires the skills of observation and communication, as well as the wear and tear of adjusting to unfamiliar climates and surroundings.

ANTIQUE DEALER

Ranking: 140
Score: 12.00
Basic Day: 10.0 Hours

Long hours, much road travel and patient searching for antiques are part of this profession. A considerable amount of time and effort is spent talking with fellow dealers, professionals and networking with clients. Dealers must be able to make quick, knowledgeable evaluations often working under the pressure of the fast pace of an auction or show. Good communication skills are a definite asset as well as the ability to describe items in a clear and accurate manner to customers. The ability to make and close a deal is essential. Strenuous physical activity is minimal, although much driving, standing and walking over long periods is part of the day to day existence.

APPLIANCE REPAIRER

Ranking: 165
Score: 14.39
Basic Day: 9.5 Hours

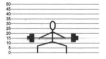

Work weeks for home appliance repairers may occasionally include weekend and evening hours, in order to accommodate some customers. Those who work in customers' homes spend some time on the road. Lifting and carrying is required in this work, as well as reaching for and handling tools and electrical parts. Good eyesight and coordination are needed in order to locate malfunctions and perform repairs correctly and safely. Home appliance repairers must guard against electrical shocks and cuts from tools.

ARCHAEOLOGIST

Ranking: 101

Score: 9.09

Basic Day: 9.0 Hours

Archeologists spend much of their time at excavation sites and are often subject to inclement weather and foreign climates. Manual dexterity is required, as archeologists, working with trowels and other tools, uncover precious artifacts which must be handled with great care. Archeologists also spend time sitting at desks, writing papers based upon their research. They need stamina, not only to conduct research in the field, but to travel great distances to present papers at conferences and meetings.

ARCHITECT

Ranking: 70

Score: 7.56

Basic Day: 9.5 Hours

Architects spend most of their time sitting at desks in pleasant offices, but sometimes they go on-site during construction to view progress on their projects. They need good mental stamina, to work overtime in order to meet deadlines. Architects must have manual dexterity to handle precision drawing instruments. They must also have the communication skills to convey their ideas and designs to clients and contractors.

ARCHITECTURAL DRAFTER

Ranking: 51

Score: 6.92

Basic Day: 9.0 Hours

Architectural drafters who are salaried work regular 40-hour weeks with occasional overtime; those who work free-lance make their own schedules. They spend their work day sitting at drawing tables, working with precision drawing instruments such as protractors and compasses. They may also work at computer terminals. Drafting calls for good hand-eye coordination and manual dexterity. Eye and back strain can result from sitting in one place for long periods of time doing detailed work.

ARTIST (COMMERCIAL)

Ranking: 46

Score: 6.85

Basic Day: 9.0 Hours

Commercial and graphic artists, whether freelance or salaried, usually work sitting at desks. They must have good hand-eye coordination as they perform very exacting work. A commercial artist usually works under strict deadline requirements, and often has to work overtime. Free-lancers have to have good communication and salesmanship skills in order to solicit to potential employers. They must have the stamina to work long days and to manage the stress of irregular hours and pay.

ARTIST (FINE ART)

Ranking: 116

Score: 9.85

Basic Day: 9.0 Hours

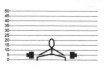

Artistic painters work irregular hours, setting their own schedules for the progress of work. In addition to artistic talent, artists must possess manual dexterity, coordination, and visual acuity. Artists handle, mix and apply paint and other substances, and construct and treat canvases or other surfaces. This work can be physically strenuous. Studios must be well- ventilated to minimize exposure to harmful fumes. Since most artistic painters hold other jobs to help support themselves, stamina is needed to perform effectively at both occupations.

ASTROLOGER

Ranking: 1

Score: 3.00

Basic Day: 8.0 Hours

Professional astrologers who work in storefronts or for publications normally perform their jobs while sitting. Since income for many astrologers depends on the volume of walk-in business, many must work long hours to earn moderate incomes. Astrologers and fortune tellers who are employed in traveling shows may be required to assist in setting up and breaking down their equipment.

ASTRONAUT

Ranking: 207

Score: 20.73

Basic Day: 8.5 Hours

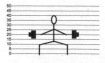

As a large majority of astronauts are members of the military, they are required to undergo the rigors of basic training and maintain excellent physical conditioning. Even non-military astronauts must be fit in order to handle the demands of space flight. All astronauts are put through an intense battery of physical tests, including subjection to high gravity forces, zero-gravity, and oxygen deprivation to determine the body's reaction under simulated flight conditions. Excellent eyesight, manual dexterity, and quick reflexes are also necessary for astronauts. In short, only the most well-conditioned and healthy individuals qualify to become astronauts.

ASTRONOMER

Ranking: 12

Score: 4.98

Basic Day: 9.0 Hours

Astronomers spend considerable time working in offices or classrooms, but they do some of their work in the evenings, in observatories. In order to make use of powerful telescopes and other related facilities, or to have the proper geographic position, astronomers are sometimes required to travel to remote observation points. Sharpness of vision is essential to astronomers. Also important, are good communication skills, since astronomers must write papers and give lectures.

ATTORNEY

Ranking: 39

Score: 6.09

Basic Day: 10.0 Hours

Lawyers usually work very long hours, in offices, courtrooms, and libraries. Attorneys often travel to appear in court, conduct research, and meet with clients, colleagues, and government officials. Since a client's future often depends on a lawyer's ability to persuade judge and jury, effective communication skills are essential for attorneys. During important cases, stamina is required to work under pressure for extended periods. Attorneys' schedules are often very hectic.

AUDIOLOGIST

Ranking: 68

Score: 7.43

Basic Day: 8.5 Hours

Audiologists work in offices at schools, hospitals, clinics, and speech and hearing centers. They are required to speak and listen with exceptional skill, as they work with people who have language and hearing disabilities. Good communication skills are especially essential for those audiologists who are involved in counseling, advising administrators, parents, and educators. Audiologists must be able to handle the mental stress which comes from the great concentration their jobs demand.

AUTHOR (BOOKS)

Ranking: 46

Score: 6.85

Basic Day: 9.0 Hours

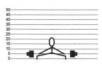

Full-time writers work a regular week, with some overtime required to meet deadlines. Free-lance writers often set their own hours. Travel may be required for writers, depending upon the writing assignment or book subject. In addition to excellent writing talent, verbal communication skills are essential for effective performance in this occupation, especially for those who conduct research through interviews. Writers commonly experience eye, back, muscular and skeletal strain.

AUTOMOBILE ASSEMBLER

Ranking: 157

Score: 13.53

Basic Day: 8.5 Hours

Automotive assemblers need the manual dexterity to handle machine parts with speed and precision. Some assembly positions call for heavy lifting. The environment in which assemblers work is noisy, and may involve some risk of bodily harm. Assemblers are under great stress caused by the demand to keep up repetitive tasks, at steady rates of speed. This work calls for endurance, and tolerance for rotating shifts and overtime hours.

AUTOMOBILE BODY REPAIRER

Ranking: 194

Score: 17.57

Basic Day: 9.5 Hours

Automotive body repairers work in noisy, dusty body shops, where they are required to do heavy lifting and carrying. Therefore, strength and stamina are needed. Body repairers work in awkward positions, stooping, kneeling and reaching. Manual dexterity and good eyesight are necessary to accurately and safely handle power tools and

welding torches. Precautions must be taken to avoid injuries as well as the effect of paint fumes.

AUTOMOBILE MECHANIC

Ranking: 209

Score: 21.57

Basic Day: 9.5 Hours

Automotive mechanics work in repair shops or garages, which may be noisy, grimy, or filled with hazardous exhaust fumes. Mechanics are required to stand, crouch, bend, lie, and reach, and to lift and carry moderately heavy objects and tools. These workers must possess mechanical aptitude, coordination, and strength, to use hand and power tools safely in diagnosing and repairing problems. Mechanics are at risk of physical injury from cuts, shock, and moving engine parts, and from working underneath vehicles which are supported by jacks. Protective gear, such as safety glasses and gloves, are often worn by mechanics.

AUTOMOBILE PAINTER

Ranking: 216

Score: 23.57

Basic Day: 9.5 Hours

Automotive painters use small machinery, such as power sanders and paint spray guns, in their work. Close attention and good hand-eye coordination are essential for mixing paint and doing detail work. Automotive painters are required to have steady hands, and to stoop, kneel, crawl or crouch while painting, sanding, or making inspections. They have to wear protective masks to prevent exposure to the harmful fumes caused by paint and particles.

AUTOMOBILE SALESPERSON

Ranking: 135

Score: 11.58

Basic Day: 9.5 Hours

Automobile salespersons generally work 40 hours per week, including some weekend and evening hours. Depending on the type of establishment, salespersons may work either indoors or outdoors. Communication skills are vital in this line of work, in order to persuade potential customers to make a purchase, and otherwise to handle customer relations smoothly. Auto salespersons spend much time standing or walking. Because these salespersons work on commission, stamina is required to deal with the pressure to make sales.

BANK OFFICER

Ranking: 10

Score: 4.76

Basic Day: 10.0 Hours

Bank officers work regular hours, in pleasant offices, but they also work a fair amount of overtime, in order to attend meetings, continuing education classes, or community functions. It is important for a bank officer to be able to listen, speak, and write well, in order to promote a good image for the bank and to advise clients and employees. Stress may be experienced as a result of the many responsibilities of bank officers.

BANK TELLER

Ranking: 33

Score: 6.03

Basic Day: 8.0 Hours

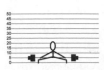

Most bank tellers work regular 40 hour weeks, but there are some who work part-time, evenings, or weekends. Bank tellers are required to stand in one place for a better part of their shifts. Excellent concentration and computation skills are needed to handle monetary transactions and keep accurate records. Bank tellers need good communication skills in order to deal well with customers and meet their needs.

BARBER

Ranking: 103

Score: 9.22

Basic Day: 8.0 Hours

Barbers usually work in comfortable surroundings, often more than 40 hours per week. The busiest times for a barber are during the lunch hour and on weekends. Barbers work standing with their arms raised to shoulder level most of the time. A barber requires manual dexterity in order to maneuver sharp scissors close to a customer's face, or administer a close shave without causing injury. Good communication skills are needed in order to determine customers' wishes and make them comfortable.

BARTENDER

Ranking: 149

Score: 13.00

Basic Day: 7.5 Hours

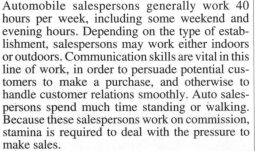

Bartenders work irregular hours, including evenings, late nights, and weekends. They are on their feet most of the time. Bartenders need manual dexterity, good eyes, and a good short-term memory to prepare many mixed drinks accurately and in rapid succession. Good communication skills are necessary, since socializing with customers is an important aspect of tending bar. Bartenders who own their own establishments must have the stamina to run the business and supervise the staff as well as tend bar.

BASEBALL PLAYER (MAJOR LEAGUE)

Ranking: 245

Score: 37.00

Basic Day: 6.0 Hours

Baseball is one of the less-demanding of the major professional sports, since players spend a good deal of the game sitting on the bench or staying inactive. Still, to be competitive at the major league level requires good physical conditioning, in addition to refined baseball skills. During the game, players must run, jump, slide, and bat, throw and catch balls. Some positions require foot speed, while others require a strong throwing arm or great overall stamina. The best players have a combination of these and other athletic skills. The long baseball season can cause wear and tear on the bodies of even the best- conditioned athletes, and injuries to joints, limbs and muscles are common. Many players undergo weight training as part of an off-season regimen.

BASEBALL UMPIRE (MAJOR LEAGUE)

Ranking: 238

Score: 33.00

Basic Day: 6.0 Hours

Though major league umpires are not required to be as well- conditioned as players, they must nevertheless run, throw, and stand for long periods of time. Unlike players, umpires are on the field for the entire game, which can last over three hours. Umpires must be quick and agile enough to achieve proper positioning to make calls and to avoid batted balls. This job requires excellent eyesight and quick judgment. Extensive travel, combined with night games, can be fatiguing for umpires over the course of the season. In the summer months, games may be played in extreme heat and humidity. In the spring and fall, night games in northern cities are often played in the cold.

BASKETBALL COACH (NCAA)

Ranking: 181

Score: 15.73

Basic Day: 8.5 Hours

Though most are former players, college basketball coaches have to undergo only a few of the physical demands placed on players. This job does entail some running and throwing during practices. However, coaching skills, knowledge of basketball strategy, and the ability to identify and develop talent are much more important in coaching than is physical conditioning. Most coaches travel extensively to attend games and scout talent, and this can cause fatigue over the course of a season.

BASKETBALL PLAYER (NBA)

Ranking: 246

Score: 38.00

Basic Day: 6 Hours

Players in the National Basketball Association are some of the best conditioned athletes in professional sports. During games, players are constantly running, jumping, throwing, and jostling each other for position. The best players have a combination of good foot speed, excellent jumping ability, stamina, and hand-eye coordination. The constant pounding and twisting on hardwood floors may cause extensive injury to the feet, ankles and knees. Weight training is part of many off-season conditioning regimens.

BIOLOGIST

Ranking: 75

Score: 7.98

Basic Day: 9.0 Hours

Biological scientists usually work regular hours, in labs or offices. Biologists in some fields, however, spend time conducting research in remote areas without modern conveniences. Biological scientists must have manual dexterity to handle sensitive instruments when conducting research on animals, plants, microorganisms, or genes. They are often exposed to dangerous substances and must exercise caution. Good communication skills are needed by those scientists who teach or present papers.

BOILERMAKER

Ranking: 215

Score: 23.39

Basic Day: 9.5 Hours

Boilermakers should have strong constitutions as they often work overtime, in cramped, and sometimes dangerous conditions. They crouch inside boilers or other large vessels, handling heavy welding or riveting equipment. They require manual dexterity, as well as strength, for handling sensitive instruments of measurement and metal working tools. Boilermakers must remain constantly alert to hazards on the job and must wear many types of protective gear.

BOOKBINDER

Ranking: 99

Score: 8.98

Basic Day: 9.0 Hours

Bookbinders work in large, noisy rooms, in which they are exposed to the smells of paper, ink, and adhesives. They work with machines, and are on their feet most of the day. They are required to do moderate lifting. Some bookbinders work independently and do everything by hand, but most bookbinders work in assembly-line fashion, doing repetitive tasks at machines which perform only a part of the entire bookbinding process. Work in this field calls for manual dexterity and visual acuity.

BOOKKEEPER

Ranking: 23

Score: 5.18

Basic Day: 8.0 Hours

Full-time bookkeepers work regular hours in offices. Part-time bookkeepers often work in the evenings or on their own schedules. Bookkeeping calls for good organization and computation skills to handle large amounts of numerical calculations and to keep accurate records. Long days at a computer or looking over record books can cause eye and lower back strain. The physical demands of this job are few.

BRICKLAYER

Ranking: 237

Score: 32.85

Basic Day: 9.0 Hours

Bricklayers spend most of their work day outdoors in a standing or crouching position. Their work schedule is irregular because of the fluctuation in demand for brick laying, and delays due to inclement weather. The tasks of a bricklayer, such as mixing mortar, and lifting bricks and scaffolding, call for strength and good physical stamina. Often working in high places, bricklayers risk the possibility of bodily injury. Bricklayers are also subject to dust and noxious fumes.

BROADCAST TECHNICIAN

Ranking: 94

Score: 8.79

Basic Day: 9.0 Hours

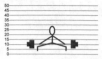

Broadcast technicians usually work indoors in comfortable surroundings, although field technicians set up equipment outside the studio. The broadcast day consists of three shifts, since broadcasting is done around the clock. Broadcast technicians' hours vary weekly, as they are often required to work overtime to meet programming deadlines. Specialized technicians need manual dexterity and good communication skills to set up and oversee the smooth operation of cameras, microphones, control panels, transmitters, and other broadcast equipment.

BUS DRIVER

Ranking: 141

Score: 12.03

Basic Day: 8.0 Hours

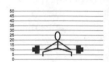

Bus drivers spend their shifts on the road. Long shifts sitting behind the wheel can cause eye and back strain. Some bus lines run 24 hours a day shifts for city or cross-country bus drivers can fall anywhere within the 24 hour time period, but school bus drivers work only during the school day. Since it is important to stay alert while driving, good concentration is necessary, as well as keen eye sight and hearing. Adverse traffic and weather conditions can cause stress and can be life-threatening.

BUTCHER

Ranking: 203

Score: 19.98

Basic Day: 9.0 Hours

Butchers are on their feet for long periods of time working in cold environments. They are required to lift heavy pieces of meat and to handle power saws and slicers. Good hand-eye coordination is essential so that the cutting is done precisely and safely. Butchers need good physical stamina to endure the extreme temperatures and physical exertion.

BUYER

Ranking: 85

Score: 8.23

Basic Day: 9.0 Hours

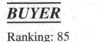

Buyers work in pleasant offices, often over 40 hours per week. Travel is often required, as well as evening and weekend work. They spend a lot of time speaking with other buyers, sales persons, and assistants, either in person, or over the telephone. A buyer must be able to make quick evaluations of the products considered for purchase. Because buyers work under pressure in a fast-paced atmosphere, they should have hearty constitutions.

CARPENTER

Ranking: 219

Score: 25.46

Basic Day: 8.5 Hours

Carpenters work both indoors and outdoors, using power tools and heavy building materials. In the course of their work, carpenters are expected to climb ladders and scaffolding, stand or crouch in uncomfortable positions, and balance on uneven surfaces high above the ground. Carpenters are subject to high noise levels at building sites, and to the risk of physical injury. Because carpenters undergo steady physical exertion on the job, they must have sound constitutions and good physical stamina.

CARPET/TILE INSTALLER

Ranking: 197

Score: 17.85

Basic Day: 9.0 Hours

Floor covering or carpet installers work regular hours in pleasant surroundings. In the course of their work, they spend a great deal of time on their knees, bending, reaching, and crouching in uncomfortable positions. They are expected to possess the strength to do heavy lifting, and the hand-eye coordination and strength to use hand and power tools. Coordination and good eyesight are required to perform the painstaking work of fitting a floor for carpet of other covering.

CARTOONIST

Ranking: 46

Score: 6.85

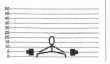

Basic Day: 9.0 Hours

In addition to a sense of humor, syndicated cartoonists must possess excellent drawing ability and overall artistic sensibility to be able to convey ideas graphically. Cartoonists normally work out of private offices or studios. Like other publishing professionals, cartoonists often work under strict deadlines, and they may be forced to spend long hours at the drawing table. Drawing requires extreme attention to detail, and this can result in eyestrain and muscle cramps.

CASHIER

Ranking: 55

Score: 7.00

Basic Day: 7.5 Hours

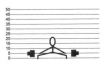

Cashiers work part-time or full-time on shifts which can fall at any time of the day or night. They usually stand in booths or behind counters. They have to handle merchandise, money, tickets, and/or receipts. Good communication skills are important for cashiers who give out information to the public. Computerized registers and other kinds of calculating machines can be noisy, and in busy establishments, the atmosphere can be hectic, especially on weekends and holidays.

CATHOLIC PRIEST

Ranking: 89

Score: 8.44

Basic Day: 10.5 Hours

Roman Catholic priests work long and often irregular hours, because they are usually on call for the members of the church. Most of their time is spent in advising individuals and communicating the precepts of the church. A priest's day consists of such activities as hearing confession, counseling, giving sermons, officiating at private ceremonies, and participating in community service. Some priests, such as those who are missionaries, may do some physical labor.

CHAUFFEUR

Ranking: 156

Score: 13.46

Basic Day: 9.5 Hours

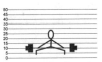

Those who work for livery services and private individuals spend a good deal of time sitting behind the wheel of limousines or vans. This can cause muscle cramps, fatigue and sometimes skin irritations. Chauffeurs for private individuals often drive comfortable, well-appointed, air-conditioned cars, while some drivers for livery services may operate less luxurious vehicles. Chauffeurs must have excellent eyesight and good overall driving skills. These workers are often required to carry, load and unload baggage for passengers.

CHEMIST

Ranking: 122

Score: 9.98

Basic Day: 9.0 Hours

Chemists work in labs or offices and generally keep regular hours. They must possess keen eyesight and manual dexterity in order to carry out precise work with chemicals and compounds, using sensitive apparatus. The substances with which they work are sometimes hazardous, so care must be taken to follow proper procedures. Mental strain and eye fatigue can be caused by this painstaking work.

CHILD CARE WORKER

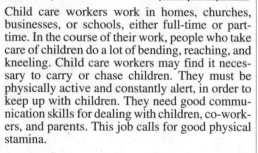

Ranking: 202

Score: 19.00

Basic Day: 7.5 Hours

Child care workers work in homes, churches, businesses, or schools, either full-time or part-time. In the course of their work, people who take care of children do a lot of bending, reaching, and kneeling. Child care workers may find it necessary to carry or chase children. They must be physically active and constantly alert, in order to keep up with children. They need good communication skills for dealing with children, co-workers, and parents. This job calls for good physical stamina.

CHIROPRACTOR

Ranking: 147

Score: 12.79

Basic Day: 10.0 Hours

Most chiropractors are self-employed, they work in pleasant offices and set their own hours. Chiropractors perform physical examinations and treatments by manually adjusting different parts of the body, especially the spine. Chiropractic work calls for strength and good physical stamina. Physical exertion for chiropractors is moderate but constant, it can be heavy in specific instances when manipulations are difficult or the patient oversized.

CHOREOGRAPHER

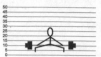

Ranking: 136

Score: 11.85

Basic Day: 9.0 Hours

Most choreographers are also dancers or former dancers, and as such are accustomed to the strenuous work and long hours professional dance demands. Since choreographers must create and teach new dances, their presence is often necessary at daily and weekend rehearsals, and at performances. This rehearsal and performance schedule can be grueling. Choreographers must be fit and agile enough to demonstrate dance moves to members of the dance company. For some choreographers, extensive travel, combined with rehearsal and performance schedules, can be fatiguing.

CIVIL ENGINEER

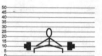

Ranking: 124

Score: 10.21

Basic Day: 9.0 Hours

Civil engineers work in offices or on building sites, where they design and oversee the construction of buildings, or transportation and water supply systems. They may, at times, be required to travel. Civil engineers require great powers of concentration for the many hours spent going over details of project plans. Civil engineers must pay careful attention to detail when analyzing plans and supervising others during the implementation of a project.

COLLEGE PROFESSOR

Ranking: 82

Score: 8.04

Basic Day: 9.0 Hours

College professors have flexible schedules, which vary according to their duties as instructors, researchers, or administrators. They usually have summers off, as well as time off during school holidays. They spend much of their day lecturing and conversing with students, so good communication skills are crucial. While teaching, college professors may be required to stand for long periods. Research and writing are also part of the college professor's job and necessitate many hours of concentration.

COMMUNICATIONS EQUIPMENT MECHANIC

Ranking: 165

Score: 14.39

Basic Day: 9.5 Hours

Communications mechanics are on call 24 hours a day, but normally work regular shifts. Mechanics stand while on the job, and are also required to crouch, bend, reach, and do some minor lifting. Manual dexterity and good eyesight are needed to follow electrical diagrams correctly, and to use hand tools, such as soldering irons, safely. Because communications mechanics often wear headsets in order to diagnose problems and make repairs, they are exposed to constant noise.

COMPOSITOR/TYPESETTER

Ranking: 127

Score: 10.82

Basic Day: 9.0 Hours

Printers, compositors and typesetters work 40-hour weeks. Most printing plants run three shifts covering 24 hours a day. Overtime to meet deadlines is common in this trade. Some minor lifting is required, as well as manipulating keyboards and other equipment and material by hand. Hand compositors work standing up; typesetters work sitting down. Shops which use monotype or linotype machines are noisy, and may be dirty. Many printers, compositors and typesetters use video display terminals. Eye and back strain may result from this details, exacting work.

COMPUTER OPERATOR

Ranking: 113

Score: 9.69

Basic Day: 8.5 Hours

Computer operators keep computer systems running, doing general maintenance and stocking computer tapes, disks, and paper. They must be alert to computer malfunctions so they can rectify problems before the system "goes down." Good communication skills are necessary, since consulting with programmers and analysts is often part of the problem-solving process. Computer operators who work for large institutions may work evening and weekend shifts.

COMPUTER PROGRAMMER

Ranking: 27

Score: 5.84

Basic Day: 9.0 Hours

Computer programmers work irregular hours, which are dictated by computer time available to them, but they generally work 40 hours per week. They spend most of their day writing and solving problems using a computer language. Eye strain may result from spending hours staring at the symbols in computer programs, evaluating each number, letter, and punctuation mark. Programmers may suffer from back strain as a result of hours spent sitting in a chair each day.

COMPUTER SERVICE TECHNICIAN

Ranking: 144

Score: 12.39

Basic Day: 9.5 Hours

Computer service technicians travel from place to place, repairing computer systems. They also install new computer equipment. Computer service technicians must be able to handle small tools and do some minor lifting as they hook up electrical connections, lay cable, and put computers in place. Electric shock or minor burns are possible, but unlikely. Because they must listen to client complaints, answer questions, and give instructions, they must have good communication skills.

COMPUTER SYSTEMS ANALYST

Ranking: 19

Score: 5.08

Basic Day: 9.0 Hours

Computer systems analysts work regular hours, but occasional overtime may be required in order to meet deadlines. Analysts talk at length with clients to determine the problems to be solved in a particular organization's computer system, so good communication skills are essential. They must be able to conduct research and prepare complex analyses, before finally implementing or changing a computer system. The physical demands on a computer analyst are few.

CONGRESSPERSON/SENATOR

Ranking: 93

Score: 8.73

Basic Day: 8.5 Hours

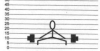

Public officials work out of comfortable, well-appointed offices and often have large staffs to perform administrative duties. Working in public office may require spending long hours in legislative sessions. In general, though, running for office is more physically demanding than the job itself. As elections approach, candidates keep very hectic campaign and fund raising schedules, which include heavy travel. The rigors of campaigning can be fatiguing for even the hardiest of candidates.

CONSERVATIONIST

Ranking: 186

Score: 15.98

Basic Day: 9.0 Hours

Conservationists spend considerable time talking with landowners, farmers, and forestry workers. They may be called upon to travel to remote areas, and work long hours when emergencies, such as brush fires, occur. Their work is physically exhausting during such times. Conservationists must have sound constitutions, as they work outdoors and are subject to the elements. They need acute powers of observation to make sound judgments regarding natural resource management.

CONSTRUCTION FOREMAN

Ranking: 206

Score: 20.72

Basic Day: 9.5 Hours

Foremen work regular hours, sometimes on a rotating shift basis. Their day is spent, for the most part, standing and walking in industrial shops or at construction sites. Observation and communication skills are important for supervising and instructing the workers, and for consulting with management. Foremen and forewomen are often exposed to a great deal of dirt, dust, noise, and vibration.

CONSTRUCTION MACHINERY OPERATOR

Ranking: 229

Score: 28.09

Basic Day: 9.0 Hours

Construction machinery operators work outdoors, operating heavy machinery that can be very dangerous if not properly run. Construction machinery operators must endure constant noise, vibration, dust, and, in some cases, toxic fumes. On some construction sites, they risk bodily injury. They must have good hand-eye coordination to measure distances and maneuver the machinery accurately.

CONSTRUCTION WORKER (LABORER)

Ranking: 241

Score: 36.41

Basic Day: 8.5 Hours

Construction laborers primarily work outdoors. This work involves a great deal of physical exertion, as laborers lift and carry heavy objects and materials, climb scaffolding, reach, stoop and bend. Construction laborers must possess the strength and coordination to handle a variety of tools and materials, from shovels to cement mixers, depending upon the job assignment. These workers are subject to noise, dust and grime. Minor falls, abrasions, and strained muscles are common in construction work.

COOK

Ranking: 174

Score: 15.00

Basic Day: 8.0 Hours

Cooks and chefs work in the kitchens of restaurants, schools, and other institutions, often on weekends, holidays and evenings. They are exposed to high temperatures and hot surfaces, and risk minor injuries from cooking accidents. They are expected to lift heavy pots and pans and to operate industrial kitchen equipment. Cooks often work under pressure to perform quickly, so effective communication with an order taker, as well as timing is important.

CORPORATE EXECUTIVE (SENIOR)

Ranking: 30

Score: 6.00

Basic Day: 10.5 Hours

Senior corporate executives work in very comfortable "corporate-style" environments with offices close to the departments under their tutelage. Long hours including evenings and weekends are mandatory, though some schedules may be fairly flexible. Extreme amounts of stress are typical, making it seem more physically demanding than it is.

CORRECTION OFFICER

Ranking: 154

Score: 13.41

Basic Day: 9.5 Hours

Correctional officers spend most of their time indoors, but some time is spend outside if they must oversee outdoor activities. A correctional officer's work schedule may include some nights, holidays, weekends, and overtime when an emergency occurs. They have direct contact with inmates, counseling or disciplining them. It is necessary for correctional officers to be in good physical condition, since they must be alert to, and prepared for, inmate disturbances.

COSMETOLOGIST

Ranking: 104

Score: 9.30

Basic Day: 8.5 Hours

Full-time cosmetologists work over 40 hours per week; weekends, lunch hours, and evenings are the busiest times. Some beauticians work part-time. Beauticians usually work in comfortable and pleasant surroundings. Cutting and styling hair calls for long periods of standing. Manual dexterity and keen eyesight are needed to perform such tasks as styling hair, applying make-up, and giving manicures or pedicures. A beautician needs good communication skills in order to meet customers' wishes.

COWBOY

Ranking: 248

Score: 41.00

Basic Day: 8.5 Hours

Cowboys and ranch hands work very long hours outdoors and are often exposed to poor weather conditions. This line of work requires physical strength and stamina. Excellent horsemanship is a necessity for cowboys. This occupation demands agility and coordination to perform a variety of tasks, such as roping cattle, while on horseback. Extensive riding can cause strain to the legs and lower back. Cowboys can suffer chafed legs and hands, and they normally develop thick calluses over time.

DAIRY FARMER

Ranking: 232

Score: 30.53

Basic Day: 10.5 Hours

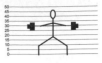

The work day for a dairy farmer normally begins long before dawn and often does not end until after dark. Tasks are often performed outdoors, in conditions ranging from extreme heat to cold, rain or snow. Though modern dairy farms are increasingly mechanized, dairy farmers must have strong hands, arms and backs to operate machinery and to lift, carry and load hay, feed and dairy produce. This can be grueling work, and stamina is required.

DANCER

Ranking: 217

Score: 23.85

Basic Day: 9.0 Hours

Dancing is an extremely strenuous profession, requiring a great deal of physical discipline. Rehearsals for performances, which often take place daily, including weekends, can be very rigorous. Training, especially for the ballet, is intense and begins at a very early age. Physical appearance is somewhat important for dancers, and body height and build normally docs not much exceed the average. Good feet, normal arches and strong legs and arms are necessary in this profession. In addition, dancers must have agility, coordination, stamina and grace. Because this profession is so demanding, many dancers transfer to related fields, such as choreography or instruction, by their mid-thirties.

DENTAL HYGIENIST

Ranking: 55

Score: 7.00

Basic Day: 8.0 Hours

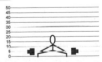

Dental hygienists generally work in dental offices, schools or hospitals. Some hygienists work full-time at one location, while others work part-time at several in order to complete a full work week. Dental hygienists sit or stand while checking and cleaning teeth. They must have manual dexterity and a good eye, so that they can be gentle and accurate as they use precision dental instruments. Good communication skills are necessary to instruct patients in oral hygiene.

DENTAL LABORATORY TECHNICIAN

Ranking: 75

Score: 7.98

Basic Day: 9.0 Hours

Dental laboratory technicians generally work 40 hour weeks, sitting in labs. They work with hand tools and specialized equipment such as metal melting torches, lathes, and grinding and polishing machines. Proper precautions must be taken to avoid minor injuries. Their work requires manual dexterity, concentration, and accuracy. Lab technicians suffer eye and back strain from long periods of finely detailed work.

DENTIST

Ranking: 121

Score: 9.96

Basic Day: 9.0 Hours

Dentists usually work in their own offices. Their work schedule often includes evenings and weekends. They must have manual dexterity and good hand-eye coordination to use dental instruments and to maneuver inside patients' mouths. Their work calls for concentration and precision. They also need patience to calm frightened children or adults. Dentists must be able to communicate with patients in order to inspire confidence and to give advice on oral health.

DIETITIAN

Ranking: 44

Score: 6.36

Basic Day: 8.5 Hours

Clinical dietitians work in offices, hospitals, nursing homes, or clinics. Their schedules may include evenings, weekends, and travel between locations. Their jobs may include hands-on work in hot kitchens and food service areas. Clinical dietitians need good communication skills to consult with doctors and other health care workers, and to advise patients, family members, and food prepares on dietary requirements.

DISHWASHER

Ranking: 212

Score: 22.00

Basic Day: 7.0 Hours

Dishwashers spend a great deal of time standing on their feet in hot, steamy kitchens. This can be tiring and uncomfortable. Dishwashers' hands and arms are exposed to hot water and detergents, and many of these workers develop calluses or dry, peeling skin. Dishwashers may be required to clear tables, and this entails lifting and carrying heavy trays filled with dishes, glasses and silverware. Workers in this occupation are often exposed to dirt, grease and unpleasant odors.

DISK JOCKEY

Ranking: 72

Score: 7.85

Basic Day: 9.0 Hours

Radio disk jockeys work in soundproof booths or studios. Since the radio is broadcast around the clock, a DJ's shift can fall anywhere within the 24 hour time period. They require excellent communication skills, as they spend their shift talking on the air, introducing songs, presenting commercials or news, or answering telephone calls. Radio disk jockeys must be alert and able to think on their feet. Pressure results from working under time limits and becoming well-known.

DRESSMAKER

Ranking: 151

Score: 13.29

Basic Day: 8.5 Hours

Dressmakers who work in garment factories spend much of their work day seated at and hunched over sewing machines. This work can be tedious and repetitive. Attention to detail is necessary for dressmakers, and eyestrain and muscle cramps may result. Cuts and other injuries from machinery are fairly common. Independent, self-employed dressmakers usually work in more comfortable environments.

DRILL-PRESS OPERATOR

Ranking: 192

Score: 17.10

Basic Day: 9.0 Hours

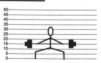

Drill press operators work in machine shops, and spend most of their time standing. The machines with which they work make a great deal of noise, so ear plugs must be worn. Drill press operators also have to wear safety glasses as protection from flying metal debris. They must have good eyesight and manual dexterity in order to monitor and control drill press operations. moderate lifting is required. Physical endurance is the key to effective performance in this field.

DRYWALL APPLICATOR/ FINISHER

Ranking: 227

Score: 27.85

Basic Day: 9.0 Hours

In the course of their work, drywall applicators and finishers are expected to stand, bend, crouch, climb ladders and balance on scaffolding. They are required to lift heavy drywall panels and use power tools. Good physical stamina is essential. Drywall applicators wear masks to protect their eyes from dust. They are exposed to a high level of noise, as they work with sanders or automatic taping tools. Work with these tools calls for a steady hand and a good eye.

ECONOMIST

Ranking: 3

Score: 4.09

Basic Day: 9.0 Hours

Economists work in many different capacities, and their schedules depend on the type of work they do. All economists work under the pressure of deadlines, which often necessitate overtime. Some economists travel in order to conduct their research. Economists who teach, require communication skills to lecture students and consult with administrators. Economists generally work at desks, looking over statistics, charts, and data reports. Eye and back strain can result from this kind of work.

ELECTRICAL ENGINEER

Ranking: 134

Score: 11.11

Basic Day: 9.0 Hours

Electrical engineers sit at desks in offices, or work on construction sites. Because they design and test new equipment, electrical engineers must have good observation skills and hand- eye coordination. Communication with co-workers is important in order to explain plans and to correct operation malfunctions. Electrical engineers endure a great amount of noise and oscillation, which can cause some hearing loss or bodily harm.

ELECTRICAL EQUIPMENT REPAIRER

Ranking: 152

Score: 13.39

Basic Day: 9.5 Hours

Electrical equipment repairers work 40-hour weeks, often on a rotating shift basis. In the course of their work, they must stand, walk, reach, crouch, and bend, sometimes in small spaces. An electrical equipment repairer may work in a noisy, dirty environment, such as a factory, or in a relatively clean, quiet place, such as a hospital. Their work environment varies with the repairs being undertaken. The work of locating and repairing electrical malfunctions demands the visual acuity and manual dexterity.

ELECTRICAL TECHNICIAN

Ranking: 143

Score: 12.13

Basic Day: 9.0 Hours

Electrical technicians work regular hours in offices, labs, or industrial plants. They are expected to have good hand-eye coordination to handle complex measuring and testing tools. Eye strain results from close, detailed work and from work with computers. Some electrical technicians supervise production workers, a responsibility which requires good powers of observation and communication.

ELECTRICIAN

Ranking: 213

Score: 22.01

Basic Day: 9.0 Hours

Electricians work both indoors and outdoors. In the course of their work, electricians may have to climb ladders, balance on scaffolding, squat, reach, and crouch in uncomfortable positions. Their work also demands moderate lifting. The ability to distinguish between colors is necessary, since electrical wires are identified by color. Manual dexterity is required to do delicate wiring and to handle sensitive tools.

EMERGENCY MEDICAL TECHNICIAN

Ranking: 208

Score: 21.26

Basic Day: 8.5 Hours

Emergency medical technicians exert a great deal of physical energy. They work long and irregular hours, often more than 40 hours per week. In the course of their work, they have to do moderate lifting, and must be able to stoop, bend, reach, crouch and kneel. Medical technicians must have manual dexterity to handle delicate medical equipment. Emergency vehicle drivers must have good reflexes to drive safely at high speeds. Good communication is important when working with patients, bystanders, or co-workers.

ENGINEERING TECHNICIAN

Ranking: 75

Score: 7.98

Basic Day: 9.0 Hours

Civil, industrial and mechanical engineering technicians work regular hours in offices, labs, or industrial plants. If they are service representatives, they may travel to consult with clients. Their work requires good powers of observation and the capacity to perform exacting work, using drawing instruments and machine models. Because they spend hours concentrating on are fine detailed drawings or models, eye and back strain can be a problem for engineering technicians.

EXECUTIVE SEARCH CONSULTANT

Ranking: 5

Score: 4.00

Basic Day: 9.0 Hours

Executive search consultants work in comfortable "corporate-style" environments. They may travel in order to network, meet potential candidates or attend corporate meetings, which is the most physically taxing activity they engage in.

FARMER

Ranking: 240

Score: 34.53

Basic Day: 10.5 Hours

Farmers who grow crops, work only about half the year, but those who raise livestock, work all year. Farmers have to be in good physical shape to work long hours outside and to walk, climb, stoop, kneel, lift heavy farm implements, and to maneuver large farm vehicles. They are often exposed to hazardous pesticides and the diseases of farm animals, so they must have hearty constitutions in order to remain healthy. The machines with which they work are often noisy and potentially dangerous.

FASHION DESIGNER

Ranking: 116

Score: 9.85

Basic Day: 9.0 Hours

Fashion designers work on schedules which usually include some nights and weekends. The self-employed work longer hours. Before each fashion season, designers inevitably work overtime. A fashion designer must have a good color sense as well as the ability to make attractive sketches to represent their designs. Communication skills are essential in the promotion of designs to clients, superiors, and to the public, and in the supervision of the workers who sew the garments.

FASHION MODEL

Ranking: 157

Score: 13.53

Basic Day: 8.5 Hours

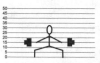

Physical appearance is more important in fashion modeling than in almost any other profession, since fashion models reflect society's ideal of beauty, grace and glamour. Though standards for models change somewhat with the times, models normally must be attractive and in excellent physical shape, with little excess body weight. Aerobics and other exercises are common in a model's conditioning regimen, and most follow some diet plan. In high fashion modeling and commercial advertising, models may be required to hold poses for long periods of time in uncomfortable positions, until the desired effect is achieved. Work days can be long, schedules hectic, and travel requirements heavy in this profession.

FILE CLERK

Ranking: 87

Score: 8.27

Basic Day: 8.5 Hours

Office clerks work full- or part-time, usually on regular schedules. Work takes place in comfortable offices. These workers sit at desks, or stand while filing or operating office machines. Manual dexterity, good vision, and physical coordination are needed, in order to handle many papers, records, files, and other office materials, and to operate office machines, such as calculators. Eye and back strain is a common result of detailed work, especially for those office clerks who work on computers.

FINANCIAL PLANNER

Ranking: 14

Score: 5.00

Basic Day: 10 Hours

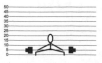

Basically a desk job with some travel means that planners work in comfortable office environments. Although they tend to work some overtime, it may be incorporated into their flexible schedule. The physical demands, though miniscule, seem to mount up as they travel in order to network, research or to meet potential clients.

FIREFIGHTER

Ranking: 249

Score: 43.23

Basic Day: 11.0 Hours

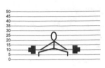

Firefighters generally work 50 hours per week on irregular shifts. In the firehouse there are few physical demands. However, when there is a fire, day or night, they are required to perform very strenuous activities at a moment's notice. In the course of their work they are required to do heavy lifting, climbing, balancing, or crawling. They must remain alert for many hours at a time to avoid injury in hazardous circumstances. They risk bodily injury from fire, smoke, or falling debris.

FISHERMAN

Ranking: 231

Score: 29.87

Basic Day: 9.0 Hours

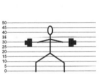

Fishermen must have strength and stamina in order to endure the long hours required in this occupation. Strength is necessary for casting and hauling in heavy lines and nets and for operating hoists and other machinery. Fishermen develop calluses on hands from working extensively with ropes, and they may suffer skin chafing and burns from working outdoors and being exposed to wind, saltwater and sun. Members of this profession must be hardy and healthy and accustomed to working on the open seas, even in poor weather conditions.

FLIGHT ATTENDANT

Ranking: 123

Score: 10.03

Basic Day: 8.0 Hours

Flight attendants stand up on the job, spending up to 85 hours per month in the air, including evenings, weekends, and holidays. They have to lift luggage, reach for things, and maneuver in tight spaces. Good powers of observation and communication are necessary to meet the needs of the passengers. On short flights, work can be hectic, and speed is required. Flight attendants are ex-

posed to airplane noise and vibration, and may experience ear problems from constantly changing altitudes.

FLORIST

Ranking: 116

Score: 9.85

Basic Day: 9.0 Hours

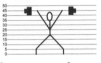

Florists work regular hours, but during holiday seasons, overtime is often required. They must be manually adept to handle flowers, greenery, and related items with care. A florist must have a good color and design sense in order to create appealing floral arrangements. They are sometimes exposed to extremes in temperature and humidity in shops equipped with greenhouse and refrigeration facilities.

FOOTBALL PLAYER (NFL)

Ranking: 250

Score: 43.73

Basic Day: 8.5 Hours

Football is perhaps the most dangerous and most demanding of professional sports. Almost all players suffer bumps, bruises, muscle pulls or other minor injuries during the course of a game. More serious injuries, including torn ligaments and fractured bones, can result from a single hit or from wear and tear over the course of a season. The most common injuries are to the knees, shoulders, and other joints. Football players are required to run, catch, throw, tackle and block. At some positions, athletic skills such as foot speed, hand-eye coordination and agility are important, while at other positions, brute physical strength is the dominant factor. For all players, conditioning is crucial in performance and in avoiding injury. For this reason, players undergo grueling practice sessions before and during the season. Weight training is an essential part of most players' conditioning regimen.

FORK-LIFT OPERATOR

Ranking: 162

Score: 14.09

Basic Day: 9.0 Hours

Industrial truck operators work in warehouses and manufacturing plants, or at outdoor lumber yards or other storage facilities. These workers must possess dexterity to drive and maneuver fork-lifts safely, and good eyesight to judge distances accurately. Strength is necessary in this occupation, since carrying and lifting are also called for on the job. Industrial truck operators risk injuries from driving accidents, and from falling objects. Operators may be exposed to noise, vibration, or harmful fumes.

FURNITURE UPHOLSTERER

Ranking: 168

Score: 14.41

Basic Day: 8.5 Hours

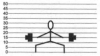

Furniture upholsterers are on their feet throughout the day, working in factories or industrial shops. In the course of their work, they are required to crouch, bend, and reach, and to do some heavy lifting. Upholsterers should have good hand-eye coordination and manual dexterity in order to cut and match fabrics and to use hand tools and sewing machines. Furniture upholsterers may be exposed to airborne dust which can be a health hazard. For those who consult with customers, communication skills are important.

GARBAGE COLLECTOR

Ranking: 242

Score: 36.55

Basic Day: 8.5 Hours

In the course of their duties, garbage collectors must lift, carry and dump heavy trash bins and cans. Arm and hand strength are important in this occupation. Trash collection normally begins early in the morning and must be carried out in all weather conditions. Collectors have to become accustomed to working in extreme heat or cold, as well as in rain or snow. Workers in this occupation are exposed to dirt, filth and grime.

GEOLOGIST

Ranking: 148

Score: 12.98

Basic Day: 9.0 Hours

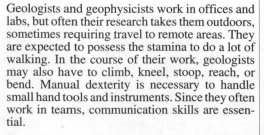

Geologists and geophysicists work in offices and labs, but often their research takes them outdoors, sometimes requiring travel to remote areas. They are expected to possess the stamina to do a lot of walking. In the course of their work, geologists may also have to climb, kneel, stoop, reach, or bend. Manual dexterity is necessary to handle small hand tools and instruments. Since they often work in teams, communication skills are essential.

GLAZIER

Ranking: 200

Score: 18.85

Basic Day: 9.0 Hours

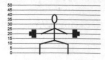

Glaziers often work outdoors; they spend a lot of time on their feet, sometimes at great heights, balanced upon scaffolding. In the course of their work, they are required to lift, climb, bend and crouch. Glaziers must have the manual dexterity and coordination to handle and install panes of glass. They are exposed not only to the noise and hazards of power tools, but also to the risk of bodily injury from broken glass or falls.

GUARD

Ranking: 146

Score: 12.55

Basic Day: 8.5 Hours

Guards patrol buildings and grounds on foot, or they sit at security desks. They work regular hours, often on a rotating shift basis. Guards must have excellent powers of observation for monitoring surveillance screens, checking people as they come and go, and making sure security systems are functioning. This work necessitates keen eyesight and hearing. A guard must be physically fit and ready for immediate response in the event of an emergency. Guards are constantly at risk of possible personal danger.

HEATING/REFRIGERATION MECHANIC

Ranking: 204

Score: 20.05

Basic Day: 9.0 Hours

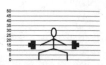

Heating and refrigeration mechanics often work in uncomfortable environments. Since air-conditioning or heating equipment is usually broken on the job site, conditions can be extremely hot or cold. In addition, work spaces can be cramped, and equipment hard to reach. Mechanics must be able to communicate effectively by radio or telephone, in order to give and receive information about jobs. These workers travel to job sites in equipped trucks. Repairs require mechanics to stoop, reach, kneel, lift, carry, and climb to high places. Heating and refrigeration mechanics endure noise, dust, and fumes, and are at risk of injury from burns, electric shocks, and lifting heavy objects.

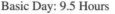

HIGHWAY PATROL OFFICER

Ranking: 195

Score: 17.63

Basic Day: 9.5 Hours

State highway patrol officers work a regular week. Schedules include holidays, nights and weekends. State troopers spend much time driving, and therefore need coordination and good eyesight. Patrolling the highways requires, quick judgment, in addition to excellent vision, to see and evaluate events on the road. Verbal skills are important in this occupation, for effective communication with motorists in a variety of situations. State police officers face hazardous and potentially volatile situations in dealing with lawbreakers.

HISTORIAN

Ranking: 20

Score: 5.09

Basic Day: 9.0 Hours

Historians normally work at desks in offices or libraries, doing a great deal of reading, writing, and research. Most historians teach in addition to doing research, and thus effective communication skills are essential in this profession. Some historical research involves much personal interviewing, and therefore travel may be required to meet with interview subjects. Historians may also travel to conduct research in other countries on otherwise inaccessible documents or material, or to attend conferences and meetings. The stamina to follow an idea persistently and systematically is necessary. The intellectual rigors of this exacting work can be physically draining.

HOME ECONOMIST

Ranking: 142

Score: 12.04

Basic Day: 9.0 Hours

Home economists normally work 35 to 40 hours per week. Those who teach in secondary schools often work or attend conferences and meetings after school hours. Home economists spend a good deal of time on their feet. These workers should have good communication skills, as well as knowledge of homemaking methods and health and nutrition. In addition, cooking skills are important in this profession.

HOSPITAL ADMINISTRATOR

Ranking: 43

Score: 6.31

Basic Day: 9.5 Hours

Hospital administrators often work long hours. The work environment for members of this profession is comfortable. Managerial activities are not physically strenuous, but managers should have the stamina to speak at length, with many different kinds of people, and to endure the long hours this position entails. Hospital administrators talk with patients or residents of health care establishments, and with finance directors, personnel officers, and other health care administrators. Thus, the ability to communicate effectively is essential to individuals in this occupation. Administrators occasionally must travel to conduct inspections of facilities, to give speeches, and to attend meetings.

HOTEL MANAGER

Ranking: 52

Score: 6.97

Basic Day: 9.0 Hours

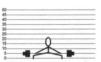

Most hotel managers work 40 hours per week, including nights and weekends, in pleasant surroundings. Overtime, especially during busy holiday and vacation seasons brings up their average working hours considerably. They can suffer from physical exhaustion from having to coordinate a variety of duties which are spread over large physical areas to which they must walk.

INDUSTRIAL DESIGNER

Ranking: 46

Score: 6.85

Basic Day: 9.0 Hours

Industrial designers work regular hours, sitting in pleasant offices. Overtime is occasionally required in this profession. Industrial designers must have the drawing talent to create clear, easily understood designs for manufactured products. Communication skills, and creativity are needed to conduct research and develop innovative products for consumer use. Those industrial designers who work in teams have an even greater need to communicate effectively.

INDUSTRIAL ENGINEER

Ranking: 83

Score: 8.21

Basic Day: 9.0 Hours

Industrial engineers do their work at desks, often using computers. Because their research includes taking surveys, they may have to do some traveling. They spend a lot of time designing, and evaluating plans, statistics, and related documents, so visual acuity is important. Eye strain can result from many hours of staring at a computer screen or concentrating on plans and documents.

INDUSTRIAL MACHINE REPAIRER

Ranking: 188

Score: 16.39

Basic Day: 9.5 Hours

Industrial machinery repairers normally work 40-hour weeks, but may put in overtime on weekends or at night, in the event of emergencies. Repair work requires a moderate amount of lifting and carrying, and crouching, kneeling, and bending. Repairers may have to climb and balance themselves on ladders. Manual dexterity is needed in this occupation, in order to use precision tools, such as micrometers and drills. Depending on the type of equipment in need of maintenance, industrial machinery repairers may be exposed to some degree of noise, vibration, dust, and grime.

INSURANCE AGENT

Ranking: 36

Score: 6.05

Basic Day: 9.0 Hours

Insurance agents or brokers often work long hours, including local or overnight travel to meet with clients or managers. The work of insurance agents is not physically taxing, since this job mainly entails sitting and talking. Agents speak with clients and potential customers, over the telephone and in person, so good communication skills are essential for effective performance. Stamina and persistence are required to locate and keep clients, and to cope with a hectic schedule.

INSURANCE UNDERWRITER

Ranking: 59

Score: 7.12

Basic Day: 9.0 Hours

Insurance underwriters normally work 40-hour weeks. Duties are usually performed at office desks, but some travel, for instance to attend conferences, is called for in this profession. The majority of an underwriter's time is spent paging through actuarial tables and other information sources, analyzing data, and communicating findings. Only limited physical activity is required in this occupation. However, eye and back strain may result from this detailed work. Communication skills are needed to interact effectively. wi

IRONWORKER

Ranking: 243

Score: 36.85

Basic Day: 9.0 Hours

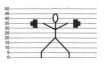

Ironworkers labor outdoors, in a variety of weather conditions. Members of this trade may have to travel significant distances in order to find work. Ironworkers perform heavy labor, which entails lifting, carrying, climbing, reaching, and bending. Manual dexterity, strength, and good physical coordination are required to use specialized equipment, such as cranes, spud wrenches, and plumb bobs. Ironworkers must endure noise and vibration while on the job. These workers wear hard-hats and safety harnesses t for protection.

JANITOR

Ranking: 187

Score: 16.16

Basic Day: 8.0 Hours

Most janitors work full-time hours, both indoors and outdoors, often at night. In the course of their work, custodians walk, reach, bend, lift, and carry. These workers need the strength and coordination to manipulate various kinds of cleaning equipment, from brooms to floor polishing machines. Those in charge of maintenance may be responsible for fairly sophisticated equipment and materials, including toxic chemicals. Depending upon specific duties and equipment used, janitors are exposed to noise, vibration, unpleasant odors, fumes, and dirt.

JEWELER

Ranking: 34

Score: 6.04

Basic Day: 9.0 Hours

Jewelers work irregular schedules, which fluctuate seasonally. Their detailed, precise work requires excellent manual dexterity and good eyesight. Jewelers sometimes wear magnifying glasses to aid in perfecting their work. Good coordination is needed to handle such instruments as pliers, precision engraving tools, and soldering irons. Eye and back strain can result from this exacting work. Jewelers who supervise shops, or who are involved in sales, need good communication skills and a personable manner.

JOCKEY

Ranking: 235

Score: 30.85

Basic Day: 9.0 Hours

Certain physical characteristics are common to most professional jockeys. Since speed is of the essence in horse racing, and as horses run more quickly carrying less weight, jockeys are normally smaller than average in build and height. Despite their diminutive stature, jockeys, like other athletes, must have strength, stamina and coordination. Controlling the horse at racing speeds requires excellent equestrian skills. The long racing season can cause physical wear and fatigue for members of this profession. Jockeys can suffer bruises and broken bones in spills during races or training.

JUDGE (FEDERAL)

Ranking: 20

Score: 5.09

Basic Day: 10.0 Hours

Federal judges work in quiet, comfortable surroundings in courtrooms and well-appointed chambers. The case load for federal judges varies depending on the time of year and the type of court over which the judge presides. Most judges can dictate their workloads to some extent, delegating a degree of research and writing duties to judicial clerks. Still, judges' case loads can be heavy and schedules hectic.

LIBRARIAN

Ranking: 70

Score: 7.56

Basic Day: 8.5 Hours

Librarians work 40-hour weeks, often including some evenings and weekends. Handling books and other library materials requires walking, reaching, kneeling, bending, and lifting. Good eyesight is required to utilize computer databases and catalogs, to read large amounts of information, and to file books and documents properly. Reference librarians talk with patrons, on the telephone or in the library, and some librarians give speeches or read in front of groups. Therefore, communication skills are important in this profession.

LITHOGRAPHER/ PHOTOENGRAVER

Ranking: 71

Score: 7.82

Basic Day: 9.0 Hours

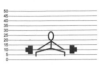

Lithographers and photoengravers work regular weeks, sometimes on night shifts. Overtime is occasionally required in this trade to meet deadlines. Lithographers and photoengravers stand while working. These workers are required to do some reaching, and to have the manual dexterity to handle detailed work using chemicals and precision instruments. Exposure to some chemicals used in lithography can cause skin and respiratory irritations. Eye and muscle strain can result from this exacting work.

LUMBERJACK

Ranking: 247

Score: 38.87

Basic Day: 9.0 Hours

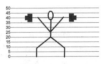

Lumberjacks generally work outdoors in varying weather, often in remote areas of the country. Overtime is required during emergencies, such as forest fires. Close observation and careful attention to visual information is required. Very heavy lifting is required which involves equipment and, at times, harvested timbers, and debris. This job involves some walking, reaching, driving, and careful handling of tools and equipment.

MACHINE TOOL OPERATOR

Ranking: 172

Score: 14.86

Basic Day: 9.0 Hours

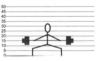

Machine tool operators work regular hours, sometimes on night shifts. These workers spend much time on their feet, and are required to perform some moderate lifting and carrying. This occupation calls for manual dexterity, to place machine tools properly, and to use precision instruments, such as micrometers, accurately. Good eyesight and observational skills are necessary to monitor machines effectively. Machine tool operators must wear protective gear to minimize the possibility of bodily injury, and to guard against damage to hearing from excessive noise.

MACHINIST

Ranking: 193

Score: 17.46

Basic Day: 9.5 Hours

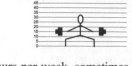

Machinists work 40 hours per week, sometimes on evening or night shifts. Work is performed in industrial shops with noisy equipment. Machinists spend much of their work time standing, and they must lift, carry, and handle moderately heavy objects. Hand-to-eye coordination is required to follow specifications, to plan operations adequately, and to finish and test pieces correctly. Safety gear must be worn in this trade, to prevent hearing loss and bodily injury.

MAID

Ranking: 190

Score: 17.00

Basic Day: 7.5 Hours

Maids and house cleaners often work part-time for several employers. These workers perform a variety of physically strenuous activities, including climbing, reaching, bending, kneeling, pushing, lifting and carrying. Maids are exposed to minor noise from using equipment such as vacuum cleaners. Frequent contact with water, detergents, and chemical cleaning compounds in this occupation may result in skin irritation. A good deal of stamina is required to perform this job effectively.

MAIL CARRIER

Ranking: 225

Score: 26.86

Basic Day: 9.0 Hours

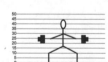

Mail carriers work 40 hours per week in all weather, including rain, snow, and extreme heat. Some mail carriers work from 4 a.m. to the early afternoon. Carriers spend most of their time walking, or driving. Those who travel routes on foot push carts or carry large bags of mail. Some mail carriers need the coordination and good eyesight to drive drive postal vehicle safely. Attention to detail is required in this occupation, for accurate reading of addresses and correct delivery.

MARKET RESEARCH ANALYST

Ranking: 6

Score: 4.09

Basic Day: 9.0 Hours

Market research analysts normally work regular hours, although overtime may occasionally be required to meet deadlines. These professionals sometimes travel to attend meetings with clients and colleagues, and to gather information. Market research analysts spend much of their time examining data and statistics, and writing reports, while sitting at desks. Communication skills are essential for effective presentations of reports to management and clients. These skills are also important when market research analysts work in teams.

MATHEMATICIAN

Ranking: 3

Score: 3.97

Basic Day: 9.0 Hours

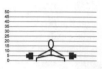

Mathematicians sit at desks, and use computers and calculators, so visual acuity is needed in this profession. Mathematicians also work with scientists or researchers, and teamwork on research and problem solving requires the ability to communicate effectively. Those mathematicians who teach spend much time standing and talking before groups, and must reach up to write on blackboards. Working with extremely detailed calculations can cause eye strain.

MAYOR

Ranking: 53

Score: 6.98

Basic Day: 9.0 Hours

Mayors of large cities normally work very hectic schedules and carry the heavy burden of administrative duties. These mayors must be accustomed to long hours, an extremely fast pace, and extensive travel. In smaller cities and towns, mayoral duties may be diminished, and thus less fatiguing. Big city mayors have the additional burden of dealing with sensitive racial issues.

MECHANICAL ENGINEER

Ranking: 125

Score: 10.28

Basic Day: 9.5 Hours

Mechanical engineers work in offices analyzing or drawing plans, and conducting research. Manual dexterity and hand-eye coordination are required when mechanical engineers test or maintain equipment. For engineers who are involved in sales, operations, or management, communication skills are an additional requirement. When certain types of machinery are involved, such as refrigerators or internal combustion engines, mechanical engineers may be exposed to extreme temperatures.

MEDICAL LABORATORY TECHNICIAN

Ranking: 64

Score: 7.26

Basic Day: 8.5 Hours

Medical laboratory technicians work 40-hour weeks, which often include nights, holidays, and weekends. Technicians work in a sterilized environment, and stand while carefully handling specimens and equipment. Visual acuity and manual dexterity are important for accurate work. Since the lives of patients may depend on the work of medical lab technicians, these workers may experience fatigue from the pressure of having to perform accurately and quickly. Safety precautions must be followed to avoid exposure to infectious substances.

MEDICAL RECORDS TECHNICIAN

Ranking: 64

Score: 7.26

Basic Day: 8.5 Hours

Medical record technicians work full- or part-time, and shift work is common in this occupation. Records technicians are required to do much reaching and handling as they retrieve and code records. Work may be performed while seated in front of microfilm machines or computers, compiling and analyzing information. Eyestrain and muscle tension can result from this detailed work. For those medical record technicians who are supervisors, communication skills are important.

MEDICAL SECRETARY

Ranking: 37

Score: 6.06

Basic Day: 8.0 Hours

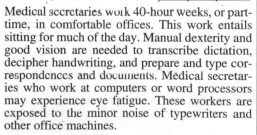

Medical secretaries work 40-hour weeks, or part-time, in comfortable offices. This work entails sitting for much of the day. Manual dexterity and good vision are needed to transcribe dictation, decipher handwriting, and prepare and type correspondences and documents. Medical secretaries who work at computers or word processors may experience eye fatigue. These workers are exposed to the minor noise of typewriters and other office machines.

MEDICAL TECHNOLOGIST

Ranking: 64

Score: 7.26

Basic Day: 8.5 Hours

Medical technologists work regular hours, including nights, holidays and weekends. Their work is performed in sterile environments, in order to prevent contamination from dirt and bacteria. These workers need to possess the visual acuity and manual coordination to conduct complex tests, using microscopes and other instruments. Medical technologists must take precautions against the hazards of working with harmful bacteria. For those in this occupation who teach or supervise, communication skills are important.

METEOROLOGIST

Ranking: 53

Score: 6.98

Basic Day: 9.0 Hours

Meteorologists work normal 40-hour weeks. Schedules often include nights, on a rotating shift basis. Meteorologists are required to have the visual skills needed to analyze data, weather maps, and graphs, often on computers. Manual dexterity and attention to detail are required in this profession, in order to make precise weather maps and graphs. Eye and back strain can result from such exacting work. Physical exertion is limited in this occupation.

METER READER

Ranking: 220

Score: 25.67

Basic Day: 8.5 Hours

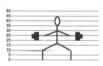

Meter readers are occasionally required to perform their jobs in cramped, stuffy, or otherwise uncomfortable spaces. Many utility meters are outdoors, and meter readers can be subjected to poor weather conditions, including rain and snow, in the course of their duties. Workers in this occupation spend a moderate amount of time on their feet, and they may also be required to drive vehicles.

MILITARY (COMMISSIONED OFFICER)

Ranking: 131

Score: 11.00

Basic Day: 8.0 Hours

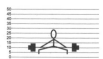

Commissioned officers in the U.S. Armed Forces perform a wide- variety of jobs and duties. Some are in combat roles, while others support overall military operations in support fields. The work place for an officer can range from a battlefield, a base in some remote region of the world, to a comfortable office. All officers undergo the rigors of basic training, and they must be proficient in military skills, including marksmanship. Military personnel of all ranks must maintain some standard of physical fitness, though this requirement is frequently not enforced. Officers perform less strenuous tasks than lower-ranking soldiers, but they must nevertheless have strength, stamina and agility to succeed on the battlefield.

MILITARY (ENLISTED PERSON)

Ranking: 222

Score: 26.00

Basic Day: 8.0 Hours

Enlisted members of the U.S. Armed Forces have to first undergo a grueling period of basic training in order to be shaped into well-conditioned soldiers. Trainees rise very early in the morning. The physical regimen includes calisthenics, running, drilling, and long marches with heavy backpacks. Enlistees must become proficient in basic soldiering skills, including marksmanship and operation of a variety of weapons. After training, enlisted personnel are assigned to any number of duties. A high standard of physical fitness is required of all soldiers, as conditioning and training can mean the difference between life and death in combat. Enlisted members of the armed forces must have strength, stamina and agility. Indeed, because combat infantry have to face such rigors, they have been given the nickname of "grunts."

MILITARY (WARRANT OFFICER)

Ranking: 174

Score: 15.00

Basic Day: 8.0 Hours

Warrant officers in the military, like other military personnel, must normally undergo the rigors of basic training. This regimen includes physical conditioning, weapons training, and preparation for more responsible duties. Warrant officers may be required to perform a number of different tasks, and even non-combat military personnel must meet a standard for physical fitness. Basic seamanship training is necessary for warrant officers in the Navy.

MILLWRIGHT

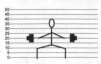

Ranking: 226

Score: 27.39

Basic Day: 9.5 Hours

Millwrights work regular hours. Some travel is required in this line of work, in order to install machinery. Millwrights have to climb ladders, balance on scaffolding, stoop, reach, bend, and lift and carry heavy machinery and tools. These workers must have manual dexterity and coordination to handle power tools, such as cutting torches and lathes, safely. Millwrights are exposed to noise and vibration, and risk falls and minor injuries. Members of this trade wear safety devices at all times while on the job.

MOTION PICTURE EDITOR

Ranking: 60

Score: 7.16

Basic Day: 9.0 Hours

Motion picture editors perform their jobs while sitting and operating splicing machines and other devices. Manual dexterity and attention to detail are required to match frames of film precisely. Editors must have some understanding of the director's intentions, as well as a degree of artistic sensibility. Long hours, including overtime, may be required to meet production deadlines in this profession. Since film editors are normally subordinate to directors, a particular movie episode may have to be edited a number of times in order to satisfy a director.

MUSEUM CURATOR

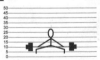

Ranking: 109

Score: 9.56

Basic Day: 8.5 Hours

Museum curators work in offices, although sometimes their research requires them to travel in order to make museum purchases and conduct specialized research for upcoming exhibits. They meet with administrators of the various museum departments and must be able to articulate their ideas clearly. In some museums, curators may also be involved in supervising the installation of exhibits, in cases like these, some minor physical exertion may be required.

MUSICAL INSTRUMENT REPAIRER

Ranking: 106

Score: 9.39

Basic Day: 9.5 Hours

Repairers generally work regular hours in music stores, shops, homes, or schools. Repairers must possess a great deal of manual dexterity and visual acuity to perform this detailed, exacting work. Repairers use precision tools, and other materials, such as sandpaper and varnish. Good hearing and a musical ear are required in order to test the tonal quality of repaired instruments. Repairers face a small possibility of minor injuries, such as cuts or burns.

MUSICIAN

Ranking: 182

Score: 15.85

Basic Day: 9.0 Hours

Musicians work in many environments, depending on the style of music they play, and the level of success they have attained. Nightclubs can be dark, smoky, and hot, while orchestra halls are normally quite pleasant. Musicians usually work nights and weekends, often on a part-time basis. Travel is sometimes required. Agile hands, strong lungs, and stamina may be required, depending on the type of instrument. Musicians often stand while performing. Those who play from sheet music need good eyesight. Stage presence is important for musicians in live performances. Rock musicians may be exposed to extremely high noise levels.

NEWSCASTER

Ranking: 46

Score: 6.85

Basic Day: 9.0 Hours

Radio and television newscasters generally work 40-hour weeks, which often include nights, weekends, and holidays. Work is performed in quiet, comfortable studios, or in noisy news rooms. Overtime or unpredictable schedules may be called for in this profession, since "the news never stops," and occasionally newscasters broadcast "on location" to cover stories or special events. Good communication skills are essential in newscasting. Work is not physically strenuous, but television newscasters face an extremely fast-paced environment, and may be exposed to dangerous situations in covering the news.

NEWS WRITER (RADIO/TV)

Ranking: 72

Score: 7.85

Basic Day: 9.0 Hours

Radio and television news writers work a regular week in noisy, bustling news rooms. Overtime is often required in this occupation to meet production deadlines. Sometimes travel is necessary in order to do research, conduct interviews, and cover stories. News writers work extensively on telephones, and often in libraries. Good communication skills, and the ability to write effectively and concisely, are essential in this line of work. Physical exertion is not demanded, but back strain may result from sitting and writing for long periods.

NUCLEAR ENGINEER

Ranking: 41

Score: 6.21

Basic Day: 9.0 Hours

Nuclear engineers spend most of their time conducting research and sitting at desks, but they are also required to go on site to observe or maintain the operations of nuclear facilities. They are expected to have the manual dexterity and visual acuity to draw plans and build models. Nuclear engineers, like anyone working with nuclear power, suffer the risk of contamination from radiation.

NUCLEAR PLANT DECONTAMI-NATION TECHNICIAN

Ranking: 205

Score: 20.13

Basic Day: 9.0 Hours

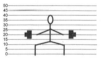

Nuclear plant decontamination technicians must wear protective suits, often lead-lined, during the course of their jobs. These suits can become hot, heavy and cumbersome after spending extended periods in them. Decontamination technicians normally carry equipment, which can be heavy, and they may be required to climb up to or descend into various hard-to-reach areas of power plants while carrying this equipment. This job requires strength, stamina and caution.

NURSE (LICENSED PRACTICAL)

Ranking: 174

Score: 15.00

Basic Day: 8.0 Hours

Licensed practical nurses work normal 40-hour weeks, which usually include some nights, holidays and weekends. These nurses spend a great deal of time on their feet, and some physical exertion is required in the course of caring for patients, for instance in lifting or guiding them into beds or wheelchairs. Nurses need hand-to-eye coordination and manual dexterity to perform injections and handle medical instruments. These workers also must possess communication skills to deal with patients sensitively. Stamina is required to maintain compassionate, safe care in often unpleasant circumstances.

NURSE (REGISTERED)

Ranking: 150

Score: 13.15

Basic Day: 8.0 Hours

Registered nurses normally work slightly more than 40-hours per week, including weekends, holidays, and nights. A good deal of standing and walking is required in this occupation. Registered nurses sometimes travel in order to treat patients or attend conferences. Some lifting and carrying is called for in the course of patient care. Manual dexterity and observation and communication skills are needed to care for patients and supervise workers effectively. Registered nurses must possess physical and mental stamina to provide compassionate and capable care to patients on a continuing basis.

NURSE'S AIDE

Ranking: 190

Score: 17.00

Basic Day: 8.0 Hours

Nursing aides work regular 40-hour weeks. Schedules include holidays, nights and weekends. Nursing aides spend much of their time walking, standing, and lifting or guiding patients. Observation, communication skills and coordination are important in caring for patients, including feeding and bathing patients, and making beds. When changing bed pans, nursing aides are exposed to unpleasant odors. Those employed in psychiatric wards face danger and stress from working with potentially violent or disorderly patients. Stamina is essential for effective performance in this occupation.

OCCUPATIONAL SAFETY/ HEALTH INSPECTOR

Ranking: 173

Score: 14.98

Basic Day: 9.0 Hours

Occupational safety and health inspectors often work long hours or irregular schedules, and are required to travel to the sites of inspection. De-

pending upon the nature of the inspection, these workers climb, crouch, stoop, reach, bend and lift objects on the job. Inspectors may be exposed to hazardous environmental conditions, indoors or outdoors. Members of this profession should possess the ability to observe closely and communicate effectively, in order to make accurate appraisals and recommendations.

OCCUPATIONAL THERAPIST

Ranking: 88

Score: 8.43

Basic Day: 8.5 Hours

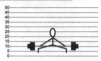

Occupational therapists work 40 hours per week, sometimes including nights and weekends. These workers must spend long periods on their feet, and may have to do some moderate lifting. Manual dexterity and the ability to communicate effectively are essential in providing therapy, such as instruction in motor skills. Physical demands in this occupation vary depending on the needs of the individuals in therapy, and the equipment or machines uses in treatment. Stamina is required in this profession to prevent frustration. Work environments for occupational therapists can be noisy.

OCEANOGRAPHER

Ranking: 139

Score: 11.98

Basic Day: 9.0 Hours

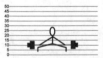

When conducting research on shore, oceanographers work in comfortable office or laboratory settings. Much research, however, is conducted underwater and on board ships. Researchers often lift, carry and operate their own equipment, including scuba gear, which is heavy when carried above water. Even under water, gear can be bulky and cumbersome. Underwater research calls for extensive training, as well as agility, good lung capacity and, of course, swimming ability. Work in this environment is extremely strenuous, and only the most physically fit researchers can spend extended periods of time working below the surface.

OFFICE MACHINE REPAIRER

Ranking: 145

Score: 12.41

Basic Day: 9.5 Hours

Office machine repairers work regular weeks. Repairers usually travel to several offices in one day. Dexterity and hand-eye coordination are necessary in using hand tools to make accurate tests and repairs on photocopiers, typewriters, and other office machines. Office machine repairers may be exposed to moderate amounts of noise, vibration, dust or grime. Good eyesight and communication skills are important in order to diagnose and correct machine malfunctions.

OPTICIAN

Ranking: 86

Score: 8.26

Basic Day: 8.5 Hours

Dispensing opticians may work up to 50 hours per week, including weekends and evenings. Much of an optician's time is spent talking with customers and helping them to choose and fit their eyeglasses, so communication and visual skills are important. Manual dexterity is also needed for members of this profession. For those dispensing opticians who also work in labs, safety measures must be made to prevent exposure to glass dust and hazardous chemicals.

OPTOMETRIST

Ranking: 115

Score: 9.79

Basic Day: 10.0 Hours

Optometrists work flexible schedules, often putting in long hours, including some evenings and weekends. Optometrists are required to push, pull, and lift complex optometric instruments and equipment. Members of this profession spend much time looking into the eyes of patients, talking with patients, and diagnosing their visual abilities. Therefore, communication skills and good eyesight are required for effective performance. Eye and back strain are common results of this detailed, exacting work.

ORTHODONTIST

Ranking: 98

Score: 8.96

Basic Day: 9.0 Hours

Regular work weeks for orthodontists often exceed 40 hours, and may include some weekends and evenings. Orthodontists sit in offices to process paperwork, and stand to perform their dental work. Manual dexterity, good eyesight, and coordination are required to apply braces gently and accurately to a patient's teeth, and to inspect the progress of orthodontic treatment. Communication skills are needed to converse with patients

and supervise the work of dental assistants effectively.

OSTEOPATH

Ranking: 184

Score: 15.90

Basic Day: 11.0 Hours

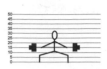

Osteopaths often work long hours and irregular schedules. Work is performed in clean, comfortable offices. Osteopaths are required to talk with and examine patients, and therefore must have communication and visual skills. In addition, coordination and manual dexterity are required in treating patients, since treatment often involves the careful manipulation of the patient's muscle and skeletal systems. Osteopaths must have stamina to endure the long hours and moderate physical exertion this profession demands.

PAINTER

Ranking: 222

Score: 26.00

Basic Day: 8.0 Hours

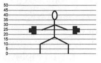

House painters often work irregular hours. House painters working on building exteriors labor outdoors. Painters and paperhangers must climb ladders, balance on scaffolding, reach, bend, and crouch. Good eyesight and manual dexterity are needed for the accurate application of paint or wallpaper. This work involves contact with solvents, sealers and other solutions, and exposure to potentially harmful fumes. Painters and paperhanger must take precautions against dangerous slips and falls on the job site.

PARALEGAL ASSISTANT

Ranking: 26

Score: 5.79

Basic Day: 9.0 Hours

Legal assistants usually work a regular 40-hour week, although sometimes long hours may be called for as court dates approach. Paralegals sit in offices and libraries, and sometimes have to lift heavy law books, and wade through lengthy files and documents. Often, legal assistants travel locally to deliver and pick up documents at courthouses, or to gather information. Good communication skills are necessary to converse effectively with lawyers, clients, and members of the public. Legal assistants must be able to write clearly and concisely, and to summarize detailed and lengthy opinions and research.

PAROLE OFFICER

Ranking: 45

Score: 6.47

Basic Day: 8.5 Hours

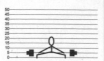

Parole officers work full-or part-time, often including nights and weekends. This work involves a moderate amount of travel to visit parolees at their homes or workplaces. Physical exertion is rarely required. Parole officers spend much of their time talking with parolees, other parole officers, and members of the community, so speaking and listening skills are essential for effective job performance.

PERSONNEL RECRUITER

Ranking: 27

Score: 5.84

Basic Day: 10.0 Hours

Personnel recruiters usually work at desks in quiet, comfortable offices. Recruiters also travel in order to attend meetings, and to interview potential employees, for instance at university campuses. Recruiters spend a great deal of time talking with prospective employees, either in person or on the telephone. Personnel recruiting also involves checking references, giving tests, and recommending job candidates to employers. Therefore, the ability to evaluate people and to communicate effectively is essential to members of this profession.

PETROLEUM ENGINEER

Ranking: 83

Score: 8.21

Basic Day: 9.0 Hours

Petroleum engineers must have coordination and dexterity to handle the complex equipment used to drill for oil and gas. They develop and conduct research, so they also spend time working on plans for new designs. Good communication skills are essential in order to supervise others and to insure safety during drilling operations. Petroleum engineers wear hard hats when on a drilling site. Those who work offshore are exposed to greater danger, because they are surrounded by water.

PHARMACIST

Ranking: 97

Score: 8.86

Basic Day: 10.0 Hours

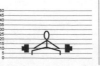

The work of pharmacists must take place in a clean, well-lit environment. Pharmacists work longer than average days and include some holidays, nights and weekends. Pharmacists stand on their feet for most of the work day, and often must stretch, stoop, or bend to reach drugs and related merchandise. Hand-to-eye coordination, concentration, and good eyesight are necessary to dispense merchandise carefully, and to properly fill prescriptions. Pharmacists occasionally wear masks or gloves for protection against harmful substances.

PHILOSOPHER

Ranking: 34

Score: 6.04

Basic Day: 9.0 Hours

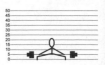

Philosophy is perhaps the least physically demanding of all occupational fields. By its very nature, it is essentially an intellectual profession and thus entails almost no physical labor. However, the long hours of reading and research this discipline requires can lead to eyestrain and muscle cramps. Philosophy faculty members normally enjoy extremely comfortable teaching schedules. Grading and publishing deadlines can result in working long hours.

PHOTOGRAPHER

Ranking: 128

Score: 10.85

Basic Day: 9.0 Hours

Still photographers work irregular, sometimes long hours, both in comfortable photography studios and outdoors. They require keen eyesight, good hand-eye coordination, and manual dexterity in order to handle cameras and developing equipment. Good communication skills are needed in order to invoke the desired response from subjects, and to direct assistants during a photo shoot.

PHOTOGRAPHIC PROCESS WORKER

Ranking: 75

Score: 7.98

Basic Day: 9.0 Hours

Photographic process workers work regular hours in a photography lab. For those in commercial labs, overtime is generally required during holiday seasons and in the summer. Manual dexterity and concentration are important in this job; it entails fast, repetitive, hand work. Processors work in darkrooms with chemicals which irritate the skin and produce noxious fumes. Good ventilation guards against overexposure to chemical fumes. Eye strain may result from close, exacting work.

PHOTOJOURNALIST

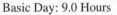

Ranking: 182

Score: 15.85

Basic Day: 9.0 Hours

Photojournalists usually work long, irregular hours in many different environments. They often have to travel in order to cover a story. Photojournalists must have good vision and hand- eye coordination in order to handle a camera. They must be quick on their feet to catch action shots and not be caught under foot. For those who conduct interviews or report news, communication skills are important. There may be a chance of personal danger if the story being photographed involves a natural disaster, war, or other violence.

PHYSICAL THERAPIST

Ranking: 179

Score: 15.43

Basic Day: 8.5 Hours

Physical therapists schedule their hours around their patients' needs, they usually work some weekends and evenings. Physical therapists must be strong and agile, they have to help patients to stand up, turn, walk, and move their bodies in other ways, so some lifting may be required. Good communication skills and powers of observation are necessary to evaluate and proscribe therapy for patients. Stamina is required to continue the proper and careful treatment of patients.

PHYSICIAN (GENERAL PRACTICE)

Ranking: 130

Score: 10.90

Basic Day: 11.0 Hours

General practitioners with private practices usually work long and irregular hours. Those who work for health maintenance organizations and clinics work regular 40-hour weeks. Doctors must have strong constitutions, as they work long hours and are constantly exposed to disease. They also need a good command of their sense faculties which are essential for examining and diagnosing patients' conditions. Doctors must have good communication skills to instill confidence in patients and give advice.

PHYSICIAN ASSISTANT

Ranking: 105

Score: 9.36

Basic Day: 8.5 Hours

Physician assistants work in a clean environment and are subject to varying physical demands depending upon duties assigned. Manual dexterity and coordination are required for handling lab equipment, sterilizing instruments, or accurately conducting tests. These skills are also needed for the careful tasks of drawing blood or applying dressings. The ability to communicate is important when performing clerical duties or dealing with patients.

PHYSICIST

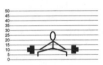

Ranking: 75

Score: 7.98

Basic Day: 9.0 Hours

Physicists work regular hours in labs, offices, or classrooms. Some travel may be required in order to access specialized facilities such as particle accelerators. Physicists are expected to possess good hand-eye coordination and powers of observation to perform complex experiments on such subjects as the nature of atomic particles, lasers, or microwaves. Physicists who teach or present papers need good communication skills.

PHYSIOLOGIST

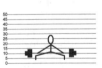

Ranking: 75

Score: 7.98

Basic Day: 9.0 Hours

Physiologists generally work a regular week in a laboratory or office. Some specialists in this field, such as geophysicists, may perform research outdoors. In field or laboratory research, physical scientists often have to walk, climb, crouch, and do some lifting and carrying. Good vision and physical coordination are necessities in properly and safely handling research equipment, chemicals, and precision instruments. For those physical scientists who teach, or who work in teams, effective communication skills are essential.

PIANO TUNER

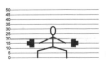

Ranking: 152

Score: 13.39

Basic Day: 9.5 Hours

Piano tuners work in homes, music stores, schools or other buildings that house pianos. Tuners must travel from client to client. In the course of their work, piano tuners are required to stoop, bend, and stand on the job. They must have the manual dexterity and coordination to handle hand tools as tuning hammers or repinners, and to make minute adjustments to piano stings. Acute hearing is important, since piano tuners must differentiate between minute pitches.

PLASTERER

Ranking: 221

Score: 25.85

Basic Day: 9.0 Hours

Plasterers work indoors for the most part, although if they are applying stucco, they work outdoors. In the process of applying plaster, they do a lot of standing, climbing, crouching, and lifting. Plasterers need manual dexterity, good coordination, strength, and stamina in order to mix and apply plaster materials and to use hand tools. They are exposed to wet plaster, dust, dirt and chemical fumes, all of which may cause eye and skin irritation.

PLUMBER

Ranking: 211

Score: 21.80

Basic Day: 9.0 Hours

Plumbers work long hours, and they often have to respond to emergencies at odd hours. In the course of their work, they often do moderate lifting, and must be capable of bending, stooping, crouching, crawling, and reaching. Often they have to stand in uncomfortable positions, for long periods of time, in unpleasant surroundings. Good hand-eye coordination and strength are required, in order to handle heavy hand tools. Plumbers risk injuries, such as cuts from sharp tools or burns from hot pipes.

PODIATRIST

Ranking: 126

Score: 10.79

Basic Day: 10.0 Hours

Podiatrists work in clean offices, on flexible schedules which usually amount to 40 hours per week. During examination and diagnosis a podiatrist must handle and inspect patients' feet, so manual dexterity and good observation skills are necessary. Good communication skills are important when discussing patients' conditions with

them during the diagnostic process. Podiatrists who perform surgery require steady hands and good eyesight.

POLICE OFFICER

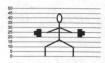

Ranking: 214

Score: 22.63

Basic Day: 9.5 Hours

Police officers work 40 hours per week, which includes some nights, weekends and holidays. They must be physically fit as their work entails a great deal of physical activity, and they must be ready to act at a moment's notice. Police require excellent powers of observation in order to detect trouble and avert danger. Strength is important to police officers as they must be able to restrain criminals and defend themselves. Police officers constantly risk grave personal danger.

POLITICAL SCIENTIST

Ranking: 39

Score: 6.09

Basic Day: 9.0 Hours

Political scientists may work both regular hours in offices and irregular hours in the field gathering research data. Some overtime may be required in order to meet deadlines. Travel, both domestic and foreign, is essential to investigate the workings of governments or to conduct surveys. Political scientists spend considerable time at meetings and conferences, discussing and analyzing political issues, so good communication skills are important.

POSTAL INSPECTOR

Ranking: 114

Score: 9.76

Basic Day: 10.0 Hours

Postal inspectors work irregular hours, and sometimes have to travel in order to observe the mechanism of the postal system. Postal inspectors require good communication skills and strong powers of observation in order to investigate possible cases of mail theft or fraud. Physical exertion is not required, but staying-power is required to endure the stress that results from dealing with difficult people and situations.

PRECISION ASSEMBLER

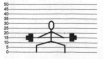

Ranking: 157

Score: 13.53

Basic Day: 8.5 Hours

Assemblers usually work regular 40 hour weeks, but some plants may require rotating shifts, or occasional overtime. Precision assembling calls for great accuracy, workers in this field must have exceptional hand-eye coordination. Conditions vary, depending upon the industry, but most precision assemblers must perform repetitive motions at a rapid pace. They are exposed to mechanical noise and vibration, and sometimes work in potentially dangerous situations.

PRESIDENT (U.S.)

Ranking: 164

Score: 14.20

Basic Day: 13.0 Hours

The vast demands of the presidential duties as well as the magnitude of the administrative tasks involved will no-doubt result in physical and mental strain. The President needs an enormous amount of physical stamina to meet the continual pressures and complex schedule he must keep. When running for office or re-election, the presidential candidate's schedule will increase, adding more physical stress to an already high- pressured position.

PROTESTANT MINISTER

Ranking: 69

Score: 7.44

Basic Day: 10.5 Hours

Protestant ministers work irregular hours, since they are always on call to serve members of the congregation. Ministers spend a great deal of time reading, conducting research, and writing. Good vision and attention to detail are thus important in this work. The ability to communicate effectively is also necessary, as ministers advise and counsel others, give sermons, teach classes, and conduct religious ceremonies. Sunday mornings can be exhausting for ministers, especially when churches have more than one service.

PSYCHIATRIST

Ranking: 138

Score: 11.90

Basic Day: 11.0 Hours

Psychiatrists work irregular schedules, sometimes spending long hours in offices. Members of this profession are required to be good listeners and observers. Communication skills are essential for psychiatrists to perform effectively. Communication skills are also important in consulting with colleagues, and for teaching in schools of psychiatry. Little physical exertion is required in this profession, but psychiatrists need stamina to continue to treat patients disturbed by mental illness compassionately.

PSYCHOLOGIST

Ranking: 58

Score: 7.09

Basic Day: 9.0 Hours

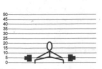

Psychologists, depending on their specialty, work regular or irregular hours, which often include weekends or evenings. Some psychologists travel in order to go to conferences or to do research. Good communication skills are essential to psychologists in the course of conducting clinical studies, tests, interviews, counseling sessions, etc. The ability to communicate is also important for those psychologists who train others or give oral reports of their research.

PUBLIC RELATIONS EXECUTIVE

Ranking: 62

Score: 7.24

Basic Day: 9.0 Hours

Though public relations executives officially maintain a 40 hour week at the office, overtime is often required to meet deadlines. In most cases, travel is necessary in order to participate in promotional or publicity tours of their clients.

PUBLICATION EDITOR

Ranking: 11

Score: 4.85

Basic Day: 9.0 Hours

Editors work regular hours, although some overtime may be required during production periods. They spend a great deal of time talking with writers and consulting with personnel in charge of the various phases of production. The responsibilities of hiring and firing, drawing up contracts, and other administrative tasks demand excellent communication skills. An editor should have a good design sense to evaluate designs and layouts for publication.

PURCHASING AGENT

Ranking: 61

Score: 7.23

Basic Day: 9.0 Hours

Purchasing agents work regular hours in offices, although sometimes they travel to trade shows or to visit suppliers. Because the success of their work relies upon relationships with with suppliers and vendors, and with other employees such as shipping personnel, purchasing agents must be good communicators. Good powers of observation and discernment are important when inspecting new products and watching demonstrations of equipment before making decisions to buy.

RABBI

Ranking: 89

Score: 8.44

Basic Day: 10.5 Hours

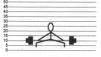

Rabbis work irregular schedules, and frequently long hours, since they are always on call for the members of their congregation. This work occasionally calls for travel within the community, for instance to visit and administer to the sick. Much of a rabbi's day is spent sitting, studying religious texts and conducting research. Eye and back strain can result from this work. Effective communication skills are essential in preparing and delivering sermons, counseling members of the congregation, meeting with community leaders, and conducting other related duties.

RACE CAR DRIVER (INDY CLASS)

Ranking: 235

Score: 30.85

Basic Day: 9.0 Hours

Race car drivers must have a great deal of stamina to endure distance races of up to 500 miles. Controlling the vehicle for long periods of time, at speeds often in excess of 200 miles per hour, requires extremely quick reflexes and good coordination, strength, timing and judgment. Accidents at such high speeds can be disastrous, even fatal. Drivers wear protective suits and helmets, which, in the cramped and hot cockpit of the car, can become uncomfortable.

RAILROAD CONDUCTOR

Ranking: 170

Score: 14.77

Basic Day: 10.0 Hours

Rail conductors and engineers may be required to work evenings and weekends, and they must become accustomed to odd hours. Conductors on passenger trains spend a good deal of time on their feet while moving through cars to collect tickets and fares from passengers. Over long journeys, fatigue can set in for both conductors and engineers. This can create hazardous situations, as conductors and engineers must be alert at all times in order to handle emergencies, such as equipment failures or track obstructions.

REAL ESTATE AGENT

Ranking: 92

Score: 8.58

Basic Day: 9.5 Hours

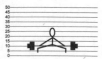

Real estate agents and brokers usually work over 40 hours per week, including some weekend and evening hours in order to accommodate their clients. This work involves a moderate amount of travel to sales properties in the community. Brokers and agents talk with clients and evaluate property, so good communication and observational skills are needed in order to perform effectively. Agents spend much time on their feet, showing properties to prospective buyers.

RECEPTIONIST

Ranking: 30

Score: 6.00

Basic Day: 8.0 Hours

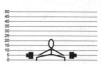

Receptionists sit at desks, usually in pleasant, comfortable office settings. Work weeks in this occupation are normally 40 hours, although many receptionists work part-time. In the course of a receptionist's duties, manual dexterity is required in order to reach, manipulate, and handle numerous objects, materials, and pieces of office equipment. Good communication skills and a personable manner are important in order to answer telephone calls and greet office visitors.

RECREATION WORKER

Ranking: 199

Score: 18.47

Basic Day: 8.5 Hours

Recreation workers generally put in 40 hours per week on the job, sometimes including nights or weekends. Much of a recreation worker's time is spent outdoors, depending upon the nature of the recreational activities being supervised. Communication skills are essential in this line of work, in order to instruct, lead and oversee others effectively and safely. Recreation workers, especially those who are employed as camp counselors or coaches, are involved in numerous physically strenuous activities, which may include running, swimming, or playing various sports.

REPORTER

Ranking: 116

Score: 9.85

Basic Day: 9.0 Hours

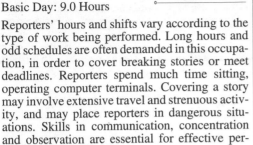

Reporters' hours and shifts vary according to the type of work being performed. Long hours and odd schedules are often demanded in this occupation, in order to cover breaking stories or meet deadlines. Reporters spend much time sitting, operating computer terminals. Covering a story may involve extensive travel and strenuous activity, and may place reporters in dangerous situations. Skills in communication, concentration and observation are essential for effective performance in this occupation.

RESPIRATORY THERAPIST

Ranking: 155

Score: 13.43

Basic Day: 8.5 Hours

Respiratory therapists work 40 hours per week, including nights and weekends. These workers are required to spend a great deal of time on their feet. Manual dexterity and good vision are required in this work in order to operate special equipment safely and accurately. Gases used in respiratory therapy are stored under pressure, and therapists must take precautions to avoid mishaps or injuries. Therapists should have stamina to work efficiently under stressful situations, such as dealing with the ill, and with emergencies.

ROOFER

Ranking: 239

Score: 33.46

Basic Day: 8.5 Hours

Roofers are required to do frequent lifting and carrying, as well as climbing, kneeling, reaching and bending. These workers must be accustomed to laboring in poor weather conditions. Roofers face the risk of injuries from falls, slips, or burns. Roofers use various tools to perform construction and repairs, applying materials such as insulation, asphalt, tar, and slate. Manual dexterity and good vision are needed in this work. Roofers must wear protective gear to fend off dust and harmful fumes.

ROUSTABOUT

Ranking: 244

Score: 36.89

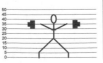

Basic Day: 10.0 Hours

Roustabouts who work offshore put in 12-hour days, on schedules alternating a week of work with a week off. Those on land work a more regular schedule. Roustabouts work in all kinds of weather conditions. Heavy lifting, climbing, bending, stooping, and reaching are required. Strength and coordination are needed to handle safely such equipment as motorized lifts, cranes, trucks and power tools. Roustabouts face a great risk of injury from falls, falling objects, and exposure to hazardous chemicals.

SALES REPRESENTATIVE (WHOLESALE)

Ranking: 110

Score: 9.58

Basic Day: 9.5 Hours

Wholesale representatives work irregular schedules, which often include weekends and evenings. This work involves some travel to visit potential buyers at companies and establishments within a sales territory. Wholesale trade salespeople must be able to communicate effectively, in order to explain products to buyers, offer them advice, and close deals. No strenuous activity is demanded in this occupation, but this work entails a good deal of standing and walking. Some wholesale salespersons spend long periods sitting at desks, writing reports, processing paperwork, and making sales appointments.

SALESPERSON (RETAIL)

Ranking: 131

Score: 11.00

Basic Day: 8.0 Hours

Retail salespeople work full- or part-time, including some weekend or evening hours, and overtime during holiday and discount periods. Normal full-time work weeks in this occupation are 37.5 to 40 hours. Retail sales personnel spend a good deal of time on their feet. These workers need to possess dexterity to demonstrate merchandise, and communication skills and a personable manner to describe the features of sales items, to persuade customers to buy merchandise, and to process sales. Stamina is required to perform effectively.

SCHOOL PRINCIPAL

Ranking: 25

Score: 5.62

Basic Day: 9.5 Hours

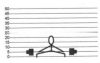

School principals regularly work over 40 hours per week, attending civic functions, school board meetings, and parent- teacher association meetings after school hours, or handling school emergencies. Principals spend a moderate amount of time sitting at desks processing paperwork. Communication skills and tact are required in advising and disciplining students, in supervising faculty and staff, and in meeting with civil leaders to negotiate school budgets and discuss curricula. This profession requires physical stamina to endure the long hours, and mental stamina to handle the pressure of criticism from various sides.

SEAMAN

Ranking: 234

Score: 30.77

Basic Day: 10.0 Hours

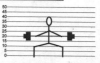

Depending on cargo destination, sailors may spend long stretches of time at sea, and they must be accustomed to working on board ship in all weather conditions. Living quarters for crew members are usually somewhat cramped, as are most spaces aboard ships. Sailors can be required to perform a number of tasks, including loading and unloading cargo, operating machinery, and working with heavy ropes and cables. These jobs require strength and manual dexterity. Engine room workers can be subjected to hot, uncomfortable conditions. Sailors who work on deck can develop sunburn, chafed skin and calluses from exposure to the elements.

SECRETARY

Ranking: 37

Score: 6.06

Basic Day: 8.0 Hours

Secretaries work regular hours in full- or part-time positions. Most of a secretary's day is spent sitting at a desk. Manual dexterity is required to operate office machines and handle paperwork. Good typing is usually a necessity for secretaries. Excellent vision is needed to decipher handwriting and documents, and in working at computer terminals. Eyestrain and back pain are common in this occupation. Secretaries should have good communication skills and pleasant speaking voices for effective interaction with clients on the telephone, and in the office.

SET DESIGNER

Ranking: 95

Score: 8.85

Basic Day: 9.0 Hours

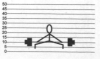

Set designers work irregular schedules, often putting in long hours in movie or television studios, or in theaters. These workers occasionally need to lift heavy set pieces and equipment. Set designers spend extended periods of time on their feet. This profession requires communication, observational, and manual skills in order to create theatrical sets, and direct their assembly. Set designers must possess physical and mental stamina to deal with the pressures associated with this job, such as having to make design changes on short notice.

SEWAGE PLANT OPERATOR

Ranking: 198

Score: 18.18

Basic Day: 9.0 Hours

Sewage plant operators work regular hours. Shifts, including weekends and holidays, are common in this line of work, and overtime may be called for during emergencies. The safe use of hand tools and special sampling devices in this profession demands manual dexterity and good vision. This work involves some lifting and carrying. Sewage plant operators occasionally face hazardous work situations. These workers may be exposed to slippery conditions, noise, unpleasant odors, or toxic fumes. The potential for equipment malfunction presents an added danger for sewage plant operators.

SHEET METAL WORKER

Ranking: 233

Score: 30.73

Basic Day: 8.5 Hours

Sheet metal workers normally work indoors, but spend some time outdoors at construction sites. These workers are required to lift, carry, bend, stoop, reach, and climb. Members of this trade often have to work in uncomfortable positions for extended periods. The safe operation of tools and equipment in this line of work calls for good vision and manual dexterity. The construction site is a noisy work environment. Sheet metal workers face the risk of injuries, including burns and cuts, while on the job. Stamina and strength are required in this occupation.

SHIPPING/RECEIVING CLERK

Ranking: 112

Score: 9.67

Basic Day: 8.5 Hours

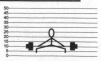

Shipping and receiving clerks work in warehouses, and also spend time on outdoor loading docks. Members of this profession work regular hours, unless overtime is called for to meet shipping or production deadlines. Clerks are required to stand, reach, bend, lift and carry. Communication skills are needed in this occupation to ensure proper handling of merchandise and packages, and to supervise other shipping procedures. Strength, manual dexterity, and good vision are required for the safe performance of duties in this line of work.

SHOE MAKER/REPAIRER

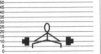

Ranking: 108

Score: 9.53

Basic Day: 8.5 Hours

Shoe repairers work a normal week. Repairers employed in large shops often work in crowded and noisy surroundings. Those who own their own businesses generally enjoy more comfortable work conditions. This occupation demands good eyesight and manual dexterity to effect repairs safely and accurately. Often, the working environment is poorly ventilated, and if so, the smells of leather dyes and stains must be tolerated. Because shoe repairers spend most of the day standing up, stamina is required for this exacting work.

SINGER

Ranking: 160

Score: 13.85

Basic Day: 9.0 Hours

Professional singers generally work in the evenings and on weekends. Singers are often required to travel in order to perform. Hours can be long and schedules irregular in this profession. Rehearsal schedules often demand extensive time commitments. Good articulation and breath control are important in singing. Care must be taken to keep the voice and lungs in good condition. Stamina is needed to maintain hectic rehearsal and performance schedules, especially for those singers who hold other jobs to make ends meet.

SOCIAL WORKER

Ranking: 24

Score: 5.47

Basic Day: 8.5 Hours

Social workers usually put in regular, 40-hour weeks. Schedules for these workers may include weekends or evenings. Some social work posi-

tions are part-time. Overtime is occasionally required in the event of emergency. Social workers often travel to visit homes, or to attend meetings. Good listening and speaking skills are essential in this line of work, to interact effectively with individuals and groups in need of service, and to work with employees of social service organizations.

SOCIOLOGIST

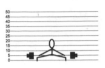

Ranking: 20

Score: 5.09

Basic Day: 9.0 Hours

Sociologists normally work a 40-hour week, which may include nights and weekends. Sociologists occasionally travel, in order to conduct research or attend conferences. These professionals spend the majority of their work day sitting at desks, reading, writing, and talking on the telephone. Eyestrain and back pain can result from long hours spent seated, conducting research. Sociologists, especially those who are teachers, must be able to communicate forcefully and effectively.

SOFTWARE ENGINEER

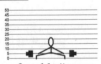

Ranking: 14

Score: 5.00

Basic Day: 10.0 Hours

Software engineers work in comfortable "corporate-style" environments. Although they tend to work overtime, they are involved in a creative and rewarding field where physical demands are few. They may suffer from "computer ailments" associated with eye strain, back strain or wrist aches. Deadlines are far apart and can be anticipated resulting in lower stress levels than other executive office positions. Work is possible from home via modem hookups allowing for some flexibility and resulting in less pressure when under deadlines.

SPEECH PATHOLOGIST

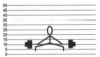

Ranking: 107

Score: 9.43

Basic Day: 8.5 Hours

Speech pathologists work regular hours in offices, sitting at tables or desks. Manual dexterity and visual skills are needed in this occupation to manipulate devices which test hearing, and to interpret results of tests. Exceptional speaking and listening abilities are required for effective performance in this line of work. To maintain patience and a high level of concentration, speech pathologists need physical and mental stamina.

SPORTS INSTRUCTOR

Ranking: 180

Score: 15.47

Basic Day: 8.5 Hours

The normal work week for sports instructors is slightly more than 40 hours. Instruction takes place at various types of indoor and outdoor facilities. Sports instructors sometimes work weekends. A great deal of time is spent walking and standing in this occupation. Depending upon the sport, this work can be physically strenuous. In order to perform effectively, instructors must be in excellent physical condition, and must possess good speaking and listening skills.

STATIONARY ENGINEER

Ranking: 224

Score: 26.18

Basic Day: 9.0 Hours

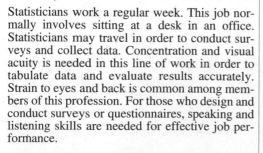

Stationary engineers work a regular week, sometimes on a shift basis. On the job, these workers are required to reach, crawl, stoop, and kneel. This work requires good vision in order to make accurate assessments and adjustments. Stationary engineers need manual dexterity in handling power tools. Workers in this occupation are exposed to a great deal of noise, as well as grease, dirt, fumes, and heat. Stationary engineers must take precautions against the danger of electric shock, burns and other injuries.

STATISTICIAN

Ranking: 2

Score: 3.95

Basic Day: 9.0 Hours

Statisticians work a regular week. This job normally involves sitting at a desk in an office. Statisticians may travel in order to conduct surveys and collect data. Concentration and visual acuity is needed in this line of work in order to tabulate data and evaluate results accurately. Strain to eyes and back is common among members of this profession. For those who design and conduct surveys or questionnaires, speaking and listening skills are needed for effective job performance.

STENOGRAPHER/COURT REPORTER

Ranking: 57

Score: 7.03

Basic Day: 8.0 Hours

Stenographers work regular, 40-hour weeks in offices, courtrooms, or legislative chambers. Members of this profession perform their jobs while seated. Operating stenographic machines to transcribe office communications and judicial and legislative proceedings accurately requires manual dexterity, and good listening skills. Stenographers must be able to communicate effectively to read back transcripts quickly. Eye, muscular, and skeletal strain may accompany this work. The pressure of having to perform duties with speed may cause physical fatigue and stress.

STEVEDORE

Ranking: 228

Score: 28.03

Basic Day: 8.0 Hours

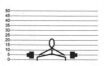

Stevedores do a great deal of heavy lifting in loading and unloading cargo. This job also involves operating hoists and other equipment and machinery. Consequently, stevedores must have strength and manual dexterity to perform the strenuous tasks required in this occupation. Work is normally performed outdoors, and stevedores may be exposed to poor weather conditions. These workers can suffer from pulled muscles and other physical impairments in the course of their jobs.

STOCKBROKER

Ranking: 63

Score: 7.25

Basic Day: 9.0 Hours

Stockbrokers usually work regular hours, mainly seated behind desks in offices or cubicles. Some leave the office to meet with clients, or to attend meetings or civic functions. Stockbrokers need to possess both good vision and excellent verbal skills, in order to monitor stock prices and other information over office computer terminals, and then to communicate quickly by telephone with clients and floor representatives. Stockbrokers must take care to avoid the distraction of noise from other workers.

SURGEON

Ranking: 184

Score: 15.90

Basic Day: 11.0 Hours

Surgeons work irregular schedules, and sometimes long hours. These professionals spend a great deal of time on their feet. Surgeons are required to have steady hands, calm nerves, excellent vision, and good communication skills, in order to treat patients and to perform surgery effectively and safely. Health and stamina are necessary to members of this profession, in order to handle the pressures of being directly responsible for the lives of patients.

SURVEYOR

Ranking: 218

Score: 24.11

Basic Day: 9.0 Hours

Surveyors work a regular week, although some overtime may be required during good weather conditions in the summer. This profession demands physical exertion, including climbing, hiking, carrying heavy equipment and instruments, reaching, and stooping. Surveyors must have good eyesight to make accurate measurements and calculations, and the ability to communicate effectively with other members of the surveying team.

SYMPHONY CONDUCTOR

Ranking: 171

Score: 14.85

Basic Day: 9.0 Hours

For most established symphony conductors, rehearsal and performance schedules are comfortable and allow a good deal of time for other endeavors, such as composing or recording. However, extra rehearsal time may be required if the rendition of a piece is not progressing properly. Many symphony orchestras periodically go on tour, and travel and performance schedules in some cases can be fatiguing. The training regimen can be intense for those wishing to enter the profession.

TAX EXAMINER/COLLECTOR

Ranking: 75

Score: 7.98

Basic Day: 9.0 Hours

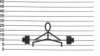

Tax examiners and collectors often work irregular schedules and long hours. This work can involve travel to meet with taxpayers. Examiners and collectors spend much of their time driving and walking, so stamina, health and good driving skills are needed. The ability to communicate effectively is essential in performing the tasks required in this profession. Tact and forcefulness may be needed in dealing with taxpayers who must be threatened with fines or criminal charges.

TAXI DRIVER

Ranking: 169

Score: 14.46

Basic Day: 9.5 Hours

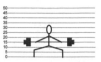

Since income for taxi drivers depends to a large extent on the number of fares they receive, many in this profession work long shifts, often up to twelve hours a day. Many taxi drivers work odd hours, including late nights and weekends. Cabbies must have excellent driving skills and the temperament to cope with traffic and troublesome passengers. Taxi drivers often assist passengers with luggage. Fatigue can become a problem for those moonlighting as drivers.

TEACHER

Ranking: 137

Score: 11.87

Basic Day: 9.0 Hours

Teachers usually work 10 months out of the year. Although the work day is less than 8 hours, teachers also have to take work home, as well as attend meetings with parents, other teachers and administrators after school hours. Teachers need stamina to handle this workload, and to sustain long periods of time spent standing and talking. Teachers who work with young children may do a good deal of stooping and kneeling.

TEACHER'S AIDE

Ranking: 67

Score: 7.41

Basic Day: 8.5 Hours

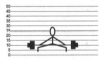

Teacher aides generally work part-time. Some physical exertion, including walking, standing, stooping, kneeling, and reaching, is demanded in this line of work. In addition to a strong speaking voice, this position calls for manual dexterity and good vision to help set up or demonstrate equipment, or to help the teacher with a variety of other instructional projects. Teacher aides must possess stamina in working with active, rambunctious children.

TECHNICAL WRITER

Ranking: 29

Score: 5.85

Basic Day: 9.0 Hours

Full-time technical writers and copy writers generally work a regular week, but are sometimes asked to work overtime in order to meet deadlines. These writers spend much of their work time at a desk in an office, but travel is occasionally required to conduct research. Good vision, manual dexterity, and effective communication skills are needed in this profession to perform duties, which involve reading, interviewing, and writing. "Computer fatigue" often must be dealt with.

TELEPHONE INSTALLER/ REPAIRER

Ranking: 178

Score: 15.39

Basic Day: 9.5 Hours

Telephone installers and repairers work in all weather conditions, and are on call at all times. Overtime is required in the event of an emergency. Repairers climb ladders and poles, and perform some of their work at dangerous heights. Lifting, crawling, and kneeling are also necessary to perform some repairs and installations. Manual dexterity and visual acuity are needed in this occupation, in order to operate special equipment, follow safety procedures, and make proper adjustments or repairs.

TELEPHONE OPERATOR

Ranking: 100

Score: 9.00

Basic Day: 8.0 Hours

Telephone operators work a regular week, on a shift basis. These workers spend the day sitting at telephone consoles. Operators must possess manual dexterity and visual skills to refer calls to the proper parties rapidly and correctly, using a switchboard and pushing the proper buttons. Good listening and speaking skills are essential for effective performance in this line of work. Eye and back strain are common for telephone operators, especially those who work at computer terminals.

TICKET AGENT

Ranking: 14

Score: 5.00

Basic Day: 8.0 Hours

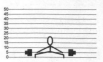

Reservation and ticket agents work full-time at irregular hours, including weekends and nights. Agents perform their jobs either standing or sitting at ticket windows or stations. These workers constantly deal with the public, either over the telephone or in person. Therefore, good communication skills, patience, and a personable manner are necessary for effective performance, especially during busy holiday periods, or when customers are irate over delays or canceled airline flights.

TOOL-AND-DIE MAKER

Ranking: 189

Score: 16.87

Basic Day: 10.0 Hours

Tool-and-die makers work regular 40-hour weeks. These workers spend much of their time standing or stooping. Members of this trade are required to do some moderate to heavy lifting. Manual dexterity, good vision, and attention to detail are important in this job, in order to use the necessary tools for precise and painstaking work. Tool-and-die makers must take precautions to avoid the dangers of flying metal, loose objects, or clothing getting caught in machinery. Tool-and-die shops are noisy work environments.

TRAVEL AGENT

Ranking: 30

Score: 6.00

Basic Day: 8.0 Hours

Travel agents normally work a regular week, although some overtime may be called for during peak travel periods. Agents spend most of their time sitting at a desk in a travel office. Communication skills and a personable manner are necessary in this line of work, in order to discuss travel plans with customers in person and on the telephone, and to work out arrangements with reservations clerks from airlines and hotels.

TRUCK DRIVER

Ranking: 210

Score: 21.68

Basic Day: 9.5 Hours

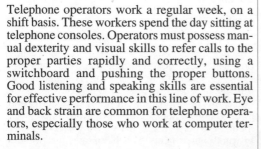

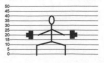

Truck drivers sometimes work over 45 hours per week, and often up to 60 hours in a 7-day period. Truck drivers who are responsible for loading and unloading cargo must do some lifting and carrying. Good reaction time, accurate vision, and excellent driving skills are needed in this occupation to cover long distances safely. To maintain alertness on the road, truck drivers need stamina.

TYPIST/WORD PROCESSOR

Ranking: 18

Score: 5.03

Basic Day: 8.0 Hours

Typists and word processors work a regular week. Many typists work part-time, or for personnel pools or temporary agencies. Most of the work day in this occupation is spent sitting at desks in offices. Manual dexterity and good vision are needed for quick and accurate typing. Eye, back, and muscular strain are common in this line of work, especially for those working at computer terminals. Both typists and word processors are exposed to noise from typewriters and printers.

UNDERTAKER

Ranking: 177

Score: 15.15

Basic Day: 10.0 Hours

As morticians have to keep body temperatures of the deceased low in order to prevent decomposing, they must become accustomed to working in a cool environment. Members of this profession must exert caution when working with chemical embalming solutions and when dealing with the potential for disease from bodies. This job requires attention to detail, and above all, sensitivity when dealing with the family of the deceased.

URBAN/REGIONAL PLANNER

Ranking: 12

Score: 4.98

Basic Day: 9 Hours

Those a basic 45 hour week is average, often late hours are necessary in order to attend civic meetings at night. Most of a planner's work is sedentary, but some standing and walking is done when making inspections. Extensive documentation of plans often necessitates carrying heavy brief cases or presentations.

VENDING MACHINE REPAIRER

Ranking: 165

Score: 14.39

Basic Day: 9.5 Hours

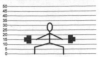

As many vending machines operate around the clock, vending machine repairers must occasionally work evenings and weekends. This occupation requires mechanical aptitude and attention to detail. When servicing machines in the field, repairers must bend and stoop frequently. Repairers are subject to such hazards as electrical shocks and cuts from sharp tools or objects.

VETERINARIAN

Ranking: 196

Score: 17.79

Basic Day: 10.0 Hours

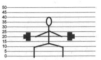

Veterinarians work irregular schedules, and sometimes long hours. Veterinarians specializing in care to farm or ranch animals may have to drive mobile clinics, and perform some of their work outdoors. Manual dexterity and accurate vision are needed in effective animal care. Depending upon the circumstances, some kneeling, stooping, and moderate lifting or carrying may be necessary in this line of work. Veterinarians risk exposure to disease from animals. Stamina is required for members of this occupation to perform lengthy veterinary procedures safely.

VOCATIONAL COUNSELOR

Ranking: 91

Score: 8.56

Basic Day: 8.5 Hours

College or employment counselors work in private offices. They keep regular hours, although some overtime may be required during special recruiting periods. Counselors benefit from having good communication skills, as they spend most of their time talking with students, parents, teachers, social workers, and others in their field. Sometimes they conduct tests, group counseling sessions, or training seminars. Physical exertion is minimal, but the mental and emotional involvement can be taxing.

WAITER/WAITRESS

Ranking: 131

Score: 11.00

Basic Day: 7.0 Hours

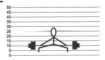

Waiters and waitresses work part- or full-time, often on a shift basis that will change weekly. Schedules for these workers include nights, weekends and holidays. This work requires a good deal of physical exertion, especially during very busy periods. Waiters and waitresses spend the work day on their feet, often having to carry many plates or trays of food and drink at once. Communication skills are important in this line of work, to take and fill orders accurately. Personality and efficiency in service can bring larger tips for waiters and waitresses.

WELDER

Ranking: 230

Score: 29.08

Basic Day: 9.0 Hours

Welders work in noisy, sometimes hazardous conditions. Workers in this trade are required to lift and carry heavy tools and equipment, and to reach, stoop, and bend on the job. Welders must have good eye-to-hand coordination in order to perform safely and effectively. These workers must take precautions to avoid eye injuries, burns, and toxic fumes. Dirt and grease are common in the work place for welders.

ZOOLOGIST

Ranking: 163

Score: 14.19

Basic Day: 10.0 Hours

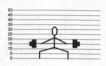

Zoologists normally work regular hours in labs or offices, although sometimes field research and study is performed in natural animal habitats. Zoologists spend a good deal of time on their feet, and may do quite a bit of walking, hiking, reaching, and bending during their work outdoors. Manual dexterity and good vision are needed to observe and study animal behavior accurately. Zoologists must take precautions in the lab if toxic materials are used, and in the field when working with wild animals.

Security

The idea that you can spend a lifetime working for one company is a nostalgic vision out of the past. American workers are learning a painful lesson: Companies no longer regard their employees as family. The managerial ideal today is a company with as few workers as possible.

The saving grace for people with an eye on career security is a new strategy: making sure that their job skills are in demand in a wide variety of related fields. It might be a fanciful notion to have a job waiting in the wings if your current one disappears, but it's not as illusory for some workers as for others. No job — that is, no position at a *particular* company — is completely secure. More and more, career security involves indulging in a once unheard-of strategy: following a career path in which there are more available positions than qualified workers. Naturally, specific occupational choices are the key to making this blueprint work; the vast majority of unemployed are eager to work — but do they have the skills now deemed valuable in a rapidly transforming economic environment? There is no survival strategy as effective as the occupational choice you make. The field in which you work, or in which you aspire to work, is the most likely determiner of whether you will be employed next month or next year.

THE THREE SECURITY FACTORS

What exactly is job security? In compiling rankings for each of our 250 occupations, we treated security as a composite of several factors: (1) anticipated employment growth or decline through the year 2005; (2) recent unemployment rates; and (3) physical hazards that could impair one's ability to work, including possible life-threatening situations on the job.

In previous editions of the *Jobs Rated Almanac*, the level of unionization in a field was a further security-related factor. Increasingly, however, the most unionized jobs tend to have the highest unemployment rates — a result to some degree of the fact that heavily unionized professions traditionally are those in heavy industry, an economic sector that has fared poorly compared to others in the transition to an information-based economy. Unions continue to serve as a softening factor for laid-off or fired workers, and in some professions they remain strong forces in regard to job security. However, looking at the working world as a whole, the issue of unionization is too complex to assign this factor either positive or negative weight across the board in our security rankings. Therefore, it has been eliminated as a factor in ranking the 250 jobs in the security category.

Each factor was assigned a range of points, and each job was given a point-value based on the degree to which that factor affects security within the given occupation. The scoring system is as follows:

(1) Unemployment rates from 1993 and 1994, based on an index of one to five: one being very low, two being low, three moderate, four high, and five very high. Unemployment is regarded as a negative factor,

and the points assigned were multiplied by negative 50, hence the lowest achievable mark was -250; the highest, -50.

(2) Expected employment growth through the year 2005, as forecast by the Department of Labor. It, too, was factored, so that the highest achievable score was 250. However, if employment growth is forecast as negative, this score could fall below zero, and in many cases it did.

(3) The degree to which one is required to do physical tasks is also a factor, because physical labor can cause injuries and because physical health is a requisite for work. Job conditions that put a worker at risk of injury were regarded as well. In certain fields — professional sports and manual labor being prime examples — physical health, or the lack thereof, can be the decisive factor in job security. The degree to which physical health can affect job performance was assigned a score based on an index similar to the unemployment factor. Achievable points, therefore were between -50 and -250.

The point totals derived in the three categories were added together, and the resulting figure serves as a basis for the security rankings. This method of scoring presupposes that all jobs have some negative security factors. Naturally, this method reaped primarily negative scores, and only a few jobs scored above zero. Nevertheless, even jobs that scored below zero can be regarded as secure relative to those that score larger negative values.

COMMON THREADS

Add the need to keep records to the old adage about death and taxes, and put them into your security plan when considering a career field. Death may be certain, but jobs in medicine keep the reaper at arm's length for a longer and longer duration — hence jobs in health care are among the highest-ranked in this chapter. Computer-based, high-tech recordkeepers and information compilers (including accountants) can expect some stability even in turbulent times. For other workers, social and economic turbulence in and of itself can be a boon to employment. Jobs in law enforcement, security, and legal professions ranked highly.

Lowest in the security rankings are jobs in professional sports, where a rookie is always out for a veteran's job, and an injury can instantly end a career. Also among the most precarious of modern career paths are certain romantic jobs that helped form the mosaic of American history—cowboys, lumberjacks, and seamen.

Though the system used to rank security employs what most regard as the key factors, one weakness is that the forecasts are based on current conditions and recent trends; and social, political, and economic factors affecting projected employment patterns aren't always so easy to gauge. For instance, the construction trades do not rank as poorly as they did in previous editions of the *Jobs Rated Almanac*. Few expected the precipitous drop in interest rates that has sparked new building. Military careers, on the other hand, fare worse compared to earlier editions; if only we had foreseen the crumbling of the old Soviet empire, which has resulted in the current move toward military downsizing.

In short, the least secure jobs are not always the jobs with most unstable histories; instead, they are the jobs that have a declining employment base, or those that are vulnerable to sudden changes in political or fiscal conditions, or to rapid technological innovations. Social and physiological factors do not change as rapidly, and thus professions whose status is linked more closely with such factors tend to be more stable.

250 Jobs Ranked by Security Scores

RANK		SCORE	RANK		SCORE
1	COMPUTER SYSTEMS ANALYST	150	33	MEDICAL TECHNOLOGIST	-94
2	PHYSICAL THERAPIST	48	35	JUDGE (FEDERAL)	-95
3	PARALEGAL ASSISTANT	44	36	OCEANOGRAPHER	-96
4	AUDIOLOGIST	15	37	TECHNICAL WRITER	-98
5	MEDICAL SECRETARY	1	37	URBAN/REGIONAL PLANNER	-98
6	PAROLE OFFICER	-10	39	NURSE'S AIDE	-99
7	OCCUPATIONAL THERAPIST	-15	40	TRAVEL AGENT	-101
8	SOFTWARE ENGINEER	-28	40	HOTEL MANAGER	-101
9	SPEECH PATHOLOGIST	-35	42	TEACHER'S AIDE	-103
10	MEDICAL RECORDS TECHNICIAN	-37	42	DIETICIAN	-103
11	CORRECTION OFFICER	-42	44	NURSE (REGISTERED)	-105
12	CHILD CARE WORKER	-51	45	ENGINEERING TECHNICIAN	-107
13	DENTAL HYGIENIST	-53	46	TAX EXAMINER/ COLLECTOR	-109
14	RESPIRATORY THERAPIST	-60	47	BANK OFFICER	-110
15	PODIATRIST	-67	47	NURSE (LICENSED PRACTICAL)	-110
16	OPTICIAN	-69	49	INDUSTRIAL ENGINEER	-112
17	PSYCHIATRIST	-71	49	SPORTS INSTRUCTOR	-112
17	PHYSICIAN (GENERAL PRACTICE)	-71	51	OPTOMETRIST	-114
17	SURGEON	-71	52	COMPUTER SERVICE TECHNICIAN	-116
17	AGENCY DIRECTOR (NONPROFIT)	-71	53	ANTIQUE DEALER	-118
21	PHYSICIAN ASSISTANT	-73	54	WAITER/WAITRESS	-119
22	ACCOUNTANT	-78	54	ADVERTISING ACCOUNT EXECUTIVE	-119
23	ATTORNEY	-80	54	EMERGENCY MEDICAL TECHNICIAN	-119
24	COMPUTER PROGRAMMER	-82	57	HOSPITAL ADMINISTRATOR	-121
24	CATHOLIC PRIEST	-82	57	AIRPLANE PILOT	-121
24	PROTESTANT MINISTER	-82	59	RECEPTIONIST	-123
27	PHARMACIST	-85	60	VETERINARIAN	-126
27	ACTUARY	-85	61	VOCATIONAL COUNSELOR	-128
27	GUARD	-85	61	FASHION MODEL	-128
30	SYMPHONY CONDUCTOR	-89	63	PHYSIOLOGIST	-130
31	MEDICAL LABORATORY TECHNICIAN	-91	64	TICKET AGENT	-132
32	PSYCHOLOGIST	-92			
33	BIOLOGIST	-94			

RANK		SCORE	RANK		SCORE
64	MATHEMATICIAN	-132	97	CHIROPRACTOR	-169
66	FLIGHT ATTENDANT	-135	97	PERSONNEL RECRUITER	-169
67	DENTIST	-139	99	COSMETOLOGIST	-171
68	REPORTER (NEWSPAPER)	-141	99	OSTEOPATH	-171
68	NEWSCASTER	-141	101	TEACHER	-173
68	PUBLIC RELATIONS EXECUTIVE	-141	102	STOCKBROKER	-176
			103	ASTROLOGER	-177
68	HISTORIAN	-141	104	STATISTICIAN	-180
72	DENTAL LABORATORY TECHNICIAN	-143	105	AUTOMOBILE BODY REPAIRER	-182
73	ELECTRICAL ENGINEER	-146	105	POSTAL INSPECTOR	-182
			107	ORTHODONTIST	-189
73	CIVIL ENGINEER	-146	108	BROADCAST TECHNICIAN	-191
73	CASHIER	-146	108	COLLEGE PROFESSOR	-191
73	INSURANCE UNDERWRITER	-146	108	PHOTOGRAPHIC PROCESS WORKER	-191
77	MAIL CARRIER	-148	108	SECRETARY	-191
77	NEWSWRITER (RADIO/TV)	-148	108	ARCHITECT	-191
77	CARTOONIST	-148	113	DISK JOCKEY	-194
77	ARTIST (COMMERCIAL)	-148	113	ECONOMIST	-194
77	AUTHOR (BOOKS)	-148	113	FINANCIAL PLANNER	-194
77	SCHOOL PRINCIPAL	-148	113	EXECUTIVE SEARCH CONSULTANT	-194
83	NUCLEAR ENGINEER	-150			
84	MECHANICAL ENGINEER	-155	117	METEOROLOGIST	-196
84	SOCIOLOGIST	-155	118	MOTION PICTURE EDITOR	-198
84	POLITICAL SCIENTIST	-155	118	ELECTRICAL TECHNICIAN	-198
84	MAID	-157	118	PUBLICATION EDITOR	-198
84	INDUSTRIAL DESIGNER	-157	121	GEOLOGIST	-200
89	SHIPPING/RECEIVING CLERK	-159	121	ASTRONAUT	-200
			123	STENOGRAPHER/COURT REPORTER	-202
89	UNDERTAKER	-159	124	BUS DRIVER	-203
91	SOCIAL WORKER	-160	124	FASHION DESIGNER	-203
92	MILITARY (WARRANT OFFICER)	-161	124	CHEMIST	-203
92	MILITARY (ENLISTED PERSON)	-161	124	LITHOGRAPHER/ PHOTOENGRAVER	-203
92	MILITARY (COMMISSIONED OFFICER)	-161	124	CHAUFFEUR	-203
95	AGRICULTURAL SCIENTIST	-168	129	BARBER	-205
			129	ARCHEOLOGIST	-205
95	MARKET RESEARCH ANALYST	-168	129	ANTHROPOLOGIST	-205
			129	ASTRONOMER	-205

RANK	SCORE	RANK	SCORE
129 HOME ECONOMIST	-205	165 HEATING/REFRIGERATION MECHANIC	-235
129 PHILOSOPHER	-205		
135 AEROSPACE ENGINEER	-207	167 BASKETBALL COACH (NCAA)	-239
135 FILE CLERK	-207		
135 JEWELER	-207	167 STATIONARY ENGINEER	-239
138 MUSEUM CURATOR	-209	169 SINGER	-244
138 BANK TELLER	-209	169 MUSICIAN	-244
138 SEWAGE PLANT OPERATOR	-209	169 CONSTRUCTION FOREMAN	-244
141 FIREFIGHTER	-212	169 CHOREOGRAPHER	-244
142 RECREATION WORKER	-214	169 PHOTOJOURNALIST	-244
142 COOK/CHEF	-214	169 PHOTOGRAPHER	-244
144 INSURANCE AGENT	-216	175 AUTOMOBILE MECHANIC	-248
145 SALES REPRESENTATIVE (WHOLESALE)	-218	176 MAYOR	-250
		176 IRONWORKER	-250
145 FLORIST	-218	178 SALESPERSON (RETAIL)	-253
145 PURCHASING AGENT	-218	178 REAL ESTATE AGENT	-253
145 BOOKBINDER	-218	180 PETROLEUM ENGINEER	-255
145 HIGHWAY PATROL OFFICER	-218	181 JANITOR	-257
		181 PHYSICIST	-257
150 DISHWASHER	-219	183 DRESSMAKER	-259
150 ADVERTISING SALESPERSON	-219	184 NUCLEAR PLANT DECONTAMINATION TECHNICIAN	-261
150 SURVEYOR	-221		
150 JOCKEY	-221	185 BARTENDER	-268
150 CORPORATE EXECUTIVE (SENIOR)	-221	185 AUTOMOBILE SALESPERSON	-268
		187 SET DESIGNER	-271
150 POLICE OFFICER	-221	187 BUYER	-271
156 CONSERVATIONIST	-223	187 AIRCRAFT MECHANIC	-271
156 OCCUPATIONAL SAFETY/ HEALTH INSPECTOR	-223	187 STEVEDORE	-271
		191 LIBRARIAN	-273
157 ARCHITECTURAL DRAFTER	-225	192 FURNITURE UPHOLSTERER	-275
		193 OFFICE MACHINE REPAIRER	-282
159 AIR TRAFFIC CONTROLLER	-227	194 FORKLIFT OPERATOR	-284
160 ACTOR	-228	195 TYPIST/WORD PROCESSOR	-286
161 MUSICAL INSTRUMENT REPAIRER	-230	196 RAILROAD CONDUCTOR	-287
		197 COMPUTER OPERATOR	-288
161 PIANO TUNER	-230	198 FISHERMAN	-289
163 ZOOLOGIST	-232	198 RACE CAR DRIVER (INDY CLASS)	-289
163 RABBI	-232		
165 PAINTER	-235	200 APPLIANCE REPAIRER	-291

RANK	SCORE	RANK	SCORE
200 TRUCK DRIVER	-291	226 MACHINE TOOL OPERATOR	-338
202 CONSTRUCTION MACHINERY OPERATOR	-292	228 BASEBALL UMPIRE (MAJOR LEAGUE)	-339
203 CONGRESSPERSON/ SENATOR	-293	229 COWBOY	-341
203 BOOKKEEPER	-293	229 CONSTRUCTION WORKER (LABORER)	-341
203 VENDING MACHINE REPAIRER	-293	231 DANCER	-344
203 ELECTRICAL EQUIPMENT REPAIRER	-293	232 DAIRY FARMER	-347
203 ARTIST (FINE ART)	-298	233 AUTOMOBILE PAINTER	-348
208 CARPET INSTALLER	-300	234 TELEPHONE INSTALLER/REPAIRER	-354
208 METER READER	-300	235 CARPENTER	-355
208 PRESIDENT (U.S.)	-300	236 SEAMAN	-361
208 ROOFER	-300	237 SHEET METAL WORKER	-362
212 MACHINIST	-302	238 PLASTERER	-364
213 TAXI DRIVER	-303	238 PRECISION ASSEMBLER	-364
214 INDUSTRIAL MACHINE REPAIRER	-307	240 DRYWALL APPLICATOR/ FINISHER	-367
307 ELECTRICIAN	-307	241 DRILL-PRESS OPERATOR	-377
216 BOILERMAKER	-309	242 COMMUNICATIONS EQUIPMENT MECHANIC	-386
217 TELEPHONE OPERATOR	-313	243 BRICKLAYER	-391
218 TOOL-AND-DIE MAKER	-316	244 SHOE MAKER/ REPAIRER	-395
219 AUTOMOBILE ASSEMBLER	-318	245 LUMBERJACK	-416
220 GARBAGE COLLECTOR	-325	246 ROUSTABOUT	-424
221 COMPOSITOR/ TYPESETTER	-329	247 BASEBALL PLAYER (MAJOR LEAGUE)	-439
222 MILLWRIGHT	-330	247 BASKETBALL PLAYER (NBA)	-439
223 PLUMBER	-332	247 FOOTBALL PLAYER (NFL)	-439
223 BUTCHER	-332	250 FARMER	-447
223 GLAZIER	-332		
226 WELDER	-338		

THE UNEMPLOYMENT LINE

Elected officials who are voted out of office, though technically "unemployed," usually can find jobs doing something else. Aside from them, the jobs below traditionally have the highest rates of unemployment. At right of the job title is the security rank.

ACTOR	160	CONSTRUCTION MACHINERY OPERATOR	202
ARTIST (FINE ART)	203	CONSTRUCTION WORKER (LABORER)	229
BOILERMAKER	216		
BOOKKEEPER	203	DANCER	231
BRICKLAYER	243	DRYWALL APPLICATOR/ FINISHER	240
BUYER	187		
CARPENTER	235	FARMER	250
CARPET INSTALLER	208	GLAZIER	223
CHOREOGRAPHER	169	LUMBERJACK	245
CONSTRUCTION FOREMAN	169	PLASTERER	238
		SHEET METAL WORKER	237

LOWEST UNEMPLOYMENT

The very lowest unemployment is enjoyed by nonelected workers at government jobs at all levels. Those jobs aside, the one's below traditionally have the lowest rates of unemployment. At right of the job title is the security rank.

AUDIOLOGIST	4	OCCUPATIONAL THERAPIST	7
CHILD CARE WORKER	12	OPTICIAN	16
COMPUTER SERVICE TECHNICIAN	52	OPTOMETRIST	51
		PHARMACIST	27
COMPUTER SYSTEMS ANALYST	1	PHYSICAL THERAPIST	2
DENTAL HYGIENIST	13	PHYSICIAN (GENERAL PRACTICE)	17
DENTAL LABORATORY TECHNICIAN	72		
DENTIST	67	PHYSICIAN ASSISTANT	21
		PODIATRIST	15
EMERGENCY MEDICAL TECHNICIAN	54	PROTESTANT MINISTER	24
ENGINEERING TECHNICIAN	45	PSYCHIATRIST	17
		RESPIRATORY THERAPIST	14
MAID	84	SOFTWARE ENGINEER	8
MEDICAL LABORATORY TECHNICIAN	31	SPEECH PATHOLOGIST	9
		SURGEON	17
MEDICAL RECORDS TECHNICIAN	10	SYMPHONY CONDUCTOR	30
MEDICAL SECRETARY	5	UNDERTAKER	89
MEDICAL TECHNOLOGIST	33	VETERINARIAN	60

ACCOUNTANT

Ranking: 22

Score: -78

Job Growth: 72%

Unemployment: Low

Accountants enjoy a high degree of geographic mobility. Tax accountants are affected by seasonal fluctuations in demand for their services. Employment opportunities in accounting should increase faster than the average, due to growth in the financial sector. Accountants' jobs are not as adversely affected by economic downturns as other occupations, because their services are indispensable to the business sector, even in bad years. Additionally, many facets of an accountant's job are related to tax matters, therefore down cycles do not eliminate the need for their services.

ACTOR/ACTRESS

Ranking: 160

Score: -228

Job Growth: 122%

Unemployment: Very High

Actors enjoy little geographic mobility, as most acting jobs originate in major cities such as New York, Los Angeles, and Chicago. The number of jobs in the entertainment industry is expected to increase faster than the average, but the field of acting is highly competitive, and will remain so. Job security in this field is contingent upon landing parts in long-running shows.

ACTUARY

Ranking: 27

Score: -85

Job Growth: 65%

Unemployment: Low

Actuaries enjoy moderate geographic flexibility. Employment prospects for actuaries are projected to increase faster than the average, through the next decade. This profession appears to be very stable. Increased demand for statistical calculations and answers to complex insurance problems should keep actuaries in high demand.

ADVERTISING ACCOUNT EXECUTIVE

Ranking: 54

Score: -119

Job Growth: 81%

Unemployment: Moderate

Advertising executives enjoy some geographic flexibility, but most jobs in advertising are found in major cities. Employment opportunities for these executives should increase as fast as the average, through the next decade, because of growth in the advertising industry. The advertising business is traditionally very competitive.

ADVERTISING SALESPERSON

Ranking: 150

Score: -219

Job Growth: 81%

Unemployment: High

Job growth for ad sales representatives will be average over the next ten years, though the advertising field expands and diversifies. Competition for jobs with major publications and stations is strong, and these positions usually require successful sales experience at smaller media outlets. Failure to meet sales quotas can mean a quick exit for advertising sales representatives.

AEROSPACE ENGINEER

Ranking: 135

Score: -207

Job Growth: 43%

Unemployment: Moderate

The demand for aerospace engineers is expected to grow in the coming years, and the number of jobs in this profession is expected to rise at a rate faster than the average in the coming decade. However, the aerospace industry is highly dependent on government defense contracts, and significant cutbacks in defense spending have limited the growth of job opportunities for aerospace engineers.

AGENCY DIRECTOR (NON-PROFIT)

Ranking: 17

Score: -71

Job Growth: 29%

Unemployment: Moderate

Non-profit employers look for precise qualifications and experience in their focal areas; those wishing to switch from corporate to non-profit sectors will find it difficult because of the tighter job market. Non-profits are not risk taking organizations, nor are they interested in experimentation for they are eager to remain stable in volatile times. Because they are at the top, the agency directors can get all of the blame as easily as all of the credit. With tax-exempt status and a base of public support, non-profits are watched closely and the highly visible director answers for the organization. However when all is going well, this is a stable position for those who are well qualified and have a previous track record. Fund raising performance and an ability to work well with directors and volunteers will also influence job security.

AGRICULTURAL SCIENTIST

Ranking: 95

Score: -168

Job Growth: 32%

Unemployment: Low

Agricultural scientists enjoy moderate geographic mobility. Employment opportunities in agricultural science should increase as fast as the national average, through the next decade. The number of jobs in the private sector should increase dramatically, while the number of teaching and research positions with universities is expected to decrease, because of declining enrollments and funding cutbacks.

AIR TRAFFIC CONTROLLER

Ranking: 159

Score: -227

Job Growth: 23%

Unemployment: Moderate

Air traffic controllers, enjoying good geographic freedom, are employed at airports across the country. Despite growth in the air transportation industry, job growth in the field of air traffic control will be minimized, due to improved radar and communications technology. Constant high stress is a hazard of this profession that can impair job security.

AIRCRAFT MECHANIC

Ranking: 187

Score: -271

Job Growth: 29%

Unemployment: Moderate

Aircraft mechanics have moderate geographic flexibility. Employment opportunities will remain stable in this field through The next decade. The state of the commercial airline industry affects job prospects in this profession. Aircraft mechanics work with or near heavy machinery, high powered equipment, and flammable fuels, creating a hazardous work environment.

AIRPLANE PILOT

Ranking: 57

Score: -121

Job Growth: 79%

Unemployment: Moderate

Commercial pilots enjoy little geographic mobility. Jobs for pilots should increase faster than the national average, over the next decade, because of growth in the air transportation industry. The commercial pilot's job presents both physical and mental hazards to job security.

ANTHROPOLOGIST

Ranking: 129

Score: -205

Job Growth: 45%

Unemployment: Moderate

Anthropologists enjoy moderate geographic flexibility. There will be few employment opportunities for anthropologists over the next decade. Declining university enrollments, especially in the social sciences, will decrease the number of teaching positions available. Gaining tenure is the sole determinant of job security.

ANTIQUE DEALER

Ranking: 53

Score: -118

Job Growth: 32%

Unemployment: Low

Knowledge of a particular market and staying abreast of collectors' interests is essential for maintaining a good position within this industry. The nation's passion for collecting has soared in recent years and the explosion of new stores, in particular antique malls, has merely fueled this growth. In turn, the field is becoming more competitive as more dealers vie for sources to replenish their inventories. Establishing an expertise and knowledge in a particular field helps to ensure the respect and trust of clients and fellow dealers.

APPLIANCE REPAIRER

Ranking: 200

Score: -291

Job Growth: 9%

Unemployment: Moderate

Home appliance repairers enjoy moderate geographic freedom. The increasing use of solid-state technology, and of microprocessors, will make appliances more reliable, and thus lessen the need for repairs. Repairers face hazards from shocks, burns, and cuts.

ARCHEOLOGIST

Ranking: 129

Score: -205

Job Growth: 45%

Unemployment: Moderate

Archeologists enjoy little geographic mobility. Teaching and research positions at universities will be adversely affected by declining university enrollments, which are expected to produce budget cuts in low enrollment programs, such as anthropology and archeology. A tenured position assures job security for archeologists.

ARCHITECT

Ranking: 108

Score: -191

Job Growth: 59%

Unemployment: High

Architects enjoy excellent geographic flexibility. Employment opportunities for architects are projected to increase, though no higher than the national average of all occupations. The field of architecture appears relatively stable, but competition for jobs is fierce and is expected to remain that way. The recent slump in new building has closed many architectural offices and re-employment opportunities are bleak.

ARCHITECTURAL DRAFTER

Ranking: 157

Score: -225

Job Growth: 25%

Unemployment: High

Architectural drafters enjoy moderate geographic flexibility. The employment outlook for draftsmen will remain stable over the next decade, but until the economy, more specifically real estate, returns to higher employment, security is poor. Industrial growth, and increasingly complex architectural designs, will create a growing demand for skilled drafters. However, innovations in computer design systems will limit any growth in opportunities for drafters.

ARTIST (COMMERCIAL)

Ranking: 77

Score: -148

Job Growth: 52%

Unemployment: Moderate

Some commercial artists work as free-lancers and enjoy excellent geographic freedom, however, most jobs originate in major cities. Increased demand for commercial art in advertising, public relations, and in-house use by businesses should keep employment secure for commercial artists, with jobs growing faster than the average, through the 1990s. Competition among commercial artists is keen and can be a hazard to job security.

ARTIST (FINE ART)

Ranking: 203

Score: -298

Job Growth: 52%

Unemployment: Very High

Artistic painters are free to work where they wish. Employment opportunities for these artists are expected to grow faster than average in the next decade. However, the market will continue to support only a very small number of the available professional artists. Competition for available jobs for artists will remain extremely strong.

ASTROLOGER

Ranking: 103

Score: -177

Job Growth: 23%

Unemployment: Moderate

Astrologers enjoy moderate geographic flexibility, although large metropolitan areas offer the greatest employment potential. The success of an astrology practice can be extremely tenuous, fluctuating with public perceptions of the profession. Employment opportunities for astrologers are expected to increase with the general growth of the U.S. population.

ASTRONAUT

Ranking: 121

Score: -200

Job Growth: 0%

Unemployment: Low

Most astronauts are military personnel and are geographically limited. Although space explora-

238

tion is expected to increase over the next decade, the field is highly competitive, and growth in job opportunities will be unable to sustain the number of applicants. Space exploration presents extreme physical and mental hazards.

ASTRONOMER

Ranking: 129

Score: -205

Job Growth: -5%

Unemployment: Moderate

Astronomers enjoy little geographic flexibility. The number of teaching positions for astronomers is expected to decrease, over the next ten years, because of declining university enrollments and funding cutbacks. New jobs will grow from private industry, due to the drive for renewed space exploration.

ATTORNEY

Ranking: 23

Score: -80

Job Growth: 70%

Unemployment: Low

Attorneys enjoy excellent geographic freedom. The number of jobs for attorneys will increase much faster than the average, as the amount of litigation in society continues to rise. Competition in this profession will remain stiff. The current high enrollment in law schools across the country indicates a glut of new lawyers in the market over the next decade.

AUDIOLOGIST

Ranking: 4

Score: 15

Job Growth: 115%

Unemployment: Very Low

Audiologists enjoy excellent geographic flexibility, they can work in any area of the country. Job opportunities for audiologists are projected to increase as fast as the national average, through the next decade. The general growth in the U.S. population insures the increase of job opportunities in this profession.

AUTHOR (BOOKS)

Ranking: 77

Score: -148

Job Growth: 52%

Unemployment: Moderate

Book writers enjoy excellent geographic freedom. Because of growth in the publishing industry, job opportunities for writers should increase faster than the average through the 1990s. Employment in this field is highly competitive, as there are far more job seekers than the writing market can sustain. Most authors work on a freelance basis, and their job security depends on maintaining a succession of independent projects.

AUTOMOBILE ASSEMBLER

Ranking: 219

Score: -318

Job Growth: 32%

Unemployment: High

Auto assemblers enjoy little geographic flexibility. Although population growth should greatly increase the demand for cars, improved automation will keep growth in this field on a par with the average through the next decade.

AUTOMOBILE BODY REPAIRER

Ranking: 105

Score: -182

Job Growth: 68%

Unemployment: Low

Autobody repairers enjoy good geographic flexibility. The number of jobs for auto repair workers will grow at a steady rate through the 1990s. An increased numbers of cars on the road is expected to create greater demand for autobody repairers, especially those with expertise in foreign automobile repair. Automotive repairers work with dangerous power tools, and are often exposed to toxic fumes.

AUTOMOBILE MECHANIC

Ranking: 175

Score: -248

Job Growth: 52%

Unemployment: Moderate

Automotive mechanics can find employment in any part of the country. As the number of cars on the road continues to rise, the demand for automotive mechanics will remain high. Consequently, job growth in this field will far surpass the average through the 1990s. Auto mechanics risk injury from working with dangerous machinery, equipment and fuels.

AUTOMOBILE PAINTER

Ranking: 233

Score: -348

Job Growth: 2%

Unemployment: High

Full-time job openings for painters is declining as more cars are being imported. Some opportunity remains the next decade as the number of cars, trucks, and buses damaged in traffic accidents grow with the U.S. automotive population. Most experienced painters can expect steady work through all economic conditions. Employment of assembly-line painters however, may be strongly affected by recessions and other cyclical downturns.

AUTOMOBILE SALESPERSON

Ranking: 185

Score: -268

Job Growth: 32%

Unemployment: High

Automobile salespeople suffer few geographic limitations on employment. Local population density has an affect on a dealership's profits. The continued American slump in automotive sales plagues the profession. Employment opportunities in automotive sales will grow faster than the average through the next decade. Competition in auto sales will remain extremely strong and only the strong survive.

BANK OFFICER

Ranking: 47

Score: -110

Job Growth: 90%

Unemployment: Moderate

Bank officers enjoy excellent geographic freedom, because of the wide distribution of banking facilities across the country. Growth in the banking industry is expected to increase employment opportunities for bank officers faster than the average, through the next decade. Although generally stable, positions in this field can be undermined by major economic recessions.

BANK TELLER

Ranking: 138

Score: -209

Job Growth: -9%

Unemployment: Moderate

Bank tellers have excellent geographic mobility, because their skills are adaptable to any banking institution. Increased automation will result in below-average job growth for tellers, through the 1990s.

BARBER

Ranking: 129

Score: -205

Job Growth: -5%

Unemployment: Moderate

Barbers enjoy moderate geographic flexibility. Job growth in barbering is expected to decline through the 1990s. Shifts in consumer preference for use of hair stylists over barbers has seriously affected this profession.

BARTENDER

Ranking: 185

Score: -268

Job Growth: -18%

Unemployment: Moderate

Bartending offers excellent geographic mobility. Employment prospects for bartenders are projected to increase very slightly through the 1990s. The decline in restaurant and entertainment facilities due to the recession has hurt the profession greatly.

BASEBALL PLAYER (MAJOR LEAGUE)

Ranking: 247

Score: -439

Job Growth: 11%

Unemployment: High

Baseball players enjoy moderate geographic freedom. With the little growth in new teams likely, employment opportunities will be moderate. The field of baseball is highly competitive and should remain so in the future.

BASEBALL UMPIRE (MAJOR LEAGUE)

Ranking: 228

Score: -339

Job Growth: 11%

Unemployment: Low

Major league umpires enjoy good geographic freedom. Employment opportunities for umpires are expected to increase only slightly over the next decade. The pool of umpires will remain relatively small and very competitive.

BASKETBALL COACH (NCAA)

Ranking: 167

Score: -239

Job Growth: 11%

Unemployment: Moderate

College basketball coaches enjoy good geographic freedom. Coaching is highly competitive, and a coach's job security frequently depends on a team's performance. Job turnover is high at many colleges and universities, and the field is expected to remain highly competitive, with little job growth.

BASKETBALL PLAYER (NBA)

Ranking: 247

Score: -439

Job Growth: 11%

Unemployment: High

Basketball players enjoy moderate geographic freedom. Slow job growth is projected in basketball through the next decade, and competition among basketball players will be as fierce as ever. Physical injuries can seriously impair job security in this field.

BIOLOGIST

Ranking: 33

Score: -94

Job Growth: 56%

Unemployment: Low

Biologists enjoy moderate geographic mobility. The field of biology appears to be growing, with job prospects increasing faster than the average, through the next decade. Most new jobs for biologists will spring from private industry, while university positions will decline because of low enrollment.

BOILERMAKER

Ranking: 216

Score: -309

Job Growth: 9%

Unemployment: High

Boilermakers enjoy excellent geographic freedom, they can work in any area of the country. Improved automation and construction should curb prospects for boilermakers. Boilermakers are subject to a variety of physical hazards which can impair job security.

BOOKBINDER

Ranking: 145

Score: -218

Job Growth: 32%

Unemployment: Moderate

Bookbinders enjoy little geographic freedom, although small binderies can be found throughout the country, most jobs for binders are found in the Northeast. Larger populations will increase the demand for books, nevertheless, greater use of automated production equipment will keep the number of jobs in bookbinding growing only as fast as the average. Bookbinders work with high-powered machinery that is hazardous and can impair job security.

BOOKKEEPER

Ranking: 203

Score: -293

Job Growth: 7%

Unemployment: Very High

Bookkeepers enjoy excellent geographic mobility. The number of jobs in bookkeeping has declined sharply due to the generally poor health in the economy. Increases in the use of automated accounting systems are primarily responsible for the slow growth in this field.

BRICKLAYER

Ranking: 243

Score: -391

Job Growth: 59%

Unemployment: Very High

Bricklayers generally can work in any geographic area. Bricklaying work is seasonal in many parts of the country. Job growth in this trade is expected to increase as fast as the overall national employment market over the next decade. The employment outlook follows the ups and downs of the construction industry as a whole. Bricklayers work with and around dangerous heavy machinery.

BROADCAST TECHNICIAN

Ranking: 108

Score: -191

Job Growth: 9%

Unemployment: Low

Employment opportunities for broadcast technicians are most prevalent in major metropolitan areas. Technicians can expect moderate employment growth over the next ten years. Tightened budgets among the major media companies will produce heavy competition for technical jobs in broadcasting.

BUS DRIVER

Ranking: 124

Score: -203

Job Growth: 47%

Unemployment: Moderate

Bus drivers have moderate geographic flexibility. Job growth for drivers should remain steady over the next decade. Drivers in major cities are safer from layoffs. However, for bus drivers working with schools or other government-related institutions, the employment outlook can be affected by budget constraints. Heavy traffic or poor weather can add to the normal road hazards bus drivers face.

BUTCHER

Ranking: 223

Score: -332

Job Growth: -32%

Unemployment: Moderate

Butchers currently enjoy excellent geographic flexibility. The demand for butchers is expected to decline over the next decade, as more cutting and boxing is done at large meat packing plants. Butchers work with sharp cutting machines, and other dangerous equipment, which often causes minor injuries and inability to work.

BUYER

Ranking: 187

Score: -271

Job Growth: 29%

Unemployment: Very High

Wholesale and retail buyers are occasionally limited to seasonal work. Retail and wholesale buying offers moderate geographic flexibility. Job growth in this profession is expected to keep pace with the average over the next decade. The field will remain highly competitive. Buyers sometimes must take substantial business risks.

CARPENTER

Ranking: 235

Score: -355

Job Growth: 45%

Unemployment: Very High

Carpenters enjoy excellent geographic flexibility. Employment opportunities for carpenters are expected to increase over the next decade. However, many carpenters can expect stretches of unemployment, due to the short-term nature of projects. The equipment used in carpentry, such as high-powered saws, contributes to a hazardous work environment.

CARPET/TILE INSTALLER

Ranking: 208

Score: -300

Job Growth: 50%

Unemployment: High

Since carpeting is a luxury item for most consumers, employment in this field is sensitive to downturns in the economy. With the office market overbuilt in the 1980s and residential construction scaled back, moderate unemployment is likely over the next decade.

CARTOONIST

Ranking: 77

Score: -148

Job Growth: 52%

Unemployment: Moderate

Cartoonists enjoy moderate geographic flexibility. Employment opportunities in cartooning are expected to grow faster than the average, through the next decade, because of growth in publishing and advertising. Competition is high among cartoonists, and although there will be growth in the field of cartooning, job candidates will continue to outnumber available positions.

CASHIER

Ranking: 73

Score: -146

Job Growth: 54%

Unemployment: Moderate

Cashiers can generally find employment opportunities in any area of the country. As a result of the expansion of the service sector, job growth for cashiers is expected to increase faster than average over the next ten years. The demand for cashiers sometimes follows seasonal patterns.

CATHOLIC PRIEST

Ranking: 24

Score: -82

Job Growth: 68%

Unemployment: Very Low

The great shortage of priests will continue into the mid-1990s. The number of available positions in the priesthood will far surpass that of seminary graduates through the next decade. Although funding in poorer parishes may run low, priests are free from layoffs or other economic concerns.

CHAUFFEUR

Ranking: 124

Score: -203

Job Growth: 47%

Unemployment: Moderate

Chauffeurs can work in any area of the country, although job opportunities for drivers are greater in major metropolitan areas. Increases in the nation's upper-class population should increase the demand for chauffeurs, and keep employment opportunities growing steadily through the 1990s.

CHEMIST

Ranking: 124

Score: -203

Job Growth: 47%

Unemployment: Moderate

Job prospects for chemists are not limited geographically. Sluggish growth in the chemical industry will result in a slower than average increase in employment opportunities in chemistry over the next decade. Employment of professional chemists in universities is expected to decline sharply through the 1990s.

CHILD CARE WORKER

Ranking: 12

Score: -51

Job Growth: 149%

Unemployment: Very Low

There are few geographic limitations on employment for child care workers. Job growth in the child care field will soar over the next decade, due to the increased number of working mothers of preschool children. Economic factors, such as government funding for day care, have a strong impact on the child care profession.

CHIROPRACTOR

Ranking: 97

Score: -169

Job Growth: 81%

Unemployment: Low

Chiropractors are free to work anywhere in the country. Competition between individual practices can be stiff. The chiropractic profession is expected to be one of the fastest growing over the next ten years. Modifications in health insurance plans may lead to instability in the field. Chiropractors must contend with the growing cost of malpractice insurance.

CHOREOGRAPHER

Ranking: 169

Score: -244

Job Growth: 56%

Unemployment: High

Choreographers enjoy little geographic freedom, most jobs for choreographers originate in major metropolitan areas. Employment opportunities in choreography should increase faster than the average, through the 1990s, because of a greater demand for dance productions. Competition among choreographers is intense, and although the number of jobs may increase, job candidates will continue to outnumber available positions.

CIVIL ENGINEER

Ranking: 73

Score: -146

Job Growth: 54%

Unemployment: Low

An expanding national economy will create a greater demand for civil engineers. The number of jobs for civil engineers will increase at a faster-than-average pace over the next decade. However, the employment situation for civil engineers within the construction industry can be erratic, due to fluctuations in building trends.

COLLEGE PROFESSOR

Ranking: 108

Score: -191

Job Growth: 59%

Unemployment: Moderate

Colleges and universities are located throughout the country, and employment for professors and instructors is relatively free from geographic restraints. Government cutbacks on funding for higher education will make college teaching precarious over the next ten years. Competition for academic positions is intense.

COMMUNICATIONS EQUIPMENT MECHANIC

Ranking: 242

Score: -386

Job Growth: -86%

Unemployment: High

Communications mechanics enjoy excellent geographical freedom. Job growth in this field will be limited in the coming decade. Although the demand for installation of new equipment will be greater, advances in communication technology will make installation easier, requiring fewer workers. In addition, communication equipment will be more reliable, and in need of less frequent service.

COMPOSITOR/TYPESETTER

Ranking: 221

Score: -329

Job Growth: -29%

Unemployment: High

Printers, compositors, and typesetters enjoy moderate geographic flexibility. Employment prospects in these trades over the next decade are somewhat uncertain. Increased growth in the printing industry should create new printing jobs at a rate as fast as the average into the 1990s. However, technological advances such as low cost "desktop publishing" make certain specialty trades in printing such as this one obsolete.

COMPUTER OPERATOR

Ranking: 197

Score: -288

Job Growth: -88%

Unemployment: Low

Computer operators enjoy a high degree of geographic flexibility. As the computerization of the workplace continues, the demand for qualified computer operators will be strong in all sectors of the economy. Consequently, this will be one of the fastest growing occupations over the next ten years. However, operators who work with large systems face slower job growth, due to technological advances in this area.

COMPUTER PROGRAMMER

Ranking: 24

Score: -82

Job Growth: 68%

Unemployment: Low

The employment outlook for computer programmers is excellent. Programmers enjoy moderate geographic flexibility. Continuing demand for computer related tasks and the general trend toward a computerized society, will give computer programming the fastest job growth of any occupation in the country over the next decade.

COMPUTER SERVICE TECHNICIAN

Ranking: 52

Score: -116

Job Growth: 34%

Unemployment: Very Low

As with most computer-related professions, the computer service field should undergo faster-than-average growth over the next decade. Employment prospects for trained computer service technicians are bright. Most technicians are safe from layoffs during economic recessions.

COMPUTER SYSTEMS ANALYST

Ranking: 1

Score: 150

Job Growth: 250%

Unemployment: Very Low

Employment opportunities for computer systems analysts should be excellent over the next decade. The number of jobs for systems analysts will grow much faster than the average through the 1990s. Many jobs will be available, but analysts can expect some stiff competition for better positions.

CONGRESSPERSON/SENATOR

Ranking: 203

Score: -293

Job Growth: 7%

Unemployment: Very High

Congressmen and senators serve a particular geographic constituency, and spend much of their time in the nation's capital. The great competition for the few positions in this prestigious and powerful field severely limits job opportunities. While in office, congressmen and senators must satisfy their voting constituents, who decide whether or not to return the office-holders for another term. Campaign financing is a constant concern for any congressman considering running for re-election.

CONSERVATIONIST

Ranking: 156

Score: -223

Job Growth: 27%

Unemployment: Moderate

Conservationists and range managers are hampered by limited geographic flexibility. Employment growth in conservation will be slower than the average over the next decade. Conservationists and range managers must contend with forest fires and other natural disasters which can hamper their ability to continue working if injured or destruction to property is severe enough to cause closure of their work site. The possibility of lower government funding is an omnipresent threat.

CONSTRUCTION FOREMAN

Ranking: 169

Score: -244

Job Growth: 106%

Unemployment: Very High

Supervisors have moderate geographic flexibility. Employment opportunities will grow at a rate higher than the overall national average over the next decade. Supervisors are generally safe from layoffs during economic recessions. However, employment in the construction trades is subject to economic fluctuations. Supervisors face hazards working with heavy machinery.

CONSTRUCTION MACHINERY OPERATOR

Ranking: 202

Score: -292

Job Growth: 108%

Unemployment: Very High

Construction machinery operators suffer from the seasonal nature of the construction industry. Employment growth for construction- related occupations follows the ups and downs of the national economy. Machinery operators can expect job growth in their field to conform to the national average over the next ten years.

CONSTRUCTION WORKER (LABORER)

Ranking: 229

Score: -341

Job Growth: 59%

Unemployment: Very High

Frequent periods of unemployment are common. With office space having been overbuilt and residential construction down in the early 1990s employment stability will be limited. Some skilled construction trade workers have been filling unskilled positions to obtain work, therefore the unskilled construction laborer will suffer.

COOK

Ranking: 142

Score: -214

Job Growth: 86%

Unemployment: Moderate

Cooks and chefs can generally find employment in any area of the country. The demand for cooks and chefs will be high over the next ten years, and faster-than-average employment growth is expected in this profession through the 1990s. Competition for higher-paying culinary positions will remain strong.

CORPORATE EXECUTIVE (SENIOR)

Ranking: 150

Score: 221

Job Growth: 29%

Unemployment: Low-Moderate

There is a growing demand for effective senior corporate executives, but extensive competition exists. The market and abrupt changes in economic conditions could affect prospects, but at this high level continued success equates to an even higher level of financial reward. The greatest demand is for senior operations, marketing, sales and research executives, as well as those in the areas of high technology, health care and non-profits.

CORRECTION OFFICER

Ranking: 11

Score: -42

Job Growth: 158%

Unemployment: Low

As the U.S. prison population grows, the number of jobs for correction officers is expected to increase much faster than the average over the next decade. The potentially volatile conditions inside prisons create high-risk job situations for correction officers.

COSMETOLOGIST

Ranking: 99

Score: -171

Job Growth: 79%

Unemployment: Moderate

Cosmetologists enjoy excellent geographic mobility. Increased consumer demand for hair-styling and body-care should cause an increase in employment opportunities for cosmetologists through the next decade.

COWBOY

Ranking: 229

Score: -341

Job Growth: -41%

Unemployment: Moderate

Cowboys enjoy little geographic mobility. Ranch hands are subject to seasonal fluctuation in demand for their services. Increased automation and slow industry growth are expected to cause a decline in job prospects for cowboys. Work with live animals presents numerous physical hazards which impair job security.

DAIRY FARMER

Ranking: 232

Score: -347

Job Growth: -47%

Unemployment: Moderate

The trend toward automated dairy conglomerates creates a grim employment picture for the small dairy farmer through the next decade. Dairy farmers have little geographic mobility. Strenuous physical labor, and the abundance of machinery used in dairy production, makes for a hazardous work environment.

DANCER

Ranking: 231

Score: -344

Job Growth: 56%

Unemployment: Very High

Because most dance companies are located in major metropolitan areas, dancers face extremely limited geographic flexibility. Employment should grow faster than the average through the 1990s, but competition for jobs in dance, as in most artistic fields, is extremely strong, and will remain so. Professional dancers often experience physical injuries, and mental stress.

DENTAL HYGIENIST

Ranking: 13

Score: -53

Job Growth: 97%

Unemployment: Very Low

Population increases and improved dental insurance plans are expected to help maintain faster-than-average growth in the number of jobs for dental hygienists over the next decade. Rapid technological advances in dentistry, however, may disturb this growth pattern. Employment for dental hygienists is free of geographic limitations.

DENTAL LABORATORY TECHNICIAN

Ranking: 72

Score: -143

Job Growth: 7%

Unemployment: Very Low

Dental laboratory technicians enjoy excellent geographic mobility. Workers in this profession will see stable growth in in the number of jobs the next decade. Employment opportunities in dental laboratories should not be affected adversely by technological advances. Prospects for technicians who open their dental laboratories will be good.

DENTIST

Ranking: 67

Score: -139

Job Growth: 11%

Unemployment: Very Low

Population growth, and improved dental insurance programs, should produce a greater demand for dental services. Dentists can expect average job growth in employment opportunities through the coming decade. However, major technological advances could alter the job picture for dentists. Dentistry will become a much more competitive field over the next ten years.

DIETITIAN

Ranking: 42

Score: -103

Job Growth: 97%

Unemployment: Low

Clinical dietitians have moderate geographic flexibility. Hospitals, nursing homes, and state and federal social programs will need to staff a rising number of qualified dietitians in the near future, and the demand for dietitians is expected to grow accordingly. As a result, the number of jobs for dietitians will increase faster than the average through the coming decade.

DISHWASHER

Ranking: 150

Score: -219

Job Growth: 81%

Unemployment: Moderate

Dishwashers can work almost anywhere. Job opportunities should increase faster than average, through the next decade. Although the restaurant industry is expected to grow steadily, automation will cause some unemployment.

DISK JOCKEY

Ranking: 113

Score: -194

Job Growth: 56%

Unemployment: Moderate

The employment outlook is relatively stable for disk jockeys, and should remain so in the coming decade. As new radio stations are licensed, the number of jobs for disk jockeys will increase. The growing number of job candidates will force stronger competition for available positions.

DRESSMAKER

Ranking: 183

Score: -259

Job Growth: -9%

Unemployment: Moderate

Dressmaker's jobs are highly skewed to the Northeast. Employment growth within this field is expected to be low over the next decade, because of cutbacks in the industry and increases in automation. Machine inflicted injuries are a hazard of dressmaking that can impair job security.

DRILL-PRESS OPERATOR

Ranking: 241

Score: -377

Job Growth: -27%

Unemployment: High

Employment prospects for drill-press operators are limited to the major manufacturing centers of the nation. Employment growth is dependent on the health of state and national economies which have been poor recently. Accidents involving high-powered machinery can cause severe physical injury to drill-press operators.

DRYWALL APPLICATOR/ FINISHER

Ranking: 240

Score: -367

Job Growth: 83%

Unemployment: Very High

Many drywall applicators work seasonally, and applicators and finishers often experience periods of unemployment between projects. Employment opportunities in this trade are limited by localized trends in the construction industry. Job growth for drywallers will be better than average over the next decade. Drywall workers are susceptible to falls, and to other construction-related mishaps.

ECONOMIST

Ranking: 113

Score: -194

Job Growth: 56%

Unemployment: High

The growing complexity of state and national economies will create a rising demand for economists in the coming years. Consequently, employment opportunities for economists will increase in the coming decade. However, budget constraints will force universities to curtail employment of economists sharply. Competition among economists for positions will be strong.

ELECTRICAL ENGINEER

Ranking: 73

Score: -146

Job Growth: 54%

Unemployment: Low

Employment prospects for electrical engineers will be excellent over the next decade. The number of jobs in this field will increase at a rate much faster than the average through the 1990s. Recent government spending cutbacks could darken the employment outlook for electrical engineers working in the defense industry.

ELECTRICAL EQUIPMENT REPAIRER

Ranking: 203

Score: -293

Job Growth: 7%

Unemployment: High

Electrical equipment repairers enjoy moderate geographic flexibility. Employment opportunities in this field are expected to increase must slower than the overall national average. Electrical workers must contend with the potential for shocks and other injuries.

ELECTRICAL TECHNICIAN

Ranking: 118

Score: -198

Job Growth: 52%

Unemployment: Moderate

Technological innovation in electronics is expected to cause rapid expansion in job opportunities for electrical technicians. This will be one of the fastest growing occupations in the nation over the next decade. Many jobs are related to the defense industry, and major cutbacks in government defense spending could cloud the job outlook for electrical technicians somewhat.

ELECTRICIAN

Ranking: 307

Score: -307

Job Growth: 43%

Unemployment: High

Employment for electricians occasionally follows seasonal patterns. These workers suffer from somewhat limited geographic flexibility. The employment outlook for electricians is expected to remain stable throughout the next decade. Electricians face the potential for injury from electrical shocks.

EMERGENCY MEDICAL TECHNICIAN

Ranking: 54

Score: -119

Job Growth: 81%

Unemployment: Very Low

Emergency medical technicians enjoy good geographic flexibility. The rising number of elderly in the nation will create an increased need for emergency medical services, funds for training and support for EMTs, consequently, job growth will be extremely good through the 1990s.

ENGINEERING TECHNICIAN

Ranking: 45

Score: -107

Job Growth: 43%

Unemployment: Very Low

Employment opportunities for engineering technicians exist throughout the country, and job prospects should be excellent through the 1990s. The call for better productivity and improved designs, combined with greater government and private sector spending for defense and high technology research, should keep the demand for engineering technicians growing faster than the average.

EXECUTIVE SEARCH CONSULTANT

Ranking: 113

Score: -194

Job Growth: 56%

Unemployment: High

Executive search consultants enjoy moderate geographic flexibility. There is increasing demand for effective search consultants but high competition exists. The market and abrupt changes in economic conditions could affect prospects, but as awareness of the benefits and services expand, so will the scope of opportunities.

FARMER

Ranking: 250

Score: -447

Job Growth: -47%

Unemployment: Very High

Most farmers are limited to seasonal work, and, tied down as they are to their particular farm, have practically no geographic mobility. As the trend toward larger, more efficient, automated farms continues, the demand for farmers will dwindle. Thus, farmers can expect a steady decline in employment opportunities through the next decade. Farmers work with hazardous, high-powered machinery. The agricultural sector is highly susceptible to economic downswings.

FASHION DESIGNER

Ranking: 124

Score: -203

Job Growth: 47%

Unemployment: Moderate

Most employment opportunities for fashion designers are located in major cities, such as New York and Los Angeles. Some designers are limited to seasonal work. The number of jobs in this field is expected to grow at a faster-than-average pace through the next decade, as consumer spending on clothing increases. Competition among members of this occupation will remain extremely strong.

FASHION MODEL

Ranking: 61

Score: -128

Job Growth: 122%

Unemployment: Moderate

Fashion models enjoy little geographic flexibility, as most modeling jobs are found in major cities. Many models experience a seasonal fluctuation in the demand for their services. Employment opportunities in modeling should increase as fast as the national job growth average. The field of fashion modeling is highly competitive, and it consistently attracts more job candidates than it can support.

FILE CLERK

Ranking: 135

Score: -207

Job Growth: 43%

Unemployment: Moderate

Office clerks experience moderate geographic mobility. Employment opportunities in the clerical field are expected to grow at a slower-than-average rate through the next decade. Increased office automation, particularly computer technol-ogy, will make many jobs obsolete, or necessitate retraining for a large part of the clerical work force.

FINANCIAL PLANNER

Ranking: 113

Score: -194

Job Growth: 56%

Unemployment: High

With the increasing number of investment options available, there is a growing demand for expert advice, but high competition exists. Abrupt changes in the securities market could affect the profession in adverse ways. As awareness of planners' services grows, it is likely that the scope of their services will also increase.

FIREFIGHTER

Ranking: 141

Score: -212

Job Growth: 38%

Unemployment: Very Low

Firefighters have very limited geographic flexibility. The increase in population will keep the number of jobs for firefighters growing at an average rate through the next decade. Firefighters encounter extreme hazards on the job, such as exposure to flame and extreme heat, danger from falling debris, and the threat of smoke inhalation during a fire.

FISHERMAN

Ranking: 198

Score: -289

Job Growth: 11%

Unemployment: Moderate

Limited geographic flexibility, highly seasonal work and increased automation, all combine to create a dismal employment outlook for small-scale commercial fishing. The number of jobs for fishermen should decrease through the next decade. Independently-operating small boat owners will find competition with the larger companies tough. Working on the open seas, especially in poor weather conditions, presents a danger to fishermen.

FLIGHT ATTENDANT

Ranking: 66

Score: -135

Job Growth: 115%

Unemployment: Moderate

Flight attendants have relatively limited geographic flexibility. Employment opportunities in this field will increase much faster than the average over the next decade, as commercial transportation needs rise. Airline accidents are a constant danger for flight attendants.

FLORIST

Ranking: 145

Score: -218

Job Growth: 32%

Unemployment: Moderate

Florists enjoy excellent geographic flexibility. The demand for florists and floral services is seasonal. The poor national economy and a general decrease in consumer spending has plagued the profession. Because many florists operate their own businesses, competition in this field can be strong.

FOOTBALL PLAYER (NFL)

Ranking: 247

Score: -439

Job Growth: 11%

Unemployment: High

Football players enjoy little geographic flexibility. There will be few employment opportunities in football playing. Not only is the field of football highly competitive, but little job growth is expected through the next decade. Serious physical injuries are common to football players and can threaten job security, which depends on daily performance and contract terms.

FORK-LIFT OPERATOR

Ranking: 194

Score: -284

Job Growth: 16%

Unemployment: Moderate

Employment opportunities in this field will decline through the next decade, as the use of computerized, automated handling equipment increases. Truck operators are also subject to layoffs during economic downturn.

FURNITURE UPHOLSTER

Ranking: 192

Score: -275

Job Growth: 25%

Unemployment: Moderate

Employment opportunities in this field will decrease through the next decade. Upholsterers who work in large metropolitan areas where those effected by the poor economy choose to reupholster, should have the best prospects for continued prosperity.

GARBAGE COLLECTOR

Ranking: 220

Score: -325

Job Growth: 25%

Unemployment: Moderate

Garbage collectors enjoy excellent geographic flexibility. Due to the use of automatic collection systems, job growth in this field will not keep up with increases in population. The physical hazards of the job can result in cuts, burns, and infections, and can endanger job security.

GEOLOGIST

Ranking: 121

Score: -200

Job Growth: 50%

Unemployment: Moderate

Geologists and geophysicists enjoy a moderate amount of geographic freedom in employment. Job growth in this profession will be stable through the next ten years. Employment for geological scientists in universities will drop drastically, as educational budgets tighten. Economic fluctuations in the oil industry affect many geologists and geophysicists.

GLAZIER

Ranking: 223

Score: -332

Job Growth: 68%

Unemployment: Very High

Glaziers enjoy moderate geographic flexibility. Some members of this profession are limited to seasonal work. A rise in business and residential construction will create greater demand for glazier services in the coming years, and employment opportunities in this field will grow at a faster-than-average pace through the 1990s. Glaziers work at great heights, and also face danger from sharp equipment.

GUARD

Ranking: 27

Score: -85

Job Growth: 115%

Unemployment: Low

Security guards are not generally hampered by geographic constraints on employment. Job growth in this occupation will be faster than the average over the next ten years, due to increasing concern over security in retail stores and in industry. Security guards can encounter dangerous, even life-threatening situations in the course of their work.

HEATING/REFRIGERATION MECHANIC

Ranking: 165

Score: -235

Job Growth: 65%

Unemployment: Moderate

Some heating and refrigeration mechanics are limited to seasonal work, although geographic flexibility is good. Employment should be stable through the next decade because of increases in population and construction rates. Electrical shocks and burns are job hazards that can impair security. Mechanics are less affected by economic downturns than other construction professionals.

HIGHWAY PATROL OFFICER

Ranking: 145

Score: -218

Job Growth: 32%

Unemployment: Low

Growth in job opportunities for state highway patrol officers will keep pace not with the average through the next decade. Employment prospects for state troopers can be affected by state and federal budget cutbacks. Highway patrol officers face volatile, and even life-threatening, situations on the job.

HISTORIAN

Ranking: 68

Score: -141

Job Growth: 59%

Unemployment: Moderate

Employment opportunities in this field will grow moderately through the next decade, as enroll-ments at the nation's colleges and universities continue to fall. Experienced graduates of prestigious universities should have the best prospects for continued employment.

HOME ECONOMIST

Ranking: 129

Score: -205

Job Growth: 45%

Unemployment: Moderate

Although they have adequate geographic flexibility, job prospects for home economists are projected to decrease significantly over the next ten years. Many jobs are expected to become obsolete because of budget cutbacks and changing research techniques.

HOSPITAL ADMINISTRATOR

Ranking: 57

Score: -121

Job Growth: 79%

Unemployment: Low

Population increases and greater demand for health care are expected to keep employment of hospital administrators growing much faster than the average in the coming decade. However, competition for most jobs should be intense. The trend toward consolidation of hospital facilities may stunt job growth and eliminate many lower-level jobs.

HOTEL MANAGER

Ranking: 40

Score: -101

Job Growth: 99%

Unemployment: Moderate

Hotel managers enjoy good geographic flexibility. Hiring in this profession can be seasonal. Both tourist and business travel will be on the rise in the coming years. As a result, the number of jobs in hotel management will grow at a rate much faster than the average over the next ten years.

INDUSTRIAL DESIGNER

Ranking: 84

Score: -157

Job Growth: 43%

Unemployment: Moderate

The growing consumer market will create demand for improved, more sophisticated products and equipment, thus keeping the number of jobs for industrial designers growing in the coming decade. Competition in this profession for available positions will continue to be strong.

INDUSTRIAL ENGINEER

Ranking: 49

Score: -112

Job Growth: 38%

Unemployment: Low

The trend toward an automated workplace, and demands for greater efficiency in business and industry, will enhance employment prospects for industrial engineers. This profession will undergo average growth over the next decade.

INDUSTRIAL MACHINE REPAIRER

Ranking: 214

Score: -307

Job Growth: -7%

Unemployment: Moderate

Employment opportunities for industrial machinery repairers are concentrated in major manufacturing and industrial centers. Improved, highly-automated industrial equipment will need less maintenance in the coming years. Thus, job growth for machine repairers will lag behind the average over the next decade. Workers in this occupation face physical hazards from working with heavy machinery and high-powered equipment.

INSURANCE AGENT

Ranking: 144

Score: -216

Job Growth: 34%

Unemployment: Moderate

Although they have moderate geographic flexibility, future employment of agents and brokers is projected to increase slower at the overall national average in the coming decade because of increased sales of group policies and telemarketing. The highly competitive nature of the field can seriously threaten job security.

INSURANCE UNDERWRITER

Ranking: 73

Score: -146

Job Growth: 54%

Unemployment: Moderate

Insurance underwriters are expected to benefit from increased use of group policies and employment should grow faster than average throughout the next ten years. Because insurance is a necessity for individuals and businesses, underwriters are safer from economic recessions and others in the insurance industry.

IRONWORKER

Ranking: 176

Score: -250

Job Growth: 50%

Unemployment: Moderate

Ironworkers are limited by seasonal work and they are required to have moderate geographic flexibility. The decline in construction has seriously hampered job opportunities. Working with heavy equipment, often from high places, is a potential job-threatening factor.

JANITOR

Ranking: 181

Score: -257

Job Growth: 43%

Unemployment: Moderate

Janitors can generally work in any area of the country. Employment rates should grow about as fast as the average, except with contracting firms, where jobs will greatly increase. Although no major technological advances are expected to impair job security, economic downturns can lead to layoffs.

JEWELER

Ranking: 135

Score: -207

Job Growth: 43%

Unemployment: High

Jewelers enjoy moderate geographic flexibility. Employment opportunities for jewelers will increase at a slower-than-average rate over the next ten years, due to foreign competition and growing use of automation during processing. Seasonal consumer trends, and economic downswings, can hamper job opportunities in this profession. During recessions, consumer spending on luxury items drops. This decline in demand can result in layoffs for jewelers.

JOCKEY

Ranking: 150

Score: -221

Job Growth: 29%

Unemployment: Low

Jockeys enjoy little geographic flexibility. The field of professional racehorse driving is small and highly competitive, little employment growth is expected over the next decade. Work with race horses presents physical hazards, which can seriously endanger job security.

JUDGE (FEDERAL)

Ranking: 35

Score: -95

Job Growth: 5%

Unemployment: Very Low

Federal judges enjoy little or no geographic flexibility, because of the nature of their appointments. Although they may come under fire for decisions rendered, federal judges enjoy excellent job security.

LIBRARIAN

Ranking: 191

Score: -273

Job Growth: 27%

Unemployment: High

Librarians have moderate geographic flexibility. Constraints on state and local budgets will limit hiring of librarians in public institutions. As a result, the number of jobs in this profession is expected to grow slower than the average over the next decade. However, this decline will be offset to some extent by an increase in demand for researchers and librarians in the private sector.

LITHOGRAPHER/ PHOTOENGRAVER

Ranking: 124

Score: -203

Job Growth: 47%

Unemployment: High

Employment opportunities for lithographers are concentrated in large commercial and industrial centers. The development of less expensive printing equipment will lower the cost of lithography and photoengraving, and increase demand for these services. As a result, job growth in this field will decline over the next ten years. Advanced, automated systems could jeopardize the jobs of workers in some specialized areas of lithography.

LUMBERJACK

Ranking: 245

Score: -416

Job Growth: -16%

Unemployment: Very High

Job opportunities for lumberjacks and loggers are limited geographically. Advances in automation in the lumber industry, coupled with political pressure on the industry from conservation movements, should minimize job growth in this field through the next decade. A greater worldwide demand for paper and wood products, however, may offset these negative factors somewhat. Lumberjacks and loggers face great hazards from working with high-powered saws, and with other dangerous equipment.

MACHINE TOOL OPERATOR

Ranking: 226

Score: -338

Job Growth: -38%

Unemployment: High

Employment opportunities for machine tool operators are generally concentrated in major manufacturing areas of the country. As foreign competition increases, the demand for skilled machine tool operators will decline . Consequently, job growth in this field will decline dramatically in the coming decade. Workers in this profession face physical hazards from working with high-powered equipment.

MACHINIST

Ranking: 212

Score: -302

Job Growth: -2%

Unemployment: Moderate

Jobs opportunities for machinists are limited to centers of manufacturing and industry. Employment in this profession will grow at a less than average rate over the next decade. Increasing use of technologically advanced automation in manufacturing will keep the number of new jobs in this profession down. Machinists face the potential for injury when working with high-powered equipment.

MAID

Ranking: 84

Score: -157

Job Growth: 43%

Unemployment: Very Low

Maids enjoy excellent geographic flexibility. Employment opportunities for house cleaners will grow as fast as the national overall average through the the 1990s. Job opportunities for maids with private contracting firms are expected to increase more rapidly. Maid service is considered a luxury to some, and in recessions, consumers tend to limit spending on such services. As a result, economic downswings can hinder employment prospects in this field.

MAIL CARRIER

Ranking: 77

Score: -148

Job Growth: 2%

Unemployment: Very Low

The U.S. Postal Service operates throughout the country, and mail carriers enjoy excellent geographic flexibility. A greater flow of mail will create an increase in job opportunities for mail carriers over the next decade.

MARKET RESEARCH ANALYST

Ranking: 95

Score: -168

Job Growth: 32%

Unemployment: Moderate

Market research analysts will be in great demand through the 1990s, because of the growing complexity of consumer spending and market trends. Employment opportunities in this profession will increase slightly faster than the overall national average during the next decade. Analysts have moderate geographic flexibility. Most jobs are located in major metropolitan areas.

MATHEMATICIAN

Ranking: 64

Score: -132

Job Growth: 18%

Unemployment: Low

Mathematicians enjoy a moderate degree of geographic flexibility. In contrast with most other academic fields, the demand for mathematicians will be moderate through the 1990s. Employment growth in this profession will not keep pace with the average over the next decade. Those with degrees in applied mathematics will have better employment prospects than those who specialize in theoretical work.

MAYOR

Ranking: 176

Score: -250

Job Growth: 0%

Unemployment: High

Prospective mayors are limited to working in one city or county, because it takes several years to build political support. Very few new mayoral positions are expected through the next decade, and competition for existing posts is stiff. Financial backing and public support are necessary elements in a successful mayoral campaign.

MECHANICAL ENGINEER

Ranking: 84

Score: -155

Job Growth: 45%

Unemployment: Low

Mechanical engineers have moderate geographic flexibility. The need for improved, more efficient production designs will keep demand for mechanical engineers very high in the coming years. This profession will grow at an average over the next decade. Cutbacks in defense spending will have a significant effect on job opportunities for mechanical engineers employed in the defense industry.

MEDICAL LABORATORY TECHNICIAN

Ranking: 31

Score: -91

Job Growth: 59%

Unemployment: Very Low

Medical laboratory technicians enjoy excellent geographic freedom. New laboratory processes and increased health-care needs of the elderly will keep demand for technicians high in the coming years. Workers in this profession can be exposed to hazardous contagions, such as bacteria and viruses.

MEDICAL RECORDS TECHNICIAN

Ranking: 10

Score: -37

Job Growth: 113%

Unemployment: Very Low

The rise in population, and the growing need for health care services and personnel, will cause the number of jobs for medical records technicians to grow at a rate much faster than the average over the next decade. Advances in technology are unlikely to substantially affect the employment picture in this field.

MEDICAL SECRETARY

Ranking: 5

Score: 1

Job Growth: 101%

Unemployment: Very Low

Medical secretaries have few, if any, geographic restraints on employment. As the nations medical needs continues to increase the the demand for medical secretaries will increase dramatically.

MEDICAL TECHNOLOGIST

Ranking: 33

Score: -94

Job Growth: 56%

Unemployment: Very Low

Medical technologists enjoy wide geographic flexibility. Employment prospects in this occupation will grow considerably as doctors increasing run tests on their patients, partially as result of the liability crisis in the medical profession. Technologists face dangers from accidental exposure to contagious diseases, and hazardous bacteria and viruses.

METEOROLOGIST

Ranking: 117

Score: -196

Job Growth: 54%

Unemployment: Moderate

Moderate geographic flexibility marks the profession. Employment growth will increase rapidly in the next decade, with most jobs opening up in private industry as companies realize the value of accurate weather predictions.

METER READER

Ranking: 208

Score: -300

Job Growth: 0%

Unemployment: High

Meter readers enjoy excellent geographic freedom. The number of jobs should decrease over the next decade, because of increased technology in which utilities can monitor usage by means other than remote meters.

MILITARY (COMMISSIONED OFFICER)

Ranking: 92

Score: -161

Job Growth: -11%

Unemployment: Very Low

With the Cold War now ended, cutbacks in the military are commonplace and many officers with low seniority are being involuntarily retired. Those with advanced academic degrees and technical training will be in particular demand as military jobs become more specialized and complex.

MILITARY (ENLISTED PERSON)

Ranking: 92

Score: -161

Job Growth: -11%

Unemployment: Very Low

Cutbacks in the military are likely to mean that the Armed forces will favor higher-ranking, higher seniority officers and may involuntarily retire those who have not achieved higher rank in a prescribed time period.

MILITARY (WARRANT OFFICER)

Ranking: 92

Score: -161

Job Growth: -11%

Unemployment: Very Low

Warrant officers enjoy little geographic freedom. Employment growth for this occupation is expected to be slower than the average, through the next decade, because of budget cutbacks. Many aspects of being a warrant officer, including combat duty, are extremely hazardous.

MILLWRIGHT

Ranking: 222

Score: -330

Job Growth: 20%

Unemployment: High

Job opportunities for millwrights will increase at a rate much slower than the average over the next decade. Employment trends in this occupation are generally unstable. Growing foreign competition, and implementation of advanced, automated equipment, will cause a significant drop in the demand for millwrights. This work involves operating heavy equipment and machinery, and can be hazardous.

MOTION PICTURE EDITOR

Ranking: 118

Score: -198

Job Growth: 52%

Unemployment: High

Video editors enjoy moderate geographic flexibility, because of increased demand for video production by private industry. Employment opportunities for motion picture editors are expected to increase faster than the average, during the next decade. Even with increased job opportunities, competition in video production will remain stiff, as this field consistently attracts more job candidates than it can support.

MUSEUM CURATOR

Ranking: 138

Score: -209

Job Growth: 41%

Unemployment: Moderate

Curators enjoy moderate geographic flexibility. Job opportunities in this profession will increase over the next decade. The continuing decline in funding of museums and archives, combined with an overabundance of qualified candidates, will force greater competition for this position.

MUSICAL INSTRUMENT REPAIRER

Ranking: 161

Score: -230

Job Growth: 20%

Unemployment: Moderate

Since musical instrument tuning and repair are luxury services for most consumers, employment in this field is extremely sensitive to downturns in the economy. Repairers who operate their own practices or are employed by large, urban-based repair shops will have the best prospects for continued prosperity.

MUSICIAN

Ranking: 169

Score: -244

Job Growth: 56%

Unemployment: High

Job opportunities for professional musicians exist throughout the country, but are heavily concentrated in major cities. The amount of leisure time available to the population will grow, as will disposable income. This will spur growth in the entertainment industry.

NEWSCASTER

Ranking: 68

Score: -141

Job Growth: 59%

Unemployment: Moderate

Newscasters enjoy good geographic flexibility. Job growth in this profession will keep pace with the average through the next decade. However, competition for available positions for newscasters is extremely tight, and will remain so in the coming years. Job prospects are better in radio broadcasting, especially in smaller markets. Newscasters are generally safe from the effects of economic downswings, though employees at some larger networks may face layoffs during corporate restructuring.

NEWS WRITER (RADIO/TV)

Ranking: 77

Score: -148

Job Growth: 52%

Unemployment: Moderate

Broadcast news writers have moderate geographic flexibility, although the higher paying jobs are located in major metropolitan areas. With the opening of more local and cable stations, job opportunities for broadcast news writers should increase faster than average in the next decade. Competition for jobs will continue to be intense.

NUCLEAR ENGINEER

Ranking: 83

Score: -150

Job Growth: 0%

Unemployment: Low

Geographic flexibility in employment is moderate for nuclear engineers. The number of jobs in this profession will grow slowly over the next ten years. Job opportunities for nuclear engineers in the defense industry are highly dependent on federal defense budgets, which are declining.

NUCLEAR PLANT DECONTAMINATION TECHNICIAN

Ranking: 184

Score: -261

Job Growth: -11%

Unemployment: Moderate

Decontamination technicians enjoy moderate geographic flexibility. Prospects for these technicians should increase faster than the overall nation average, through the next decade, because of increased use of nuclear power. The job security of a nuclear decontamination technician can easily be endangered by the many physical hazards of the profession.

NURSE (LICENSED PRACTICAL)

Ranking: 47

Score: -110

Job Growth: 90%

Unemployment: Very Low

Licensed practical nurses enjoy excellent geographic freedom. Current medical trends, emphasizing acute care and high-technology are expected to continue the high growth in number of jobs in nursing. Nurses face stressful emergency situations, and potential exposure to disease.

NURSE (REGISTERED)

Ranking: 44

Score: -105

Job Growth: 95%

Unemployment: Very Low

Registered nurses enjoy excellent geographic flexibility, with hospitals and health care institu-

tions spread across the country. The rising demand for medical services and personnel will create a greater call for qualified registered nurses in the coming years. Consequently, job growth in this occupation will be much faster than the average through the 1990s. Exposure to disease and illness is a constant threat to nurses.

NURSE'S AIDE

Ranking: 39

Score: -99

Job Growth: 101%

Unemployment: Very Low

The large number of hospitals and medical clinics across the country give nursing aides excellent geographic flexibility. The rising need for medical care among all segments of the growing population will keep the demand for qualified nursing aides high. As a result, employment opportunities in this occupation will grow at a rate faster than the average through the next decade. Nursing aides sometimes work with the seriously ill, and can become exposed to contagious disease.

OCCUPATIONAL SAFETY/ HEALTH INSPECTOR

Ranking: 156

Score: -223

Job Growth: -23%

Unemployment: Low

Safety and health inspectors have moderate geographic flexibility. Employment opportunities for inspectors will increase over the next decade. Tightened state and federal budgets will be responsible for the hiring slowdown. As government workers, health and safety inspectors are usually protected against the threat of layoffs.

OCCUPATIONAL THERAPIST

Ranking: 7

Score: -15

Job Growth: 135%

Unemployment: Very Low

Occupational therapists enjoy excellent geographic freedom. Employment opportunities in occupational therapy should increase at a pace much faster than the average through the mid-1990s. The growing population will create a great demand for health care professionals. Job prospects for therapists abound with public and private institutions.

OCEANOGRAPHER

Ranking: 36

Score: -96

Job Growth: 104%

Unemployment: Low

Oceanographers enjoy moderate geographic flexibility. The increasing demand for undersea exploration and development of marine resources should keep job growth in oceanography near the overall national average through the next decade. Researchers are susceptible to dangers from working in an unexplored or unfamiliar marine environment.

OFFICE MACHINE REPAIRER

Ranking: 193

Score: -282

Job Growth: 18%

Unemployment: High

Office machine repairers can find employment opportunities in any area of the country. The majority of positions are located in major metropolitan areas. The mounting paperwork produced by business and government, and the increasing dependence on office machines to handle this burden, will create a growing demand for qualified service technicians. Economic downturns severely effect near-term job prospects and security.

OPTICIAN

Ranking: 16

Score: -69

Job Growth: 81%

Unemployment: Very Low

The increasing population will create a greater demand for optical services. Dispensing opticians can look forward to faster-than-average job growth in their profession through the next decade. The job outlook for opticians is often affected by medical insurance policies in force at the time.

OPTOMETRIST

Ranking: 51

Score: -114

Job Growth: 36%

Unemployment: Very Low

The growing number of middle-aged persons in America is expected to produce a greater demand for optometrists and other eye care professionals. Employment opportunities for optometrists will increase over the next decade. Large-scale, group insurance plans will make optometry services available to a much wider range of people than before.

ORTHODONTIST

Ranking: 107

Score: -189

Job Growth: 11%

Unemployment: Low

Orthodontists enjoy good geographic flexibility, but an overabundance of orthodontic practices in one locality can affect business success in this profession. Improved group health care plans will determine job growth for orthodontists over the next decade.

OSTEOPATH

Ranking: 99

Score: -171

Job Growth: 79%

Unemployment: Low

Job opportunities for osteopaths should increase over the next decade, due to expansion of group health plans for a growing population. The current high medical school enrollment means greater competition for jobs in osteopathy in the near future. Like other professionals in medicine, osteopaths face the rising cost of malpractice insurance.

PAINTER

Ranking: 165

Score: -235

Job Growth: 65%

Unemployment: High

Job opportunities for painters are spread throughout the country. Instability in the home construction industry have caused recent high unemployment. Painters are vulnerable to physical hazards, such as falls and burns.

PARALEGAL ASSISTANT

Ranking: 3

Score: 44

Job Growth: 194%

Unemployment: Low

Legal assistants enjoy good geographic flexibility. Employment prospects in this occupation over the next ten years are excellent. Continued expansion of legal services will drive up the demand for qualified paralegals. Consequently, this will be one of the fastest growing professions in the coming decade. However, competition among legal assistants is strong, and will continue to be so, as the number of job candidates in this field rises. Hiring of paralegals can also be affected by economic downturns.

PAROLE OFFICER

Ranking: 6

Score: -10

Job Growth: 90%

Unemployment: Very Low

Job prospects for parole officers are very limited geographically. Employment opportunities for parole officers and other social workers should increase faster than the average in the coming decade. Rising crime rates, and a shortage of available prison space, will fuel the demand for parole officers, offsetting the effects of state and national budget constraints on employment in this profession.

PERSONNEL RECRUITER

Ranking: 97

Score: -169

Job Growth: 81%

Unemployment: High

Personnel recruiters enjoy moderate geographic flexibility. Increasing demand for effective personnel decisions in the business sector should cause job growth in personnel recruitment the mid-1990s. The competitiveness of the market, and changes in economic conditions, can affect job prospects for personnel recruiters.

PETROLEUM ENGINEER

Ranking: 180

Score: -255

Job Growth: -5%

Unemployment: Moderate

Employment opportunities for petroleum engineers are somewhat limited geographically. This work can be seasonal. The demand for improved, more efficient recovery methods of oil and natural gas will create average job growth for petroleum engineers over the next ten years. Employment in this profession can be affected by foreign economic circumstances, such as artificial oil price levels set by OPEC.

PHARMACIST

Ranking: 27

Score: -85

Job Growth: 65%

Unemployment: Very Low

A growing abundance of available prescription drugs, and the rising health care demands of the nation's elderly population, employment opportunities for pharmacists will grow through the next decade. Diminished hospital budgets, and sluggish economic performance for pharmacies, is expected to hamper job prospects.

PHILOSOPHER

Ranking: 129

Score: -205

Job Growth: 45%

Unemployment: Moderate

Philosophers enjoy moderate geographic flexibility. Job prospects at universities are expected to decline through the next decade, because of declining enrollments and budget cutbacks. Low enrollments should create a glut of potential philosophy teachers. Only with a tenured position, is job security a reality for philosophers.

PHOTOGRAPHER

Ranking: 169

Score: -244

Job Growth: 56%

Unemployment: High

Still photographers enjoy a moderate degree of geographic flexibility. Employment opportunities for still photographers are expected to increase faster than the average through the next decade, reflecting the growing need for photographic services in the business sector. Photography remains a highly competitive profession, especially for those interested in the artistic aspects of the field.

PHOTOGRAPHIC PROCESS WORKER

Ranking: 108

Score: -191

Job Growth: 59%

Unemployment: Moderate

The rise in personal income will boost consumer spending on still photography. As a result, the number of jobs for photographic process workers is expected to increase. Employment prospects for photographic processors can be affected by seasonal economic trends, and by rapid technological advances.

PHOTOJOURNALIST

Ranking: 169

Score: -244

Job Growth: 56%

Unemployment: High

Photojournalists who work free-lance enjoy excellent geographic flexibility. Employment opportunities should grow at a steady rate into the next decade. Competition for jobs in photojournalism will remain very strong. News photographers are often asked to work in war zones, cover natural disasters, and otherwise expose themselves to dangerous situations.

PHYSICAL THERAPIST

Ranking: 2

Score: 48

Job Growth: 198%

Unemployment: Very Low

The employment outlook for physical therapists is excellent. Job opportunities for therapists throughout the country are fairly wide-ranging. The rising need for medical services, combined with more sophisticated health care plans, will keep physical therapists in high demand through the coming decade. As a result, physical therapy should be one of the fastest-growing professions in the nation over the next ten years.

PHYSICIAN (GENERAL PRACTITIONER)

Ranking: 17

Score: -71

Job Growth: 79%

Unemployment: Very Low

The rising number of elderly in the nation, and liberalization of medical insurance plans, is expected to keep the demand for medical services high. Employment opportunities for doctors will grow faster than the average in the next decade. An upsurge in the number of medical school graduates will create greater competition, and could glut the market with doctors. Medical professionals face the mounting cost of malpractice insurance.

PHYSICIAN ASSISTANT

Ranking: 21

Score: -73

Job Growth: 77%

Unemployment: Very Low

Physician assistants enjoy better than average geographic freedom. The field of physician assistants is very stable and employment growth is projected to increase much faster than the average through the 1990s. Growth in procedures those in the field are allowed to perform has increased demand.

PHYSICIST

Ranking: 181

Score: -257

Job Growth: -7%

Unemployment: Moderate

The hiring of physicists by universities will be curtailed by state and federal budget cutbacks. An increase in the number of jobs for physicists in private-sector research and development will somewhat offset the decline in academic positions, but employment growth in this profession will still lag behind the average over the next decade.

PHYSIOLOGIST

Ranking: 63

Score: -130

Job Growth: 70%

Unemployment: Low

Physiologists enjoy moderate geographic flexibility. The number of positions for physiologists should increase faster than the national average, through the next decade. Most jobs for physiologists will come from private industry, while declining university enrollments will shut the door for job growth in the education sector. Tenure at a university affords the job security for physiologists.

PIANO TUNER

Ranking: 161

Score: -230

Job Growth: 20%

Unemployment: Moderate

Employment opportunities for piano tuners are somewhat scarce. The time and expense needed to train an apprentice is considerable. Job growth for piano tuners will be slower than the average over the next ten years. The profession is very susceptible to economic swings. When the economy is poor, consumers tend to put off luxury expenditures, such as piano tuning.

PLASTERER

Ranking: 238

Score: -364

Job Growth: 36%

Unemployment: Very High

Many plasterers are limited to seasonal work. Employment opportunities in the plastering profession are expected to be severely limited through the 1990s The increasing use of drywall, as opposed to plaster, has caused job opportunities for plasterers to dwindle. However, the possibility of a shift back to the more durable plaster in the near future, does bring some brightness to the job outlook for workers in this trade. The plastering trade is also affected by fluctuations in the construction industry.

PLUMBER

Ranking: 223

Score: -332

Job Growth: 18%

Unemployment: High

The demand for plumbers is strong nationwide, and will remain so. New construction, and necessary maintenance on older plumbing systems, should keep job growth in the plumbing trade at, or near, the average through the next decade. Plumbers face physical hazards from burns, shocks, and exposure to toxic fumes.

PODIATRIST

Ranking: 15

Score: -67

Job Growth: 83%

Unemployment: Very Low

The growing need for health care, especially among the elderly, will force an increase in demand for podiatrist's services through the next decade. The trend toward physical fitness also will create a rising need for podiatrists. As a result, podiatry will be one of the fastest growing professions in the coming years.

POLICE OFFICER

Ranking: 150

Score: -221

Job Growth: 29%

Unemployment: Low

Police protection is a necessity in every area of the country, and officers enjoy good geographic flexibility. Rising crime rates will help keep the demand for police officers steady. Metropolitan police workers are relatively safe from layoffs. As the overall population grows, employment opportunities for police officers will increase as fast as the average through the next decade. In dealing with the criminal element, police often face extremely volatile, and even life-threatening, situations.

POLITICAL SCIENTIST

Ranking: 84

Score: -155

Job Growth: 45%

Unemployment: Moderate

Limits on state and federal budgets for education, combined with dropping student enrollment, will cause a hiring slowdown for political scientists in colleges and universities. As a result, the number of jobs for political scientists will grow at a rate much slower than average over the next decade. Competition for available political science positions will be strong.

POSTAL INSPECTOR

Ranking: 105

Score: -182

Job Growth: 18%

Unemployment: Low

Postal inspectors enjoy moderate geographic flexibility. Slow growth in government programs is expected to keep employment opportunities for postal inspectors down in the coming years. The number of jobs for inspectors will rise at a rate slower than the average over the next decade. Competition for positions in this field will continue to be stiff.

PRECISION ASSEMBLER

Ranking: 238

Score: -364

Job Growth: -14%

Unemployment: High

Precision assemblers are geographically limited to production areas of specific products. Employment opportunities in the field of precision manufacturing will decline considerably through the next decade, because of increased automation and improved production techniques.

PRESIDENT (U.S.)

Ranking: 208

Score: -300

Job Growth: 0%

Unemployment: Very High

Odd as it may sound, four of the five living men elected to the White House can no longer get their old job back. Once inaugurated, the President, like all other civil officers may be removed from office only on impeachment for reasons of treason, high crimes, bribery or misdemeanors. However, since 1963, one President was assassinated, one did not run for re-election because of public pressure, one resigned because of impending impeachment proceedings and three were voted out of office.

PROTESTANT MINISTER

Ranking: 24

Score: -82

Job Growth: 68%

Unemployment: Very Low

Protestant ministers have moderate geographic flexibility in employment. Job growth for ministers will be limited over the next decade by a decline in the sizes of congregations, and by inadequate funding. The greatest growth in opportunities for ministers will exist with youth centers and counseling programs.

PSYCHIATRIST

Ranking: 17

Score: -71

Job Growth: 79%

Unemployment: Very Low

Mental health professionals enjoy good geographic flexibility. An increase in the demand for mental health services will help maintain stable growth in job opportunities for psychiatrists through the 1990s. As public awareness increases about the treatability of mental illnesses, demand for psychiatric care will increase considerably.

PSYCHOLOGIST

Ranking: 32

Score: -92

Job Growth: 108%

Unemployment: Low

Psychologists enjoy good geographic flexibility. As the population increases, the demand for psychologists will continue to rise. Job opportunities for professional psychologists will grow at a much higher-than-average rate through the next decade. Some health insurance plans will broaden coverage to include the expenses of psychotherapy, further enhancing the job outlook for psychologists.

PUBLIC RELATIONS EXECUTIVE

Ranking: 68

Score: -141

Job Growth: 59%

Unemployment: Moderate

Jobs for public relations specialists are located primarily in major metropolitan areas. Employment opportunities for PR specialists will grow over the next decade. An increasing emphasis on media and public relations in the business sector, will keep demand for PR professionals high. In addition, private institutions will employ PR specialists to improve fund raising efforts, as budgets tighten in the coming decade.

PUBLICATION EDITOR

Ranking: 118

Score: -198

Job Growth: 52%

Unemployment: High

Technological advances in printing and publishing are expected to open up greater employment opportunities for editors. The number of editorial jobs will increase faster than the average in the next ten years, as new and more sophisticated publications crop up. The fields of trade and technical publishing will experience especially strong growth. As the number of job candidates mounts, competition for most editing positions will continue to be very strong.

PURCHASING AGENT

Ranking: 145

Score: -218

Job Growth: 32%

Unemployment: High

Employment opportunities for purchasing agents extend throughout the country. Job growth in this occupation should match the average over the next decade. In times of economic turmoil, the profession is highly unstable and is severely affected by recessions.

RABBI

Ranking: 163

Score: -232

Job Growth: 68%

Unemployment: High

Rabbis have broad options in choosing where they wish to work. Employment prospects for rabbis through the next decade will vary between the different branches of Judaism. Orthodox rabbis will face the toughest competition for jobs, as the number of new graduates from orthodox schools increases. Many rabbis fail to win posts as heads of congregations and work in teaching or scholarly aspects of the field, in which unemployment is high.

RACE CAR DRIVER (INDY CLASS)

Ranking: 198

Score: -289

Job Growth: 11%

Unemployment: Moderate

Race car drivers are subject to heavy travel schedules on the racing circuit. The seasonal nature of race car driving can limit earnings for those unable to compete in foreign countries. Driving high-speed precision vehicles is very dangerous. Job security in the field of racing depends on individual performance and the ability to avoid serious injuries.

RAILROAD CONDUCTOR

Ranking: 196

Score: -287

Job Growth: 63%

Unemployment: High

Conductors and engineers have extremely limited geographic flexibility. The number of jobs in the railroad industry is expected to decline through the next decade, as advanced automation in rail transport makes many jobs obsolete. The industry will experience very little growth overall, but some small, highly localized rail lines may emerge.

REAL ESTATE AGENT

Ranking: 178

Score: -253

Job Growth: 47%

Unemployment: High

Real estate agents and brokers can find employment opportunities in any area of the country. Job growth in realty is expected to be slightly below the overall national average through the next decade. The long slump in construction of new properties will somewhat lessen the demand for agents and brokers. This should spark increased competition for available positions in realty.

RECEPTIONIST

Ranking: 59

Score: -123

Job Growth: 77%

Unemployment: Moderate

Employment opportunities for receptionists are not geographically limited. Job growth for this occupation is expected to be up considerably through the 1990s. Weak economic conditions can cause layoffs and other disruptions in employment patterns for receptionists.

RECREATION WORKER

Ranking: 142

Score: -214

Job Growth: 86%

Unemployment: High

Recreational work offers excellent geographic flexibility. Employment in recreation is occasionally seasonal. The amount of leisure time available to the population will increase in the coming years. As a result, recreation workers can look forward to a faster-than-average growth in job opportunities over the next decade.

REPORTER

Ranking: 68

Score: -141

Job Growth: 59%

Unemployment: Moderate

Employment opportunities for reporters are confined primarily to major metropolitan areas. Job growth in newspaper, radio, and television reporting will match the average through the next decade. The establishment of new radio and television stations, and technological advances in the print media, should help to open up new positions for both broadcast and print journalists. The continuing high number of journalism graduates will keep competition for jobs among reporters strong.

RESPIRATORY THERAPIST

Ranking: 14

Score: -60

Job Growth: 90%

Unemployment: Very Low

Respiratory therapists can find employment opportunities at hospitals and clinics across the country. The rising number of elderly in the nation, and an increase in the population in general, will keep the demand for medical personnel growing steadily in the coming years. Accordingly, job growth in respiratory therapy will be much faster than the average through the next decade.

ROOFER

Ranking: 208

Score: -300

Job Growth: 50%

Unemployment: High

Roofing work is highly seasonal. This occupation offers excellent geographic mobility. The need for roof repairs, combined with new construction of buildings and homes, will result in a continued demand for qualified roofers through the next decade. Job growth in roofing will keep pace with the average over this period of time. Unlike many construction workers, roofers are not as effected as others from downswings in the construction industry.

ROUSTABOUT

Ranking: 246

Score: -424

Job Growth: -74%

Unemployment: High

The oil industry is highly unstable, and is subject to foreign economic and political circumstances. Increased mechanization, combined with the uncertain outlook in the energy sector, will keep the number of new jobs down over the next decade. Strenuous physical labor with heavy machinery results in a very high rate of injury among oil workers.

SALES REPRESENTATIVE (WHOLESALE)

Ranking: 145

Score: -218

Job Growth: 32%

Unemployment: Moderate

Advertising sales offers moderate geographic flexibility. Job growth in this occupation will be faster than average through the 1990s, assuming recessionary pressures do not continue through the decade. It will continue to be a very competitive profession. Employment prospects are greatly affected by economic swings.

SALESPERSON (RETAIL)

Ranking: 178

Score: -253

Job Growth: 47%

Unemployment: High

Hiring in retail sales is often seasonal. The number of temporary sales positions in retail stores rises in the months before Christmas. Though retail sales are expected to increase in the coming years, the trend toward computerized, self-service check-out systems will keep job growth for salespeople to slightly above the overall national average. Retail sales will remain a competitive employment field. Salespeople have moderate geographic flexibility.

SCHOOL PRINCIPAL

Ranking: 77

Score: -148

Job Growth: 52%

Unemployment: Moderate

Employment opportunities for school principals range throughout the country. Competition for jobs is stiff, and should remain so in the future. Unlike teachers principals are usually safe from layoffs and other effects of budgetary constraints.

SEAMAN (SAILOR)

Ranking: 236

Score: -361

Job Growth: -11%

Unemployment: High

Seamen work in all coastal areas, enjoying moderate geographic freedom. Seamen are subject to seasonal fluctuation in the demand for their services. Even though more ships will be built in the coming decade, jobs for seamen will decline because of technological advances. Working conditions at sea can be hazardous and impair job security.

SECRETARY

Ranking: 108

Score: -191

Job Growth: 9%

Unemployment: Moderate

Secretaries can find employment opportunities in any area of the country. The increasing use of word processors and other automated office machines has lessened the demand for secretarial services. Consequently, secretaries face a slower-than-average growth in the number of jobs in their occupation through the coming decade.

SET DESIGNER

Ranking: 187

Score: -271

Job Growth: 29%

Unemployment: High

Employment opportunities for set designers are most abundant in major metropolitan areas. The number of jobs for set designers is expected to increase faster than the average through the coming decade. However, the most qualified candidates for positions in set design will continue to outnumber job openings by a wide margin. Competition among set designers for available positions will be extremely strong.

SEWAGE PLANT OPERATOR

Ranking: 138

Score: -209

Job Growth: 41%

Unemployment: Low

Sewage plant operators enjoy good geographic flexibility. Employment opportunities in waste management should grow at the average rate over the next ten years, but the possibility of city and state budget cutbacks somewhat clouds the job outlook for waste management professionals. Sewage plant operators face hazards from exposure to toxic gases and chemicals.

SHEET METAL WORKER

Ranking: 237

Score: -362

Job Growth: 38%

Unemployment: Very High

Sheet metal work offers good geographic flexibility. The number of job opportunities in this trade is expected to rise steadily through the next decade, though unforeseen downswings in the construction industry could alter the employment prospects for workers in this occupation. Sheet metal workers face potential injury from the dangerous power tools they must use. The construction site is a hazardous work environment.

SHIPPING/RECEIVING CLERK

Ranking: 89

Score: -159

Job Growth: 41%

Unemployment: Moderate

Shipping and receiving clerks are occasionally limited to seasonal employment. Increased automation in shipping and receiving is expected to cause job growth in this field to lag behind the average through the next decade. Employment prospects for shipping and receiving clerks will also be limited by somewhat sluggish expansion in the manufacturing and wholesale industries.

SHOEMAKER/REPAIRER

Ranking: 244

Score: -395

Job Growth: -45%

Unemployment: Very High

Shoe repair will be one of the most rapidly declining occupations in the coming decade. Increasing automation in shoe repair will cut the demand for qualified repairers drastically over the next ten years. The jobs that are available for shoe repairers will not be geographically limited.

SINGER

Ranking: 169

Score: -244

Job Growth: 56%

Unemployment: High

As the entertainment industry expands over the next decade, employment opportunities for singers will increase greatly. Competition for top jobs will be strong. The number of professional singers will remain much higher than the number of available jobs for vocalists. Singers have moderate geographic flexibility. Vocalists are occasionally limited to seasonal employment.

SOCIAL WORKER

Ranking: 91

Score: -160

Job Growth: 90%

Unemployment: High

Social workers enjoy moderate geographic freedom. The increase in population will create a greater demand for social services, and social workers should see faster-than-average job growth in their profession through the next decade. However, many social workers are employed by government agencies, which are extremely dependent on state and federal funding. Deep cuts in budgets for social services has seriously hampered employment prospects.

SOCIOLOGIST

Ranking: 84

Score: -155

Job Growth: 45%

Unemployment: Moderate

Declining university enrollment nationwide, and tightened education budgets, will force a drop in university hiring of sociologists over the next decade. Growth in employment opportunities for sociologists within the private sector will help to offset the decline in academic positions in this field.

SOFTWARE ENGINEER

Ranking: 8

Score: -28

Job Growth: 72%

Unemployment: Very Low

The current shortage of software engineers coupled with the increasing demand from almost every business sector means the outlook for employment is better than excellent. The constantly evolving nature of this profession will provide security and great opportunities into the next century. As a science in relative infancy, there is likely to be an increased demand for those who keep pace with technical innovations and new software. Those certified by the major software publishers will have the most secure jobs.

SPEECH PATHOLOGIST

Ranking: 9

Score: -35

Job Growth: 115%

Unemployment: Very Low

Speech pathologists enjoy excellent geographic freedom. Employment growth in speech pathology will keep pace with the average in the coming decade. Broader health care programs, and a general increase in population will keep the demand for speech pathologists rising steadily.

SPORTS INSTRUCTOR

Ranking: 49

Score: -112

Job Growth: 88%

Unemployment: Moderate

As the amount of leisure time available to the population increases, the nationwide need for sports instructors will grow. As a result, the number of job opportunities for sports instructors will increase faster than the average over the next decade. However, budget cuts could affect the job outlook for instructors employed by public schools. Sports instruction is a very seasonal profession.

STATIONARY ENGINEER

Ranking: 167

Score: -239

Job Growth: 11%

Unemployment: Low

Employment prospects for stationary engineers look grim. Increased use of automated equipment should cut the demand for stationary engineers. As a result, job growth in this occupation will be slower than the average over the next ten years. Stationary engineers risk injury from burns and explosions while on the job.

STATISTICIAN

Ranking: 104

Score: -180

Job Growth: 20%

Unemployment: Moderate

Statisticians have moderate geographic freedom. The number of jobs for qualified statisticians has leveled off considerably. In the private sector, the fields of market research and quality control will offer the best employment opportunities for professional statisticians. Those with backgrounds in computer science generally enjoy better job prospects.

STENOGRAPHER/COURT REPORTER

Ranking: 123

Score: -202

Job Growth: -2%

Unemployment: Moderate

The future looks grim for stenography. Improved office automation is expected to make the stenographer's work increasingly obsolete over the next decade. Consequently, stenography will be one of the most rapidly declining occupations of the 1990s. Stenographers currently have moderate geographic freedom.

STEVEDORE

Ranking: 187

Score: -271

Job Growth: 29%

Unemployment: Moderate

Stevedores are geographically limited to coastal areas. Employment prospects for stevedores should increase slower than the average, through the next decade, because of cutbacks in the shipping industry and increases in automation. The physical hazards of working with heavy machinery and cargo can seriously threaten job security.

STOCKBROKER

Ranking: 102

Score: -176

Job Growth: 74%

Unemployment: High

Employment opportunities for stockbrokers are distributed nationally. The number of positions in the brokerage profession is expected to grow much faster than average over the next ten years. This highly competitive occupation is very susceptible to economic ups and downs. Stockbrokers can expect an increased emphasis on ethical concerns in the financial sector through the next decade.

SURGEON

Ranking: 17

Score: -71

Job Growth: 79%

Unemployment: Very Low

The need for medical services is nationwide, and consequently surgeons enjoy good geographic freedom. The growing number of elderly in the population will cause the demand for qualified surgeons to rise in the near future. Thus, the number of jobs for surgeons should increase faster than the average over the next decade. However, an expected overabundance of medical school graduates may offset any gains in employment opportunities caused by this growing demand for surgeons.

SURVEYOR

Ranking: 150

Score: -221

Job Growth: 29%

Unemployment: Moderate

Surveyors are often limited to seasonal work. This occupation enjoys moderate geographic flexibility. The employment situation for surveyors, and for most other workers in the construction sector, is strongly affected by economic factors, such as fluctuating interest rates.

SYMPHONY CONDUCTOR

Ranking: 30

Score: -89

Job Growth: 11%

Unemployment: Very Low

Symphony conductors enjoy moderate geographic flexibility. Employment opportunities should increase slower than the national average, through the next decade, because of budget cutbacks in the arts. The field of orchestra conducting is very competitive and tends to draw an overabundance of job seekers, though once appointed to a top spot, few conductors are dismissed before retirement, though many leave to accept better positions.

TAX EXAMINER/COLLECTOR

Ranking: 46

Score: -109

Job Growth: 41%

Unemployment: Very Low

Geographic mobility for these government workers is moderate. Job growth is expected to lag behind the average through the next decade, due to state and federal budget constraints.

TAXI DRIVER

Ranking: 213

Score: -303

Job Growth: 47%

Unemployment: High

Taxi drivers enjoy moderate geographic flexibility, although major metropolitan areas offer the greatest money-making potential. The number of job openings for taxi drivers will increase considerably through the next decade, due to the expansion of urban populations. Regardless of job growth, competition between drivers in major cities will remain fierce.

TEACHER

Ranking: 101

Score: -173

Job Growth: 77%

Unemployment: Moderate

Job growth will match the average through the next decade, as student enrollment increases. Employment opportunities are expected to grow most rapidly in the southern and the western areas of the country. Constraints on government budgets for education often have an impact on the teaching profession.

TEACHER'S AIDE

Ranking: 42

Score: -103

Job Growth: 97%

Unemployment: Moderate

Teacher's aides enjoy excellent geographic flexibility. Higher enrollment in elementary schools over the next decade will create a greater demand for teaching assistants, and aides can expect a steady increase in job opportunities through the 1990s. However, budget cutbacks for education, as well as population movement, will somewhat curtail job opportunities for teacher's aides in certain parts of the country.

TECHNICAL WRITER

Ranking: 37

Score: -98

Job Growth: 52%

Unemployment: Low

Because of a greater emphasis on precise and effective communication in both the technical and advertising fields, technical writers and copywriters can expect a rapid increase in the demand for their services in the near future. Job opportunities for specialized writers will grow faster than the average through the next decade. Advertising copywriters face stiff competition for jobs within their profession.

TELEPHONE INSTALLER/ REPAIRER

Ranking: 234

Score: -354

Job Growth: -54%

Unemployment: High

Employment prospects for telephone installers are rather bleak. The use of advanced communications technology, such as fiber optics, will create longer-lasting, and more reliable, phone systems. As a result, the demand for telephone installers and repairers will drop drastically over the next decade. Phone installers and repairers face physical hazards from working with high-voltage wiring, which can cause shocks and burns.

TELEPHONE OPERATOR

Ranking: 217

Score: -313

Job Growth: -63%

Unemployment: High

The increased use of automation has drastically reduced the need for telephone operators. More recent innovations such as calling cards and menu-driven telephone user options continue to reduce employment opportunities.

TICKET AGENT

Ranking: 64

Score: -132

Job Growth: 68%

Unemployment: Moderate

Ticket and reservation agents are occasionally limited to seasonal employment. Agents enjoy moderate geographic flexibility. Job growth in this occupation is expected to lag behind the average through the next decade, as new computer reservation and ticketing processes are implemented. The travel and entertainment industry is highly vulnerable to fluctuations in the economy.

TOOL-AND-DIE MAKER

Ranking: 218

Score: -316

Job Growth: -16%

Unemployment: Moderate

Tool-and-die makers experience moderate geographic mobility. Employment opportunities for these tradesmen will grow at a rate much slower than the overall national average through the next decade, as a result of foreign competition and technological innovation. The growing preference for non-metal replacement parts in design and construction of machinery, will also lead to a drop in the demand for tool-and-die makers.

TRAVEL AGENT

Ranking: 40

Score: -101

Job Growth: 149%

Unemployment: High

As the population's standard of living improves, and as its amount of leisure time expands, the demand for travel agents will sharply increase. Consequently, this will be one of the fastest growing occupations over the next decade. Relying as it does on consumer spending, the travel industry is often affected by domestic economic fluctuations. In addition, foreign political and economic factors, such as the value of the dollar overseas, can affect the travel industry.

TRUCK DRIVER

Ranking: 200

Score: -291

Job Growth: 59%

Unemployment: High

Trucking offers excellent geographic flexibility. Drivers can look forward to an increased demand for transportation of goods by truck, which will contribute to a growth rate for truck driving jobs that matches the average through the 1990s. The field is generally very competitive. Truckers face fatiguing work, and poor weather conditions can add to normal road hazards.

TYPIST/WORD PROCESSOR

Ranking: 195

Score: -286

Job Growth: -36%

Unemployment: High

Typists and word processors enjoy excellent geographic mobility. Increased office automation will lead to a decline in job opportunities for these office workers over the next ten years. Employment prospects will be much better for those trained on, and familiar with, word processing equipment and programs.

UNDERTAKER

Ranking: 89

Score: -159

Job Growth: 41%

Unemployment: Very Low

Undertakers enjoy good geographic flexibility, although most jobs are located near major metropolitan areas. Employment opportunities in undertaking should increase though not as fast as the overall national average. This is a very old, relatively stable occupation, and it is expected to remain so in the future.

URBAN/REGIONAL PLANNER

Ranking: 37

Score: -98

Job Growth: 52%

Unemployment: Low

Limits on local government spending will hinder job growth for urban and regional planners. Professionals in this field can expect a an average increase in employment opportunities over the next ten years. Competition for jobs in urban and regional planning is high. There are many more available candidates than there are positions as planners.

VENDING MACHINE REPAIRER

Ranking: 203

Score: -293

Job Growth: 7%

Unemployment: Moderate

Vending machine repairers enjoy moderate geographic flexibility. Jobs for repairers should increase as fast as the average, through the next decade. Greater demand for vending machines will be offset by improved machine technology, keeping job growth slightly below the overall national average. Typical job injuries include burns and shocks, hazards that can threaten job security.

VETERINARIAN

Ranking: 60

Score: -126

Job Growth: 74%

Unemployment: Very Low

Veterinary positions are readily available throughout the country. Veterinarians can expect an increase in the nation's domestic animal population over the next ten years, and the demand for veterinary services will rise accordingly. As a result, employment opportunities for veterinarians will grow at a rate faster than the average through the next decade.

VOCATIONAL COUNSELOR

Ranking: 61

Score: -128

Job Growth: 72%

Unemployment: Low

Employment opportunities in this field will decline slightly through the next decade, as school enrollments continue to fall. Employees of large school districts and well-funded private institutions should have the best prospects for advancement and continued employment.

WAITER/WAITRESS

Ranking: 54

Score: -119

Job Growth: 81%

Unemployment: Low

As the service sector expands, job opportunities for restaurant workers, waiters, and waitresses will grow at a pace faster than the average through the 1990s. Waiters and waitresses enjoy excellent geographic flexibility. Competition for positions at the more prestigious establishments is intense.

WELDER

Ranking: 226

Score: -338

Job Growth: -38%

Unemployment: Moderate

Welders have moderate geographic flexibility. The number of jobs in this trade should increase as fast as the average through the next decade. However, the employment outlook for welders can be hampered by economic fluctuations in the construction industry. Welders face numerous hazards from working with powerful torches, and at great heights.

ZOOLOGIST

Ranking: 163

Score: -232

Job Growth: 18%

Unemployment: Moderate

Zoologists can look forward to a moderate amount of geographic flexibility. Job opportunities for zoologists are expected to grow as fast as the average through the next ten years, producing a relatively stable employment outlook. An increase in zoological research, especially in the field of genetics, should create many new positions. As in many other research professions, competition within zoology for government and private funds will remain tight.

Stress

There may be relative calm in the sheep-herding business in rural Scotland, but in corporate America stress is everywhere, at every level, in every department. Stress, fear, anxiety—the feeling goes by many names, but in the workplace foreboding of some kind is as commonplace as Post-it Notes and coffee cups.

Noted management psychologist Dr. David Thompson has written: "Freud's theory doesn't hold up; sex is not man's primary driver—it is fear. Our greatest instinct is for survival, far surpassing our need to procreate or engage in physical or sexual pleasure." Thompson maintains that at most U.S. companies today, the majority of workers, from top to bottom, see their employment situation as a game of survival.

For most people, a *little bit* of stress is better than none at all. Florists and janitors—workers whose job fields scored among the lowest in our stress survey — certainly do not encounter the same kinds of challenges and the same excitement that astronauts, stockbrokers, or police officers do—the latter group being jobs that involve high levels of stress. Some people feed off an adrenalin high; others flee from it. But most would admit that a little pressure on the job can enhance the working day.

It comes as no surprise that jobs such as that of a senior corporate executive, firefighter, and President of the U.S. score highest in the stress category out of our list of 250. Why is it, then, that when you meet one of these people, he or she frequently is a model of composure? Most likely several factors come into play. Emotional constitution is one, for a person rarely is selected for a high-stress position if he shows outward signs of anxiety. Additionally, most such workers have learned to cope with stress, to adjust their emotional response to anxiety-producing situations. For them, stress is a catalyst for appropriate action to hostile forces.

Adversity in the work environment, then, is not always such a bad thing—for some. Nevertheless, stress in general is a contaminant of the workplace, and it springs from many sources. Measuring these contaminant factors, then, is how the stress rankings were compiled.

THE 21 STRESS FACTORS

The amount of stress a worker experiences can be predicted, in part, by looking at the typical demands and crises inherent in his or her job. The *Jobs Rated Almanac*'s ranking system for stress considered 21 job demands that can reasonably be expected to evoke stress (*see list below*). Each demand was assigned a range of points. A high score was awarded if a particular demand was a major part of the job, fewer points were awarded if the demand was a small part of the job, and no points were awarded if that demand was not normally required. For example "deadlines" was one job demand measured. Journalists, who often face daily deadlines, received the maximum of nine points in this category. In comparison, biologists, who seldom face deadlines, received no points.

The demands measured, and the point ranges assigned to each area, are as follows:

Quotas	0-5
Deadlines	0-9
Advocacy	0-5
Win or lose situations	0-5
Working in the public eye	0-5
Competitiveness	0-15
Lifting required	0-5
Physical demands (stooping, climbing, etc.)	0-14
Environmental conditions	0-13
Machines or tools used	0-5
Speed required	0-5
Hazards encountered	0-5
Own life at risk	0-8
Life of another at risk	0-10
Precision required	0-5
Initiative required	0-5
Stamina required	0-5
Outdoor work	0-5
Confinement	0-5
Detail	0-5
Meeting the public	0-8

In computing scores for each occupation, points were added together for all 21 factors. This subtotal was then adjusted to reflect a job's average work hours per week. Exceeding 40 hours a week served to boost a job's stress ranking, while working less than 40 hours served to lower scores. Calculations involved multiplying subtotal scores by the average weekly work hours, and then dividing by 40, the hours in a normal American work week.

GRAPHICS REPRESENTATIONS

The scores are shown on a thermometer-like graphic beside each entry. For the five jobs that had scores exceeding 100, the graphic representation "hits the top;" that is, it registers the maximum. These 100-plus stressful jobs are (in order of increasing stress): taxi driver, Indy-class race car driver, senior corporate executive, firefighter, and President of the U.S.

To illustrate how this ranking system works, take the case of a firefighter, second only to President in stress. Firefighters scored maximum or near-maximum points in exertion, physical demands, speed, stamina, working conditions, hazards, outdoor work, risk of one's own death, and a risk of the death others. Firefighting scored three points in the categories of machines used, meeting the public, and instructing. One point was assigned for precision. When the score was adjusted to reflect a firefighter's long average work week of 56.2 hours, the total was 110.936.

These scores, of course, reflect only a typical stress profile for any given occupation. For individual workers, of course, stress can vary greatly, depending on the particular working conditions, the boss and co-workers, one's own mental outlook, and a multitude of other factors that play a part in producing or limiting stress, but that are less quantifiable.

250 Jobs Ranked by Stress Scores

RANK		SCORE	RANK		SCORE
1	MEDICAL RECORDS TECHNICIAN	15.488	33	COSMETOLOGIST	25.944
2	JANITOR	16.320	34	HOME ECONOMIST	25.979
3	FORKLIFT OPERATOR	18.180	35	FINANCIAL PLANNER	26.250
4	MUSICAL INSTRUMENT REPAIRER	18.776	36	FURNITURE UPHOLSTERER	26.269
5	FLORIST	18.806	37	TEACHER'S AIDE	26.288
6	ACTUARY	20.187	38	PAROLE OFFICER	26.463
7	APPLIANCE REPAIRER	21.123	39	COMPUTER PROGRAMMER	26.508
8	MEDICAL SECRETARY	21.147	40	ARCHITECTURAL DRAFTER	26.754
9	LIBRARIAN	21.400	41	DENTAL LABORATORY TECHNICIAN	26.940
10	BOOKKEEPER	21.462	42	BIOLOGIST	26.946
11	FILE CLERK	21.719	42	CONSERVATIONIST	26.946
12	PIANO TUNER	22.297	44	INDUSTRIAL MACHINE REPAIRER	26.991
13	PHOTOGRAPHIC PROCESS WORKER	22.450	45	TELEPHONE OPERATOR	26.993
14	DIETICIAN	22.990	46	LITHOGRAPHER/ PHOTOENGRAVER	27.556
15	PARALEGAL ASSISTANT	23.084	47	PETROLEUM ENGINEER	27.636
16	VENDING MACHINE REPAIRER	23.470	48	NURSE'S AIDE	27.776
17	BOOKBINDER	23.573	49	STATISTICIAN	27.975
18	BARBER	23.621	50	ASTRONOMER	28.069
19	MEDICAL LABORATORY TECHNICIAN	23.748	51	TELEPHONE INSTALLER/ REPAIRER	28.164
20	ELECTRICAL TECHNICIAN	23.972	52	COMPUTER OPERATOR	28.230
21	TYPIST/WORD PROCESSOR	24.096	53	OFFICE MACHINE REPAIRER	28.242
22	BROADCAST TECHNICIAN	24.184	54	RECEPTIONIST	28.369
23	MATHEMATICIAN	24.673	55	MAID	28.418
24	DENTAL HYGIENIST	24.719	56	HISTORIAN	28.419
25	JEWELER	24.860	57	INSURANCE UNDERWRITER	28.513
26	COMPUTER SYSTEMS ANALYST	24.965	58	PURCHASING AGENT	28.856
27	ASTROLOGER	25.000	59	VOCATIONAL COUNSELOR	28.890
27	SOFTWARE ENGINEER	25.000	60	MEDICAL TECHNOLOGIST	28.910
29	CASHIER	25.117	61	WAITER/WAITRESS	28.944
30	DISHWASHER	25.326	62	METEOROLOGIST	29.192
31	COMPUTER SERVICE TECHNICIAN	25.817	63	POSTAL INSPECTOR	29.292
32	PHARMACIST	25.877			

RANK		SCORE	RANK		SCORE
64	RECREATION WORKER	29.638	99	SPEECH PATHOLOGIST	34.757
65	NEWSWRITER (RADIO/TV)	29.869	100	PAINTER	34.799
66	GUARD	29.918	101	TAX EXAMINER/ COLLECTOR	34.805
67	BANK TELLER	30.120	102	SALESPERSON (RETAIL)	34.851
68	PHYSICIST	30.314	103	ELECTRICIAN	34.906
69	BARTENDER	30.352	104	MILITARY (WARRANT OFFICER)	35.000
69	SHIPPING/RECEIVING CLERK	30.352	105	AUTOMOBILE ASSEMBLER	35.170
71	ANTIQUE DEALER	30.375	106	POLITICAL SCIENTIST	35.239
72	PHILOSOPHER	30.497	107	BANK OFFICER	35.395
73	HEATING/REFRIGERATION MECHANIC	30.544	108	PUBLICATION EDITOR	35.400
74	PRECISION ASSEMBLER	30.907	108	SET DESIGNER	35.400
75	SHOE MAKER/REPAIRER	30.929	110	RAILROAD CONDUCTOR	35.409
76	DRYWALL APPLICATOR/ FINISHER	30.989	111	SEWAGE PLANT OPERATOR	35.565
77	DRESSMAKER	31.073	112	ZOOLOGIST	35.672
78	ACCOUNTANT	31.138	113	OCEANOGRAPHER	35.928
79	CHILD CARE WORKER	31.259	114	SPORTS INSTRUCTOR	35.989
80	AGRICULTURAL SCIENTIST	31.437	115	TICKET AGENT	36.195
80	CHEMIST	31.437	116	COOK/CHEF	36.242
80	PHYSIOLOGIST	31.437	117	DRILL-PRESS OPERATOR	36.416
83	FARMER	31.596	118	ELECTRICAL ENGINEER	36.448
84	AUDIOLOGIST	31.598	119	TECHNICAL WRITER	36.506
85	INDUSTRIAL DESIGNER	32.081	120	CARPET INSTALLER	36.523
86	FLIGHT ATTENDANT	32.120	121	CIVIL ENGINEER	36.848
87	GEOLOGIST	32.560	122	OPTICIAN	37.170
88	COMMUNICATIONS EQUIPMENT MECHANIC	32.858	123	MUSEUM CURATOR	37.450
89	CONSTRUCTION MACHINERY OPERATOR	32.951	124	PHOTOGRAPHER	37.613
			125	PLASTERER	37.630
90	ANTHROPOLOGIST	32.966	126	OCCUPATIONAL THERAPIST	37.917
91	STENOGRAPHER/ COURT REPORTER	33.132	127	CHIROPRACTOR	37.929
92	ELECTRICAL EQUIPMENT REPAIRER	34.032	128	METER READER	37.940
			129	MECHANICAL ENGINEER	38.288
93	ARCHEOLOGIST	34.103	130	PLUMBER	38.518
93	SOCIOLOGIST	34.103	131	COMPOSITOR/ TYPESETTER	38.579
95	SECRETARY	34.238			
96	MOTION PICTURE EDITOR	34.335	132	ECONOMIST	38.650
97	AEROSPACE ENGINEER	34.545	133	RESPIRATORY THERAPIST	38.970
97	INDUSTRIAL ENGINEER	34.545	134	NUCLEAR ENGINEER	39.151

RANK	SCORE	RANK	SCORE
135 BUS DRIVER	39.156	168 SURVEYOR	46.709
136 URBAN/REGIONAL PLANNER	39.296	169 UNDERTAKER	46.962
137 TOOL-AND-DIE MAKER	39.496	170 EXECUTIVE SEARCH CONSULTANT	47.250
138 HOSPITAL ADMINISTRATOR	39.585	171 CONSTRUCTION WORKER (LABORER)	47.306
139 DISK JOCKEY	39.825	172 BUYER	47.324
140 AUTOMOBILE BODY REPAIRER	40.673	173 MUSICIAN	47.569
141 ARTIST (COMMERCIAL)	40.931	174 SOCIAL WORKER	47.633
142 BRICKLAYER	40.950	175 WELDER	47.660
142 GLAZIER	40.950	176 PODIATRIST	47.717
144 BUTCHER	41.533	176 VETERINARIAN	47.717
145 OCCUPATIONAL SAFETY/ HEALTH INSPECTOR	41.542	178 AUTOMOBILE PAINTER	47.850
146 PROTESTANT MINISTER	41.768	179 NURSE (LICENSED PRACTICAL)	48.000
147 PERSONNEL RECRUITER	41.812	180 RABBI	48.294
148 MARKET RESEARCH ANALYST	42.060	181 CONSTRUCTION FOREMAN	48.590
149 MACHINE TOOL OPERATOR	42.085	182 MAIL CARRIER	48.708
150 STATIONARY ENGINEER	42.448	183 CARTOONIST	49.781
151 CHAUFFEUR	42.561	184 PSYCHOLOGIST	50.017
152 ENGINEERING TECHNICIAN	42.646	185 NUCLEAR PLANT DECONTAMINATION TECHNICIAN	50.226
153 GARBAGE COLLECTOR	42.760	186 IRONWORKER	50.911
154 MILITARY (COMMISSIONED OFFICER)	43.000	187 TEACHER	51.003
154 MILITARY (ENLISTED PERSON)	43.000	188 STEVEDORE	51.217
156 AIRCRAFT MECHANIC	43.485	189 AGENCY DIRECTOR (NONPROFIT)	51.250
157 DENTIST	43.670	190 SEAMAN	51.282
158 OPTOMETRIST	44.046	191 SCHOOL PRINCIPAL	51.718
159 PHYSICAL THERAPIST	44.237	192 ARTIST (FINE ART)	51.994
160 SHEET METAL WORKER	44.752	192 NEWSCASTER	51.994
161 HOTEL MANAGER	44.840	194 BASEBALL PLAYER (MAJOR LEAGUE)	52.500
162 CARPENTER	45.494	195 ORTHODONTIST	52.628
163 CATHOLIC PRIEST	45.684	196 BOILERMAKER	52.807
164 TRUCK DRIVER	45.990	196 MILLWRIGHT	52.807
165 MACHINIST	46.117	198 TRAVEL AGENT	52.826
166 ROOFER	46.552	199 CHOREOGRAPHER	53.100
167 JUDGE (FEDERAL)	46.676	200 AUTOMOBILE MECHANIC	53.831
		201 COLLEGE PROFESSOR	54.216

RANK		SCORE	RANK		SCORE
202	SALES REPRESENTATIVE (WHOLESALE)	55.108	228	LUMBERJACK	67.603
			229	AIRPLANE PILOT	68.727
203	BASKETBALL PLAYER (NBA)	56.250	230	FISHERMAN	69.820
			231	STOCKBROKER	71.656
204	AUTOMOBILE SALESPERSON	56.294	232	CONGRESSPERSON/ SENATOR	72.056
205	FASHION MODEL	56.511	233	PHOTOJOURNALIST	73.013
206	AUTHOR (BOOKS)	57.525	234	REAL ESTATE AGENT	73.063
207	BASEBALL UMPIRE (MAJOR LEAGUE)	57.750	235	ADVERTISING ACCOUNT EXECUTIVE	74.555
208	SINGER	58.631	236	BASKETBALL COACH (NCAA)	75.331
209	ADVERTISING SALESPERSON	59.888	236	JOCKEY	76.331
210	COWBOY	60.046	238	MAYOR	77.470
211	PSYCHIATRIST	61.313	239	PUBLIC RELATIONS EXECUTIVE	78.523
212	NURSE (REGISTERED)	62.144	240	HIGHWAY PATROL OFFICER	80.651
213	ACTOR	63.056			
213	FASHION DESIGNER	63.056	241	AIR TRAFFIC CONTROLLER	83.138
213	SYMPHONY CONDUCTOR	63.056	242	FOOTBALL PLAYER (NFL)	92.799
216	INSURANCE AGENT	63.322	243	POLICE OFFICER	93.893
217	OSTEOPATH	64.037	244	ASTRONAUT	99.349
217	PHYSICIAN (GENERAL PRACTICE)	64.037	245	SURGEON	99.463
219	DANCER	64.162	246	TAXI DRIVER	100.491
220	ATTORNEY	64.337	247	RACE CAR DRIVER (INDY CLASS)	101.775
221	DAIRY FARMER	64.509	248	CORPORATE EXECUTIVE (SENIOR)	108.625
222	CORRECTION OFFICER	64.694	249	FIREFIGHTER	110.936
223	REPORTER (NEWSPAPER)	65.269	250	PRESIDENT (U.S.)	176.550
224	ROUSTABOUT	65.548			
225	PHYSICIAN ASSISTANT	65.835			
226	ARCHITECT	66.920			
227	EMERGENCY MEDICAL TECHNICIAN	67.113			

THE COMPETITORS

At some jobs competition is as much a part of the landscape as the field is for the farmer. Below are the jobs which received the maximum allowable points for competitiveness in the ranking system. At right of the job title is the stress rank.

ACTOR	213	CORPORATE EXECUTIVE (SENIOR)	248
ADVERTISING ACCOUNT EXECUTIVE	235	DANCER	219
ASTRONAUT	244	DISK JOCKEY	139
ATTORNEY	220	FASHION DESIGNER	213
AUTOMOBILE SALESPERSON	204	FASHION MODEL	205
BASEBALL PLAYER (MAJOR LEAGUE)	194	FOOTBALL PLAYER (NFL)	242
BASKETBALL COACH (NCAA)	236	JOCKEY	236
BASKETBALL PLAYER (NBA)	203	MAYOR	238
CHOREOGRAPHER	199	NEWSCASTER	192
CONGRESSPERSON/SENATOR	232	PHOTOJOURNALIST	233
		PRESIDENT (U.S.)	250

CLOCK WATCHERS

Some jobs require completion by a "drop-dead date." Others have stringent quotas. Below are the jobs that scored the maximum allowable points in three categories: Deadlines, Quotas and Time Sensitive-levels. At right of the job title is the cumulative points scored for these categories.

CORPORATE EXECUTIVE (SENIOR)	17	PUBLIC RELATIONS EXECUTIVE	12
STENOGRAPHER/COURT REPORTER	14	REAL ESTATE AGENT	12
AIR TRAFFIC CONTROLLER	14	REPORTER (NEWSPAPER)	12
PRESIDENT (U.S.)	14	INSURANCE UNDERWRITER	12
COMPOSITOR/TYPESETTER	14	NURSE (REGISTERED)	12
STOCKBROKER	13	PURCHASING AGENT	12
STEVEDORE	13	SECRETARY	12
MOTION PICTURE EDITOR	12	SOCIAL WORKER	12
TECHNICAL WRITER	12	TEACHER	12
AUTHOR (BOOKS)	12	TYPIST/WORD PROCESSOR	12
PHOTOJOURNALIST	12	CARTOONIST	11
		DAIRY FARMER	11

ACCOUNTANT

Ranking: 78

Score: 31.138

Hours per Day: 9

Time Pressure: Moderate-High

Competition: Moderate

Accountants often work irregular hours. When they are under pressure to meet project deadlines, the long hours of concentrated, detailed work can be stressful. Accountants also must work effectively on a team with representatives from other departments or companies. Most tax accountants work longer hours under heightened pressure to meet stringent deadlines.

ACTOR

Ranking: 213

Score: 63.056

Hours per Day: 9

Time Pressure: Moderate

Competition: Very High

Actors face irregular employment and long working hours. Auditions, rehearsals, and performances demand physical and mental stamina. There is pressure to be creative, but also to compromise when necessary. Acting is a highly competitive field and every project is important. Actors are vulnerable to the criticism and rejection of the public. Some actors must deal with environmental conditions associated with "on location" filming.

ACTUARY

Ranking: 6

Score: 20.187

Hours per Day: 9

Time Pressure: Moderate

Competition: Low

Actuaries usually work regular hours, but certain projects may call for significant overtime. Because actuaries work with statistical data, constant attention to detail is necessary. They must be precise in their calculations, and they must carefully analyze large amounts of data. In addition, actuaries are often required to meet project deadlines.

ADVERTISING ACCOUNT EXECUTIVE

Ranking: 235

Score: 74.555

Hours per Day: 9.5

Time Pressure: Moderate

Competition: Very High

Although not physically demanding in itself, a position as an advertising account executive is an emotionally and mentally stressful one. Due to competition among firms and the pressure of acquiring and maintaining major accounts, executives in this field must deal with the strain of working long and irregular hours, traveling frequently, and making presentations. The work requires a consistently high level of creativity, the meeting of deadlines, a close attention to detail, and self-motivation.

ADVERTISING SALESPERSON

Ranking: 209

Score: 59.888

Hours per Day: 9.5

Time Pressure: Moderate

Competition: Very High

Advertising sales is a fast-paced field. Since advertising revenue is a major source of income for most periodical publishers, and the primary source for most broadcasters, the pressure on sales workers to succeed can be intense. Closing deals successfully depends in large part on a salesperson's negotiation and presentation skills. Individuals in this occupation face sales quotas, publishing or broadcast deadlines, and heavy contact with the public.

AEROSPACE ENGINEER

Ranking: 97

Score: 34.545

Hours per Day: 9

Time Pressure: Moderate

Competition: Moderate

Aerospace engineers solve detailed problems related to design and construction. Many engineers work under the pressure to develop creative new designs within a specified time limit. Conscientious attention to detail is necessary, because testing and construction are very expensive. Aerospace engineers bare the additional stress of having indirect responsibility for the safety of those who use their products.

AGENCY DIRECTOR (NON-PROFIT)

Ranking:189

Score: 51.250

Hours per Day: 10

Time Pressure: High

Competition: High

In addition to a regular working week, many after hours appearances and presentations need to be made at fund raising events and other agency related events. Because this is a highly competitive field, agency directors are often under pressure to work quickly and creatively to meet deadlines. Dealing with the board of directors is often the most stressful and critical part of a director's role. Added pressures include supervision and maintenance of a volunteer and administrative staff.

AGRICULTURAL SCIENTIST

Ranking: 80

Score: 31.437

Hours per Day: 9

Time Pressure: Low

Competition: Low

Agricultural research demands attention to detail; a small mistake can jeopardize an entire project. Most agricultural scientists work in research labs or classrooms, but some work outdoors under potentially stressful environmental conditions. Because most scientists in this field conduct their research under minimal supervision, they must remain continually motivated.

AIR TRAFFIC CONTROLLER

Ranking: 241

Score: 83.138

Hours per Day: 9

Time Pressure: High

Competition: Low

Air traffic controllers may be required to work unusual or irregular hours. They must make important decisions quickly and without error. Excellent verbal communication skills are necessary to safely direct aircraft, both in the air and on the ground. Controllers must function as part of a team in order to manage potentially disastrous situations.

AIRCRAFT MECHANIC

Ranking: 156

Score: 43.485

Hours per Day: 9

Time Pressure: Moderate-High

Competition: Low

Aircraft mechanics at many airports work late at night, or on weekends and holidays. They are required to work in all types of weather, in potentially hazardous positions. Because they are responsible for maintaining equipment which supports human life, their work calls for extreme precision and close attention to detail. In busy airports, teamwork and efficiency are essential to meet scheduled departure times.

AIRPLANE PILOT

Ranking: 229

Score: 68.727

Hours per Day: 9

Time Pressure: Moderate

Competition: Low

Airplane pilots are under a great deal of pressure to guarantee the comfort and safety of passengers while staying within flight schedules. This can prove especially difficult when flying in inclement weather conditions and during peak travel seasons. In addition to often working irregular hours and varying routes, pilots must often layover in other cities and deal with jet lag and frequent delays.

ANTHROPOLOGIST

Ranking: 90

Score: 32.966

Hours per Day: 9

Time Pressure: Low

Competition: Moderate

Anthropologists are sometimes required to work long hours during conferences or periods of field work. Some anthropologists balance teaching and research responsibilities. Researchers must pay close attention to detail. Anthropologists must possess strong initiative, because their work is not closely supervised. They are often placed under pressure to complete projects quickly, and to publish significant articles.

ANTIQUE DEALER

Ranking: 71

Score: 30.375

Hours per Day: 9

Time Pressure: Moderate

Competition: High

Working in this highly competitive field requires detailed knowledge of one's area of interest and the ability to predict future trends and to satisfy customer need. Dealers must be able to establish professional contacts easily and to network effectively. Along with the benefit of independence, those working alone have the risks and stress of no sales, no pay. However, as an extension of one's personal interests, this is a profession that can be a rewarding passion.

APPLIANCE REPAIRER

Ranking: 7

Score: 21.123

Hours per Day: 9.5

Time Pressure: Low-Moderate

Competition: Low

Making repairs during evening and weekend hours is commonplace for many home appliance repairers. Because broken appliances frequently have electrical problems, repairers have to be extremely cautious to avoid burns or shocks. Another possible stress factor for home appliance repairers is dealing with disgruntled customers. Successful repairers work quickly and efficiently.

ARCHEOLOGIST

Ranking: 93

Score: 34.103

Hours per Day: 9

Time Pressure: Low

Competition: Low

Archeologists work fairly regular hours, except during occasional conferences or during periods of field work. Many archeologists, however, combine the rigors of research with the burdens of teaching. Because they work in a competitive field, successful archeologists are highly motivated to perform research and publish their findings. Archeologists who do field research must sometimes deal with difficult cultural, physical, and climatic conditions.

ARCHITECT

Ranking: 226

Score: 66.920

Hours per Day: 9.5

Time Pressure: Moderate

Competition: High

Architects often work irregular hours, including evenings and weekends, to complete projects on time. They must use their creativity to solve unique practical problems. Their work requires patience and attention to detail. Architects must also possess skills for communicating and cooperating with clients, contractors and zoning board. Because architecture is a highly competitive field, architects may be required to sell their ideas to prospective clients, building inspectors and zoning boards.

ARCHITECTURAL DRAFTER

Ranking: 40

Score: 26.754

Hours per Day: 9

Time Pressure: Moderate

Competition: Low

Architectural drafters sometimes work evenings and weekends in order to meet project deadlines. They are often required to do extremely detailed work for long periods of time, and much of their work is repetitive. Because drafters must combine information from several sources to prepare accurate drawings, a facility for teamwork is often necessary. Drafters need skills of organization and discipline in order to coordinate concurrent projects.

ARTIST (COMMERCIAL)

Ranking: 141

Score: 40.931

Hours per Day: 9

Time Pressure: Moderate

Competition: High

Project deadlines often result in irregular working hours for both free-lance and salaried commercial artists. Nearly half of all commercial artists work as free-lancers, which requires that they sell their talent and ideas to prospective employers. Successful commercial and graphic artists are consistently creative and highly motivated. They also must deal with public response to their work.

ARTIST (FINE ART)

Ranking: 192

Score: 51.994

Hours per Day: 9

Time Pressure: Low-Moderate

Competition: High

Artistic painters generally work erratic hours and are consistently under pressure to be creative in their designs. Because they work in a highly competitive field, successful artists are self-disciplined and give extreme attention to detail in their work. Speed is sometimes a necessity to complete and sell projects. Other major stress factors for artistic painters are facing public criticism of their work and being in the public spotlight.

ASTROLOGER

Ranking: 27

Score: 25.000

Hours per Day: 8

Time Pressure: Low

Competition: Moderate

Astrologers must take many fine details into consideration when calculating horoscopes. Additional stress is caused by advising clients on intimate, personal matters and by dealing with a public which is generally skeptical and scornful of astrology. Most astrologers work independently and are thus solely dependent upon the income from their business.

ASTRONAUT

Ranking: 244

Score: 99.349

Hours per Day: 8.5

Time Pressure: Moderate

Competition: Very High

Working in a highly visible and competitive field, astronauts must push themselves to the physical, emotional, and mental limits of human endurance. Much of their time in preparing for space flights requires strenuous physical conditioning, analysis of complex aeronautical and engineering problems, and training for meeting mission objectives. Test flights and actual space flights are not only extremely hazardous but place the astronaut in a constant, stressful, and closely scrutinized work environment. Many astronauts also work as representatives of the space industry, frequently appearing in public and speaking to groups across the country.

ASTRONOMER

Ranking: 50

Score: 28.069

Hours per Day: 9

Time Pressure: Low

Competition: Moderate

Astronomers generally work regular hours, but scheduling changes are sometimes required for research at remote observation facilities. Their work demands creativity, patient attention to detail, and strong personal initiative. Astronomers affiliated with universities are under considerable pressure to publish scientific papers, and an astronomer's career is often judged according to the success of a single, long-term project.

ATTORNEY

Ranking: 220

Score: 64.337

Hours per Day: 10

Time Pressure: Moderate

Competition: Very High

Attorneys tend to work long and erratic hours when preparing important cases. Their work calls for detailed research and creative thought, as well as skills of speech and writing. Lawyers require strong initiative to finish their work on schedule. Most lawyers have a high degree of contact with the public and must sometimes work with disagreeable clients. Successful lawyers consider serious matters, and bear partial responsibility for their resolution.

AUDIOLOGIST

Ranking: 84

Score: 31.598

Hours per Day: 8.5

Time Pressure: Low-Moderate

Competition: Low

Due to constant attention to detail and the intense concentration involved with helping clients with speech, language, and hearing problems, audiologists can experience great mental strain. They must also demonstrate patience and excellent communication skills in instructing clients and conferring with physicians, psychologists, and other professionals. Another important stress factor might include the frustration involved with a client's slow progress.

AUTHOR (BOOKS)

Ranking: 206

Score: 57.525

Hours per Day: 9

Time Pressure: Moderate-High

Competition: High

Book writers generally choose their own hours, and although writing is not physically demanding, mental pressures can cause significant stress. Writers have to be extremely careful with details, highly motivated, and able to meet deadlines. Writing consistently attracts many more potential writers than the market can sustain. Successful writers are self-disciplined and good salespersons. Creative demands can also be a significant stress factor for writers.

AUTOMOBILE ASSEMBLER

Ranking: 105

Score: 35.170

Hours per Day: 8.5

Time Pressure: High

Competition: Low

Assembly line work is necessarily monotonous, as each employee repeatedly performs only one particular job within the total production. Automative assemblers must nevertheless work with speed, consistency, and precision in order meet production quotas while maintaining a high level of quality. They must also adjust to working in shifts, including nights and weekends.

AUTOMOBILE BODY REPAIRER

Ranking: 140

Score: 40.673

Hours per Day: 9.5

Time Pressure: Moderate-High

Competition: Low

Automotive body repairers use many potentially dangerous tools, such as metal cutting devices and torches. The work calls for good physical stamina and body repairers must constantly be alert to avoid injury from flying or broken pieces of metal or other hazards. Much of their work is done in cramped spaces. Automotive body repairers are expected to work quickly under deadline pressures.

AUTOMOBILE MECHANIC

Ranking: 200

Score: 53.831

Hours per Day: 9.5

Time Pressure: Moderate-High

Competition: Low

Many automotive mechanics work evening and weekend hours, or are available after closing for emergency repairs. They are required to make quick, accurate diagnoses of automotive problems, and to work with potentially hazardous equipment, such as torches and jacks. Auto mechanics work in a confined area, in frequently uncomfortable positions. Some mechanics are under pressure to sell parts and accessories to customers. Handling disgruntled customers is another possible source of stress.

AUTOMOBILE PAINTER

Ranking: 178

Score: 47.850

Hours per Day: 9.5

Time Pressure: Moderate

Competition: Low

Automotive painters work indoors, usually in a confined area, and may be exposed to hazardous paint fumes. Good physical stamina is required to handle a heavy work day. They must pay careful attention to detail when mixing and applying paint, but speed is essential to success, as many automotive painters work on a commission basis. The combination of speed and precision over a long period of time is a foolproof formula for stress.

AUTOMOBILE SALESPERSON

Ranking: 204

Score: 56.294

Hours per Day: 9.5

Time Pressure: Moderate

Competition: Very High

Automobile and vehicle salespersons generally are required to work evenings and weekends. Successful salespersons are able to handle even the most unpleasant customers politely. Because they work independently, salespersons must be self-motivated. Automobile sales are highly competitive and salespersons who are unable to meet sales quotas often lose their jobs. Dealing with the public's negative stereotype of automobile salespersons can also cause stress.

BANK OFFICER

Ranking: 107

Score: 35.395

Hours per Day: 10

Time Pressure: Low-Moderate

Competition: Moderate

Mortgage loan officers need to assess the solvency of potential clients with accuracy. They must stay familiar with the financial market and the policies of their company. Lack of teamwork between banking specialists can cause considerable stress and a loss of efficiency. Mortgage loan officers are usually under pressure to meet loan quotas by securing as many clients as possible. Officers should possess strong powers of persuasion and a talent for handling a variety of personalities.

BANK TELLER

Ranking: 67

Score: 30.120

Hours per Day: 8

Time Pressure: Low-Moderate

Competition: Low

Bank tellers are usually confined to a fairly small area for the duration of their shifts. They must pay close attention to every transaction that they handle. Tellers spend the majority of their time interacting with the public, and are expected to deal effectively with customers of all temperaments. Their work is highly repetitive, and tellers may be required to work in the evenings or on the weekends.

BARBER

Ranking: 18

Score: 23.621

Hours per Day: 8

Time Pressure: Low-Moderate

Competition: Moderate

As their income depends largely on customer satisfaction, barbers are constantly under pressure to enhance a customer's appearance and to deal with the public in a tactful manner. Since more than half own their shops, barbers have the added stresses associated with running a business. The work itself is somewhat repetitive and requires good physical stamina.

BARTENDER

Ranking: 69

Score: 30.352

Hours per Day: 7.5

Time Pressure: Moderate

Competition: Low

As a large part of their income derives from tips, bartenders must always be courteous, even when dealing with inebriated and unruly customers. Although monotonous, work requires efficiency and precision under pressure. Some physical stamina is needed, as bartenders must work quickly to fill orders and in irregular shifts, often late into the night and on weekends.

BASEBALL PLAYER (MAJOR LEAGUE)

Ranking: 194

Score: 52.500

Hours per Day: 6

Time Pressure: Moderate-High

Competition: Very High

Professional baseball players constantly face the possibility of physical injury, and they work schedules which include evenings, weekends, and holidays. Batting and fielding demand extreme precision, and players must maintain a high level of quality and intensity during a long season in order to guarantee job security. The work is highly competitive and requires being in the public spotlight.

BASEBALL UMPIRE (MAJOR LEAGUE)

Ranking: 207

Score: 57.750

Hours per Day: 6

Time Pressure: Low-Moderate

Competition: Moderate

Baseball umpires need to be in good physical shape, as they must stay on their feet throughout the game and work in all weather conditions. They must remain constantly alert and make hundreds of decisions quickly and accurately. Other stress factors include working erratic hours, being in the public spotlight, and dealing with players, managers, and fans who disagree with their decisions.

BASKETBALL COACH (NCAA)

Ranking: 236

Score: 75.331

Hours per Day: 8.5

Time Pressure: Moderate

Competition: Very High

Athletic coaches must assume a number of responsibilities simultaneously in this highly competitive field, including designing strategies, training and evaluating players, viewing game films, and dealing with the public and the press. As schools depend in part on the revenue generated from successful athletic programs, coaches are under a great deal of pressure to amass winning records. Losing seasons may result in much public criticism and, ultimately, dismissal. A number of sports are played in inclement weather conditions which can increase stress.

BASKETBALL PLAYER (NBA)

Ranking: 203

Score: 56.250

Hours per Day: 6

Time Pressure: Moderate

Competition: Very High

Professional basketball players must constantly perform at high levels during a season which extends over several months. Work requires an extensive and erratic traveling schedule and results in close public scrutiny on both a professional and personal level. With little job security, players face the constant possibility of injury, competition from fellow players, and the pressure to meet expectations in each game.

BIOLOGIST

Ranking: 42

Score: 26.946

Hours per Day: 9

Time Pressure: Low

Competition: Low

Biological scientists frequently carry out field research in potentially stressful environments. Those employed by academic institutions are forced to balance teaching and research schedules, and they must compete for funding and fellowships. Professors also have to deal with the pressure to publish and bring recognition to their institutions. Research requires organization, a close attention to detail, patience, and the meeting of deadlines.

BOILERMAKER

Ranking: 196

Score: 52.807

Hours per Day: 9.5

Time Pressure: Moderate

Competition: Low

In addition to having to make accurate calculations in repairing and building, boilermakers must frequently work under hazardous conditions with potentially dangerous tools, such as acetylene torches. Boilermakers are sometimes called in at irregular hours to make emergency repairs, often in cramped boilers. They must work quickly and with precision to return boilers to full operation within a short amount of time.

BOOKBINDER

Ranking: 17

Score: 23.573

Hours per Day: 9

Time Pressure: Moderate-High

Competition: Low

Although frequently performing only one or two monotonous tasks, bookbinders must work both quickly and accurately in order to meet production quotas. Some work with fast-moving, potentially dangerous equipment, such as paper cutters, while others who are employed in hand binderies must pay extremely close attention to detail.

BOOKKEEPER

Ranking: 10

Score: 21.462

Hours per Day: 8

Time Pressure: Moderate

Competition: Low

Many bookkeepers specialize in specific tasks, and their work can be extremely repetitive. Bookkeepers need to be fastidious in making their calculations. They must be able to analyze large amounts of data at once, and to concentrate for long periods of time.

BRICKLAYER

Ranking: 142

Score: 40.950

Hours per Day: 9

Time Pressure: Moderate

Competition: Low

Bricklayers work outdoors, sometimes in potentially hazardous locations, such as atop high scaffolds or ladders. The work requires good physical stamina and teamwork. Erecting walls, chimneys, or columns, and laying stone, demands close attention to detail, and successful bricklayers work quickly and with precision. As with most construction jobs, bricklayers are frequently under pressure to complete projects on time.

BROADCAST TECHNICIAN

Ranking: 22

Score: 24.184

Hours per Day: 9

Time Pressure: Moderate

Competition: Low

As most stations transmit programming twenty-four hours a day, broadcast technicians must often work long and extended shifts. Operating electronic equipment requires the ability to concentrate for extended periods of time, and technicians have to perform a number of tasks, often in highly pressured situations. Speed and the ability to meet deadlines are essential.

BUS DRIVER

Ranking: 135

Score: 39.156

Hours per Day: 8

Time Pressure: Moderate

Competition: Low

Bus drivers sometimes work split morning and evening shifts, when demand is highest and traffic heaviest. They are responsible to perform safely, yet are under considerable pressure to keep to schedule. Monotony can become a problem, particularly if a limited local route is repeated each day. It is also important to remember that bus drivers, trained in operating a large piece of machinery, not in public relations, are in constant contact with people, wrong change, and traffic.

BUTCHER

Ranking: 144

Score: 41.533

Hours per Day: 9

Time Pressure: Low-Moderate

Competition: Low

Butchers use sharp cleavers and power tools, and work much of the time in refrigerated rooms. Work is often repetitive, and requires both endurance and precision to avoid injuries. Many butchers have frequent contact with the public and must handle unusual client demands. Speed is an important factor in many meat packing operations. Butchers who operate their own businesses may also be responsible for tasks such as management and bookkeeping.

BUYER

Ranking: 172

Score: 47.324

Hours per Day: 9.5

Time Pressure: Moderate

Competition: Very High

Wholesale and retail buyers must frequently work long, irregular hours and make decisive and often risky decisions quickly. Working in this highly competitive field requires a detailed knowledge of various products and the ability to predict future consumer trends and to satisfy customer need. Buyers must be able establish professional contacts easily and work effectively with others.

CARPENTER

Ranking: 162

Score: 45.494

Hours per Day: 8.5

Time Pressure: Moderate

Competition: Low

In addition to occasionally working in inclement weather, carpenters must frequently use high-powered tools, often while standing on scaffolds, ladders, or support beams. The job requires good physical stamina, a careful attention to detail, speed, and economy of effort. Independent carpenters must cope with the additional pressures associated with managing their own businesses.

CARPET/TILE INSTALLER

Ranking: 120

Score: 36.523

Hours per Day: 9

Time Pressure: Moderate

Competition: Low

Installers sometimes are required to work evening and weekends on rush jobs. Their work calls for accurate measurements and the ability to work under deadline pressure. Tasks can be repetitive, and installers occasionally must deal with dissatisfied customers. Some installers have the added responsibility of working as sales representatives.

CARTOONIST

Ranking: 183

Score: 49.781

Hours per Day: 9

Time Pressure: Moderate-High

Competition: High

Cartoonists must be consistently creative while meeting regular deadlines. Like many artistic fields, this profession is highly competitive and has a surplus of skilled candidates. Although they have little contact with the public, cartoonists must face public criticism.

CASHIER

Ranking: 29

Score: 25.117

Hours per Day: 7.5

Time Pressure: Moderate

Competition: Low

Cashiers are required to perform highly repetitive tasks quickly and accurately, while remaining courteous and tactful to the public. They are sometimes confined to small booths or stations and work irregular hours. Other stress factors include handling a high volume of merchandise and dealing with large crowds during peak shopping periods.

CATHOLIC PRIEST

Ranking: 163

Score: 45.684

Hours per Day: 10.5

Time Pressure: Moderate

Competition: Low

Roman Catholic priests work very erratic and frequently long hours, carrying out numerous responsibilities, including holding services, counseling, attending to the sick, and various personal and parish emergencies. Sermons and teaching duties demand creativity, personal initiative, and the ability to communicate effectively with large groups of people. Priests have to deal with the stress of being closely scrutinized on both a professional and personal level.

CHAUFFEUR

Ranking: 151

Score: 42.561

Hours per Day: 9.5

Time Pressure: Moderate

Competition: Low

Chauffeurs must drive safely and obey traffic laws while picking-up and delivering passengers quickly. An accident can result in dismissal. The work can become repetitive, and drivers may have to work erratic hours and deal with unruly passengers. Other stress factors include driving in heavy traffic and dealing with dispatchers.

CHEMIST

Ranking: 80

Score: 31.437

Hours per Day: 9

Time Pressure: Low

Competition: Low

Carrying out research, chemists concentrate on highly detailed information in working on analytical and technical problems. Those employed in the industry sector often work in very competitive research environments.

CHILD CARE WORKER

Ranking: 79

Score: 31.259

Hours per Day: 7.5

Time Pressure: Moderate

Competition: Low

Child care workers must have a good deal of patience and physical stamina in order to work constantly with active children. They also have to deal with disgruntled parents and handle staff conflicts. The attrition rate is high, and employees frequently work irregular hours, including evenings and weekends.

CHIROPRACTOR

Ranking: 127

Score: 37.929

Hours per Day: 10

Time Pressure: Low-Moderate

Competition: Moderate

Chiropractors must work closely with ailing patients, some of whom suffer from chronic and painful sicknesses, and make accurate diagnoses. Additional stress factors include dealing with the potential of malpractice lawsuits and handling the pressures associated with running a business.

CHOREOGRAPHER

Ranking: 199

Score: 53.100

Hours per Day: 9

Time Pressure: Moderate

Competition: Very High

Choreographers work under the pressure of planning a performance and training a troupe of dancers within a certain deadline, frequently resulting in long, irregular work days. They must closely observe the production details, noticing a dancer's miscue or bad timing, and be patient with troupe members. With little job security, choreographers work with the stress of knowing that further employment is dependent upon the success of a production.

CIVIL ENGINEER

Ranking: 121

Score: 36.848

Hours per Day: 9.5

Time Pressure: Moderate

Competition: Low

Civil engineers need excellent analytical and technical skills. Their work is highly detailed, and mistakes in calculation can be very costly. Many civil engineers are required to perform as managers within their companies. Successful civil engineers are highly motivated and effectively handle the pressure to complete projects on schedule.

COLLEGE PROFESSOR

Ranking: 201

Score: 54.216

Hours per Day: 9

Time Pressure: Moderate

Competition: Very High

Although actually teaching only a few hours a day, college professors must combine instruction schedules with research, administrative, and advising responsibilities. They have to prepare material for presentation and lead discussion in classes ranging in size from as many as several hundred students to as few as five. The greatest stress, however, comes from the pressure to write and publish original work and thereby gain tenure and job security.

COMMUNICATIONS EQUIPMENT MECHANIC

Ranking: 88

Score: 32.858

Hours per Day: 9.5

Time Pressure: Moderate

Competition: Low

Communications mechanics are under pressure to quickly and accurately locate technical problems, and to fix them. Some stay on call throughout the night. Because of the complexity of most communications equipment, knowledge and flexibility are essential. Most communications mechanics need to interact effectively with unfamiliar or disgruntled clients.

COMPOSITOR/TYPESETTER

Ranking: 131

Score: 38.579

Hours per Day: 9

Time Pressure: High

Competition: Low

Compositors and typesetters generally work odd hours, including evenings and weekends. Much of their work is rather monotonous and demands both precision and attention to detail. They must work quickly but remain alert to avoid easily made mistakes. Deadlines can cause considerable stress for compositors and typesetters, especially those affiliated with newspapers or magazines.

COMPUTER OPERATOR

Ranking: 52

Score: 28.230

Hours per Day: 8.5

Time Pressure: Moderate

Competition: Low

Computer operators must be able to concentrate for long periods of time while working quickly and accurately, even when performing such repetitive operations as rote data entry. As a number of companies run their computer systems for sixteen to twenty-four hours a day, some computer operators are required to work evening or night shifts. Work is often closely supervised, and employees are frequently confined to single terminals for the duration of their shifts.

COMPUTER PROGRAMMER

Ranking: 39

Score: 26.508

Hours per Day: 9

Time Pressure: Moderate

Competition: Low

Computer programmers frequently work unusual hours, as when equipment is difficult to access during the day. Programmers concentrate on extremely detailed information, often under pressure to meet a deadline. Because small mistakes in a program can be difficult to find, programmers must review their work many times before it is ready for application.

COMPUTER SERVICE TECHNICIAN

Ranking: 31

Score: 25.817

Hours per Day: 9.5

Time Pressure: Moderate-High

Competition: Low

Computer service technicians are often on call during the night for emergency repairs. They must locate problems quickly, because computers are often essential to the daily operations of a business. Technicians work without supervision in situations which are sometimes unfamiliar. Computer technicians should be self-motivated, patient, and capable of communicating effectively with their clients.

COMPUTER SYSTEMS ANALYST

Ranking: 26

Score: 24.965

Hours per Day: 9

Time Pressure: Moderate-High

Competition: Low

Computer systems analysts must be able to work on a number of complex problems simultaneously. Since clients need non-functioning systems back in operation as soon as possible, analysts must be available at all times of the day and work both quickly and accurately in returning a computer to its full capability. As many systems analysts work as consultants, they must deal with the added pressures of acquiring new clients and running their own businesses.

CONGRESSPERSON/SENATOR

Ranking: 232

Score: 72.056

Hours per Day: 8.5

Time Pressure: Moderate

Competition: Very High

Senators and congresspersons tend to work odd hours, including evenings and weekends when they are in session. Speeches, travel, meetings, and other events can cause considerable fatigue for politicians. Senators and congresspersons must pay close attention to the demands of their constituents to remain in office beyond a single term. Competitiveness, personal initiative, and the ability to work under pressure in the public spotlight are essential for success.

CONSERVATIONIST

Ranking: 42

Score: 26.946

Hours per Day: 9

Time Pressure: Low-Moderate

Competition: Low

Many conservationists work long hours, often in remote areas, under a wide variety of weather conditions. Some conservationists risk injury by fighting fires or other threats to nature. Their work calls for physical stamina and the ability to work with others. Conservationists need to possess strong initiative, and the verbal ability necessary to support their actions and opinions.

CONSTRUCTION FOREMAN

Ranking: 181

Score: 48.590

Hours per Day: 9.5

Time Pressure: Moderate

Competition: Low

Foremen sometimes work night or weekend shifts, depending upon the industry. They must continually solve problems related to employee management, such as absenteeism. Because they often face project deadlines, supervisors must be highly motivated and able to enforce leadership and organization upon their subordinates. Some supervisors face the added pressures of mediating conflicts between workers and management.

CONSTRUCTION MACHINERY OPERATOR

Ranking: 89

Score: 32.951

Hours per Day: 9

Time Pressure: Low-Moderate

Competition: Low

Construction machinery operators must perform specific functions accurately and precisely while working with potentially dangerous machinery. Work is done outdoors, often in inclement weather conditions. Operators are confined to a small cab and control console, and even though work is frequently repetitive, operators must be alert at all times to prevent accidents.

CONSTRUCTION WORKER (LABORER)

Ranking: 171

Score: 47.306

Hours per Day: 8.5

Time Pressure: Low-Moderate

Competition: Low

Construction laborers work alongside potentially hazardous equipment, such as cranes, bulldozers and power tools. Although most workers execute a variety of tasks, some laborers perform highly repetitive work. Much of their work is done outdoors, sometimes in bad weather conditions. Teamwork and physical stamina are essential to avoid injury in hazardous situations.

COOK

Ranking: 116

Score: 36.242

Hours per Day: 8

Time Pressure: Low-Moderate

Competition: Low

Cooks work under the pressure of filling a variety of orders quickly while preparing high quality food, a task which can be especially demanding during peak service periods. Good physical stamina is required in standing in small, hot areas and doing the numerous tasks needed to prepare orders. Close attention to detail is needed, and cooks must be alert when working with potentially dangerous utensils and appliances. Other stress factors include working irregular shifts and dealing with employee conflicts.

CORPORATE EXECUTIVE (SENIOR)

Ranking: 248

Score: 108.625

Hours per Day: 11

Time Pressure: High

Competition: High

Working in this highly competitive field requires a detailed knowledge of the financial community, economic trends as well as technological developments and implications. Senior corporate executives require excellent communication skills and the ability to work with important customers, high-level corporate boards and CEO's. Needing to excel in many fields, senior corporate executives wearing many hats often face a great deal of stress. They must be able to develop, articulate and implement decisions, be financially minded and convey their directives well with all levels of staff.

CORRECTION OFFICER

Ranking: 222

Score: 64.694

Hours per Day: 9.5

Time Pressure: Low-Moderate

Competition: Low

Correction officers work in shifts, including nights, weekends, and holidays. Because they oversee criminals and people who have been accused of committing crimes, correction officers often face hazardous, possibly life threatening situations. They must pay close attention to the movements and moods of inmates, and work within the limitations of their powers to enforce institutional rules. A failure to cooperate with other officers, or to follow security procedures, can be dangerous.

COSMETOLOGIST

Ranking: 33

Score: 25.944

Hours per Day: 8.5

Time Pressure: Low-Moderate

Competition: Moderate

Generally, cosmetologists work irregular hours, including evenings and weekends. Though their work is frequently repetitive, beauticians must work with care and precision. Like the producers of other services, beauticians should pay special attention to the customer's satisfaction. Beauticians deal directly with the public, and should project confidence and competence.

COWBOY

Ranking: 210

Score: 60.046

Hours per Day: 8.5

Time Pressure: High

Competition: Low

Although much of their work is repetitive, cowboys are under pressure to work quickly and carefully in order to avoid injury and to complete projects on time. They must often work in inclement weather and in irregular schedules, including evenings, weekends, and holidays. Increased automation has lessened some of the physical demands of the profession, but good stamina is still essential in working with unpredictable animals.

DAIRY FARMER

Ranking: 221

Score: 64.509

Hours per Day: 10.5

Time Pressure: High

Competition: Low

In addition to working long hours, dairy farmers face the constant task of feeding, milking, and maintaining their cows three hundred and sixty-five days a year. As many dairy farmers run their own farms independently, they face the added pressures of hiring and supervising workers, sell-

ing and shipping their product, and meeting delivery deadlines and production quotas. Added stress factors include competition and dealing with market fluctuations.

DANCER

Ranking: 219

Score: 64.162

Hours per Day: 9

Time Pressure: Low-Moderate

Competition: Very High

During periods of employment, dancers work long, irregular hours. Successful dancers must stay in excellent physical condition, take instruction well, and work productively as part of a group—skills which do not come easily to most people. Because dancing is a highly competitive field, dancers should demonstrate confidence and initiative. The potential for physical injury can also be a cause of stress.

DENTAL HYGIENIST

Ranking: 24

Score: 24.719

Hours per Day: 8

Time Pressure: Low-Moderate

Competition: Low

Dental hygienists provide direct patient care, which demands concentration and attention to detail. They must work well with the public while maintaining a reassuring, professional manner. Their work is often repetitive, but it requires that they take special care with every appointment, as when cleaning dental implements. Dental hygienists are required to work effectively as a team with dentists and dental assistants.

DENTAL LABORATORY TECHNICIAN

Ranking: 41

Score: 26.940

Hours per Day: 9

Time Pressure: Moderate

Competition: Low

Dental laboratory technicians must be extremely precise in following dentists' instructions, and much of their work is repetitive. They often need to coordinate their activities with other specialists in the lab. Dental technicians are commonly under pressure to work quickly and efficiently.

DENTIST

Ranking: 157

Score: 43.670

Hours per Day: 9

Time Pressure: Low-Moderate

Competition: Moderate

Dentists use precise technical skills, and must communicate with anxious patients. Most dentists are required to manage a dental hygienist and a dental assistant. Dentists are often responsible throughout their careers for the practical aspects of their business, which include building a clientele and finding a good location for their office. Dentists also risk hurting their patients or being the target of malpractice suits.

DIETITIAN

Ranking: 14

Score: 22.990

Hours per Day: 8.5

Time Pressure: Low-Moderate

Competition: Low

Clinical dietitians must analyze large amounts of detailed data, and instruct clients according to their findings. They are required to interact with doctors and administrators, as well as with patients and their families. Initiative and organizational skills are vital for dietitians handling multiple clients. Some dietitians balance administrative and clinical duties.

DISHWASHER

Ranking: 30

Score: 25.326

Hours per Day: 7.5

Time Pressure: Low-Moderate

Competition: Low

Because of the large number of dishes restaurants need in serving their customers, dishwashers are frequently under pressure to work quickly and efficiently. Work is highly repetitive and requires good physical stamina, as employees must transport stacks of dishes and stay on their feet. Other stress factors include exhaustion from working in a hot kitchen and in irregular and often long shifts, including evenings, weekends, and holidays.

DISK JOCKEY

Ranking: 139

Score: 39.825

Hours per Day: 9

Time Pressure: Low-Moderate

Competition: Very High

Disk jockeys work unusual hours, including weekends and holidays. They are restricted to small broadcast booths for the duration of their shift. Their program must usually follow a fairly tight broadcasting schedules. Because radio is an extremely competitive field, there is great pressure to develop a distinctive on-air personality. Radio work often requires precise timing and a talent for dealing with unexpected mistakes.

DRESSMAKER

Ranking: 77

Score: 31.073

Hours per Day: 8.5

Time Pressure: Moderate.

Competition: Low

Although their work is repetitive, dressmakers must work both precisely and quickly to meet production quotas while maintaining a high level of quality. Work requires a close attention to detail for hours at a time and demands careful handling of high- powered machinery to avoid injury. Most dressmakers are confined to a single machine for the duration of a shift.

DRILL-PRESS OPERATOR

Ranking: 117

Score: 36.416

Hours per Day: 9

Time Pressure: Low-Moderate

Competition: Low

Drill-press operators work with potentially dangerous machinery, and are sometimes required to make urgent mechanical adjustments. The combination of immobility, standing for long periods, and machine noise can be somewhat stressful. Drill-press work calls for physical stamina, precision, speed, and a tolerance for repetition. Most operators are closely supervised, and must follow a strict schedule.

DRYWALL APPLICATOR/ FINISHER

Ranking: 76

Score: 30.989

Hours per Day: 9

Time Pressure: Low-Moderate

Competition: Low

Drywall applicators and finishers commonly use potentially hazardous power-tools, and sometimes work in a cloud of drywall dust. Their work can be monotonous because their limited duties are repetitive. As in most construction jobs, measurements and installations must be precise. Workers are under continual pressure to complete jobs on time. Finishers frequently work in the presence of paint fumes and chemical compounds.

ECONOMIST

Ranking: 132

Score: 38.650

Hours per Day: 9

Time Pressure: Moderate

Competition: Moderate

Economists affiliated with the academic community must coordinate teaching, research, and administrative schedules. They typically analyze large amounts of highly detailed data, and are often under deadline pressure. Some economists must sell the results of their research to business or the government. Economists work in a very speculative discipline; nonetheless, they are often held responsible for the losses of their employers.

ELECTRICAL ENGINEER

Ranking: 118

Score: 36.448

Hours per Day: 9

Time Pressure: Moderate

Competition: Low-Moderate

Electrical engineers work with large amounts of detailed technical information. Because many projects take several months to complete, engineers must possess patience and self-discipline. Some electrical engineers have the additional stress of administrative responsibilities. Engineers need to keep up with technological advances in their field, which is quite competitive.

ELECTRICAL EQUIPMENT REPAIRER

Ranking: 92

Score: 34.032

Hours per Day: 9.5

Time Pressure: Low-Moderate

Competition: Low

Some electrical equipment repairers work in shifts or are held on call overnight. Successful repairers diagnose problems quickly, and work with great precision. Because a given repairer often works in unfamiliar environments, he or she must be especially cautious in order to avoid burns or electrical shock. Repairers should be able to work with little supervision and to interact well with the public.

ELECTRICAL TECHNICIAN

Ranking: 20

Score: 23.972

Hours per Day: 9

Time Pressure: Low-Moderate

Competition: Low

Electrical technicians are required to concentrate for long hours on detailed projects. Most technicians specialize in a limited area of electronics, and must work in teams in order to complete large projects. Technicians who work as sales representatives are in frequent contact with the public, and are expected to combine technical expertise with communication and marketing skills.

ELECTRICIAN

Ranking: 103

Score: 34.906

Hours per Day: 9

Time Pressure: Low-Moderate

Competition: Low

Electricians handle dangerous levels of electric current, and must remain alert in order to avoid accident and injury. They must be precise, efficient, and careful. Electricians often coordinate their effort with that of a partner. Many electricians are in frequent contact with the public; some must cope with the pressures of managing their own businesses.

EMERGENCY MEDICAL TECHNICIAN

Ranking: 227

Score: 67.113

Hours per Day: 8.5

Time Pressure: Moderate

Competition: Low

Emergency medical technicians live with the greatest pressure of all—saving people's lives. While on duty, they must be prepared at all times of the day and night to respond to calls and arrive at the scene quickly. Emergency crews have to make split-second diagnoses and give medical assistance immediately in order to stabilize injured parties and rush them to medical facilities. The job frequently involves working on-site in dangerous and hazardous situations, such as in fire areas.

ENGINEERING TECHNICIAN

Ranking: 152

Score: 42.646

Hours per Day: 9

Time Pressure: Moderate

Competition: Moderate

In constructing experimental equipment, engineering technicians must work with precision and concentrate for long periods of time. As work often involves handling potentially hazardous equipment, such as power-tools, from ladders or scaffolds, they must remain alert to avoid injury. Technicians have to work both accurately and quickly in order to complete quality projects under production deadlines. Additional stress factors include working with team members.

EXECUTIVE SEARCH CONSULTANT

Ranking: 170

Score: 47.250

Hours per Day: 9

Time Pressure: Moderate

Competition: High

Working in this highly competitive field requires detailed knowledge of one's area of interest and the ability to locate appropriate candidates. Executive search consultants need excellent communication skills and the ability to work with high level corporate boards or management. Many consultants face stress from making quotas, closing a certain number of deals quickly, or selecting an inappropriate candidate.

FARMER

Ranking: 83

Score: 31.596

Hours per Day: 10.5

Time Pressure: Low-Moderate

Competition: Low

Many types of farm work are seasonal in nature, but the operation of meat or dairy farms requires year-round vigilance. Owner/operations of farms are subject to a wide variety of work hazards. They can contract diseases from handling and inhaling pesticides; they may be injured by gasoline powered planting and reaping machinery; or they may become ill or impaired from near-constant exposure to severe or inclement weather. Additionally, farmers face the less tangible but constant dangers of crop spoilage, commodity supply gluts (and accompanying price devaluations), and mortgage default.

FASHION DESIGNER

Ranking: 213

Score: 63.056

Hours per Day: 9

Time Pressure: Moderate

Competition: Very High

Some fashion designers work long hours before shows or when creating a new line of clothing. Because they work in a highly competitive field, successful designers need to predict the public's tastes and demands. They must work diligently to complete projects within firm time constraints. Designers must balance the need for creativity and a distinctive look with the requirements of affordable production.

FASHION MODEL

Ranking: 205

Score: 56.511

Hours per Day: 8.5

Time Pressure: Moderate

Competition: Very High

Fashion models work irregular and frequently long hours. While often repetitive, the work in prepping and shooting can be physically demanding and tiring. Other pressures associated with the job include traveling between jobs, waiting for set-ups, satisfying a number of clients, dealing with the criticism of agents and designers, and working to acquire accounts in this highly competitive field.

FILE CLERK

Ranking: 11

Score: 21.719

Hours per Day: 8.5

Time Pressure: Moderate-High

Competition: Low

Many perform very mundane, repetitive tasks, such as filing, typing and running errands. They may be confined to a desk or room throughout the workday. Filing and other tasks often call for accuracy and attention to detail. They are required to work effectively with secretaries and other office personnel. Some clerks are responsible for more detailed tasks such as bookkeeping and stenography.

FINANCIAL PLANNER

Ranking:35

Score: 26.250

Hours per Day: 10

Time Pressure: Moderate

Competition: Moderate

Critical decision-making in this field can be especially stressful adding to the pressures of keeping pace with economic trends. Planners need excellent communication skills and the ability to work with high net-worth individuals. Many face the stress which may arise from a financial crisis or unstable economy. The pressures involving finding new clients, collecting receivables and running a small business (for the high percentage that are self-employed) add to the stress potential.

FIREFIGHTER

Ranking: 249

Score: 110.936

Hours per Day: 11

Time Pressure: Very High

Competition: Low

Firefighters frequently work irregular or unusual hours, or remain on call throughout the night. They risk heat exhaustion, smoke inhalation, and serious injury while on the job. The state of anticipation preceding a major threat can be quite stressful in itself. Firefighters are sometimes required to spend long hours outdoors in bad weather.

FISHERMAN

Ranking:230

Score: 69.820

Hours per Day: 9

Time Pressure: Moderate

Competition: Moderate

Livelihood depends upon the size of the catch, therefore fishermen deal with the uncertainty of their trade, supply and customer demand, bad seasons, inclement weather conditions, and market price fluctuations. Although often monotonous, work can be hazardous and physically demanding. Fisherman are confined to a boat for the day and have to deal with the pressure of meeting promised quotas and selling the catch to buyers.

FLIGHT ATTENDANT

Ranking: 86

Score: 32.120

Hours per Day: 8

Time Pressure: Low-Moderate

Competition: Low

Flight attendants are subject to unscheduled delays and sometimes work erratic hours. Most of their time on the job involves contact with the public, and calls for a pleasant, professional attitude. Much of a flight attendant's stress comes from regular contact with rude or sick passengers. Flight attendants may also worry about, or even face, life-threatening situations.

FLORIST

Ranking: 5

Score: 18.806

Hours per Day: 9

Time Pressure: Moderate

Competition: Low

Florists usually are required to work heavy overtime during holiday seasons. Filling and delivering orders promptly is essential. Much of a florist's work involves direct contact with the public, which calls for good communication skills and a thorough knowledge of the product line. Because many florists run their own businesses, they face the added pressures of bookkeeping, employee management, and advertising.

FOOTBALL PLAYER (NFL)

Ranking: 242

Score: 92.799

Hours per Day: 8.5

Time Pressure: Moderate

Competition: Very High

Working in a highly competitive field, professional football players are under pressure to perform at high levels for the length of a season while avoiding injury. With little job security, players realize that poor performance, injury, and a ready surplus of talented recruits can lead to dismissal. Practices, games, and traveling schedules result in irregular hours. Players must also face frequent criticism and close public scrutiny on both a professional and and private level.

FORK-LIFT OPERATOR

Ranking: 3

Score: 18.180

Hours per Day: 9

Time Pressure: Low-Moderate

Competition: Low

Industrial truck operators are vulnerable to dangerous accidents; they must stay alert to avoid injuring themselves or others on the road. Their work can be monotonous, and operators are confined to a small cab for the duration of their shifts. Responsibility for the handling of expensive goods and equipment can also cause stress. Many industrial truck operators are required to keep detailed records of their operations.

FURNITURE UPHOLSTERER

Ranking: 36

Score: 26.269

Hours per Day: 8.5

Time Pressure: Moderate

Competition: Low

Furniture upholsterers perform tasks that can be both repetitive and highly detailed. Some must work quickly to meet production quotas. Because the majority of furniture upholsterers are self-employed, they often face the additional pressures associated with managing a small business. Upholsterers who work with fine and antique furniture have to meet exacting standards.

GARBAGE COLLECTOR

Ranking: 153

Score: 42.760

Hours per Day: 8.5

Time Pressure: Moderate

Competition: Low

Garbage collectors have to work quickly and efficiently in order to complete daily routes. Much of their work is repetitive and physically demanding, and handling garbage can expose workers to contagious diseases. Conflict between drivers and workers can be stressful, and workers have to deal with the public's lack of respect for their profession.

GEOLOGIST

Ranking: 87

Score: 32.560

Hours per Day: 9

Time Pressure: Moderate

Competition: Low

Many geologists and geophysicists divide their time between outdoor research and lab work indoors. Research frequently necessitates travel to remote and potentially stressful environments. Geological problems are often theoretical, and geologists must be precise in their calculations to successfully solve complex problems. Quality research demands self-regulation, strong motivation, and close attention to detail. Geologists or geophysicists affiliated with universities face pressure to publish academic articles of high quality.

GLAZIER

Ranking: 142

Score: 40.950

Hours per Day: 9

Time Pressure: Moderate

Competition: Low

Glaziers must stay alert when they work. They use potentially hazardous equipment, such as power tools and glass cutters, and they often stand on high ladders or scaffolds. Weather conditions can cause stress, because glaziers often work outdoors. Glaziers usually work in groups, and teamwork is essential for success. Stress can also be caused by the repetitiveness of the work, and the pressure to meet project deadlines.

GUARD

Ranking: 66

Score: 29.918

Hours per Day: 8.5

Time Pressure: Low-Moderate

Competition: Low

Guards must sometimes work late at night or during the weekend. Their work can often be lonely and monotonous, but they are expected to be prepared at all times for an emergency situation. Some guards have frequent contact with the public. Many face the possibility of managing dangerous situations. Guards are often assigned to protect valuable property or equipment, and must shoulder great responsibility.

HEATING/REFRIGERATION MECHANIC

Ranking: 73

Score: 30.544

Hours per Day: 9

Time Pressure: Moderate

Competition: Low

Heating and refrigeration mechanics are sometimes called for emergency repairs in the middle of the night. They can be required to work outdoors in bad weather conditions and must remain alert to avoid electrical shocks or torch burns. Some mechanics work from ladders or in extremely confined conditions. Because many heating and refrigeration mechanics work alone, they are expected to be self-reliant and self-motivated.

HIGHWAY PATROL OFFICER

Ranking: 240

Score: 80.651

Hours per Day: 9.5

Time Pressure: Moderate

Competition: Low

State highway patrol officers work in shifts, including graveyard hours, weekends, and holidays. They generally have heavy contact with the public, patrol a large territory, and are required to drive in even the worst weather conditions. Patrol officers face many potential hazards, such as high-speed chases and gun-toting citizens. Investigative work requires good physical stamina, close attention to detail, teamwork and personal initiative. Officers have the added stresses of handling life-threatening situations and being in the public eye.

HISTORIAN

Ranking: 56

Score: 28.419

Hours per Day: 9

Time Pressure: Low

Competition: Low

Historians perform detailed research, which often calls for long hours of concentration. Many historians balance research and teaching responsibilities. The majority of the historian's work is accomplished without supervision, under conditions demanding initiative and discipline. Historians working for universities are frequently pressured to publish original papers or books of high quality.

HOME ECONOMIST

Ranking: 34

Score: 25.979

Hours per Day: 9

Time Pressure: Moderate

Competition: Low

Irregular work hours are common for home economists. Quality research demands careful examination of details and strong personal initiative. Home economists are often pressured by deadlines. Advocating a research opinion can create considerable stress for home economists, especially if their opinion is proven false.

HOSPITAL ADMINISTRATOR

Ranking: 138

Score: 39.585

Hours per Day: 9.5

Time Pressure: Moderate

Competition: Moderate

Hospital administrators generally work erratic hours, and can be called in at any hour to handle emergency situations. Administrators are frequently under pressure to creatively manage problems of finance and personnel. Their work calls for close attention to detail, strong initiative, and the ability to manage people effectively. The work of administrators is often scrutinized by higher management. Pressure to meet deadlines can also cause considerable stress.

HOTEL MANAGER

Ranking: 161

Score: 44.840

Hours per Day: 9

Time Pressure: Moderate-High

Competition: High

Hotel managers often work evenings and weekends, or face the added pressure of staying on call to handle emergencies. They are responsible for managing staff members and for addressing customer complaints. Staff schedules, reservations, and bookkeeping call for careful attention to detail. Some hotel managers are also responsible for increasing profits through advertising or other promotions.

INDUSTRIAL DESIGNER

Ranking: 85

Score: 32.081

Hours per Day: 9

Time Pressure: Moderate

Competition: Moderate

Industrial designers are consistently under pressure to create appealing and high quality product designs in a short amount of time. With the development of new products being costly, designers have to face the possibility of financial failure. An additional stress factor is handling adverse public reaction to work.

INDUSTRIAL ENGINEER

Ranking: 97

Score: 34.545

Hours per Day: 9.5

Time Pressure: Moderate

Competition: Moderate

Industrial engineers are required to continually solve problems with a blend of information from both technical and administrative sources. Industrial engineering demands good interpersonal communication skills, self-motivation, and a talent for managing personnel. Other possible stress factors include deadline pressure and implementing innovative systems or programs.

INDUSTRIAL MACHINE REPAIRER

Ranking: 44

Score: 26.991

Hours per Day: 9.5

Time Pressure: Low-Moderate

Competition: Low

Repairers of industrial machinery are sometimes summoned in the evenings or on weekends to perform emergency repairs. They work with complex machinery under potentially hazardous conditions. Repairers are required to diagnose a great variety of problems with precision and care. Because broken machinery can be costly to stricken businesses, repairers are frequently under great pressure to work quickly.

INSURANCE AGENT

Ranking: 216

Score: 63.322

Hours per Day: 9

Time Pressure: Moderate

Competition: Very High

Insurance agents and brokers often work unusual hours to facilitate their client's schedules. Much of their work demands accurate financial calculations. Agents and brokers are constantly in contact with the public and must deal with a wide variety of personalities. Because they work in a highly competitive field, successful agents and brokers possess initiative and perseverance.

INSURANCE UNDERWRITER

Ranking: 57

Score: 28.513

Hours per Day: 9

Time Pressure: Moderate-High

Competition: Low

Insurance underwriters devote long hours to tasks requiring concentration and close attention to detail. Underwriters need to analyze large amounts of data before project deadlines expire. They must assess the potential demands of their clients with as much accuracy as possible. Bearing responsibility for decisions which can cost their employer large sums of money can also lead to stress.

IRONWORKER

Ranking: 186

Score: 50.911

Hours per Day: 9

Time Pressure: Low-Moderate

Competition: Low

Ironworkers generally work outdoors in every kind of weather. Much of their work involves large, potentially hazardous equipment. Ironworkers who construct bridges or buildings must be careful to avoid falls. Their activity demands physical stamina and cooperation between workers on a team. Ironworkers may need to seek further employment upon the completion of a major project.

JANITOR

Ranking: 2

Score: 16.320

Hours per Day: 8

Time Pressure: Low-Moderate

Competition: Low

Some janitors are required to work late at night, when buildings are quiet and free from traffic and use. Cleaning and maintaining the same areas every day can be monotonous. Janitors sometimes are forced to work in unpleasant environments, such as bathrooms or garbage rooms. Janitors may be required to handle potentially hazardous cleaning fluids and heavy tools or machines.

JEWELER

Ranking: 25

Score: 24.860

Hours per Day: 9

Time Pressure: Low-Moderate

Competition: Moderate

Jewelers need to deal with a wide variety of clients. Their work demands intense concentration and a high degree of precision. Quality jewelers work quickly and carefully with little supervision. They often must change their designs in order to satisfy customer demand. Managing, bookkeeping, and advertising skills are essential for jewelers who own their own businesses.

JOCKEY

Ranking: 236

Score: 76.331

Hours per Day: 9

Time Pressure: High

Competition: Very High

In addition to investing long hours in training, traveling, and racing, jockeys have to work under close supervision and deal with the constant pressure to win racing events. Added stresses include handling animals, which can be unpredictable, and working under close public scrutiny. As there is little job security, jockeys must remain successful and stay in top form to guarantee employment.

JUDGE (FEDERAL)

Ranking: 167

Score: 46.676

Hours per Day: 10

Time Pressure: Low-Moderate

Competition: Low

In presiding over a number of cases a day, federal judges must review the information in detail, research pertinent legal precedents, and in many situations make a decision that will determine the fate of another individual. The nature and level of their work also requires judges to have considerable contact with the press and public. Other major stress factors include making decisions that will become precedents for the lower courts to follow.

LIBRARIAN

Ranking: 9

Score: 21.400

Hours per Day: 8.5

Time Pressure: Low-Moderate

Competition: Low

Many librarians are in constant contact with the public, which can cause considerable stress. Librarians are required to work with highly detailed systems of classification and retrieval. Some librarians specialize in computer research, and face long hours of concentration at their terminal. Librarians in supervisory positions face stress from managing the staff and budget.

LITHOGRAPHER/ PHOTOENGRAVER

Ranking: 46

Score: 27.556

Hours per Day: 9

Time Pressure: Moderate

Competition: Low

Lithographers and photoengravers sometimes work late at night or during the weekend in order to meet publishing deadlines. Platemakers work with toxic chemicals and must be careful to avoid injury. Lithographers and photoengravers must be extremely precise in their drawings and measurements. Working with fine detail for long periods of time can be tiring.

LUMBERJACK

Ranking: 228

Score: 67.603

Hours per Day: 9

Time Pressure: Moderate

Competition: Low

Although their work is repetitive, lumberjacks must work both carefully and quickly in order to avoid injury and to meet quotas. The job includes working in inclement weather and with potentially dangerous machinery and high-speed power equipment. The job calls for good physical stamina and speed. Working in potentially life-threatening environments can also be stressful.

MACHINE TOOL OPERATOR

Ranking: 149

Score: 42.085

Hours per Day: 9

Time Pressure: Moderate

Competition: Low

Machine tool operators work with machinery that can cause permanent injury. Although much of their work is repetitive, operators must remain alert at all times in order to prevent an accident. Most machine tool operators spend their entire shift working with one machine in a small area. Constant attention to detail can also cause considerable stress. Most machine tool operators face pressure to meet production quotas every day.

MACHINIST

Ranking: 165

Score: 46.117

Hours per Day: 9.5

Time Pressure: Moderate

Competition: Low

Machinists use potentially dangerous power tools. Loud shop noises and loose pieces of hot metal can also be extremely hazardous. Machinists produce parts which often demand extreme precision and attention to detail. Skilled machinists work quickly, with little supervision, and can consistently meet production quotas.

MAID

Ranking: 55

Score: 28.418

Hours per Day: 7.5

Time Pressure: Low-Moderate

Competition: Low

Maids generally work irregular hours, accommodating their schedules to match those of their clients. Successful maids work quickly and efficiently. Those employed by hotels are often under heightened pressure and must deal with the public. Some maids are occasionally required to clean up unpleasant messes.

MAIL CARRIER

Ranking: 182

Score: 48.708

Hours per Day: 9

Time Pressure: Moderate

Competition: Low

Mail carriers work in shifts, sometimes beginning as early as 4 a.m. They work outdoors, even in the worst weather conditions, and sometimes must handle vicious animals. Working the same route each day can cause significant stress. Meeting the public demands an outgoing personality and the ability to listen patiently to disgruntled customers. Personal initiative and speed are essential, because most carriers work by themselves.

MARKET RESEARCH ANALYST

Ranking: 148

Score: 42.060

Hours per Day: 9

Time Pressure: Moderate-High

Competition: Very High

Market researchers enhance sales through an on-going analysis of public opinion. Accurate measurement of these opinions requires careful attention to detail. Market researchers often work with large amounts of data at once, yet they must complete projects with precision and care. Because researchers have considerable contact with the public, they should pay careful attention to their conduct.

MATHEMATICIAN

Ranking: 23

Score: 24.673

Hours per Day: 9

Time Pressure: Low

Competition: Low

Many mathematicians balance teaching and research schedules. Their work requires constant problem solving, frequently under pressure from project deadlines. Most mathematicians work alone and are required to exercise initiative and self-regulation. The academic pressures to teach, publish, and secure tenure can be very stressful.

MAYOR

Ranking: 238

Score: 77.470

Hours per Day: 9

Time Pressure: Moderate

Competition: Very High

Campaigning and attending meetings and civic and social functions result in long and irregular work days. Mayors have the added pressures of working with diverse special interest groups in formulating policy, dealing with a city council, and maintaining a positive public profile. The job requires frequent contact with the press and being closely scrutinized by the public on both a professional and personal level. The field is small and competitive, and campaigning for office is a long and often grueling process.

MECHANICAL ENGINEER

Ranking: 129

Score: 38.288

Hours per Day: 9.5

Time Pressure: Moderate

Competition: Moderate

Mechanical engineers are likely to have periods when long hours are required and deadline pressure is heavy. Lapses in analytic precision can be expensive to repair. Successful mechanical engineers possess self-discipline and strong powers of concentration. Mechanical engineers in management positions are under economic pressure to market their ideas and make difficult business decisions.

MEDICAL LABORATORY TECHNICIAN

Ranking: 19

Score: 23.748

Hours per Day: 8.5

Time Pressure: Low-Moderate

Competition: Low

Medical laboratory technicians frequently specialize in one area of research, and their duties can be repetitive. Because they work with infective specimens, accidental illness is a potential hazard. Their findings must be extremely accurate to ensure proper medical treatment of patients by the physician. Teamwork, and the ability to take orders from a medical technologist, are essential.

MEDICAL RECORDS TECHNICIAN

Ranking: 1

Score: 15.488

Hours per Day: 8.5

Time Pressure: Low-Moderate

Competition: Low

Some medical research technicians handle specific tasks, and much of their work can be repetitive. They may be required to manage other employees, or to coordinate massive research programs. Careful attention to detail is vital in order to ensure proper identification and treatment of patients. In the course of research, some technicians analyze patterns in large bodies of data.

MEDICAL SECRETARY

Ranking: 8

Score: 21.147

Hours per Day: 8

Time Pressure: Moderate

Competition: Low

Medical secretaries often perform highly repetitive tasks. They are confined to their desk all day, and their work is constantly interrupted by the telephone. They are under pressure to finish letters, memos, and transcriptions with speed and precision. Working with demanding doctors and nurses can also be stressful.

MEDICAL TECHNOLOGIST

Ranking: 60

Score: 28.910

Hours per Day: 8.5

Time Pressure: Moderate

Competition: Low

Some medical technologists work as researchers and teachers at the same time. Researchers may suffer stress from performing highly repetitive tests. Bodily specimens sent to labs are often diseased, and medical technologists must be careful to avoid contaminating themselves. Because the findings of the technologist often influence the doctor's treatment of a patient, careful attention to detail is necessary at all times.

METEOROLOGIST

Ranking: 62

Score: 29.192

Hours per Day: 9

Time Pressure: Moderate

Competition: Low

Meteorologists employed at weather stations work in shifts, including late nights and weekends. Much of their work involves research demanding close attention to detail and fine analytical skills. At small research facilities, meteorologists usually work alone and must be highly motivated and exercise self-regulation. Being in the public spotlight can also cause stress for meteorologists who work for television or radio stations.

METER READER

Ranking: 128

Score: 37.940

Hours per Day: 8.5

Time Pressure: Moderate

Competition: Low

Meter readers must deal with the monotony of their jobs and still meet daily quotas. Other stress factors include working in inclement weather conditions and facing unpleasant drivers. Good physical stamina is needed as meter readers walk most of the day.

MILITARY (COMMISSIONED OFFICER)

Ranking: 154

Score: 43.000

Hours per Day: 8

Time Pressure: Low-Moderate

Competition: Moderate

Commissioned officers must lead and train large numbers of lower-rank personnel and answer for their performance. Responsibilities include planning and participating in all-night maneuvers and strenuous training drills, which can be especially demanding during officers' training camp. Active duty combat is extremely physically and emotionally taxing, and officers are under constant pressure to prevent the loss of their lives and those of their troops. Throughout their careers members of the armed forces must also deal with the adjustments associated with frequent relocation.

MILITARY (ENLISTED PERSON)

Ranking: 154

Score: 43.000

Hours per Day: 8

Time Pressure: Low-Moderate

Competition: Low

Enlisted personnel are required to participate in strenuous training and maneuvers, which are physically demanding and often take place in inclement weather conditions. Members often work irregular hours, especially during basic training and guard duty shifts. In placing military personnel in life-threatening situations, active combat is both extremely physically and emotionally difficult.

MILITARY (WARRANT OFFICER)

Ranking: 104

Score: 35.000

Hours per Day: 8

Time Pressure: Moderate

Competition: Low

Warrant officers tend to work irregular hours, including evenings and weekends. Because they are frequently in charge of enlisted personnel, warrant officers constantly have to exhibit leadership and problem solving skills. Outdoor maneuvers frequently take place in bad weather conditions and can be hazardous. Combat duty is highly stressful and necessitates teamwork between military personnel.

MILLWRIGHT

Ranking: 196

Score: 52.807

Hours per Day: 9.5

Time Pressure: Moderate

Competition: Low

Millwrights work with a variety of potentially harmful machinery, such as torches, soldering guns, and power tools. Many millwrights work in hazardous environments, such as coal mines or factories. Millwrights must work with precision and flexibility on a variety of tasks. A facility for teamwork ensures safety and efficiency when working with unfamiliar groups. Pressure to complete projects on time can also cause stress.

MOTION PICTURE EDITOR

Ranking: 96

Score: 34.335

Hours per Day: 9

Time Pressure: High

Competition: Moderate

Motion picture editors work long and irregular hours and concentrate on a number of details for long periods of time. The job also requires working under the pressure of meeting project deadlines and dealing with criticism from directors and producers. As most editors work independently, they must continually seek new employment.

MUSEUM CURATOR

Ranking: 123

Score: 37.450

Hours per Day: 8.5

Time Pressure: Moderate

Competition: Moderate

Some curators have heavy contact with the public, teaching classes and lecturing on specialized topics. Many curators have the added responsibility of managing fund raising campaigns along with their administrative duties. Purchasing new entries for a museum's collection calls for careful attention to detail, especially an eye for authenticity. Curators generally work independently and are expected to be self-motivated and able to meet deadlines. Disagreements with the museum's board of directors concerning purchases or funding can also cause considerable stress for curators.

MUSICAL INSTRUMENT REPAIRER

Ranking: 4

Score: 18.776

Hours per Day: 9.5

Time Pressure: Low-Moderate

Competition: Low

Repairing precision instruments demands careful attention to detail. Repairers generally concentrate for long hours on a single aspect of an instrument's design. Initiative is necessary because repairers usually have little supervision. Repairers also face the possibility of seriously damaging fragile and often expensive instruments.

MUSICIAN

Ranking: 173

Score: 47.569

Hours per Day: 9

Time Pressure: Low-Moderate

Competition: High

Musicians work irregular hours, often during evenings and weekends. Some musicians split their time between performing and teaching. Long hours of practice and performance can be stressful. Musicians must possess physical stamina and an engaging stage presence to perform in front of crowds. Competing for opportunities to play can be another source of stress. Teamwork is essential for success when working in a group of any size.

NEWSCASTER

Ranking: 192

Score: 51.994

Hours per Day: 9

Time Pressure: Moderate

Competition: Very High

Radio and television newscasters work long, irregular hours, which may include evenings and weekends. Because they work in a very competitive field, successful newscasters need to project confidence and ability in order to stay on the air. Deadline pressure is a major source of stress for newscasters. Sharing their work with huge audiences can also invoke considerable pressure.

NEWS WRITER (RADIO/TV)

Ranking: 65

Score: 29.869

Hours per Day: 9

Time Pressure: High

Competition: Moderate

Broadcast news writers generally work long, erratic hours, especially when treating major stories. News writers face considerable pressure to be accurate and creative in their work. They must work effectively in groups, even when under pressure to meet rigorous deadlines. The instability of media programming occasionally forces writers to seek further employment. Some writers are also responsible for the delivery of their ideas to the public.

NUCLEAR ENGINEER

Ranking: 134

Score: 39.151

Hours per Day: 9

Time Pressure: Moderate

Competition: Moderate

Nuclear engineers work in a technically demanding and politically volatile field. They must be accurate in their calculations, and capable of concentrating for long periods of time on extremely detailed information. Since construction is very expensive, and radiation is extremely hazardous, extreme care is required to prevent mistakes at the design stage. Some nuclear engineers are also responsible for managerial and marketing tasks.

NUCLEAR PLANT DECONTAMINATION TECHNICIAN

Ranking: 185

Score: 50.226

Hours per Day: 9

Time Pressure: Moderate

Competition: Low

Nuclear plant decontamination technicians are on call at all times of the day and night for emergency services. The work requires extreme precision and alertness to minute changes in radiation levels that could preview disasters. Technicians must also deal with the pressure of facing potentially dangerous situations on a daily basis.

NURSE (LICENSED PRACTICAL)

Ranking: 179

Score: 48.000

Hours per Day: 8

Time Pressure: Low-Moderate

Competition: Low

Licensed practical nurses (LPNs) should possess skills of communication to interact well with patients. Because they frequently work with unwell people, LPNs routinely face the hazard of self-contamination. Performing medical duties and keeping accurate records both require care and precision. LPNs sometimes handle patients with bad tempers or other behavioral problems. Also stressful is the emotional aspect of seeing others in constant pain.

NURSE (REGISTERED)

Ranking: 212

Score: 62.144

Hours per Day: 8

Time Pressure: High

Competition: Low

Registered nurses work in shifts which span the entire day. Because they come into contact with a variety of diseased patients, registered nurses face the possibility of becoming sick themselves. Injections, measurements, and medical tests demand precision to avoid injuring the patient or biasing the results. Emotional resiliency is necessary to deal consistently with sick or dying patients. Handling sudden or serious emergencies can also be stressful.

NURSE'S AIDE

Ranking: 48

Score: 27.776

Hours per Day: 8

Time Pressure: Low-Moderate

Competition: Low

Nursing aides are frequently required to perform distasteful tasks, such as removing soiled linens. Their work can be repetitive and simple. Aides face the danger of contamination from unwell patients. Nursing aides must handle patients who are in pain or distress. Taking orders from nurses and doctors can also be stressful. Orderlies are routinely involved with emotional situations involving suffering or death.

OCCUPATIONAL SAFETY/HEALTH INSPECTOR

Ranking: 145

Score: 41.542

Hours per Day: 9

Time Pressure: Low-Moderate

Competition: Low

Safety and health inspectors usually work irregular hours, and they spend much of their time traveling to inspection sites. They face many of the same hazards as the workers that they investigate, such as exposure to harmful chemicals. Field research demands careful attention to detail and excellent communication skills. Self-discipline is essential, because most inspectors work without direct supervision.

OCCUPATIONAL THERAPIST

Ranking: 126

Score: 37.917

Hours per Day: 8.5

Time Pressure: Low-Moderate

Competition: Low

Occupational therapists design recovery programs which must suit the individual patient. They need to cooperate with other health professionals, and with a variety of patients. Occupational therapists sometimes face stress from working with anxious or frustrated people. Most therapists work with little supervision, and must be diligent and highly motivated.

OCEANOGRAPHER

Ranking: 113

Score: 35.928

Hours per Day: 9

Time Pressure: Moderate

Competition: Low

Oceanographers have to balance research, teaching, and administrative responsibilities. Research demands careful attention to minute details and self-motivation, and the oceanographers associated with universities are under pressure to publish articles based on this research in order to gain tenure and job security. Having to work in the ocean can also be stressful.

OFFICE MACHINE REPAIRER

Ranking: 53

Score: 28.242

Hours per Day: 9.5

Time Pressure: Low-Moderate

Competition: Low

Office machine repair demands care to avoid electrical shock and other hazards. Many repairers service a wide variety of equipment, necessitating flexibility and creativity. Many face the stress of performing repetitive and routine repairs. Office machine repairers must be precise and efficient in their work. Dealing with confused or anxious customers can be a source of tension.

OPTICIAN

Ranking: 122

Score: 37.170

Hours per Day: 8.5

Time Pressure: Moderate

Competition: Moderate

Dispensing opticians spend considerable time working with customers, instructing them on eye care and helping them to choose appropriate frames. Some dispensing opticians do their own lab work, and use small instruments to perform delicate adjustments. They must be precise in following the instructions of the optometrist. Many dispensing opticians are under pressure to sell as many frames as possible.

OPTOMETRIST

Ranking: 158

Score: 44.046

Hours per Day: 9.5

Time Pressure: Low-Moderate

Competition: Low

Optometrists affiliated with universities often shoulder teaching, research, and administrative responsibilities. Their work demands attention to minute details and the accurate diagnosis of a variety of eye problems. Like other medical professionals, optometrists work directly with patients, and sometimes encounter difficult or unfriendly people. The risk of misdiagnosing a patient's condition can also cause considerable stress.

ORTHODONTIST

Ranking: 195

Score: 52.628

Hours per Day: 9

Time Pressure: Low-Moderate

Competition: Moderate

Orthodontists need to work with speed and precision. Because some procedures can be painful, orthodontists must often placate patients under stress. Ambition is essential for most orthodontists, because they need to build a clientele and retain it. The routine difficulties of finance and personnel can also be a source of considerable stress.

OSTEOPATH

Ranking: 217

Score: 64.037

Hours per Day: 11

Time Pressure: Moderate

Competition: Moderate

Osteopaths, like many physicians, work long and irregular hours. Because they are responsible for the health of others, osteopaths are required to make accurate diagnoses, pay close attention to detail, and work with extreme precision. A lack of teamwork between osteopaths and other medical professionals can cause a great deal of tension. Dealing with a variety of patients with respect and courtesy can also be difficult.

PAINTER

Ranking: 100

Score: 34.799

Hours per Day: 8

Time Pressure: Moderate

Competition: Low

Painters have to deal with the repetitive nature of their work while still working quickly and accurately in order to meet deadlines. They must also be careful and alert when using power-tools such as torches and sanders, often while working from high scaffolds or ladders. Good physical stamina is also required.

PARALEGAL ASSISTANT

Ranking: 15

Score: 23.084

Hours per Day: 9

Time Pressure: Moderate

Competition: Low

Legal assistants sometimes work long hours of overtime under heavy deadline pressure. Their research demands close attention to detail and excellent analytical skills. Some legal assistants face stress from monotonous projects that call for little or no personal input. Often, legal assistants meet with clients and must be remain objective at all times. Faulty research can destroy a lawyers case, and get the legal assistant fired.

PAROLE OFFICER

Ranking: 38

Score: 26.463

Hours per Day: 8.5

Time Pressure: Low-Moderate

Competition: Low

Parole officers have to deal with the pressures associated with working with convicted criminals. Case loads can be large, and the work can require long and erratic hours. Officers have heavy contact with the public and have to advise on life-threatening situations.

PERSONNEL RECRUITER

Ranking: 147

Score: 41.812

Hours per Day: 10

Time Pressure: Moderate

Competition: High

Personnel recruiters must know how to handle people. Because they interview extensively and perform research on individuals, they are required to be attentive to even the smallest fact or inconsistency. Excellent communication between personnel specialists and management is a necessity to fill a position with the best candidate. Many personnel recruiters face stress from mandatory interview quotas and the possibility that an employee recommendation they make could turn out to be an absolute mistake.

PETROLEUM ENGINEER

Ranking: 47

Score: 27.636

Hours per Day: 9

Time Pressure: Moderate

Competition: Low

Some petroleum engineers are required to work at wells or derricks in all types of weather conditions. Their work calls detailed technical analysis and accurate calculation. Many petroleum engineers work with little supervision and must be self-motivated. The push to complete projects as well as to perform the necessary administrative duties on time can cause additional pressure.

PHARMACIST

Ranking: 32

Score: 25.877

Hours per Day: 10

Time Pressure: Low-Moderate

Competition: Low

Some pharmacists are required to work late-night, weekend and holiday shifts. Many pharmacists are confined behind a counter for the duration of their shifts. Because they work with medicines, pharmacists are under pressure to make accurate measurements and follow prescription orders to the letter. Other possible stress factors include advising physicians on prescriptions and the possibility of making a life-threatening mistake when filling out a prescription.

PHILOSOPHER

Ranking: 72

Score: 30.497

Hours per Day: 9

Time Pressure: Low

Competition: Moderate

Most philosophers are employed by universities and thus have to balance the demands of teaching, researching and writing, and handling administrative tasks. The work demands close attention to theoretical details and self-discipline for writing. University philosophers also have to speak to large classes of students regularly and have to deal with the pressures associated with publishing and working for tenure.

PHOTOGRAPHER

Ranking: 124

Score: 37.613

Hours per Day: 9

Time Pressure: Moderate

Competition: High

Many still photographers work highly irregular hours, sometimes shooting at dawn and then again in the middle of the night. Because they use intricate cameras and developing equipment, photographers are required to work with precision. Setting up a photograph demands patience and careful attention to detail. Handling unpleasant personalities, deadlines, and working in a highly competitive field are other possible stress factors.

PHOTOGRAPHIC PROCESS WORKER

Ranking: 13

Score: 22.450

Hours per Day: 9

Time Pressure: Moderate

Competition: Low

Photographic process workers are required to work a lot of overtime following major holidays. Workers at larger, fast-paced operations perform highly repetitive tasks and must work in a small area throughout a shift. Employees at smaller facilities are responsible for more complex tasks that call for a great deal of accuracy and attention to detail. Additional stress is caused in having to meet production quotas.

PHOTOJOURNALIST

Ranking: 233

Score: 73.013

Hours per Day: 9

Time Pressure: High

Competition: Very High

Because news stories break at all times of the day, photojournalists must be ready to work highly erratic hours. Work in this highly competitive field requires facing the constant pressure of meeting deadlines and dealing with criticism. As many photojournalists work as free-lancers, they have to handle the added business stresses of selling their pictures. The job is extremely hazardous for those who work in war zones or other turbulent areas of the world.

PHYSICAL THERAPIST

Ranking: 159

Score: 44.237

Hours per Day: 8.5

Time Pressure: Low-Moderate

Competition: Low

Physical therapists must deal with the pressures of aiding a number of physically and mentally impaired patients a day. Work may additionally involve supervising assistants in carrying out treatment plans. Independent physical therapists are frequently required to work evening and weekend hours, depending on the needs of their patients. Additional stresses include assisting difficult patients and dealing with staff conflicts.

PHYSICIAN (GENERAL PRACTICE)

Ranking: 217

Score: 64.037

Hours per Day: 11

Time Pressure: Moderate-High

Competition: Low

Physicians work long and irregular hours, often during evenings and weekends. They are required to make important decisions quickly, and to communicate effectively with sick or nervous patients. Dealing with unwell people every day can be emotionally trying. The responsibility for a patient's health, and the risk of worsening that person's pain, can also cause stress.

PHYSICIAN ASSISTANT

Ranking: 225

Score: 65.835

Hours per Day: 8.5

Time Pressure: Moderate-High

Competition: Moderate

Physician assistants have to deal with the pressure of working with patients, most of whom are generally afraid of medical personnel. Those assisting doctors in surgery must work quickly and efficiently, and they are often confronted with the anxiety of life and death situations. The job often requires working irregular hours, including evenings and weekends.

PHYSICIST

Ranking: 68

Score: 30.314

Hours per Day: 9

Time Pressure: Low

Competition: Low

Physicists affiliated with universities have to balance the demands of teaching and research. Because of the highly theoretical nature of their work, physics research demands great attention to detail, and physicists face the pressures of researching and developing new hypotheses. Additional stress factors include meeting project deadlines and, for university physicists, publishing in order to gain tenure.

PHYSIOLOGIST

Ranking: 80

Score: 31.437

Hours per Day: 9

Time Pressure: Low

Competition: Low

Quality physiological research demands critical attention to detail for long periods of time and constant personal initiative. Those associated with universities are often under pressure to carry out significant research and to publish in order to gain tenure. While most researchers employed in the private sector work regular hours, university physiologists have to balance the demands of teaching, researching, and carrying out administrative duties.

PIANO TUNER

Ranking: 12

Score: 22.297

Hours per Day: 9.5

Time Pressure: Low-Moderate

Competition: Low

Piano tuning requires intense concentration, often for long periods of time. Tuners must analyze instruments in detail and make extremely accurate adjustments to bring the instrument back to its proper sound. Most piano tuners work independently and thus have to handle the pressures associated with running a business.

PLASTERER

Ranking: 125

Score: 37.630

Hours per Day: 9

Time Pressure: Moderate

Competition: Low

Although work can be repetitive, plasterers have to work both precisely and quickly in order to do quality work within project deadlines. Additional stress comes from having to work in potentially dangerous situations, as on high scaffolds and ladders. Plasterers who work on more creative projects have to be especially attentive to intricacies of design.

PLUMBER

Ranking: 130

Score: 38.518

Hours per Day: 9

Time Pressure: Moderate

Competition: Low

Plumbers have to be available at all times of the day and night in order to make emergency repairs. Work includes using potentially dangerous tools, such as torches and drills, and working in cramped spaces and outdoors in inclement weather. Sewer gas explosions and burns from hot pipes are some of the possible hazards plumbers face. Other possible stress factors include handling disgruntled customers and meeting project deadlines.

PODIATRIST

Ranking: 176

Score: 47.717

Hours per Day: 10

Time Pressure: Low-Moderate

Competition: Low

Podiatrists are under pressure to make a number of accurate diagnoses a day. Other stress factors include handling a potentially large flow of patients, many of whom may be in great pain, and dealing with concerns about malpractice. Many podiatrists work independently and thus face the added strains associated with running a business.

POLICE OFFICER

Ranking: 243

Score: 93.893

Hours per Day: 9.5

Time Pressure: Moderate

Competition: Low

Police officers face potentially life-threatening situations daily. Shifts can be long and strenuous, especially when dealing with emergency situations, and work requires a great deal of physical and emotional stamina. Other possible stress factors include interacting with the public and providing medical attention to injured parties.

POLITICAL SCIENTIST

Ranking: 106

Score: 35.239

Hours per Day: 9

Time Pressure: Moderate

Competition: High

Political scientists affiliated with universities have to balance the demands of teaching, research, student advising, and administration. Having to lecture to large groups of students on a regular basis can also be stressful. Additional pressures include carrying out significant research projects and publishing in order to gain tenure.

POSTAL INSPECTOR

Ranking: 63

Score: 29.292

Hours per Day: 9.5

Time Pressure: Moderate

Competition: Low

Postal inspectors work highly irregular hours, sometimes investigating incidents in the middle of the night. Criminal investigations can be hazardous, as inspectors are often involved in raids against those breaking postal laws. An additional stress factor is having to complete investigations within deadlines.

PRECISION ASSEMBLER

Ranking: 74

Score: 30.907

Hours per Day: 8.5

Time Pressure: Moderate

Competition: Low

Precision manufacturing assembly demands both accuracy and speed because of the detailed nature of its products. Excellent coordination and teamwork are essential for many precision assemblers. The tasks are highly repetitive, and workers are confined to one area throughout their shifts. In addition, most precision manufacturing assemblers are required to meet daily quotas.

PRESIDENT (U.S.)

Ranking: 250

Score: 176.550

Hours per Day: 13

Time Pressure: High

Competition: Very High

As Commander-in-Chief, the President is considered on duty 24 hours a day and holds the power and responsibility to formulate and direct military strategy. As with members of the Senate and Congress, the President works long days in order to carry out the executive powers voted him, including formulating policy and working with his aides, speaking at civic functions and fund raisers, and conferring with foreign officials and colleagues. The President, traveling extensively, is constantly under the unique pressure involved with his duties. Also, there is the insistent public scrutiny on both personal and professional levels.

PROTESTANT MINISTER

Ranking: 146

Score: 41.768

Hours per Day: 10.5

Time Pressure: Low-Moderate

Competition: Moderate

Protestant ministers usually work irregular hours, and are prepared at all times to assist others in an emergency. Dealing with troubled or desperate people can cause considerable stress. Ministers of large congregations are often responsible for handling matters of finance and personnel. Ministers must be confident and highly motivated. Being in the public spotlight can be another source of stress.

PSYCHIATRIST

Ranking: 211

Score: 61.313

Hours per Day: 11

Time Pressure: Low-Moderate

Competition: Moderate

Psychiatrists must concentrate for long periods of time and handle the mental and emotional pressures associated with helping others with emotional problems. Since they work very intensely with their patients, psychiatrist must deal with the hazards of becoming too involved in a crisis and losing objectivity. Psychiatrists also often work irregular hours, tailoring their work schedules around patient needs. Other stress factors include becoming involved in patient suicide attempts and handling the responsibility of instructing individuals on important personal matters.

PSYCHOLOGIST

Ranking: 184

Score: 50.017

Hours per Day: 9

Time Pressure: Moderate

Competition: Moderate

Psychologists have to deal with the pressures associated with helping clients with personal problems. In accommodating patient schedules, many psychologists work erratic hours, including evening and weekends. School psychologists have to handle the demands of teaching, research, and counseling. Other stress factors include dealing with a client's slow progress and handling patient suicide attempts.

PUBLIC RELATIONS EXECUTIVE

Ranking: 239

Score: 78.523

Hours per Day: 9

Time Pressure: High

Competition: Very High

Some public relations specialists are required to attend banquets to make speeches and presentations in the evening and on weekends. Because public relations is a highly competitive field, specialists are often under pressure to work quickly and creatively to meet deadlines. Public relations specialists sometimes lose their jobs for advocating programs that fail. Many public relations specialists face the added pressures of supervising assistants and other office workers.

PUBLICATION EDITOR

Ranking: 108

Score: 35.400

Hours per Day: 9

Time Pressure: High

Competition: High

Editors often work long or irregular hours, usually under pressure to meet deadlines. Their work calls for excellent writing skills, and a sensitivity to the demands of style and sense. Successful editors are well disciplined and able to manage writers and editorial assistants. Some editors also write articles for publication.

PURCHASING AGENT

Ranking: 58

Score: 28.856

Hours per Day: 9

Time Pressure: High

Competition: Moderate

Purchasing agents must often work with large amounts of detailed information in making quick decisions. Because most agents face a variety of choices, they are required to make extensive contacts with sellers and judge the sellers' operations. They also have to work quickly in order to meet deadlines.

RABBI

Ranking: 180

Score: 48.294

Hours per Day: 10.5

Time Pressure: Moderate

Competition: Low

Rabbis, like most clergy, have to be available at all times of the day and night in order to quickly administer to the sick or help in other emergencies. Work requires instructing individuals, appearing in front of large congregations, conducting research, and teaching groups of students. Rabbis have a great deal of contact with the public and the added pressures of being under close public scrutiny on both a professional and personal level.

RACE CAR DRIVER (INDY CLASS)

Ranking: 247

Score: 101.775

Hours per Day: 9

Time Pressure: Moderate

Competition: Very High

Race car drivers work highly erratic hours due to travel schedules, practices and race times. A race car driver's life depends on the stability of his automobile and his own driving skills and the skills of his fellow racers. The work is extremely hazardous; a single wrong turn can result in a career-ending injury, or death. Other possible stress factors for race car drivers include working in an extremely competitive field, being in the public spotlight and lack of teamwork with a pit crew.

RAILROAD CONDUCTOR

Ranking: 110

Score: 35.409

Hours per Day: 10

Time Pressure: Moderate

Competition: Low

Although their work is monotonous, railroad conductors are under pressure to work both quickly and efficiently in keeping trains running both safely and on time. As trains run at all hours of the day and night, work hours are often long and erratic. In addition, conductors occasionally have to confront unruly passengers.

REAL ESTATE AGENT

Ranking: 234

Score: 73.063

Hours per Day: 9.5

Time Pressure: High

Competition: Very High

Real estate agents and brokers generally work long, erratic hours, spending much of their time outside the office, showing properties to clients. Because they work one-on-one with customers, they are required to give close attention to the details of a property and a client's needs. Agents and brokers must be extremely independent and able to handle sales quotas and deadline pressures. Because they work in an extremely competitive field, successful agents and brokers are expert salespersons.

RECEPTIONIST

Ranking: 54

Score: 28.369

Hours per Day: 8

Time Pressure: Low-Moderate

Competition: Low

Handling the monotony of answering phones and greeting the public can become strenuous for receptionists. They are usually confined to a desk throughout the workday and are required to be pleasant to an often demanding public. Scheduling appointments and taking phone messages demand close attention to detail. Receptionists have to interact effectively with managers and other staff personnel. Constantly being viewed by the public can also cause stress.

RECREATION WORKER

Ranking: 64

Score: 29.638

Hours per Day: 8.5

Time Pressure: Low-Moderate

Competition: Low

Evening and weekend activities generally give recreation workers erratic hours. Many recreation workers act as group leaders and must have a creative working knowledge of what they teach. Recreation workers sometimes work in groups and are required to interact effectively to complete a program. Because they have a high degree of public contact and often fill leadership roles, their jobs can be stressful.

REPORTER

Ranking: 223

Score: 65.269

Hours per Day: 9

Time Pressure: High

Competition: Very High

Reporters work highly irregular hours, often covering stories that break in the middle of the night. Investigative reporting demands an assertive personality and extreme attention to detail. Supervision is at a minimum when reporters are working on a story so self-motivation is mandatory. Deadlines can be a major cause of stress for reporters. Those who are well known face the added pressures of public scrutiny. Misrepresentation, or similar mistakes can ruin a reporter's career. One of the most stressful factors is the strictly enforced deadlines for reporting timely news events.

RESPIRATORY THERAPIST

Ranking: 133

Score: 38.970

Hours per Day: 8.5

Time Pressure: Moderate

Competition: Low

Some respiratory therapists are required to work late night and weekend shifts because hospitals run around the clock. Much of their work entails emergency treatment of patients, and respiratory therapists must move with speed and precision to save lives. Lack of teamwork between respiratory therapists and other medical personnel can cost a patient's life.

ROOFER

Ranking: 166

Score: 46.552

Hours per Day: 8.5

Time Pressure: Low-Moderate

Competition: Low

Roofers have to remain alert to avoid burns from sealing compounds and cuts from sharp tools. Their work is hazardous, especially when working on slanted roofs. Parts of their job can become monotonous and they are required to work outdoors in all weather conditions. Stamina and teamwork are essential for success on roofing projects. Most roofers work without ropes or supports and face the constant threat of falling and breaking a neck, or worse.

ROUSTABOUT

Ranking: 224

Score: 65.548

Hours per Day: 10

Time Pressure: Moderate

Competition: Low

Roustabouts generally work in shifts, sometimes alternating between day and night hours. Most of their work is highly repetitive and necessitates excellent stamina. Because they usually work with large, high-powered machinery, roustabouts must remain alert to avoid serious injuries. Working in stressful weather conditions is fairly common in this profession. On most jobs, lack of teamwork can cause considerable stress, and endanger the lives of a work crew.

SALES REPRESENTATIVE (WHOLESALE)

Ranking: 202

Score: 55.108

Hours per Day: 9.5

Time Pressure: Moderate-High

Competition: Very High

Wholesale trade sales representatives generally work long, erratic hours. Working with large amounts of highly detailed product information can be stressful. Sales representatives spend the majority of their time making sales contacts and attempting to meet quotas. Wholesale trade is very competitive and sales representatives have to be independent and display a very shrewd, outgoing personality.

SALESPERSON (RETAIL)

Ranking: 102

Score: 34.851

Hours per Day: 8

Time Pressure: Low-Moderate

Competition: Moderate

Many retail salespeople work evening and weekend hours. The duties of a salesperson can easily become monotonous and they are required to spend considerable time on their feet. Handling irate or indecisive customers is a major stress factor for salespeople. Because many salespeople work on commission, they face stiff competition from other stores and from fellow employees. Meeting sales quotas is another important stress factor for salespeople.

SCHOOL PRINCIPAL

Ranking: 191

Score: 51.718

Hours per Day: 9.5

Time Pressure: Moderate

Competition: Low

School principals are required to attend board meetings, after school conferences, and other evening and weekend activities. Some principals teach classes and have the added responsibilities of grading papers and making lesson plans. The administrative duties of a school principal, such as analyzing budgets, evaluating teachers and other employees, and working with the school board, demand careful attention to detail. Princi-

pals also face stress from deadlines, special interest groups, and from being in the public eye.

SEAMAN

Ranking: 190

Score: 51.282

Hours per Day: 10

Time Pressure: Moderate-High

Competition: Low

Seamen generally work 2 four-hour shifts, day or night, in a 24-hour period, with 8 hours rest between work details. Seamen work in even the worst weather conditions, sometimes alternating from hot boiler rooms to frozen decks. Much of a seaman's duties can be highly repetitive. High winds, weather conditions and other factors make this position fairly hazardous. Working quickly and efficiently with other crew members is essential for safety.

SECRETARY

Ranking: 95

Score: 34.238

Hours per Day: 8

Time Pressure: High

Competition: Moderate

Some secretaries are required to put in heavy overtime hours. Their tasks can quickly become repetitive and they are usually confined behind a desk all day. Typing, filing, and other duties call for speed and accuracy. Many secretaries have heavy contact with the public and must have excellent communication skills. Quality secretaries work efficiently and complete projects on time.

SET DESIGNER

Ranking: 108

Score: 35.400

Hours per Day: 9

Time Pressure: Moderate

Competition: Moderate

Set designers may be required to work late evening and weekend hours. They must communicate effectively with directors and other staff to produce the right result. Their work often calls for delicate artistic skills and fine attention to detail. Deadline and creative pressures can cause significant stress for set designers. Some set designers also are responsible for managing their assistants.

SEWAGE PLANT OPERATOR

Ranking: 111

Score: 35.565

Hours per Day: 9

Time Pressure: Low-Moderate

Competition: Low

Sewage plant operators work in shifts, including late nights, weekends, and holidays. Emergency situations can call for long overtime hours. Sewage plant operators may be exposed to chlorine gas, or other hazardous substances. They work both indoors and out, even in bad weather conditions. Measuring gauges and analyzing data require close scrutiny of detailed information.

SHEET METAL WORKER

Ranking: 160

Score: 44.752

Hours per Day: 8.5

Average Work Week: 43.66

Time Pressure: Low-Moderate

Competition: Low

Sheet metal workers use a variety of potentially hazardous equipment, such as chain saws, presses, and other power-tools. They sometimes work high above the ground on ladders or scaffolds and must remain alert to avoid injury. Precision is required for building and installing sheet metal. Completing projects on time can also cause stress for sheet metal workers.

SHIPPING/RECEIVING CLERK

Ranking: 69

Score: 30.352

Hours per Day: 8.5

Time Pressure: High

Competition: Low

Shipping and receiving clerks in some industries work late-night or weekend hours. They often work with large, potentially hazardous machinery, such as fork-lifts. Much of their work can be monotonous and they generally spend long hours on their feet. Accuracy is essential for recording shipping and receiving documents. Shipping clerks are usually under pressure to work quickly to keep up with deadlines.

SHOEMAKER/REPAIRER

Ranking: 75

Score: 30.929

Hours per Day: 8.5

Time Pressure: Moderate-High

Competition: Low

Shoe repairers often work with sharp tools and must be careful to avoid injury. Doing repetitive tasks in cramped working conditions can cause considerable stress. Many repairers have heavy contact with the public and must deal with unpleasant personalities. Because many shoe repairers own their own businesses, strong personal drive and managerial skills are essential for success. Shoe repairers have to work quickly to meet deadlines and satisfy their customers.

SINGER

Ranking: 208

Score: 58.631

Hours per Day: 9

Time Pressure: Low-Moderate

Competition: Very High

Performances and rehearsals generally require singers to work highly erratic hours. Good physical stamina is essential and singers have a high degree of public contact. Singers who write their own songs can face considerable creative pressure. Lack of teamwork between singers and musicians can easily ruin a performance. Singers also face the added stresses of working in a competitive field and being in the public spotlight.

SOCIAL WORKER

Ranking: 174

Score: 47.633

Hours per Day: 8.5

Time Pressure: Moderate-High

Competition: Low

Social workers sometimes have to balance their schedules around their client's needs. There is a high degree of employee burn-out in social work. Their work demands a great deal of emotional stamina, because they are required to involve themselves in their client's problems and still remain objective. Social workers counsel clients, and interact heavily with other professionals. Some social workers face the added stress of time constraints and counseling quotas.

SOCIOLOGIST

Ranking: 93

Score: 34.103

Hours per Day: 9

Time Pressure: Moderate

Competition: Low

Sociologists have to balance teaching, research and administrative duties. Some research projects require long hours of heavy contact with the public. Quality research demands fine attention to detail and strong personal initiative. Teaching duties can require a sociologist to lecture to hundreds of students at one time. Universities often demand that sociologists write and publish several research articles before they are given tenure.

SOFTWARE ENGINEER

Ranking: 27

Score: 25.000

Hours per Day: 10

Time Pressure: Moderate

Competition: Moderate

Software engineers are under the unique pressure of combining creativity with analytic skills. Designing and developing large software systems in a fast-changing and rapidly growing industry, software engineers must keep current by continually expanding upon their educational background.

SPEECH PATHOLOGIST

Ranking: 99

Score: 34.757

Hours per Day: 8.5

Time Pressure: Low-Moderate

Competition: Low

Speech pathologists must have good communication skills to instruct patients and consult with other medical professionals effectively. Because they sometimes work with technical equipment, precision is required. Diagnosing a patient's condition and determining a treatment plan demands extreme attention to detail. An added stress for speech pathologists is the slow rate at which many patients progress.

SPORTS INSTRUCTOR

Ranking: 114

Score: 35.989

Hours per Day: 8.5

Time Pressure: Low-Moderate

Competition: Low

Evening and weekend classes often require sports instructors to work irregular hours. Some sports are played outdoors, even in bad weather conditions. Instructors should have good physical stamina and the ability to lead groups of students. Because they work with little supervision, sports instructors have to be self-reliant and capable of handling injuries or other emergency situations.

STATIONARY ENGINEER

Ranking: 150

Score: 42.448

Hours per Day: 9

Time Pressure: Moderate

Competition: Low

Stationary engineers can be called in during the night to make emergency repairs on equipment. They must remain alert to avoid electrical shocks, burns and other hazards of working with powerful equipment. Because they generally work in hot, dusty rooms, the job requires significant physical stamina. Reading gauges, analyzing equipment, and keeping records of daily activities call for close attention to detail.

STATISTICIAN

Ranking: 39

Score: 27.975

Hours per Day: 9

Time Pressure: Moderate

Competition: Low

Statisticians have to regularly analyze and tabulate large amounts of detailed information, often for extended periods of time. Work requires performing a number of tasks, including gathering information, designing surveys, and computing statistics for projects. Those affiliated with universities are under pressure to carry out research projects and publish in order to gain tenure and job security. Other stress factors include traveling to gather information and dealing with individuals in preparing and conducting surveys.

STENOGRAPHER/COURT REPORTER

Ranking: 91

Score: 33.132

Hours per Day: 8

Time Pressure: High

Competition: Low

The repetitive nature of their work can cause significant stress for stenographers. Most stenographers are confined to a desk for the majority of their workday. Taking dictation and transcribing notes calls for great accuracy and precision. They must work quickly and efficiently to complete projects on time. Some stenographers have the added responsibilities of answering phones, filing, and typing.

STEVEDORE

Ranking: 188

Score: 51.217

Hours per Day: 8

Time Pressure: High

Competition: Low

Stevedores generally work in shifts, including evenings, weekends, and holidays. Working with heavy machinery such as cranes and fork-lifts can be hazardous. Outdoor work, even in bad weather, is common for stevedores and good physical stamina is essential. Some duties assigned to stevedores can become monotonous. Teamwork between crew members is a necessity to insure a safe, efficient workday. Deadlines can also create stress for stevedores.

STOCKBROKER

Ranking: 231

Score: 71.656

Hours per Day: 9.5

Time Pressure: High

Competition: Very High

Stockbrokers generally work irregular hours, including evenings and weekends. Some brokers are responsible for advising their clients on sales and purchases. Keeping abreast of the stock market requires careful, up-to-the-minute scrutiny of trading and market trends. Brokers usually handle several accounts at one time and have to communicate effectively with their clients. Successful stockbrokers work quickly, analyze large amounts of data at one time, have a keen selling

ability and are able to meet sales quotas and deadlines.

SURGEON

Ranking: 245

Score: 99.463

Hours per Day: 11

Time Pressure: Moderate

Competition: High

Surgeons are sometimes required to operate at odd hours. Many operations take several hours to complete and demand intense concentration. Surgeons face the threat of self-contamination during operations or while examining patients. Operating calls for extreme precision and attention to detail. Because they often deal with life-threatening situations, surgeons must make quick decisions and communicate effectively with nurses and assistants. Rising malpractice insurance costs are a major cause of stress for many surgeons.

SURVEYOR

Ranking: 168

Score: 46.709

Hours per Day: 9

Time Pressure: Moderate

Competition: Low

Surveyors generally work outdoors, sometimes in bad weather conditions. Because they work with highly detailed information, their measurements and calculations must be extremely precise. Lack of teamwork between surveyors and other building professionals can destroy a project. Since their work is generally the first part of any construction project, surveyors are often under pressure to complete projects on schedule.

SYMPHONY CONDUCTOR

Ranking: 213

Score: 63.056

Hours per Day: 9

Time Pressure: Moderate

Competition: Very High

Symphony conductors generally work long, highly irregular hours, dividing their time between rehearsals, writing time, and supervisory activities. This is a high-stress position that demands extreme attention to detail, precise communication with the orchestra, and the ability to meet deadlines and handle the pressures of being in the public spotlight. Competition within the field is intense, and mistakes by musicians during a performance can cause considerable stress for conductors.

TAX EXAMINER/COLLECTOR

Ranking: 101

Score: 34.805

Hours per Day: 9

Time Pressure: Moderate

Competition: Low

Some tax examiners and collectors are required to work odd hours, sometimes waiting until businesses close for the day to examine financial records. Because this position demands intense concentration on detailed information, mental stamina is a must. Occasionally, the outcome of a tax examination will determine the financial future of a business or individual; thus, calculations by examiners have to be precise. Deadline pressure is common in this field.

TAXI DRIVER

Ranking: 246

Score: 100.491

Hours per Day: 9.5

Time Pressure: Moderate

Competition: Moderate

Taxi drivers generally work highly erratic hours, including late-nights, evenings, and weekends. Their safety depends on the stability of their automobile and their driving skills. Because taxi drivers are frequently in a rush to please their customers, driving in traffic, especially in major cities, is quite dangerous. They are confined to their vehicle all day and drive in bad weather conditions. Handling obnoxious or cheap customers can cause considerable stress for taxi drivers.

TEACHER

Ranking: 187

Score: 51.003

Hours per Day: 9

Time Pressure: Moderate-High

Competition: Low

Instructing students can cause considerable stress for teachers. Their work is physically and emotionally exhausting and calls for good physical stamina. Teachers must observe students and their work very closely. Working with parents, administrative personnel, and other teachers can be a significant stress factor. Teachers should be self-

motivated, creative, and able to handle public scrutiny.

TEACHER'S AIDE

Ranking: 37

Score: 26.288

Hours per Day: 8.5

Time Pressure: Low-Moderate

Competition: Low

Many teacher's aides instruct students in small groups or in front of the entire class. Because their duties vary in each school district, some teacher's aides have to perform mundane tasks such as grading papers, keeping attendance, typing, and filing. Working with children is physically and emotionally draining. Lack of teamwork between a teacher and teacher's aide can be a major stress factor for everyone in the classroom.

TECHNICAL WRITER

Ranking: 119

Score: 36.506

Hours per Day: 9

Time Pressure: Moderate-High

Competition: Moderate

Technical writers must consistently be attentive to details. Successful technical writers are self-disciplined and able to work effectively with specialized personnel. Those employed in advertising or working for publications face high-stress deadlines and creative pressures. Many copy writers have the added responsibility of selling their ideas to management personnel. Deadlines can be a major stress factor for both types of writers.

TELEPHONE INSTALLER/ REPAIRER

Ranking: 51

Score: 28.164

Hours per Day: 9.5

Time Pressure: Low-Moderate

Competition: Low

Telephone installers and repairers sometimes have to make emergency repairs at odd hours of the day or night. Some installers and repairers work near electrical equipment and must be alert to avoid shocks or other hazards. Cutting, splicing, and laying telephone lines demands precision. Repairers sometimes are required to face irritated customers. Speed is essential for installers and repairers.

TELEPHONE OPERATOR

Ranking: 45

Score: 26.993

Hours per Day: 8

Time Pressure: Moderate

Competition: Low

Telephone operators work in shifts, including late nights, weekends and holidays. Their work is extremely repetitive, and demands considerable speed in operating the equipment. They are confined to a console for the duration of their shift and have to consistently be pleasant with the public. Productivity is highly supervised and job performance evaluated on a regular basis.

TICKET AGENT

Ranking: 115

Score: 36.195

Hours per Day: 8

Time Pressure: Moderate-High

Competition: Low

Some reservation and ticket agents are required to work late night and weekend hours because many transportation companies operate 24 hours a day. Overtime work is common during holiday seasons. Agents must communicate effectively because their job involves constant public contact. Filling out tickets can be repetitive and agents generally remain at a phone or counter throughout their shifts. Handling irate customers can cause significant stress. The importance of speed and accuracy are other possible stress factors.

TOOL-AND-DIE MAKER

Ranking: 137

Score: 39.496

Hours per Day: 10

Time Pressure: Low-Moderate

Competition: Low

Tool-and-die makers generally work in shifts, and sometimes have to work overtime to meet production quotas. Because they work around powerful, high-speed machinery, they must be alert to avoid pieces of flying metal and other hazards. Their work demands precision workmanship, speed, and long hours of concentration on detailed material. Tool-and-die makers generally work in one small area throughout their shift and have to be on their feet most of the time.

TRAVEL AGENT

Ranking: 198

Score: 52.826

Hours per Day: 8

Time Pressure: Moderate

Competition: Very High

Some travel agents work erratic hours, balancing their schedules around their client's needs. Because they generally work on a commission basis, travel agents walk a fine line between being travel planners and salespeople. Analyzing travel schedules, fares, and other data demands close scrutiny. They have to handle dissatisfied or obnoxious customers with tact and diplomacy. Another major stress factor for travel agents is the competitive nature of the business.

TRUCK DRIVER

Ranking: 164

Score: 45.990

Hours per Day: 9.5

Time Pressure: Moderate

Competition: Low

Truck drivers work highly irregular hours, often driving in the middle of the night. Driving in bad weather can create considerable hazards for truck drivers. Good physical stamina is important for drivers making long hauls. Other stress factors include the repetitive nature of the work, and confinement to a cab for extended periods of time. Truck drivers, especially those who are self-employed, often face the added pressures of tight schedules and small profit margins.

TYPIST/WORD PROCESSOR

Ranking: 21

Score: 24.096

Hours per Day: 8

Time Pressure: Moderate

Competition: Low

The highly repetitive nature of their responsibilities can create considerable stress for typists and word processors. They are confined at a typewriter or console throughout the workday. Accuracy and close attention to detail are essential. Typists or word processors who cannot work quickly under deadline pressure frequently lose their jobs.

UNDERTAKER

Ranking: 169

Score: 46.962

Hours per Day: 10

Time Pressure: Moderate

Competition: Low

Undertakers generally work irregular hours, depending on daily workloads. Preparing a body for funeral arrangements and burial demands good physical stamina and a great deal of objectivity. Working with dead bodies can be hazardous because of communicable diseases. Undertakers have considerable contact with the public and have to be compassionate to grieving relatives. Completing projects on time can be highly stressful for workers in this profession.

URBAN/REGIONAL PLANNER

Ranking: 136

Score: 39.296

Hours per Day: 9

Time Pressure: Moderate

Competition: Moderate

Urban or regional planners are sometimes required to attend evening or weekend board meetings and civic activities. Their research involves analyzing large amounts of detailed data. Many planners have heavy contact with the public and face the stresses of public speaking. Planners work with little supervision and are frequently under pressure to complete their research on time. Selling a potentially risky idea to a community can create considerable stress.

VENDING MACHINE REPAIRER

Ranking: 16

Score: 23.470

Hours per Day: 9.5

Time Pressure: Low-Moderate

Competition: Low

Vending machine repairers often work irregular hours, sometimes on-call for late-night repairs. Because they work with heavy, electrical machinery, electrical shocks and cuts are some potential hazards. Although repairers can face a wide array of problems, many techniques can become monotonous. Generally, repairers work independently and self-reliance and self-motivation are essential.

VETERINARIAN

Ranking: 176

Score: 47.717

Hours per Day: 10

Time Pressure: Low-Moderate

Competition: Low

Veterinarians, especially those who work in rural areas, work irregular hours because of emergencies that may occur in the middle of the night. Because they frequently work with diseased animals, they run the risk of being contaminated. Operations call for good physical stamina, precision with surgical instruments, and a keen eye for detail. Most veterinarians are frequently in the public eye and face the added stresses of working in life-threatening situations.

VOCATIONAL COUNSELOR

Ranking: 59

Score: 28.890

Hours per Day: 8.5

Time Pressure: Low-Moderate

Competition: Low

Employment counselors are sometimes required to work irregular hours or overtime, especially during recruiting periods. Successful counselors are able to interact effectively with a wide variety of personalities. They also must be sympathetic and patient enough to examine unique problems in detail. Dealing honestly with a client's real possibilities and limitations can be somewhat stressful.

WAITER/WAITRESS

Ranking: 61

Score: 28.944

Hours per Day: 7.5

Time Pressure: Moderate

Competition: Low

Some waiters and waitresses work late night and weekend shifts. Their work can be monotonous and calls for good physical stamina because they spend all of their shift running around on their feet. Waiting on rude or angry customers is a major stress factor for waiters and waitresses. Waiters and waitresses have to work quickly and communicate efficiently with cooks, busboys, and management.

WELDER

Ranking: 175

Score: 47.660

Hours per Day: 9

Time Pressure: Moderate

Competition: Low

Welding torches and gas canisters are extremely hazardous and welders have to be alert at all times to avoid burns, explosions, or eye damage. Much of their work is repetitive, but demands precision and close attention to detail. They often work outdoors, sometimes from great heights. Speed and physical stamina are essential. As in most construction jobs, deadline pressure is common.

ZOOLOGIST

Ranking: 112

Score: 35.672

Hours per Day: 10

Time Pressure: Moderate

Competition: Low

Many zoologists must budget their time between research, teaching, and administrative duties. Quality research demands strong self-initiative and careful scrutiny of details. Research deadlines can be stressful for zoologists. Those employed by universities face the added pressures of writing and publishing research articles to gain tenure. Also, teaching may require speaking before hundreds of students at one time.

Extras, Perks and Amenities

Perks just keep getting harder to find. There are jobs, however, at which perks are a part of the compensation package. The jobs reviewed in this chapter are confined to those.

In healthy, happy postwar America, when the Man in the Grey Flannel Suit was the career ideal to strive for, the key to the executive washroom stood as the symbol of success — the magical instrument that unlocked a secret door, behind which a select few undertook decisions that moved and shook America. Gaining entrance to that chamber was a rite of passage signifying one's advancement to elite status.

By the go-go '80s, perks had become more diverse, more expansive, and a little more fun. Condos in Vail, membership in exclusive country clubs, catered lunches, chauffered limos, fully stocked bars, helicopters to the Hamptons, villas in Mexico — these were the goodies at the top of the corporate heap, the trickle-up blessings of Reaganomics. In time, those perks took on a life of their own. What began as symbols of success, as motivation on the climb up the corporate ladder, became things to be expected of the potential employer. What, no luxury box for the local NFL team? No corporate health club? No personal assistant? Sorry, I'll take my career elsewhere.

But a funny thing happened on the way to the summit — something you might remember, called the recession. Now everybody's working harder, and everybody's playing less. Has all the down-sizing, all the restructuring, all the rethinking meant an end to the perk, the most cherished of stick-borne carrots?

Not necessarily. What the new career climate of the '90s has done is made companies a little more aware of where their money is being spent. Businesses are reevaluating *all* their expenses, and perks — both big and little — naturally are coming in for close scrutiny. Is the beach house really necessary? Does that water cooler increase productivity, or hinder it? Do we really need all those magazine subscriptions? Maybe our sales reps can stay at the two-star hotel, instead of the three. How about finger sandwiches and fruit juice instead of caviar and champagne at the gala banquet to launch the new product line?

Even elements that employees see as normal and necessary to the work environment can be recast as perks by scrupulous bean-counters. Writing implements may not seem like amenities to an office worker, but one well-known company that places temporary computer operators charges its employees for extra pens if they lose the one they're given. Similarly, most professionals view a telephone as an indispensible piece of business equipment — but does that mean employees must, or should, have unlimited access to that equipment? Indeed, for many cost-conscious companies, individual access codes for each employee to the company's long-distance service are becoming increasingly popular as a means of preventing abuse of phone privileges. Just print up a list of who called where, and a boss can track whether that call was made for business or personal purposes.

The perk isn't dead, but it is being viewed in a new light — the light of reason in the cost-conscious, post-recession '90s. As Nobel Prize-winning economist Milton Friedman pointed out, there's no such thing as a free lunch. The money going toward perks has to come from somewhere. Might that money better be spent on something that more directly influences the bottom line?

Even the beneficiaries of presumed perks may start to see them differently. It's common for sports teams to provide journalists with complimentary food and beverages at games, but most often the bounty isn't of the healthiest variety — hotdogs, fried chicken, pizza. To someone watching his her or weight, the complimentary buffet isn't a perk any longer. Employees of a company or a non-profit organziation that seems to spend an inordinate amount of its funds on baubles to keep the workers happy, may begin to question the direction of the company or the mission of the organization. And in the new hands-on corporate environment, some top executives are moving out of their plush, wood-paneled corner offices and back into cubicles out on the floor to become more involved in the everyday workings of the business and its employees.

As people reevaluate their place in the world — both in their careers and in life outside the job — they may begin also to reevaluate the worth and the necessity of the freebies that have become part and parcel of the commercial environment. Whereas once it may have been common to accept gifts from potential clients or customers, the new business-ethical climate has begun to call some of that palm-greasing into question. We hold our elected representatives to high standards in terms of receiving gifts as a way to influence decisions; should the decision-makers in the business world be held similarly accountable? You may be trying to decide between two companies with similar products or services. Is the value of those products or services truly reflected in the size of a company's vacation retreat or corporate jet? Maybe the young, hungry company that hasn't yet established itself enough to indulge in such perquisites is the one you'd rather work with.

Still, perks, amenities, and benefits will continue to be a drawing card for workers deciding on new careers, or evaluating job offers. Our advice? Don't let the glitter of those attractive baubles sway you from your prime concern, which should be: Is this the right job for me? Will I enjoy doing this job day in and day out? Will I be personally rewarded — not just financially, not just with advancement, and not just with certain amenities and privileges, but with a feeling of self-fulfillment? That, ultimately, is the best perk of all.

ADVERTISING ACCOUNT EXECUTIVE

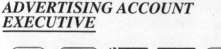

Advertising professionals frequently dine with clients in three- or four-star restaurants to discuss campaign proposals and revisions. They typically are provided with expense accounts, small private offices, and often have a private, or shared secretary. Bigger agencies commonly offer excellent health insurance plans. Senior executives frequently get city club or country club memberships. Some agencies offer child-care benefits.

AGENCY DIRECTOR (NONPROFIT)

Private offices, good benefits, modest expense accounts and frequent social engagements are part of non-profit agency directors' perks. There are standard to excellent health insurance benefits, vacation time, and professional conferences and meetings.

ANTIQUE DEALER

Many antiques/collectibles dealers need to make frequent trips, incurred at the business' expense. Although their clients may be in the same geographic region, travel to other regions, internationally and to more exotic locales is often essential to service their client's needs and requests. A company car is almost standard fare.

ARCHITECT

Senior employees of large architectural firms, who frequently entertain clients and travel to inspect on-going construction projects, are typically provided with generous expense accounts. Senior architects are occasionally rewarded with stock options and the use of company cars.

ASTRONAUT

Astronauts are provided with specially balanced meals, accommodations while training for flights, base-to-base transportation, and medical and dental insurance by NASA, the U.S. space agency.

ARCHAEOLOGISTS AND ANTHROPOLOGISTS

Anthropologists and archaeologists are often provided with free or subsidized housing, meals, and automotive transportation while on assignment "in the field." At home — at museums, universities and research organizations — workers in this field are usually assigned private offices and have regular access to department secretaries and other administrative aids. Those working abroad often have access to child-care benefits.

ATTORNEY

Senior employees of large firms or corporate legal departments are frequently provided with company cars, personal secretaries and paralegals, life insurance, health insurance, and generous in-town and traveling expense accounts. Large, prestigious firms offer city club and country club memberships for those who have "partner status" at their firms.

BANK OFFICER

Upper level officers of commercial banks frequently entertain major depositors, travel to recruit new customers, and attend seminars and conventions and are usually given substantial expense accounts. Senior bank officers are typically provided with company cars and yearly profit-based bonuses. A few are rewarded with memberships in city clubs and country clubs.

BASEBALL PLAYER (MAJOR LEAGUE)

During the regular baseball season, the play-offs, and the World Series, major league players are provided with first class transportation and accommodations. Players are offered health insurance plans, free tickets to games, and year-round access to team training and recreational facilities.

BASEBALL UMPIRE

The major leagues provide transportation and lodging for their umpires during the regular baseball season, the play-offs, and the World Series. Umpires also receive comprehensive health care and life insurance.

BASKETBALL COACH (NCAA)

Coaches at colleges with nationally-ranked basketball programs usually negotiate comprehensive packages of perquisites and bonuses. These often include housing, club membership and health insurance, as well as an automobile. An expense account to entertain recruits is common.

BASKETBALL PLAYER (NBA)

During basketball season and the post season championship, starting players for NBA teams are provided with free first-class transportation and accommodations, as well as excellent per diem meal allowances. Players arc also offered health insurance, free tickets to games, and year-round access to team training and recreational facilities.

CLERGYMAN

Religious congregations provide for many of the day-to-day needs of their spiritual leaders, including housing (rectories etc.), automobiles, health insurance and occasional meals and entertainment.

CORPORATE EXECUTIVE (SENIOR)

At this level, the most common perks for a senior corporate executive include company car, use of any corporate-owned homes and vacation facilities, country and health club memberships, personal financial counseling, partial accounting services, low-interest loans, spouse travel expenses, full insurance coverage and a pension. Senior corporate executives are usually provided with plush private offices, as well as personal secretaries and administrative assistants.

CONGRESSPERSON/SENATOR

Congresspersons and senators are provided with nominal subsidies for the extensive expenses they usually incur in commuting between Washington, D.C. and their home state. Most legislators, however, are assigned a bevy of administrative assistants — as well as unpaid, "all purpose" interns — to ease the strains of day-to-day professional and personal obligations.

COWBOY

Modern ranches provide for most of their employees' essential needs. Unmarried cowboys sleep in bunkhouses, eat at a central mess hall, and drive ranch-owned trucks and jeeps. Married hands are usually provided with small private cabins or tract houses, as well as a monthly ration of free beef. Most ranches also provide comprehensive medical insurance (or on-site treatment) for employees and their families.

ENGINEER

Employees of established engineering firms are usually provided with private offices, as well as regular access to department secretaries and other technical and administrative assistants. Those with "partner status" are often rewarded with yearly profit-based bonuses. Insurance benefits are also common.

EXECUTIVE SEARCH CONSULTANT

Those employed by successful recruiting firms are usually provided with private offices, as well as having access to department or personal secretaries and administrative assistants. Expense accounts and health insurance benefits are common. The very best at large firms often get city- and country-club memberships.

FINANCIAL PLANNER

Financial planners in the corporate environment are usually provided with private offices, as well as access to department or personal secretaries and administrative assistants. Insurance benefits are common. Many have in-town expense accounts to entertain clients.

GEOLOGIST

While "in the field," geologists are often provided with free or subsidized housing, meals, and automotive transportation. While at home — at mineral exploration firms, universities and research organizations — geologists are usually assigned private offices and have regular access to department secretaries, computer simulation technicians and other technical and administrative aids. Health insurance benefits are common. Those working abroad often have access to child-care facilities.

HOTEL MANAGER

Hotel managers, some would say, enjoy a perpetual vacation environment. They are usually provided with complimentary on-site accommodations and meals, as well as use of hotel vehicles and facilities. Employees of three- and four-star hotels may also be provided with generous expense allowances, travel to other hotels within their chain and some are provided with housing within their hotel.

INSURANCE AGENT

Insurance agents, who make frequent trips within their sales territories, are usually provided with modest expense accounts, and they are sometimes given access to company-owned or rental cars. Experienced, successful agents are often rewarded with quarterly cash or travel bonuses. Health insurance is standard fare.

NUCLEAR PLANT DECONTAMINATION TECHNICIAN

Decontamination technicians are given a per diem meal and lodging allowance, as they travel from plant to plant nearly ten months out of every year. Additionally, they are usually provided with complete health care and life insurance coverage.

PHOTOJOURNALIST

Photojournalists make frequent domestic and international trips. While on assignment for newspapers and magazines, they are usually provided with modest expense accounts, and their transportation is often prepaid.

PRESIDENT (U.S.)

The President of the U.S. is provided with a most unique home, the White House, with its full staff, as well as having most of his expenses, travel and entertainment covered by the taxpayers. Administrative and personal aides support the President, to help ease the strain of the most rigorous of professional obligations. As Commander-in-Chief, the President's health care needs are attended to by the military. In addition, a full staff of aircraft and limousines are at the President's disposal, including the famous Air Force One.

PUBLIC RELATIONS EXECUTIVE

Public relations professionals frequently dine with clients at three- or four-star restaurants to discuss campaign proposals and revisions. They typically are provided with expense accounts, private offices, automobiles and secretaries. High-level executives frequently get city- and country-club memberships.

REPORTER

Some reporters occasionally entertain "sources" and interviewees. The most senior ones travel periodically and are provided with expense ac-

counts. They typically work in noisy newsrooms, and are allowed regular access to staff secretaries and other technical and editorial assistants. Larger publications frequently offer excellent health insurance plans.

SALES REPRESENTATIVE (WHOLESALE)

Many sales representatives are provided with company cars and expense accounts. Those who travel the most extensively are often provided with membership in airline VIP clubs, and city clubs. Health insurance is a common. benefit for those who work at large companies. Many smaller companies, which compensate salespeople on a commission basic only, provide no benefits at all.

SOFTWARE ENGINEER

Like other engineering disciplines, those employed by well- established firms are usually provided with private or semi- private offices, as well as regular access to department secretaries and other technical and administrative assistants. A few outstanding senior workers are rewarded with yearly profit-based bonuses. Many software engineers are often given home computers and software programs to link them to the office. Health insurance is common.

STOCKBROKER

Senior employees of large securities firms frequently entertain clients, travel to recruit new investors, and attend educational and promotional seminars, and are typically provided with generous expense accounts. Outstanding workers in this field are occasionally rewarded with increased commission rates, membership in athletic and social clubs, and company cars.

TRAVEL AGENT

Experienced agents take periodic complimentary or subsidized airline and ocean voyages to evaluate current travel market offerings. Senior workers are sometimes rewarded with equity interests in their firms. Larger agencies often provide health insurancel plans.

Travel Opportunities

Do you long for the glamour and excitement of the high-powered, jet-setting business traveler? Well, consider for a moment the peacefulness you feel in the airport departure lounge as you await your vacation flight to some interesting or exotic destination, anticipating the relaxation and the fun that lies ahead. Then think of the guilty pleasure you feel when you emerge briefly from your reverie to notice the harried businessmen and businesswomen scurrying through the terminal as they rush to make their flights to Toledo, Tulsa, Tallahassee, or some other mundane metropolis.

For some, business travel is the spice that makes a job intriguing. But for many others it's a burden to be endured, a necessary evil that disrupts family life and grinds down both body and mind. Jet lag. Connecting flights. Shaky commuter planes. Airline food. Weather woes. Miserable airport traffic that can cause you to be late for your appointment or your flight. It's enough to make some frequent fliers long for the moment they can plant their feet firmly on the ground and their seats firmly behind a desk.

This is not to say that business travel always is distasteful — far from it. A handful of trips a year can offer a welcome break from the monotony of the work day. In addition, business travelers meet new colleagues, make new friends — and often establish networks of contacts that can be valuable in a future job search. The willingness to travel often is a sign to the employer that you'll "pay your dues" to the company; some bosses see it as a test of loyalty and commitment.

Business travel also can benefit your private life. Most corporate travelers accumulate frequent flier miles on their individual accounts, a perk that can pay off down the road with free airline tickets, rental cars, and hotel rooms that can be applied to personal vacations (if there ever is time for a vacation). For those enterprising or flexible enough, business travel schedules sometimes can be reworked to allow for visits with far-off family and friends, or a little sightseeing. For instance, instead of forcing a worker to fly out Friday morning and returning later that night, many bosses will allow you to stay in town a few weekend days, if you so desire, and perhaps fly back on Sunday — although the employee likely will have to foot the bill for expenses incurred beyond those related to business.

A welcome trend in the business world is the growing popularity of destination resorts that cater to conventions and large corporate gatherings. Savvy executives know that holding the annual branch managers' meeting in Aspen or Palm Springs — rather than at corporate headquarters in, say, Pittsburgh — can be a big morale boost. There's nothing like a little skiing or golf to lift spirits and liven up those boring seminars.

More often, however, business travel leaves little time to experience the ambiance and take in the special sights of particular destinations. Marathon meetings with clients can leave executives with a desire to do little other than head back to the hotel, order up room service, and hit the sack early. What's more, the growing worldwide popularity of office complexes near large airports means that on a three-day trip to "Munich," you might never get closer than 20 miles from the Bavarian delights of that colorful city. Looking for local color at one of those small, quaint hotels? Given the international expansion of the big hotel chains — and the barter deals companies increasingly are negotiating with such chains — your room in suburban London might look an awful lot like the bland digs on your last trip to Chicago or Charlotte. The best most business travelers can do is sample a restaurant or two; the normal itinerary — back and forth from airport to hotel to office to airport — usually won't give you a real feel for a city or a region.

Business travel comes in a wide range of styles—from road trips in one's own car, with sleepovers at the roadside budget motel, to first-class airline and hotel accommodations with a service staff that pamper the traveler and goodies that flow freely. But even the beneficiaries of the most luxurious business travel—for instance, professional athletes, who fly on chartered or team-owned planes and stay in four-star hotels—can grow weary of the grind. A rookie NBA player probably will revel in the attention lavished on him by obsequious hotel staffers and flight attendants on the team's private jet. He'll probably love the nice per-diems for meals, and he likely will enjoy sampling the night life in each city he visits. On the other hand, veterans who have seen and done it all usually grow jaded in regard to the fast lane of life on the road, and long to get back home to their families.

The jobs discussed in this chapter are meant to serve as a selection of the jobs that involve the most travel, not as a comprehensive list of careers that involve travel. Obviously, the individual circumstances will dictate whether a particular employment situation involves travel. Indeed, even positions you wouldn't expect to entail taking a trip or two can offer that opportunity. For instance, waiters and waitresses aren't normally counted among the globe-trotters of the working world—but it's certainly not unusual for a large specialty chain that is launching a new restaurant in another city to send experienced staffers from an established location to the new site on a temporary basis, to help train personnel and get things organized for the opening.

So take a look at this chapter to get an overall feel for the nature of business travel. You may not find the particular field you are considering; if not, try to find the career most similar to yours, and get an idea of the amount of travel various career areas and experience levels entail. You may be someone who loves to fly and to stay in hotels; on the other hand, you may despise traveling or be unwilling to risk the loss of family time business excursions often require. Whatever the field, however, the guiding principle of business travel is: Smaller doses usually are better.

ADVERTISING ACCOUNT EXECUTIVE

Style: First Class

Frequency: Moderate-High

Advertising professionals make frequent inter-city trips to present campaign proposals and revisions to clients, and to arrange the strategic plans for their client's campaigns. Account executives typically travel by air, in coach class seats, and stay in three-star ("excellent") hotels. The average duration of their business trips is two to three days.

AGENCY DIRECTOR (NON PROFIT)

Style: Deluxe

Frequency: Low-Moderate

Agency directors usually take several short trips annually to attend conferences, conventions and important fund raising events. In the interests of their non-profit status, travel expenses are encouraged to be minimal.

ANTIQUE DEALER

Style: Deluxe

Frequency: Moderate-High

Dealers travel locally by car for research and finding antiques for inventory. Many deal exclusively with clients within their own geographic region. More established and specialized dealers travel extensively to service clients in other regions, sometimes internationally or to more exotic locales. Dealers traveling to and selling at shows often drive hundreds of miles to their destinations along with their inventory and display equipment, requiring long road trips and setting up of displays.

AIRLINE PILOT

Style: Deluxe

Frequency: Very High

Since the nature of their work is to move people and cargo from place to place, airplane pilots naturally spend a large amount of time traveling. Airline pilots normally fly an average of 80 hours per month. Most flights, both domestic and international, involve layovers, for which airlines usually provide pilots with three-star ("excellent") accommodations and expense allowances.

ANTHROPOLOGISTS AND ARCHAEOLOGISTS

Style: Modest

Frequency: High-Very High

Anthropologists and archeologists spend roughly half their work year "in the field," studying the customs, artifacts and social structures of foreign and archaic cultures. Their research often takes them to other nations and continents. Anthropologists often prefer primitive, native food and accommodations to commercial alternatives. Typical excavations and field surveys last several months, though some continue for years.

ARCHITECT

Style: First Class

Frequency: Moderate

Architects make periodic inter-city trips to present design proposals and revisions to clients, and to oversee construction projects. They travel primarily by air, in coach class seats, and stay in two-star ("good") hotels.

ASTRONAUT

Style: Deluxe

Frequency: Moderate

Astronauts and astronaut candidates make frequent overnight and two day trips, to various Air Force installations, flying their own jets to hone their piloting skills. Although food and accommodations are provided by the military, these are usually of two-star ("good") quality.

ATTORNEY

Style: First Class

Frequency: Moderate

Travel opportunities in this field vary greatly, but a typical attorney makes several overnight trips each year to consult with clients, file legal actions and attend conventions. Employees of corporations or large legal firms are usually provided with company cars. For longer trips, attorneys fly first class, and they are often provided with memberships in airline VIP clubs.

BANK OFFICER

Style: Deluxe

Frequency: Moderate

Bank officers make frequent short trips to meet with officers of branch banks, attend conferences and seminars, and lobby legislators. Many bank officials fly business-class, and are often provided memberships in airline VIP clubs. On overnight trips, bank officers are provided with four-star ("top-of-the-line") meals and accommodations, as well as hefty expense accounts and luxury ground transport.

BASEBALL PLAYER (MAJOR LEAGUE)

Style: First Class

Frequency: Very High

Major league players spend about a month and a half at pre-season training camp in warm-weather locales. Teams play a minimum of 81 "away" games during the regular season in major league cities. Series usually are three to five games. Players fly first- or business-class or on chartered flights, and stay in four-star ("top-of-the-line") hotels. Teams also provide a per diem meal allowance to players.

BASEBALL UMPIRE

Style: First Class

Frequency: Very High

Baseball umpires work in crews of four, and crews travel from city to city to work three to five games in a series. Umpires, like players, are normally provided four-star ("top-of-the-line") accommodations in the major cities which house big league baseball teams.

BASKETBALL PLAYER (NBA)

Style: First Class

Frequency: Very High

Starting players for NBA teams spend roughly one week a year at pre-season training camp, and attend a minimum of 41 one-day "away" games. Basketball players always fly first class, and are usually provided with four-star ("top-of-the-line") accommodations. While traveling, most players are given a per diem meal allowance of $40-$60.

BASKETBALL COACH (NCAA)

Style: First Class

Frequency: High

In addition to dozens of "away" games, coaches spend approximately six additional weeks on recruiting trips. For team trips of less than 200 miles, coaches travel with their players in chartered or university-owned buses. For longer stretches, they fly in coach class on commercial carriers. While traveling, division I coaches are

usually provided with four-star ("top-of-the-line") food and accommodations.

CLERGYMAN

Style: Deluxe

Frequency: Moderate

Most members of the clergy make several trips per year to meet with other church officials, attend religious conferences, and administer church and charity programs. Styles of travel and types of accommodations for clergy members vary. High-ranking church officials travel overseas on occasion, and enjoy deluxe accommodations. Lower-level clergy normally are provided with less luxurious accommodations on short overnight trips.

CONGRESSPERSON/SENATOR

Style: Deluxe/First Class

Frequency: High

Congressman and senators spend much of their time between sessions commuting between Washington, D.C. and their home states. Surprisingly, most congressmen and senators fly in coach-class seats and make frequent overnight trip in their personal automobiles. Occasional travel overseas on diplomatic or fact-finding junkets is part of the regime.

CORPORATE EXECUTIVE (SENIOR)

Style: First Class

Frequency: High

Travel is extensive. Senior corporate executives may travel within office locations to monitor operations or confer with other executives. To network with their international counterparts many will travel overseas. There may be frequent business lunches, dinners and strategy sessions with clients and business contacts which would likely occur at three- or four-star restaurants. Senior corporate executives will attend meetings, conferences and educational events which provide the opportunity to keep on top of current technological, political and organizational developments.

ENGINEER

Style: Deluxe

Frequency: Moderate

Structural, hydraulic and highway engineers frequently make extended car trips to inspect and oversee work sites. Many engineers are provided with company or rental cars, and stay in deluxe motels or hotels.

EXECUTIVE SEARCH CONSULTANT

Style: Deluxe

Frequency: Moderate

Travel to interview candidates and meet hiring authorities is done on a limited basis. Usually business can be conducted on the telephone, however many consultants feel that personal visits are more effective, particularly to large companies which have the power to hire for several positions simultaneously. Lunches and dinners with clients are common. Some convention travel can be part of the regime.

FINANCIAL PLANNER

Style: First Class

Frequency: Moderate

Some travel will be necessary, particularly for those planners with an international client base. Though generally planner's clients are local, many travel to meet well-heeled prospects and attend social or business functions where they are likely to congregate. Investment conventions are also part of the travel regime.

FLIGHT ATTENDANT

Style: Deluxe

Frequency: Very High

Not surprisingly, flight attendants make the most trips per year of any workers, since the amount of time they spend in the air is not regulated by law, as it is for pilots. On domestic routes, attendants may work more than one flight per day, and stay overnight in cities away from home. On long domestic and international routes, layovers may last several days, allowing attendants the opportunity for sightseeing or short vacations. Like pilots, flight attendants normally are given three-star ("excellent") accommodations.

FOOTBALL PLAYER (NFL)

Style: First Class

Frequency: High

NFL players spend roughly three weeks a year at pre-season training camp, and attend 10-15 one-day "away" games. Football players fly first-class or on chartered jets, and are usually provided with four-star ("top-of-the-line") accommodations.

GEOLOGIST

Style: Modest-Deluxe

Frequency: Moderate-High

Geologists often travel to remote sites, by helicopter or jeep, where meals and accommodations are rudimentary. Exploration geologists frequently travel overseas, and geological oceanographers may spend significant time at sea.

HOTEL MANAGER

Style: First Class

Frequency: Moderate

Hotel managers take several short trips a year to attend hoteliers conventions, arrange important affairs and evaluate the accommodations of their competitors. Managers usually travel by business-class air, and are generally provided with four-star ("top- of-the-line") meals and accommodation by their employers.

INSURANCE AGENT

Style: Deluxe

Frequency: Low-Moderate

Insurance agents frequently travel on short day- or overnight trips in order to meet with clients and examine claims. Independent agents often use their own auto, while those with large agencies may be provided with company cars. Insurance agents usually stay in two-or three-star ("good" to "excellent") hotels, and may have modest expense accounts.

NUCLEAR PLANT DECONTAMINATION TECHNICIAN

Style: Modest-Deluxe

Frequency: High

Decontamination technicians spend nearly ten months out of every year traveling from plant to plant, as demand for their highly-specialized services arises. Technicians usually travel by bus or train, even on extended trips, and they are given a nominal per diem meal and lodging allowance.

PHOTOJOURNALIST

Style: Deluxe

Frequency: High

Many journalists take ground trips of 200 miles or less, as often as once a week. Longer, overnight junkets, however, are much less common. While on traveling assignments, photojournalists occupy coach class airplane seats, and are provided with three-star meals and lodging. A few workers in this field routinely travel overseas.

PRESIDENT

Style: First Class+

Frequency: High

In directing the foreign policy of the U.S., the President frequently makes trips overseas on diplomatic efforts. The President is a significant player in any major global political conference and as such spends a significant portion of his term in office representing the United States around the world, along with members of his cabinet. Nationally, the President often travels on promotional venues or to support other members of his political party. In an election year, the President and the First Lady would make numerous trips, mostly within the United States.

PUBLIC RELATIONS EXECUTIVE

Style: First Class

Frequency: Moderate-High

Many public relations professionals deal exclusively with clients within their geographic region, but a substantial minority travel extensively to service clients in other regions. These workers travel primarily by business-class air, and are provided with three-star ("excellent") accommodations.

REPORTER

Style: Modest-Deluxe

Frequency: Low

Most reporters work a strictly local "beat," but a substantial minority travel periodically to cover major stories. For trips under 300 miles, reporters generally take their own cars, and they fly coach-class for longer journeys. Depending on the relative size and success of their publications, reporters are usually provided modest to deluxe meals and accommodations.

SALES REPRESENTATIVE (WHOLESALE)

Style: Deluxe

Frequency: High

Sales representatives take frequent ground trips in personal or company cars within their "sales territories." On longer trips, they usually fly in coach-class seats, and they are often provided with membership in airline VIP clubs or city-clubs. Sales representatives typically receive either a per diem allowance for their meals and lodging or they have reimbursable expense accounts which cover those expenses.

STOCKBROKER

Style: First Class

Frequency: Low

Stockbrokers make frequent short trips to consult with important clients, recruit new investors, and attend educational and promotional seminars. Brokers travel almost exclusively by business-class air, but when ground transport is required, they are usually provided with company cars. Brokers typically describe their meals and accommodation as four-star ("top-of-the-line").

TRAVEL AGENT

Style: First Class

Frequency: Low-Moderate

Travel agents take periodic complimentary or subsidized trips to evaluate current travel market offerings. They usually travel by air, although they are occasionally invited on sea voyages (cruises) for promotional purposes. Agents are usually provided with the best available accommodations and meals.

250 Jobs Ranked by Cumulative Scores

In the overall ranking system, it is assumed that each of six categories (Environment, Income, Outlook, Physical Demands, Security, and Stress) is equally important. Scores are derived by adding together the individual rank that each job has received in those categories. Because a high rank in an individual category means it is more desirable than a low rank, this ranking system translates to the lowest score being the most desirable. For example, the top ranked job in the "Overall Rankings" below, actuary, scored points as follows: 2 for its 2nd rank in Environment, 29 for its 29th rank in Income, and so on.

RANK		SCORE	RANK		SCORE
1	ACTUARY	118	31	OCCUPATIONAL THERAPIST	414
2	SOFTWARE ENGINEER	124	32	PHARMACIST	421
3	COMPUTER SYSTEMS ANALYST	131	33	PHILOSOPHER	428
			34	BANK OFFICER	431
4	ACCOUNTANT	218	35	AGENCY DIRECTOR (NONPROFIT)	439
5	PARALEGAL ASSISTANT	222			
6	MATHEMATICIAN	223	36	POSTAL INSPECTOR	441
7	MEDICAL SECRETARY	230	37	OPTICIAN	451
8	COMPUTER PROGRAMMER	263	38	ELECTRICAL ENGINEER	452
9	PAROLE OFFICER	279	39	VOCATIONAL COUNSELOR	457
10	MEDICAL RECORDS TECHNICIAN	294	40	ASTRONOMER	468
			40	FINANCIAL PLANNER	468
11	DIETICIAN	310	42	OCEANOGRAPHER	470
12	MEDICAL TECHNOLOGIST	335	43	PUBLICATION EDITOR	471
13	STATISTICIAN	336	44	ASTROLOGER	474
14	AUDIOLOGIST	342	45	NUCLEAR ENGINEER	476
15	HOSPITAL ADMINISTRATOR	349	46	CIVIL ENGINEER	485
16	DENTAL HYGIENIST	350	46	POLITICAL SCIENTIST	485
17	MEDICAL LABORATORY TECHNICIAN	365	48	AEROSPACE ENGINEER	491
18	URBAN/REGIONAL PLANNER	367	49	TAX EXAMINER/COLLECTOR	494
19	BIOLOGIST	370	50	ECONOMIST	496
20	SOCIOLOGIST	374	51	NEWSWRITER (RADIO/TV)	498
21	HISTORIAN	379	51	MECHANICAL ENGINEER	498
22	METEOROLOGIST	388	53	BROADCAST TECHNICIAN	499
23	PHYSIOLOGIST	390	54	OPTOMETRIST	502
24	DENTAL LABORATORY TECHNICIAN	392	55	PODIATRIST	512
			56	MOTION PICTURE EDITOR	514
25	INDUSTRIAL ENGINEER	396	57	PROTESTANT MINISTER	515
26	TECHNICAL WRITER	399	58	ATTORNEY	531
27	JUDGE (FEDERAL)	402	59	CHIROPRACTOR	535
28	INSURANCE UNDERWRITER	403	60	HOTEL MANAGER	536
29	INDUSTRIAL DESIGNER	408	61	COMPUTER SERVICE TECHNICIAN	538
30	SPEECH PATHOLOGIST	410			

RANK		SCORE
62	PHYSICIST	549
62	SCHOOL PRINCIPAL	549
64	ENGINEERING TECHNICIAN	551
65	GEOLOGIST	560
66	ANTHROPOLOGIST	562
67	PERSONNEL RECRUITER	563
68	PHYSICAL THERAPIST	566
69	PSYCHOLOGIST	570
70	COSMETOLOGIST	576
71	PETROLEUM ENGINEER	578
72	TEACHER'S AIDE	579
73	AGRICULTURAL SCIENTIST	588
74	CASHIER	589
75	RESPIRATORY THERAPIST	590
76	ARCHITECTURAL DRAFTER	593
76	ELECTRICAL TECHNICIAN	593
78	CHEMIST	597
79	JEWELER	604
79	ADVERTISING ACCOUNT EXECUTIVE	604
81	TICKET AGENT	606
82	RECEPTIONIST	607
83	MUSEUM CURATOR	608
84	ARTIST (COMMERCIAL)	610
85	SECRETARY	613
86	PHOTOGRAPHIC PROCESS WORKER	614
87	MILITARY (COMMISSIONED OFFICER)	617
88	LITHOGRAPHER/ PHOTOENGRAVER	623
88	SOCIAL WORKER	623
90	DENTIST	626
91	PURCHASING AGENT	630
92	FLORIST	631
93	CATHOLIC PRIEST	634
94	ARCHEOLOGIST	634
95	MARKET RESEARCH ANALYST	635
96	PHYSICIAN (GENERAL PRACTICE)	638
97	LIBRARIAN	639

RANK		SCORE
98	WAITER/WAITRESS	641
99	PSYCHIATRIST	645
100	EXECUTIVE SEARCH CONSULTANT	649
101	FILE CLERK	651
102	COLLEGE PROFESSOR	654
103	GUARD	655
104	ZOOLOGIST	663
105	ANTIQUE DEALER	664
106	SHIPPING/RECEIVING CLERK	673
107	HOME ECONOMIST	676
108	TYPIST/WORD PROCESSOR	680
108	FLIGHT ATTENDANT	680
110	MUSICAL INSTRUMENT REPAIRER	682
110	VETERINARIAN	682
110	AIRPLANE PILOT	682
113	CARTOONIST	688
114	NURSE (REGISTERED)	695
115	BOOKBINDER	696
116	PHYSICIAN ASSISTANT	697
117	CHILD CARE WORKER	699
118	BOOKKEEPER	700
118	ORTHODONTIST	700
120	NURSE'S AIDE	702
120	SYMPHONY CONDUCTOR	702
122	MILITARY (WARRANT OFFICER)	706
123	STENOGRAPHER/COURT REPORTER	711
124	SURGEON	714
125	BARBER	723
126	NEWSCASTER	731
126	PUBLIC RELATIONS EXECUTIVE	731
128	FASHION MODEL	732
129	RABBI	742
130	SET DESIGNER	745
130	UNDERTAKER	745
132	BANK TELLER	748
133	CONSERVATIONIST	751

RANK		SCORE	RANK		SCORE
133	TRAVEL AGENT	751	168	SALES REPRESENTATIVE (WHOLESALE)	902
135	MAID	759	169	AIRCRAFT MECHANIC	903
136	AUTHOR (BOOKS)	765	170	RECREATION WORKER	904
137	TEACHER	779	171	ASTRONAUT	905
138	APPLIANCE REPAIRER	783	172	CHOREOGRAPHER	912
139	STOCKBROKER	789	173	DISHWASHER	914
140	FORKLIFT OPERATOR	795	173	EMERGENCY MEDICAL TECHNICIAN	914
141	AUTOMOBILE BODY REPAIRER	803	175	AUTOMOBILE ASSEMBLER	923
142	CORRECTION OFFICER	804	176	PHOTOGRAPHER	924
143	PIANO TUNER	810	177	MUSICIAN	926
144	NURSE (LICENSED PRACTICAL)	812	177	MILITARY (ENLISTED PERSON)	926
145	INDUSTRIAL MACHINE REPAIRER	816	179	TELEPHONE INSTALLER/ REPAIRER	927
145	OCCUPATIONAL SAFETY/ HEALTH INSPECTOR	816	180	ADVERTISING SALESPERSON	928
147	OSTEOPATH	819	181	BUYER	935
148	INSURANCE AGENT	821	182	BUS DRIVER	937
149	HEATING/REFRIGERATION MECHANIC	834	183	TELEPHONE OPERATOR	939
149	FASHION DESIGNER	834	184	RACE CAR DRIVER (INDY CLASS)	944
151	ARCHITECT	837	185	ELECTRICAL EQUIPMENT REPAIRER	945
152	REPORTER (NEWSPAPER)	838	186	SALESPERSON (RETAIL)	954
153	SEWAGE PLANT OPERATOR	841	187	TOOL-AND-DIE MAKER	955
154	JANITOR	842	188	SINGER	957
155	CHAUFFEUR	843	189	BARTENDER	958
156	SPORTS INSTRUCTOR	845	190	CONSTRUCTION FOREMAN	960
157	CORPORATE EXECUTIVE (SENIOR)	845	191	COMPOSITOR/TYPESETTER	963
158	OFFICE MACHINE REPAIRER	847	192	CONGRESSPERSON/ SENATOR	976
159	COMPUTER OPERATOR	859	193	SURVEYOR	977
159	COOK/CHEF	859	194	PLUMBER	979
161	DISK JOCKEY	864	195	DRESSMAKER	993
162	VENDING MACHINE REPAIRER	867	196	SHOE MAKER/REPAIRER	996
163	FURNITURE UPHOLSTERER	875	197	GLAZIER	999
164	MAIL CARRIER	881	198	ARTIST (FINE ART)	1001
165	AIR TRAFFIC CONTROLLER	898	199	COMMUNICATIONS EQUIPMENT MECHANIC	1006
166	STATIONARY ENGINEER	899	200	HIGHWAY PATROL OFFICER	1011
167	RAILROAD CONDUCTOR	900			

RANK		SCORE	RANK		SCORE
201	BASEBALL UMPIRE (MAJOR LEAGUE)	1014	226	BASKETBALL PLAYER (NBA)	1127
201	FIREFIGHTER	1014	227	PRESIDENT (U.S.)	1129
203	CARPET INSTALLER	1016	228	NUCLEAR PLANT DECONTAMINATION TECHNICIAN	1137
203	REAL ESTATE AGENT	1016			
205	PRECISION ASSEMBLER	1017	229	IRONWORKER	1150
206	MACHINIST	1022	230	STEVEDORE	1151
207	BASKETBALL COACH (NCAA)	1031	231	BUTCHER	1153
208	ELECTRICIAN	1035	232	BOILERMAKER	1162
208	CONSTRUCTION MACHINERY OPERATOR	1035	233	CARPENTER	1172
			234	BRICKLAYER	1175
210	ACTOR	1040	235	MILLWRIGHT	1190
211	PLASTERER	1045	236	METER READER	1199
211	AUTOMOBILE MECHANIC	1045	237	WELDER	1206
211	POLICE OFFICER	1045	238	DAIRY FARMER	1216
214	DRILL-PRESS OPERATOR	1049	239	FARMER	1232
215	PHOTOJOURNALIST	1055	240	GARBAGE COLLECTOR	1235
216	PAINTER	1056	241	SEAMAN	1252
217	TRUCK DRIVER	1095	242	AUTOMOBILE PAINTER	1262
218	AUTOMOBILE SALESPERSON	1102	243	ROOFER	1280
			244	FISHERMAN	1297
219	BASEBALL PLAYER (MAJOR LEAGUE)	1113	245	TAXI DRIVER	1301
			246	ROUSTABOUT	1319
220	MAYOR	1116	247	COWBOY	1329
220	FOOTBALL PLAYER (NFL)	1116	248	CONSTRUCTION WORKER (LABORER)	1342
222	DRYWALL APPLICATOR/ FINISHER	1117			
			249	DANCER	1357
223	MACHINE TOOL OPERATOR	1119	250	LUMBERJACK	1440
223	JOCKEY	1119			
225	SHEET METAL WORKER	1125			

250 Jobs Ranked Within Categories

Category Rank		Overall Rank	Category Rank		Overall Rank
	AGRICULTURE			**BUSINESS/FINANCE**	
1	AGRICULTURAL SCIENTIST	73	1	ACCOUNTANT	4
2	DAIRY FARMER	238	2	PARALEGAL ASSISTANT	5
3	FARMER	239	3	INSURANCE UNDERWRITER	28
4	SEAMAN	241	4	BANK OFFICER	34
5	FISHERMAN	244	5	AGENCY DIRECTOR (NONPROFIT)	35
6	COWBOY	247	6	VOCATIONAL COUNSELOR	39
	THE ARTS		7	FINANCIAL PLANNER	40
			8	ECONOMIST	50
1	MOTION PICTURE EDITOR	56	9	ATTORNEY	58
2	ARCHITECTURAL DRAFTER	76	10	PERSONNEL RECRUITER	67
3	MUSEUM CURATOR	83	11	CASHIER	74
4	ANTIQUE DEALER	105	12	RECEPTIONIST	82
5	SYMPHONY CONDUCTOR	120	13	SECRETARY	85
6	FASHION MODEL	128	14	PURCHASING AGENT	91
7	SET DESIGNER	130	15	MARKET RESEARCH ANALYST	95
8	FASHION DESIGNER	149	16	EXECUTIVE SEARCH CONSULTANT	100
9	ARCHITECT	151	17	FILE CLERK	101
10	CHOREOGRAPHER	172	18	TYPIST/WORD PROCESSOR	108
11	MUSICIAN	177	19	BOOKKEEPER	118
12	SINGER	188	20	BANK TELLER	132
13	ARTIST (FINE ART)	198	21	STOCKBROKER	139
14	ACTOR	210	22	INSURANCE AGENT	148
15	DANCER	249	23	CORPORATE EXECUTIVE (SENIOR)	157
	ATHLETICS		24	SALES REPRESENTATIVE (WHOLESALE)	168
1	SPORTS INSTRUCTOR	156	25	BUYER	181
2	RACE CAR DRIVER (INDY CLASS)	184	26	SALESPERSON (RETAIL)	186
3	BASEBALL UMPIRE (MAJOR LEAGUE)	201	27	REAL ESTATE AGENT	203
4	BASKETBALL COACH (NCAA)	207	28	AUTOMOBILE SALESPERSON	218
5	BASEBALL PLAYER (MAJOR LEAGUE)	219		**COMMUNICATIONS**	
6	FOOTBALL PLAYER (NFL)	220			
7	JOCKEY	223	1	TECHNICAL WRITER	26
8	BASKETBALL PLAYER (NBA)	226	2	PUBLICATION EDITOR	43

Category Rank		Overall Rank	Category Rank		Overall Rank
3	NEWSWRITER (RADIO/TV)	51	5	AUDIOLOGIST	14
4	BROADCAST TECHNICIAN	53	6	HOSPITAL ADMINISTRATOR	15
5	ADVERTISING ACCOUNT EXECUTIVE	79	7	DENTAL HYGIENIST	16
6	ARTIST (COMMERCIAL)	84	8	MEDICAL LABORATORY TECHNICIAN	17
7	CARTOONIST	113	9	PHYSIOLOGIST	23
8	NEWSCASTER	126	10	DENTAL LABORATORY TECHNICIAN	24
9	PUBLIC RELATIONS EXECUTIVE	126	11	SPEECH PATHOLOGIST	30
10	AUTHOR (BOOKS)	136	12	OCCUPATIONAL THERAPIST	31
11	REPORTER (NEWSPAPER)	152	13	PHARMACIST	32
12	DISK JOCKEY	161	14	OPTICIAN	37
13	PHOTOGRAPHER	176	15	OPTOMETRIST	54
14	ADVERTISING SALESPERSON	180	16	PODIATRIST	55
15	PHOTOJOURNALIST	215	17	CHIROPRACTOR	59
			18	PHYSICAL THERAPIST	68

CONSTRUCTION TRADES

			19	PSYCHOLOGIST	69
1	CONSTRUCTION FOREMAN	190	20	RESPIRATORY THERAPIST	75
2	SURVEYOR	193	21	DENTIST	90
3	GLAZIER	197	22	PHYSICIAN (GENERAL PRACTICE)	96
4	CARPET INSTALLER	203			
5	CONSTRUCTION MACHINERY OPERATOR	208	23	PSYCHIATRIST	99
6	PLASTERER	211	24	VETERINARIAN	110
7	PAINTER	216	25	NURSE (REGISTERED)	114
8	DRYWALL APPLICATOR/ FINISHER	222	26	PHYSICIAN ASSISTANT	116
9	SHEET METAL WORKER	225	27	ORTHODONTIST	118
10	IRONWORKER	229	28	NURSE'S AIDE	120
11	CARPENTER	233	29	SURGEON	124
12	BRICKLAYER	234	30	NURSE (LICENSED PRACTICAL)	144
13	ROOFER	243	31	OSTEOPATH	147
14	CONSTRUCTION WORKER (LABORER)	248	32	EMERGENCY MEDICAL TECHNICIAN	173

HEALTH CARE/MEDICINE

MATH/SCIENCE

1	MEDICAL SECRETARY	7	1	ACTUARY	1
2	MEDICAL RECORDS TECHNICIAN	10	2	MATHEMATICIAN	6
3	DIETICIAN	11	3	STATISTICIAN	13
4	MEDICAL TECHNOLOGIST	12	4	BIOLOGIST	19
			5	METEOROLOGIST	22
			6	INDUSTRIAL ENGINEER	25

Category Rank		Overall Rank
7	ASTRONOMER	40
8	OCEANOGRAPHER	42
9	ASTROLOGER	44
10	PHYSICIST	62
11	GEOLOGIST	65
12	CHEMIST	78
13	ZOOLOGIST	104

PERSONAL SERVICES

1	COSMETOLOGIST	70
2	CHILD CARE WORKER	117
3	BARBER	125
4	UNDERTAKER	130
5	MAID	135
6	CHAUFFEUR	155
7	TAXI DRIVER	245

PRODUCTION/ MANUFACTURING

1	INDUSTRIAL DESIGNER	29
2	ELECTRICAL ENGINEER	38
3	NUCLEAR ENGINEER	45
4	CIVIL ENGINEER	46
5	AEROSPACE ENGINEER	48
6	MECHANICAL ENGINEER	51
6	MECHANICAL ENGINEER	51
7	ENGINEERING TECHNICIAN	64
8	PETROLEUM ENGINEER	71
9	PHOTOGRAPHIC PROCESS WORKER	86
10	LITHOGRAPHER/ PHOTOENGRAVER	88
11	SHIPPING/RECEIVING CLERK	106
12	BOOKBINDER	115
13	FORKLIFT OPERATOR	140
14	FURNITURE UPHOLSTERER	163
15	AUTOMOBILE ASSEMBLER	175
16	TOOL-AND-DIE MAKER	187
17	COMPOSITOR/TYPESETTER	191
18	DRESSMAKER	195
19	PRECISION ASSEMBLER	205
20	MACHINIST	206
21	DRILL-PRESS OPERATOR	214
22	MACHINE TOOL OPERATOR	223
23	STEVEDORE	230
24	BUTCHER	231
25	BOILERMAKER	232
26	MILLWRIGHT	235
27	WELDER	237
28	AUTOMOBILE PAINTER	242
29	ROUSTABOUT	246
30	LUMBERJACK	250

PUBLIC SECTOR

1	PAROLE OFFICER	9
2	URBAN/REGIONAL PLANNER	18
3	JUDGE (FEDERAL)	27
4	POSTAL INSPECTOR	36
5	TAX EXAMINER/COLLECTOR	49
6	SCHOOL PRINCIPAL	62
7	TEACHER'S AIDE	72
8	MILITARY (COMMISSIONED OFFICER)	87
9	SOCIAL WORKER	88
10	LIBRARIAN	97
11	COLLEGE PROFESSOR	102
12	MILITARY (WARRANT OFFICER)	122
13	STENOGRAPHER/COURT REPORTER	123
14	CONSERVATIONIST	133
15	TEACHER	137
16	CORRECTION OFFICER	142
17	OCCUPATIONAL SAFETY/ HEALTH INSPECTOR	145
18	SEWAGE PLANT OPERATOR	153
19	MAIL CARRIER	164
20	AIR TRAFFIC CONTROLLER	165
21	ASTRONAUT	171
22	MILITARY (ENLISTED PERSON)	177

Category Rank		Overall Rank
23	BUS DRIVER	182
24	CONGRESSPERSON/ SENATOR	192
25	HIGHWAY PATROL OFFICER	200
26	FIREFIGHTER	201
27	POLICE OFFICER	211
28	MAYOR	220
29	PRESIDENT (U.S.)	227
30	NUCLEAR PLANT DECONTAMI- NATION TECHNICIAN	228
31	METER READER	236
32	GARBAGE COLLECTOR	240

SOCIAL SCIENCES

1	SOCIOLOGIST	20
2	HISTORIAN	21
3	PHILOSOPHER	33
4	POLITICAL SCIENTIST	46
5	ANTHROPOLOGIST	66
6	ARCHEOLOGIST	94
7	HOME ECONOMIST	107

TECHNICAL/REPAIR

1	SOFTWARE ENGINEER	2
2	COMPUTER SYSTEMS ANALYST	3
3	COMPUTER PROGRAMMER	8
4	COMPUTER SERVICE TECHNICIAN	61
5	ELECTRICAL TECHNICIAN	76
6	MUSICAL INSTRUMENT REPAIRER	110
7	APPLIANCE REPAIRER	138

Category Rank		Overall Rank
8	AUTOMOBILE BODY REPAIRER	141
9	PIANO TUNER	143
10	INDUSTRIAL MACHINE REPAIRER	145
11	HEATING/REFRIGERATION MECHANIC	149
12	OFFICE MACHINE REPAIRER	158
13	COMPUTER OPERATOR	159
14	VENDING MACHINE REPAIRER	162
15	AIRCRAFT MECHANIC	169
16	TELEPHONE INSTALLER/ REPAIRER	179
17	ELECTRICAL EQUIPMENT REPAIRER	185
18	PLUMBER	194
19	SHOE MAKER/REPAIRER	196
20	COMMUNICATIONS EQUIPMENT MECHANIC	199
21	ELECTRICIAN	208
22	AUTOMOBILE MECHANIC	211

TRAVEL/FOOD SERVICE

1	HOTEL MANAGER	60
2	TICKET AGENT	81
3	WAITER/WAITRESS	98
4	FLIGHT ATTENDANT	108
5	AIRPLANE PILOT	110
6	TRAVEL AGENT	133
7	COOK/CHEF	159
8	RAILROAD CONDUCTOR	167
9	DISHWASHER	173
10	BARTENDER	189
11	TRUCK DRIVER	217